Springer Textbooks in Law

Springer Textbooks in Law compiles high-quality educational content aimed at undergraduate and graduate students in all areas of law. All self-contained volumes are authored by accomplished academics and suitable for use in class as well as individual study. Many of them include chapter abstracts, definitions of technical terms, cases and self-assessment exercises, as well as recommended reading sections. This series is an invaluable resource for students and lecturers alike and spans the full range of topics in international and European law, including fundamentals of law and comparative law. Special attention is paid to current and emerging topics such as IT law, intellectual property, human rights as well as dispute resolution, mediation, arbitration – and many more.

George Mousourakis

Traversing Legal Traditions

Perspectives on Comparative Law and Legal History

Second Edition

With Contributions by Matteo Nicolini

Springer

George Mousourakis
School of Law and Graduate School
of Humanities and Social Sciences
Hiroshima University
Hiroshima, Japan

ISSN 2509-999X ISSN 2510-0009 (electronic)
Springer Textbooks in Law
ISBN 978-3-031-94668-4 ISBN 978-3-031-94669-1 (eBook)
https://doi.org/10.1007/978-3-031-94669-1

This Springer imprint is published by the registered company Springer Nature Switzerland AG
The registered company address is: Gewerbestrasse 11, 6330 Cham, Switzerland

Dedicated to the memory of Professor Jim Evans, a remarkable teacher and a true friend, whose guidance and wisdom continue to inspire

Preface

In recent decades, there has been an increasing tendency among legal academics and professionals to look beyond their own legal borders. While much of the growing interest in foreign legal systems can be attributed to the effects of globalization and the consequent rise in transnational economic activities, this empirical parameter accounts for only part of the explanation. The other part involves a desire to gain a deeper understanding of law as a social phenomenon and fresh insights into the current state and future direction of one's own legal system.

Comparative law enables legal scholars and professionals to explore the dominant features and developmental trends of diverse legal systems and to integrate their knowledge of law into a cultural panorama extending well beyond their own country. In this way, they can develop the standards and cultivate the analytical skills necessary to address the challenges presented by a rapidly changing world. The accumulated experiences of different legal systems offer a vast pool of resources for legal policymakers, members of the judiciary, and other stakeholders, which they can use to enrich and advance both domestic and international legal frameworks.

In response to the growing internationalization of legal practice and academic research, law schools worldwide have expanded their comparative law programs. Most law schools have integrated one or more comparative law courses into the first-year curriculum to help students gain an understanding of the nature, goals, and methodology of comparative legal studies. Additionally, there is an increased focus on comparative legal analysis within core legal subjects, alongside greater attention to the impact of global developments on domestic laws. As an integral component of contemporary legal education, comparative law plays a pivotal role in shaping a new generation of academic and practicing lawyers who recognize and appreciate the importance of cultural and legal diversity, as well as what societies and legal systems share in an ever-changing and interconnected world.

This book is designed for undergraduate and postgraduate students studying comparative and transnational law, legal history, and legal theory. Its main objective is to provide clear and informed accounts of central topics in comparative law. The text is organized into two main parts.

The first part addresses foundational issues related to the nature, scope, and historical evolution of comparative law, as well as its interactions with other fields of legal study. It examines the role of legal comparatism from classical antiquity through the early modern age, with a particular focus on the contributions of eighteenth- and nineteenth-century thinkers who were instrumental in developing the discipline of comparative law. Additionally, it outlines and appraises the uses of comparative law in current domestic and international law-making and judicial processes, along with key aspects of comparative law methodology. In this context, the topics of harmonization and convergence of laws, as well as the methodological challenges associated with the comparative study of legal systems, are discussed and explained.

Following a discussion of theories regarding the classification of the world's legal systems into various families, the second part of the book examines the historical evolution and defining characteristics of several major legal traditions. These include the Roman and civil law tradition, the English common law tradition, the Islamic legal tradition, indigenous legal traditions, and, in connection with the topic of legal transplantation, the Japanese legal tradition. The book concludes with a list of bibliographical references for further reading, along with the titles of the studies that formed the foundation for the work.

The various chapters of the book can be read in conjunction or on their own. As long as it is remembered that the book is not intended to be an all-encompassing textbook on comparative law and is therefore likely to be used alongside other resources, it is hoped that it will make the study of comparative law and legal traditions more accessible to readers across various fields of legal learning.

The impetus for this book originated from a series of undergraduate and postgraduate lectures I delivered at universities in Australia, New Zealand, Japan, and Europe over the past several years. Portions of this work have also been presented at conferences and academic colloquia, where feedback from commentators and audiences has frequently helped me clarify some of my ideas. I am particularly indebted to the contributing author of this book, Professor Matteo Nicolini of the University of Verona, for his extensive efforts in preparing his chapter and his cooperation in bringing this volume to fruition.

I must acknowledge the excellent work of Professor Csaba Varga of the Pázmány Péter Catholic University and the Institute for Legal Studies of the Hungarian Academy of Sciences, whose publications I relied on in certain areas. Additionally, I wish to thank Professor Reinhard Zimmermann, Director of the Max Planck Institute for Comparative and International Private Law in Hamburg; Professor Thomas Duve, Director of the Max Planck Institute for Legal History and Legal Theory in Frankfurt; Professor Johannes Platschek, Director of the Leopold Wenger Institute at the University of Munich; Professor Nikolaus Benke of the University of Vienna; Professor Guido Pfeifer of the University of Frankfurt; Dr David Kohout of Charles University, Prague; and Ms. Christina Schmid, Director of the Swiss Institute of Comparative Law in Lausanne, for their generosity in granting me access to their library resources and other research facilities. I would also like to extend my gratitude to Ms. Lucy Stroud and Mr. Ian McIntosh, who have been exceptional editors and have provided numerous valuable suggestions for improvement.

Special mention must also be made of my long-time friends and colleagues: Professor Nobuhito Yoshinaka, Dean of Law at Hiroshima University; Emeritus Professor Katsunori Kai of the Institute of Comparative Law at Waseda University; Emeritus Professor Koshi Yamazaki of Kanagawa University; Professor Alberto Cadoppi of the University of Parma; Emeritus Professor Peter Watts and Professor Kenneth Palmer of the University of Auckland; Emeritus Professor Nigel Simmonds of the University of Cambridge; Emeritus Professor Martin Wasik of Keele University; Emeritus Professor Alexander McCall Smith of the University of Edinburgh; Emeritus Professor Joshua Dressler of the Ohio State University; and Emeritus Professor Roger Clark of Rutgers University, for their encouragement and support.

Finally, I wish to express my gratitude to the Graduate School of Humanities and Social Sciences at Hiroshima University and the Institute of Comparative and Transnational Law for the financial grants they provided in support of this project and to my publishers for their cooperation and courteous assistance.

Hiroshima, Japan
March 2025

George Mousourakis

Competing Interests The authors have no competing interests to declare that are relevant to the content of this manuscript.

Contents

Chapter 1
Charting the Domain of Comparative Law

1.1 Introduction

Although the question 'what is law?' can be answered in various ways and on different levels, we can begin with the assumption that law consists of a body of binding rules regulating the behaviour of citizens in their interactions with one another and society as a whole. The term 'system of law' refers to the framework of laws, procedures, institutions, and legal actors that make up the legal environment of a specific country or jurisdiction. This term expresses the fact that, in a broad sense, law is composed of diverse, interconnected elements that should be considered from the perspective of their functional interdependence as parts of a cohesive and comprehensive whole. Key components of a legal system include: the sources of law, such as constitutions, statutes and case law; legal institutions that create, interpret and enforce the laws, such as legislatures, courts and administrative agencies; and legal processes for enacting laws, resolving disputes and administering justice.

Related to but distinct from the term 'legal system' is the term 'legal order'. The later term refers to the overarching normative framework that ensures the regulation and organization of society through law. This framework embraces: fundamental principles and values, such as equality, justice and freedom; the norms and standards that govern behaviour, resolve disputes and ensure social order; the principles underpinning the legitimacy and authority of legal institutions; and the logical and systematic arrangement of laws and legal norms, which ensures they are consistent and work together in an orderly fashion. In essence, the legal order is the philosophical and conceptual foundation of the law, while the legal system is the practical manifestation of these concepts in a given jurisdiction. The legal system operates within the context of the legal order, and the effectiveness and legitimacy of the legal system depend on the strength and coherence of the legal order.

Legal scholars recognize that understanding the function of law in society requires examining the factors that influence the development and substantive

G. Mousourakis, *Traversing Legal Traditions*, Springer Textbooks in Law,
https://doi.org/10.1007/978-3-031-94669-1_1

content of legal rules and institutions. These interrelated factors include historical circumstances, social and cultural values and expectations, religious beliefs, and linguistic and philosophical traditions. Legal systems must be placed in a broad historical and socio-cultural context. In this respect, concepts such as 'legal tradition' and 'legal culture' play a key role.

Legal tradition refers to a set of long-stablished, historically conditioned perspectives and attitudes regarding the essence of law, its role within society and governance, and the structure and functioning of a legal system. It encompasses fundamental principles, methodologies, and structures that steer the evolution and interpretation of laws, affect legal reasoning, and mould legal institutions.[1] According to Patrick Glenn, a legal tradition may be described as a 'pool' or network of legal information, all the elements of which are interlinked and their meaning and function informed by the whole.[2] There are national legal traditions, each with its characteristic attitudes towards law, which, according to their more general features, may be classified into broader, transnational traditions. All enduring legal traditions have a core set of foundational norms and principles that emerge through a process transcending generations and, in the case of transnational traditions, national boundaries. These norms form the essential framework of rights, duties, powers, and prohibitions necessary for maintaining social order. Over time, these basic rules can develop, adapt, and become more sophisticated, but the evolving laws build upon this fundamental structure.[3] Legal traditions evolve in pursuit of efficiency, order, and societal consensus and, as the values and circumstances of society change, a tradition's norms will tend to adapt accordingly. However, it is intrinsic to the nature of a tradition that the change is piecemeal: traditions evolve, and progress occurs continually over generations, with each generation building on the heritage of its predecessors.[4] Legal traditions do not exist in isolation but contribute to one another through a continuous exchange of information, ideas, and models. The more intense and pervasive forms of communication today have made the boundaries of legal traditions more permeable than at any time in the past.

[1] In the words of John Henry Merryman, a legal tradition is an expression of "deeply rooted, historically conditioned attitudes about the nature of law … the role of law in … society and the polity, the proper organization and operation of a legal system, and about the way law is, or should be made, applied, studied, perfected and taught. The legal tradition relates the legal system to the culture of which it is a partial expression." Merryman (1985), p. 2. And see Krygier (1986), pp. 240–251.

[2] Glenn (2014), pp. 13–14. This understanding of legal tradition is generally consistent with the manner in which contemporary social science describes culture. See, e.g., Cuche (2004).

[3] In the domain of law, the past serves as a source of ongoing authority and guidance, but it is construed through the lens of the present. What matters most is not what the law was in the past, but how authoritative interpreters have reinterpreted it to meet contemporary needs. As Martin Krygier has remarked, legal traditions are characterized by "a dialectical interplay between inherited layers which pervade and mould the present, and the constant renewals and reshaping of these inheritances, in which authorized interpreters and guardians of the tradition and lay participants indulge and must indulge." Krygier (1991), p. 68.

[4] See Berman (1983), p. 5.

'Legal culture' is a multi-dimensional term employed in sociological and anthropological studies of law. It refers to the attitudes, values, beliefs and opinions held in society regarding law and legal institutions.[5] It involves the public's perception of the legal system, their trust in legal institutions, and their expectations of justice and fairness. It also encompasses how legal professionals, such as judges, lawyers, and legal scholars, conduct themselves and how laws are applied and enforced. Viewing law as culture implies that law is more than simply a body of rules or institutions; it is also a social practice within a legal community. It is this social practice that shapes the actual meaning of the rules and institutions, their relative weight, and the way they are implemented and operate in society. Understanding law presupposes knowledge of the social practice of the legal community and this, in turn, implies familiarity with the general culture of the society in which the legal community is a part.[6] One might say that law is an element of the culture of a society that both impacts upon culture and is permeated by it.[7] According to Lawrence Friedman, legal culture can be seen as embodying two aspects: an 'external' (lay) and an 'internal' (professional).[8] External legal culture embraces the opinions, judgments, conceptions and beliefs of the general population regarding the legal system and its actual rules and institutions.[9] Internal legal culture, on the other hand, encompasses the ideology, principles, values, and knowledge of legal terminology and interpretations of those members of society who perform specialized legal tasks, such as advocates, judges and legal scholars. Legal specialists perform a twofold function: they are influenced by and reproduce the legal culture to which they belong and, at the same time, may give rise to new attitudes or values about law, thus creating legal culture. It should be noted further that diverse legal cultures can coexist within the same society. The term 'legal pluralism' is used to describe this situation.[10] Friedman defines legal pluralism as the existence of distinct legal systems or cultures within a single political community. He then distinguishes between *horizontal* legal pluralism, when subcultures or subsystems have equal status and legitimacy (as in a

---

[5] Friedman (1977), p. 103. See also Friedman (1994). John Bell defines legal culture as "a specific way in which values, practices, and concepts are integrated into the operation of legal institutions and the interpretation of legal texts." Bell (1995), p. 70. Erhard Blankenburg and Freek Bruinsma define legal culture in terms of the interplay of all four levels of legal phenomena: law in the books, comprising both substantive and procedural law; the institutional infrastructure (judicial system and legal profession); patterns of legally relevant behaviour (e.g. legal transactions); and legal consciousness. Blankenburg and Bruinsma (1991), pp. 8–9.

[6] See van Hoecke and Warrington (1998), p. 498.

[7] As Merryman observes, "Law is, among other things, a cultural expression; ideas about law are a deeply rooted, historically conditioned component of the culture. Such ideas powerfully limit and direct thinking about what law is and about the proper composition and operation of the legal system. Legal culture can be thought of as the inner logic of the legal system." Merryman (1998), p. 776. See also Visegrády (2001), pp. 204–205; Ehrmann (1976), pp. 6 ff.

[8] See Friedman (1977), p. 76.

[9] What Friedman refers to as 'claims consciousness' pertains to the eagerness or reluctance of the general population to involve themselves in litigation.

[10] For a closer look at legal pluralism consider Hooker (1975) and Griffiths (1986).

federal state), and *vertical* legal pluralism, when subcultures or subsystems are arranged in a hierarchical order (as in colonial or imported legal systems).[11]

We may conclude at this point that while legal tradition focuses on the historical and philosophical foundations of a legal system, legal culture focuses, largely, on the contemporary attitudes, practices, and behaviours related to law. Furthermore, while the concept of legal tradition is broad and general, pertaining to the entire legal system at a structural level, that of legal culture is more specific and localized, relating to how laws are interpreted, applied, and perceived in daily life.[12] Legal tradition provides the foundational basis of a legal system and, as such, it is more stable and enduring over time, whereas legal culture describes the living, evolving practices and attitudes towards law within a society and, as such, it is more dynamic and subject to change.

1.2 Defining Comparative Law

Comparative law can be defined as the study and analysis of different legal systems, legal traditions and legal cultures or aspects thereof with a view to obtaining knowledge that may be used for a variety of theoretical and practical purposes.[13] It involves comparing and contrasting the laws, legal institutions, and legal principles of various countries or regions to understand their similarities, differences, and underlying normative structures. Comparative law also involves the study of methodological problems and challenges encountered in cross-border and transnational legal research.[14] The primary purpose of comparative law is to gain insights into how different legal systems operate, how they address similar problems, and how they influence each other. The knowledge thus obtained can be used to improve legal systems, inform law reform, facilitate international cooperation, and enhance the understanding of foreign legal systems for better cross-border interactions and transactions. It is important to note here that the scope of comparative law extends beyond the mere study of legal rules and institutions. It also involves examining law as a broader social phenomenon, and considering the historical, social, economic, political, and cultural contexts in which laws and legal institutions emerge and develop. Given the vastness of its scope, the subject matter of comparative law can never be exhaustively treated, as it is impossible to imagine all the potential purposes and dimensions of legal comparison.

[11] Friedman (1975), pp. 196–197.

[12] According to Merryman, one can use the term 'legal culture' when referring to a specific legal system, and 'legal tradition' when referring to a historically related group of legal systems (e.g., the civil law tradition). Merryman (1998), p. 776.

[13] In the words of Konrad Zweigert and Hein Kötz, comparative law is "an intellectual activity with law as its object and comparison as its process." Zweigert and Kötz (1987), p. 2.

[14] Bogdan (1994), p. 18. And see Samuel (2014), pp. 8 ff.

To be considered comparative, a study must make explicit comparisons between two or more legal systems or aspects thereof. Anyone studying a foreign legal system will inevitably compare foreign legal institutions with those of their own country. Thus, any examination of foreign law can be considered implicitly comparative, as it aims to make one legal system intelligible to those trained in another. However, intuitive or implicit comparisons, as well as incidental and disconnected comparisons found in legal literature, can hardly qualify as comparative law. For a study to be recognized as a comparative study, it must explicitly adopt a comparative approach to the legal systems, institutions, or rules being examined. As Michael Bogdan has pointed out, "one cannot begin to speak about comparative law until the purpose with the work is to ascertain (and possibly also to further process) the similarities and differences between the legal systems, i.e., when the comparison is not merely an incidental by-product. …It is the comparison that is the central element of the comparative work."[15] Framing the inquiry in clearly comparative terms makes one think hard about each legal system being compared and about the precise ways in which they are similar or different. This does not, of course, mean that the independent study of foreign law is unprofitable. Indeed, besides being a valuable form of legal scholarship in its own terms, such study is an important starting point for any comparative inquiry. In this respect, an important aim of comparative law is to provide the tools that allow one to access foreign law with relative certainty and to derive the information needed to address a particular legal problem. Besides the study of foreign law, comparative law also includes the results or conclusions of comparative inquiries. Insofar as these results confirm the existence of general principles of law recognized by the legal systems of the world, one might view comparative law as a potential source of a transnational body of legal norms and standards. This body of law can be viewed as a *sui generis* form of positive law—a unique system of valid legal norms which, unlike those established by national legislators, derives its authority from its universal recognition among nations.[16]

1.2.1 Comparative Law: Method or Science?

Modern comparative law has evolved through various stages. In the nineteenth century, influenced by advancements in social and biological sciences and a renewed interest in history and linguistics, comparatists focused on the historical development of legal systems. They aimed to trace broad patterns of legal progress common to all societies. The concept of the organic evolution of law as a social phenomenon

[15] Bogdan (1994), pp. 21, 57. According to Konrad Zweigert and Hein Kötz, for a study to be regarded as a comparative law inquiry there must be "specific comparative reflections on the problem to which the study is devoted." Zweigert and Kötz (1977), p. 5. Consider also Reitz (1998), p. 618.

[16] This common body of law is listed among the sources of public international law in the Statute of the International Court of Justice.

led scholars to search for fundamental structures, or a 'morphology', of law and other social institutions. They sought and constructed evolutionary patterns to uncover the essence of the idea of law. As Franz Bernhöft remarked, "comparative law seeks to teach how peoples of common heritage elaborate the inherited legal notions for themselves; how one people receives institutions from another and modifies them according to their own views; and finally, how legal systems of different nations evolve even without any factual interconnection according to the common laws of evolution. It searches, in short, within the systems of law, for the idea of law."[17] In the late the nineteenth century, the French scholars Édouard Lambert and Raymond Saleilles, motivated by a universalist vision of law, advocated the search for what they referred to as the 'common stock of legal solutions' from amongst all the advanced legal systems of the world. This idea was introduced at the First International Congress of Comparative Law, held in Paris in 1900, which also adopted the view of comparative law as an independent and substantive science concerned with unravelling the patterns of legal development common to all advanced nations.[18]

However, in the first half of the twentieth century, scholars widely regarded comparative law as merely a *method* to be employed for various purposes in the study of law.[19] According to this view, comparative law is simply a means to an end, and thus the purpose for which the comparative method is utilized should define comparative law as a subject. This approach represented a shift in emphasis from comparative law as a distinct field of science and academic discipline to the uses of the comparative method within the study of law.[20] By focusing on the uses of the comparative method, comparatists categorized their activities into several distinct areas:

1. *Descriptive Comparative Law or Comparative Nomoscopy*: This category involves the mere description of foreign laws.
2. *Comparative Nomothetics*: This involves the comparative analysis of the strengths and weaknesses of different legal systems.
3. *Comparative Nomogenetics or Comparative History of Law*: This focuses on the evolution of legal concepts and institutions across various systems.
4. *Legislative Comparative Law*: This refers to the process whereby foreign laws are used as references for drafting new national laws.

---

[17] Bernhöft (1878) pp. 36–37. And see Rothacker (1957), p. 17. According to Giorgio del Vecchio, "many legal principles and institutions constitute a common property of mankind. One can identify uniform tendencies in the evolution of the legal systems of different peoples, so that it may be said that, in general, all systems go through similar phases of development." del Vecchio (1950), p. 688.

[18] See Dannemann (2019) p. 392.

[19] The co-called 'method theory' has been advocated by several eminent comparatists, including Frederick Pollock, René David, and Harold Cooke Gutteridge. See Siems (2018), pp. 6–7. Consider also Hall (1963), pp. 7–10.

[20] Scholars who regard comparative law as a mere method and empty of content of its own draw attention to the fact that in some languages the relevant subject is referred to as 'comparison of laws' (*Rechtsvergleichung*) or 'law compared' (*droit comparé*) and argue that the term 'comparative law' should be abandoned. See Örücü (2004), p. 14.

5. *Comparative Jurisprudence*: This perspective aims to assist in constructing general legal theories or tracing the origins and development of legal concepts and institutions, aiding legal philosophers and historians.[21]

Such divisions do not undermine the fundamental unity of the comparative method. As Harold Gutteridge noted, comparative law is not fragmented; it is not merely a collection of independent inquiries connected only by their focus on different legal systems. The core characteristic of comparative law, as a method, is its applicability to all types and fields of legal inquiry. It is used by legal philosophers, legal historians, judges, practitioners, and law teachers, encompassing both public and private law.[22]

One might say that those who view comparative law as a method and those who consider it a science approach it from different perspectives. When speaking of 'laws' and 'rules', the former typically refer to normative 'laws' and 'rules'—the kinds that legal professionals commonly work with. The latter, on the other hand, tend to perceive law primarily as a social and cultural phenomenon, seeing the relationship between law and society as governed by 'laws' that transcend any particular legal system. As John Henry Merryman observed, there is a notable distinction between 'professional' and 'academic' comparative law. Professional comparative law embraces "the sort of work that is principally of interest and value to lawyers, judges and legislators professionally engaged in dealing with concrete legal questions. Academic [comparative law] can be divided into humanistic and scientific. Humanistic scholarship is in the tradition of philosophical, historical, and literary description, narrative, interpretation, analysis, and criticism. ... scientific [refers to] scholarship that seeks to educe generalizations that can be used as the basis for explanations of and predictions about social-legal behaviour. These are categories of convenience and are not mutually exclusive."[23] One might assert that, at its simplest level, that of the description of differences and similarities between legal systems, the comparative method enables a better understanding of the characteristic features of specific legal institutions or rules. However, as the comparative method becomes more sophisticated, such as when it incorporates the socioeconomic and political structures, historical backgrounds, and cultural patterns underpinning legal institutions and rules, it starts to produce explanations based on interrelated variables. These explanations become progressively more scientific in nature.[24] One might argue that creating a sharp dichotomy between science and method can be epistemologically dangerous, as there is no science without method. The link

[21] See in general Gutteridge (1946), p. 4. See also Gutteridge (1953), p. 20.

[22] Consider Langrod (1957), pp. 363–369.

[23] Merryman (1998), p. 772.

[24] Among the leading scholars who advocated the intrinsic value of comparative law as a science and as an academic discipline is Ernst Rabel. According to him, "comparative law can release the kernel of legal phenomena from the shell of their formulae and superstructures and maintain the coherence of a common legal structure." Cited in Coing (1956), p. 670. On the view that comparative law constitutes both a science and a method consider Winterton (1975).

between the two is the model, which aims to relate real-world experiences to an abstract scheme of elements and relationships. As Anselm von Feuerbach has remarked, "The richest source of all discoveries in every empirical science is comparison and combination. Only by manifold contrasts the contrary becomes completely clear; only by the observation of similarities and differences and the reasons for both may the peculiarity and inner nature be recognized in an exhaustive manner. Just as the comparison of various tongues produces the philosophy of language, or linguistic science proper, so does a comparison of laws and legal customs of the most varied nations, both those most nearly related to us and those farthest removed, create universal legal science, i.e., legal science without qualification, which alone can infuse real and vigorous life into the specific legal science of any particular country."[25]

One might say, then, that comparative law is a branch of legal science, using the term 'science' to describe a discourse that operates simultaneously within the realm of facts and the conceptual framework that constitutes science. The objective of legal comparison, as a science, is to illuminate the similarities and differences between legal systems and to contribute to a deeper understanding of these systems.[26] Scientific comparative law is distinctive among the branches of legal science due to its primary reliance on the comparative method. In contrast, other branches may place greater emphasis on other methods of cognition, such as empirical induction or a priori speculation. Nonetheless, comparative law supports other branches of legal science and is, in turn, supported by them.[27]

Now, comparative legal inquiries can be approached from three distinct perspectives: *idealistic*, *realistic*, and *particularistic*. Idealistic theories of law posit that the validity of law is derived from an idea, principle or purpose inherent in law, such as justice, fairness, and the social good. These theories assert that enacted law can only be seen as an attempt to realize these ideals, with varying degrees of success. In contrast, realistic theories of law adopt an empirical view of law, relying on empirical evidence and hypotheses tested against real-world conditions. These theories are often developed within the interdisciplinary tradition of socio-legal studies, incorporating historical and sociological insights into the nature and functioning of law. Both idealistic and realistic approaches address the issue of generalization. The comparative study of legal systems reveals numerous differences and similarities. Idealistic universalism aims to identify the ideal form of law, while realistic

[25] A von Feuerbach, *Blick auf die deutsche Rechtswissenschaft, Vorrede zu Unterholzner, Juristische Abhandlungen* (München 1810), in *Anselms von Feuerbach kleine Schriften vermischten Inhalts* (Osnabrück 1833) 163; cited in Hug (1932), p. 1054. Consider also Barreau (1995), p. 51.

[26] See on this Sacco (1991a), p. 8; And see Sacco (1991b); Samuel (1998).

[27] Contemporary comparatists acknowledge the important relationship between law, history, and culture, and proceed from the assumption that every legal system is the product of several intertwining and interacting historical and socio-cultural factors. Alan Watson, for instance, defines comparative law as "the study of the relationship between legal systems or between rules of more than one system … in the context of a historical relationship … [the study of] the nature of law and the nature of legal development." Watson (1974), pp. 6–7.

universalism seeks to uncover the sociological laws that govern legal phenomena. Despite their theoretical differences, both approaches share the common goal of universalism: they strive to go beyond mere description to systematize and discover general explanatory principles that apply to legal phenomena across different times and places. Those who advocate for a particularistic approach to comparative law argue that general frameworks are too abstract to serve as study goals. This approach tends to reduce comparative law to a detailed description of various legal systems, viewing comparison as merely the translation of diverse legal rules into a single language. However, in most cases, an intermediate position between universalism and particularism is sought, insofar as it is recognized that every legal system has both specific and general characteristics.[28]

At this point, some reference to the distinction between legal dogmatics and legal theory may be useful. Legal dogmatics refers to a branch of legal scholarship that systematically analyses, interprets, and organizes existing legal norms and principles. It involves the detailed study and exposition of laws, legal concepts, and legal systems with the aim of providing clarity, coherence, and consistency to legal texts and practices.[29] Legal dogmatics plays a critical role in maintaining the stability and predictability of the legal system by offering authoritative interpretations and frameworks for understanding the law. As such, it is closely tied to legal practice, assisting judges, lawyers, and other legal practitioners in understanding and applying the law in specific cases. Legal theory, also known as jurisprudence, is a broader and more abstract study of law. It employs philosophical, sociological, and interdisciplinary approaches to address fundamental questions about the nature, purposes, and underlying principles of law and legal systems. Legal theory is more abstract and philosophical, concerned with the underlying principles and concepts of law, while legal dogmatics is more practical and concrete, dealing with the law as it exists. Although the scope of comparative law is broader than that of legal dogmatics, it is narrower than that of legal theory. Indeed, comparative law can be seen as an intermediate link between legal dogmatics and legal theory. While legal theory aims for a universal understanding of law, comparative law is inherently positioned between the particular and the general. The comparative law approach can be described as dialectical, as it focuses on the interplay between general explanatory principles and specific legal frameworks that have evolved over time.

Comparative law inquiries involve various levels of concretization or abstraction. Depending on the level at which a comparative study is conducted, distinctions are made between institutional or primary comparison, systematic comparison, and global comparison. Institutional or primary comparison focuses on the description, analysis, and evaluation of a specific legal institution or rule. A legal institution may be examined from several perspectives: historical—when one investigates the development of the institution over time; sociological—when one considers the

---

[28] This reflects the Aristotelian view of the legal order as a result partly of natural regularities and laws, and partly of the human will.

[29] Although an exposition of this kind may embody sociological, philosophical, moral, historical, and other considerations, its focus is on the interpretation and systematization of current law.

operation of the institution in different socio-cultural environments; and normative-dogmatic, when the focus of the inquiry is on semantic and juristic aspects of the institution. Systematic comparison involves a comparative examination of a set of legal institutions or rules within a particular branch of the law (e.g., private law). In this type of study, special attention is given to the interrelationships and interactions between the institutions under consideration and the general principles governing the relevant legal field. Finally, global comparison is concerned with the comparison of entire legal systems or legal traditions. John Henry Merryman distinguishes between text-centred and system-centred approaches to comparative law. The former, also known as 'rule-comparison', identifies law with authoritative texts and focuses on legal rules or norms. In this respect, a legal institution (e.g., the institution of property, the institution of contract) is understood as a structured body of rules in force within a particular jurisdiction. On the other hand, system-centred comparative law understands a 'legal system' as "the complex of social actors, institutions and processes referred to by members and observers of a society as 'legal' or 'juridical' or as directly related to or forming part of 'law' or 'the legal system' or the 'juridical order'. These interrelated people, institutions and processes constitute a social subsystem that is the society's legal system."[30]

By distinguishing various levels of comparison, scholars can gain a deeper understanding of the complexities and nuances of legal systems and institutions across different contexts. Elucidating the similarities and differences between legal systems requires considering a variety of exogenous and endogenous to the systems factors, both permanent and transient.[31] These factors are interrelated and interdependent, and their scale and complexity vary from society to society and country to country.

1.3 Comparative Law and Theoretical and Contextual Legal Studies: A Closer Look

Comparative law provides invaluable models, experiences, and resources to scholars and practitioners across diverse legal fields. Exploring the relationship between comparative law and other legal disciplines enhances our understanding of comparative law as a distinct field. It also clarifies how it interacts with, contributes to, benefits from, and overlaps with other areas of legal study. In this context, the relationship between comparative law and disciplines such as legal philosophy or jurisprudence, legal sociology, and legal history merits special attention.

---

[30] Merryman (1998), p. 775.

[31] See Rodière (1979), pp. 4 ff; Agostini (1988), pp. 10 ff.

1.3.1 Comparative Law and Legal Philosophy

Broadly speaking, legal philosophy, also known as jurisprudence or legal theory, is the theoretical study of law. It is concerned with fundamental questions about the nature of laws and legal systems, and their relationship to other social institutions. Legal philosophy seeks to provide a deeper understanding of law's role in society, its ethical implications, and its impact on human behaviour. The theoretical study of law focuses on four interrelated sets of questions:

1. *Questions of Authority*: These questions explore how the authority of law is established and maintained as a means of social control.[32]
2. *Questions of Value and Order*: This area is concerned with finding a measure to assess and order the diverse practices of law, whether through politics or ethics.
3. *Questions of Legal Judgment*: Legal philosophy dedicates significant effort to explaining the nature of judicial decision-making and the conditions that must be met for a judgment to be considered lawful.[33]
4. *Questions of Force and Justice:* Much of legal philosophy examines the intricate relationship between force or violence and the necessity for, and practice of, law.[34]

Legal philosophy operates at the level of describing, explaining, and evaluating laws and legal practices. It examines the workings of legal doctrine and connects law to other discourses such as philosophy, sociology, history, anthropology, and psychology.[35]

Three main schools of thought or traditions in legal philosophy can be discerned: (a) conceptual or analytical reasoning about law; (b) normative (axiological) or value-based reasoning about law; and (c) contextual (historical or sociological)

[32] The question 'is this a valid law?' is a question of authority.

[33] Questions of legal judgment focus, among other things, on the norms governing the practice of adjudication.

[34] Such force or violence could be immediate and physical (e.g., being arrested by a member of the police), or it could be the violence that follows from a judicial decision (e.g., sending a person to prison, or fining them). Furthermore, the notion of force can refer to the historical violence that establishes a political-legal regime.

[35] Continental European jurists draw a distinction between general theory of law and legal philosophy (in a narrow sense). The former focuses on the basic concepts, methods, classification schemes and instruments of the law; the latter examines the values that underpin legal systems, institutions, and rules. As Jean-Louis Bergel remarks, "the general theory of law starts out from the observation of legal systems, from research into their permanent elements, from their intellectual articulations, so as to extract concepts, techniques, main intellectual constructions and so on; the philosophy of law, on the other hand, is more concerned with philosophy than law for it tends to strip law of its technical covering under the pretext of better reaching its essence so as to discover its meta-legal signification, the values that it has to pursue, its meaning in relation to an all-embracing vision of humanity and the world." Bergel (1989), p. 4. Furthermore, the term legal science (*scientia juris*) is used to denote positive law organized in such a way that it rationalizes, scientifically, law as an empirical object. See on this Orianne (1990), pp. 73 ff.

analysis about law. These schools of thought differ in their construction of the subject-matter of legal philosophy but are not necessarily incompatible with one other. Conceptual or analytical jurisprudence claims to operate in the name of scientific rationalism, focusing on the logic of law. It articulates law as an abstract scheme of axiomatic principles, which may be peculiar to law or derived from social institutions. Much of analytical jurisprudence is concerned with clarifying the meaning of the term 'law' and terms embodying fundamental legal concepts, such as rights, duties, ownership, contracts, torts, and legal personality.[36] Analytical jurisprudence is associated with legal positivism—the theory that claims that there is no necessary connection between law and morality. Normative jurisprudence seeks to provide an ethical framework for evaluating legal practices in both general and specific contexts. From this perspective, the foundation of law is rooted not so much in a system of logic but in a system of values. In other words, this school of thought emphasizes the moral knowledge underlying the law. Normative analyses of law explore its grounding in moral, social, or political values.[37] Finally, contextual (historical and sociological) analyses of law view law as a system that exists and evolves within specific social and historical contexts. Sociological theories of law, in particular, emphasize that legal norms cannot be fully understood unless they are examined in light of social facts, including the intentions, interests, and evaluations of social agents.

Despite their differences, all types of legal theory share a common element: universalism. They aim to systematize and find a general means of explanation that would enable the understanding of legal phenomena regardless of time and place. Even if it is acknowledged that different legitimate approaches to legal phenomena exist, there is often an assumed starting point, typically declared as the ontological essence of law. The questions 'what is law?', 'how is law cognizable?', and 'what methods can be used for testing propositions concerning law?' must be coherent in some way. There is an intrinsic link between the ontology, epistemology, and methodology of law. Different possible ontologies exist: law as norms (a normativist ontology) or law as a social or psychological phenomenon (a realist ontology). Regardless of whether law is considered a matter of norms or facts, it must be

[36] In the English-speaking world, the systematic analysis of legal concepts was begun by the eighteenth century philosopher Jeremy Bentham (author of *The Principles of Morals and Legislation* (1789) and *The Limits of Jurisprudence Defined* (1782)) and was developed further by his student John Austin in his works *The Province of Jurisprudence Determined* (1832) and *Lectures on the Philosophy of Law* (1863). Modern forms of analytical jurisprudence have been developed by H.L.A. Hart, by the German jurist Hans Kelsen, author of *The General Theory of Law and State*, and by jurists influenced by the philosophy of language.

[37] Normative jurisprudence is primarily concerned with questions of 'ought', not just with questions of 'is'. In philosophy, questions of ought are sometimes called 'teleological' (from the Greek word *telos*, which means end), deontological (from the Greek word *deon*: ought to be done), ethical, or are grouped under theories of justice or theories about the purpose of law. Normative jurisprudence asks questions such as: Are the state's claims of authority to lay down legal rules and enforce them always justified or warranted? What direction should decisions aimed at law reform take? Can a person legitimately refuse to comply with the law?

acknowledged that it involves values. Law reflects certain values or serves as a means for achieving specific desired social states or goals. Thus, one might declare that law has three aspects: rules, behaviour (social context), and values. These aspects must be interconnected in some manner for a claim of universality to have substance, and different theories seek to attain this in different ways.[38]

Commentators agree that comparative law is highly valuable for empirically testing the propositions of legal philosophy.[39] These propositions can be assessed by reference to concrete comparative material, as there is a dialectical relationship between theory and practice that transcends beyond the confines of a single legal order—most legal theorists tend to assume a deductive universality in their analyses.

The starting point of comparative law is often the identification of common social problems across different legal systems. The key question is whether there are similarities or, conversely, differences in how these problems are regulated within these diverse legal frameworks. How should these similarities or differences be explained? Comparative law operates on two key assumptions:

(a) Law is not merely a manifestation of will but is also socially established. Therefore, legal regulations cannot be compared on a purely formal basis without considering their social context.
(b) While law originates from social relations, it cannot be entirely reduced to them, for otherwise the focus would shift from comparing laws to comparing the underlying social facts that laws express.

Law involves intentional elements; its 'facts' are institutional rather than mere 'brute facts' and should be interpreted within their social context.[40] Intentional

[38] In a number of theories, the uniting factor is derived from the existentialist concept of experience. This aligns with a school of thought in epistemology known as empiricism, which asserts that all knowledge (or at least all knowledge of matters of fact, as distinct from purely logical relations between concepts) is obtained through sensory experience and inductive reasoning. Empiricism has characteristically seen the acquisition of knowledge as a slow, piecemeal process, endlessly self-correcting and limited by the possibilities of experiment and observation. The development in the seventeenth and eighteenth centuries of what is referred to as the British empiricist school of philosophy (represented by John Locke, George Berkeley, and David Hume) was closely connected with the growth of experimental science. Much of contemporary British legal theory has its roots in the tradition of philosophical empiricism. In this context normativity, both in law and morals, is understood and explained in terms of social practices observable in the world. The nineteenth century jurist John Austin, for example, defined law in terms of a command supported by a sanction and as presupposing the habitual obedience of the bulk of a community to the commands of a sovereign himself not habitually obedient to anyone else. See Austin (1995). Similarly, HLA Hart's conception of legal obligation, although somewhat more complex, derived from the observation of people's actual practices analysed in terms of 'the internal point of view' crucial to their comprehension of and participation to these practices. Consider Hart (2012).

[39] Consider, e.g., Lawson (1977), p. 59.

[40] According to Ota Weinberger, "Institutional facts…are in a peculiar way complex facts: *they are meaningful normative constructs and at the same time they exist as elements of social reality.* They can only be recognised when understood as normative mental constructs and at the same time conceived of as constituent parts of social reality. As a meaningful normative construct, the law is the object of hermeneutic analysis. The real existence of the legal system is conditioned by a mul-

actions can be understood through a framework that includes goals—states of affairs with properties perceived as valuable—and epistemic conditions, which encompass knowledge about social structures, possible means, and means-goals relationships. Simply comparing the form and factual content of a legal institution to a similar one in another legal order is insufficient. There is an evaluative component attached to facts and concepts and this should not be ignored. Additionally, analysing social power is crucial when using an intentional model to understand and explain legal institutions. It is essential to ask: which social group has the power to impose its worldview—its knowledge, beliefs, and desires regarding society—as the basis for legal norms and their application? Once this question is addressed, one can analyse the factors that have led to the normative modelling of society through law in a particular way.

Comparative law provides additional perspectives for a more comprehensive understanding of law by highlighting both the commonalities and differences among various legal systems. It introduces new concepts, styles, organizations, and categorizations, thereby expanding the very notion of law and enabling jurists to address their concerns more effectively. Comparatists, in turn, cannot fully grasp laws and legal systems without understanding their underlying values, notions of justice, and general mentalities. Consequently, they should pay considerable attention to philosophical studies of law in their work. As the scope of comparative law extends beyond mere description to encompass broader theoretical issues, it inevitably overlaps with legal philosophy, despite their different emphases. As Richard Tur remarks, "The unity of general jurisprudence and comparative law consists in the unity of form and content; they are essential moments of legal knowledge, different sides of the same coin. General jurisprudence without comparative law is empty and formal; comparative law without general jurisprudence is blind and non-discriminating. General jurisprudence with comparative law is real and actual; comparative law with general jurisprudence is selective and clear-sighted."[41]

1.3.2 Comparative Law and Sociology of Law

In the late nineteenth century, a strand of thought emerged that identified law as a fundamentally social phenomenon and sought to investigate the various and evolving social forms in which law has appeared. Law was subsumed within broader social and historical structures, which were variously referred to as 'primitive,' 'matriarchal,' 'patriarchal,' 'civilized,' 'modern,' 'capitalist,' 'Protestant,' and so

titude of different circumstances: the law exists in the consciousness of people, meshes in with interconnections of behaviour-patterns and expectations, has standing relationships towards social institutions and observable events." MacCormick and Weinberger (1986), p. 113. Consider also Searle (1969), p. 51; Anscombe (1958).

[41] Tur (1977), p. 249. For an interesting perspective on the relationship between comparative law and legal philosophy see Ewald (1998). And see Ewald (1995).

on. Additionally, there was a focus on analysing law in relation to specific empirical and local social and institutional contexts. The sociological study of law, developed by classical sociologists of the late nineteenth and early twentieth centuries, paved the way for the sociology of law—a specialty devoted to studying law within the discipline of sociology.

The sociology of law is defined as the study of the relationship between law, legal institutions, and society. It examines how law and legal systems influence and are influenced by social norms, values, behaviours, and structures.[42] Key aspects of the sociology of law include:

(a) *Law in Social Context*: This area explores how laws are created, implemented, and enforced within specific social, cultural, and historical contexts.
(b) *Social Control and Order*: This looks at how laws function to maintain social order and control, addressing issues such as crime, deviance, and punishment. This includes studying how laws contribute to social stability and how they are used to manage conflicts.
(c) *Legal Institutions*: The sociology of law examines the roles and functions of various legal institutions such as courts, police, and correctional facilities. It investigates how these institutions operate and their impact on society.
(d) *Legal Culture*: This area focuses on the cultural dimensions of law, including how legal concepts, practices, and institutions are understood and interpreted by different social groups. It explores the symbolic aspects of law and its role in shaping social identities and relations.
(e) *Law and Social Change*: This perspective investigates the dynamic relationship between law and social change, including how legal reforms can drive social transformation and how social movements influence the development of new laws.

Legal sociology transcends national frameworks, examining the social functions of law to uncover the common and unique social conditions across diverse countries. Ideas from this field of study have influenced the development of other social sciences, shaping their approaches to law and bringing diverse perspectives together under the banner of a broader law and society tradition.

A key difference between legal sociology and comparative law is that the former is primarily descriptive and analytical, while the latter also addresses normative questions about how the law ought to be.[43] Nevertheless, there are many points of

---

[42] Roger Cotterrell describes the sociology of law as "the systematic, theoretically grounded, empirical study of law as a set of social practices or as an aspect or field of social experience." Cotterrell (2007), p. 1413. According to this author, scholars interested in the study of law have often turned "to sociology of law to escape the narrow disciplinary outlook of academic law." Cotterrell (2006), p. 6.

[43] Zweigert and Kötz (1977), pp. 9–10. Consider also Watson (1974), p. 183. However, this way of looking at the two disciplines has been called into question. While the sociology of law is mainly concerned with describing and understanding the relationship between law and society, normative questions and critiques can and do emerge within the field. For an interesting discussion of the relationship between comparative law and legal sociology see Riles (2019).

overlap between the two disciplines, as both explore how law influences and shapes human behaviour and the role law plays in society. Therefore, it is unsurprising that comparatists need legal sociology as much as legal philosophy and legal history. In seeking to understand the similarities and differences between legal systems and the practical operation of legal rules and institutions, comparative law can benefit significantly from a sociological approach. This approach invites one to consider not only the law in books but also the law in action, helping comparatists understand legal rules, institutions, and processes as products of social conditions, political structures, and economic realities. In short, it highlights the social contingency of law. However, the extent to which comparative law benefits from legal sociology depends on the comparatist's view of law. If this view is fundamentally positivist and doctrinal, construing law as a system of rules and principles, the distance between the two disciplines tends to increase, and legal sociology may be of little use to comparative law. Conversely, if the comparatist's approach to law is pragmatic and sociological, the distance between the two fields diminishes, making a sociological perspective integral to comparative law.[44]

In recent decades, comparatists have increasingly drawn on sociological perspectives in a variety of contexts. These include the study of non-Western and traditional legal systems, the comparative examination of legal cultures, and the role of customary norms, particularly in countries with a colonial history. There has been significant debate on the efforts to export Western concepts of legality and the rule of law to developing nations, as well as on the relative autonomy of law in the context of the 'legal transplants' theory. More recently, scholarship has focused on global legal pluralism and the role of supranational and non-state law.

1.3.2.1 Comparative Law and Comparative Lawyering

With the growing interest in legal sociology, particular attention has been given to the operation of groups and institutions related to law and social behaviour, such as lawyers and law offices. Decisions made by lawyers in their offices and the ways these decisions affect behaviour are significant aspects of the legal system. The rise of preventive law underscores the importance of the lawyering function. Lawyers, when appropriately consulted, make decisions that guide clients in ways that can prevent or minimize the risk of litigation. Although the preventive role of lawyers is difficult to measure, they play a crucial part in the dispute resolution process, often resolving more disputes outside of court than within it. This is achieved through negotiation, mediation, and arbitration, which help settle cases amicably and

---

[44] One should note here that much of the comparative method is derived from the work of Max Weber, one of the founders of modern sociology. Weber's theory has influenced the work of many distinguished comparatists, including Max Rheinstein, who declared that whenever comparative law delves into the social function of law, it becomes legal sociology. Rheinstein (1987), p. 28. For a closer look at Weber's views on legal sociology see Weber (1978), pp. 641–900. And see White (2001).

efficiently. Each settlement reached without judicial intervention reduces the burden on the court system, allowing it to focus on more complex cases that require formal adjudication. This process not only enhances the efficiency of the legal system but also contributes to a more orderly society by resolving conflicts in a timely and less adversarial manner.

The growing awareness of the importance of the lawyering function has significantly impacted the scope of comparative law. Comparative lawyering refers to the study and analysis of how lawyers operate in different legal systems and cultures around the world. This field examines the variations in legal practice, ethical standards, professional conduct, and the roles lawyers play in society across different jurisdictions. Key aspects of comparative lawyering include: (a) comparing how lawyers are educated and trained in different countries, including the requirements for becoming a lawyer, the structure of legal education, and the types of qualifications needed; (b) analysing the ethical standards and codes of conduct that govern lawyers' behaviour in various legal systems, and how these standards are enforced; (c) understanding the different roles lawyers play in various legal systems, such as advocates, advisors, negotiators, and mediators; (d) exploring how cultural, social, and historical factors influence the practice of law and the perception of lawyers in different societies; and (e) examining the effects of globalization on the legal profession, including the rise of multinational law firms, cross-border legal practice, and the harmonization of legal standards.

On a practical level, comparative research on the legal profession across different countries can uncover methods to improve the lawyering function. For example, it may suggest ways to reduce the cost of legal services, thereby enhancing the role of law offices in extrajudicial dispute resolution. On a theoretical level, the comparative study of legal practices in diverse societies can provide valuable insights into how these practices reflect the influence of various social and cultural norms. This approach can elucidate the relationship between positive or enacted law and custom, and between positive law and social behaviour. Additionally, it can be useful in evaluating the utility and potential social impact of proposed legal reforms. Comparative lawyering is a highly intellectual endeavour that encompasses a wide range of issues, including the criteria by which the lawyering function should be evaluated. As society constantly evolves, the relevant inquiries are continuous and perpetually enlightening.[45]

[45] For a discussion of the role of the legal profession see, in general, Abel and Lewis (1995) and Cain and Harrington (1994).

1.3.3 Comparative Law and Legal History

It has long been recognized that law and history are closely intertwined. The history of Western civilization, in particular, would be inconceivable without the influence of law. As Carl Joachim Friedrich remarked, "from feudalism to capitalism, from Magna Carta to the constitutions of contemporary Europe, the historian encounters law as a decisive factor."[46]

Legal history is the study of how law and legal systems have evolved over time and how they have shaped and been shaped by social, political, economic, and cultural contexts. Contemporary legal historians view legal systems as complex networks of norms, institutions, actors (such as judges, legislators, and lawyers), and symbols. They consider how these elements interact with other social forces to change, adapt, resist, or promote certain aspects of human society. Legal history is closely intertwined with the history of civilizations, operating within the broader context of social and cultural history. It encompasses both the history of individual legal systems and the legal histories of multiple societies, contributing to a universal history of law. Key aspects of legal history include: (a) tracing the origins and evolution of different legal traditions, such as civil law, common law, religious law, and customary law; (b) analysing how significant historical events, such as wars, revolutions and social movements, have influenced legal changes; (c) studying the contributions of influential judges, lawyers, legislators, and scholars in shaping the law; (d) understanding how legal doctrines and principles have developed and changed over time; (e) examining how laws have affected society, including issues of justice, rights, and equality; and (f) comparing the legal histories of different countries or regions to identify common patterns and differences. Legal history is interdisciplinary, drawing on methods and insights from general history, law, political science, sociology, and other fields. It provides a deeper understanding of the present legal system by illuminating its historical roots and evolution.

The role of the comparative method in the field of legal history cannot be overstated. As Frederic William Maitland pointed out, "history involves comparison and the … lawyer who knew nothing and cared nothing for any system but his own hardly came in sight of legal history. (…) an isolated system cannot explain itself, still less explain its history."[47] By comparatively examining legal systems at different stages of development, legal historians aim to trace the evolution of legal institutions and uncover historical connections between legal orders. The comparative method is also used for diachronic comparisons within a single legal order. A comparative perspective is as essential to the historical study of law as legal history is to the study and comparison of contemporary legal systems. Without the insights gained from historical-comparative studies, it is impossible to fully understand

[46] Friedrich (1963), pp. 233–234.

[47] Maitland (1911), pp. 488–489.

contemporary legal institutions, as they are significantly shaped by historical conditions, borrowings, and mutual influences of past legal systems in the past.[48]

Notwithstanding the interrelationship between legal history and comparative law, it is important to observe the significant differences between these fields regarding both their methodology and objectives. With respect to methodology, legal history and historiography exhibit a high degree of sophistication and consistency, whilst comparative law remains largely underdeveloped. This disparity can be attributed to the fact that legal historians generally receive extensive training and adhere to high professional standards, in contrast to comparative lawyers, who often lack graduate training in comparative law. Regarding objectives, legal history primarily focuses on understanding the past (and, by reflection, the present), with little emphasis on the practical utility of its findings for current legal practice. In contrast, the comparative study of law is pursued not only for the sake of knowledge but also for its practical applications, such as legal reform or the international harmonization of law. One might say that legal history is methodologically advanced but of limited practical use, while comparative law is methodologically unsophisticated but practically significant. The differences in methodology and objectives pose a significant obstacle to integrating the two disciplines and developing a true comparative history of law.[49]

1.4 Globalization, Legal Transnationalism, and Comparative Law

Over the past few decades, academic writings on globalization have proliferated. While many issues and interpretations are contested, globalization can broadly be defined as the process of bringing the world together through various forms of transnational activity: economic, political, cultural, demographic, technological, and more. The result of globalization is a more unified and interactive planet. The forces of globalization are closely interwoven and reinforce each other in powerful ways, leading to complex interactions at multiple levels, from the global to the very local. The forces of economic globalization include multinational corporations, global economic institutions (such as the World Trade Organization, the International Monetary Fund, and the World Bank), as well as global economic policies like free trade that these institutions support and promote. From a political science perspective, globalization focuses on issues such as the demarcation of the globe into nation-states, shifting territorial configurations, and novel forms of supranational social, economic, and legal regulation. The cultural dimension of globalization has

[48] As commentators have observed, comparative legal history is 'vertical comparative law', while the comparison of modern systems is 'horizontal comparative law'. Consider on this Ewald (1995), p. 1944.

[49] For a closer look at the relationship between comparative law and legal history consider Gordley (2019).

also been widely discussed and debated by scholars. Traditionally, cultural anthropologists viewed culture as something that differentiated one group of people from another, identifying otherness. Today, however, cultural anthropologists also study how global economic and political forces affect local cultures, including domestic legal cultures. They argue that one cannot adequately understand a particular culture by looking at it solely through a local perspective.

As a result of globalization and, in particular, the growing interconnectedness between national economic systems, the domestic insularity in which lawyers once practiced their profession is no longer sustainable. This interconnectedness extends beyond the domain of the economy to encompass environmental issues, human rights, migration, and transnational crime. The integration of the global economy, the rise of transnational problems like climate change and terrorism, and the need for governments to collaborate on regulating increasingly mobile people, money, and goods all point toward legal transnationalism. Today's lawyers must be equipped to provide advice on antitrust and competition, consumer protection, environmental, and employment law issues for each country where their clients operate. Transactional lawyers are expected to follow their clients across borders, negotiating mergers among internationally active companies and securing goods and services from global suppliers. Tax and estate lawyers must be ready to interpret—and, when appropriate, recommend—investments and holdings outside their clients' home states. Even family law, once the exclusive domain of domestic legal systems, has become internationalized in the context of transnational custody disputes. In the public sector, we have witnessed a proliferation of international conventions and agreements in international trade, human rights, and criminal law. A notable effect of globalization has been the growth of what is commonly referred to as 'transnational law.' Initially, transnational law encompassed public and private international law, as well as all domestic and foreign law related to cross-border issues.[50] In recent years, the term is often used to denote the amalgamation of common legal principles from domestic and international legal systems or the multidimensional international legal order resulting from globalization.

The internationalization of legal practice and the rise of transnational law present new challenges to comparative law. Firstly, comparative law must extend beyond the traditional framework of coexisting nation-states and address the more intricate and fluid relationships among multiple overlapping and intersecting legal orders. Secondly, its scope must broaden to include the study of international, transnational, and supranational regimes, such as the United Nations, the European Union, human rights frameworks, the global trade system, and environmental protection mechanisms.[51] Thirdly, comparative law must also consider non-state legal norms—rules, standards, and practices not created or enforced by formal state institutions—which

[50] On this issue, see Jessup (1956), p. 2; Shapiro (1993).

[51] For more on this issue see Reimann (2001).

play an increasingly significant role in today's world.[52] To effectively describe, explain, and help coordinate the world's diverse legal orders, comparative law must rethink many of its traditional dichotomies, such as the distinctions between national and international law or between private and public law. These dichotomies are insufficient to capture the complexity of the contemporary global legal environment.[53]

Addressing the challenges posed by globalization and the expansion of transnational law necessitates the development of a more scientific form of scholarship than what traditional comparative law has typically offered. This new scholarship should place greater emphasis on theory, understood broadly as the conceptual structures that serve as the principal mechanisms for perceiving, understanding, and structuring reality. Rethinking comparative law from a global perspective will involve all the main tasks of legal theory, including synthesis, the construction and elucidation of concepts, the development of both empirical and normative models, and the critical analysis of the assumptions and presuppositions that underpin legal discourse. Moreover, substantial work is needed on the question of the transferability of legal concepts across different cultures, especially since the harmonization of global legal statistics requires reasonably transferable concepts. In this respect, understanding diversity is vitally important in a world increasingly driven by trends toward global law. It is necessary to define tools that will prevent or minimize what is sometimes referred to as 'Western hegemonic thinking.' Comparative law scholars must develop the skills necessary to navigate, interpret, and critique laws and legal institutions while remaining aware of the dangers of uncritically projecting their own values and assumptions about law onto other societies.[54]

In response to the challenges posed by a more interconnected world, comparative law is diversifying and becoming increasingly sophisticated, moving beyond the outdated notion of a neatly compartmentalized world consisting solely of nation-states. However, truly integrating international and transnational regimes into the comparative law agenda requires more than merely cataloguing them alongside national legal systems. It necessitates a deeper understanding of how law functions across national, transnational, and international contexts. Additionally, it calls for an exploration of the dynamic interplay between these contexts, illuminating the complexities and interconnections that shape contemporary legal landscapes.[55]

---

[52] Unlike state law, which is enacted and enforced by governmental entities, non-state legal norms derive their authority from other forms of social or cultural recognition and adherence, such as social custom, religion, and principles established by international organizations or agreements. Non-state legal norms can be particularly significant in areas where state law is weak or absent, or in communities that maintain strong cultural or religious identities. Consider on this matter Teubner (1997).

[53] For a fuller discussion, see Biddulph and Nicholson (2008), Muir Watt (2019), Glenn (2001) and von Mehren (2001).

[54] See Werro (2001), pp. 1230–1232; Eberle (2009), pp. 485–486; Gerber (2001); Demleitner (1998).

[55] As Thijmen Koopmans has remarked, "For a long time it looked as though comparative law was a matter for academic research, difficult and, surely, very interesting, beautiful to know something about, but not immediately relevant to the daily life of the law. Over the last ten or fifteen years the

References

Abel RL, Lewis PSC (eds) (1995) Lawyers in society: an overview. University of California Press, Berkeley
Agostini E (1988) Droit comparé. Presses universitaires de France, Paris
Anscombe GEM (1958) On brute facts. Analysis 18(3):69–72
Austin J (1995) In: Rumble WE (ed) The province of jurisprudence determined. Cambridge University Press, Cambridge. (original work published 1832)
Barreau H (1995) L' épistémologie, 3rd edn. Presses universitaires de France, Paris
Bell J (1995) English law and French law – not so different? Curr Leg Probl 48:63–101
Bergel J-L (1989) Théorie générale du droit, 2nd edn. Dalloz, Paris
Berman H (1983) Law and revolution: the formation of the Western legal tradition. Harvard University Press, Cambridge
Bernhöft F (1878) Über Zweck und Mittel der vergleichenden Rechtswissenschaft. Zeitschrift für vergleichende Rechtswissenschaft 1:1–38
Biddulph S, Nicholson P (2008) Expanding the circle: comparative legal studies in transition. In: Nicholson P, Biddulph S (eds) Examining practice, interrogating theory: comparative legal studies in Asia. Martinus Nijhoff, Leiden, pp 9–23
Blankenburg E, Bruinsma F (1991) Dutch legal culture. Kluwer Publishers, Deventer
Bogdan M (1994) Comparative law. Kluwer, Deventer
Cain M, Harrington CB (eds) (1994) Lawyers in a postmodern world; translation and transgression. Open University Press, Buckingham
Coing H (1956) Das deutsche Schuldrecht und die Rechtsvergleichung. Neue Juristische Wochenschrift 569
Cotterrell R (2006) Law, culture and society: legal ideas in the mirror of social theory. Ashgate, Aldershot
Cotterrell R (2007) Sociology of law. In: Clark DS (ed) Encyclopedia of law and society: American and global perspectives. Sage, Thousand Oaks, pp 1413–1420
Cuche D (2004) La notion de culture dans les sciences sociales, 3rd edn. Le Decouverte, Paris
Dannemann G (2019) Comparative law: study of similarities or differences? In: Reimann M, Zimmerman R (eds) The Oxford handbook of comparative law, 2nd edn. Oxford University Press, Oxford, pp 390–422
del Vecchio G (1950) L' unité de l' esprit humain comme base de la comparaison juridique. Revue international de droit comparé 2(4):686–691
Demleitner N (1998) Challenge, opportunity and risk: an era of change in comparative law. Am J Comp Law 46(4):647–655
Eberle EJ (2009) The method and role of comparative law. Wash Univ Glob Stud Law Rev 8(3):451–486
Ehrmann HW (1976) Comparative legal cultures. Prentice-Hall, Englewood Cliffs
Ewald W (1995) Comparative jurisprudence (1): what was it like to try a rat? Univ Pa Law Rev 143:1889–2149
Ewald W (1998) The jurisprudential approach to comparative law: a field guide to 'rats'. Am J Comp Law 46:701–707
Friedman LM (1975) The legal system: a social science perspective. Russell Sage Foundation, New York
Friedman LM (1977) Law and society: an introduction. Prentice-Hall, Englewood Cliffs

legal climate seems to be changing. This evolution may be influenced by the process of European integration; it may also result from the fact that we are living closer together (the 'global village' situation); it may finally be an autonomous process, occasioned by the lawyer's search for fresh perspectives, in particular when completely new legal problems are to be solved." Koopmans (1996), p. 545.

Friedman LM (1994) Is there a modern legal culture? Ratio Juris 7(2):117–131
Friedrich CJ (1963) The philosophy of law in historical perspective. University of Chicago Press, Chicago
Gerber DJ (2001) Globalization and legal knowledge. Tulane Law Rev 75:949–975
Glenn HP (2001) Comparative law and legal practice: on removing the borders. Tulane Law Rev 75:977–1002
Glenn HP (2014) Legal traditions of the world: sustainable diversity in law, 5th edn. Oxford University Press, Oxford
Gordley J (2019) Comparative law and legal history. In: Reimann M, Zimmermann R (eds) The Oxford handbook of comparative law, 2nd edn. Oxford University Press, Oxford, pp 754–771
Griffiths J (1986) What is legal pluralism? J Leg Plur Unoff Law 18(24):1–55
Gutteridge HC (1946) Comparative law: an introduction to the comparative method of legal study and research. Cambridge University Press, Cambridge. repr. 2015
Gutteridge HC (1953) Le droit comparé, Introduction à la méthode comparative dans la recherche juridique et l'étude du droit. Librairie générale de droit et de jurisprudence, Paris
Hall J (1963) Comparative law and social theory. Louisiana State University Press, Baton Rouge
Hart HLA (2012) The concept of law, 3rd edn. Oxford University Press, Oxford. (original work published 1961)
Hooker MB (1975) Legal pluralism: an introduction to colonial and neo-colonial laws. Clarendon Press, Oxford
Hug W (1932) The history of comparative law. Harv Law Rev 45(6):1027–1070
Jessup P (1956) Transnational law. Yale University Press, New Haven
Koopmans T (1996) Comparative law and the courts. Int Comp Law Q 45:545–556
Krygier M (1986) Law as tradition. Law Philos 5:237–262
Krygier M (1991) Thinking like a lawyer. In: Sadurski W (ed) Ethical dimensions of legal theory. Rodopi, Amsterdam, pp 67–90
Langrod G (1957) Quelques réflexions méthodologiques sur la comparaison en science juridique. Revue internationale de droit compare 9(2):353–369
Lawson FH (1977) The comparison: selected essays, vol II. North-Holland Publishing Co, Amsterdam
MacCormick N, Weinberger O (1986) An institutional theory of law: new approaches to legal positivism. Reidel, Dordrecht
Maitland FW (1911) Collected papers. Cambridge University Press, Cambridge
Merryman JH (1985) The civil law tradition: an introduction to the legal systems of Western Europe and Latin America, 2nd edn. Stanford University Press, Stanford
Merryman JH (1998) Comparative law scholarship. Hastings Int Comp Law Rev 21(4):771–784
Muir Watt H (2019) Globalization and comparative law. In: Reimann M, Zimmermann R (eds) The Oxford handbook of comparative law, 2nd edn. Oxford University Press, Oxford, pp 599–623
Orianne P (1990) Apprendre le droit: Eléments pour une pédagogie juridique. Éd. Frison-Roche, Paris
Örücü E (2004) The enigma of comparative law. Springer, Dordrecht. repr. 2013
Reimann M (2001) Beyond national systems: a comparative law for the international age. Tulane Law Rev 75:1103–1120
Reitz JC (1998) How to do comparative law. Am J Comp Law 46(4):617–636
Rheinstein M (1987) Einführung in die Rechtsvergleichung. Beck, Munich
Riles A (2019) Comparative law and socio-legal studies. In: Reimann M, Zimmerman R (eds) The Oxford handbook of comparative law, 2nd edn. Oxford University Press, Oxford, pp 772–804
Rodière R (1979) Introduction au droit comparé. Dalloz, Paris
Rothacker E (1957) Die vergleichende Methode in den Geisteswissenschaften. Zeitschrift für vergleichende Rechtswissenschaft 60:13–33
Sacco R (1991a) La comparaison juridique au service de la connaissance du droit. Economica, Paris
Sacco R (1991b) Legal formants: a dynamic approach to comparative law. Am J Comp Law 39(1):1–34

Samuel G (1998) Comparative law and jurisprudence. Int Comp Law Q 47(4):817–836
Samuel G (2014) An introduction to comparative law theory and method. Hart Publishing, Oxford
Searle JR (1969) Speech acts. Cambridge University Press, Cambridge
Shapiro M (1993) The globalization of law. Indiana J Glob Leg Stud 1:37–64
Siems M (2018) Comparative law, 2nd edn. Cambridge University Press, Cambridge
Teubner G (ed) (1997) Global law without a state. Dartmouth, Aldershot
Tur R (1977) The dialectic of general jurisprudence and comparative law. Juridical Rev 22(2):238–249
van Hoecke M, Warrington M (1998) Legal cultures, legal paradigms and legal doctrine: towards a new model for comparative law. Int Comp Law Q 47:495–536
Visegrády A (2001) Legal cultures in the European Union. Acta Juridica Hungarica 42:203–217
von Mehren A (2001) The rise of transnational legal practice and the task of comparative law. Tulane Law Rev 75:1215–1224
Watson A (1974) Legal transplants: an approach to comparative law. Scottish Academic Press, Edinburgh
Weber M (1978) In: Roth G, Wittich C (eds) Economy and society: an outline of interpretive sociology. University of California Press, Berkeley
Werro F (2001) Notes on the purpose and aims of comparative law. Tulane Law Rev 75:1225–1233
White AA (2001) Max Weber and the uncertainties of categorical comparative law. In: Riles A (ed) Rethinking the masters of comparative law. Hart Publishing, Oxford, pp 40–57
Winterton G (1975) Comparative law teaching. Am J Comp Law 23(1):69–118
Zweigert K, Kötz H (1977) An introduction to comparative law. North Holland Publishing, Amsterdam
Zweigert K, Kötz H (1987) An introduction to comparative law, 2nd edn. Clarendon Press, Oxford

Chapter 2
Legal Comparatism in Antiquity, the Middle Ages, and the Early Modern Era

2.1 Introduction

Modern comparative law emerged in the nineteenth century as a response to the diversification of national legal systems in Europe. Its principal goal was to restore a measure of legal unity and lay the foundations for a science of law with the universal character of a genuine science. Additionally, the comparative study of legal systems aimed to assist national legislators in formulating and implementing laws and legal institutions that could meet the needs of a rapidly changing industrial society. However, this does not mean that legal comparison, as a form of cognition involving the study of foreign laws, had no place in earlier civilizations. Since ancient times, people have observed that the legal norms of different societies were not identical, and these diverse norms were sometimes considered when new laws and legal institutions were created.

This chapter outlines the role of legal comparatism in ancient, medieval, and early modern European legal thought and practice, with the aim of tracing key ideas that contributed to the rise of comparative law discourse. Special attention is given to the development of the comparative approach to law during the Renaissance and Enlightenment eras, periods marked by the emergence of scientific rationalism and the rise of modern nation-states and national legal systems.

2.2 Legal Comparatism in Greek and Roman Antiquity

In ancient Greece, the comparison of different legal systems served as a source of inspiration for statesmen, lawmakers and philosophers. In the realm of legislative practice, numerous examples demonstrate the frequent adoption of laws and legal institutions by one Greek city-state from another. Notable instances include the

G. Mousourakis, *Traversing Legal Traditions*, Springer Textbooks in Law,
https://doi.org/10.1007/978-3-031-94669-1_2

homicide laws of Athens,[1] which were emulated by several other Greek cities; the legislation of Charondas, a renowned lawgiver from Catania in Sicily,[2] which influenced several Greek colonies in Sicily and Southern Italy; the legislation of Solon in Athens,[3] elements of which were incorporated into the laws of Alexandria; and certain marriage laws from the city of Naucratis, which were adopted by Antinoopolis in Egypt.[4] References to legal comparison can also be found in the works of philosophers. For instance, Plato (429–348 BC), in his *Laws*, discussed the laws of several Greek and other states to formulate the basic political structure and laws of an ideal city-state named Magnesia.[5] Similarly, in his *Politics*, Aristotle (384–322 BC) examined the constitutions of 158 Greek city-states[6] before settling on his three preferred forms of government (monarchy, aristocracy, and constitutional government or 'polity') and their corrupt versions (tyranny, oligarchy, and democracy).[7] Although it is unclear whether the conclusions of Aristotle's work were based on extensive study of factual material or were largely speculative, there is little doubt that his general approach was empirical, rooted in observations on how people actually governed themselves. Aristotle relied on the comparative method, and what he and his students were doing may be regarded as an early form of comparative constitutional law.[8]

The idea that comparative material can serve as a basis for justifying positive law was embraced by Greek philosophers, such as Plato and Aristotle, in response to the prevailing legal particularism in the Greek world at that time. Each city-state (*polis*) had its own legal system, leading some thinkers, notably the Sophists, to conclude that law is a voluntary creation of man, entirely dependent on public opinion within

[1] See in general Gagarin (1979, 1981) and Phillips (2008).

[2] See Adcock (1927); Gagarin (1989), pp. 51 ff; Papakonstantinou (2008).

[3] On Solon's legislation see Leão and Rhodes (2015). Consider also Gagarin (1989), pp. 65 ff; Lewis (2007), pp. 64 ff; Owens (2010); Phillips (2013).

[4] See Bowman and Crowther (2020), p. 62; Bell (1940).

[5] The third book of the *Laws* discusses the origins and evolution of political systems and attempts to draw lessons for the legislator from the histories of several actual states, including Athens, Sparta, Argos, Crete, and Persia.

[6] As stated in this work, "Our purpose is to consider what form of political community is best of all for those who are most able to realize their ideal life. We must therefore examine not only this but other constitutions, both such as actually exist in well-governed states, and any theoretical forms which are held in esteem, in order to ascertain which features of them are good and useful." *Politics*, Bk 2, 1.

[7] Of this work, probably composed by members of Aristotle's school, only a small part has survived (the 'Athenian Constitution'). For a closer look see Bodenheimer (1974), pp. 6–10 and 13–14; Mulgan (1977), pp. 60–77 and 116–138.

[8] In this connection, reference should also be made to Theophrastus (372–287 BC), a student of Aristotle, who composed a work containing an exposition of the laws of Athens as compared with those of other city-states. This work was entitled '*peri nomon kata stiheion*' ('concerning the laws by reference to their subject-matter'). From the fragment of this work that has come down to us, it appears that Theophrastus' approach was quite modern in a sense, as it involved an attempt to bring to light the broad principles underpinning the various laws and then draw attention to particular rules that conflicted with them. See Zweigert and Kötz (1998), p. 49.

each particular *polis*. According to this view, there is no notion of law being grounded in a divine natural order; all law is positive law, a product of popular opinion in a specific time and place.[9] Aristotle's perspective on law represents a synthesis of sophistical legal thinking, with its inherent voluntarism, and Platonic natural law, which allows for the philosophical deduction of a rational, ideal law. Aristotle conceives of law as an ontologically unitary phenomenon: all law is the law of the *polis*.[10] However, the comparative study of law reveals certain common features across diverse legal systems. These features, though not incidental, indicate that under similar circumstances, it would be rational to enact similar laws.[11]

In the Hellenistic and Roman periods, the concept that juridical life was confined to the *polis* gradually waned under the influence of Stoic philosophy and concurrent socio-political developments. The Stoics envisioned a *cosmopolis*, a universal community governed by a divine, rational principle (*Nous*, *Logos*), in which all human beings are equal and equally capable of achieving a perfect moral life. According to them, natural law, founded on divine reason, is universally valid, immutable, and has the force of law *per se*, independently of human positivisation. Adhering to its

---

[9]This approach drew support from the doctrine of the Sophist philosopher Protagoras, who stated that "man is the measure of all things". This is understood to mean that all knowledge is relative to the person seeking it. What *seems* true to each person *is* true as far as they are concerned. Reality exists only in relation to one's own feelings and convictions. The Sophists pointed out that customs and standards of behaviour previously accepted as universal, absolute, and divinely created were, in fact, local and relative. It was against this view that Plato's work was directed. Plato objected to the general tendency in Sophist thinking to relativize the very norms that should possess absolute binding force. For him, law and laws are objects of free philosophical speculation, and they can be derived only from reason and the idea of the good. Every right law is merely an approximation of the eternal truths—an imperfect reproduction of the idea of law and justice. From this notion (associated with Plato's famous theory of forms) derives the strand of natural law thinking that regards values as having an eternal existence and eternal veracity.

[10]Greek thinkers believed that the concept of a state (*polis*) is inconceivable without simultaneously considering the concept of law (*nomos*). This implies that the state is identified with a specific type of legal order and is defined by its laws. This connection is evident in the close relationship between the laws and the community of citizens, which possesses a common will expressed through the legal order. The law is integral to the state because it makes it an object of knowledge. It can be described as the mould that imparts regularity and normality to the life of a given society. In this respect, the origin of law is inseparable from the development of the community as a whole, suggesting that legal development is fundamentally a social process. At the same time, the development of the community is inherently rational, as it can be understood through its legal order. This account perfectly agrees with the analysis of the origin and development of the law in Plato's *Laws* III.

[11]As Aristotle elaborates in Book 5 of the *Nichomachean Ethics* (1134b 8-24): "There are two kinds of political justice, one natural and the other legal. The natural is that which has the same validity everywhere and does not depend upon acceptance; the legal is that which in the first place can take one form or another indifferently, but which, once laid down, is decisive (…) [L]aws that are not natural but man-made are not the same everywhere, because forms of government are not the same either; but everywhere there is only one natural form of government, namely that which is best". Although Aristotle seems to have accepted that there is a natural and universal right and wrong, apart from any human ordinance or convention, he fell short of developing a natural law theory.

principles is essential for attaining justice, which is the essence of law in a broad sense. In this context, the universal recognition of a legal principle among nations, as revealed through the comparative study of laws, can be considered *prima facie* evidence that such a principle originates from natural law. As Carl Joachim Friedrich states, "the most that can be admitted is that there is a presumption in favour of the contention that a legal institution found in diverse *civitates* is part of the law of nature."[12]

A well-known example of alleged foreign influence on the drafting of legislation from early Roman history concerns the Law of the Twelve Tables, the oldest compilation of Roman law, enacted in the mid-fifth century BC. Writings by the orator and philosopher Cicero (106–43 BC) and the jurist Gaius (second century AD) suggest that they believed a legend stating that, before work on the law code began, a three-member commission was sent to Greece to learn from the laws of the famous Athenian lawgiver Solon and other Greek city-states. However, modern historians consider it unlikely that such a delegation was ever sent to Greece. This scepticism is supported by the fact that the preserved fragments of the Law of the Twelve Tables show very little direct Greek influence, although certain parallels with the laws of other early societies can be observed.[13] Nevertheless, as the story of the Twelve Tables indicates, the influence of the Greek civilization on Roman culture is undeniable.

The prevailing tendency among Roman jurists was to focus exclusively on the domestic law of Rome.[14] They aimed to preserve and develop this law by devising new practical applications for its doctrines and institutions. However, they did not consider their tasks to include analysing law from ethical, historical, or other general viewpoints, nor were they directly interested in the laws and customs of other nations. They maintained a conservative attitude and demonstrated an almost total lack of interest in legal concepts and norms originating externally or differing from the Roman legal system. Nevertheless, comparative inquiries into the laws and customs of different peoples appear to have influenced the formation of the so-called 'law of nations' (*ius gentium*), the body of Roman law that regulated economic relations between Roman citizens and foreigners.

From an early period, as Rome expanded its sphere of influence, the Romans realized that certain institutions of their own domestic law (*ius civile*) also existed in the legal systems of other nations. Contracts of sale, service, and loan, for

---

[12] Friedrich (1963), p. 32.

[13] The Law of the Twelve Tables shares some elements with Athenian law. According to Cicero, the relevant provisions derived from Solon's laws primarily address the resolution of disputes between neighbours, the right to form associations (*collegia*), and restrictions on funeral displays. See Cicero *de leg*. 2. 23. 59; 2. 25. 64. For more on the Law of the Twelve Table see Mousourakis (2007), pp. 24 ff.

[14] Like other ancient peoples, the Romans observed the principle of the personality of the laws, whereby each person lived according to the law of their community. Thus, the Roman *ius civile* (the civil law of the Roman state) applied exclusively to Roman citizens, and the term *ius civitatis* denoted the legal rights to which only Roman citizens were entitled.

example, were recognized by many systems, leading to the assumption that the principles governing these were universally applicable in the same manner. The Romans deemed that those institutions that Roman law had in common with other legal systems belonged to the law of nations (*ius gentium*) in a broad sense. However, this understanding of the *ius gentium* held little practical value for the Roman lawyers, as the specific rules governing such generally recognized institutions varied from one legal system to another. When the Romans began to trade with foreigners, they realized that their own domestic law was an unsuitable basis for developing trading relations. Foreigner traders were similarly disinclined to conform to the tedious formalities of the Roman *ius civile*. Consequently, some common ground had to be established as the basis for a common court that could adjudicate legal disputes involving citizens of different states. This common ground was found in the *ius gentium*, or the law of nations in a narrow, practical sense.

In contrast to the *ius civile* as the law that applied exclusively to Roman citizens, the term *ius gentium*, in a narrow, practical sense, came to signify that part of Roman law governing relations between citizens and foreigners, and between foreigners belonging to different states. This body of law was constructed from the edicts of the *praetor peregrinus*, the special magistrate dealing with legal disputes involving foreigners and, to a lesser degree, from the edicts of provincial governors. Addressing disputes involving people of diverse national backgrounds would have been difficult without employing rules based on common sense, expediency, and fairness that were confirmed by general and prevalent usage among many communities. In contrast to the *ius civile*, the *ius gentium* was characterized by its simplicity, adaptability, and emphasis on substance rather than form. For that reason, not only foreigners but also Roman citizens often relied on it as a means for resolving legal disputes. Moreover, elements of the *ius gentium* entered the edict of the *praetor urbanus* (the magistrate in charge of the administration of the *ius civile*) and thereby the domain of the domestic Roman law. However, it was only in the classical period of Roman law (the imperial period) that the further development of the *ius gentium* was influenced by comparative inquiries, and therefore was denationalized and turned into a form of 'universal law'. This was accomplished by a combination of comparative jurisprudence and rational speculation.[15] It was now claimed that the Roman *ius gentium* was binding upon all inhabitants of the empire because it was also natural law based on natural reason.[16]

The second-century AD jurist Gaius declared that Roman law was partly based on the law of nations (*ius gentium*), which he defined as "the law that natural reason establishes among all mankind [and] is observed by all peoples alike." He further explained that "the Roman people observe partly their own particular law [and] partly that which is common to all peoples."[17] Although Gaius did not provide a

[15] See Mommsen (1887), p. 606.

[16] For more on the concept of *ius gentium* see Kaser (1976), pp. 134 ff; Kaser (1971), pp. 202 ff; Schiller (1978), pp. 528–529.

[17] Gaius, *Institutes*, 1. 1. Consider also the *Digest of Justinian*, 41. 1. 1 pr., 9. 3 (Gaius).

detailed schema to distinguish which legal institutions belong to each category, he offered enough markers for us to reasonably understand what he considered domestic Roman law (*ius proprium Romanorum*) and what he considered *ius gentium* (or *ius commune*). For instance, acquiring title by delivery (*traditio*) from the owner was an institution of the *ius gentium* (which he identified with *ius naturale*), while acquiring title by mancipation (*mancipatio*) was an institution of domestic Roman law (*ius civile*).[18] Furthermore, the partnership (*societas*) that was contracted by simple agreement (*consensus*) among the parties was an institution of the *ius gentium*, while the partnership among heirs, which prevailed in early Rome, pertained only to Roman citizens.[19] Gaius' and other jurists' remarks suggest a comparative effort. Unfortunately, the process by which these comparisons were made was not recorded or, if it was, it has not survived. It is probable that this process occurred before Gaius' time, and he merely reported some of the conclusions.

A notable comparative work from the later imperial age is the *Lex Dei quam praecipit Dominus ad Moysen* ("The Divine Law Which the Lord Commanded unto Moses"), also known as *Collatio legum mosaicarum et romanarum* ("A Comparison between Mosaic and Roman Laws"). The exact date of this work is unclear, but the main body of the text appears to have been compiled in the first half of the fourth century.[20] The work is divided into titles, each beginning with a quotation from the first five books of the Old Testament (particularly the maxims of Moses), followed by extracts from the classical Roman jurists Paulus, Ulpianus, Papinianus, Modestinus, and Gaius, as well as imperial constitutions from the Gregorian and Hermogenian Codes.[21] Ostensibly, the primary purpose of this work was to compare selected Roman norms, mainly of a penal character, with related norms of Mosaic law to demonstrate that Roman law, in its basic principles, was consistent with Mosaic law and, in some sense, implemented it.[22]

---

[18] Gaius, *Institutes*, 2. 65. The *mancipatio* was a highly formal procedure employed when ownership over certain types of property, referred to as *res mancipi*, was transferred. *Res mancipi* included land and buildings situated in Italy, slaves, and draft animals, such as oxen and horses. All other objects were *res nec mancipi*. The ownership of *res nec mancipi* could be passed informally by simple delivery (*traditio*).

[19] Gaius, *Institutes*, 3.154–154a.

[20] The *Collatio legum mosaicarum et romanarum* was first edited in the sixteenth century but more materials were added later based on two manuscripts discovered in the nineteenth century. The standard modern edition is that of Theodor Mommsen included in his *Collectio librorum iuris anteiustiniani* (1890) III. And see Riccobono et al. (1968), pp. 543–589. For commentary consider Volterra (1930); Barone-Adesi (1992).

[21] The Gregorian Code (*Codex Gregorianus*, *c.* AD 291) contained imperial constitutions (mostly rescripts) spanning the reigns of Hadrian (AD 117–130) to Diocletian (AD 284–305); the Hermogenian Code (*Codex Hermogenianus*, *c.* AD 295) was a supplementary collection of constitutions that were issued during the reign of Diocletian. Although both these codes were unofficial collections, evidence suggests that their production was approved or authorized by Diocletian's government.

[22] The author of this work remains unknown, although the attempted comparison of Roman and Mosaic law suggests that he was probably of Jewish origin. For a closer look at the role of legal comparatism in Greek and Roman antiquity consider Donahue (2019), pp. 3–7.

2.3 Legal Comparatism in the Middle Ages

After the demise of the Roman Empire in the West in the fifth century, the once universal system of Roman law was replaced by a plurality of legal systems. The Germanic tribes that settled in the lands of the former Roman Empire lived according to their own laws and customs, while the Roman portion of the population and the clergy remained governed by Roman law. This marked a return to the ancient principle of the personality of law: the law applicable to a person was determined not by the territory they inhabited but by the people or ethnic group to which they belonged.[23] To facilitate the administration of law in their territories, some Germanic kings ordered the compilation of legal codes containing the personal Roman law that regulated the lives of many subjects. Among the most important compilations of Roman law that appeared during this period were the *Lex Romana Visigothorum* (AD 506), the *Edictum Theodorici* (late fifth century AD) and the *Lex Romana Burgundionum* (AD 517).

The coexistence of Roman and Germanic laws within the same territory led to an awareness of the differences between these systems and provided an opportunity for comparison. Evidence of such legal comparison is found in the influence that Roman law had on various Germanic legal codes that emerged in the West during this period. The most significant of these codes include the *Codex Euricinianus*, enacted about 480 by Euric, the Visigothic king, and drafted with the assistance of Roman jurists; the Salic Code (*Pactus legis Salicae*) of the Franks, composed in the early sixth century; the *Lex Ribuaria*, promulgated in the late sixth century for the Franks of the lower and middle Rhine region; and the *Lex Burgundionum*, issued in the early sixth century for the inhabitants of the Burgundian kingdom. Among these codes, the Visigothic and Burgundian Codes exhibit a stronger Roman influence compared to the Salic and Ripuarian Codes.

Over time, as the Roman and Germanic elements of the population fused, the division of people based on their ethnic origin began to dissolve. The system of personal laws was gradually replaced by the idea of law tied to a specific territory. A common body of customary norms, blending debased Roman and Germanic law, now governed all persons within a given territory. Thus, the diversity of laws no longer persisted as an intermixture of personal laws but as a variety of local customs. Despite this shift, awareness of different sources of law and occasional efforts to juxtapose these sources continued throughout the Early Middle Ages.[24]

---

[23] When Emperor Justinian reincorporated Italy into his empire in 553, his legislation was introduced to this region. However, its validity was short-lived, as most of the Byzantine territories in Italy fell to the Lombards in 568. After this period, Justinian's legislation only applied in those parts of Italy that remained under Byzantine control. The rest of Italy followed a pattern similar to that of Gaul and Spain, where Roman law persisted through the application of the principle of the personality of laws.

[24] In this connection reference should be made to the so-called 'code' of the Anglo-Saxon King Alfred (849–899). See Wormald (1999), pp. 265–285.

From the early eleventh century, the growth of trade, commerce, and industry, along with the restoration of some order in Europe, sparked a renewed interest in the study of law. Initially, this legal revival focused on the systematic exposition of native Germanic, particularly Lombard law.[25] However, it also encompassed feudal law,[26] canon law, and elements of pre-Justinianic Roman law, which were already integral to the Western European legal landscape. By the end of the eleventh century, the jurists known as the *antiqui*, who were primarily interested in Germanic law, were replaced by the *moderni*, who focused on Roman law. From the eleventh to the thirteenth century, the systematic analysis and interpretation of Justinian's Roman law became the primary concern of the jurists at the renowned law school of Bologna, known as the school of the Glossators.[27]

During the same period, the law of the Church, or canon law, became the object of systematic study. The task of the canonists was to amalgamate and harmonize the mass of canons contained in earlier canonical collections, which involved eliminating contradictions and updating matters as necessary. Their aim was to develop, expand, and systematise canon law as an independent body of law and not merely as a set of rules for ecclesiastics. The work that succeeded in transforming canon law into a complete system was the *Decretum*, also known as *Concordia discordantium canonum*, composed by Gratian, a Bolognese monk, around the middle of the twelfth century. The *Decterum Gratiani*, as this work became known, was both a code and a treatise on canon law. It systematically presented the rules governing priesthood, ecclesiastical jurisdiction, Church property, marriage, and the sacraments and services of the Church, without inconsistencies and contradictions. Gratian's method of arranging the materials was similar to that followed by the drafters of Justinian's Institutes.[28] Although it was published as an unofficial private work, Gratian's *Decretum* was soon recognized as an authoritative statement of canon law as it stood in his era. Like the codification of Justinian, it became the object of systematic study in universities. Students could obtain their degrees either in civil law or in canon law, or they could qualify as bachelors of both civil and canon law. In carrying out their work, the canonists relied heavily on Roman law, especially in areas where the basic canonical sources were deficient. As the Church was held to live by Roman law, it is unsurprising that whole branches of Roman law

[25] After the annexation of the Lombard kingdom by the Frankish Empire during the reign of Charles the Great (742–814), Lombard law continued to apply in northern Italy. At Pavia, the centre of Lombard Italy, a school of Lombard law was established, probably as early as the ninth century. The study of Lombard law was based primarily upon the *Liber Papiensis*, a work composed probably in the early years of the eleventh century. This compilation contained materials dating back to the Edict of Rothari, the foundational statement of Lombard Law, published in 643. Additionally, reference should be made to the *Lombarda* or *Lex Langobarda* and the *Expositio ad Librum Papiensem*, which combined materials drawn from both Lombard and Roman sources, with particular reference to the Institutes, the Code, and the Novels of Justinian.

[26] During this period, a sourcebook of feudal law, referred to as *Libri feudorum*, was used for study in Northern Italy.

[27] For further information on the school of the Glossators see Chap. 7 below.

[28] For more on this code see Winroth (2000).

were incorporated into the canonical system. A particularly noteworthy development of this period was the creation of a system of Romano-canonical procedure. This system, the result of a combined effort of canonist and civilian jurists, furnished the basis of the procedural system prevailing in civil law systems today.[29]

From the thirteen century a new breed of jurists, known as Post-Glossators or Commentators, sought to develop contemporary law by adapting Roman law, as expounded by the Glossators, to the social and economic conditions of their own era. The positive law enforced by the courts at that time comprised Roman law, the customary law of Germanic or feudal origin, the statute law of the Holy Roman Empire of the German nation (established in the tenth century) and self-governing municipalities, and canon law. The integration of these bodies of law into a unitary system was the concern of the Commentators. The result was the creation of a system of law in which the non-Roman elements were, so to speak, Romanized. In carrying out their work, the Commentators examined the statutes and customs of diverse states, and when they found it impossible to reconcile them with their learning, they simply recognized the differences. However, the Commentators did not rest content with merely acknowledging the existence of differing bodies of law; they also sought to explain why such differences existed and, on this basis, develop a system to address conflicts of laws.[30]

Medieval jurists regarded contemporary legal particularism as a problem, which they aimed to eliminate by adopting Roman law as the common foundation of European legal science. Their method involved both authority (*auctoritas*) and reason (*ratio*), but in this context, *ratio* does not refer to natural reason but to Aristotelian logical inference. As true medieval scholars, they interpreted Justinian's texts in the same manner that theologians interpreted the Bible or contemporary philosophers interpreted the works of Aristotle. Just as Aristotle was considered infallible and his statements applicable to all circumstances, so too were the texts of Justinian regarded by jurists as sacred and as the repository of all wisdom.[31] The law developed by the Glossators and the Commentators, resulting from a synthesis between non-Roman elements and glossed Roman law, achieved universal validity as *ratio scripta* and was received in nearly all European countries. Thus, it became the 'common law' (*ius commune*) of Continental Europe. Like the Latin language and the universal Church, the *ius commune* represented an aspect of the unity of the West during a time when there were no strong centralized political administrations or unified legal systems, but rather a perpetual contest among the competing and often overlapping jurisdictions of local, feudal, ecclesiastical, mercantile, and royal authorities.

The universal *ius commune* was juxtaposed with the *ius proprium*, the local laws of the diverse medieval political entities. Local law sometimes took the form of

[29] See on this van Caenegem (1973), vol. 16, chapter 2.

[30] For more on the school of the Commentators see Chap. 5 below.

[31] In the realm of philosophy this period corresponded with the full flowering of medieval scholasticism. The scholastic method, as applied to law, sought to expose the general principles of law so as to erect a comprehensive theory of law.

statutes or, especially in earlier times, evolved from custom. However, the universal and local laws were not necessarily antithetical; they were complementary and influenced each other. Statutory enactments, created to address situations not covered by the *ius commune*, were often formulated and interpreted according to the concepts developed by scholars of the *ius commune*. These scholars, in turn, considering concrete social and commercial issues and the need to address existing laws, incorporated local law into their analyses. In their roles as judges, lawyers, and state officials, jurists trained in Roman law regarded local law as an exception to the *ius commune* and therefore subject to restrictive interpretation. They tended to interpret local law using concepts and terminology derived from Roman law, thereby harmonizing it with the *ius commune*.[32]

In the sixteenth and subsequent centuries, the medieval feudal nobility was defeated by a central authority that represented the interests of the expanding urban class and the lower gentry. As a result, legislation gained prominence as a means of enforcing centripetal policy. Furthermore, the concept of national social consensus, or the belief that members of a nation had common interests, emerged as a fundamental assumption. During this period, the nascent idea of the nation-state and the increasing consolidation of centralized political administrations had diverse effects on the relationship between received Roman law and local legal systems.

2.4 Pioneers of Comparative Law in the Early Modern Era

In the sixteenth century, the homologation of customary law in France[33] prompted jurists to employ the comparative method in the study of law. This method had already been prevalent among the French humanists, who are also credited with inventing of the modern historical method.[34] Guy Coquille's work *Institution au*

[32] For a closer look at the role of legal comparatism in the Medieval age see Donahue (2019), pp. 7 ff.

[33] Homologation of customary law refers to the official recognition and validation of customary laws, which varied significantly from one region to another, by the state or judicial authorities. Homologation sought to integrate these customs into the formal legal framework, providing them with legal authority and ensuring their consistent application. An important starting-point in this process was King Charles VII's Ordinance of Montils-les-Tours, issued in 1453, which mandated the codification of customary laws in various regions of France. This was an attempt to bring uniformity to the diverse legal practices across the kingdom and make the legal system more consistent and predictable. Although this attempt proved largely ineffectual, it was repeated by subsequent monarchs and a large part of the customary law had been committed to writing by the end of the sixteenth century. Although the publication of the customs removed much of the confusion caused by local differences, legal unity was not fully achieved. In addition to the differences between Northern and Southern France, considerable regional diversity persisted even within each of the main territorial divisions until the enactment of the Napoleonic Code in 1804. See Robinson et al. (1994), pp. 200–201.

[34] The method adopted by the humanist scholars in France became known as *mos gallicus* (in contradistinction with the *mos italicus* of the Bolognese jurists) or *Elegante Jurisprudenz*. For more on

droit des Francois, an extensive commentary on French customary law published in 1607, is particularly noteworthy in this context.[35] The *Institution* begins with the titles of the homologated customs of Nivernais, stating the rules for each title and comparing them with relevant rules from other regions. For instance, in the section on marital property, Coquille notes that in Nivernais, a married woman must obtain her husband's consent to make a testament. He then points out that the same rule applies in Burgundy, while in Rheims, Auxerre, Berry, and Poitou, the rule is the opposite. Once the conflict is identified, Coquille, like other jurists of this era, proceeds to ask: what is the 'true rule' that should apply in such cases? His argues that the correct rule is that a testament cannot depend on the will of another person, as this is the nature of a testament. He justifies this view by referencing certain passages in the Digest of Justinian. Although this interpretation does not invalidate the customs of Nivernais or Burgundy, it limits the scope of the relevant rule: if the custom is abolished, then the rule has no force because the *ius commune* provides otherwise. Coquille does not deny the existence of customs contrary to the *ius commune* but insists that such customs must be clearly stated and considers them applicable only in those exceptional situations to which they pertain.[36] Occasionally, Coquille argues that a customary rule is flat-out wrong, either because it goes against higher principles or because it does not correspond with social reality (though this argument is usually only hinted at). Fifteenth-century Italian jurists, on the other hand, rarely employ arguments of this type. However, Coquille and other French jurists of this period went beyond earlier Italian jurists in another respect: they sought to find common principles that underpinned the divergent French customs when no reference to the *ius commune* could be made. Additionally, they utilized principles and methods of the *ius commune* in analysing a customary system of law that was not regarded as being founded on the *ius commune*.[37]

In the seventeenth and eighteenth centuries, as national systems of law began to burgeon, European jurists focused on the study and mastery of their own domestic laws. Despite the absence of a systematic practice of comparative law, several scholars emphasized the importance of examining foreign legal systems to make a true assessment of their own. The English philosopher Francis Bacon (1561–1626), for example, proposed developing a system of universal justice to assess and improve

---

the humanist movement see Chap. 5 below.

[35] Coquille (1523–1603) was a prominent jurist and legal scholar, best known for his contribution to the development and systematization of French customary law. He studied humanities in Paris and law in Padua and Orleans and practiced law in the customary courts of Nivernais, where he worked as an advocate for the local *Parlement*. (The *parlements* were regional judicial and legislative bodies in France's *Ancien Regime*: the social and political system that prevailed in France under the late Valois and Bourbon dynasties from the fifteenth century to the time of the French Revolution in the later eighteenth century.) See Robinson et al. (1994), p. 202.

[36] A similar approach was followed by the Italian jurists of the fifteenth century when they were faced with statutes that were contrary to the *ius commune*: such statutes were narrowly construed.

[37] For a closer look at sixteenth-century French legal thought and the role of legal comparatism see Donahue (2019), pp. 13 ff. And see Seong-Hak Kim (2021).

the legal system of one's country.[38] However, although Bacon asserted that the propositions of this system should be based, at least to some extent, on the study of diverse legal systems, he set them down without supporting them with foreign legal material. The German philosopher Gottfried Wilhelm von Leibniz (1646–1716) proposed creating a 'legal theatre' (*theatrum legale*) where the legal systems of all nations at different times could be portrayed and compared, though this idea was never realized.[39] Hugo Grotius (1583–1645), a leading representative of the School of Natural Law, employed the comparative method to place the ideas of natural law on an empirical footing.[40] Believing that the universal propositions of natural law could be proved not only by mere deduction from reason but also by recognition of certain legal rules and institutions in diverse legal systems, Grotius used legal material from different countries and ages to illustrate and support his system of natural law. Other members of the Natural Law School who utilized this method include John Selden (1584–1654), Samuel von Pufendorf (1632–1694), and Christian von Wolff (1679–1754).

Selden, a celebrated jurist whose legal opinions were highly esteemed by his contemporaries, emphasized the importance of the comparative study of laws. He believed this should be based on a profound understanding of the history of legal institutions across different countries and eras. His work is regarded as marking the beginning of comparative legal history.[41] Pufendorf was the first modern legal philosopher to elaborate a comprehensive system of natural law that encompassed all branches of law.[42] His work significantly influenced the structure of later legal codifications, particularly the 'general part' commonly found at the beginning of civil codes, where the basic principles of law are laid out. Drawing on the work of Leibniz and Pufendorf, Wolff proposed a system of natural law that aimed to make law a rigorously deductive science. His system had considerable influence on the eighteenth and nineteenth-century German codifiers and jurists, as well as on legal education in German universities.[43] Although Pufendorf and Wolff had different

[38] Bacon, *De dignitate et augmentis scientiarum* (1623) bk. Viii, c.3. And see Dauchy et al. (2016), pp. 170 ff; Scarciglia (2023), p. 17.

[39] Leibniz, *Nova Methodus discendae docendaeque Jurisprudentiae* (1667). For a closer look see Wigmore (1917).

[40] On the rise and influence of the School of Natural law see Chap. 7 below.

[41] Selden explored the influence of Roman law on the common law of England and applied the comparative method in the *History of Tithes*, one of his best-known works, and in his treatises on Eastern legal systems. And see Scarciglia (2023), pp. 17–18; Robinson et al. (1994), p. 220.

[42] Pufendorf is best known for his book *De jure naturae et gentium* (On the Law of Nature and Nations, 1672). His earlier work *Elementa jurisprudentiae universalis* (Elements of a Universal Jurisprudence, 1660) led to his being appointed to a chair in the Law of Nature and Nations especially created for him at the University of Heidelberg. According to Erik Wolf, "Pufendorf combines the attitude of a rationalist who describes and systematizes the law in the geometrical manner with that of the historian who rummages through the archives and who explores historical facts and personalities." Wolf (1944), p. 298. And see Dauchy et al. (2016), pp. 219 ff; Robinson et al. (1994), pp. 214–216.

[43] Robinson et al. (1994), p. 216.

methods, both sought to base their theories partly on deduction and partly on the observation of facts. While their approach differs from that employed by modern comparatists, some aspects of their work can be described as comparative, as they occasionally relied on examples from diverse legal systems to support the premises. Elements of the comparative method can also be found among Enlightenment thinkers, such as Robert-Joseph Pothier (1699–1772), who were only partially aligned with the Natural Law School, as well as among scholars not belonging to this school, such as Giovanni Battista Vico (1668–1744) and, notably, Charles-Louis de Secodat, baron de la Brède et de Montesquieu (1689–1755), who is probably the most important precursor of modern comparative law.

Pothier was born and studied in Orleans, where he served as a judge and, from 1749, as a university professor. His first major work, *La coutume d'Orléans avec des observations nouvelles*, published in 1740,[44] focused on the customary law of his hometown. His next significant work was a comprehensive treatise on Roman private law titled *Pandectae justineaneae in novum ordinem digestae cum legibus codicis et novellae* (1748–1752). This was followed by a series of writings on various legal institutions.[45] In his works, Pothier aimed to address the issues in legal practice caused by the fragmentation of the law in France by systematically restating fundamental legal concepts and principles.[46] Through this approach, he greatly contributed to the unification of private law in France. His work is considered the final expression of legal doctrine in France before the Revolution and, due to the high regard in which he was held, inevitably influenced the compilers of the Napoleonic Civil Code of 1804.[47]

Although Pothier was not a particularly original thinker, he possessed immense knowledge and demonstrated a thorough familiarity with the writings of

[44] A revised edition of this work was published in 1760.

[45] These included his *Traité des obligations I et II* (1761–1764); *Traité du contrat de vente* (1762); *Traité des retraits* (1762); *Traité du contrat de constitution de rente* (1763); *Traité du contrat de louage*; (1764); *Traité du contrat de société* (1764); *Traité de cheptels* (1765); *Traité du contrat de prêt de consomption* (1766); *Traité du contrat de dépôt et de mandat* (1766); *Traité du contrat de natissement* (1767); *Traité du contrat de mariage I et II* (1766); *Traité du droit de domaine de propriété* (1772); and *Traité de la possession et de la prescription* (1772). Pothier's works were widely used by jurists and lawyers throughout the eighteenth and nineteenth centuries. An important collection of these works in 11 volumes was published by Dupin in 1824/1825.

[46] For example, in his treatise on the institution of ownership, Pothier demonstrates how the fundamental Roman law concept of property could theoretically resolve many of the discrepancies within a feudal system that encompassed various forms of property and related entitlements.

[47] The Civil Code adopted numerous legal solutions proposed by Pothier, particularly in the area of the law of obligations. Additionally, the drafters of the Code embraced the systematic structure favoured by Pothier. This structure, rooted in the work of the classical Roman jurist Gaius and latter followed by Justinian, categorizes the law into three main divisions: persons, things (including obligations and succession), and actions.

Commentators such as Bartolus,[48] Humanists like Cujas,[49] and Natural Lawyers such as Pufendorf. He devoted his enormous energy and organizing ability to gaining a profound understanding of French law as it existed in the period preceding the Revolution. Pothier went beyond mere description, giving new dimensions to French law, particularly in the fields of property law and the law of obligations. In these areas, it is unsurprising that the superior methodology of Roman law, with which Pothier was so thoroughly acquainted, came to dominate the largely disorganized and fragmented customary law. This, however, does not mean that he neglected customary law. Although he holds a central place in the mainstream of the civilian tradition, he adopted a great deal from customary law. Like medieval jurists, Pothier cited and accurately reported rules and principles derived from various legal systems: divine law, natural law, Roman law, Salic law, and the customary law of France. Nevertheless, he was not concerned with exploring and explaining the differences and similarities between these systems. Rather, his primary effort was directed at reconciling all these systems into one coherent whole. Thus, in contrast to other thinkers of his period, it is difficult to see a clear connection between Pothier and modern comparatists.[50]

Vico was born in Naples, Italy, and spent most of his professional life as a professor of rhetoric at the University of Naples. Though trained in jurisprudence, he read widely in classics, philology, and philosophy, which significantly influenced his original views on history, historiography, and culture. His thought is most fully expressed in his mature work, *Scienza Nuova* (*The New Science*), first published in 1724.

Initially, Vico adopted the methods of Grotius and Descartes but later departed from them to develop his own theory of *scienza* (science or knowledge). Contrary to Cartesian philosophy, which emphasizes clear and distinct ideas—the simplest elements of thought from which all knowledge could be derived a priori through deductive rules—Vico argued that full knowledge of anything involves discovering *how* it came to be as a product of human action. He criticized Descarte's hypothetico-deductive method for reducing phenomena that cannot be expressed logically or mathematically to mere illusions. Vico maintains that phenomena can only be known through their origins or causes. In *The New Science*, he seeks to develop a conception of science that allows understanding the facts of the human world without reducing them to mere contingency or explaining them through speculative ideas generated by traditional metaphysics. To this end, he introduces a distinction between 'the true' (*il vero*) and 'the certain' (*il certo*): the former, being eternal and universal, is the object of knowledge (*scienza*), while the latter, connected with human consciousness (*coscienza*), is particular and individuated. From this

[48] Bartolus of Saxoferrato (1314–1357) was the most influential of the Commentators and one of the greatest jurists of all time.

[49] Jacques Cujas (Cuiacius, 1522–1590), probably the greatest of the French Humanists, taught at Cahors, Valence, Paris and Bourges.

[50] For more on Pothier's contribution see Donahue (2019), pp. 24–26; Descamps (2019), pp. 245–258; Stein (1999), pp. 114–115; Robinson et al. (1994), p. 256.

perspective, he argues that philosophy contemplates reason, which leads to knowledge of the true, while history, in a broad sense, observes the empirical phenomena of the world arising from human choice: the languages, customs, and actions of people that make up civil society. When combined, philosophy and history can yield a full knowledge of both the universally true and the individually certain.

In his work Vico endeavours to develop a science that, by drawing on the history of human ideas, customs, and deeds, would reveal the universal principles governing human nature. This requires tracing human society back to its origins to uncover a common human nature and a universal pattern through which all nations progress. Although nations may not develop at the same pace, they all pass through certain distinct stages and evolve through a consistent and uninterrupted order of causes and effects. Vico emphasizes the cyclical nature of historical development: society progresses towards perfection but never fully attains it, as it is periodically interrupted by a regression to a more primitive condition.[51] From this reversal, history begins anew, albeit from a higher point than previously reached.

Moreover, Vico observes that nations independently adopt largely identical norms based on the common sense of mankind (*senso comune del genero umano*). This observation is founded on an anthropological theory suggesting that under certain circumstances, people tend to act similarly. In many respects, Vico's approach is akin to that of modern comparatists, who do not merely compare legal rules and institutions but also examine the broader historical and socio-cultural context in which these rules and institutions are born and evolve.[52] For Vico, the historical and comparative study of diverse cultures and nations is crucial for understanding the processes through which civilizations emerge, develop, and decline.[53]

2.4.1 Montesquieu

Montesquieu studied law at the University of Bordeaux and, from 1716, held the office of Président à Mortier in the Parlement of Bordeaux, a body primarily responsible for judicial and administrative function at the time. In 1748 he published his

[51] See Berlin (2000), p. 47.

[52] On the epistemological foundations of Vico's thought see le Moigne (1999), p. 49.

[53] In his conception of history, Vico employs what may be described as an early version of the so-called 'reification theory', based on the concept of 'alienation' (*Entfremdung*). According to this theory, people are dominated for long periods by entrenched beliefs, especially religious ones, as well as laws and institutions. Although these constructs are created by human beings, they derive their authority from the illusion that they are objective, eternal, and universal, much like the laws of nature. Vico argues that the 'common mind' or collective consciousness of each people or nation regulates social life in a manner reflecting these prevailing beliefs. See on this Berlin (2000), pp. 135–136; Scarciglia (2023), pp. 19–20.

seminal work *On the Spirit of the Laws* (*de l'esprit des lois*), in which he aimed to elucidate the nature of laws and legal institutions.[54]

According to Montesquieu, positive law is oriented towards the idea of justice. However, since positive law constitutes only an approximation of justice rather than a realization of it, the question arises on what basis such an approximation can be envisaged. In addressing this question, Montesquieu departs from the natural law tradition, which sought to provide a universal answer, and proposes that each society must formulate its laws in accordance with its own particular spirit. This spirit is shaped by the environmental, historical, cultural, political, and economic conditions in which a society develops. From this perspective, the key to understanding different legal systems is to recognize that they should be adapted to a variety of diverse factors. Specifically, laws should be tailored "to the people for whom they are framed, to the nature and principle of each government, to the climate of each country, to the quality of its soil, to its situation and extent, to the principal occupation of the natives… [Laws] should have relation to the degree of liberty the constitution will bear, to the religion of the inhabitants, to their inclinations, riches, numbers, commerce, manners, and customs…. [Laws] have relations to each other, as also to their origin, to the intent of the legislator, and to the order of things on which they are established; in all of which different lights they ought to be considered."[55]

Montesquieu further asserts that laws are relative and that there are no inherently 'good' or 'bad' laws in the abstract. Each law must be evaluated in relation to its context, including its background, surroundings, and antecedents. A law can only be regarded as good if it fits well into this framework. Montesquieu's relativistic approach to laws and legal systems was influenced by sixteenth-century French thought, particularly that of *Huguenot scholars who questioned the universal authority of Roman law and the universal power of the Roman Catholic Church.*[56] *Furthermore,* unlike seventeenth-century Natural Law School writers, Montesquieu's work is characterized by a significant increase in the cultural and geographical diversity of the examples used. This is undoubtedly a result of the greater knowledge European had acquired about countries like China, Japan, and India.

[54] Montesquieu's work represents an early attempt to construct a theory of positive law and a veritable science of legal history. See Rabello (2000).

[55] *De l'esprit des lois,* Book 1, Ch. 3. As Harold Gutteridge has remarked, it was Montesquieu "who first realized that a rule of law should not be treated as an abstraction but must be regarded against a background of its history and the environment in which it is called upon to function." Gutteridge (1949), p. 6. It should also be noted here that, according to contemporary scholars, Montesquieu's work set the foundations of modern sociology. As Leopold Pospisil has pointed out, "With his ideas of the relativity of law in space as well as in time, and with his emphasis on specificity and empiricism, [Montesquieu] can be regarded as the founder of the modern sociology of law in general and of the field of legal dynamics in particular." Pospisil (1971), p. 138. Consider also Launay (2001); Donahue (2019), pp. 22–24; Kelly (1992), pp. 273–274.

[56] The Huguenots were French Protestants who, due to religious persecution, were forced to flee France to other countries in the sixteenth and seventeenth centuries.

Consequently, less emphasis is placed on examples from antiquity, although these are certainly not absent.[57]

Montesquieu identified three types of government: republican (ruled by an elected leader), monarchical (ruled by a king or queen), and despotic (ruled by a dictator). These types are grouped based on whether they are founded on law: republican and monarchical governments rest on law, whereas despotic ones do not. Montesquieu's doctrine of the separation of powers, whether applied in a monarchical or republican context, requires that the powers be clearly delineated by the basic law and fixed with respect to their respective functions and domains. Only when these conditions are met can political freedom be ensured.[58] Montesquieu's critique of absolute monarchy, as articulated in *The Spirit of the Laws*,[59] stems from the implicit conflict between the French *parlements* and the monarchy.[60] He sought to defend the *parlements* and the interests of the aristocracy they represented by comparing France and Western Europe with other societies and historical forms of government. His primary aim was to demonstrate the superiority of European political systems, particularly constitutional monarchy, over Asian absolutism and other 'primitive' systems.[61] However, he did not support European territorial ambitions, as he believed such ambitions were characteristic of absolutism.[62]

In his work, Montesquieu combines a rational principle—that of the constitutional state—with various laws of nature to interpret the legal system of each society as an expression of its 'spirit'. This 'spirit' is not elevated to the status of an absolute principle, as in Hegel's philosophy, but remains relative and, ultimately, subject to the abstract measure of rational justice.[63] It is important to note, however, that Montesquieu seeks to detach laws from the constraints of rationalism[64] and explain them by reference to the nature of things on the ground and in terms of their

---

[57] See Launay (2001), p. 24.

[58] Kelly (1992), pp. 278–279.

[59] See Launay (2001), pp. 25–26.

[60] The great majority of the members of these bodies belonged to the French aristocracy and tended to react with hostility whenever the monarchy introduced measures taken to undermine their own privileges.

[61] It should be noted here that not all of Montesquieu's contemporaries subscribed to his notion of 'Asian despotism', and this may be explained by reference to the political differences that prevailed among different classes in society. For instance, Voltaire, who opposed the privileges of the aristocracy and steadfastly supported the monarchy against the power of the *parlements*, spoke very highly of China and other Asian systems of government. See Launay (2001), p. 37.

[62] It is thus unsurprising that Montesquieu regarded the conquest of America by the Spanish as disastrous for both Spain and the peoples of that continent and opposed similar actions by the Europeans in Asia and Africa.

[63] Montesquieu's notion of the spirit of a nation bears a certain resemblance to Rousseau's concept of the general will and to some extent corresponds to the modern notion of a system of values or beliefs. According to him, one should not attempt to change the habits and customs of a people by means of laws, for such laws would appear too tyrannical. *On the Spirit of the Laws* XIX, 14.

[64] The notion that one can arrive at substantial knowledge about the nature of the world by pure reasoning alone and without appeal to any empirical premises.

functions. He identifies nine different kinds of law: the law of nature; divine law; ecclesiastical law; international law; general constitutional law; special constitutional law; the law of conquest; civil law; and family law. These forms of law are seen as disparate legal orders whose principles must be clearly differentiated to create sound legal rules. From this general assumption, Montesquieu develops a series of important distinctions between diverse fields of law.[65] The basis of these distinctions appears to be the legislative power of establishing the constitution or basic law. In *The Spirit of the Laws*, Montesquieu emphasizes the importance of the comparative study of the laws of diverse nations for legislators. He declares that "to determine which of the systems [under comparison] is most agreeable to reason, we must take them each as a whole and compare them in their entirety."[66] He adds that "as the civil laws depend on the political institutions, because they are made for the same society, whenever there is a design of adopting the civil law of another nation, it would be proper to examine beforehand whether both [nations] have the same institutions and the same political law".[67]

Montesquieu's ideas found genuine resonance among later philosophers both in France and abroad. A prominent case in point is Hegel who, in his *Philosophy of Right*, pays tribute to the French thinker in many ways while simultaneously adapting Montesquieu's views to fit his own absolute idealism. In his discussion of the character of law and its relation to the 'nature of things', Hegel asserts that natural law, or law from the philosophical point of view, is distinct from positive law. However, he emphasizes that interpreting their difference as an opposition and contradiction would be a gross misunderstanding. He then acknowledges that Montesquieu proclaimed the true historical view and the genuinely philosophical position, namely that law, both in general and in its particular provisions, should be treated not as something isolated and abstract but rather as a subordinate moment in a whole, interconnected with all the other features that constitute the character of a nation and an epoch. It is only when viewed in this interconnectedness that laws acquire their true meaning and justification.[68] Later, in the section on constitutional law, Hegel reiterates the praise by stating that Montesquieu, above all, highlighted both the interconnectedness of laws and the philosophical principle of always treating the part in relation to the whole.[69]

---

[65] However, these distinctions are not rigid, for particular social institutions may feature in more than one legal sphere depending on the possibility of their possessing different legally relevant aspects.

[66] *On the Spirit of the Laws*, Book XXIX, 11.

[67] *On the Spirit of the Laws*, Book XXIX, 13. See Scarciglia (2023), p. 19.

[68] Hegel (2001), p. 24.

[69] Hegel (2001), pp. 199–200.

References

Adcock FE (1927) Literary tradition and early Greek code-makers. Camb Hist J 2(2):95–109
Barone-Adesi G (1992) L'età della Lex Dei. Jovene, Naples
Bell HI (1940) Antinoopolis: a Hadrianic foundation in Egypt. J Roman Stud 30(2):133–147
Berlin I (2000) Three critics of the enlightenment: Vico, Hamann, Herder. Pimlico, London
Bodenheimer E (1974) Jurisprudence: the philosophy and method of the law. Harvard University Press, Cambridge
Bowman A, Crowther C (2020) The epigraphy of Ptolemaic Egypt. Oxford University Press, New York
Dauchy S, Martyn G, Musson A et al (eds) (2016) The formation and transmission of Western legal culture. Springer, Cham
Descamps O (2019) Robert-Joseph Pothier: (1699-1772). In: Descamps O, Domingo R (eds) Great Christian jurists in French history. Cambridge University Press, Cambridge
Donahue C (2019) Comparative law before the Code Napoléon. In: Reimann M, Zimmermann R (eds) The Oxford handbook of Comparative Law, 2nd edn. Oxford University Press, Oxford, pp 3–28
Friedrich CJ (1963) The philosophy of law in historical perspective. University of Chicago Press, Chicago
Gagarin M (1979) The prosecution of homicide in Athens. Greek Roman Byzantine Stud 20(4):301–323
Gagarin M (1981) Drakon and early Athenian homicide law. Yale University Press, New Haven
Gagarin M (1989) Early Greek Law. University of California Press, Berkeley
Gutteridge HC (1949) Comparative law: an introduction to the comparative method of legal study and research, 2nd edn. Cambridge University Press, Cambridge
Hegel GWF (2001) Philosophy of right. Dyde SW (trans). Batoche Books, Kitchener
Kaser M (1971) Das römische Privatrecht, 2nd edn. Beck, Munich
Kaser M (1976) Römische Rechtsgeschichte. Vandenhoeck & Ruprecht, Göttingen
Kelly JM (1992) A short history of western legal theory. Clarendon Press, Oxford
Launay R (2001) Montesquieu: the specter of despotism and the origins of comparative law. In: Riles A (ed) Rethinking the masters of comparative law. Hart, Oxford, pp 22–38
Le Moigne J-L (1999) Les epistimologies constructivistes, 2nd edn. PUF, Paris
Leão DF, Rhodes PJ (2015) The laws of Solon: a new edition with introduction, translation and commentary. IB Tauris, London
Lewis JD (2007) Early Greek lawgivers. Bristol Classical Press, London
Mommsen T (1887) Romisches Staatsrecht. S Hirzel, Leipzig
Mousourakis G (2007) A legal history of Rome. Routledge, New York
Mulgan RG (1977) Aristotle's political theory: an introduction for students of political theory. Clarendon Press, Oxford
Owens R (2010) Solon of Athens. Sussex Academic Press, Brighton
Papakonstantinou Z (2008) Lawmaking and adjudication in Archaic Greece. Duckworth, London
Phillips DD (2008) Avengers of blood: homicide in Athenian law and custom from Draco to Demosthenes. Franz Steiner Verlag, Stuttgart
Phillips DD (2013) The law of ancient Athens. University of Michigan Press, Ann Arbor
Pospisil L (1971) Anthropology of law: a comparative theory. Harper and Row, New York
Rabello AM (2000) Montesquieu et la codification du droit privé (le code Napoléon). Revue internationale de droit comparé 52(1):147–156
Riccobono S, Baviera G, Ferrini C, Furlani G, Arrangio-Ruiz V (eds) (1968) Fontes iuris romani anteiustiniani II, 2nd edn. AG Barbera, Florence
Robinson OF, Fergus TD, Gordon WM (1994) European legal history, 2nd edn. Butterworths, London
Scarciglia R (2023) Methods and legal comparison. Edward Elgar, Cheltenham
Schiller AA (1978) Roman law: mechanisms of development. Mouton, Hague

Seong-Hak Kim M (2021) Custom, law, and monarchy: a legal history of early modern France. Oxford University Press, Oxford
Stein P (1999) Roman law in European history. Cambridge University Press, Cambridge
van Caenegem RC (1973) History of European civil procedure (Chapter 2). In: Cappelletti (ed) International encyclopedia of comparative law, vol 16. Mohr, Tübingen
Volterra E (1930) Collatio legum mosaicarum et romanarum. Bardi, Rome
Wigmore JH (1917) Nova Methodus discendae docendaeque Jurisprudentiae. Harv Law Rev 30(8):812–829
Winroth A (2000) The making of Gratian's Decretum. Cambridge University Press, Cambridge
Wolf E (1944) Grosse Rechtsdenker der deutschen Geistesgeschichte. Mohr, Tübingen
Wormald P (1999) The making of English law: King Alfred to the twelfth century. Blackwell, Oxford
Zweigert K, Kötz H (1998) An introduction to comparative law, 3rd edn. Oxford University Press, Oxford

Chapter 3
The Evolution of Modern Comparative Law: Early Milestones

3.1 Introduction

The development and consolidation of the nation-state during the eighteenth and nineteenth centuries, along with the growth of national legislation, ended the era of legal unity in Europe. National ideas and the movement towards the codification of law gave rise to a sources-of-law doctrine that tended to exclude legal rules and institutions lacking explicit recognition by national legislators or judiciaries. Whether one emphasized the will of the nation as a source of law or believed that law expressed the organic development of the national spirit, law came to be viewed as a national phenomenon. In this context, foreign law was not regarded as authoritative; it could only provide, through the medium of legal science, examples and technical models for national legislators. The nationalization of legal sources was driven not only by ideological factors but also by social and economic factors. Industrialization and the form of capitalism that emerged in the late eighteenth century were key conditions contributing to this development.[1]

The industrial revolution in Europe spurred an extraordinary growth in legislative activity, driven by the need to modernize the state and address new problems generated by scientific, technological and economic developments. In drafting legal codes, national legislators increasingly relied on large-scale legislative comparisons that they undertook or mandated. Interest in the comparative study of laws, especially in the fields of commercial and economic law, was also precipitated by the

[1] It should be noted here that a certain degree of universalism was characteristic of the nineteenth-century laissez-faire economic theory, which advocated free trade. Regarding internal economic policy, empirical data was utilized regardless of its origin. However, while the interests of industry and trade were partially international, the fundamental assumption was a strong liberal state capable of ensuring internal discipline.

G. Mousourakis, *Traversing Legal Traditions*, Springer Textbooks in Law,
https://doi.org/10.1007/978-3-031-94669-1_3

expansion of economic activities and the growing need to develop rules facilitating commercial transactions at a transnational level.[2]

By the end of the nineteenth century, comparative law was associated with a grand ambition: the unification of law or the development of a common law for all civilized mankind (*droit commun de l'humanité civilisée*). This vision was articulated at the first International Congress of Comparative Law held in Paris during the summer of 1900. At the Congress, the renowned French comparatist Raymond Saleilles asserted that the primary aim of comparative law is to discover, through the study of diverse legal systems, norms and principles common to all civilized societies. These universal norms and principles could serve as the foundation for a relatively ideal law akin to a flexible natural law.

The ideal of legal unification was reiterated at the twentieth anniversary of the International Association for Comparative Law and National Economics, held in Berlin on the eve of the First World War. It was proclaimed that the association should continue to strive for the harmonization of law under the principle through legal comparison towards legal unification. Believing in the basic unity of human nature and reason, many jurists sought to identify the best solutions to legal problems through the comparative study of laws. They argued that the differences in laws and legal codes indicated that not all drafters fully understood the principles of reason concerning certain common issues. Therefore, they saw their primary task as eliminating confusion and highlighting the legal solutions that rational thought would support.[3]

A second strand of universalism, associated with the development of comparative law, was historicism, which in the nineteenth century became the fundamental paradigm of nearly all sciences. The primary objective of legal-historical comparatism was to uncover the objective laws governing the process of legal development and, following the pattern of the Darwinian theory of evolution, to extend the scope of these laws to other social phenomena. The concept of the organic evolution of law as a social phenomenon led jurists to seek out fundamental structures, or a 'morphology', of law and other social institutions. They aimed to construct

[2] The growing interest in comparative law during this period is reflected in the establishment of various organizations and scholarly societies dedicated to the comparative study of laws. These include the Société de Législation Comparée in France; the Internationale Vereinigung für vergleichende Rechtswissenschaft und Volkswirtschaftslehre in Germany; and the Society for Comparative Legislation in England. The growth of interest in comparative law is also manifested by the increasing emphasis on comparative law as a subject in legal education.

[3] Notwithstanding the decline of the idea of natural law, many scholars still believed in a universal truth, hidden behind historical and national variations, which could be brought to light through the comparative study of laws. In the words of the German philosopher Wilhelm Dilthey, "As historicism rejected the deduction of general truths in the humanities by means of abstract constructions, the comparative method became the only strategy to reach general truths." Rothacker (1957), p. 15. In 1852, Rudolf von Jhering deplored the degradation of German legal science to "national jurisprudence", which he regarded as a "humiliating and unworthy form of science" and called for comparative legal studies to restore the discipline's universal character. See von Jhering (1955), p. 15. See in general David (1950), p. 111; Stolleis (1998), pp. 7–8, 12, 24; Zweigert and Kötz (1987), pp. 52 ff. Consider also Hug (1932), p. 1069.

evolutionary patterns that would enable them to uncover the essence of the 'idea of law'.[4]

The efforts of nineteenth-century scholars, who aimed to explain legal phenomena through a historical-comparative lens, laid the foundation for the recognition of comparative law as a distinct branch of legal science and an academic discipline. This approach was significantly influenced by other sciences that employed the comparative method of analysis. Similar to comparative religion, comparative philology, and later, comparative linguistics, comparative law became part of a broad group of disciplines based on the comparative method. The rapid growth of comparative law during this period, however, should primarily be attributed to historical realities. Developments such as the proliferation of national legislation, often involving the borrowing of legal models from one country to another, the expansion of transnational trade and commerce, and the spread of European colonialism around the world, compelled jurists to look beyond national legal frameworks, thus giving further impetus to comparative legal studies.

3.2 The Development of Comparative Law in Germany

By the end of the sixteenth century, Roman law had become firmly established as the common law of Germany.[5] Germanic law had largely been rejected in favour of the more advanced Roman system, and German jurisprudence had essentially become Roman jurisprudence.[6] However, in some parts of Germany, such as Saxony,

[4] The influence of this school of though is reflected in more recent discussions of the nature and aims of the comparative study of laws. According to Mario Rotondi, comparison is one of two methods (the other being the historical method) whose combination can provide a comprehensive understanding of law as a universal social phenomenon. Legal science relies upon these methods to detect and construe the (natural) laws governing the evolution of this phenomenon. In searching for relations between different legal systems or families of legal systems, one seeks to discover, to the extent possible, certain stable features in this evolutionary process that may allow for the foreshadowing of future developments regarding the character and orientation of legal systems and branches of law. Rotondi (1968), p. 13. According to Hessel Yntema, comparative law, following the tradition of the *ius commune* (*droit commun*), embodies a deep-rooted humanist vision concerning the universality of justice. It is based on the study of historical phenomena and seeks to discover and rationally construe the common elements of human experience related to law and justice. In today's world, the primary task of comparative law is to elucidate the conditions under which economic and technological development can occur within the framework of the Rule of Law. Yntema (1958), p. 698. Giorgio del Vecchio remarks that "many legal principles and institutions constitute a common property of mankind. One can identify uniform tendencies in the evolution of the legal systems of different peoples, so that it may be said that, in general, all systems go through similar phases of development." del Vecchio (1950), p. 688. See also Bernhöft (1878), pp. 36–37. And see Rothacker (1957), p. 17.

[5] German scholars use the phrase '*Rezeption in complexu*' (full reception) to describe this development.

[6] The Roman law that was received embodied the Roman law of Justinian, especially the Digest or Pandects, as interpreted and modified by the Glossators and the Commentators. This body of law

Germanic customary law survived, and certain institutions of Germanic origin were retained in the legislation of local princes and cities. From the sixteenth to the eighteenth century, legal practitioners and jurists executed the process of moulding Roman and Germanic law into a single system. This effort led to the development of a new approach to the analysis and interpretation of Roman law, known as *Usus modernus Pandectarum* (modern application of the Pandects/Digest).

In the early years of the nineteenth century, the French Civil Code, enacted under Emperor Napoleon in 1804, garnered significant attention in Germany. As Napoleon extended his rule over Europe, parts of Germany adopted this law code. However, the rise of German nationalism during the wars of independence compelled many scholars to emphasize the necessity of a uniform law code to unite Germany under one system of law and aid in its political unification. The Historical School, led by the influential jurist Friedrich Carl von Savigny (1779–1861), argued that the introduction of a German Code should be postponed until the historical circumstances that shaped the law in Germany were fully understood and the current needs assessed.[7] The influence of the Historical School, coupled with the lack of an effective central government, resulted in the abandonment of early proposals for codification. Scholarly attention shifted from the largely ahistorical natural law approach to a historical examination of the two main sources of law in Germany: Roman law and Germanic law. Scholars divided into two main groups, one concentrating on Germanic law and the other on Roman law, delving beyond the *ius commune* into the *Corpus Iuris Civilis* and other ancient sources. The latter group, known as the Pandectists, set themselves the task of studying Roman law to uncover its 'latent system' and adapt it to contemporary needs. In executing this task, these jurists elevated the study of the *Corpus Iuris Civilis*, particularly Justinian's Digest, to its highest level, producing an elaborate and systematic body of law (*Pandektenrecht*) for nineteenth century Germany.

The dominance of the Historical School and the conceptual jurisprudence of the pandectists account for the relative neglect of comparative law in Germany, particularly during the period 1840–1870.[8] In the early part of the nineteenth century, comparative law attracted the interest of several jurists, the most eminent of whom was

---

was further modified by German jurists to fit the conditions of the times and thereby a Germanic element was introduced into what remained a basically Roman structure. And see Chap. 7, below.

[7] Savigny elaborated his thesis in a pamphlet entitled 'On the Vocation of our Times for Legislation and Legal Science' (*Vom Beruf unserer Zeit für Gesetzgebung und Rechtswissenschaft*). von Savigny (1814).

[8] Nineteenth-century German legal positivists tended to discount the value of comparative law as a branch of legal science. In the words of Ernst Rudolf Bierling, comparative law is "of little or no use for learning the principles of law." Bierling (1894), p. 33. Even after German legal positivism yielded to the neo-Kantian search for 'just law' in the early twentieth century, some German jurists rejected the notion that comparative law could be relied upon as a means of discovering the just law. They argued that the comparative study of laws that were factually conditioned could never enable us to grasp those unconditionally valid modes of thought needed for the scientific study of law. Consider Stammler (1922), p. 11.

Eduard Gans (1798–1839).[9] Gans studied law at Berlin, Göttingen, and finally Heidelberg, where he attended Hegel's lectures and became thoroughly imbued with the principles of Hegelian philosophy. In his famous work on the law of inheritance,[10] Gans attempted a comparison of a diversity of legal systems, including Ancient Greek and Roman, Scandinavian, Scottish, Portuguese, Chinese, Indian, Hebrew, and Islamic, in the spirit of *Universalrechtsgeschichte*, or Universal History of Law.

From a philosophical standpoint, the origins of German comparative law can be traced to Hegel's work, particularly his notion of the variety and asymmetry of human civilizations and their constituent institutions, such as law and ethics. According to Hegel, law and ethics are expressions of a historical evolution that is the manifestation of a national spirit, and the various national spirits collectively manifest the world spirit. However, Hegel's view of law should not be confused or equated with that of the Historical School. Although both Hegel and the Historical School adopted the notion of national spirit, their uses of this concept were fundamentally different. In the Historical School's theory, the national spirit served as a rather nebulous unifying principle, providing a general framework for studying the development of legal institutions. In contrast, in Hegel's philosophy, the national spirit was given the function of expressing universal freedom, a principle designated as the manifestation of the world spirit.[11]

A revival of interest in comparative law occurred in the later part of the nineteenth century. This resurgence was driven partly by a practical interest in studying foreign laws for legislative purposes and was closely linked to the movement for the codification and unification of law in Germany.[12] Extensive comparative law research preceded the German Civil Code of 1900 and other enactments,[13] as well as legislative reforms in the field of criminal law. This period saw a significant increase in historical, sociological, and anthropological scholarship related to comparative law. Particularly noteworthy was the rise of ethnological jurisprudence, a field combining the perspectives of ethnology and comparative law, focusing on discovering the origins and early stages of law in relation to particular cultural

---

[9] See Franklin (1954).

[10] Gans (1824–1835).

[11] Philosophy, Hegel says, "concerns itself only with the glory of the idea mirroring itself in the history of the world. [It] escapes to the calm region of contemplation from the weary strife of the passions that agitate the surface of society; that which interests it is the recognition of the process of development which the idea has passed through in realizing itself, the idea of freedom whose reality is the consciousness of freedom and nothing short of it." See Friedrich (1954), pp. 157–158.

[12] The practical aims of comparative law were highlighted in the world's first journal devoted to comparative law, which was founded by Karl Salomo Zachariä and Karl Joseph Anton von Mittermaier in 1829. See *Kritische Zeitschrift Für Rechtswissenschaft und Gesetzgebung Des Auslandes* No. 1 (1829), p. 25.

[13] Reference should be made here to the General German Negotiable Instruments Law enacted in 1848 and the General German Commercial Code of 1861, both of which drew on comparative studies not only of the laws of different regions of Germany but also of the relevant laws of other European countries, such as the Dutch Commercial Code of 1838.

phenomena. Leading figures in this field included Albert Hermann Post (1839–1895), Franz Bernhöft (1852–1933), and Josef Kohler (1849–1919).

Post pursued his legal studies at the Universities of Heidelberg, Göttingen, and Berlin, where he developed a keen interest in the comparative study of legal systems. His academic career included professorships and lectureships at several German universities, where he influenced many students and future scholars in the field of law. His most notable work is his exploration of primitive law and his efforts to systematically compare different legal traditions across various cultures. His seminal book, *Grundriss der ethnologischen Jurisprudenz* (Outline of Ethnological Jurisprudence), published in 1881, laid the foundation for the comparative study of legal systems, particularly those of non-European societies. This work was groundbreaking in its approach, combining legal theory with ethnological research to understand the evolution and functioning of law in different social contexts. Post's legacy lies in his pioneering approach to understanding law as a cultural phenomenon, and his work remains influential in the fields of legal anthropology and comparative law.

Post's starting point was the assumption that society is defined through the evolution of the law and its symbolic practices. If the legal order played a major part in shaping societal culture as a whole, as contemporary anthropologists recognized, then a historical approach to the study of law could engender a truly scientific model of explanation only if it was able to integrate indigenous legal practices into a universal theory of legal evolution. Post's scholarly endeavours focused on constructing a general science of law grounded in anthropology. He described what he referred to as "the universal law of mankind" in terms of diverse forms of social organization, positing that the law is a function of social formations associated with the spirit or mentality of a people. The historical and comparative study of laws received considerable impetus through ethnology, which Post described as "that new science which deals with the life of all nations according to a method arising purely from natural sciences and which has embraced into its realm all peoples on earth."[14] According to him, comparative ethnology enabled jurists to discover "far-reaching parallels in the laws of all peoples on earth, which could not be reduced to accidental correspondence, but which could only be regarded as emanations of the common nature of mankind."[15] Ethnological jurisprudence thus focuses on discovering those legal norms and institutions found among all peoples of the world.[16] It should be noted that although Post adopts a functional view of law as a product of a particular socio-psychological order, his work is more concerned with the

---

[14] Post (1894), p. 2.

[15] Post (1894), p. 4.

[16] Post (1894), p. 7. Post views law as a universal phenomenon. He observes that "There is no people on earth without the beginnings of some law. Social life belongs to human nature and with every social life goes a law." Post (1894), p. 8.

systematic ordering of the bewildering multitude of customary laws than with explaining the evolution of legal systems.[17]

Bernhöft was a prominent jurist and legal historian known for his significant contributions to the study of ancient legal systems, particularly Roman law, and their influence on modern jurisprudence. His work often focused on the historical development of legal concepts and institutions, exploring how ancient Roman legal principles had shaped contemporary legal thought and practices. Throughout his career, Bernhöft was recognized for his meticulous research and his ability to contextualize ancient legal texts within broader historical and cultural frameworks. His legacy continues to be felt in the fields of legal history and Roman law studies.

Bernhöft emphasized the importance of broadening the scope of comparative jurisprudence beyond the Roman and Germanic legal systems, which were the primary focus of the German Historical School. He argued that a legal science based solely on the study of these two systems would be incomplete, much like a science of comparative linguistics based on the study of only two languages. Moreover, Bernhöft highlighted the value of comparing foreign laws as an aid to legislation, particularly, the codification of law in Germany. However, he believed that the ultimate goal of comparative jurisprudence was to uncover the general laws governing the development of legal systems and apply these insights to the historical evolution of individual nations. In Bernhöft's words, "[C]omparative law wants to teach how peoples of common heritage elaborate the inherited legal notions for themselves, how one people receives institutions from another one and modifies them according to their own views, and finally how legal systems of different nations evolve even without any factual interconnection according to the common laws of evolution. It searches, in a nut-shell, within the systems of law, for the idea of law."[18] It is crucial to note that Bernhöft's definition of comparative jurisprudence was limited to positive law. From this perspective, customs were viewed as belonging to a preliminary stage in the development of law, relevant only to the extent that they contributed to the formation of positive law.

Kohler studied law at the University of Heidelberg, where he completed his doctoral dissertation, and later became a professor at the University of Würzburg and the University of Berlin. He is best known for his contributions to the understanding of intellectual property rights and his interpretation of civil law within a broader cultural and social context. Throughout his career, Kohler also engaged in comparative law studies, exploring legal systems from different cultures and epochs. He believed that understanding diverse legal traditions could enhance the development of a more universal legal science.

Initially, Kohler's work in comparative law focused on comparing German law with the legal systems of other European states and the United States. Additionally, he examined the legal structures of non-independent territories, particularly those

[17] For an in-depth discussion of Post's work within the framework of nineteenth century scientific thinking consider Kiesow (1997). And see Lyall (2008).

[18] Bernhöft (1878), pp. 36–37.

under the protection of the German Reich (*Schutzgebieten*).[19] Although Kohler initially adhered to Post's theory of legal evolution, which posited that the European legal systems represented the pinnacle of 'natural' legal development, he later departed from this view. He recognized that law evolves in diverse ways, functioning as an interdependent element of a people's mental and material culture.[20] According to Kohler, constructing a 'universal' science and history of law necessitates a broader study encompassing the laws and customs of peoples from all parts of the world. This approach required considering the development of diverse legal systems on a comparative basis. In his extensive body of work, which includes more than 2300 scientific publications, Kohler described and explored the laws of peoples across the globe.[21] He aimed to lay the foundation for a truly universal science of law by including as many societies as possible, regardless of how 'primitive' or 'advanced' they appeared. However, Kohler's scholarly efforts faced significant challenges, partly due to the scarcity of reliable sources on the laws and customs of non-European peoples at the turn of the nineteenth century.

Kohler's work in ethnological jurisprudence was further developed by distinguished scholars who shared his historical-comparative outlook, such as Richard

[19] Consider Grossfeld and Wilde (1994).

[20] Nevertheless, he often expressed the view that non-European peoples should adopt and evolve according to the European model. See Grossfeld and Wilde (1994), p. 73.

[21] Of special interest are Kohler's works on the laws of indigenous peoples, such as the Indians, Aztecs and Papuans. In a well-known article on the law of the Australian Aborigines he expressed the view that these people, however 'primitive' their economic life may be, "possess law. They have legal institutions that are put under the sanction of the general public, for law exists before any organization of the state, before any court or any executory performance exists: it exists in the hearts of the people as a feeling of what should be and what should not be. …Although it may be left to the single individual to obtain justice for himself, and although there may be no possibility to obtain a formal decision on the question of right or wrong, law manifests itself in that the community as a whole not only approves or disapproves of the act of the individual, but also supports the one who is believed to have justice on his side in his pursuance and exercise of law." Kohler (1887), p. 321. Consider also Kohler (1895).

Thurnwald (1869–1954), regarded as the founder of modern anthropology of law,[22] Leonhard Adam (1891–1960),[23] and Hermann Trimborn (1901–1986).[24]

3.2.1 Ernst Rabel

The recognition of comparative law as an academic discipline in Germany can be largely attributed to the efforts of Ernst Rabel (1874–1955), who is regarded as one of the world's most eminent legal comparatists. Rabel was born and raised in Vienna, a city known for its vibrant artistic and intellectual movements at the turn of the twentieth century. He studied law at the University of Vienna, where he was profoundly influenced by Ludwig Mitteis, a leading legal historian and expert in Roman law.[25] From Mitteis, Rabel learned the significance of the historical-comparative study of law and acquired the methodological tools necessary to engage the comparative study of legal systems.[26] After graduation, he worked as an apprentice in his father's law office and also completed his doctorate in law under Mitteis's supervision. In 1899, Rabel followed Mitteis to Leipzig, where he completed his *Habilitation* in 1902 and subsequently taught Roman law and German Private Law.

In 1906, Rabel was appointed to a professorship in Basel, where he had the opportunity to familiarize himself with the new Swiss civil law. Following his tenure in Basel, his academic career led him to Kiel (1910), Göttingen (1911), Munich

[22] Thurnwald was an anthropologist and sociologist renowned for his comparative studies of social institutions. His views on social anthropology stemmed from his extensive knowledge of various societies, acquired during field expeditions to the Solomon Islands and Micronesia, New Guinea, and East Africa. Although he briefly taught at several prominent U.S. universities, his main position from 1924 was at the University of Berlin, where he taught anthropology and sociology. In 1925, he founded and edited the *Zeitschrift für Völkerpsychologie und Soziologie* (Journal of Popular Psychology and Sociology), later renamed *Sociologus*. He also edited journals on anthropology and comparative law.

[23] Born in Berlin, Adam pursued law and became a legal scholar, but his interests soon shifted towards anthropology. His work focused on the material culture and legal systems of indigenous peoples, particularly in Australia and the Pacific Islands. Throughout his life, Adam published numerous articles and books on anthropology and indigenous art, leaving a lasting impact on the field. His interdisciplinary approach combined legal studies with anthropological research, making his work unique and influential.

[24] Trimborn pursued his education in anthropology and ethnology, eventually becoming a professor at the University of Bonn. His extensive research work focused on the history, culture, and languages of indigenous peoples, and he made significant contributions to the understanding of pre-Columbian civilizations, especially in Peru and Mexico. His publications, such as "The Ancient Cultures of Peru" and "The Aztecs," are well-regarded in the field. Trimborn's meticulous fieldwork and scholarly contributions have left a lasting impact on the study of indigenous cultures.

[25] Mitteis' seminal work *Reichsrecht und Volksrecht in den östlichen Provinzen des römischen Kaiserreichs*, published in Leipzig in 1891, is regarded as a turning-point in contemporary Roman law scholarship. This work went beyond the confines of classical Roman law to the comparative study of other legal systems of antiquity, especially Greek law. See on this Zimmerman (2001).

[26] See on this Gerber (2001), p. 192.

(1916),[27] and finally to Berlin (1926), where he established the Kaiser Wilhelm Institute for Comparative and International Private Law.[28] Additionally, Rabel served as a judge both in Germany and on the international level. He was a member of the German-Italian Mixed Arbitral Tribunal (1921–1927), which heard reparation claims against the German Reich and private contract claims arising out of wartime conditions. Furthermore, he served as an ad hoc judge at the Permanent Court of International Justice in the Chorzow Cases (1925–1927) and as a member of the Permanent German-Italian (1928–1935) and German-Norwegian (1929–1936) Arbitral Commissions. This blend of German and foreign, as well as academic and judicial experience, shaped Rabel's work, which, from an early stage, utilized the comparative method.

From 1927 to 1936, Rabel edited the Journal of Foreign and International Private Law (*Zeitschrift für ausländisches und internationales Privatrecht*), which now bears his name. During this period, he produced several significant works in comparative law, particularly in the field of the law of sales. In 1928, Rabel proposed to the League of Nations' Institute for the Unification of Private Law (now UNIDROIT) that the unification of the law of international sales of goods be adopted as one of its principal projects. The Institute entrusted Rabel and his colleagues at the Berlin Institute for Comparative and International Private Law with the task of conducting an extensive comparative law investigation aimed at developing a uniform sale of goods law for worldwide application. The first draft of this law was published in 1935. A year later, Rabel published the first volume of his seminal work, *Das Recht des Warenkaufs* (The Law of the Sale of Goods), which provided a comprehensive analysis of his findings in this field.

Rabel's career took a downward turn after the National Socialists came to power in 1933. Being of Jewish descent, he became a target of the new regime, which stripped him of various positions, including the directorship of the Kaiser Wilhelm Institute, and prohibited him from publishing scholarly works. To escape persecution, he immigrated to the United States in 1939 at the age of 65. There, he continued his work as a research scholar with the support of the American Law Institute. For this Institute, he authored a monumental four-volume work titled "The Conflict of Laws: A Comparative Study," a true masterpiece at the intersection of comparative law and private international law.[29] He also held research positions at the University of Michigan Law School, which published his "Conflict of Laws" as part

---

[27] In 1917 he established the Institute for Comparative Law at the University of Munich, the first of its kind in Germany.

[28] The Institute undertook basic research, reporting on current legal developments in diverse jurisdictions, and also furnished practical advice to the German legislature, government departments and agencies, the courts and bar, and companies engaged in international trade. Rabel's Institute is today the Max Planck Institute for Comparative and International Private Law in Hamburg.

[29] The first edition dates are: Volume 1 (1945); Volume 2 (1947); Volume 3 (1950); and Volume 4 (1958).

of its Legal Studies series,[30] and at Harvard University, where he completed the fourth volume of the aforementioned work. Apart from his treatise on the conflict of laws, Rabel's comparative law scholarship in English is not very extensive. Nevertheless, he made a significant contribution to the development of comparative law and conflict of laws studies in the United States. Some of his students, such as Max Rheinstein and Friedrich Kessler, became leading figures in the field of comparative law in the country.[31] In 1950, Rabel returned to Germany and settled in Tübingen, where he was made an honorary professor at the local university. He also spent time at the Free University of Berlin, which appointed him professor emeritus.[32]

Rabel's scholarship spans a wide range of topics, including Roman law, Egyptian papyrology, German legal history, private law, public international law, private international law, and, most notably, comparative law. He believed that comparative law offered a diverse set of tools to address the fundamental legal problems facing Europe in general and Germany, in particular. Rabel identified three distinct yet interconnected aspects of comparative law:

(a) The first aspect focuses on the historical evolution of legal systems and their interrelations.[33]
(b) The second aspect involves the study of contemporary legal orders and the elucidation of their differences.[34]
(c) The third aspect, which integrates legal history, legal doctrine, and the philosophy of law, aims to uncover profound truths about the development and social impact of laws.[35]

---

[30] During his stay at this university, he received advice and editorial assistance from Hessel Yntema, a distinguished comparative law scholar, and other members of the Law School. See Thieme (1986), p. 268.

[31] See Gerber (2001), pp. 207–208. Both Rheinstein and Kessler immigrated to the United States after the National Socialists came to power in Germany. The former was appointed professor of law at the University of Chicago, and the latter held a professorship at Yale University.

[32] For a closer look at Rabel's career see Kegel (1990); Kleinheyer and Schröder (1983), pp. 346 ff; Rheinstein (1956).

[33] This was the focus of Rabel's work during the earlier part of his career.

[34] This was the focus of his research after 1916.

[35] In a paper published in 1919, Rabel remarked that this third aspect "penetrated philosophy, where historical and systematic legal science, together with legal philosophy, examine the deepest issues of the evolution and impact of law." Rabel (1919), p. 2. In an article discussing the reach and functions of comparative law, Rabel remarks that "the subject matter of thinking about legal problems must be the law of the entire world, past and present, the law's interrelation with soil, climate and race, with the historical destiny of peoples (war, revolution, the formation of states, subjugation), with religious and ethical beliefs, the ambition and creativity of individuals; the needs of production and consumption; the interests of strata, parties, classes. Intellectual trends of every kind are at work ...the congruity of adapted paths of law, and not least the search for an ideal state and an ideal law. All of these are mutually dependent in social, economic and legal design. The law of every developed people dazzles and trembles under the sun and the wind in a thousand hues. All these vibrating bodies together form a whole which nobody has yet perceived and understood." Rabel (1924), p. 283.

However, Rabel never fully developed the third aspect of comparative law.

Rabel maintained that the principal goal of comparative law is 'pure science.' This central tenet implies that all specific applications of comparative law, as a form of 'applied' science, emanate from this foundational principle. Although Rabel was not always precise about what he meant by 'science', he often construed the term broadly as the self-conscious and disciplined search for knowledge (*Erkenntnis*). For him, the subject of the relevant scientific inquiry was the legal rule (*Rechtssatz*).[36] As he explains, "legal comparison means that the legal rules of one state (or other law-prescribing community) are analysed in connection with those of another legal order or a number of legal orders from the past and the present."[37]

While Rabel viewed comparative law as a science, he also emphasized the practical utility of its methods. This blend of academic rigor and practical application shaped his approach and distinguished it from those of past and contemporary comparatists. Rabel aimed to develop methods and tools that would enable lawyers to better understand and effectively address foreign legal problems. His scholarly endeavours also encouraged students to immerse themselves in the specifics of legal situations, thereby gaining valuable knowledge of how such situations were handled in diverse legal systems. Moreover, his methods were sought to produce better law through the clarification of legal concepts and the improvement of solutions to societal problems available to decision-makers.

It is important to note that for Rabel, the formal language of legal rules and principles divulged little about how problems are actually solved. Reliance on language alone is likely to obscure rather than illuminate what is happening in practice. The correct way to acquire information about a foreign legal system is to ask how the relevant rules and principles relate to and address a concrete factual situation. In this way, Rabel shifted the methodological focus of comparative law to the specific societal functions of rules, thereby laying the foundation for what is now regarded as the basic methodological principle of comparative law: the principle of functionality.[38]

---

[36] The term *Rechtssatz* does not have a direct translation in English. The closest translation is probably 'legal rule', understood here in the broader sense of authoritative legal proposition. See Rabel (1937).

[37] Rabel (1924), p. 280.

[38] It should be noted that, although Rabel often emphasizes the importance of method in the broad sense of a carefully devised plan about how one achieves a set of goals, he did not elaborate a detailed methodology. What he proposes as a methodology consists of some generally defined principles that would serve the goals of comparative law as he identified them. In form, his methodology has many elements in common with the historicist methodology in the social sciences that prevailed in Germany from the 1880s until the First World War. From this viewpoint, 'method' was a matter of in-depth examination of trends and patterns in the evolution of society and economy, and not a matter of theoretical construction of methodological principles. Consider on this Gerber (2001), pp. 198–199.

3.3 The Growth of Comparative Legal Studies in Britain

During the nineteenth century, Great Britain, as a dominant colonial power, inevitably encountered interactions between its domestic and foreign laws. The Judicial Committee of the Privy Council, based in London, served as the highest court of appeal for all countries and territories of the British Empire, excluding Britain itself. This court not only handled appeals from other common law jurisdictions but also from regions applying diverse legal systems, such as Hindu and Islamic laws (India); Sinhalese and Tamil laws (Ceylon); Chinese law (Hong Kong, the Malay States, Sarawak and Borneo); Roman-Dutch law (Ceylon, South Africa and Rhodesia); elements of the French Napoleonic Code embodied in the Canadian Civil Code of 1866 (Quebec); Norman customs (The Channel Islands); and Asian and African customary laws. It is important to note that, according to the English model of colonial governance, imperial control was largely indirect. Existing local laws and customs were generally retained, except where they were specifically overridden by English legislation, which primarily occurred in the fields of public and criminal law.[39] Under these circumstances, there was a need for "a more ready access to the sources from whence an acquaintance might be derived with those systems of foreign jurisprudence, which [were] most frequently presented to the consideration of an English tribunal."[40]

Among the earliest attempts at applying the comparative method to practical aspects of law are William Burge's *Commentaries on Colonial and Foreign Laws*, written for legal practitioners and published in 1838,[41] and Leone Levi's *Commercial Law* (1852), an extensive treatise comparing the commercial laws of Britain with those of other mercantile countries, including ancient Rome.[42] In 1848, the House of Commons' Select Committee proposed the establishment Chairs in international, comparative, administrative, and English law at universities. However, it was several years before this proposal was implemented. By the late nineteenth century, as common law became entrenched, particularly within the broader Commonwealth, comparative law began to be recognized as a form of science, although it never acquired the profound scientific character of its Continental counterpart.

---

[39] Although indigenous legal systems continued to apply, they were in the course of time profoundly influenced by English law. The same occurred in countries under the control of other Western colonial powers, such as France and Holland. On the issue of Western legal expansion see Mommsen and de Moor (1992) and Benton (2002). Where settlements were established in previously uninhabited lands—a rather curious concept—English (or Western) law was considered to be imported by the settlers themselves. Consequently, indigenous populations and their local laws were essentially ignored by nearly all European powers, including England, when establishing territorial laws.

[40] Burge (1838), v.

[41] According to Rabel, the range and quality of Burge's work made it useful as a substitute for a basic text on comparative private law.

[42] Levi (1850–1852). See also Levi (1854). It should be noted that Levi was the first scholar to propose the international unification of commercial law through the method of comparative law.

Of significant importance to the development of comparative law in England was Sir Henry Maine's work on the laws of ancient peoples, particularly his book *Ancient Law*, published in 1861. In this work, Maine applied the comparative method to the study of the origins of law, a method similar to the one Charles Darwin employed in his *Origin of the Species* (1859). Maine (1822–1888), regarded as the founder of the English Historical School of Law, was born in Scotland and educated at Cambridge University. After graduating in 1844, he accepted a position as a tutor at Trinity College, which he held until his appointment as a professor of civil law at Cambridge in 1847. In 1850, Maine was called to the bar, and 2 years later, he became a reader in Roman law and jurisprudence at the Inns of Court. He also served as a legal member of the council of the Viceroy of India from 1863 to 1869 and as vice-chancellor of the University of Calcutta. Upon returning to England in 1869, Maine was appointed to the chair of historical and comparative jurisprudence at the University of Oxford, a position he held until 1877. Subsequently, he was elected master of Trinity Hall, Cambridge, and concluded his career as a professor of international law at Cambridge.

Maine was one of the first scholars to argue that law and legal institutions must be studied historically to be properly understood.[43] In his work *Ancient Law*, he proposed an evolutionary theory of law, complete with a growth pattern to which all systems—despite being geographically or chronologically remote from one another—could be shown to conform. By drawing on knowledge of Greek, Roman, biblical, and other ancient legal systems, as well as the native institutions of contemporary India, he concluded that different societies tend to develop their legal systems by passing through certain universal stages.

He asserted that the earliest stage was in one sense pre-legal, where king-priests delivered judgments about actual disputes, which contained a strong religious element. The next stage involved crystallizing these judgments into customs, of which the oligarchies that had succeeded the early monarchs acted as custodians. The third stage, usually associated with a popular movement to overcome the oligarchic monopoly of expounding the law, is that of the codes.[44] At this point, some societies cease to progress further, as their legal institutions are unable to evolve new dimensions beyond the bounds of their petrified codes. Maine referred to these societies as 'static', in contrast to 'dynamic' societies, which had the ability to adapt their legal systems to novel circumstances.

To meet the needs derived from such circumstances, dynamic societies employ three mechanisms of change: fictions, equity, and legislation. Although Maine's

[43]As commentators have observed, Maine's approach reflects the influence of Carl von Savigny's theory of the genesis and foundation of law, as well as the contemporary interest in evolution, spurred by the publication of Charles Darwin's masterpiece, *The Origin of Species*, in 1859. A further, remoter influence has been Hegel's philosophy of history, which may have suggested to Maine the notion of uniform principles of development. See Stone (1966), p. 120. And see Janssen (2000), pp. 164–165.

[44]Examples of such codes include the Greek codes of Draco and Solon and the Twelve Tables of Rome.

scheme has been criticized by later scholars for relying on evidence too weak to support such far-reaching generalizations, some of his insights have been particularly enlightening. Perhaps the most celebrated of these is his view of how dynamic or progressive societies evolve:

> The movement of the progressive societies has been uniform in one respect. Through all its course it has been distinguished by the gradual dissolution of family dependency, and the growth of individual obligation in its place. The Individual is steadily substituted for the Family, as the unit of which civil laws take account. The advance has been accomplished at varying rates of celerity, and there are societies not absolutely stationary in which the collapse of the ancient organization can only be perceived by careful study of the phenomena they present. ...Nor is it difficult to see what is the tie between man and man which replaces by degrees those forms of reciprocity in rights and duties which have their origin in the Family. It is Contract. Starting, as from one terminus of history, from a condition of society in which all the relations of Persons are summed up in the relations of Family, we seem to have steadily moved towards a phase of social order in which all these relations arise from the free agreement of Individuals.[45]

In this way, Maine arrives at his often-quoted conclusion that the evolution of dynamic societies has been characterized by a shift from Status to Contract. In a status-based society, an individual's condition is fixed, lacking will and opportunity.[46] Legal relations are entirely dependent on birth, family group, or caste, reflecting a socio-cultural order where the group, rather than the individual, is the primary unit of social life. As society evolves, this condition gradually transitions to one based on contract. According to Maine, a progressive society is marked by the emergence of the independent, free, and self-determining individual, where achieved status becomes the central element of social life.[47] In such a society, the emphasis on individual achievement and voluntary contractual relations sets the stage for a more advanced legal system that uses legislation as the principal means of harmonizing society and law.

---

[45] Maine (1931), pp. 139–140.

[46] In this kind of society, the conditions necessary for individuality to emerge and thrive were largely absent. Individuals defined themselves through a limited set of clearly prescribed social roles and functions, which fixed their identities. The personality of each group member remained relatively amorphous and lacked a definite structure, at it could only attach itself to the immediately available roles within the group. In such a social environment, a person's life path was largely predetermined, limiting their opportunities for choice. They were heavily dependent on the traditions and norms of their group, which hindered their ability to make independent decisions, assert themselves consciously, and pursue their own goals.

[47] The gradual collapse of the medieval social structure in Europe set in motion a significant historical process, leading to the emergence of a new form of society that fostered the growth of individuality. This transformation fundamentally altered the relationship between individuals and their social environment. No longer firmly attached to a particular group—such as an extended family, village community, manor or guild—the individual was no longer bound by fixed social roles and moral commitments predetermined by these associations. Instead, personal identity became paramount. Individuals were increasingly required to make their own decisions amidst a variety of competing views and lifestyles. By the nineteenth century, individualism had become a central element of moral belief in European societies, embraced and propagated by numerous thinkers and philosophers.

Commentators have described Maine as a defender of laissez-faire economic individualism.[48] However, the transformation of liberal laissez-faire governments into social welfare states and the resultant increase in social legislation, which increasingly restricted the freedom of contract in the later decades of the nineteenth century, suggested that the process Maine discerned had begun to reverse. Although Maine's vision of social evolution did not align with reality, his contributions to anthropology and comparative law remain unquestionable. By establishing a link between law, history, and anthropology, he highlighted the role of the comparative method as a valuable tool in legal science. Maine believed that while comparative law, as an application of the comparative method to the study of legal phenomena, could only play a secondary or supporting role, the true science of law was historical and comparative in character. Whereas comparative law analyses legal systems at a specific point in time, historical-comparative jurisprudence focuses on development and dynamics of law over time.[49]

Frederick Pollock, a disciple and successor of Maine in his scientific endeavours, sought to elucidate the interrelationship between the 'static' perspective of comparative law in its narrow sense and the 'dynamic' approach of historical jurisprudence. According to Pollock, true jurisprudence, or science of law, must be both historical and comparative. In this regard, comparative law plays more than just a subsidiary role; it occupies a distinct and significant place within the system of legal sciences.[50]

In 1894, a Chair of Legal History and Comparative Law was founded at the University College London. Shortly afterward, the English Society of Comparative Legislation was established, resulting in the formation of several similar societies on both sides of the Channel. Beyond the establishment of research institutes, scholarly journals, and a national committee on comparative law, a significant parliamentary initiative aimed at promoting the comparative study of laws occurred in 1965 with the enactment of the Law Commissions Act. This Act created two law reform commissions, the English and the Scottish Law Commissions. Their function includes obtaining information from foreign legal systems to facilitate the systematic development and reform of the law.[51]

[48] See, e.g., Janssen (2000), p. 168.

[49] For more on Maine's contribution to legal thought see Cocks (1988), Feaver (1969), Diamond (2006) and Landauer (2003).

[50] As Pollock remarked, "It makes no great difference whether we speak of historical jurisprudence or comparative jurisprudence, or, as the Germans seem inclined to do, of the general history of law." Pollock (1903), p. 76.

[51] See s 3(1) Law Commissions Act 1965.

3.4 The Evolution of Comparative Law in France

Nineteenth-century French legal scholarship significantly contributed to the rise of modern comparative law. Important turning points in the development of comparative law in France include the establishment of a chair of comparative legal history at the College of France in 1831; the creation of a chair of comparative criminal law at the University of Paris in 1846; and the founding of the French Society of Comparative Legislation (*Société française de législation comparée*) in Paris in 1869.[52] In 1876, the French Ministry of Justice set up an office of foreign and international law (*Office de législation étrangère et de droit international*), which employed the comparative method in the investigation of problems of private international law. In the 1890s, comparative civil law began to be taught in Paris,[53] and in 1900, the first International Congress of Comparative Law was organized by Raymond Saleilles and Édouard Lambert in the context of the Paris World Fair.

Special reference should be made to a group of jurists, known as *juristes inquiets* or 'anxious jurists,' who, despite their political differences, shared a common concern (*inquiétude*) about the growing discrepancy between the formalism and extreme conceptualism of the traditional legal system and a rapidly changing social reality. These jurists challenged the dominant Exegetic School, which emphasized strict adherence to the text of the law, arguing instead for a more interpretative and sociologically informed approach to legal studies. The *juristes inquiets* played a crucial role in laying the groundwork for modern comparative law and critical legal studies. Their ideas contributed to the evolution of legal theory by promoting a more dynamic and pragmatic approach to understanding and applying the law. Among the principal representatives of this group were François Gény (1861–1959) and Raymond Saleilles (1855–1912).

François Gény studied law at the University of Nancy, where he later became a professor. In 1930, he was appointed as a corresponding member of the Academy of Moral and Political Sciences. Gény is renowned for his advocacy of 'free scientific research' (*libre recherche scientifique*) in legal theory and his critique of legal positivism, promoting a more holistic and interdisciplinary approach to understanding and applying legal principles. He emphasized the importance of judicial discretion in law-making and challenged the traditional belief that the Napoleonic Civil Code of 1804 had resolved all legal issues, including unforeseen ones. Gény argued that courts should have the freedom to make their own rules when existing written or unwritten laws are insufficient. He believed that the law is shaped by applying juristic techniques, or 'constructions' (*construits*), to the given data (*donnés*) of the social sciences. His seminal works, particularly *Méthode d'interprétation et sources*

[52] The Society's periodical, now called *Revue internationale de droit comparé*, is still in existence today.

[53] A Chair of comparative civil law was founded in 1902. Other similar professorships established during the same period included a Chair of comparative maritime and commercial law (1892) and a Chair of comparative constitutional law (1895).

en droit privé positif and *Science et technique en droit privé positif*, have exercised a strong influence on legal scholars and practitioners worldwide.[54]

Raymond Saleilles initially taught legal history at the Universities of Grenoble in 1884 and Dijon from 1885 to 1895. In 1895, he moved to Paris where he first held the chair of comparative criminal law and later the newly created chair of comparative civil law.[55] Saleilles introduced French jurists to the laws and legal cultures of various countries, significantly advancing comparative law in France. He viewed comparative law as an essential methodological tool and a means to illuminate law as a social and historical phenomenon transcending national boundaries. Moreover, he believed that familiarity with diverse legal systems and their developmental processes enables a more comprehensive understanding of one's own legal system. It also opens up new and unexpected possibilities for national legislators and judges in addressing concrete legal problems.[56]

Saleilles was familiar with several civil law and common law systems, but was particularly conversant with German legal thinking, especially the spirit and methodology of the German Historical School, which he introduced in France through his teaching and extensive writings.[57] According to Saleilles, the Historical School successfully demonstrated that law evolved through the adaptation of legal rules and principles to the demands of social reality. In this respect, the judiciary is entrusted with the important function of adjusting the law to constantly changing socio-economic conditions.[58]

Saleilles further believed that changes in the field of law also reflected the interests of, and ongoing conflicts among, diverse social, economic, and political groups, according to what he saw as 'laws of evolution'.[59] A defining moment in the development of his thought came when he recognized the inadequacy of the socio-historical determinism of the German Historical School for legal science. He realized that the relationship between social reality and legal institutions was not merely one of cause and effect. Rather, legal institutions were unavoidably value-laden and, as such, had to correspond not only to material interests and related conflicts in society but also to prevailing ideals and values. These ideals and values exhibit an internal logic and consistency, and as a consequence, legal institutions are not simply determined by social forces but themselves help to shape the social value system. Furthermore, Saleilles dismissed the rigid dogmatism and exaggerated conceptualism of the German Historical School, which he criticized for neglecting

[54] For more on Gény's career and legacy see Mayda (1978) and Tanzi (1990).

[55] For an overview of Saleilles career consider Gaudemet (1912) and Beudant et al. (1914).

[56] See Saleilles (1905), p. 68 ff.

[57] Reference may be made here to his *Essai d'une théorie générale de l'obligation d'après le projet de code civil allemand*, which appeared in 1890, and his *De la déclaration de volonté: contribution à l'étude de l'acte juridique dans le Code civil allemand*, published in 1901. In 1901 Saleilles commenced work on an annotated translation of the German Civil Code (BGB).

[58] It is thus unsurprising that Saleilles referred to the common law judges, whom he regarded as the true heirs of the Roman jurists, as the ideal prototypes.

[59] See Saleilles (1902), pp. 94–95.

fundamental principles of justice and equity in favour of logical abstraction and precise conceptualization.[60]

3.4.1 The Paris International Congress of Comparative Law

An important landmark in the development of modern comparative law was the International Congress of Comparative Law, organized by the French Society of Comparative Legislation (*Société française de législation comparée*). This event was held in Paris from July 31 to August 4, 1900, coinciding with the Paris World Fair and the International Congress of Higher Education. The regulations prepared by the Society divided the program into six sections, with the greatest emphasis placed on general theory and method.[61] French was selected as the official language of the Congress.[62] The French jurist Édouard Lambert, a former student of Raymond Saleilles and a professor at the Faculty of Law at Lyon, was entrusted with the task of elaborating the theoretical and methodological aspects of the new discipline.

The Congress was declared to have four principal objectives.[63] First, from the perspective of comparative legal science, it aimed to identify the most effective methods for analysing diverse legislative systems. Comparative law addresses this task in three stages: observation, comparison, and adaptation. Observation is based on the premise that legislative texts are meaningless without interpretation, and that interpretation itself is meaningless without considering its consequences. Therefore, comparative law must look beyond the letter of the law to illuminate these consequences. In the second stage, comparative law examines the rational rapprochement among different national legislative systems, considering their technical-juridical forms and concepts, as well as their practical implications. Based on this analysis, a predominant type can be identified and used as a model for other national legislatures. In the third stage, comparative law adapts the selected model to national, social, and environmental conditions, as well as significant cultural traditions. Historical knowledge plays an important supplementary role here, aiding in identifying examples of inadequate legislation and artificial adaptations, and highlighting the conditions and methods that enable successful integration of legislation into existing national law and the life of the people. These techniques can also be utilized to develop new theoretical models and justify the legitimacy of judicial

[60] For a closer look at this argument, see Saleilles (1902). For a closer look at Saleilles' career see Sabbioneti (2019).

[61] Article 8.

[62] Reports and other materials not in French were to be translated or summarized into French (article 11). It should be noted here that only one English scholar, Sir Frederick Pollock, participated in the proceedings as a representative of the English legal tradition, whereas all other participants were from Continental Europe.

[63] These objectives were stated in a report prepared by Saleilles and addressed to the organizing commission of the Congress. See Saleilles (1900).

construction of legal rules. When applied to legislation, legal doctrine, and judicial interpretation, the aforementioned three stages of comparative law might contribute, at least in part, to the development of a 'common law of civilized mankind' ('*droit commun de l'humanite civilisee*').

The second objective of the Congress was to determine the role of comparative law as a method of instruction. The third objective was to ascertain how the outcomes of comparative law should be utilized, whether through legislative action, judicial interpretation, or international conventions. The fourth and final objective of the Congress was to identify and organize techniques and mechanisms for obtaining information about the sources of foreign law and its theoretical elaboration.

The program of the Congress included both theoretical and practical components. Additionally, its scope was considered broad enough to encompass a variety of legal fields, such as private law, private international law, commercial law, public law, and criminology.

Édouard Lambert presented a report on general theory and method during the first part of the Congress. He also summarized various reports that highlighted the importance of foreign law translations, particularly for lawyers dealing with matters of private international law. It was acknowledged, however, that while translation work is an essential prerequisite for legal comparison, comparative law requires much more than just knowledge of foreign law.

Lambert then proceeded to comment on the issue of comparative law methodology, drawing on the work of Franz Bernhöft, a professor at the University of Rostock and a leading representative of German ethnological jurisprudence. According to Bernhöft, there is no single uniform comparative law method but rather three interconnected principal methods: the ethnological, the historical, and the dogmatic.

The ethnological method is characterized by its universality, as it is concerned with observing the legal life of all peoples and nations. Through the examination of diverse legal cultures, ethnological comparative law reveals the dependence of law on social and economic relations and the striking uniformity of nations at the same level of civilization. The historical method essentially extends legal history, exploring the evolution of legal systems over time. Lastly, the dogmatic method, particularly popular in the latter half of the nineteenth century, focuses on the relationship between law and contemporary life. It aims to elucidate the needs of commerce and ethical views that demand satisfaction from the law and to create legal forms capable of addressing those demands. Achieving these goals requires an in-depth knowledge of a nation's general social, political, and economic life.

Lambert informed the participants that, according to Congress commentators, comparative law should employ both social science methods, such as comparative institutional history, and legal science methods. He expressed his agreement with this approach. Lambert used the term 'comparative legislation' (*législation comparée*) to describe the entire body of legal norms applicable in a country, including those derived from scholarly doctrine and judicial jurisprudence. He argued that studying different countries' laws can reveal a unity of general purpose that transcends each system's particularities. Therefore, it is possible to discern a common foundation of legal institutions and a 'common legislative law' (*droit commun législatif*).

According to Lambert, comparative law, as a branch of legal science, serves three practical purposes. First, it can influence legal policy and legislation. Second, it can enhance existing national legislation by shaping scholarly doctrine and judicial jurisprudence. Third, it can foster the convergence of legal systems by eliminating accidental differences in the laws of societies at similar stages of development. As Lambert stated:

> [C]omparative law must resolve the accidental and divisive differences in the laws of peoples at similar stages of cultural and economic development, and reduce the number of divergences in law, attributable not to the political, moral or social qualities of the different nations but to historical accident or to temporary or contingent circumstances.[64]

Lambert also addressed the issue of legal education reform, arguing that the teaching of comparative law should receive the same attention as domestic civil law. He asserted that understanding living law requires illuminating its historical development, its conceptual connections with the laws of neighbouring countries, and the social and economic reasons that underlying its rules.[65]

Raymond Saleilles, in his commentary on the general meaning and definition of comparative law and in the final report delivered at the Congress' closing session, expressed the view that comparative law could be conceptually approached into two distinct ways. First, it could be regarded as a subsidiary science to each branch of law. In this context, concerning national legislation, the primary task of comparative law scholars would be to study foreign laws with the aim of formulating proposals for the adoption of better legal enactments or the improvement of existing domestic legislation. This goal could be accomplished through scholarly doctrine, disseminated by means of legal instruction and scholarly publications, or through judicial interpretation embodied in published court decisions.[66]

Second, comparative law could be viewed as an independent science with its own objectives, rules of operation, and methods. Saleilles observed a general and gradual convergence in legal evolution around the world and pointed out that history and sociology offer useful insights for comparative law methodology. As an independent discipline, comparative law is concerned not with what law should be but with discovering fundamental similarities among diverse national legal systems. In Saleilles's words: "[the goal of comparative law] should be to retrieve from the mass of particular legal institutions a common fund, that is, the points of rapprochement

---

[64] Lambert (1905), p. 26.

[65] It should be noted that Lambert viewed comparative law as pertaining primarily to private law. Although it has not reached the scale he envisioned, comparative private law (*droit privé comparé*) is now considered highly significant in France.

[66] According to Jamin, both Saleilles and Lambert saw comparative law as the principal means for the renewal and enhancement of French legal thought. See Jamin (2000), p. 743. Consider also Jamin (2002).

that may be discovered from apparently diverse elements. These points constitute the essential identity of universal legal life."[67]

The principal difference between Saleilles and Lambert lies in their perspectives on the universality of legal principles. Saleilles believed that it is possible to identify a common foundation among all civilized societies (*fond commun de l'humanité civilisée*), which could serve as a replacement for the outdated concept of natural law. He argued that a thorough examination of all legal systems, across different times and places, would uncover the general laws that explain the emergence, evolution, and decline of legal institutions.

In contrast, Lambert refuted the notion that universal and eternal laws could be discovered. He maintained that comparative legislation (*législation comparée*) can only identify a common basis among countries that have reached a similar level of social and economic development. According to Lambert, to discover a 'common legislative law' (*droit commun législatif*), it is sufficient to study existing legal systems that are at a comparable stage of development. It is important to note that Lambert considered the codification of law as a hallmark of a highly developed legal system. Therefore, it is unsurprising that he expressed doubts about including non-codified or common law systems, such as the English system, in comparative law studies.[68]

According to Saleilles, the distinct science of comparative law analyses the law-making function in three stages. In the first stage, it critically examines each selected foreign enactment from a social and economic perspective. In the second stage, it seeks to discover common elements susceptible to an evolutionary process observable in many countries. Finally, in the third stage, it attempts to determine one or more 'ideal forms' for a given legal institution, which would inform and direct the development of legal policy in diverse nations with similar social and economic conditions. This approach could lead to the formation of a 'common law of civilized mankind' (*droit commun de l'humanité civilisée*). In other words, it would gradually construct a unitary law out of diverse legal particularities.

It should be noted that several jurists at the Congress expressed the view that a uniform law, or a common law of civilized humanity, is unattainable because diversity and competition are inevitable facts of life. According to André Weiss, probably Saleilles' most ardent critic, "the uniformity of laws is not feasible, nor is it desirable… It is a chimera today to impose a single law for all men, a dangerous chimera. A law is not an abstract formula, forged a priori, appropriate without distinction for all; it is a concrete rule destined to apply to a specific situation, obliged to take account of certain conditions, which are not the same in all places, as well as differences in races and social institutions."[69]

---

[67] *Session du Congrès: Procès-verbaux sommaires (Séance générale de clôture du 4 août 1900)*. In 1 *Congrès international de droit comparé, Procès-verbaux des séances et documents* 21–25 (1905), p. 143.

[68] See on this Michaels (2002), p. 101.

[69] Weiss (1900), p. 420.

Other participants argued that comparative law, by working with differences, has the potential to promote a competitive and gradual adaptation of law. In this respect, different countries might be seen as 'laboratories of experience' for other countries. Legislation, legal doctrine, and judicial jurisprudence in each nation could progress toward a common process leading to a universal legal science. However, it is important to correctly identify and engage with the areas and issues where unification is feasible.[70]

Notwithstanding the objections to the notion of a 'common law of civilized mankind', commentators agree that the positions advanced at the Paris Congress marked a new beginning for the discipline of comparative law.[71] Until that time, jurists were familiar only with codified legal systems or systems based on English common law. The codification of law was envisioned as a product of jurisprudential rationalism, and reason was naturally perceived as unique, universal, and non-contradictory. Although law codes diverged, this divergence was attributed to the fact that not all code drafters had fully grasped the precepts of reason. Jurists before the 1900 Congress believed that if there were more than one codified solution to a legal problem, only one of them was rational and therefore correct (usually the one adopted by the legal system of the jurist concerned). In areas where the Romano-canonical legal tradition prevailed and was respected, some degree of diversity was permitted, allowing for divergent interpretations of a text to arise and persist. However, such differences could be reconciled through jurisprudential analysis, enabling the identification of the best solution and a return to a unitary idea: the *Ius Unum*. The notion of unity in the law tends to prevail when one views comparative law as a pathway to the unification or standardization of law. According to Rodolfo Sacco, this unitary and universalistic mentality is characteristic of comparative scholarship at its earliest stage of development.

[70] For an account of the conference proceedings and the positions advanced at the Paris Congress see Clark (2001).

[71] As X Blanc-Jouvan has remarked, the Paris Congress of 1900 "still remains the inescapable reference point for all comparatists, inasmuch as it marked, if not the birth of comparative law (which had long existed before that date), at least the beginning of a true reflection on this new branch of the legal science. It gave a tremendous impetus to the study of foreign and comparative law throughout all the century. Its success was due, to a large extent, to the participation of the most important jurists of the time… They considered all of the main aspects of this discipline: its aims, its uses (and misuses), its means and its functions, its relationship to other branches of law, the way it should be taught, and its impact on the practice of law.… The opinions expressed at the 1900 Congress were, in fact, much more advanced than we often assume, so much so that we are naturally led to wonder whether, in spite of all appearances and in spite of countless colloquia, books, and articles, we have made any real progress in this field." Blanc-Jouvan (2001), p. 862. Other commentators have argued, however, that the notion of comparative law adopted at the Congress was excessively narrow in its focus. In the words of Mathias Reimann, "the concept of comparative law that the Paris Congress bequeathed to the twentieth century was extremely narrow. It was the science of a "*droit commun législatif*." This meant, essentially, the comparison of the private law codes and statutes of continental European countries with the purpose of legal harmonization and unification. Most importantly in our present context, it meant reducing the discipline to the comparison of national legal systems." Reimann (2001), p. 1105.

In contrast, a comparative law that recognizes legal diversity does not align with the 'unitary theorem'.[72] However, the pluralistic mentality, which embraces diversity, did not yet exist when Saleilles and Lambert advanced their proposals. After the Paris Congress, the narrow comparative approach, which focused on written codes, judicial decisions, and conceptual definitions primarily within European legal systems, became indefensible. The norm studied in comparative law was no longer only the formalized norm; the discipline's scope broadened to include legal systems and forms outside the Western legal tradition.[73]

References

Benton L (2002) Law and colonial cultures. Cambridge University Press, Cambridge

Bernhöft F (1878) Über Zweck und Mittel der vergleichenden Rechtswissenschaft. Zeitschrift für vergleichende Rechtswissenschaft 1:1–38

Beudant R et al (1914) L'Oeuvre juridique de Raymond Saleilles. Rousseau, Paris

Bierling ER (1894) Juristische Prinzipienlehre I. Mohr, Freiburg im Br

Blanc-Jouvan X (2001) Centennial world congress on comparative law: opening remarks. Tulane Law Rev 75(4):859–864

Burge W (1838) Commentaries on colonial and foreign laws: generally and in their conflict with each other, and with the Law of England. Saunders and Benning, London

Clark DS (2001) Nothing new in 2000? Comparative law in 1900 and today. Tulane Law Rev 75(4):871–912

Cocks R (1988) Sir Henry Maine: a study in Victorian jurisprudence. Cambridge University Press, Cambridge

David R (1950) Traité élémentaire de droit civil compare: Introduction à l'étude des droits étrangers et à la méthode comparative. Librairie générale de droit et de jurisprudence, Paris

del Vecchio G (1950) L' unité de l' esprit humain comme base de la comparaison juridique. Revue internationale de droit comparé 2(4):686–691

Diamond A (ed) (2006) The Victorian Achievement of Sir Henry Maine: a centennial reappraisal. Cambridge University Press, Cambridge

Feaver G (1969) From status to contract: a biography of Sir Henry Maine 1822–1888. Longmans Green, London

Franklin M (1954) The influence of Savigny and Gans on the development of the legal and constitutional theory of Christian Roselius. Festschrift Rabel 1:141

Friedrich CJ (ed) (1954) The philosophy of Hegel. Random House, New York

Gans E (1824–1835) Das Erbrecht in weltgeschichtlicher Entwicklung. Maurer, Berlin

Gaudemet E (1912) Raymond Saleilles 1855-1912. Revue bourguignonne de l'Université de Dijon 22:161–263

Gerber DJ (2001) Sculpting the agenda of comparative law: Ernst Rabel and the facade of language. In: Riles A (ed) Rethinking the masters of comparative law. Hart Publishing, Oxford, pp 190–208

Grossfeld B, Wilde M (1994) Josef Kohler und das Recht der deutschen Schutzgebiete. Rabels Zeitschrift 58:59–75

Hug W (1932) The history of comparative law. Harv Law Rev 45(6):1027–1070

[72] See on this matter Sacco (2001), p. 1166.

[73] See on this issue Sacco (2000), p. 340; Stoffel (2001).

Jamin C (2000) Le vieux rêve de Saleilles et Lambert revisité: À propos du Congres international de droit comparé de Paris. Revue internationale de droit comparé 52(4):733–751
Jamin C (2002) Saleilles' and Lambert's old dream revisited: on the occasion of the centennial of the international congress of comparative law, Paris 1900. Am J Comp Law 50(4):701–718
Janssen H (2000) Die Übertragung von Rechtsvorstellungen auf fremde Kulturen am Beispiel des englischen Kolonialrechts: ein Beitrag zur Rechtsvergleichung. Mohr Siebeck, Tübingen
Kegel G (1990) Ernst Rabel – Werk und Person. Rabels Zeitschrift für ausländisches und internationales Privatrecht 54:1–23
Kiesow RM (1997) Das Naturgesetz des Rechts. Suhrkamp, Frankfurt am Main
Kleinheyer G, Schröder J (1983) Deutsche Juristen aus fünf Jahrhunderten. Eine biographische Einführung in die Geschichte der Rechtswissenschaft, 2nd edn. CF Müller Juristischer Verlag, Heidelberg
Kohler J (1887) Über das Recht der Australneger. Zeitschrift für vergleichende Rechtswissenschaft 7:321–368
Kohler J (1895) Das Recht der Azteken. Zeitschrift für vergleichende Rechtswissenschaft 11:1–111
Lambert E (1905) Conception générale et definition de la science du droit compare. In: Procès verbaux des séances et documents du Congrès international de droit compare 1900 I. LGDJ, Paris, pp 26–61
Landauer C (2003) Henry Summner Maine's grand tour: Roman law and ancient law. Curr Leg Issues 6:135–147
Levi L (1850–1852) Commercial law, its principles and administration, or, The mercantile law of Great Britain: compared with the codes and laws of commerce of the following mercantile countries: Anhalt, Austria ... Wurtemburg, and the Institutes of Justinian. W. Benning, London
Levi L (1854) Commercial law of the world. Smith Elder and Co, London
Lyall A (2008) Early German legal anthropology: Albert Hermann Post and his questionnaire. J Afr Law 52(1):114–138
Maine H (1931) Ancient law. Oxford University Press, London
Mayda J (1978) Francois Geny and modern jurisprudence. Louisiana State University Press, Baton Rouge
Michaels R (2002) Im Westen nichts Neues? 100 Jahre Pariser Kongreß für Rechtsvergleichung – Gedanken anläßlich einer Jubiläumskonferenz in New Orleans. Rabels Zeitschrift für ausländisches und internationales Privatrecht 66(1):97–115
Mommsen WJ, de Moor JA (eds) (1992) European expansion and law: the encounter of European and indigenous law in the 19th-and -20th-century Africa and Asia. Berg Publishers, Oxford
Pollock F (1903) The history of comparative jurisprudence. J Soc Comp Legis 5(1):74–89
Post AH (1894) Grundriss der ethnologischen Jurisprudenz. Oldenburg, Schulze
Rabel E (1919) Das Institut für Rechtsvergleichung an der Universität München. Zeitschrift für Rechtspflege in Bayern 15:2–6
Rabel E (1924) Aufgabe und Notwendigkeit der Rechtsvergleichung. Rheinische Zeitschrift für Zivil- und Prozessrecht 13:279–301
Rabel E (1937) Die Fachgebiete des Kaiser-Wilhelm-Instituts für ausländisches und internationales privatrecht (gegründet 1926) 1900-1935. In: 25 Jahre Kaiser-Wilhelm-Gesellschaft zur Förderung der Wissenschaften 3: Die Geisteswissenschaften. Springer, Berlin, pp 77–190
Reimann M (2001) Beyond national systems: a comparative law for the international age. Tulane Law Rev 75:1103–1120
Rheinstein M (1956) In memory of Ernst Rabel. Am J Comp Law 5:185–196
Rothacker E (1957) Die vergleichende Methode in den Geisteswissenschaften. Zeitschrift für vergleichende Rechtswissenschaft 60:13–33
Rotondi M (1968) Technique du droit dogmatique et droit compare. Revue internationale de droit comparé 20(1):5–18
Sabbioneti M (2019) Raymond Saleilles: (1855-1912). In: Descamps O, Domingo R (eds) Great Christian jurists in French history. Cambridge University Press, Cambridge, pp 324–341

Sacco R (2000) L'avenir du droit comparé: un défi pour les juristes du nouveau millénaire. Société de législation comparée, Paris
Sacco R (2001) One hundred years of comparative law. Tulane Law Rev 75:1159–1176
Saleilles R (1900) Rapport presente a la commission d'organisation sur l'utilite, le but et le programme du Congres. Bull. de la societe 29:228–236
Saleilles R (1902) Ecole historique et droit naturel. Revue trimestrielle de droit civil 1:80–112
Saleilles R (1905) Rapport sur la conception et l'objet de la science du droit compare. Congrès international de droit comparé tenu à Paris du 31 juillet au 4 août 1900. Société de législation comparée, LGDJ, Paris, p 68
Stammler R (1922) Lehrbuch der Rechtsphilosophie. W de Gruyter, Berlin
Stoffel WA (2001) Enlightened decision making. Tulane Law Rev 75:1195–1214
Stolleis M (1998) Nationalität und Internationalität: Rechtsvergleichung im öffentlichen Recht des 19. Jahrhunderts. Steiner, Stuttgart
Stone J (1966) Social dimensions of law and justice. Stevens and Sons, London
Tanzi A (1990) François Gény tra scienza del diritto e giurisprudenza. Giappichelli, Torino
Thieme J (1986) Ernst Rabel (1874-1955): Schriften aus dem Nachlass. Rabels Zeitschrift für ausländisches und internationales Privatrecht 50:251–281
von Jhering R (1955) Des Geist des Römischen Rechts auf den verschiedenen Stufen seiner Entwicklung I, 9th edn. Scientia-Verlag, Aalen
von Savigny FC (1814) Vom Beruf unserer Zeit für Gesetzgebung und Rechtswissenschaft. Mohr und Zimmer, Heidelberg
Weiss A (1900) Rôle, fonction et méthode du Droit comparé dans le domaine du Droit civil. Bulletin de la Société de législation comparée 12:417
Yntema H (1958) Le droit comparé et l' humanisme. Revue internationale de droit comparé 10(4):693–700
Zimmerman R (2001) In der Schule von Ludwig Mitteis: Ernst Rabels rechtshistorische Ursprünge. Rabels Zeitschrift 65:1–38
Zweigert K, Kötz H (1987) An introduction to comparative law, 2nd edn. Clarendon Press, Oxford

Chapter 4
Uses of Comparative Law in Domestic and International Lawmaking and Adjudication

4.1 Introduction

In an era of increasing global mobility and the internationalization of legal life, comparative legal studies are gaining momentum. While the widespread interest in the comparative study of laws can be largely attributed to the dramatic growth of transnational economic transactions, this factor only partially explains the trend. Another significant factor is the expectation of gaining a deeper understanding of law as a social phenomenon and obtaining fresh insights into the current state and future direction one's own legal system.

Most legal professionals operate within their native legal system and are conversant with the laws of the land they have grown up with and become accustomed to. They are familiar with the substantive and procedural rules and principles of their system and may tend to assume that the solutions it provides to legal problems are the best. Sometimes they may be right, but they are likely just as often to be wrong. Being confined to one's own legal system can be insulating and distorting. Comparative law enables lawyers and jurists to integrate their knowledge of law into a cultural panorama extending well beyond their own borders, providing them with a broader understanding of the possible range of solutions to legal problems than familiarity with a single legal system allows.[1] It allows them to view their own

[1]Zweigert and Kötz argue that the study of only one legal system cannot not reach the level of a true academic inquiry: "It may indeed be that the mere interpretation of positive rules of law in the way traditionally practised by lawyers does not deserve to be called a science at all, whether intellectual or social. Perhaps legal studies only become truly scientific when they rise above the actual rules of any national system, as happens in legal philosophy, legal history, the sociology of law, and comparative law." Zweigert and Kötz (1998), p. 4. On the value of comparative law as a means of broadening legal knowledge see also: Yntema (1956), p. 901; Paton (1972), p. 41. And see Grossfeld and Eberle (2003), p. 292.

G. Mousourakis, *Traversing Legal Traditions*, Springer Textbooks in Law,
https://doi.org/10.1007/978-3-031-94669-1_4

legal system from a broader perspective and a certain distance.[2] This broader perspective helps them recognize that foreign legal concepts, institutions, and rules may significantly diverge from those in their own system and yet still be valid. They can consider how similar rules may produce different effects and how different rules may lead to identical results in diverse national contexts due to different interpretations and applications of these rules.[3] Although they will naturally focus on the mainstream features and substantive and procedural rules of their own system, recognizing the diversity in legal reasoning and having a wider knowledge of possible solutions to legal problems gleaned from other jurisdictions will better prepare them to deal with new and complex legal issues.[4]

In this context, reference must be made to the traditional *de lege lata* and *de lege ferenda* comparison. In legal parlance, the latter term means 'the law as it should be' and is often used when comparing an existing law (*lex lata*) to a proposed one. This comparison involves inquiries concerned with formulating new legal rules and instruments at a domestic or international level. The comparative study of legal systems is also valuable when courts and other authorities interpret and apply the rules of their legal system or face the task of filling gaps in legislation or case law.

This chapter will explore some of the principal applications of comparative law, both as a method and as an academic discipline. Its aim is to highlight the general utility of comparative law as vital tool for addressing the challenges that lawmakers, judges, and legal practitioners encounter in a rapidly evolving world of unforeseen connections.

4.2 Comparative Law as an Aid to Legislation and Law Reform

Comparative law holds significant importance in the legislative field, especially when proposing new laws or modifying existing ones.[5] In today's complex society, lawmakers often face challenging problems. Instead of relying on conjecture and risking suboptimal outcomes, they can draw on the vast wealth of legal experience that comparative legal studies offer. As Rudolf Jhering aptly noted, "the reception of

[2] See, in general, Fletcher (1998) and Muir-Watt (2000).

[3] As Zweigert and Kötz have remarked, "it is the general educational value of comparative law that is most important: it shows that the rule currently operative is only one of several possible solutions; it provides an effective antidote to uncritical faith in legal doctrine; it teaches us that what is often presented as pure natural law proves to be nothing of the sort as soon as one crosses a frontier, and it keeps reminding us that while doctrine and categories are essential in any system, they can sometimes become irrelevant to the functioning and efficacy of the law in action and degenerate into futile professional games." Zweigert and Kötz (1998), pp. 21–22. Consider also Siems (2018), pp. 2–3. For a closer look at the role of comparative law in legal education see Reimann (2012), pp. 14–15; Demleitner (2019); Péteri (2002); Gordley (2001).

[4] Consider Siems (2018), p. 28; Schadbach (1998).

[5] Dannemann (2019), pp. 408–409.

a foreign legal institution is not a matter of nationality, but a matter of usefulness and need. No one bothers to fetch a thing from afar when one has one as good or better at home, but only a fool would refuse a good medicine just because it did not grow in his own back garden."[6]

Therefore, it is unsurprising that legislators, when considering various approaches to resolving a particular issue, often examine how the same or similar problems have been addressed in other jurisdictions. Adopting of a foreign legal rule typically assumes that the rule has been generally effective in its country of origin and is likely to produce the desired results in the country considering its adoption. However, in most cases, adopting a foreign rule without significant modifications may prove impossible due to differences in court structures, legal processes, and legal reasoning, as well as broader socio-cultural, political, and economic disparities between the countries.

As noted in Chap. 3, the rise of modern comparative law as both a science and an academic discipline was largely driven by the desire of national authorities to study foreign laws as a means of designing or improving domestic legislation.[7] A notable example of drawing inspiration from foreign law is the Prussian company law of 1843, which was partly based on the French Commercial Code of 1807, the earliest legislative enactment on companies.[8] Other examples include the concept of income tax, which originated in England and was adopted by German and other Continental European legislators in the early nineteenth century; the Austrian anti-trust law, which served as the model for the German cartel law of 1923; and the Swedish institution of the ombudsman, which has been adopted in many countries worldwide.

Moreover, the widespread adoption of civil law codes across Europe and other parts of the world during the nineteenth and twentieth centuries is a well-documented phenomenon. Notably, the French Civil Code of 1804 (*Code civil des Francais*) served as a model for the civil codes of many countries, including Italy, Spain, Portugal, Poland, Romania, Bolivia, Mexico, Quebec, and Louisiana. The Swiss Civil Code of 1907 was adopted in Turkey in 1926, and the drafts of the German Civil Code of 1900 (*Burgerliches Gesetzbuch* or BGB) influenced the civil codes of Japan, Korea, Brazil, Switzerland, Austria, Hungary, and Greece. Additionally, the civil codes of the Netherlands (1992) and Québec (1994), the German law of obligations of 2002, and the new codes in the areas of civil, commercial, and criminal law enacted in former communist countries of Central and Eastern Europe were also based on extensive comparative law research.

Furthermore, all contemporary constitutions have been inspired or influenced by foreign sources. In some countries, the adoption of foreign norms in the domain of

---

[6] von Jhering (1955), p. 8; quoted in Zweigert Kötz (1987), p. 16. And see Siems (2018), pp. 4–5.

[7] The discipline of legislative comparative law (legislation comparée), as developed by the Société de Législation Comparé (established in 1869), promoted the comparative study of foreign law codes in France and several other countries.

[8] In nineteenth century Germany a number of legal unification projects in the fields of private law, criminal law and the law of procedure drew on extensive comparative research into the laws of other countries. See on this Drobnig and Dopffel (1982).

constitutional law was preceded by a detailed and critical learning process, while in others, the process was less thorough. Generally, the tendency to borrow in this field has been more prominent during significant transitions in the legal-political system, such as after the Second World War or following the collapse of communist regimes in Eastern Europe.[9] A state drafting a new constitution is particularly susceptible to external influences, often due to a desire to abandon norms associated with overthrown political regimes or previous disappointing constitutional experiences. Borrowing from other constitutions offers the advantage of providing a fresh start, but it also carries risks. If the process of adopting foreign norms at such a formative stage is uncritical, the norms may be profoundly alien to the history and culture of the recipient country.

In general, contemporary law-making and law reform are characterized by eclecticism. This approach involves using comparative law to investigate various approaches and solutions to legal problems across multiple jurisdictions, and integrating the findings into the drafting of new legislation.[10] In Continental European countries, such research is usually initiated by the ministry of justice and carried out by experts in comparative law research institutes or suitably qualified civil servants. In the United Kingdom, comparative law is incorporated into legislative process mainly through the work of the English and Scottish Law Commissions. Section 3(1)(f) of the Law Commissions Act 1965, which created the two law reform commissions, states that one of the functions of the Law Commissions is "to obtain such information as to the legal systems of other countries as appears to the Commissioners likely to facilitate the performance of their functions," namely, systematically developing and reforming the law of England and Scotland.[11] An important aspect of the commissions' work is to inquire into the function of legal rules and the context within which they operate. After consultation with local and foreign experts, they ascertain whether the rules have been successful in achieving their intended objectives.

In the United States, the American Law Institute, established in 1932, conducts a wide range of comparative law research aimed at law reform and general restatement of laws. The Institute's Model Penal Code, for example, draws on legal experience from several jurisdictions. Similarly, in the field of competition law, the federal legislature was inspired by European legal models when reviewing the Sherman

[9] On the concept of transition see, e.g., Teitel (2002).

[10] This tendency is evident, for example, in the new Civil Code of Holland, which came into effect in 1992. In carrying out their work, the Dutch drafters relied not only on a variety of Continental European models, but also on models derived from common law countries, as well as from international treaties and conventions.

[11] Consider, e.g., the English Law Commission's report on 'Privity of Contracts: Contracts for the Benefit of Third Parties'. Besides surveying the laws of other common law countries, the Commission also recognized that a factor in support of legal reform in this field was that "the legal systems of most of the member states of the European Union recognize and enforce the rights of third-party beneficiaries under contracts." (See Law Com. No 242, 1996, 41.) The report led to the enactment of the Contracts (Rights of Third Parties) Act 1999.

Antitrust Act of 1890.[12] However, compared to European countries, the influence of foreign law on American law-making appears to be less prominent. This may be connected to the fact that inter-state comparison within the United States is regarded as more important than comparison with foreign legal systems.

We may conclude that most new legislation enacted in Europe and elsewhere is preceded by at least some comparative law research, and that every legal system in the world today embodies borrowed or imported elements. It is important to note that the most common way in which foreign legal models are integrated into national law is through academic legal writing. Legal scholars often introduce points from foreign legal systems into domestic debates, thereby bringing them to the attention of the legislative bodies in their respective countries. Legal scholarship is generally more susceptible to foreign influence than the judiciary or the legal profession. This is evidenced, for instance, by the fact that the reception of Roman law in Continental Europe first occurred in the realm of legal science.[13]

4.3 The Role of Comparative Law in the Judicial Process

Comparative law holds practical significance for courts and the judicial process, particularly when judges are tasked with interpreting legal rules or filling gaps in legislation or case law. Legal systems recognize the importance of legal certainty, which dictates that courts should decide cases according to their own domestic law. However, situations inevitably arise where statutory provisions or case law authorities do not cover specific matters. In such instances, comparative law can offer a range of approaches and potential solutions. While foreign laws and court decisions are not binding, they can be highly informative or even persuasive.[14] This is especially relevant when judges encounter legal rules, concepts, and principles borrowed or adopted from other jurisdictions. The influence of comparative law on national courts is evident in nearly every legal system, despite significant differences among countries.[15]

---

[12] For more examples see Zaphiriou (1982), pp. 71 ff.

[13] On the influence of comparative law on domestic law see, in general, Smits (2019). Consider also Harmathy (1999).

[14] Consider Siems (2018), pp. 4–5. And see Glenn (1987) and Markesinis (1990).

[15] According to Lord Steyn, former Lord of Appeal in Ordinary in the U.K., a function of comparative law "is to throw light on the competing advantages and disadvantages of feasible solutions thereby showing what in the generality of cases is the most sensible and just solution in a difficult case. It enables courts to re-examine the merits and demerits of legal institutions in a rigorous manner." Steyn (2006), p. 5. In the words of Zweigert and Kötz, "Comparative law is an 'école de vérité' which extends and enriches the 'supply of solutions' and offers the scholar of critical capacity the opportunity of finding the 'better solution' for his time and place." Zweigert and Kötz (1987), p. 15.

With the exception of the United States, where there is considerable resistance to the influence of foreign sources in the domestic legal system,[16] the exchange of legal ideas at the judicial level is generally encouraged in common law countries. Cross-citations between common law courts in different jurisdictions are frequent.[17] In these countries, the principal criterion for the selection of foreign judgments is legal family, leading to frequent references to sources from other common law systems. The accessibility of relevant legal materials in terms of language and availability further encourages judges to consider such sources first. Additionally, the standing and prestige of a foreign court can provide an additional reason for judges to take its case law into account. In this respect, judges sometimes refer to judgments from the highest courts in Germany, France, Italy, and the Netherlands. However, the problems of language and availability present significant obstacles to the use of legal materials from non-common law sources.

Compared to courts in common law jurisdictions, courts in Continental European or civil law countries are generally reluctant to seek inspiration outside their national legal framework. This can be attributed to differences in legal cultures, particularly in judicial reasoning and decision-making processes. In common law countries, the prevailing style of judicial reasoning allows judges to express their personal socio-political views freely and utilize teleological (consequentialist) arguments, including those derived from comparative law, to support their legal conclusions. Conversely, the deductive method of judicial reasoning predominant in civil law jurisdictions leaves little room for judges to look beyond their own legal system for justification. Civil law judges do not create their own legal constructions but rather

[16] In his dissenting opinion in the case of *Roper v. Simmons*, which concerned the constitutionality of the juvenile death penalty, Justice Antonin Scalia of the Supreme Court of the United States presented the following argument with regard to the use of foreign legal materials in judicial decision-making: "The basic premise of the Court's argument - that American law should conform to the laws of the rest of the world - ought to be rejected out of hand. In fact, the Court itself does not believe it. (…) To begin with, I do not believe that approval 'by other nations and peoples' should buttress our commitment to American principles any more than (what should logically follow) disapproval by 'other nations and peoples' should weaken that commitment. (…) What these foreign sources 'affirm', rather than repudiate, is the Justices' own notion of how the world ought to be, and their diktat that it shall be so henceforth in America. The Court's parting attempt to downplay the significance of its extensive discussion of foreign law is unconvincing. 'Acknowledgment' of foreign approval has no place in the legal opinion of this Court unless it is part of the basis for the Court's judgment – which is surely what it parades as today." 543 U.S. 2005, *Roper v. Simmons*, dissenting opinion of Justice Scalia, pp. 16–23. According to Alain Levasseur, with the exception of Louisiana, the relevance of foreign and comparative law in American courts "is almost nil". Levasseur (1999), p. 333. This does not mean, however, that there are no examples of state courts or of the United States Supreme Court referring to foreign legal sources. For example, in the above-mentioned case of *Roper v Simmons* the Court held that the execution of offenders who were under the age of eighteen at the time of the commission of the crime was a violation of the Eighth Amendment. According to the majority of the Court, this view drew support from the fact that executing juvenile offenders violated several international treaties and that "the overwhelming weight of international opinion [was] against the juvenile death penalty". Consider also *Roe* v. *Wade*, 410 US 113 (1972).

[17] See on this Mak (2011).

borrow from legal science. Therefore, it is primarily through legal science and scholarship that foreign law is brought to their attention.

However, it is important to note that significant differences exist among Continental European legal systems in how national courts approach foreign law. In Germany, it is not uncommon for the Federal Constitutional Court (*Bundesverfassungsgericht*) to utilize foreign legal sources to support its arguments, though the number of such cases is relatively limited. When foreign sources are cited, they usually reference jurisdictions with a shared legal heritage, such as Switzerland and Austria, with fewer instances of citations from French, Italian, English, or American law. In contrast, French case law seldom references foreign legal sources. This is unsurprising given that the decisions of the French Supreme Court (*Cour de Cassation*) are typically not extensively reasoned and often do not even include references to French legal doctrine or case law. A similar situation exists in Belgium, the Netherlands, and Greece, where references to foreign law are sparse and generally quite broad. Even when references to foreign legal systems are made, they are often limited to the interpretative analyses of statutory provisions offered by scholars. The legislative enactments related to these analyses, the socio-cultural environment in which the relevant provisions operate, and the comparison of this environment with that of the recipient country are either not considered at all or, if considered, never appear in the court's judgment.

However, one should be careful not to conclude that foreign legal sources have no relevance to judicial decision-making in these countries. In Continental European countries, which have a system of Advocates-General advising the Supreme Court, the opinions of these officials often contain comparative references to foreign and international statutory and case law. When the court explicitly references the part of the Advocate-General's opinion that includes these foreign legal sources, the influence of foreign law becomes evident.[18] Finally, it should be noted that, despite differences among European countries regarding the use of foreign and comparative law, a certain degree of convergence can be observed in the national judicial treatment of the European Court of Human Rights and European Union law.[19]

As already noted, the need to consult foreign legal sources typically arises when a court encounters a gap in the law or when the meaning of the relevant statutory enactment is unclear. Although courts could resolve such problems solely within a domestic framework using well-established interpretive techniques (textualism, intentionalism, purposivism), the increasing use of comparative arguments in recent years reflects a growing recognition among the judiciary, especially the higher courts, of the potential benefits of foreign experience. This approach is particularly useful when similar or identical problems arise in different countries.[20] For example, the question of whether 'immaterial damages' should be awarded in cases involving privacy infringement, which was not addressed by the German Civil

[18] Consider on this issue Drobnig (1999).

[19] Martinico and Pollicino (2010).

[20] Koopmans (1996), p. 549.

Code, was answered in the affirmative by the highest German civil and constitutional courts after consideration of foreign law.[21] Furthermore, the German Supreme Court ruled that statements made by an accused person during a police interview were inadmissible as evidence if the accused had not been informed of their right to remain silent and their right to legal representation. The Court supported its decision with references to the American case of *Miranda v. Arizona* (1966) and to English, French, and Dutch law.[22]

In addressing the question of whether land rights should be given to aboriginals, the High Court of Australia made extensive references to other legal systems, citing fourteen cases in favour of its decision, only three of which were Australian.[23] Similarly, the Supreme Court of Canada referred extensively to foreign, particularly American, case law when deciding which rights aboriginal people should have.[24] In *Fairchild* v. *Glenhaven Funeral Services*[25] the English House of Lords departed from the normal rules concerning causation in a case where a person suffering from a disease caused by exposure to asbestos would be unable to show which of several employers had caused his condition. Besides relying on common law authority, the House referred to legal sources from France, Germany, Norway, and the Netherlands.[26] The list of pertinent examples could easily be extended.

However, one should not infer from the foregoing that voluntary recourse to foreign legal authorities is common in difficult or controversial cases. There are numerous instances where judges do not refer to foreign law at all, even though such references could be beneficial. This phenomenon can be partly attributed to institutional factors and partly to individual approaches judges take towards judicial decision-making. A judge's personal views regarding their role in relation to the legislature and the executive inevitably influence the margin of discretion they believe they possess in a challenging case.[27] Furthermore, judges may hold differing opinions on the relevance and appropriateness of foreign laws and legal experiences in their decision-making process. These varying perspectives and attitudes are influenced by the judges' educational background, legal training, degree of interaction with colleagues and legal scholars, and their personal views on the exercise of judicial discretion in the interpretation of laws.[28]

---

[21] BGH 5 March 1963, BGHZ 39, 124 and BVerfG 14 February 1973, BVerfGE 34, 269.

[22] BGH [1992] *Neue Juristische Wochenschrift* 1463.

[23] High Court of Australia, *Mabo and Others v. State of Queensland* (1992) 107 ALR 1.

[24] *Inter alia* in *Van der Peet* v. *The Queen* (1996) 2 SCR 507.

[25] *Fairchild* v. *Glenhaven Funeral Services* [2003] 1 AC 32.

[26] See on this matter Scherpe (2004).

[27] Consider on this Barak (2006), p. 118.

[28] On the role of comparative law in judicial decision-making consider, in general, Posner (2008) and Andenas and Fairgrieve (2015).

4.4 Comparative Law and Private International Law

Private international law, also known as conflict of laws, is a branch of private law comprising rules that determine the applicable law in cases involving multiple legal jurisdictions. While these rules are primarily national in origin, they inherently possess a transnational scope and aim to promote international decisional harmony, i.e., uniformity of results regardless of the forum. The role of comparative law in relation to private international law is twofold: first, it assists legislators in drafting new conflict of laws rules; second, it is used by courts to apply foreign law or to recognize and enforce foreign judicial decisions and judgments. It can be said that the practical operation of private international law relies significantly on comparative law, thereby providing the latter with practical legitimacy.

Comparative law plays a crucial role in the drafting and codifying of national conflict of laws rules. Given the supranational and technical nature of these rules, private international lawyers and legislators regularly seek guidance from comparative law scholars who are well-versed in foreign legal systems. This practice is equally important in the creation of international conflict of laws conventions.[29] The widespread use of comparative law in the legislative process has resulted in a significant degree of international uniformity in private international law, particularly concerning basic principles and general rules. For example, in recent decades, European Union countries have moved towards harmonizing their conflict of laws rules as part of the Europeanization of private international law. The comparative study of European legal systems has been essential to this process—a natural consequence of a long-standing academic tradition that has fostered the exchange of legal ideas and concepts across the Continent.

Furthermore, when private international law rules require the application of foreign law, judges rely on comparative law to identify, understand, and correctly apply the relevant foreign laws. This is particularly true in countries that do not recognize the automatic application of the *lex fori* (the law of the country of the court) in resolving conflict of laws cases and in countries such as Germany, Austria, Switzerland, and Italy, where judges are expected to apply foreign law *ex officio*.[30] The need for comparison is acknowledged even if judges ultimately revert to the *lex fori*.

With the development of content-orientated choice of law rules, comparative analyses are often necessary to apply the forum's conflict of laws rules correctly. These rules frequently employ terms whose proper interpretation requires an understanding of their respective meanings in all the legal systems involved in a case.[31] Moreover, many private international law conventions explicitly require that courts consider how other jurisdictions have interpreted their provisions to maintain

[29] Of particular importance in this respect is the Hague Conference on Private International Law.

[30] Consider Reimann (1995), pp. 159 ff; Hartley (1996); de Boer (1996).

[31] This is referred to as the problem of 'qualification' or 'characterization'. See on this issue Rabel (1931).

uniformity of meaning. Although obtaining such knowledge does not in itself constitute comparative law in the strictest sense, the application of conflict of laws rules presupposes comparisons between different legal systems, even if these comparisons are not always made explicit in the relevant judgment.[32] Therefore, it is accurate to say that, even in its practical, day-to-day operations, "no system of private international law can escape involvement with the discipline of comparative law".[33]

4.5 Exploring the Role of Comparative Law in the Domain of Public International Law

Public international law is the body of law that governs relationships involving states, intergovernmental or supranational organizations, and other entities regarded as international legal persons. It is a vast field encompassing issues such as the use of armed force, human rights, international crimes, the law of the sea, international commercial relations, environmental protection, and even outer space. Comparative law, on the other hand, is traditionally concerned with examining legal problems and institutions originating from two or more legal systems, or with comparing entire legal systems to acquire a better understanding of them. At first glance, there seems to be little connection between these two fields. This is mainly because public international law is perceived as a relatively uniform system, providing little opportunity for comparison. Although comparing the public international law system itself with other legal regimes, including domestic ones, might be very informative, comparatists have largely focused on national systems and have, by and large, neglected public international law as an object of study. However, this does not mean that the comparative method is of no use to international law scholars and practitioners. Indeed, scholars are increasingly recognizing the importance of this method in addressing the problems of international law.[34]

In recent years, several scholars have been working to integrate the fields of comparative law and public international law, focusing particularly on comparing national approaches to international law and governance. The comparative study of

[32] Consider, for example, a situation where a judge must determine whether a will made by a citizen of a foreign country is invalid due to the testator's lack of capacity. According to the conflict of laws rules in the country of the forum, this question must be decided based on the law of the testator's country. Therefore, the judge must refer to the applicable foreign legal system to identify the rules that align, in content and substance, with the rules of their own system concerning the capacity to make a will, despite any terminological or other differences between the two systems. Similar considerations apply to the recognition and enforcement of foreign judicial decisions.

[33] See von Mehren (1978), pp. 32, 33. For a closer look at the role of comparative law in private international law consider, in general, Reimann (2012), pp. 15–18; Reimann (2019); Fauvarque-Cosson (2001); de Boer (1994).

[34] At the Centennial World Congress of Comparative Law in 2000, the leading German comparatist Mathias Reimann emphasized the need for comparative law to broaden its scope to embrace transnational and international issues. See Reimann (2001) and Dibadj (2008).

diverse national approaches to international law dates back to the early 1960s when the term 'comparative international law' was coined to describe the competing Western and Soviet perspectives on international law. Decolonization and developments in foreign policy and international relations highlighted the importance of understanding how states utilized existing international processes and norms to strengthen their positions in the global power race. A notable example of this comparative effort is the Protocol of Cooperation concluded in 1983 between the Law Faculty of the University College London and the Institute of State and Law of the USSR Academy of Sciences. This cooperation agreement led to a series of studies on the relationship between comparative and international law and the methodological challenges facing both disciplines.[35]

In the early post-Cold War era, many scholars viewed the political changes in Eastern Europe and elsewhere as marking the end of perceiving international law and its institutions as ideological battlegrounds. However, the eruption of ethnic and religious conflicts in Eastern Europe (especially the Former Yugoslavia), Asia, and Africa, along with the rise of terrorism, made it clear that international law was entering a new period of crisis. In this new and unsettled environment, the principal challenge for international law has been to address the inability of states and other international actors to create an effective multilateral framework for ensuring and promoting global security. As contemporary international law has evolved into a complex system of diverse sub-fields, institutional fragmentation, theoretical differentiation, and political pluralism have emerged as significant issues.[36] An important task of comparative law in this new setting is to address the challenges faced by public international law by considering diverse national, ethnic, religious, and cultural approaches to the role of international law and its institutions.

4.5.1 Comparative Law and General Principles of Law

The main sources of public international law are defined in Article 38(1) of the Statute of the International Court of Justice (ICJ). These sources include:

(a) International Treaties and Conventions: Formal agreements between states that are legally binding.
(b) International Custom: Practices that have developed over time and are accepted as binding by the international community. Customary international law arises from consistent and general practice by states followed out of a sense of legal obligation (*opinio juris*).

[35] Consider on this matter Butler (1989).

[36] Some scholars have associated this development with what they refer to as a split between European and American approaches to international law, both of which being subject to a comparative analysis. Consider on this issue Verdirame (2007) and Koskenniemi and Leino (2002).

(c) General Principles of Law Recognized by Civilized Nations: Fundamental principles that are common to the legal systems of the world. These principles can fill gaps in international law where no treaty or custom exists.
(d) Judicial Decisions and Scholarly Writings: While not binding sources, the judicial decisions of international courts and tribunals, as well as academic writings by leading scholars, are considered subsidiary means for the determination of the rules of international law.

These sources collectively contribute to the development and application of public international law, guiding the conduct of states and other international actors.

We now turn to Article 38(1) (c) of the Statute of the International Court of Justice, which identifies the 'general principles of law recognized by civilized nations' as one of the sources of public international law.[37] This concept inherently acknowledges a set of normative propositions that are universally valid, transcending diverse socio-political systems once stylistic, technical, and cultural differences are accounted for. Historically, general principles of law have played a vital role in the development of public international law, as norms derived from these principles were often the only ones available and acceptable to states for regulating international relations. These principles were regarded as a source of law based on the theory that when states universally applied similar principles in their domestic laws, their consent to be bound by those same principles at the international level could be inferred.

However, contemporary international law relies less on general principles of law as a source of legal norms. This shift is partly due to the extraordinary proliferation of treaties and other international legal instruments used to regulate relations between states. Additionally, many norms originally derived from general principles have, over time, been incorporated into customary international law. Furthermore, the process of international law-making through 'legislative' treaties (as opposed to merely 'declaratory' treaties) has reduced the need to resort to general principles of law to fill gaps in the international legal system. This explains why general principles are today regarded as a subordinate source compared to international treaties and custom.

General principles have been used to fill gaps in the law, particularly regarding procedural matters and issues of international judicial administration. For instance, the International Court of Justice has employed general principles to establish the international rule that reparation is due for any internationally wrongful act.[38] Additionally, it has determined that a state may be barred (estopped) from insisting on a claim resulting from its own actions;[39] that circumstantial evidence is admissible

[37] The phrase 'civilized nations' was used to indicate that the general principles were limited to those common to mature or developed legal systems, serving as a means to prevent judicial arbitrariness. However, in a post-colonial era, the reference to 'civilized nations' is considered inappropriate and can be disregarded.

[38] *Chorzow Factory (Indemnity) Case (Merits)* (1928).

[39] *Temple of Preah Vihear Case* (1962).

in determining a state's alleged wrongdoing;[40] and that a case once decided between the same parties on the same facts cannot be raised again—commonly referred to as the *res judicata* principle.[41] Equity is probably the most pertinent general principle of international law, though some scholars argue that it should be regarded as a distinct source not covered by Article 38 of the Statute of the International Court of Justice.[42] In a general sense, equity is understood to mean fairness or justice and is considered central to law, as the principal attribute of good law is its justice. In a narrower sense, within legal philosophy, 'equity' is contrasted with strict law (*ius strictum*). Once a legal rule is established, it is the judge's duty to apply it without questioning it, as justice demands certainty in the application of the law. However, no system of law can foresee all possible variations of circumstances to provide rules capable of achieving justice in every situation. Legal rules are meant to be of general application, binding in all relevant cases. Nevertheless, situations inevitably arise that the general rules cannot address. In such cases, resorting to equity, as distinct from strict law, becomes necessary. The International Court of Justice has frequently referenced equity, particularly in cases concerning maritime delimitations and the delimitation of boundaries on land.[43] The Court's position is that resorting to equity is a logical and essential part of applying substantive legal rules.[44] Furthermore, international law encompasses the general principle of *good faith*, which mandates that states must act honestly in fulfilling their international obligations.[45]

As noted by scholars, comparative law plays a role in uncovering and elucidating the 'general principles of law' that both international and, occasionally, national courts must apply.[46] Rudolf Schlesinger aptly described the phrase 'general principles of law' as referring to principles evident in the municipal laws of various

[40] *Corfu Channel Case* (1949).

[41] *Effect of Awards of the UN Administrative Tribunal Case* (1954). For more examples of cases that rely on general principles consider Shaw (2008), pp. 98 ff.

[42] Consider on this issue Cheng (1953), pp. 1–26; Thirlway (2014), pp. 104–110. It should be noted here that Article 38 (2) of the Statute of the International Court of Justice provides that the Court may reach a decision in a case on the basis of what it deems just and right (*ex aequo et bono*), if the parties to the case agree.

[43] Consider, e.g., *North Sea Continental Shelf Cases* (n. 9) paras 85–88; *Frontier Dispute (Burkina Faso v Republic of Mali)*, Judgment [1986] ICJ Per. 554, para. 150.

[44] As stated in a recent case, the role of equity in delimitation cases is to "achieve a delimitation that is equitable" and not "an equal apportionment of maritime areas." *Maritime Delimitation in the Black Sea (Romania v Ukraine)*, Judgment [2009] ICJ Rep. 61, para. 111.

[45] See on this issue Cheng (1953), pp. 103–160.

[46] Hugo Grotius (1583–1645), a leading representative of the School of Natural Law and the founder of modern international law theory, employed the comparative method to empirically ground the ideas of natural law. He believed that the universal propositions of natural law could be proven not only through mere deduction from reason but also by demonstrating that certain legal rules and institutions were recognized across all legal systems. To illustrate and support his system of natural law, Grotius utilized legal materials from diverse countries and historical periods. And see Chap. 7 below.

nations, asserting that these principles can only be ascertained through the comparative method.[47] However, the role of legal comparatism in this context should not be overstated, as conducting a comparative study to identify general principles on a global scale would be an almost impossible task. Firstly, there is the challenge of determining which legal systems should be included. Prioritizing a select few systems to the exclusion of others could raise questions about the integrity and objectivity of the relevant judicial process. Secondly, it is debatable whether certain domestic legal concepts and principles can be compared or transposed into international law decisions. Thus, it is unsurprising that the comparative method is not frequently employed in practice.[48]

The comparative method is more commonly used in specific sub-categories of international law that have developed over recent decades. For example, the European Court of Human Rights often engages in comparative studies of member state laws to interpret the European Convention on Human Rights and determine the meaning and scope of its provisions.[49] Similarly, the European Court of Justice employs the comparative method in interpreting European Union law and reaching decisions by evaluating solutions provided by various legal systems.[50]

Although it may be unclear or controversial which legal principles are universally recognized or applicable at an international level, there is sufficient material in the domestic laws of states for international judges to perform their mandate. Of particular importance in this regard is the concept of 'common core research', which seeks to identify the highest common denominator in an area of substantive law across diverse national legal systems. Common core research is a reasonably reliable method for identifying common or general legal principles and plays a significant role in projects aimed at the international or regional unification or harmonization of law.[51] This observation leads us to the next topic of the present discussion: the unification or harmonization of law through international conventions.

---

[47] Schlesinger et al. (1988), p. 36. See also Schlesinger (1957) and Kiss (1980).

[48] For a closer look see Cheng (1953), p. 392; Zimmerman et al. (2006), pp. 259–261 (notes). Consider also Bothe and Ress (1980), p. 61.

[49] See on this Mahoney (2004).

[50] In the *Nold* judgment, for instance, the Court expressed the view that "fundamental rights form an integral part of the general principles of law (…) In safeguarding these rights, the Court is bound to draw inspiration from constitutional traditions common to the Member States, and it cannot therefore uphold measures which are incompatible with fundamental rights recognised and protected by the constitutions of those States" (*Nold* v *Commission*, case 4-73, 14 May 1974, para 13). The Court has used the comparative method in diverse fields of law and in connection with a variety of legal issues. Consider, e.g., *Algera*, joined cases 7/56, 3/57 to 7/57, 12 July 1957; *Hansen and Balle* v *Hauptzollamt de Flensburg*, case 148/77, 10 October 1978; *Zelger* v *Salinitri*, case 129/83, 7 June 1984; *CECA* v *Ferriere Sant'Anna*, case 168/82, 17 May 1983; *Orkem*, case 374/87, 18 October 1989. See Kakouris (1999), pp. 100 ff; Pescatore (1980).

[51] See Schlesinger (1968).

4.5.2 The Unification or Harmonization of Law by Means of International Conventions

The comparative law method can significantly contribute to the drafting of treaties and other international legal instruments aimed at the unification or harmonization of laws. It is important to distinguish between unification, which involves replacing multiple legal systems with a single system, and harmonization, which seeks to "effect an approximation or coordination of different legal provisions or systems by eliminating major differences and creating minimum requirements or standards."[52]

Leading comparatists Zweigert and Kötz argue that legal unification or harmonization is a desirable political objective, for which comparative law provides an important foundation. They emphasize, in particular, the role of comparative law in developing a common private law for Europe.[53] According to them, unified law offers several advantages: it facilitates international legal transactions; avoids the complexities of applying private international law and foreign substantive law; and reduces legal risks in international business, thereby benefiting both business planners and judges resolving related disputes. Unified law thus enhances legal certainty and predictability.[54] A significant step towards this goal was made in 1989 when the European Parliament adopted a resolution declaring its long-term goal to develop a uniform European Code of Private Law.[55] Over the past four decades, groups of academic lawyers across Europe have been engaged in projects focusing on legal harmonization in various fields of European private law.[56]

---

[52] Kamba (1974), p. 501. Consider also Siems (2018), p. 5.

[53] Zweigert and Kötz (1998), p. 16.

[54] Zweigert and Kötz (1998), p. 25.

[55] Resolution A2159/89 of the European Parliament on action to bring into line the private law of the Member States, [1989] OJ C158/400. Reference should also be made to a report published by the Directorate General for Research of the European Parliament in 1999, under the title 'The Private Law Systems in the EU: Discrimination on Grounds of Nationality and the Need for a European Civil Code.' See European Parliament, Directorate General for Research, Working Paper, Legal Affairs Series JURI 103 EN (1999).

[56] In this context reference should be made to the *Principles of European Contract Law*, a work of several European academics working in an independent capacity (the Commission on European Contract Law or 'the Lando Commission') (see *Principles of European Contract Law*, Parts I and II Revised 2000, Part III 2003); the Study Group on a European Civil Code (the successor to the Lando Commission), which prepared several volumes of the *Principles of European Law*; the Acquis Group, focusing on the systematic arrangement of current Community law with a view to elucidating the common structures of the emerging Community private law; the Common Core of European Private Law Project, which has completed several important comparative studies on European private law; the Academy of European Private Lawyers ('The Gandolfi Project'), which has published a draft European Contract Code inspired by the Italian Civil Code, and a draft Contract Code prepared for the Law Commissions of England and Scotland; the European Group on Tort Law, which has drafted the *Principles of European Tort Law*; and the Commission on European Family Law, which carries out research concerned with the harmonization of family law in Europe.

Comparative law has played and continues to play a significant role in projects aimed at legal integration or the harmonization of laws on an international or regional level. These projects are designed to reduce or eradicate, as far as possible and desirable, discrepancies and inconsistencies between national legal systems by encouraging the adoption of uniform legal rules and practices. To achieve this objective, uniform rules are typically developed based on research conducted by comparative law experts. These rules are then incorporated into transnational or international treaties, obliging the parties to adopt them as part of their domestic law.

However, the practical effectiveness of unification or harmonization projects is necessarily limited by the legal structures, institutions, and procedures within the participating nations, which ultimately determine the degree of uniformity in the interpretation and application of the relevant rules.[57] Despite the challenges surrounding the implementation of unification or harmonization schemes, there have been notable successes. These successes are particularly evident among countries that closely cooperate, such as the member countries of the European Union, and in certain areas of law, such as international commercial law, transportation law, intellectual property law, and the law of negotiable instruments.

In general, legal unification or harmonization is pursued through the efforts of international institutions. These institutions include the International Institute for the Unification of Private Law in Rome (UNIDROIT);[58] the UN Commission on International Trade Law (UNCITRAL);[59] the European Committee on Legal Cooperation;[60] the Hague Conference on Private International Law;[61] the World

[57] Merryman and Clark (1978), p. 58.

[58] The International Institute for the Unification of Private Law is an independent intergovernmental organization focused on the harmonization and coordination of private, particularly commercial, law among states. Its mission is to develop uniform instruments, principles, and rules to achieve these objectives. Established in 1926 as an auxiliary organ of the League of Nations, UNIDROIT was re-established in 1940 based on a multilateral agreement known as the UNIDROIT Statute. For more on this organization see Bonell (2006).

[59] The UN Commission on International Trade Law serves as the primary legal body of the United Nations system in the field of international trade law. When establishing the Commission, the UN General Assembly acknowledged that disparities in national laws governing international trade created significant obstacles to the free flow of trade. Consequently, the General Assembly viewed UNCITRAL as a mechanism through which the United Nations could actively work to reduce or eliminate these barriers. UNCITRAL's primary focus is on the modernization and harmonization of rules governing international commercial transactions.

[60] The European Committee on Legal Cooperation is an intergovernmental body responsible for the standard-setting activities of the Council of Europe in both public and private law. It promotes law reform and cooperation in various fields, including administrative law, civil law, data protection, family law, information technology and law, justice and the rule of law, nationality, and issues concerning refugees and asylum seekers. The Committee fulfils its tasks through the adoption of draft conventions, agreements, protocols, and recommendations. Additionally, it organizes and supervises colloquies and conferences and monitors the implementation and functioning of international instruments within its area of competence.

[61] The Hague Conference on Private International law is an intergovernmental organization dedicated to the progressive unification of rules governing private international law. The primary method it employs to achieve this goal is through the negotiation and drafting of multilateral trea-

Intellectual Property Organization (WIPO);[62] the International Labour Organization;[63] the Comité Maritime International;[64] and the International Civil Aviation Organization (ICAO).[65] Most relevant projects pertain to matters of private law, both civil and commercial.

An important aspect of legal integration or harmonization involves the development of supranational entities and the diminishing of traditional relationships between state power and the legal regulation of society. Consider the European Union, for example. This organization embodies the concept of a non-state legislative power, whose rules and legal policy objectives take precedence over those of its individual member states. This can be seen not only as an expression of a particular interpretation of integration ideology but also as a starting point for a new perspective on legal theory.

In the background, critical questions arise concerning the relationship between law and society: What are the goals of integration, and whose interests do they serve? If it is recognized that the goals of integration reflect specific interests, should these interests be acknowledged? The general assumption is that legal integration schemes are part of a coherent plan designed to facilitate economic transactions by establishing a legal structure that encourages enterprise and reduces costs. Although the primary motive appears to be economic, the forces driving legal integration are fundamentally political, closely connected with the institutional framework in which integration occurs. The comparative method may be indispensable for designing and implementing of legal integration schemes, but understanding these schemes' purpose requires considering this institutional framework.

---

ties or conventions in various fields of private international law. These fields include international judicial and administrative cooperation; conflict of laws concerning contracts, torts, maintenance obligations, the status and protection of children, relations between spouses, wills and trusts; recognition of companies; jurisdiction; and the enforcement of foreign judgments.

[62] The World Intellectual Property Organization is a specialized agency of the United Nations dedicated to the development and promotion of an international intellectual property system. WIPO aims to harmonize national intellectual property legislation and procedures; offer services for international applications for industrial property rights; provide legal and technical assistance to countries; and facilitate the resolution of private intellectual property disputes.

[63] The International Labour Organization is a specialized agency of the United Nations dedicated to bringing together governments, employers, and workers to establish labour standards, develop policies, and design programmes. It operates through three main bodies: The International labour Conference, the Governing body, and the International Labour Office, all of which include representatives from governments, employers, and workers.

[64] The Comité Maritime International is a non-governmental organization dedicated to maritime law and associated commercial practices. Its primary objective is to promote the unification and harmonization of maritime law in all its aspects.

[65] The International Civil Aviation Organization is a specialized agency of the United Nations that aims to promote the secure and sustainable development of civil aviation through cooperation among its member states. The charter of the ICAO is the Convention on International Civil Aviation, which was drafted in Chicago in December 1944 and to which each ICAO contracting state is a party.

Legal integration, in theory, aims to create a uniform law that incorporates the best elements from diverse legal systems, benefiting all countries involved. In practice, however, there is a risk that marginal but significant and useful legal categories from smaller legal systems would be lost, and larger systems would dominate. As a result, the final outcome may resemble a form of 'legal imperialism' more than harmonization. It is unsurprising, therefore, that not all comparative law scholars, nor all lawyers, consider legal integration desirable. Some argue that as long as we can understand each other's legal systems, interpret our laws, and communicate effectively, harmonization becomes less appealing.

Regarding European legal integration, a common European private law could symbolize European unity and offer benefits for both businesses and individual citizens. However, law, as a socio-cultural phenomenon, is intrinsically linked to the culture of a particular society—legal norms and their socio-cultural context are interconnected. Replacing a historically developed and functioning national legal system with a supranational and largely alien body of law merely for symbolic reasons could weaken rather than strengthen European unity. A legal integration scheme imposed without sufficient attention to the diverse cultural traditions in which it should apply would be as meaningless and counterproductive as abolishing national languages and imposing from above a single 'official' language across Europe.

4.6 Concluding Note

The comparative study of legal systems enables legal practitioners and scholars to integrate their knowledge of law into a conceptual and institutional framework extending beyond their national borders. This study provides them with a much broader understanding of the possible range of solutions to legal problems than familiarity with a single legal system would allow. Comparative law makes it possible to perceive new features and trends in the development of legal systems, particularly in connection with scientific-technical progress, integration processes, and the growing role of transnational and international law. This broader perspective enables jurists to develop the standards and sharpen the analytical skills required to address the challenges they face in a rapidly changing social and economic landscape. The legal experience accumulated by diverse systems of law constitutes an inexhaustible source from which lawmakers may derive significant benefits when conducting reforms of national legislation. Consequently, contemporary law drafters increasingly resort to a comparative analysis of rules found in foreign legal systems. On a smaller scale, judicial and arbitral practices also rely on comparative law materials to address legal problems. Moreover, comparative law plays an increasingly important role in international and transnational law. It assists international lawyers in drafting and constructing international agreements, interpreting and applying international law in national courts, and understanding and bridging differences between regional varieties of international law.

References

Andenas M, Fairgrieve D (eds) (2015) Courts and comparative law. Oxford University Press, Oxford
Barak A (2006) The judge in a democracy. Princeton University Press, Princeton
Bonell MJ (ed) (2006) The UNIDROIT principles in practice: caselaw and bibliography on the UNIDROIT principles of international commercial contracts, 2nd edn. Transnational Publishers, Ardsley
Bothe M, Ress G (1980) The comparative method and international law. In: Butler WE (ed) International law in comparative perspective. Sijthoff & Noordhoff, Alphen aan den Rijn, pp 49–66
Butler WE (1989) On the history of international law in England and Russia. In: Butler WE (ed) The non-use of force in international law. Martinus Nijhoff, Dordrecht, pp 3–15
Cheng B (1953) General principles of law as applied by international courts and tribunals. Cambridge University Press, Cambridge (repr. 2006)
Dannemann G (2019) Comparative law: study of similarities or differences? In: Reimann M, Zimmerman R (eds) The Oxford handbook of comparative law, 2nd edn. Oxford University Press, Oxford, pp 390–422
de Boer TM (1994) The missing link: some thoughts on the relationship between private international law and comparative law. In: Boele-Woelki K, Grosheide FW, Hondius EH, Steenhoff GJW (eds) Comparability and evaluation: essays on comparative law, private international law and international commercial arbitration. Martinus Nijhoff, Dordrecht, pp 15–25
de Boer TM (1996) Facultative choice of law, the procedural status of choice-of-law rules and foreign law. Recueil des cours 257:223–427
Demleitner N (2019) Comparative law in legal education. In: Reimann M, Zimmermann R (eds) The Oxford handbook of comparative law, 2nd edn. Oxford University Press, Oxford, pp 320–344
Dibadj R (2008) Panglossian transnationalism. Stanf J Int Law 44:253–299
Drobnig U (1999) The use of comparative law by courts. In: Drobnig U, van Erp JHM (eds) The use of comparative law by courts. Kluwer Law International, The Hague, pp 3–21
Drobnig U, Dopffel P (1982) Die Nutzung der Rechtsvergleichung durch den deutschen Gesetzgeber. Rabels Zeitschrift für ausländisches und internationals Privatrecht 46:253–307
Fauvarque-Cosson B (2001) Comparative law and conflict of laws: allies or enemies? New perspectives on an old couple. Am J Comp Law 49:407–423
Fletcher GP (1998) Comparative law as subversive discipline. Am J Comp Law 46:683–700
Glenn HP (1987) Persuasive authority. McGill Law J 32:261–299
Gordley J (2001) Comparative law and legal education. Tulane Law Rev 75:1003–1014
Grossfeld B, Eberle EJ (2003) Patterns of order in comparative law: discovering and decoding invisible powers. Tex Int Law J 38:291–316
Harmathy A (1999) Comparative law and changes of the law. Acta Juridica Hungarica 40:159–167
Hartley TC (1996) Pleading and proof of foreign law: the major European systems compared. Int Comp Law Q 45(2):271–292
Kakouris CN (1999) L'utilisation de la méthode comparative par la Cour de justice des Communautés européennes. In: Drobnig U, van Erp S (eds) The use of comparative law by courts. Kluwer Law International, The Hague, pp 97–111
Kamba WJ (1974) Comparative law: a theoretical framework. Int Comp Law Q 23:485–519
Kiss AC (1980) Comparative law and public international law. In: Butler WE (ed) International law in comparative perspective. Sijthoff and Noordhoff, Alphen aan den Rijn, pp 41–48
Koopmans T (1996) Comparative law and the courts. Int Comp Law Q 45(3):545–556
Koskenniemi M, Leino P (2002) Fragmentation of international law? Postmodern anxieties. Leiden J Int Law 15:553–579
Levasseur AA (1999) The use of comparative law by courts. In: Drobnig U, van Erp JHM (eds) The use of comparative law by courts. Kluwer Law International, The Hague, pp. 315-334

Mahoney P (2004) The comparative method in judgments of the European Court of Human Rights: reference back to national law. In: Cavinet G, Andenas M, Fairgrieve D (eds) Comparative law before the courts. British Institute of International and Comparative Law, London, pp 135–150
Mak E (2011) Why do Dutch and UK judges cite foreign law? Camb Law J 70(2):420–450
Markesinis B (1990) Comparative law in search of an audience. Mod Law Rev 53:1–21
Martinico G, Pollicino O (eds) (2010) The national judicial treatment of the ECHR and EU laws: a comparative constitutional perspective. Europa Law Publishing, Groningen
Merryman J, Clark D (1978) Comparative law: Western European and Latin American legal systems. Bobbs-Merrill, Indianapolis
Muir-Watt H (2000) La fonction subversive du droit comparé. Revue internationale de droit comparé 52:503–527
Paton GW (1972) A textbook of jurisprudence. Clarendon Press, Oxford
Pescatore P (1980) Le recours, dans la jurisprudence de la Cour de Justice des Communautés européennes, à des normes déduites de la comparaison du droit des États members. Revue internationale de droit comparé 32:337
Péteri Z (2002) Teaching of comparative law and comparative law teaching. Acta Juridica Hungarica 43:243–261
Posner R (2008) How judges think. Harvard University Press, Cambridge
Rabel E (1931) Das Problem der Qualifikation. Rabels Zeitschrift für ausländisches und internationales Privatrecht 5:241–288
Reimann M (1995) Conflict of laws in Western Europe, a guide through the jungle. Transnational Publishers, Irvington
Reimann M (2001) Beyond national systems: a comparative law in the international age. Tulane Law Rev 75:1103–1120
Reimann M (2012) Comparative law and neighbouring disciplines. In: Bussani M, Mattei U (eds) The Cambridge companion to comparative Law. Cambridge University Press, Cambridge, pp 13–34
Reimann M (2019) Comparative law and private international law. In: Reimann M, Zimmermann R (eds) The Oxford handbook of comparative law, 2nd edn. Oxford University Press, Oxford, pp 1339–1370
Schadbach K (1998) The benefits of comparative law: a continental European view. Boston Univ Int Law J 16:331–422
Scherpe JM (2004) Ausnahmen vom Erfordernis eines strikten Kausalitätsnachweises im englischen Deliktsrecht. Zeitschrift für Europäisches Privatrecht 12:164
Schlesinger RB (1957) Research on the general principles of law recognized by civilised nations. Am J Int Law 51:734–753
Schlesinger RB (1968) Formation of contracts: a study of the common core of legal systems. Oceana Publications, New York
Schlesinger RB, Baade HW, Damaska MR, Herzog PE (1988) Comparative law: cases, text, materials, 5th edn. Foundation Press, Mineola
Shaw MN (2008) International law, 6th edn. Cambridge University Press, Cambridge
Siems M (2018) Comparative law, 2nd edn. Cambridge University Press, Cambridge
Smits JM (2019) Comparative law and its influence on national legal systems. In: Reimann M, Zimmermann R (eds) The Oxford handbook of comparative Law, 2nd edn. Oxford University Press, Oxford, pp 502–523
Steyn L (2006) The challenge of comparative law. Eur J Law Reform 8(1):3–11
Teitel RG (2002) Transitional justice. Oxford University Press, Oxford
Thirlway H (2014) The sources of international law. Oxford University Press, Oxford
Verdirame G (2007) The divided West: international lawyers in Europe and America. Eur J Int Law 18(3):553–580
von Jhering R (1955) Des Geist des Römischen Rechts auf den verschiedenen Stufen seiner Entwicklung I, 9th edn. Scientia-Verlag, Aalen

von Mehren A (1978) The contribution of comparative law to the theory and practice of private international law. Am J Comp Law 26:31–41

Yntema HE (1956) Comparative legal research: some remarks on 'looking out of the cave'. Mich Law Rev 54(7):899–928

Zaphiriou GA (1982) Use of comparative law by the legislator. Am J Comp Law 30:71–95

Zimmerman A, Tomuschat C, Oellers-frahm K (eds) (2006) The Statute of the International Court of Justice, a commentary. Oxford University Press, Oxford

Zweigert K, Kötz H (1987) An introduction to comparative law, 2nd edn. Clarendon Press, Oxford

Zweigert K, Kötz H (1998) An introduction to comparative law, 3rd edn. Clarendon Press, Oxford

Chapter 5
Theoretical and Methodological Aspects of Comparative Law

5.1 Introduction

Comparison is a mental process in which two or more different objects are examined to determine their possible relationships. As an element of cognition, comparison cannot be considered separately from other logical means of cognition, such as analysis, synthesis, induction, and deduction. Scientific comparison involves three interconnected aspects: a logical method of cognition, a process or cognitive activity, and a cognitive result, i.e., knowledge of a certain kind. It also includes judgment and evaluative selection, as it usually focuses on one or some aspects of the objects being compared while provisionally and conditionally abstracting others. Comparison is used in all fields of scientific inquiry, though the comparative method employed in each field has distinct features that fulfil the relevant cognitive functions. There is a distinction between the function of comparison as an element of cognition in general and the comparative method as a relatively autonomous, systematically organized means of research designed to achieve specific cognitive aims.[1]

Comparison lies at the heart of comparative law. In this context, the comparative method is employed to: (a) identify similarities and differences between two or more legal systems, rules, or institutions; (b) elucidate the factors that explain these similarities and differences; and (c) evaluate the legal systems under comparison. This method operates on both descriptive-empirical and theoretical-evaluative levels and can be applied in various comparative legal inquiries. These inquiries may concern the ideological foundations of legal institutions, the nature and hierarchy of legal sources, the scope and operation of legal rules and principles, techniques of

[1] On the nature of the comparative process see Jansen (2019).

G. Mousourakis, *Traversing Legal Traditions*, Springer Textbooks in Law,
https://doi.org/10.1007/978-3-031-94669-1_5

statutory interpretation, forms of legal procedure, and systems of legal education.[2] The selection of particular legal systems or aspects to compare depends on the aims of the comparative study and the interests of the comparatist.[3]

5.1.1 Types of Comparative Legal Inquiry

A legal comparison can be either bilateral, involving two legal systems, or multilateral, involving more than two systems, and can be diachronic or synchronic. Diachronic or historical comparison analyses the evolution of laws and legal institutions over time, comparing past and contemporary legal systems. This approach offers insights into the historical development and transformation of legal systems. In contrast, synchronic comparison examines legal systems or their components at a specific point in time. This form of comparison is static, focusing on the current state of laws across different jurisdictions without considering their historical development.

Additionally, one may choose to compare legal systems of a particular region or those of transnational or international regimes. Comparison within a single state is referred to as internal comparison, in contrast to external comparison, which involves comparing laws from different national or international legal orders. Internal comparison can pertain to both federal and unitary states and may be either diachronic or synchronic. The existence of multiple legal systems within a unitary state provides valuable material for internal comparisons. These comparisons are instrumental in elucidating the significance and potential interrelations of the various legal sub-systems.

One can further distinguish between a comparison focusing on entire legal systems, or groups of legal systems, and a comparison focusing on individual legal institutions, rules, or practices. In the first case, we refer to *macro-comparison*, or comparative law in a broad sense; in the second case, we refer to *micro-comparison*, or comparative law in a narrow sense.[4]

Macro-comparison examines the overarching characteristics that define different legal systems or transnational legal families. This type of comparison focuses on

---

[2] According to Esin Örücü, in all fields of legal study the comparative method is "an empirical, descriptive research design using 'comparison' as a technique of cognizance." Örücü (2006), p. 29.

[3] As Peter de Cruz notes, "It has been argued by many eminent scholars that systems selected for comparison must be those which are at a similar stage of development … Nevertheless, it is usually necessary to select systems or institutions which are at a similar stage of legal development, which will then ensure a baseline of similarity. However, it is not necessary that this is followed in every case, because the choice of legal systems must ultimately depend on the main aims and objectives of the particular comparative investigation." de Cruz (1993), pp. 36–37. And see Kamba (1974), p. 506 ff. According to K Zweigert and H Kötz, it is difficult to speak in general terms about how a comparative law scholar should select legal systems for comparison, as much depends on the precise topic of their research. Zweigert and Kötz (1998), p. 42.

[4] See Dannemann (2019), p. 394.

aspects such as the historical origins and evolution of legal systems; the philosophical foundations of legal systems; the sources of law and their hierarchy; the distribution of legal material into branches of law; legal reasoning and judicial decision-making; the division of labour among legal professionals; the contribution of legal scholars to the development of law; and forms of legal instruction. Macro-comparison is closely linked with structural, normative, and contextual comparisons. Structural comparison focuses on the organization and structure of legal systems, including the hierarchy of legal norms, relationships between different branches of law, and the institutional framework of the legal system. Normative comparison evaluates legal systems based on general values or criteria, such as justice, efficiency, or human rights. Contextual comparison considers the broader social, economic, political, and cultural contexts in which legal systems develop and function.

Micro-comparison, on the other hand, delves into specific legal rules, doctrines, or institutions and their operation across different systems. Examples of questions within the scope of micro-comparison include: Under what conditions is a manufacturer liable for damages caused by defective products? How is the issue of compensation addressed in the case of road traffic accidents? What are the rules governing an heir's liability for the debts of the testator? What factors are relevant in determining child custody in divorce cases? What is the basis of liability for a homeowner whose property deteriorates to the extent that tiles fall from the roof and injure a pedestrian? In this context, reference should be made to 'functional comparison', which examines how different legal systems solve similar problems or fulfil analogous functions. This type of comparison identifies the underlying social needs or functions of law and analyses how different legal systems address them.[5]

As Zweigert and Kötz point out, micro-comparative and macro-comparative inquiries are interrelated or interdependent. They assert that "it is only by discovering how the relevant rules have been created and developed by the legislature and the courts and ascertaining the practical context in which they are applied that one can understand why a foreign legal system resolves a given problem the way it does and not otherwise."[6]

5.2 Prerequisites of Comparative Legal Research

Familiarity with the legal rules and institutions being compared is essential for any meaningful comparison between legal systems. This means that the comparatist must obtain current and accurate information on the relevant aspects of the systems under consideration. However, to adequately learn the details of foreign law, one must overcome several practical and theoretical challenges. Specifically, it is

[5] And see Sect. 5.4.2 below.

[6] Zweigert and Kötz (1987), p. 5. And see Samuel (2014), p. 50.

important to remember that studying legal rules and institutions alone is insufficient; one must also consider the context within which law operates and develops. This context includes not only the material aspects of sociology, history, economy, and politics but also the ideological context of the law and what may be called the 'juridical life', which encompasses tradition and legal style or mentality.

Describing foreign law entails more than merely reporting legal rules and certainly more than simply quoting the wording of statutory enactments. First, one must determine which legal rules are in force and binding at the time of consideration. This presents a formal problem: has a particular rule been abolished or not? It also poses a problem of content: is the rule under examination compatible with a higher-level rule in the hierarchy of legal sources? If not, the rule should be considered invalid and thus non-existent in the legal order being studied. However, concluding that a relevant rule is invalid is not simply a descriptive statement; it is the conclusion of an interpretation. This demonstrates the extent to which the description and interpretation of legal rules are interrelated. Every description of the law implies a (conscious or unconscious) interpretation of the law. Facts do not simply exist; they are always perceived, described, and classified through the lens of the legal system concerned. Because a factual situation may be constructed in different ways, solutions to problems that seem possible in one legal system may not be available in another. Legal concepts, categories, and techniques, on the one hand, offer opportunities for resolving problems but, on the other, render certain solutions impossible.

As the above discussion suggests, any legal description of facts is determined by the conceptual framework and rules of a particular legal system, as systematized in legal doctrine over the years. This systematization is achieved through the interpretation of the various legal rules based on several fundamental concepts and principles. This indicates a close connection not only between description and interpretation but also between interpretation (of a specific rule) and systematization (of a set of rules). Legal doctrine, concerned with the systematization and description of the law in a particular legal system, is, along with statute law, case law, and customary law, an object of comparative study. Moreover, legal doctrine is important for comparative law because it is an area where theories, such as those concerning legal sources, are made explicit or proposed new theories are discussed.

One of the greatest challenges for a comparatist is the tendency to assume, either consciously or instinctively, that the legal concepts, norms, and institutions familiar within their own legal system also exist in the foreign system under study. For instance, a comparatist might be tempted to assume that the courts in the foreign system, similar to those in their own country, refer to preparatory legislative materials when interpreting statutory enactments. While such assumptions can sometimes align with reality, they are often incorrect. A fundamental methodological principle of comparative law is that foreign legal rules, institutions, and concepts must be considered from the perspective of the legal order to which they belong. In other words, the comparatist must distance themselves from their own legal system and its perspectives, immersing themselves in the environment of the rules or institutions under consideration.[7] They must employ the legal concepts and methods of legal analysis and interpretation used by the lawyers and jurists of the foreign system. As Zweigert and Kötz have remarked, "one must never allow one's vision to be clouded by the concepts of one's own national system."[8]

It is important to acknowledge that distancing oneself from one's own legal system when studying foreign law is challenging, as the legal education received in one's own country heavily influences one's way of thinking and approaching legal problems. False assumptions about foreign law naturally lead to poor and factually incorrect legal comparisons. However, these potential difficulties should not discourage the study of foreign law or the comparison of different legal systems. As Zweigert and Kötz have noted, "Writers often stress the number of traps, snares, and delusions which can hinder the student of comparative law or lead him quite astray. It is impossible to enumerate them all or wholly to avoid them ... [Even] the cleverest comparatists sometimes fall into error; when this happens the good custom among workers in the field is not to hound the forgivable miscreant with contumely from the profession, but kindly to put him right."[9]

It is crucial to recognize that a successful comparative study requires linguistic competence and the ability to translate one legal worldview into another. However, applying translation skills in this context is challenging. One must exercise great caution and avoid assuming that a word, concept, or idea can be perfectly translated from one legal culture to another.[10] The meaning of a word, concept, or idea must be understood within its own cultural setting before it is translated into another legal culture, whether it is the researcher's own or a different foreign culture. To effectively carry out this translation, the comparatist should be able to explain the cultural context in which the relevant word, concept, or idea is situated. Successful translation presupposes and relies on prior knowledge and mastery of diverse semiotic systems and linguistic contexts, as well as the ability to determine how to adjust and transfer a particular worldview into another. When accomplished well, translation can serve as a bridge between cultures, highlighting the differences and similarities between legal orders.[11]

---

[7] In the 1970s, some Western lawyers asserted that China lacked a legal system because it did not have attorneys in the American or European sense, no independent judiciary, and, following the Cultural Revolution, no formal system of legal education. However, this perspective judges a non-Western system by Western standards. When studying a non-Western system, it is important not to search for Western institutions, rules, or concepts, but to look for the functional equivalents of legal terms and concepts within that system. In other words, one should ask: by which institutions and methods are the four basic tasks of the law—social control, conflict resolution, adaptation to social change, and norm enforcement—being performed?

[8] Zweigert and Kötz (1987), p. 31. And see Ewald (1995), pp. 1973–1974 (noting that it is important to compare law from an internal point of view so that we can understand how lawyers think in their own legal system). Consider also Demleitner (1998), p. 652.

[9] Zweigert and Kötz (1987), p. 33.

[10] As it has been pointed out by scholars, the most evident translations of Roman legal terms accepted in different legal cultures may be misleading. See Kahn-Freund (1966), p. 52.

[11] See Grosswald Curran (1998), p. 661. And see Glanert (2014); Hoeflich (2002).

Studying foreign law requires not only proficiency in the foreign language but also a deep understanding of the legal terminology specific to the legal system being examined. As Harold Gutteridge has observed, "the pitfalls of terminology are the greatest difficulty and danger which the student of comparative law encounters in his novitiate."[12] One must keep in mind that, even within the context of the same national language, legal terminology often diverges in meaning from everyday usage. Additionally, basic legal concepts may be similar across countries, yet different legal terms are often used. This variation can occur even within the same legal family. Conversely, identical terms may have different substantive content or applications.

Take the term 'equity', for example, which is used in both civil law and common law countries (*aequitas, equité, Billigkeit*). In civil law countries, equity refers to principles of fairness and justice that can supplement or modify the strict application of legal rules within the framework of the codified legal system. Civil law judges use this concept to avoid a narrow or formal interpretation of a legal rule, particularly when they wish to adapt the rule to changing socio-economic circumstances. In contrast, in the English common law tradition, 'equity' refers to a distinct body of law that evolved separately from the common law. Other examples include 'jurisprudence', which in France primarily refers to case law or the body of court decisions, whereas in England it usually denotes the general theory or philosophy of law; 'good faith', which serves as a general principle in German law permeating various aspects of contractual and commercial relationships, but simply means honesty and fair dealing in English law, typically applied in specific contexts or types of contracts; and 'Auftrag', roughly translated as commission or mandate, which in Swiss law covers both remunerated and unremunerated commissions, while in German law, it refers only to the latter type.[13] These distinctions highlight how the same term can have varying implications within different legal systems, even those that share linguistic similarities. The list of relevant examples can easily be expanded.

As previously noted, the study of foreign law, a prerequisite for comparative law, hinges on one's ability to obtain accurate and up-to-date knowledge. This, in turn, requires access to reliable sources of information. It is crucial for a researcher to rely on primary sources of law or authoritative texts, such as statutory enactments, regulations, and judicial decisions. Depending on the goals and scope of the study, these primary materials may be supplemented with secondary sources, such as comparative law encyclopaedias, introductory textbooks, reference manuals, and journal articles. A scholar researching a foreign legal system may find it challenging to understand and utilize primary sources without adequate background knowledge of the system being studied. Introductory textbooks, besides offering an overview of the legal issues in their broader context, typically include references to authoritative texts and other essential legal sources for the researcher. Finally, it is worth

[12] Gutteridge (1938), p. 403.

[13] Remunerated commissions are referred to in German law as Dienstvertrag or Werkvertrag.

mentioning that empirical data—such as the number of cases, the duration of legal processes, and the outcomes of legal decisions—collected through statistical research studies can be relied upon to identify and compare general patterns and trends.

5.3 Stages of Comparative Legal Analysis

According to Walter Kamba, a comparative inquiry can be divided into descriptive, identification, and explanatory stages.[14] At the descriptive stage, the researcher provides a detailed account of the legal institutions, rules, and principles relevant to the study, alongside the associated social problems and solutions offered by the legal systems being examined. This description must be objective—free from critical evaluation—and both accurate and comprehensive.

It is essential to begin with a thorough description of the legal institutions under comparison, revealing their structure and intended or unintended consequences. The researcher must consider all sources of law recognized as authoritative by the legal systems in question, including statutory enactments and judicial decisions, and understand how these sources are interpreted by legislative bodies, courts, and academic scholars. Furthermore, the factual situations that the relevant legal institution is designed to address must be clearly identified.

The researcher should contextualize the institution within the entire legal system and explore its possible connections with institutions or rules in other areas of the law, such as constitutional provisions, procedural rules, or international legal requirements. Additionally, attention must be paid to socio-economic, political, ideological, cultural, and other extra-legal factors. Considering these factors is crucial for understanding the variations in how the compared institutions operate in practice.

At the identification stage, the similarities and differences between the systems being compared are identified and delineated. During this stage, the comparatist must highlight the characteristics of the legal institutions under consideration and explain how these institutions are similar or different.

Finally, at the explanatory stage, the detected similarities and differences between the legal systems under comparison are explained or accounted for. Consideration of historical, socio-economic, cultural, and other extra-legal factors can play a particularly important role at this stage. A historical analysis can reveal whether the legal institutions in question are indigenous or borrowed from another legal system. One may conclude that the relevant institutions are similar because they have a common ancestry (e.g., they both derive from Roman law) or because they have developed in parallel or converged. In the case of parallel development, the institutions acquire similar features independently, whereas in the case of convergence, they do

[14] Kamba (1974).

so through some form of contact or through the mediation of another legal institution. The differences between the institutions under consideration may be explained by the influence of extra-legal factors or by an innovative doctrinal approach adopted by a national lawmaker or judicial authority.

Although it is not necessary to always follow the specified order, all three stages must be considered at some point for the inquiry to be regarded as a comparative one. According to Kamba, the way a comparatist deals with the questions encountered at each stage of the comparative process depends on three factors: (i) the comparatist's jurisprudential outlook, i.e., their general attitude toward the study of law;[15] (ii) the socio-cultural context of the legal systems under comparison; and (iii) the legal context of the issues under examination in the case of a micro-comparative study.

As previously noted, in establishing the law in each jurisdiction under study, one should: (a) describe the typical conceptual framework of the lawyers; (b) consider all sources that a lawyer might use to form their opinion about what the law is; and (c) account for potential discrepancies between the law on the books and the law in action, as well as any gaps in the available knowledge about both.

Other important issues to consider in a comparative study include: (1) the type of legal system (national, subnational, transnational) and the legal family or transnational legal tradition to which it belongs (civil law, common law, religious law); (2) the field of law in which the issue being studied is located (public law, private law); (3) the type of sources needed (e.g., statutes, law codes, international treaties, casebooks or law reports, legal encyclopaedias, textbooks, monographs, journal articles) and the techniques used in data collection (e.g., literature searches, interviews, empirical surveys); and (4) language and translation issues. It is particularly important to state the relative weight accorded to historical, socio-economic, cultural, ideological, and political factors and their possible influence on the development and function of the legal rules or institutions under consideration.

The information collected must be critically appraised and the conclusions presented within a clearly comparative framework. The approach adopted should ultimately be assessed in the light of the purposes or goals of the comparatist. In this respect, one may ask, for example: Does the approach adopted facilitate a better understanding of one's own law? Does it help in the formulation of a well-grounded theory? Does it assist in the development of a law reform or legal unification or harmonization program?

[15] For example, a comparatist interested in legal history, or the sociology of law will usually adopt a historical or sociological approach to the legal systems, institutions, or rules under examination.

5.4 The Issue of Comparability

An essential aspect of the comparative law methodology is the issue of the comparability of legal phenomena: determining whether the legal institutions, rules, or practices under consideration are suitable for comparison. Comparatists agree that a comparison is meaningful when the objects being compared share certain common features, which can serve as a common denominator (*tertium comparationis*). Identifying these requisite common features takes place during the preliminary stage of the comparative inquiry. At this stage, one examines the structure, purposes, and functions of the legal institutions or rules one intends to compare without delving into a detailed comparative analysis. This detailed analysis occurs in the main phase of the comparative inquiry, where one considers and attempts to explain the similarities and differences between the objects being compared.

At the preliminary stage of the inquiry, certain legal institutions or rules may seem comparable. However, as the comparative process advances, significant differences can become apparent. For instance, legal institutions initially assumed to be comparable due to certain common structural characteristics may subsequently prove to operate in entirely different ways. Therefore, it is often impossible to confirm whether two or more seemingly comparable legal institutions share common characteristics (e.g., they address the same problem) until a thorough comparison is conducted.

Resolving the problem of comparability does not presuppose the full application of the comparative method, but ascertaining comparability is often challenging. Two key questions arise: What criteria should be used to identify common elements or characteristics in the objects one seeks to compare? How relevant are broader socio-economic, political, and cultural considerations in defining these criteria? The following paragraphs explore different theoretical approaches to the problem of comparability, one of the major theoretical issues in comparative law methodology.

5.4.1 The Legal-Dogmatic Method in Comparative Law

In the nineteenth and early twentieth centuries, comparatists often assumed that similar legal institutions, rules, concepts, and principles reflected general legal ideas or patterns inherent in most advanced legal systems. The so-called 'legal-dogmatic method', also known as the doctrinal method, begins with an examination of legal terms, concepts, and categories specific to one's own legal system. It is presumed that a comparable legal system employs the same terms, concepts, and categories, and that behind similar names lies a shared legal idea or pattern. The legal-dogmatic method emphasizes the internal coherence and systematic structure of legal rules and principles, seeking to understand how different parts of a legal system fit together to form a coherent whole. It focuses on the primary sources of law and the language of legal texts, heavily drawing on legal doctrines and theories developed by legal scholars. In the context of comparative law, this method involves a detailed and systematic analysis of legal texts and doctrines within the legal systems under consideration, with special attention paid to internal coherence, textual analysis, and doctrinal development. As such, it tends to be formalistic, focusing more on the 'law in the books' rather than the 'law in action', and paying less attention to broader social, economic, political, or cultural considerations.

The comparative law of the German *Begriffsjurisprudenz* (conceptual jurisprudence) preferred comparisons of conceptual forms, hoping to prove the existence of universally valid legal systematics.[16] It aimed to reveal the common core or essence (*Wesen*) of basic juridical concepts, even while recognizing that each legal order has its own system. However, criticism against this school of thought has been severe. One of the most vigorous attacks came from Rudolf Jhering, who insisted that legal theory must abandon the delusion that it is a system of legal mathematics, with no higher aim than a correct reckoning with conceptual schemes.[17] Furthermore, since the period of logical empiricism, there has been a tendency to regard questions concerning the essence of legal concepts as generally meaningless.[18] The Analytical School of law[19] typically reduces legal problems to relationships between legal facts

[16] *Bergriffsjurisprudenz*, a school of thought that emerged in the nineteenth century, is characterized by its emphasis on the logical and systematic analysis of legal concepts, often at the expense of considering the social context of law. Its aim was to develop a coherent system of law based on clear, precise, and internally consistent legal definitions and principles. See, e.g., Puchta (1841), pp. 95–108; Windscheid (1891), pp. 59–60.

[17] See Jhering (1884).

[18] Logical empiricism, also known as logical positivism, was a philosophical movement that emerged in the early trwentieth century, primarily in Europe. Its distinctive feature was its attempt to develop and systematize empiricism—the theory that all knowledge is derived from sensory experience—using the conceptual tools provided by modern research in logic and mathematical theory. The movement was largely centred around the Vienna Circle, a group of philosophers based in Vienna in the 1920s and 1930s. A central tenet of logical empiricism was the verifiability principle, which posited that a statement or proposition is only meaningful if it can be empirically verified or is analytically true. Logical empiricists distinguished between analytic statements, which are true by virtue of their meaning (e.g., all bachelors are unmarried), and synthetic statements, which are true by virtue of empirical verification. Statements that could not be empirically tested were considered meaningless. By the mid-20th century, logical empiricism began to decline, but its impact on the philosophy of science and analytic philosophy has been profound.

[19] The Analytical School of Law emphasizes the importance of analysing the structure and function of legal systems. It involves studying the language of the law, the definitions of legal concepts, and the relationships between different legal rules and principles.

(*Rechtstatbestand*)[20] and legal consequences (*Rechtsfolge*).[21] Influenced by logical empiricism, scholars who adopted the analytical method and its conceptual nominalism[22] argued that many traditional legal concepts were 'empty' and should be replaced by concepts with extensional reference. In other words, the emphasis should be on the function, not the imaginary essence, of these concepts. From this perspective, the regulation of contracts, for example, can be reduced to relationships between *legal facts* and *legal consequences*. When certain consequences do not ensue, the situation can be termed 'invalidity', but otherwise, the concept itself lacks substantive content.[23] The reaction to the formalism and extreme conceptualism of the German *Bergriffsjurisprudenz* led to the emergence of new movements in European legal thought. Examples of such movements include *Zweckjurisprudenz* (teleological jurisprudence)[24] and *Interessenjurisprudenz* (jurisprudence of

---

[20] *Rechtstatbestand* refers to the set of factual circumstances or conditions that must be present for a particular legal rule to apply. These are the specific elements or criteria defined by law that, when fulfilled, trigger the application of a legal norm. In other words, the *Rechtstatbestand* is the 'if' part of a legal norm: if certain facts are present, then the law will recognize them as satisfying the conditions for a legal consequence. Consider, for example, the provision of a contract law that states: "If a valid offer is made and accepted, a legal contract is formed." Here the *Rechtstatbestand* consists of: (a) a valid offer being made and (b) the offer being accepted.

[21] *Rechtsfolge* refers to the legal outcome that follows once the *Rechtstatbestand* is fulfilled. It represents the 'then' part of a legal norm: if the conditions set out in the *Rechtstatbestand* are met, then a certain legal effect or consequence will occur. The *Rechtsfolge* can involve the creation, modification, or termination of legal rights or duties. For example, in the aforementioned example, if the *Rechtstatbestand* (valid offer and acceptance) of a contract provision is satisfied, the *Rechtsfolge*, or legal outcome, will be the formation of a valid contract, leading to binding obligations on the parties involved.

[22] Conceptual nominalism is a philosophical theory concerning the nature of universals and abstract objects. At its core, nominalism asserts that universal entities do not exist outside of the mind. According to nominalists, only particular objects exist, and what we call 'universals' are merely names (hence 'nominalism') or labels that we apply to groups of similar objects. In other words, universals are not real entities existing independently of our minds but are concepts we create to make sense of the world around us. Conceptual nominalism emphasizes how language and labels are used to organize and communicate our experiences and perceptions.

[23] See, e.g., Aarnio (1979), p. 65 ff.

[24] *Zweckjurisprudenz*, or 'jurisprudence of ends, is a legal theory developed by the German jurist Rudolf von Jhering. This theory emphasizes the purposes or societal goals that laws and legal institutions are meant to achieve, rather than focusing strictly on abstract legal concepts and principles. *Zweckjurisprudenz* critiques purely formalistic approaches to law, which prioritize the consistency and coherence of legal rules over their practical effects. According to this theory, such formalistic approaches can lead to unjust or inefficient outcomes if they ignore the broader purposes of the law. See Jhering (1877).

interests).[25] These movements were precursors to legal realism[26] and the sociology of law.[27]

The limitations of the legal-dogmatic method have been emphasized by many contemporary comparative law scholars. This method, with its narrow focus on legal texts and formal rules, often neglects the broader socio-economic, political, and cultural contexts that significantly shape legal systems. Without this contextual understanding, comparisons can be superficial and misleading, missing dynamic changes and practical realities in different systems. The method's abstract and theoretical nature can result in outcomes that are not easily applicable in real-world contexts, lacking practical relevance for policymakers and practitioners. Moreover, because legal terms and concepts often do not have exact equivalents in different languages and legal systems, the legal-dogmatic method can struggle with translation issues, leading to misinterpretations or oversimplifications. Additionally, different legal cultures may be underpinned by distinct philosophies, making it challenging to create a coherent comparative analysis on a purely legal-dogmatic basis. Critics argue that the method often reflects a bias towards Western legal traditions, leading to an ethnocentric perspective that marginalizes or misrepresents non-Western legal systems. Addressing these issues requires incorporating more interdisciplinary, contextual, and dynamic approaches in comparative law.

---

[25] *Interessenjurisprudenz*, developed in the early twentieth century, is a legal theory that emphasizes balancing and reconciling competing interests within society when interpreting and applying the law. Unlike formalistic or rule-based perspectives, this theory views the law as a tool to balance conflicting interests and achieve fair and just outcomes by considering the needs, goals, and interests of all parties involved. *Interessenjurisprudenz* is particularly applicable in areas where conflicts of interest are pronounced, such as labour law, family law, and environmental law. It is a pragmatic approach that seeks to adapt the law to the evolving needs of society. For more on this theory consider Heck (1914).

[26] Legal realism, a legal theory that emerged in the early twentieth century, emphasizes the influence of social, economic, and other contextual factors on judicial decisions. Unlike traditional views that see the law as a collection of abstract principles and logical deductions, legal realists argue that understanding the law requires more than studying statutes and legal precedents. It must also account for the real-world impacts and the behaviours of judges and other legal actors. A prominent figure in the development of legal realism was Oliver Wendell Holmes Jr. (1841–1935), an American jurist and Supreme Court Justice. See Holmes (1881, 1897).

[27] Sociological jurisprudence is a branch of legal theory that emphasizes the social aspects of law and the impact of legal institutions on society. It argues that law should not be viewed as an isolated set of rules but as a social institution that must be understood in the context of its effects on society and vice versa. Like legal sociology, sociological jurisprudence is concerned with the relationship between law and society. However, sociological jurisprudence focuses more on the application and impact of law to achieve social purposes, while legal sociology is more about understanding law as a social phenomenon through empirical research. A key figure in the development of sociological jurisprudence was the American jurist Roscoe Pound (1870–1964). See Pound (1911–1912).

5.4.2 The Functional Method in Comparative Law

The limitations of the legal-dogmatic approach have led contemporary comparatists to adopt a perspective that emphasizes the functions of legal rules and institutions rather than their names. To ascertain the actual similarities and differences between the substantive contents of legal systems, one should focus on the functions of legal rules, i.e., the real or potential conflict situations that the rules are intended to regulate. The legal institutions being compared must be functionally comparable: they must be designed to address the same problem. This common function provides the necessary *tertium comparationis*, which makes comparison possible.

As Walter Kamba points out, the key question for the comparatist is: "What legal norms, concepts, or institutions in one system perform the equivalent functions performed by certain legal norms, concepts or institutions of another system?"[28] According to Oliver Brand, "Functionalism is so centrally relevant to contemporary comparative law because of its orientation towards the practical. It is particularly concerned with how to compare the law's consequences across legal systems and therefore allows rules and concepts to be appreciated for what they do, rather than for what they say. Functionalists believe that the 'function' of a rule, its social purpose, is the common denominator (*tertium comparationis*) that permits comparison."[29]

Functional comparison in law does not start with a legal term or norm and then look for a corresponding social fact. Instead, it begins with a social fact and examines how different legal systems regulate it. This approach does not involve comparing abstract or general legal notions, but rather how different legal systems address the same factual situations in real life. A fundamental requirement of functional legal comparison is the comparability of basic social conditions and problems. Such similarities allow us to conclude that the respective legal solutions found in different legal systems are comparable.

According to Max Rheinstein, the principle of functionality necessitates that comparative inquiries "go beyond the taxonomic description or technical application of one or more systems of positive law… every rule and institution has to justify its existence under two inquiries: First, what function does it serve in present society? Second, does it serve this function well or would another rule serve it better?"[30]

Zweigert and Kötz explain: "The basic methodological principle of all comparative law is that of functionality. From this basic principle stem all the other rules which determine the choice of laws to compare, the scope of the undertaking, the creation of a system of comparative law, and so on. Incomparables cannot usefully be compared, and in law the only things which are comparable are those which fulfil

[28] Kamba (1974), p. 517.

[29] Brand (2007), p. 409.

[30] Rheinstein (1938), pp. 617–618.

the same function."[31] The authors emphasize that "function is the start-point and basis of all comparative law. It is the *tertium comparationis*, so long the subject of futile discussion among earlier comparatists. For the comparative process this means that the solutions we find in the different jurisdictions must be cut loose from their conceptual context and stripped of their national doctrinal overtones so that they may be seen purely in the light of their function, as an attempt to satisfy a particular legal need. It means also that we must look to function in order to determine the proper ambit of the solution under comparison"[32]

The resolution of specific social problems can be achieved through diverse legal mechanisms across different legal systems. For instance, the institution of trust or trust ownership in English law[33] has no direct counterpart in Romano-Germanic legal systems. Instead, these systems use direct representation by a legal representative to fulfil similar functions for individuals lacking dispositive legal capacity.[34] This illustrates that different legal mechanisms can be employed to achieve the same legal and social objectives, such as protecting the interests of those without dispositive legal capacity. The absence of a direct equivalent of a legal institution in one system compared to another does not indicate a gap in the law or render the systems incomparable regarding their solutions to particular social and legal issues. Functional comparison can be defined as the study of legal means and methods used by different legal systems to address similar or identical socio-legal problems. Such a comparison serves both theoretical-scientific and practical purposes, thereby enhancing the understanding and evaluation of legal institutions within one's own legal system.[35]

Functionalism rests on three interconnected premises. The first premise involves the realist view of law as an instrument for guiding human behaviour, resolving conflicts, and advancing societal interests. This premise embodies the

---

[31] Zweigert and Kötz (1987), p. 31.

[32] Zweigert and Kötz (1987), p. 42. And see Siems (2018), p. 31 ff; Samuel (2014), p. 65 ff; Michaels (2019).

[33] A trust is a legal arrangement where one party (the trustee) holds and manages property for the benefit of another party (the beneficiary). The settlor, the person who creates the trust by transferring property to the trustee, outlines the terms and conditions of the trust in a document known as the trust deed. The trustee has the responsibility to manage the property according to the terms of the trust deed and in the best interests of the beneficiaries. The beneficiary holds an equitable interest in the property, meaning they are entitled to enjoy the benefits and income generated from it. The institution of trust in English law plays a crucial role in various contexts, including estate planning, asset protection, and charitable activities.

[34] Direct representation refers to a legal concept where an individual, the representative (*Vertreter*), acts on behalf of another person, the principal (*Vertretene*), and their actions directly affect the legal sphere of the principal. The authority to act on behalf of the principal can be granted explicitly through a power of attorney or can be implied from the circumstances. Direct representation ensures that the principal can engage in legal transactions through the actions of another, facilitating business and personal legal matters by allowing for the delegation of authority.

[35] In this context, it should be noted that some scholars argue that the functional approach fully addresses the problem of comparability, as the social needs that legal institutions and rules aim to meet are largely similar across most systems. See Ancel (1982), p. 5.

'problem-solution' approach advocated by functionalists. Comparatists who follow this approach begin their comparisons by selecting a specific practical problem or social conflict. They then analyse how different legal systems address this problem. Finally, in the third stage, they identify, explain, and assess the similarities and differences between the solutions offered by the systems under consideration.

The second premise of functionalism is that most of the problems the law seeks to resolve are similar, if not identical, across diverse legal systems. The third premise relates to the assumption that legal systems tend to resolve practical problems in the same way. The German comparatist Konrad Zweigert cites many examples from various legal systems to argue that in 'unpolitical' areas of private law, such as commercial and property transactions and business dealings, the similarities in the substantive contents of legal rules and the practical solutions they lead to are so significant that one may speak of a 'presumption of similarity' (*praesumptio similitudinis*).[36] This presumption, Zweigert claims, can serve as a useful tool in the comparative study of different legal systems. If, at the end of a comparative study, the comparatist concludes that the solutions offered by the examined systems are identical or compatible, this may be regarded as confirmation that the systems have been understood and compared correctly. Conversely, the discovery of substantial differences indicates that an error may exist, necessitating the repetition of the process and careful verification of the results.[37] This 'presumption of similarity' supports the idea that it might be possible to develop, based on comparative research, a system of general legal principles that could gain international recognition. In Zweigert's words:

> [The international unification of law] cannot be achieved by simply conjuring up an ideal law on any topic and hoping to have it adopted. One must first find what is common to the jurisdictions concerned and incorporate that in the uniform law. Where there are areas of difference, one must reconcile them either by adopting the best existing variant or by finding, through comparative methods, a new solution which is better and more easily applied than any of the existing ones. Preparatory studies in comparative law are absolutely essential here; without them one cannot discover the points of agreement or disagreement in the different legal systems of the world, let alone decide which of the actual or proposed solutions is the best.[38]

It is important to note that Zweigert, in both publications where he elaborates on the idea of a 'presumption of similarity', refers only to the field of private law, specifically the law of contract and the law of tort, excluding family law. Furthermore, he

---

[36] See, e.g., Zweigert (1966); Zweigert and Kötz (1987), p. 36. And see Dannemann (2019), pp. 394–395.

[37] In the words of K Zweigert and H Kötz, "The comparatist can rest content if his researches … lead to the conclusion that the systems he has compared reach the same or similar practical results, but if he finds that there are great differences or indeed diametrically opposite results, he should be warned and go back to check again whether the terms in which he posed his original question were indeed purely functional, and whether he has spread the net of his researches quite wide enough." Zweigert and Kötz (1998), p. 40.

[38] Zweigert and Kötz (1987), p. 23.

acknowledges significant differences between legal systems in how they achieve their solutions. It is the solutions to societal problems that are often similar.

Based on the aforementioned premises, functionalists aim to explain the similarities and differences between legal norms in diverse jurisdictions and how these norms are expressed through different or similar types of legal rules. They emphasize the importance of neutrality in studying legal systems and institutions and the necessity of avoiding the perspective of one's own legal system when approaching foreign laws. In other words, functionalists pay little attention to differences in the technical-juridical construction of rules, stressing that "the solutions [found] in the different jurisdictions must be cut loose from their conceptual context and stripped of their national doctrinal overtones so that they may be seen purely in the light of their function, as an attempt to satisfy a particular legal need."[39]

In this respect, the functional approach marks a significant departure from the methods of nineteenth and early twentieth-century scholars, who tended to focus on the wording, structure, and systematic classification of legal rules and institutions rather than the social purposes they were meant to serve. This approach has been adopted by comparatists in Europe, the United States, and other regions, and continues to play a crucial role in comparative law research today.[40] There is a universalist trend inherent in functionalism, as this approach assumes that "the legal system of every society faces essentially the same problems and solves these problems by quite different means though very often with similar results."[41]

However, despite its merits, functionalism is not without its challenges. These challenges stem from the basic assumptions underlying the functional method: the presence of a common legal need among the legal systems being compared and the existence of similar factual circumstances. The functional approach posits that a meaningful comparison can only occur if the relevant problem is defined in similar practical terms by the legal systems in question. In other words, a problem that holds different social significance in one of the systems under examination cannot be addressed, as there would be no basis for comparing legal rules or principles of similar function.

The difficulty arises because legal functions can vary significantly across different levels and cultures, making it challenging to ascertain 'common need' or 'function' and 'similarity' concerning factual circumstances, even within familiar socio-economic environments. As Gunter Frankenberg notes, "the functional approach runs the risk of simplifying complex reality by assuming that similarity of problems produces similarity of results."[42] The diverse functions of the law – social, political, economic, religious, spiritual, symbolic – are often difficult to detect,

[39] Zweigert and Kötz (1998), p. 44. And see Reitz (1998), pp. 621–622.

[40] The recent trend of combining comparative law and economics can be seen as a narrower form of functionalism. This approach focuses specifically on the efficiency of legal rules or institutions in economic terms, rather than on social functions in general. See Mattei (1994, 1997).

[41] Zweigert and Kötz (1987), p. 31.

[42] Frankenberg (1985), p. 436.

describe, and evaluate in terms of importance. Thus, functionality ultimately depends on the perspective adopted.[43]

Myres McDougal emphasizes that "the demand for inquiring into function is...but the beginning of insight. Further questions are: 'functional' for whom, against whom, with respect to what values, determined by what decision-makers, under what conditions, how, with what effects".[44] This suggests that the functional method must have a broad scope to account for the relativity of socio-economic and cultural circumstances under which legal institutions operate. In other words, a method that focuses on the function of law as conditioned by the socio-economic and cultural environment is necessary. Legal rules and institutions should be examined in light of their broader implications, encompassing not only legal but also social, economic, political and cultural relationships. As Janet Ainsworth remarks, "a legal order simultaneously encompasses systems of political arrangements, social relations, interpersonal interactional practices, economic processes, cultural categorizations, normative beliefs, psychological habits, philosophical perspectives and ideological values." Therefore, we must scrutinize not only rules but also legal cultures, traditions, ideals, ideologies, identities, and entire legal discourses.[45] An interdisciplinary and comprehensive approach is essential to avoid false assumptions about seemingly 'identical' societal problems and ill-founded, de-contextualized evaluations of legal solutions.[46]

As the above discussion suggests, the use of the functional method requires a comparatist to possess an extremely broad knowledge base, encompassing not only contemporary law but also sociology, anthropology, and history, among other fields. This level of expertise is highly demanding, if not impossible, for a single

---

[43] Focusing solely on economic efficiency as the basis for comparing laws, as suggested by the strict law and economics approach, represents a reductionist understanding of law and its role in society.

[44] McDougal (1980), p. 219. Consider also Gerber (2001), p. 204; Markesinis (2003), p. 39.

[45] Ainsworth (1996), p. 28.

[46] It should be noted that traditional functionalists have also called for an interdisciplinary approach, albeit in somewhat different terms. According to Pierre Lepaulle, "[I]t must be clear that a comparison restricted to one legal phenomenon in two countries is unscientific and misleading. A legal system is a unity, the whole of which expresses itself in each part; the same blood runs in the whole organism. An identical provision of the law of two countries may have wholly different moral backgrounds, may have been brought about by the interplay of wholly different forces and hence the similarity may be due to the purest coincidence – no more significant than the double meaning of a pun". Lepaulle (1922), p. 853. Similarly, Rabel, one of the founders of functionalism, points out that "The material of reflection about legal problems must be the law of the entire globe, past and present, the relation of the law to the land, the climate, and race, with historical fates of peoples, - war, revolution, state-building, subjugation -, with religious and moral conceptions; ambitions and creative power of individuals; need of goods production and consumption; interests of ranks, parties, classes. Intellectual currents of all kinds are at work... Everything is conditioned on everything else in social, economic and legal design". *Rabel* (1925), p. 5. See also Rothacker (1957), p. 31; Siems (2018), p. 44. For a critical assessment of functionalism see also Brand (2007); Graziadei (2003).

comparatist to achieve.[47] Consequently, functional legal comparison is typically conducted by international teams of experts. Specific socio-legal problems are assigned to national rapporteurs according to a preliminary scheme designed to facilitate comparative analysis. Each representative of a national legal system then submits a report explaining how the law in their system addresses the specific issue under consideration. This collective approach to functional comparison offers considerable advantages, though it often incurs significant costs and necessitates substantial organizational effort and time.

5.5 Explaining Similarities and Differences Between Legal Systems

As previously noted, comparative law often begins with the recognition of common social problems across different legal systems. The key question is whether these legal systems exhibit common features or differences in their regulation of these issues and how these similarities or differences can be explained. Addressing this question requires examining the factors that influence the development, structure, and substantive content of these systems. The similarities and differences between these factors often result in the observed variations in legal domains. Relevant factors include physical and geographical conditions, historical circumstances, economic structure, political system and ideology, religion, and other cultural elements. Compiling a comprehensive list of all contributing factors is challenging, as some may be unknown or incidental. Additionally, the various factors are not independent but are interrelated and interdependent. Law can be viewed as the product of a synthesis of both exogenous factors, such as physical and geographical conditions, and endogenous elements, such as legislative processes and judicial decision-making. The impact of these factors varies significantly across different contexts.[48]

The content of laws is often directly influenced by physical conditions such as geography, climate, and the availability or lack of natural resources. For example, regulations governing night work in Arctic regions differ significantly from those in equatorial countries. Similarly, legal frameworks for water supply vary greatly between the desert areas of North Africa and the water-abundant regions of Scandinavia. Climatic conditions also shape laws related to food supply and distribution. In areas with high seismic activity, construction standards are designed to mitigate earthquake risks. The discovery of new energy sources, such as oil or

[47] As John Reitz remarks, "good comparatists should be sensitive to the ever-present limitations on information available about foreign legal systems and should qualify their conclusions if they are unable to have access to sufficient information or if they have reason to suspect that they are missing important information. If the gaps are too large, the study should not be undertaken at all because its conclusions about foreign law will be too uncertain to be useful." Reitz (1998), p. 631.

[48] As previously noted, what Montesquieu refers to as the 'spirit of the laws' (*De l'Esprit des lois*) is the result of the combined influences of these factors. See Chap. 2 above.

natural gas, necessitates the creation of regulations for their exploitation.[49] Physical conditions not only shape specific legal rules designed to address particular needs but also influence the broader character of a legal system. For instance, they can affect the mentality and temperament of the population, impacting a country's economy and, consequently, its legal development, given the significant influence of economic circumstances on the law.[50]

An interrelationship exists between economic and legal development, where the content of specific legal rules reflects underlying economic patterns. The economic structure sets the boundaries for decision-making regarding both the legal system as a whole and its detailed rules. Essentially, the economy underpins and defines the limits of the law while also providing the framework within which economic activity occurs. Countries with differing economic systems, such as free market economies and centrally planned economies, or at various stages of economic development, will naturally have different legal rules within the economic domain. For instance, antitrust legislation becomes necessary only within the context of a free market economy and assumes a certain level of economic power concentration. Additionally, the economic structure influences other aspects of social life, such as criminality and family life, thereby indirectly affecting criminal law and family law. Despite its central significance, the economic system should be regarded as one of several interrelated factors that shape the character and development of the law.[51]

To thoroughly understand of a country's legal system and its development, it is essential to examine the nature of its political system. The political system encompasses the processes, practices, and structures through which a society organizes and administers public policies and affairs. The key elements of a political system include: (a) the government, including the different branches of government (executive, legislative, and judicial) and their respective functions and powers; (b) political institutions, such as parliaments, courts, and administrative agencies, through which political power is exercised and decisions are made; (c) political processes and methods through which policies are formulated, implemented, and enforced; (d) political culture, including the attitudes, beliefs, and values that shape the behaviour and practices of individuals and groups within the political system; (e) individuals

---

[49] See Grossfeld (1990), p. 75 ff; Rodière (1979), p. 8.

[50] See Wahl (1973).

[51] The Marxist theory of the state and law emphasizes the relationship between the state, law, and the economic base of society. Law and state are phenomena of the so-called superstructure, while the base consists of 'real' relations of production and exchange, including labour, means of production, and relationships between workers and owners. The superstructure serves to maintain and legitimize the base. The state arises from and serves to manage class conflict, functioning to protect the interests of the ruling class by maintaining the existing class structure. Legal systems reinforce existing economic relations and class structures. Critics argue that the Marxist view oversimplifies the state's functions and underestimates the state's relative autonomy. It is also argued that law is not solely determined by the economic base but is relatively independent: it not only expresses socio-economic relations but also influences them. Law has both explicit and latent non-intentional functions, a thesis supported by German functionalist sociologists of law, such as Niklas Luhmann. For more on this perspective, see Luhmann (1974, 2004).

and groups who participate in the political process and whose actions and interactions shape the dynamics of the political system; and (f) the body of laws, such as constitutions, statutes and judicial precedents, that govern the functioning of the political system.

Political systems can be broadly categorized into several principal types. In a democracy, power is vested in the people, either directly or through elected representatives. A monarchy features a single ruler (the monarch) who governs based on hereditary right or divine mandate. An oligarchy concentrates political power in the hands of a small, elite group, often based on wealth, family ties, or military control. Authoritarianism is characterized by power concentrated in a single leader or a small group. Totalitarianism, an extreme form of authoritarianism, seeks to control nearly every aspect of public and private life. In a theocracy, religious leaders control the government, claiming to rule on behalf of a divine authority. The nature and functioning of a political system are influenced by historical, cultural, economic, and social factors, and they can evolve over time in response to internal and external pressures.

The political system and social structure impose ideological boundaries on legal regulation. Legislation can be viewed as an expression of a worldview, reflecting how certain societal groups perceive the current state of affairs and how they believe society should be organized both now and in the future. A worldview comprises two types of elements: factual-theoretical and normative-ideological. While these elements are intricately intertwined, they can be considered separately at an abstract level. The factual-theoretical element encompasses beliefs about both actual and possible states of affairs. These beliefs are primarily rooted in everyday experience, which complements systematic theoretical knowledge and provides its interpretative basis. The normative-ideological element, on the other hand, includes opinions on how society should be structured. It addresses states of affairs that have not yet been realized but they are considered desirable. This element provides criteria for assessing that the current state of affairs is inadequate and articulates the means necessary for rectifying the situation. A worldview is articulated through legal norms and functions as the dominant ideology, explaining and legitimizing these norms. The use of a particular worldview to legitimize legal norms presupposes that a social group believes in this worldview and possesses sufficient social power to advance its inherent goals. Therefore, an analysis of social and state power is essential to understand and explain legal institutions. One must ask: which social groups have the power to impose their worldview or ideology—their knowledge, beliefs, and desires regarding society—as the foundation for creating and applying legal norms? After addressing this question, one can analyse the factors that led to the normative modelling of society through law in a specific manner.

The political-ideological perspective is instrumental in explaining the differences between the legal systems of democratic and non-democratic states, particularly in the areas of constitutional, criminal, and administrative law.[52] Furthermore,

[52] See on this Friedmann (1972), pp. 22–23.

the close connection between a country's political system and its economic structure provides a general explanatory background for economic activity as a framework for specific observations.[53] Although a particular type of ideology typically underpins an economic and political system, ideological differences can exist even between countries with similar political and economic systems. For instance, differences in the prevailing views in two countries regarding the position of women in society are reflected not only in family law but also in other branches of law, such as employment law and the law of succession. These ideological differences can be explained by cultural, religious, and historical factors.

However, comparative law scholars caution against the significant error of conflating the political and ideological underpinnings of a legal rule with its juridical function. While two legal systems may fundamentally differ in their ideological goals, the juridical functions of specific rules can be similar or compatible.[54] For instance, no former socialist country eradicated the use of money as a means of exchange for goods and services. Consequently, the distribution of goods and services to citizens was facilitated through a market system regulated by legal rules (concerning, e.g., sales, leases, and loans) that were functionally similar to those in capitalist countries. A citizen in former East Germany purchasing goods in a state-owned department store engaged in a similar activity as a citizen of West Germany buying goods in a privately-owned store. Although the former individual could theoretically be considered a part-owner of the state-owned store, and state-owned stores in socialist countries aimed to serve broader social needs than profit, these differences were so remote from the actual transaction that they did not significantly impact the practical legal issues arising from the purchase. As a result, the legal rules governing such transactions were similar in both countries, sharing many common features. This similarity extends to many rules governing relationships in other fields of private law.

The study of cultural history reveals the significant role religions have played in the development of legal systems. The influence of religion on law is evident not only in early societies, where religious, moral, and legal norms often overlapped, but also in modern ones. In countries of the Muslim world, for instance, religious norms have either directly attained the status of legal norms or have been indirectly incorporated into the legal system. Similarly, in Western countries, religious beliefs and attitudes have impacted the development of the law, especially in the areas of family and criminal law. Additionally, as Zweigert and Kötz have noted, religious or quasi-religious beliefs[55] can uniquely influence the style of a legal system and

---

[53] Political decision-making may be described as the uniting link between economic conditions and legal norms.

[54] See, e.g., Bogdan (1978), pp. 1, 2, 93, 95; Bogdan (1994), p. 61 ff; Zweigert and Kötz (1987), p. 37 ff.

[55] A quasi-religious belief refers to a set of convictions or principles that resemble or mimic aspects of religious beliefs but are not necessarily tied to any formal religion or deity. These beliefs often encompass rituals, moral codes, and a sense of purpose or meaning similar to those found in traditional religions.

people's attitudes toward it.[56] For example, Confucian ethics in Asian countries contribute to a general aversion to laws and judicial proceedings, emphasizing compromise and conciliation for resolving private disputes. The role of law varies significantly across different societies, as it can have a broader or narrower scope and encompass a larger or smaller portion of intentional human behavior. This variation can often be attributed to cultural and religious influences. It is essential, however, to examine the effects of religious factors on a particular legal culture within the context of the historical processes that shaped the era in which that culture emerged. This analysis should always consider the interplay between these religious factors and the prevailing socio-economic and political influences.

Law can only be properly understood when placed in a broad historical context. The defining features of a legal system are products of historical processes, especially those shaping the epoch during which the system was formed. Historical factors can elucidate a country's constitutional structure, the hierarchy of legal sources, the organization of its court system, and the enactment of specific laws.[57] For instance, consider the phenomenon of codification of law—a distinctive feature of civil law systems. Codification denotes an authoritative statement of the whole law in a coherent and systematic way. This tradition originates from the rationalist tendencies that dominated European philosophy during the eighteenth and nineteenth centuries, with roots tracing back to the comprehensive codification of Roman law by Emperor Justinian in the sixth century AD. One can trace back to Justinian the idea that a code overrides all legal sources, offering a fresh start to the law. The historical relationship between legal orders and the issue of the transferability of legal institutions and norms is also crucial to address. Countries like Canada, Australia, New Zealand, India, and Singapore share many common legal characteristics due to their historical inheritance from British colonialism. However, it is essential to recognize that despite this shared heritage, the legal rules and institutions inherited from the colonial power have often been modified or replaced to better suit local conditions and needs.

Many similarities among different legal systems are attributed to the phenomenon of legal convergence. According to Rudolf Schlesinger, legal convergence occurs when different legal systems, starting from distinct stated rules, evolve to meet at a middle ground.[58] This convergence can occur at substantive, institutional,

[56] Zweigert and Kötz (1987), p. 73.

[57] Insofar as law is a product of the authoritative power of the state, it is unsurprising that legislative enactments have historically been influenced by the personal preferences or priorities of individuals in positions of great authority. For example, certain family law rules in early 19th-century France were shaped by considerations related to Napoleon Bonaparte's own family situation during the introduction of the French Civil Code. Generally, however, a legislator's choices are seldom entirely arbitrary. Typically, a legislator will adopt one of several possible solutions to a problem arising from a conflict of interests, choosing the solution that appears most reasonable under the circumstances. Nonetheless, another legislator might find a different solution preferable.

[58] Schlesinger (1995).

or procedural levels, and sometimes across all these levels.[59] Legal convergence assumes that societies, as they evolve through similar stages of development, encounter similar needs and exhibit a natural tendency towards imitation. This tendency may be driven by a desire to accelerate progress or pursue specific political and socio-economic objectives.[60]

While each legal system is shaped by a unique combination of socio-cultural and historical factors, it is also true that collective cultural identities are formed through interaction with others, and no culture can claim to be entirely original. If legal rules emerge in response to social needs, as the socio-functional view of law suggests, the development of a global society will almost inevitably lead to a greater convergence among legal systems.[61] Factors driving legal convergence include the transplantation and borrowing of legal ideas and norms,[62] increased international cooperation among states, the operation of international organizations, and a growing awareness of shared global concerns such as environmental pollution and climatic change.

Legal convergence through international and transnational law results in the harmonization of legal systems across different jurisdictions. This process is driven by several factors, including formal international agreements, the influence of international organizations, private regulations, the activities of non-governmental organizations (NGOs), professional networks, and cross-border litigation.

International law encompasses a set of rules and principles that govern the relationships and interactions between states and other international actors. It includes treaties, conventions, customs, and judicial decisions of international courts. Countries often sign and ratify international treaties and conventions, thereby agreeing to adopt similar legal standards and practices. Organizations such as the United Nations create frameworks that promote legal convergence by encouraging member states to adopt common regulations and standards. International initiatives aimed at harmonizing laws in specific areas, such as environmental protection or intellectual property, promote convergence by establishing uniform standards and practices that

---

[59] See Sacco (1991).

[60] According to Giorgio del Vecchio, "the basic unity of human spirit makes possible the effective communication between peoples. Law is not only a national phenomenon; it is, first and foremost, a human phenomenon. A people can accept and adopt as its own a law created by another people because, in the nature of both peoples, there exist common demands and needs which [often] find expression in law". del Vecchio (1960), p. 497. See on this Levi-Strauss (2001), p. 103 ff. On the so-called 'law of imitation' and its role in the evolution of social institutions see Tarde (1890). And see Allen (1964), p. 101 ff.

[61] See King (1997); Ferrari (1990); Markesinis (1994); Zimmerman (1995). For a critical perspective on this issue see Legrand (1996). A number of scholars have raised the question of whether or not 'natural convergence' is simply a euphemism for what they call 'Western legal imperialism'. See on this issue von Mehren (1971); Knieper (1996); J. Whitman (2009).

[62] The phenomenon of legal transplantation has garnered significant attention in recent years, especially since the 1974 publication of Alan Watson's book *Legal Transplants: An Approach to Comparative Law*. According to this author, the term 'legal transplants' refers to "the moving of a rule (…) from one country to another, or from one people to another". Watson (1974), p. 21. And See Chap. 12 below.

countries incorporate into their domestic legal systems. Additionally, decisions by international courts, such as the International Court of Justice or the European Court of Human Rights, can influence national legal systems by setting precedents that member states are encouraged to follow.[63]

Transnational law comprises legal norms and practices that transcend national borders, without necessarily originating from formal international agreements. It includes regulations and standards set by non-governmental organizations (NGOs), multinational corporations, and other non-state actors. Legal convergence through transnational law occurs in various ways. Non-governmental organizations and other civil society organizations play a significant role in promoting legal convergence by advocating for the global adoption of certain legal standards and practices. For instance, environmental NGOs may push for the implementation of similar environmental laws and regulations across different countries. Multinational corporations often establish codes of conduct and standards that apply across their operations in multiple countries. These private regulations can influence national legal systems by setting *de facto* standards that countries adopt to attract business and investment. Transnational professional networks, such as the International Bar Association (IBA), promote the exchange of ideas and best practices among legal professionals, leading to the adoption of similar legal frameworks in different countries. Additionally, cross-border litigation involving parties from various jurisdictions frequently necessitates that courts consider foreign laws and precedents. This process can result in the incorporation of foreign legal principles into domestic legal systems, thereby fostering convergence.

There is a continuous competition between factors that promote similarity or convergence and those that foster differentiation or divergence among legal systems. The ultimate outcome is shaped by the relative significance ascribed to these various factors within different historical, social, political, economic, cultural, and legal contexts.

5.6 Concluding Remarks

In legal science, attempts have been made to reduce social relations to individual right-duty relationships, which are the objects of legal regulation.[64] These frameworks enable the clear articulation of similarities and differences in legal regularities.

---

[63] See Chap. 4 above.

[64] For example, the jurist Wesley Hohfeld devised a system in which all legal relations can be expressed using 'fundamental legal conceptions.' He proposed that legal relations can be systematically categorized into a set of basic elements, which he called 'jural relations.' These are structured in pairs and opposites, allowing for a precise analysis of legal interactions. The basic relations are: right—duty; privilege (or liberty)—no right; power—liability; and immunity—disability. A legal right is a claim that one party (the right-holder) has against another party (the duty-bearer). Corresponding to the right, a duty is an obligation imposed on the duty-bearer to act or refrain from

Although legal relations under these frameworks may appear abstract, they are intrinsically connected to social reality. Legal roles and relations reflect deeper, more fundamental social positions. This does not imply that analysing legal relations lacks value. Even purely formal schemes serve as useful starting points. The process begins with describing abstract legal relations, followed by examining whether they can be explained through more fundamental social relations. Legal relations and the behaviours they model are based on an experimental shaping of social relations. This shaping is not purely empirical and cognitive; it also includes evaluative reactions where certain states of affairs are chosen based on axiological grounds as consciously pursued goals. This process involves a set of juristic forms that are neither incidental nor unique to specific cases. Instead, they originate from the historical development of legal doctrines and ideas. Axiological and teleological considerations must be examined in conjunction with the doctrinal history of legal concepts and their systematic treatment.[65] It is crucial to recognize that an evaluative element is inherent in all intentional decision-making, including lawmaking and the application of laws. This element is also present in concepts used to convey regulatory information. Therefore, it is insufficient to merely compare the form and factual content of a legal institution with a similar institution in another legal system. The evaluative component embedded within facts and concepts must not be ignored.

In conclusion, the common elements that form the requisite *tertium comparationis* can appear at various levels, including language, conceptual framework, structure, functions, values, goals, and outcomes of legal rules and institutions. These elements often manifest simultaneously across multiple levels. Depending on the nature, scope, and purposes of the comparative inquiry, various criteria of comparability may be employed, either in combination or alternatively. While comparative law extends beyond merely comparing legal elements, its ultimate focus remains on law. The methodological challenges of comparative law cannot be addressed solely at the linguistic level, as these issues are not exclusively semiotic. Accurate translation of legal terms is crucial but insufficient on its own. Similarly, the mere presence of comparable social relationships does not suffice for a meaningful comparison. A

acting in a certain way towards the right-holder. A privilege or liberty is the freedom of an individual to act or not act in a certain way without a corresponding duty. If person A has a privilege, person B has a no-right in relation to that privilege. A legal power is the ability of an individual to change legal relations, either their own or those of others. Corresponding to the power, a liability is the condition of being subject to having one's legal relations changed by the exercise of someone else's power. Immunity is a protection against having one's legal relations altered by another party. Corresponding to immunity, a disability is the lack of legal power to alter someone else's legal relations. By breaking down complex legal relationships into these fundamental components, Hohfeld's system aids in the clarification of legal disputes and enhances the precision of legal discourse. See Hohfeld (1917).

[65] Historically, juridical forms and their systematic organization predate the norms of present law. General doctrines play a crucial role as a framework for comparative legal studies. This significance arises partly from common legal challenges and partly from historical traditions. For example, Roman law has served as common foundational basis for many contemporary legal systems. Therefore, the conceptual framework of Roman law can be seen as an apt *tertium comparationis*, a common denominator for legally organized relationships in life.

sufficient similarity in social function is necessary for meaningful legal comparison, but a form of conceptual commensurability is also required. One of the primary objectives of comparative law as a branch of legal science is to explore and elucidate these issues. Achieving this objective necessitates a method with a solid theoretical foundation; otherwise, comparative law risks remaining at the level of mere description or falling into speculative traps.

References

Aarnio A (1979) Denkweisen der Rechtswissenschaft. Springer, Vienna and New York
Ainsworth JE (1996) Categories and culture: on the 'rectification of names' in comparative law. Cornell Law Rev 82:19–42
Allen CK (1964) Law in the making. Clarendon Press, Oxford
Ancel M (1982) Le probléme de la comparabilité et la méthode fonctionelle en droit *compare*. Festschrift für Imre Zajtay. Mohr Siebeck, Tubingen, pp 1–6
Bogdan M (1978) Different economic systems and comparative law. Comparative Law Yearb 2:89–115
Bogdan M (1994) Comparative law. Kluwer, Deventer, p 2000
Brand O (2007) Conceptual comparisons: towards a coherent methodology of comparative legal studies. Brooklyn J Int Law 32:405–466
Dannemann G (2019) Comparative law: study of similarities or differences? In: Reimann M, Zimmerman R (eds) The Oxford handbook of comparative law, 2nd edn. Oxford University Press, Oxford, pp 390–422
de Cruz P (1993) A modern approach to comparative law. Kluwer, Devender
del Vecchio G (1960) Les bases du droit comparé et les principes généraux du droit. Revue internationale de droit compare 12:493–499
Demleitner N (1998) Challenge, opportunity and risk: an era of change in comparative law. Am J Comp Law 46(4):647–655
Ewald W (1995) Comparative jurisprudence (1): what was it like to try a rat? Univ Pa Law Rev 143:1889–2149
Ferrari V (1990) Socio-legal concepts and their comparison. In: Oeyen E (ed) Comparative methodology: theory and practice in international social research. Sage, London, p 63 ff
Frankenberg G (1985) Critical comparisons: re-thinking comparative law. Harv Int Law J 26(2):411–455
Friedmann W (1972) Law in a changing society, 2nd edn. Stevens, London
Gerber DJ (2001) Sculpting the agenda of comparative law: Ernst Rabel and the facade of language. In: Riles A (ed) Rethinking the masters of comparative law. Hart Publishing, Oxford, pp 190–208
Glanert S (2014) Translation matters. In: Glanert S (ed) Comparative law: engaging translation. Routledge, Abingdon, pp 1–19
Graziadei M (2003) The functionalist heritage. In: Legrand P, Munday R (eds) Comparative legal studies: traditions and transitions. Cambridge University Press, Cambridge, pp 100–128
Grossfeld B (1990) The strength and weakness of comparative law. Oxford University Press, New York
Grosswald Curran V (1998) Dealing in difference: comparative law's potential for broadening legal perspectives. Am J Comp Law 46(4):657–668
Gutteridge HC (1938) The comparative aspects of legal terminology. Tulane Law Rev 12:401–411
Heck P (1914) Gesetzesauslegung und Interessenjurisprudenz. Archiv für die civilistische Praxis 112:1–318

Hoeflich MH (2002) Translation and the reception of foreign law in the antebellum United States. Am J Comp Law 50(4):753–775

Hohfeld WN (1917) Fundamental legal conceptions as applied in judicial reasoning. Yale Law J 26(8):710–770

Holmes OW (1881) The common law. Little, Brown, & Co., Boston

Holmes OW (1897) The path of the law. Harv Law Rev 10:457–478

Jansen N (2019) Comparative law and comparative knowledge. In: Reimann M, Zimmermann R (eds) The Oxford handbook of comparative law, 2nd edn. Oxford University Press, Oxford, pp 291–319

Jhering R (1877) Der Zweck im Recht. Breitkopf & Härtel, Leipzig

Jhering R (1884) Scherz und Ernst in der Jurisprudenz. Breitkopf & Härtel, Leipzig

Kahn-Freund O (1966) Comparative law as an academic subject. Law Quart Rev 82:40–61

Kamba WJ (1974) Comparative law: a theoretical framework. Int Comp Law Quart 23(3):485–519

King M (1997) Comparing legal cultures in the quest for law's identity. In: Nelken D (ed) Comparing legal cultures. Aldershot, pp 119–134

Knieper R (1996) Rechtsimperialismus? Zeitschrift für Rechtspolitik 29:64–67

Legrand P (1996) European systems are not converging. Int Comp Law Quart 45:52–81

Lepaulle P (1922) The function of comparative law with a critique of sociological jurisprudence. Harv Law Rev 35:838–858

Levi-Strauss C (2001) Race et histoire. Albin Michel, Paris

Luhmann N (1974) Rechtssystem und Rechtsdogmatik. W Kohlhammer, Stuttgart

Luhmann N (2004) Law as a social system. Oxford University Press, Oxford

Markesinis B (ed) (1994) The gradual convergence: foreign ideas, foreign influences, and English law on the eve of the 21st century. Clarendon Press, Oxford

Markesinis B (2003) Comparative law in the courtroom and in the classroom: the story of the last thirty-five years. Hart Publishing, Oxford

Mattei U (1994) Efficiency in legal transplants: an essay in comparative law and economics. Int Rev Law Econ 14(1):3–19

Mattei U (1997) Comparative law and economics. University of Michigan Press, Ann Arbor

McDougal MS (1980) The comparative study of law for policy purposes: value clarification as an instrument of democratic world order. In: Butler WE (ed) International law in comparative perspective. Sijthoff & Noordhoff, Maryland, p. 191 ff

Michaels R (2019) The functional method of comparative law. In: Reimann M, Zimmermann R (eds) The Oxford handbook of comparative law, 2nd edn. Oxford University Press, Oxford, pp 345–389

Örücü E (2006) Methodological aspects of comparative law. Eur J Law Reform 8(1):29–42

Pound R (1911–1912) The scope and purpose of sociological jurisprudence. Harv Law Rev 24 (June 1911):591–619; 25 (December 1911): 140–168; 25 (April 1912): 489–516

Puchta GF (1841) Cursus der Institutionen I. Breitkopf & Härtel, Leipzig

Rabel E (1925) Aufgabe und Notwendigkeit der Rechtsvergleichung. Max Hueber, Munich

Reitz JC (1998) How to do comparative law. Am J Comp Law 46(4):617–636

Rheinstein M (1938) Teaching comparative law. Univ Chicago Law Rev 5(4):615–624

Rodière R (1979) Introduction au droit comparé. Dalloz, Paris

Rothacker E (1957) Die vergleichende Methode in den Geisteswissenschaften. Zeitschrift für vergleichende Rechtswissenschaft 60:13–33

Sacco R (1991) Legal formants: a dynamic approach to comparative law. Am J Comp Law 39(1):1–34

Samuel G (2014) An introduction to comparative law theory and method. Hart Publishing, Oxford

Schlesinger R (1995) The past and future of comparative law. Am J Comp Law 43(3):477–481

Siems M (2018) Comparative law, 2nd edn. Cambridge University Press, Cambridge

Tarde G (1890) Les Lois de l'Imitation. Alcan, Paris

von Mehren A (1971) An academic tradition for comparative law? Am J Comp Law 19(4):624–632

Wahl E (1973) Influences climatiques sur l'évolution du droit en Orient et en Occident. Contribution au régionalisme en droit compare. Revue internationale de droit compare 25(2):261–276
Watson A (1974) Legal transplants: an approach to comparative law. Scottish Academic Press, Edinburgh
Whitman JQ (2009) Western legal imperialism: thinking about the deep historical roots. Theor Inq Law 10(2):305–332
Windscheid B (1891) Lehrbuch des Pandektenrechts I, 7th edn. Literarische Anstalt Bütten & Loening, Frankfurt
Zimmerman R (1995) 'Common law' und 'civil law', Amerika und Europa. In: Zimmerman R (ed) Amerikanische Rechtskultur und europäisches Privatrecht. Mohr Siebeck, Tübingen, pp 1–10
Zweigert K (1966) Des solutions identiques par des voies différentes. Revue internationale de droit comparé 18:5–18
Zweigert K, Kötz H (1987) An introduction to comparative law, 2nd edn. Clarendon Press, Oxford
Zweigert K, Kötz H (1998) An introduction to comparative law, 3rd edn. Clarendon Press, Oxford

Chapter 6
Taxonomies of Legal Systems in Comparative Law Scholarship

6.1 Introduction

Comparative law scholarship has a long-standing tradition of categorizing legal systems into broader families based on kinship and descent.[1] The foundation of these classifications lies in the observation that, while national legal systems differ significantly with respect to specific rules and procedures, these differences diminish when viewed through the lens of the broader socio-legal culture, historical origins, modes of legal thinking, and other overarching perspectives.[2] Classifying legal systems into transnational legal traditions or families facilitates comparative law studies by enabling inquiries based on the systems' general characteristics, styles, and orientations. These classifications highlight the diversity and complexity of legal systems and how they have been shaped by various cultural, religious, and historical influences. In essence, the study of transnational legal traditions is a window into the broader cultural and historical forces that have shaped human societies. The classification of legal systems into families has been a topic of scholarly discussion and debate for many years. Comparative law is not only a method of legal research but can also be regarded as a distinct branch of legal science, partly because it addresses broad theoretical issues related to the categorization of the world's legal systems.

While some scholars have attempted to base the classification of legal systems on a single criterion, such as historical origins or political and economic ideology, most comparatists today recognize that a useful classification should involve multiple criteria. According to the jurist Léontin-Jean Constantinesco, considered one of the architects of modern comparative law, several 'determinant factors' should be used together when categorizing legal systems into groups. These factors include: (a) the

---

[1] Dannemann (2019), p. 393.

[2] See Winterton (1975), p. 69.

G. Mousourakis, *Traversing Legal Traditions*, Springer Textbooks in Law,
https://doi.org/10.1007/978-3-031-94669-1_6

historical origins and evolution of a legal system, including how past events have shaped the current system; (b) the primary sources of law and their hierarchy; (c) the methodologies used in the application and interpretation of law, including procedures and techniques employed by judges and other legal professionals in legal reasoning and decision-making; (d) the organization, function, and interrelationships of legal institutions, such as legislative bodies, courts, and administrative agencies; and (e) the broader socio-economic and political context within which a legal system operates. Constantinesco's approach aims to provide a comprehensive framework for understanding and classifying legal systems, allowing for a more nuanced analysis of the complexities and unique characteristics of each system.[3] It is important to note that even when a single, broad criterion is proposed, such as a system's general 'style', this criterion usually requires the consideration of many interrelated factors.

Although traditional classifications have lost some appeal in the age of globalization, the conceptual framework of legal families remains relevant for describing the current legal landscape. This chapter reviews various classifications of legal systems proposed by both early and contemporary scholars, highlighting the criteria on which these classifications are based.

6.2 Early Approaches to the Classification of Legal Systems

From an early period, jurists and philosophers recognized that certain legal institutions inherent to their own countries also existed within the legal frameworks of other nations. This observation led to the realization that legal systems, despite their geographical and cultural differences, shared common elements. These shared legal institutions and practices became the foundation for some of the earliest efforts to classify and compare legal systems across different regions and civilizations.

Christopher St. German (c. 1460–1540), an influential English legal scholar, authored theoretically sophisticated legal works, demonstrating a profound understanding of the importance of the comparative study of legal systems.[4] In his work *Doctor and Student*, St. German discusses the nature of law and its various sources, clearly differentiating between English common law and Roman law. He emphasizes that English common law is rooted in the customs and traditions of the English

---

[3] Constantinesco (1971), pp. 262–265. Constantinesco suggests, moreover, that several legal families can together form a broader family (*Rechtskreis*). The latter constitutes an expression of one of the cultural civilizations (*Kulturkreis*) in which human societies may be divided. Consider Constantinesco (1979, 1981).

[4] Saint German's best-known work is his *Dialogus de fundamentis legum Anglie et de conscientia* (known as Dialogue in English between a Doctor of Divinity and a Student in the laws of England) (London 1528). This was a a handbook for law students, which was not superseded until the publication of Blackstone's *Commentaries* in the eighteenth century. See Plucknett and Barton (1974), Donahue (1979).

people, developed over centuries, whereas Roman law is based on the codifications and principles of ancient Roman jurists. St. German believed that English common law was more suited to the needs and circumstances of the English people and should be preserved and developed independently of Roman law influences. His distinction between English and Roman law was significant in the development of the common law tradition, underscoring the importance of local customs and judicial precedents in the English legal system.

Furthermore, St. German explains the distinction between the common law of England and canon law, the body of laws developed by the Catholic Church. He emphasized that while canon law was influential in certain areas, particularly in ecclesiastical matters, it was separate from and subordinate to the common law of the land in civil and criminal matters. St. German's work reflects the tensions and interactions between these two legal systems during his time, especially in the context of the Reformation and the increasing assertion of royal authority over ecclesiastical jurisdiction.

Additionally, St. German addressed the relationship between common law, which originated in custom and developed through judicial decisions, and equity, which comprised principles of fairness and justice developed by the Court of Chancery to supplement common law when the rigid application of rules would result in injustice. St. German extensively employed the terms 'conscience' and 'equity' in his legal writings. He argued that judges and lawyers should look to their consciences, rather than solely to the revealed authority of religion or statutory texts, to achieve a perfect understanding of how laws should be written and applied.[5]

William Fulbeck, an English legal writer of the late sixteenth and early seventeenth centuries, made significant contributions to the understanding and categorization of legal systems. In his work "A Direction or Preparative to the Study of the Law," published in 1600, Fulbeck classified legal systems based on their origins and underlying principles. He distinguished between divine law,[6] natural law,[7] and human positive law,[8] and further subdivided human positive law into three categories: civil law, which encompasses legal systems derived from Roman law and characterized by comprehensive legal codes; English common law, which is based on judicial precedents and customs rather than written codes; and canon law, developed

[5] For more on this aspect of St. German's work see Endicott (1989), Holdsworth (1915).

[6] This category includes laws believed to be given by a divine entity. These laws are considered universal and unchangeable, guiding moral and ethical behaviour. Fulbeck likely viewed these as the highest form of law, providing the foundation for justice and righteousness.

[7] Fulbeck categorized natural law as those laws derived from human nature and reason. These laws are inherent to humanity and can be discovered through rational thought and the study of human nature. Natural law principles are considered self-evident truths that form the basis for human rights and justice.

[8] This category encompasses laws created by human societies. Positive law includes statutes, regulations, and ordinances enacted by governments and legal authorities. Fulbeck recognized that these laws could vary widely between different societies and were subject to change over time based on societal needs and contexts.

by the ecclesiastical authorities of the Christian Church.[9] Fulbeck's classifications have profoundly influenced legal thought for centuries.

In 1880, Ernest Glasson, a prominent French jurist and legal historian,[10] drawing on historical sources and the common characteristics of various legal systems, classified them into three main categories: (i) those strongly influenced by Roman law, such as the Italian, Spanish, Portuguese, Romanian, and Greek legal systems; (ii) those largely immune from Roman law influence and originating in customary law, such as the English, Scandinavian, and Russian systems; and (iii) those combining Roman and Germanic (or Barbarian) influences, such as the French, German, and Swiss legal systems.[11] The principal criterion for Glasson's classification was a system's proximity to Roman law. Interestingly, Glasson grouped the English, Russian, and Scandinavian legal systems, each of which would belong to a separate legal family according to contemporary classifications, into the same category. Furthermore, he assigned the French and German systems to the same category, separate from the Spanish, Portuguese, and Italian systems, which are today considered part of the French branch of the civil law family.[12] Glasson's classification of legal systems into categories based on their proximity to Roman law remains a significant reference point for scholars studying the historical development of legal traditions.[13]

In 1884, the Japanese jurist Hozumi Nobushige, recognizing the importance of classifying legal systems as a methodological tool in comparative law, offered a classification that significantly influenced the development of Japan's modern legal framework.[14] Hozumi distinguished between traditional legal systems, based on customs, and modern legal systems, influenced by Western legal thought. He categorized legal systems into seven broad families: (i) Chinese, (ii) Indian (Hindu), (iii)

[9] See Fulbeck (1600, 1601).

[10] Glasson (1839–1907) was a professor of law at the University of Paris and a member of the prestigious French Academy of Moral and Political Sciences.

[11] Glasson (1879), cxli. And see Pargendler (2012), pp. 1047–1049; Husa (2015), p. 103.

[12] According to Constantinesco, Glasson was probably the first scholar to seek the relationship between the European legal systems in the common historical origins and development instead of their racial relationships. Constantinesco (1983), pp. 96–97.

[13] Clovis Bevilaqua, a professor of comparative law and draftsman of the Brazilian Civil Code of 1916, adapted Glasson's classification to encompass both Latin American and European countries. Unlike twentieth-century authors, however, Bevilaqua did not categorize Latin American jurisdictions as direct descendants of European systems. Instead, he identified them as a distinct fourth category, encompassing original legal systems that could not be neatly classified within existing European groupings. Bevilaqua (1897).

[14] Hozumi lived during a time when Japan was undergoing significant transformation during the Meiji Restoration (1868–1912). This period marked Japan's rapid modernization and Westernization, including the adoption of Western legal systems. He was instrumental in the drafting and implementation of the Meiji Constitution and the Civil Code of Japan. For more on Hozumi's background and contribution to the development of modern Japanese law see Aoki (2001). And see Chap. 12 below.

Islamic, (iv) Roman, (v) Germanic, (vi) Slavonic, and (vii) Anglo-Saxon.[15] He noted that as Japan was undergoing a process of modernization, Japanese law was rapidly transitioning from the Chinese legal family to the European legal family.[16]

At the 1900 International Congress on Comparative Law in Paris, the taxonomy of the world's legal systems attracted significant attention and came to be regarded as a key element of the emerging science of comparative law. At that Congress, Gabriel Tarde, a professor of Modern Philosophy at the College of France, emphasized the importance of legal family classifications as one of the principal goals of comparative law. As he pointed out, "under this new viewpoint, the task of comparative law is less to indefinitely collect exhumed laws than to formulate a natural – that is, rational – classification of juridical types, of branches and families of law."[17] Tarde's approach to the taxonomy of legal systems drew heavily on comparative linguistics and biology. It may be regarded as an early articulation of an approach that would come to dominate twentieth-century comparative law thinking. While earlier classifications were meant simply to facilitate the description of different countries' legal systems, the formulation of a proper taxonomy now became the primary goal of comparative law scholarship. This method has descriptive, analytical, and normative dimensions, providing a framework for understanding how different legal systems operate, how they can be improved, and how they relate to each other on a global scale

While Tarde himself did not propose a criterion for classifying legal systems, Adhémar Esmein, a notable French jurist and legal historian, addressed this issue in his contribution to the Paris Congress. Esmein relied on language and ethnicity as his principal classification criteria. This approach reflects a broader trend in 19th and early 20th-century scholarship, where language and ethnicity were often seen as fundamental elements shaping legal systems and cultural identities.

Language serves as a primary vehicle for the transmission of legal concepts, cultural norms, and societal values. Esmein recognized that the legal traditions and practices of a society are deeply embedded in its linguistic heritage. By analysing legal texts and traditions in their original languages, he aimed to uncover the inherent characteristics and historical evolution of different legal systems. Ethnicity, encompassing shared ancestry, cultural practices, and historical experiences, also plays a crucial role in shaping legal systems. Esmein considered ethnic background to understand the social and historical context in which legal norms developed. Ethnic groups often have distinct customs and traditions that influence their legal principles and judicial processes. By classifying legal systems based on ethnicity, Esmein aimed to highlight the cultural and historical roots of legal diversity. This

[15] Hozumi (1904).

[16] In Hozumi's words, "the new Japanese Civil Code stands in a filial relation to the European systems, and with the introduction of Western civilization, the Japanese civil law passed from the Chinese Family to the Roman Family of Law'. Hozumi (1904), p. 16. The idea of Japan as a civil law country became commonplace in the early twentieth century.

[17] Tarde (1905), pp. 439–440. And see Pargendler (2012), pp. 1049–1050.

approach provided insights into how different societies adapted and integrated foreign legal influences into their own ethnic frameworks.

On this basis, Esmein proposed dividing Western legal systems into five main groups: (i) the Latin group, which includes the legal systems of France, Belgium, Italy, Spain, Portugal, Romania, and the countries of Central and South America; (ii) the Germanic group, comprising the legal systems of Germany, Austria, Hungary, and the Scandinavian countries; (iii) the Anglo-Saxon group, encompassing the legal systems of England, the United States, and the British colonies and dominions; (iv) the Slavic group; and (v) the Muslim group.[18] Overall, Adhémar Esmein's reliance on language and ethnicity as classification criteria provided a comprehensive framework for analysing and understanding the complex interplay between legal systems, cultural identities, and historical contexts. Although his classification scheme bears some resemblance to later widely used classifications, it faced significant criticism and was soon forgotten.[19]

In the early 1910s, French comparatist Georges Sauser-Hall proposed a new ethnological taxonomy of legal systems using race as his principal classification criterion. Based on this approach, he identified four broad legal families: (i) Aryan/Indo-European, which included Hindu, Celtic, Greco–Latin, Germanic, Anglo-Saxon, and Slavic legal systems; (ii) Semitic, encompassing Jewish and Arabic-Muslim systems; (iii) Mongoloid, comprising Chinese, Indo-Chinese, and Japanese systems; and (iv) Barbarian customary, which included African, Melanesian, Indonesian, Australian, Polynesian, American, and Hyperborean native systems.[20] By taking race as an apparently immutable criterion for classification, Sauser-Hall was critical of early comparatists' universalist vision, which, according to him, ignored profound differences across peoples. Many later comparatists criticized Sauser-Hall's theory for failing to establish any causal relationship between race and law, and thus his approach was not pursued by other scholars.[21]

In the interwar period, Henry Lévy-Ullmann was the first scholar to propose a classification of legal systems according to their sources of law. He divided the world's systems into three broad groups: (i) Continental, based on written sources of law and derived from Roman law; (ii) Anglo-Saxon, based on customary law and

[18] Esmein (1905), p. 445 ff; Esmein (1909). And see Pargendler (2012), pp. 1050–1052.

[19] Esmein's classification has been criticized for its overly simplistic approach, which fails to capture the complexities and nuances of different legal traditions. Critics argue that Esmein's framework is excessively Eurocentric, focusing primarily on Western legal traditions and overlooking other significant legal systems such as Islamic law, Hindu law, and East Asian legal traditions. Notably, Esmein's classification disregards the role and importance of customary law in many societies, particularly in Africa, Asia, and the Pacific Islands, where customary practices are integral to the legal landscape. Furthermore, contemporary legal scholars have criticized Esmein's approach for not recognizing legal pluralism, where multiple legal systems, including customary, religious, and formal state laws, coexist within a single country. See Monateri (2023), pp. 15–17. For a defence of Esmein's approach see Zweigert and Kötz (1987), p. 64.

[20] Sauser-Hall (1913), p. 113 ff. See also Pargendler (2012), p. 1052; Zweigert and Kötz (1987), p. 64; Monateri (2023), pp. 18–19; Siems (2018), pp. 88–89.

[21] See, e.g., Constantinesco (1983), p. 93; David (1950), pp. 155–157.

developed through judicial decisions and case law as opposed to codified statutes; and (iii) Islamic, having a religious basis and characterized by immobility.[22] This classification was the first clear articulation by a leading comparatist of the basic civil law—common law dichotomy that prevailed in comparative law in later years. Lévy-Ullmann's approach emphasizes the historical and cultural roots of legal systems, recognizing the significant influence of Roman law, common law, and religious laws on the development of legal traditions worldwide.

In 1928, John Henry Wigmore, a prominent American legal scholar, drawing on an extensive historico-comparative study, proposed a comprehensive taxonomy of legal systems that embraced both historical and contemporary contexts. His work, *Panorama of the World's Legal Systems*,[23] categorizes legal systems into several groups, including Mesopotamian, Egyptian, Hebrew, Chinese, Hindu, Greek, Roman, Japanese, Muslim, Germanic, Romanesque,[24] and Anglican.[25] On this basis, he identified five groups of legal cultures founded on different cultural contexts: (1) primitive laws, (2) ancient laws, (3) Euro-American law, (4) religious systems, and (5) Afro-Asian systems.

Interestingly, in Wigmore's scheme, all European subdivisions of legal systems were replaced by a single family of Euro-American law, which included the United States legal system. Unlike other classification schemes that viewed Roman law as the origin of modern systems, Wigmore regarded Roman law as distant from current legal systems and categorized it under ancient laws. What emerges from this scheme is the idea of a single, extensive Euro-American legal family that encompasses American law within a predominantly European context, clearly separated from its historical origins.[26]

Finally, reference should also be made to the 'juristic-historical' classification theory proposed by the Argentinian jurist Enrique Martinez-Paz in 1934. Building on Glasson's earlier theory, Martinez-Paz began with the assumption that all legal systems initially possessed a high degree of originality. He then examined the extent to which each system's development was influenced by other systems, such as Roman law and Canon law, as well as by more recent democratic ideas. Based on this analysis, he identified four broad groups of legal systems: (i) the Barbaric-Customary group (England, Sweden, Norway); (ii) the Barbaric-Roman group (Germany, France, Austria); (iii) the Barbaric-Roman-Canonical group (Spain, Portugal, Italy); and (iv) the Roman-Canonical-Democratic group (Latin America, Russia, Switzerland). This classification is based on generic criteria related to

[22] Lévy-Ullmann (1923), pp. 85–87. And see Pargendler (2012), pp. 1052–1053; Zweigert and Kötz (1987), p. 64; Monateri (2023), pp. 17–18.

[23] Wigmore (1928).

[24] Romanesque legal systems are derived from Roman law and are known for their codified nature.

[25] Anglican law refers to the legal system that originated in England and forms the basis of the common law tradition. This legal system relies heavily on judicial decisions and precedents as the principal means of shaping the law.

[26] See Monateri (2023), pp. 19–21. And see Siems (2018), pp. 88–89, 102.

barbaric, Roman, feudal, Canonical, and democratic juristic elements.[27] Paz's approach shows that, as late as the 1930s, many comparatists tended to neglect the civil law-common law dichotomy while also being willing to group under the same label legal systems as diverse as those of Latin America, Switzerland, and Russia.

6.3 Taxonomies of Legal Systems in Post-WWII Comparative Law Scholarship

The first in a series of classifications proposed during the half-century following World War II was developed by Pierre Arminjon, Boris Nolde, and Martin Wolff. These scholars aimed to establish the theoretical and methodological foundations of comparative law as a science, moving beyond merely describing the contemporary legal world. They argued that "the task of comparative law as an autonomous science should have as its starting point the classification of the large number of the world's legal systems."[28] According to their classification theory, there exist certain 'model' or 'parent tree' systems whose legal rules and institutional structures were transplanted (often through military conquest or colonization) or adopted (due to their perceived quality and prestige) in many countries worldwide.[29] This approach, known as diffusionism and prevalent in anthropological studies, posits that similar practices in different societies result largely from diffusion rather than independent discovery or development. From this perspective, it is argued that in human history features a few original models and numerous imitations, with imitation being the typical mode of legal evolution. Based on this theory, the authors assert that the crucial criterion for the classification of legal systems is the substantive content of laws, which necessitates attention to originality, derivation, and common elements, rather than external factors such as race or geography. From this perspective, they identify seven legal families: (i) French, (ii) German, (iii) Scandinavian, (iv) English, (v) Russian, (vi) Islamic, and (vii) Hindu.[30]

Critics, however, have identified significant flaws in this approach. For instance, Åke Malmström argued that the authors failed to explicitly state that legal systems of European origin share several common ideological and other features, justifying their classification into a broader Western (European-American) group. According to Malmström, socialist legal systems, non-communist Asian systems, and African systems fall into distinct categories.[31] Zweigert and Kötz acknowledged that Arminjon, Nolde, and Wolff's scheme was the most convincing to date, particularly

---

[27] Martinez-Paz (1934), pp. 149–160.

[28] Arminjon et al. (1950), p. 42.

[29] Arminjon et al. (1950), p. 47 ff.

[30] Arminjon et al. (1950), pp. 42–63. The authors point out, however, that their proposed classification pertains primarily to private law. And see Siems (2018), pp. 89–90.

[31] See Malmström (1969), pp. 145–146. Zweigert and Kötz (1987), p. 65.

in its rejection of external factors. However, they criticized the authors for not clearly articulating the common qualities upon which the relationships between legal systems are based.[32] Furthermore, the general distinction between civil law and common law systems was not sufficiently elaborated in their scheme.

René David has offered a distinctive approach to the classification of legal systems into families. According to his theory, originally proposed in 1950, the decisive criterion for such classification is ideology or philosophical worldview. David considered ideology as a product of religion, philosophy, and political, social, and economic structures. Complementing ideology is legal technique, which David regarded as a secondary criterion related to how philosophical theories and conceptions of justice are realized in positive law.[33] Based on these criteria, David proposed dividing the world's legal systems into five groups or families:

(i) Western law: Grounded on Christian religious doctrine, liberal political philosophy, and capitalist economic theory.
(ii) Socialist law: Based on Marxist-Leninist political and economic theory and ideology.
(iii) Islamic law: Founded on the teachings of the Qur'an and the Muslim religious tradition.
(iv) Hindu law: Based on the religious, philosophical, and social system of Hinduism.
(v) Chinese law: Underpinned by the politico-religious and moral philosophy of Confucianism.[34]

Additionally, David proposed a division of the systems of the Western legal family into two sub-groups: the French and the English. However, his classification scheme notably omits the distinction between Continental European and common law traditions. David acknowledged the "inevitably arbitrary" nature of legal taxonomies in his treatise, illustrating this by referencing earlier comparatists' attempts to construct adequate classifications.[35]

An interesting perspective on the classification of legal systems was proposed by Northrop in 1959. Drawing on cultural and historical knowledge, Northrop suggested dividing the world's legal systems into three broad groups: (i) intuitive

[32] See Zweigert and Kötz (1987), pp. 65–66. And see Monateri (2023), pp. 21–22.

[33] David (1950), pp. 8 and 214–226.

[34] A similar approach to the classification of legal systems was adopted by Sola Cañizares, who identified the following legal families: (i) Western (Christian but not authoritative); (ii) Soviet (atheist and collectivist); (iii) religious (derived from religious principles and including canonical, Hindu, and Muslim laws); and (iv) Chinese (grounded on a quasi-religious philosophy in which the law is ethically coloured). See de Sola Cañizares (1954), p. 330.

[35] David (1950), p. 223. However, the author expresses his dissatisfaction with what he describes as "the traditional opposition, affirmed by all authors, between the Roman law system and the common law system." David (1950), p. 225.

mediational; (ii) those developed according to natural history; and (iii) abstract contractual systems.[36]

Intuitive mediational systems prioritize harmony, social relationships, and moral guidance over strict legal codes, employing informal and flexible approaches to resolving disputes. This category includes: (i) Confucian systems, which focus on moral virtues, hierarchical relationships, and social harmony, promoting dispute resolution through mediation and the cultivation of moral character rather than legal punishment; (ii) Buddhist systems, which emphasize compassion, non-violence, and conflict resolution through understanding and mutual respect; (iii) Taoist systems, which advocate for a natural order, balance, simplicity, and spontaneity, encouraging conflict resolution through mediation and natural harmony; and (iv) Non-Aryan Hindu systems, based on indigenous legal practices in India that are not influenced by Aryan cultural and legal traditions, prioritizing community-based dispute resolution and mediation.[37] Intuitive mediational systems reflect a cultural preference for maintaining social harmony and avoiding confrontation. They are flexible and adaptable but may lack the consistency and predictability found in more formal legal systems. These systems can be effective in societies where personal relationships and community cohesion are highly valued. However, they might struggle to address complex or large-scale legal issues due to their informal nature.

Natural history-developed systems are shaped by the historical and cultural development of a society, evolving organically over time and deeply rooted in its traditions and customs. This category encompasses: (i) Classical Chinese systems, developed through centuries of historical experience, integrating moral philosophy with legal principles that emphasize the state's role in maintaining order and justice; (ii) Ancient Indian/Aryan systems, derived from Vedic traditions[38] and ancient Indian philosophy, balancing moral and legal obligations with the goal of achieving

---

[36] Northrop (1959), p. 184.

[37] According to Northrop, in the Far Eastern mediational systems "the procedure is to push legal codes into the background, preferably dispensing with them altogether, and to bring the disputants into a warm give-and-take relationship, usually by way of a mediator, so that previously made demands can be modified gracefully, and a unique solution taking all the exceptional circumstances of the case into account is spontaneously accepted by both disputants. Codes there may be, but they are to be used only as a last resort, and even then recourse to them brings shame upon the disputants. … Not only is there no resort to a legal rule; there is also no judge. Even the mediator refuses to give a decision. Instead, the dispute is properly settled when the disputants, using the mediator merely as an emissary, come to mutual agreement in the light of all the existential circumstances, past, present, and future. … Not the abstract universals of a legal code, but the existential particularity of the concrete problematic situation is the criterion of the just and the good." Northrop (1959), pp. 184–185. As author remarks on p. 186, "behind this intuitive, mediational type of law in Asia there is a Confucian, Buddhist and pre-Aryan Hindu epistemology which affirms that full, direct and exact empirical knowledge of any individual, relation or event in nature reveals it to be unique."

[38] Vedic traditions are the religious, cultural, and philosophical practices that originate from the ancient Vedas, a large body of religious texts composed in early Sanskrit. These texts form the oldest layer of Sanskrit literature and are considered the oldest scriptures of Hinduism. The Vedic traditions have profoundly influenced Indian culture and religion.

social and cosmic order.[39] Natural history-developed systems offer a sense of continuity and legitimacy, as they are seen as extensions of long-standing traditions. However, their reliance on historical precedents can sometimes render them resistant to change and adaptation in the face of modern challenges.

Abstract contractual systems are founded on formal, codified laws and legal principles, emphasizing individual rights, obligations, and the enforcement of contracts within a well-defined legal framework. Key characteristics include: (i) comprehensive legal codes detailing rights, duties, and penalties; (ii) structured and standardized processes for dispute resolution and law enforcement; and (iii) a focus on personal freedom, property rights, and the protection of individual interests through contracts and legal agreements.[40] These systems provide clarity, predictability, and consistency in legal matters, making them well-suited for complex societies with diverse populations and advanced economies. By prioritizing individual rights and formal legal structures, abstract contractual systems can effectively manage large-scale and intricate legal issues. However, their rigidity and formalism can sometimes result in impersonal justice, where the letter of the law takes precedence over the nuances of individual cases and social relationships. Additionally, the emphasis on legalism can create barriers for those without access to legal knowledge or resources.

Northrop's classification highlights the diversity of legal systems and the influence of cultural, historical, and philosophical factors on the development of law. Each category offers distinct advantages and challenges, reflecting the values and priorities of the societies they govern.

Another approach to classifying legal systems based on a historico-cultural perspective was proposed by Adolf Schnitzer in 1961. Schnitzer introduced the term 'great cultural circle' (***große Kulturkreise***) to describe a major cultural and civilizational group sharing common historical, social, and cultural traits. Each cultural circle develops a corresponding 'circle of law' (*Rechtskreis*), meaning that the legal systems and principles within each cultural group are shaped by their unique historical and cultural contexts. According to him, five major blocks of civilization can be discerned: (i) primitive peoples, with simple social structures, oral traditions, and no written laws; (ii) ancient cultured peoples, such as those in Mesopotamia, Egypt, Ancient Greece, and Rome, noted for early writing, centralized governments, and legal systems based on written codes; (iii) European-American civilizations,

[39] Northrop observes that in Natural history-developed systems "codes are expressed in the syntactical grammar of the language of common-sense objects and relations … [T]he codes describe the biologically conceived patriarchal or matriarchal familial and tribal kinship norms of the inductively and sensuously given status quo." Northrop (1959), pp. 184–185.

[40] According to Northrop, in abstract contractual systems there is some "technical terminology permitting the construction of legal and social entities and relations while [the] identification of the ethical and the socially legal with abstractly and imaginatively constructed human norms and relations makes possible ethical and legal reform. Because [in such systems] all men are equal, they are instances of the same universals, their existential particularity is ethically irrelevant. Thereby a contractually constructed norm cannot be regarded as ethical unless if it holds for any one individual it also holds for any other." Northrop (1959), pp. 188–189. And see Varga (2012), pp. 57–58.

including Romanist, Germanic, Slavic and Anglo-American, characterized by complex legal systems rooted in Roman law, customary law, and later, codified national laws; (iv) religious civilizations, such as Christian, Islamic, and Jewish, defined by their religious foundations and the major role religion plays in shaping societal norms and laws; and (v) Afro-Asian civilizations, which are influenced by a combination of traditional customs, colonial legacies, and modern legal reforms.[41]

Schnitzer's framework underscores the interconnectedness of culture and law, suggesting that the evolution of legal systems is deeply rooted in the cultural and historical experiences of different civilizations. This approach emphasizes the diversity of legal traditions and the importance of understanding cultural context in the study of law.[42]

In 1961, Konrad Zweigert published his well-known theory of classification, which shared significant commonalities with the framework developed by Arminjon, Nolde, and Wolff in the 1950s. Zweigert's proposed criterion for grouping legal systems into families is 'style' (*Rechtsstil*), a multifaceted criterion shaped by the interaction of several factors: (a) the historical background and development of a system; (b) its predominant and characteristic mode of legal thinking; (c) its distinctive legal institutions; (d) the hierarchy and interpretation of its legal sources; and (e) the ideological background of the system.

Zweigert's classification of legal systems, later also adopted by Kötz, categorizes them into eight distinct families:

(i) The Romanistic family, which has its roots in Roman law and includes France, Italy, Spain, and other Latin countries in Europe and Latin America. This family is characterized by comprehensive codes that cover various areas of law, such as civil, commercial, and criminal law, contributing to legal predictability and uniformity.

(ii) The Germanic family, which incorporates aspects of Roman law but also emphasizes academic legal scholarship and the role of legal science in developing and interpreting the law. It includes countries like Germany, Austria, Switzerland, and the Netherlands.

(iii) The Nordic (Scandinavian) family, which includes the legal systems of Denmark, Finland, Iceland, Norway, and Sweden. While influenced by both Romanistic and Germanic legal traditions, these systems have distinct features. Nordic legal systems are less codified than their European counterparts and place a strong emphasis on case law and judicial decisions. They are known for their pragmatic approach to law, focusing on practical solutions rather than strict adherence to doctrinal purity.

(iv) The Anglo-American (common law) family, which has its origins in England and spread to other English-speaking countries, including the United States,

[41] Schnitzer (1961), p. 133 ff. And see Siems (2018), p. 90.

[42] Zweigert and Kötz have criticized Schnitzer's scheme for conflating the methods of comparative legal history and comparative law, thereby failing to serve as a foundation for a comprehensive theory of legal families. Zweigert and Kötz (1987), p. 68.

Canada, Australia, New Zealand, and India. Common law systems place significant importance on case law and the role of judges in interpreting and developing the law.

(v) The Socialist family, which encompasses the legal systems of the former Soviet Union and other socialist states like China, Cuba, and Vietnam. Socialist legal systems are heavily influenced by Marxist-Leninist ideology and emphasize the role of the state in regulating economic and social life. While many former socialist countries have transitioned to other legal systems, the legacy of socialist law still influences their legal frameworks and institutions.

(vi) The Far Eastern family, which includes the legal systems of China, Japan, and Korea. Far Eastern legal systems blend elements of civil law, common law, and traditional Confucian principles. They systems tend to emphasize harmony, social order, and the resolution of disputes through mediation and conciliation rather than litigation.

(vii) The Islamic family, based on Sharia law, derived from the Quran, Hadith (sayings of the Prophet Muhammad), and other Islamic texts. It is prevalent in countries like Saudi Arabia, Iran, and Pakistan. In many countries, Islamic law operates alongside secular legal systems, creating a complex legal landscape where religious and state laws intersect.

(viii) The Hindu family, based on the ancient legal traditions of Hinduism, as codified in texts like the Dharmashastra.[43] Hindu law primarily influences the legal system in India and traditionally governs personal matters such as marriage, inheritance, and family relations. The coexistence of Hindu law with secular legal principles reflects India's pluralistic society and the ongoing evolution of its legal system.

Zweigert's classification of legal systems into these eight families highlights the diversity of legal traditions around the world and allows scholars and practitioners to appreciate the historical, cultural, and ideological underpinnings of different legal systems. However, Zweigert emphasized that any taxonomy of legal systems is largely dependent on the particular period being considered. Consequently, the classification of the world's legal systems into families is subject to change due to legislative reforms or other significant events.[44]

In the early 1960s, David, without abandoning his original criteria, modified his earlier classification of legal systems in response to criticisms, particularly from German scholars who objected to his view that the German system should be included in the French sub-group. He reclassified the legal systems of the world into

[43] The Dharmashastra is a genre of Sanskrit texts and refers to a collection of ancient Indian legal, ethical, and moral treatises. The Dharmashastra texts are not uniform or consistent in their prescriptions; rather, they reflect the diversity and evolution of Hindu legal and moral thought over centuries.

[44] Zweigert (1961), p. 45 ff; see also Zweigert and Kötz (1987), pp. 68–75. Consider also Zweigert and Kötz (1971), pp. 69 and 74. And see Siems (2018), p. 90; Monateri (2023), pp. 24–26.

four broad families: (i) the Romano-Germanic or civil law family; (ii) the Anglo-American or common law family; (iii) the socialist family; and (iv) the family of legal systems based on religious and traditional grounds. Within the last group, he included Islamic law, Hindu law, and the indigenous legal systems of Eastern Asia and Africa.[45]

David's taxonomy is based on two mutually supplementing classification criteria: legal technique (including vocabulary, concepts, hierarchy of the sources of law, and juridical methods) and the philosophical, political, or economic principles desired to be implemented. He emphasized that "[t]he two criteria are to be used subsequently and not in isolation."[46] In this respect, one is invited to consider whether a lawyer educated in a particular legal system should be able to work without great difficulty within another legal system. If the answer is affirmative, one should conclude that the two systems probably belong to the same broader family. According to David, legal technique is subordinate to the ideological criterion. Despite their similarities in legal technique, two or more systems cannot be regarded as belonging to the same family if they are based on markedly different ideologies. Thus, while David recognizes considerable differences between civil law and common law systems, he argues that these differences exist at a technical, not an ideological, level.[47] He asserts that both systems reach essentially similar legal results through different technical methods.[48] Methodologically, David's approach to the classification of legal systems is particularly noteworthy and has been met with significant approval, as it successfully integrates historical context, legal analysis, and ideological policy considerations into a framework that captures the essence of the contemporary legal landscape.

In 1969, Åke Malmström, drawing heavily from a historical and cultural perspective, provided a framework for categorizing legal systems into four distinct groups: (i) Western legal systems, including Continental European, Latin American, Nordic, and Anglo-Saxon systems; (ii) Socialist (or Communist) systems, encompassing the legal systems of the Soviet Union, people's democracies, and China;

[45] See David and Brierley (1985), pp. 22–31, 33 ff. And see Zweigert and Kötz (1987), pp. 64–65; Monateri (2023), pp. 22–23.

[46] David (1964), p. 16.

[47] At a time when the Cold War was at its height, Gino Gorla posited that the divide between capitalist and socialist legal systems eclipsed the traditional distinction between civil law and common law. Gorla contended that the differences between Continental and Anglo-Saxon legal systems were primarily formal, while the contrast between these and socialist legal systems was substantive. In Gorla's words, "the difference between continental (or Romanist) law and common law is certainly rather formal, i.e., drawn by a criterion that distinguishes and approaches forms (structures, techniques and concepts), rather than substance." Gorla (1963), p. 9.

[48] As he notes in his earlier treatise, "the opposition between continental and common law cannot be scientifically placed at the same level as that between French and Chinese law; it permits no more than to establish a division, albeit fundamental, within a legal system whose unity is recognized and affirmed: the Western legal system. It is only by an error of perspective that Anglo-American law, and with even greater reason German law, was until now considered as constituting separate categories enjoying perfect autonomy in relation to French law." David (1950), p. 225.

(iii) Asian (non-Communist) systems; and (iv) African systems.[49] This was the most expansive scheme since David's early attempt in 1950 and the first to clearly recognize the legal systems of Latin America as part of the Western legal family. However, Malmström's classification also has its limitations. It tends to oversimplify the complexities within each category, potentially overlooking the nuances and hybrid nature of many legal systems. Thus, while Malmström's framework is a valuable starting point for comparative legal studies, it should be complemented with more detailed and context-specific analyses to fully appreciate the intricacies of each legal tradition.

In the early 1990s, following the collapse of socialist regimes in Eastern Europe, Czech comparatist Viktor Knapp argued that three distinct legal families exist: (i) the Continental European or Civil law family, which is prevalent in Europe and in regions of the world influenced by European colonialism; (ii) the Anglo-American or Common law family, primarily found in the United Kingdom, the United States, and other former British colonies; and (iii) the Islamic family. Knapp asserted that the Eastern European legal systems belong to the Continental European group.[50]

Michael Bogdan argued that Socialist law has not entirely disappeared, even while considering Chinese law a distinct system. His classification scheme differentiates between English, American, French, German, Socialist, Chinese, and Islamic legal systems.[51] Bogdan's approach acknowledges that remnants and influences of Socialist legal principles persist, especially in former Soviet states and countries influenced by Marxist-Leninist ideologies, despite the decline of traditional Socialist law. By categorizing Chinese law as a distinct system, Bogdan emphasizes the unique blend of Socialist, civil law, and indigenous elements that shape China's legal framework. This system integrates Socialist principles with Chinese characteristics, heavily influenced by the Communist Party's governance and Confucian traditions. Additionally, the distinction between English and American legal systems, despite both being rooted in common law, highlights significant divergences in procedural law, judicial review, and the role of precedent. While Bogdan's categories offer a useful starting point, they must be applied flexibly to account for ongoing changes and the emergence of new legal phenomena. Moreover, some might argue that including other influential legal systems, such as those in India or Japan, would provide a more comprehensive global perspective.

Mark van Hoecke and Martin Warrington's classification of legal families into two broad groups—Western and non-Western (Asian, Islamic, and African)—is an attempt to categorize the world's diverse legal systems into manageable categories for comparative analysis. The Western group primarily includes legal systems that have evolved from Roman law, common law, and other European legal traditions. The non-Western group comprises legal systems developed independently of these European influences, often rooted in distinct cultural, religious, and historical

[49] Malmström (1969). See also Varga (2012), p. 63.

[50] Knapp (1991), pp. 52–53, 58.

[51] Bogdan (1994), p. 245 ff.

contexts.[52] However, grouping diverse legal systems into just two categories can obscure significant differences within each group. For example, the legal systems in China, Japan, and India are vastly different despite all being classified as 'non-Western'.[53] Additionally, Van Hoecke and Warrington's classification suggests a binary distinction where Western legal systems are seen as a unified group against the heterogeneous non-Western systems. This can reinforce a Eurocentric perspective that places Western legal traditions as the normative benchmark.

A more sophisticated scheme was proposed by Patrick Glenn, who, drawing on the concept of tradition, sought to distinguish between different philosophical and historical patterns that have shaped the development of law. According to Glenn, distinctions should be made between chthonic, Talmudic, civil law, Islamic, common law, Hindu, and Asian or Confucian traditions. Each of these legal traditions reflects the unique historical, cultural, and social contexts in which they evolved.[54]

Derived from the Greek word 'chthon', meaning 'earth', chthonic law refers to indigenous legal traditions that are often unwritten and closely tied to the land and community. These systems emphasize harmony with nature, collective decision-making, and oral traditions and customs passed down through generations, typically found in indigenous cultures around the world.[55]

Talmudic law is a religious legal system based on the Torah (the Hebrew Bible) and the Talmud (a central text in Rabbinic Judaism). It is a comprehensive legal system governing all aspects of life, including religious practices, ethical behaviour, and civil matters, relying heavily on interpretation and commentary by rabbinic scholars.[56]

The civil law tradition encompasses codified legal systems originating from Roman law and further developed in Continental Europe.[57]

Islamic law, also known as Sharia, is derived from the Quran (the holy book of Islam) and the Hadith (sayings and actions of the Prophet Muhammad). It encompasses both religious and secular aspects of life, including rituals, family law, criminal law, and commercial law. Sharia is interpreted by scholars through various schools of thought (madhabs) and is implemented differently across the Muslim world.[58]

The common law tradition originated in England and is based on judicial precedents and case law rather than written statutes.[59]

Hindu law is a religious legal system derived from the ancient texts of Hinduism, such as the Vedas and Dharmashastra. It governs various aspects of life, including

[52] van Hoecke and Warrington (1998).

[53] See Varga (2012), pp. 66–67.

[54] Glenn (2004). Consider also Glenn (2019). And see Siems (2018), p. 92.

[55] Glenn (2004), pp. 59–91.

[56] Glenn (2004), pp. 92–124.

[57] Glenn (2004), pp. 125–169.

[58] Glenn (2004), pp. 170–221.

[59] Glenn (2004), pp. 222–270.

family matters, rituals, and personal conduct. Hindu law is traditionally flexible and adaptive, with a focus on dharma (moral and ethical duties).[60]

The Asian or Confucian legal tradition encompasses various legal systems in Asia, which can include elements of chthonic, civil, common and religious laws. These systems emphasize harmony, social order, and the collective well-being over individual rights.[61]

The Italian comparatist Ugo Mattei proposes three patterns that are decisive for a comprehensive classification of legal systems: law in the Western sense, politics, and philosophical and religious tradition. Based on these patterns, he suggests a tripartite taxonomy of legal families. The first legal family, associated with the Western legal tradition, is characterized by the prevalence of professional law, the separation of legal and political decision-making, and the secularisation of law. The second family is marked by the dominance of political law (law of development), which results from the interaction among law, public policy, administration, and politics. This family is described as 'unstable' and incudes former Socialist, Southern European, unestablished African, and South American systems. The third family is characterized by the preponderance of traditional law and includes Islamic, Indian, Hindu and other Asian and Confucian systems.[62]

The dominant pattern within a legal system determines the legal family to which that system belongs. According to Mattei, all three patterns may exist in any legal system, but only one is predominant. For example, he categorizes the Chinese system under traditional law, though it is developing toward the political, while the Japanese system, also influenced by traditional law, is developing towards the professional.[63] Furthermore, Mattei points out that legal systems are not internally homogenous: "The same system may belong to the rule of traditional law if we consider family law, while belonging to the rule of professional law as far as commercial law is concerned, and to the rule of political law when we look at its criminal justice system."[64]

Although Mattei's approach to classifying legal systems is useful for educational purposes, it remains very schematic and is not substantially different from some traditional classifications, despite renaming legal families. For instance, his classification places the Chinese and Japanese legal systems under the same category due to Confucian influence, although their political developments have diverged.[65]

A special category of legal systems often neglected in traditional classifications is the so-called mixed or hybrid systems, which are influenced by two or more legal

[60] Glenn (2004), pp. 271–300.

[61] Glenn (2004), pp. 301–342.

[62] See Mattei (1997). And see Siems (2018), p. 91.

[63] Mattei (1997), p. 40.

[64] Mattei (1997), p. 16.

[65] Varga (2012), pp. 67–68.

traditions.[66] Examples of these include the legal systems of Québec, Louisiana, and South Africa.

The legal system of Quebec is unique in Canada as it has been influenced by both French and English law. Quebec's private law, which includes civil matters such as contracts, property, and family law, is primarily based on the French Civil Code. This is a legacy of its history as a French colony before becoming part of the British Empire in 1763. The French influence is codified in the Civil Code of Quebec. On the other hand, public law in Quebec follows the common law tradition of England. This dual legal system allows Quebec to maintain its distinct French legal heritage while also integrating aspects of the English common law system, creating a unique blend of legal traditions.[67]

The legal system of Louisiana in the United States is influenced by both French and American law. This is largely due to Louisiana's history as a French colony before becoming part of the United States through the Louisiana Purchase in 1803. The primary legal code in Louisiana is the Louisiana Civil Code, originally enacted in 1808 and heavily influenced by the French Napoleonic Civil Code. However, over time, American common law principles have also influenced the state's legal system, particularly in areas such as criminal law and procedural law. Thus, Louisiana's legal system is a hybrid, incorporating elements of both civil law and common law, making it distinct within the United States.[68]

The South African legal system is a mixed legal system that has been significantly influenced by both Dutch and English law. This dual influence originates from the country's colonial history. When the Dutch East India Company established a settlement at the Cape of Good Hope in 1652, Dutch-Roman law (a mixture of Roman law and Dutch customary law) was introduced. Later, when the British took control of the Cape Colony in 1806, English common law and legal principles began to exert a strong influence, particularly in areas such as commercial law, maritime law, and procedural law. As a result, South Africa's legal system today combines elements of civil law (stemming from its Dutch roots) and common law (from its British colonial period). This blend creates a unique legal system where Roman-Dutch law typically governs private law matters, such as property, contract, and family law, while English law influences areas such as constitutional, administrative, and criminal law.[69]

Comparative law scholars encounter significant challenges when dealing with hybrid legal systems, as traditional comparative law methods may not be entirely applicable. This necessitates the development of new approaches and frameworks to

---

[66] For a detailed discussion of mixed legal systems see Du Plessis (2019). And see Palmer (2012), McKnight (1977), Baxter (1983), Örücü (1996), Siems (2018), p. 92.

[67] For a closer look at Quebec's legal system see Zweigert and Kötz (1987), pp. 121–122. Consider also Lemieux (1989).

[68] For a closer look at Louisiana's legal system see Zweigert and Kötz (1987), pp. 119–121. And see Osakwe (1986).

[69] For more on the South African legal system see Zweigert and Kötz (1987), pp. 240–244. Consider also Zimmermann and Visser (1996).

effectively analyse and compare these systems. Hybrid legal systems often integrate diverse legal principles and norms, resulting in conceptual ambiguity. Scholars must navigate and reconcile these often contradictory elements to comprehend the system's legal landscape. Additionally, such systems may generate normative conflicts where rules and procedures from different legal traditions clash, complicating the application of law due to the lack of clear precedence or hierarchy among the conflicting norms. Moreover, hybrid legal systems are often in a state of flux, continuously evolving in response to new social, political, and economic pressures. This dynamic nature poses a challenge for scholars attempting to provide a stable and comprehensive analysis, as the legal landscape can change rapidly. Addressing hybrid legal systems often requires interdisciplinary knowledge, as these systems intersect with various fields such as sociology, anthropology, history, and political science. Scholars must draw on insights from these disciplines to fully grasp the complexities of hybrid legal systems and adopt a multifaceted and flexible approach to navigate their intricate and evolving nature.

6.4 Concluding Remarks

The classifications of legal systems into families, as proposed by comparative law scholars, cannot be considered strict or exhaustive.[70] There is no single criterion for grouping legal systems into families. This classification primarily serves as a tool to facilitate the comparative study of laws, and its nature, scope, and purpose can vary with each study. For example, if the comparative study aims to explore the influence of religious factors on law, religion would be the primary criterion for classification. If the study focuses on indigenous or native legal systems, it may be more useful to contrast systems based on customary or unwritten law with those based on written law. Therefore, it is important to remember that grouping legal systems into families is not an end in itself; it is connected to a particular purpose, and a classification suitable for one purpose may not be helpful for another.[71]

Special issues arise concerning mixed legal systems, which have been influenced by two or more legal traditions. Many countries in Asia and Africa have legal systems that are a blend of traditional local law, religious elements, and laws imported from European countries during the colonial period or in more recent times.[72] Classification challenges also emerge regarding legal systems in transition, such as those in Eastern European countries following the demise of socialism. These considerations suggest that members of any legal family are subject to evolution, a fact not always accounted for in the various scholarly approaches to the notion of legal

[70] As Malmström notes, "it is impossible to establish a uniform system of classification which is ideal from every point of view and implies a clear distinction between families or groups." Malmström (1969), p. 138.

[71] Consider on this matter Bogdan (1994), p. 85; Schlesinger (1970), p. 252.

[72] Consider Reyntjens (1991).

families. The proposed methods of classification do not yield unanimous results, and assigning a legal system to a particular legal family can lead to serious misconceptions. The classification of East Asian legal systems exemplifies this issue.

David, Zweigert, and Kötz classify the legal systems of the People's Republic of China, Japan, Korea, and Indo-China under the Far Eastern legal Family.[73] They argue that the ancient Chinese doctrines of Confucius (551-479 BC), which emphasize social, group, or community harmony over individual interests, have significantly influenced these societies. As a result, individuals in these cultures tend to favour compromise and conciliation over litigation.[74] Their classification of the East Asian legal systems into a single legal family is based on what they consider a shared cultural heritage. However, one might argue that it is overly simplistic to emphasize culture at the expense of other factors as the primary classification criterion. Consider Japanese law, for example. The Japanese legal system has been variously classified as part of the Far Eastern legal family, described as a civil law system based on German law, and treated as a unique hybrid of different legal traditions. These differing classifications suggest that the classification process is more arbitrary, subjective, and open to manipulation than traditional comparatists might acknowledge.

Additionally, proposed classifications, which concern national systems in their entirety, do not always align with classifications specific to particular branches of law or those attempted within micro-comparative legal studies. For instance, from the perspective of constitutional law, one might distinguish between federal systems, such as those of the United States, Germany, Brazil, Canada, and Australia, and unitary systems, such as the United Kingdom, France, Japan, Italy, and New Zealand. Furthermore, the United States, Italy, Germany, Canada, and France could

---

[73] The term "Far Eastern" is said to be problematic since it implies a Eurocentric perspective. A purely geographic notion, such as "East Asian" would be more neutral and therefore preferable.

[74] Confucianism, a multifaceted system of moral, social, political, and philosophical thought, has deeply shaped East Asian culture and governance. Its core teachings prioritize education as the means for moral development, ensuring that the state is governed through virtue rather than coercion. Central to Confucianism is the concept of relationships, where individuals fulfill specific roles to achieve social harmony—the philosophy's ultimate goal. Disputes are ideally resolved through ethical conciliation and compromise, guided by both human sentiment and reason. In traditional Chinese society, two concepts underpinned this structure: *fa* (positive law, enforced by rulers) and *li* (customs, ethics, and rituals governing social behavior). While *fa* was seen as necessary for controlling those who rejected social norms or were deemed outsiders, *li* was viewed as the ideal mechanism for preserving harmony. Chinese society often regarded legal proceedings with suspicion, associating them with dishonor and punishment, which clashed with Western notions of legal justice. A parallel system existed in traditional Japan, where *giri* (social obligations) played a dominant role in maintaining order, often superseding formal legal structures. According to van Hoecke and Warrington, "[the] Asian legal culture, when interpreted from an (overtly) Western point of view, can to a certain extent be represent ted as irrational, because of the important role of morals, or religion and of the Confucianist conception of the natural order of things. Oriental people likewise may well consider Western people too rational: so caught up in their own minds and in their rational concepts that they have lost all contact with the universe which surrounds them, lost the consciousness of their place in this universe." Van Hoecke and Warrington (1998), pp. 505–506. And see Chap. 12 below.

be grouped together based on their recognition of judicial review of the constitutionality of legislative enactments. These examples indicate that a legal system may belong to one group concerning a particular branch of law while being classified differently concerning another branch.

In the field of comparative law, consideration of legal culture is crucial for defining the object of comparison, particularly when a strict comparison of legal texts proves inadequate. In recent years, traditional classifications of legal systems into families of law have lost much of their earlier appeal, highlighting the importance of studying legal culture. Typically, the notion of legal family is relied upon when comparing formal laws and legal institutions. However, this concept falls short in explaining the attitudes, perceptions, and behaviours associated with law as a sociocultural phenomenon.[75] The study of legal culture can more effectively reveal fundamental similarities and differences among legal systems, including those within the same legal family.[76]

Contemporary comparatists have embraced the view that the basic methodological principle of comparative law is functionality, according to which only legal rules and institutions that fulfil the same function can fruitfully be compared. Zweigert and *Kötz* remark that the legal system of every society has to solve essentially the same problems. Although the means by which these problems are addressed may differ, the results are often very similar.[77] This approach, however, seems to overlook the decisive role that legal culture can play in determining the outcomes. Legal rules that ostensibly fulfil the same function in different cultural settings may lead to diverse results because each cultural setting understands and applies the relevant rules differently. This observation has led some comparatists to argue that comparison among legal families should be replaced by a thorough study of different legal cultures.[78]

The study of legal culture would be particularly fruitful in relation to branches of law, such a family law and criminal law, that are closely connected to social, political, and cultural factors. As Otto Kahn-Freund has pointed out, "the use of the comparative method requires a knowledge not only of the foreign law, but also of its social, and above all its political context. The use of comparative law for practical purposes becomes an abuse only if it is performed by a legalistic spirit which ignores this context of the law."[79] Zweigert and *Kötz recognize that, in comparing legal systems rather than just legal rules, it is crucial for the comparatist to grasp the 'style' of the legal systems under consideration. According to these authors, the following factors are crucial for determining the style of a legal system: "(1) its*

[75] Lawrence Friedman has remarked that traditional classifications of legal systems can be useful in many ways, but without a knowledge and understanding of legal culture, their structures and substance are merely 'lifeless artefacts'. Friedman (1977), p. 76.

[76] See Blankenburg (1994). On the notion of global culture consider Robertson (1992). Consider also Ancel (1981). And see Varga (2007).

[77] Zweigert and Kötz (1987), p. 31.

[78] Consider, e.g., van Hoecke and Warrington (1998).

[79] Kahn-Freund (1974), p. 27.

historical background and development, (2) its predominant and characteristic mode of thought in legal matters, (3) its distinctive institutions, (4) the kind of legal sources it acknowledges and the way it handles them, and (5) its ideology."[80] *One may ask: wouldn't the style of a legal system be dependent on cultural factors as well? At the very least, the historical background, the predominant and characteristic mode of legal thinking, and the system's ideological background are all related to the cultural context. The relevance of concepts such as legal tradition and mentalité* – the collective mindset, attitudes, beliefs, values, and ways of thinking that are characteristic of a particular group, society, or era[81]—*is also emphasized by scholars.*[82] Mentality can shape decision-making, problem-solving, and interactions with others, reflecting the underlying cognitive and emotional patterns that define a person's or group's mindset.

To make a legal comparison meaningful, one must go beyond merely juxtaposing formal laws. It is essential to examine additional elements, such as how the language of a legal text is understood, the public's perception of a legal rule or institution's function, and its practical application. Effective comparison requires understanding the ideas, beliefs, and habits of the general population regarding law, which Friedman describes as the external legal culture.[83] *This necessitates that legal comparatists transcend the boundaries of their own legal training and culture.*[84] *However, surpassing one's own legal culture to gain insight into another challenging, akin to stepping outside oneself, as culture largely defines our identity. Nonetheless, this intellectual and psychological effort is crucial in any comparative study, as the principal objective of such a study is to learn from the 'other'.*

---

[80] Zweigert and Kötz (1987), pp. 68–69.

[81] 'Mentalité' is a French term that translates to 'mentality' in English but carries a broader and deeper connotation, particularly in the context of historical and social studies. This concept is often used in the study of history and anthropology to understand how people in different times and places perceived the world around them and made sense of their experiences. Mentalité encompasses the shared cultural norms, practices, and cognitive frameworks that influence how a community interprets events, traditions, and social structures. It highlights the importance of understanding the subjective experiences and collective consciousness of people in different historical and cultural contexts.

[82] See, e.g., Krygier (1986), Bell (1994), Legrand (1996–1997).

[83] As Grosswald Curran has remarked, such "cultural immersion requires immersion into the political, historical, economic and linguistic contexts that molded the legal system, and in which the legal system operates. It requires an explanation of various cultural mentalities." Grosswald Curran (1998a), p. 51. See also Grosswald Curran (1998b), pp. 659–661.

[84] Zweigert and *Kötz describe this need to eradicate all preconditions of one's own legal system when carrying out a comparative study as the negative aspect of functionality.* Zweigert and Kötz (1987), pp. 31–32.

References

Ancel M (1981) Le *comparatiste devant les systèmes* (ou "*familles*") de *droit*. In: Bernstein H, Drobnig U, Kötz H (eds) Festschrift fur Konrad Zweigert. CB Mohr, Tübingen, pp 355–362

Aoki H (2001) Nobushige Hozumi: a skillful transplanter of Western legal thought into Japanese soil. In: Riles A (ed) Rethinking masters of comparative law. Hart Publishing, Oxford, pp 129–150

Arminjon P, Nolde B, Wolff M (1950) Traité de droit comparé I. Librairie Générale de Droit et de Jurisprudence, Paris

Baxter LG (1983) Pure comparative law and legal science in a mixed legal system. Comparative Int Law J Southern Africa 16(1):84–99

Bell J (1994) Comparative law and legal theory. In: Krawietz W, MacCormick N, von Wright GH (eds) Prescriptive formality and normative rationality in modern legal systems, Festschrift for RS Summers. Duncker and Humblot, Berlin, pp 19–31

Bevilaqua C (1897) Resumo das licções de legislação comparada sobre o direito privado, 2nd edn. Bahia, Magalhães

Blankenburg E (1994) The infrastructure for avoiding civil litigation – comparing culture of legal behaviour in the Netherlands and West Germany. Law Soc Rev 28(4):789–809

Bogdan M (1994) Comparative law. Kluwer, Deventer, repr, p 2000

Constantinesco LJ (1971) Rechtsvergleichung I. Heymanns, Köln

Constantinesco LJ (1979) Über den Stil der 'Stiltheorie' in der Rechtsvergleichung. Zeitschrift für vergleichende Rechtswissenschaft 78:154–172

Constantinesco LJ (1981) Die Kulturkreise als Grundlage der Rechtskreise. Zeitschrift für Rechtsvergleichung 22:161–178

Constantinesco LJ (1983) Rechtsvergleichung III Die rechtsvergleichende Wissenschaft. Heymanns, Köln

Dannemann G (2019) Comparative law: study of similarities or differences? In: Reimann M, Zimmerman R (eds) The Oxford handbook of comparative Law, 2nd edn. Oxford University Press, Oxford, pp 390–422

David R (1950) Traité élémentaire de droit civil compare. Librairie Générale de Droit et de Jurisprudence, Paris

David R (1964) Les grands systèmes de Droit contemporains. Dalloz, Paris

David R, Brierley J (1985) Major legal systems in the world today, 3rd edn. Stevens, London

de Sola Cañizares F (1954) Iniciación al derecho comparado. Consejo Superior de Investigaciones Científicas, Barcelona

Donahue C (1979) Review of St German's Doctor and Student, eds. T.F.T Plucknett and J.L. Barton. Legal Hist Rev 47(2):182–186

du Plessis J (2019) Comparative law and the study of mixed legal systems. In: Reimann M, Zimmermann R (eds) The Oxford handbook of comparative law, 2nd edn. Oxford University Press, Oxford, pp 474–501

Endicott T (1989) The conscience and the king: Christopher St German and Thomas More and the development of English equity. Univ Toronto Law Rev 47(2):549–569

Esmein A (1905) Le droit comparé et l'enseignement du droit comparé. In: Congrès international du droit comparé tenu à Paris du 31 juillet au 4 août 1900, Procès- verbaux des séances et documents I. Librairie générale de droit de jurisprudence, Paris 445 ff

Esmein A (1909) ÉlÉments de droit constitutionnel français et comparÉ. Sirey, Paris

Friedman LM (1977) Law and society: an introduction. Prentice-Hall, Englewood Cliffs

Fulbeck W (1600) A direction or preparative to the study of the law. Thomas Wight, London

Fulbeck W (1601) A parallele or conference of the civil law, the canon law, and the common law of this realme of England. Thomas Wight, London

Glasson E-D (1879) Le mariage civil et le divorce dans les principaux pays de l'Europe, précédé d'un aperçu sur les origines du droit civil moderne: Études de législation comparée. Pedone-Lauriel, Paris

Glenn HP (2004) Legal traditions of the world: sustainable diversity in law, 2nd edn. Oxford University Press, Oxford

Glenn HP (2019) Comparative legal families and comparative legal traditions. In: Reimann M, Zimmermann R (eds) The Oxford handbook of comparative law, 2nd edn. Oxford University Press, Oxford, pp 423–441

Gorla G (1963) Intérêts et problèmes de la comparaison entre le droit continental et la Common Law. Revue internationale de Droit comparé 15:5–18

Grosswald Curran V (1998a) Cultural immersion, difference and categories in U.S. comparative law. Am J Comp Law 46(1):43–92

Grosswald Curran V (1998b) Dealing in difference: comparative law's potential for broadening legal perspectives. Am J Comp Law 46(4):657–668

Holdsworth W (1915) The early history of equity. Mich Law Rev 13(4):293–301

Hozumi N (1904) The New Japanese Civil Code, as material for the study of comparative jurisprudence. A paper read at the International Congress of Arts and Sciences, at the Universal Exposition, Saint Louis, 1904. Tokyo Printing Co. Ltd, Tokyo

Husa J (2015) A new introduction to comparative law. Hart, Oxford

Kahn-Freund O (1974) On uses and misuses of comparative law. Mod Law Rev 37(1):1–27

Knapp V (1991) Základy srovnávací právni vedy. Aleko, Prague

Krygier M (1986) Law as tradition. Law Philosophy 5:237–262

Legrand P (1996–1997) Uniformity, legal traditions and law's limits. Juridisk Tidskrift 2:306–322

Lemieux D (1989) The Quebec civil law system in a common law world: the seven crises. Jurid Rev 34:16ff

Lévy-Ullmann H (1923) Observations générales sur les communications relatives au droit privé dans les pays étrangers. In: Les transformations du droit dans les principaux pays depuis cinquante ans (1869–1919). Livre du cinquantenaire de la Société de législation comparée, Librairie Générale de Droit et de Jurisprudence, Paris, pp 85–111

Malmström A (1969) The system of legal systems, notes on a problem of classification in comparative law. Scand Stud Law 13:127–149

Martinez-Paz E (1934) Introducción al estudio del derecho civil comparado. Imprenta de la Universidad, Córdoba Argentina

Mattei U (1997) Three patterns of law: taxonomy and change in the world's legal systems. Am J Comp Law 45(1):5–44

McKnight J (1977) Some historical observations on mixed systems of law. Jurid Rev 22:177–186

Monateri PG (2023) Comparative law and the style of legal systems. In: Zander LA, Kramp-Seidel N (eds) Europe in law and literature, transdisciplinary voices in conversation. Walter de Gruyter, Berlin & Boston, pp 15–26

Northrop FSC (1959) The complexity of legal and ethical experience, studies in the methods of normative subjects. Little, Brown & Co, Boston

Örücü E (1996) Mixed and mixing systems: a conceptual search. In: Örücü E, Attwooll E, Coyle S (eds) Studies in legal systems: mixed and mixing. Kluwer Law International, London, pp 335–352

Osakwe C (1986) Louisiana legal system: a confluence of two legal traditions. Am J Comp Law 34:29–45

Palmer VV (2012) Introduction to mixed jurisdictions. In: Palmer VV (ed) Mixed jurisdictions worldwide:the third legal family, 2nd edn. Cambridge University Press, Cambridge, pp 3–18

Pargendler M (2012) The rise and decline of legal families. Am J Comp Law 60(4):1043–1074

Plucknett TFT, Barton JL (eds) (1974) Christopher St German's Doctor and Student. Selden Society Series, London, Vol. 91

Reyntjens F (1991) Note sur l'utilité d'introduire un système juridique 'pluraliste' dans la macro-comparison des droits. Revue de Droit Internationale et Droit Comparé 68:41–50

Robertson R (1992) Globalization: social theory and global culture. Sage, London

Sauser-Hall G (1913) Fonction et méthode du droit comparé, Leçon inaugurale faite à l'Université de Neuchâtel le 23 octobre 1912. A Kündig, Genève

Schlesinger RB (1970) Comparative law. Cases – texts – materials, 3rd edn. Foundation Press, Mineola New York
Schnitzer AF (1961) Vergleichende Rechtslehre I. Verlag für Recht und Gesellschaft, Basel
Siems M (2018) Comparative law, 2nd edn. Cambridge University Press, Cambridge
Tarde G (1905) Le droit comparé et la sociologie. In: Congrès international de droit comparé tenu à Paris du 31 juillet au 4 août 1900, Procès-Verbaux des Séances et Documents. Librairie générale de droit de jurisprudence, Paris, pp 439–440
Van Hoecke M, Warrington M (1998) Legal cultures, legal paradigms and legal dogmatics: towards a new model for comparative law. Int Comp Law Quart 47(3):495–536
Varga C (2007) Comparative legal cultures? Acta Juridica Hungarica 48(2):95–113
Varga C (2012) Theatrum legale mundi: on legal systems classified. In: Varga C Comparative legal cultures. Szent Istvan Tarsulat, Budapest, pp 49–76
Wigmore JH (1928) A panorama of the world's legal systems I–III. West Publishing Co, Chicago
Winterton G (1975) Comparative law teaching. Am J Comp Law 23(1):69–118
Zimmermann R, Visser D (1996) Introduction: South African law as a mixed legal system. In: Zimmermann R, Visser D (eds) Southern Cross: civil law and common law in South Africa. Clarendon Press, Oxford, pp 1–30
Zweigert K (1961) Zur Lehre von den Rechtskreisen. In: 20th century comparative and conflicts law. Legal essays in honor of Hessel E. Yntema. Sythoff, Leyden, pp. 42–55
Zweigert K, Kötz H (1971) Einführung in die Rechtsvergleichung auf dem Gebiete des Privatrechts I Grundlagen. Mohr, Tübingen
Zweigert K, Kötz H (1987) An introduction to comparative law, 2nd edn. Clarendon Press, Oxford

Chapter 7
From Rome to Modernity: The Rise of the Civil Law Tradition

7.1 Introduction

The civil law tradition is the oldest and most prevalent legal tradition in the world today, encompassing the legal systems of Continental Europe, Latin America, and many African and Asian countries. Despite significant differences in the substantive laws of civil law countries, there exists a fundamental unity among them. The most obvious element of unity in civil law systems is that they are all derived from the same sources, and their legal institutions are classified according to a commonly accepted scheme that existed before their own development, which they adopted and adapted at some stage in their history.

The civil law tradition emerged from the interaction of three principal forces: Roman law, as transmitted through the sixth-century codification of Emperor Justinian; Germanic customary law; and the canon law of the Church, which, while partly derived from Roman law, constituted a distinct system. The work of medieval jurists, who systematically studied, interpreted, and adapted Roman law to their contemporary conditions and needs, was particularly influential. Through a process known as 'Reception', Roman law, as elaborated by these jurists, provided the basis for a common body of law that applied throughout Continental Europe. From the fifteenth century onwards, the interaction between received Roman law, Germanic customary law, and canon law was increasingly influenced by the rise of nation-states and the consolidation of centralized political administrations. The rise of national law precipitated the move toward the codification of laws, resulting in the great European codifications of the eighteenth and nineteenth centuries. During this period, the civil law system began to expand beyond Continental Europe, driven partly by colonization and partly by the advantages associated with the reception of the codification techniques prevalent in Continental European legal systems of the time.

G. Mousourakis, *Traversing Legal Traditions*, Springer Textbooks in Law,
https://doi.org/10.1007/978-3-031-94669-1_7

7.2 The Legacy of Roman Law

Roman law, both in terms of its historical timeline and extensive influence, stands as the principal catalyst in the evolution of the civil law tradition. The history of ancient Roman law spans over eleven centuries. Initially the law of a small rural community, Roman law eventually became the law of a powerful city-state. Over time, it developed into the law of a multinational empire that encompassed a large part of the civilized world. Throughout its long history, Roman law underwent a remarkable process of evolution, advancing through various stages and undergoing substantial transformations in both substance and form as it adapted to societal changes, particularly those arising from Rome's expansion in the ancient world. This evolutionary process involved the interplay of custom, enacted law, and case law, leading to the creation of a highly sophisticated legal system composed of multiple layers. Notably, the great bulk of Roman law, especially Roman private law, emerged from jurisprudence rather than from legislation. This body of unenacted law was not a chaotic collection of fluctuating customs but a consistent tradition developed and maintained by specialists, initially members of the Roman priestly class and later secular jurists. In the final stages of this evolution, as law-making became increasingly centralized, jurisprudence, alongside statutory law, was systematically compiled and codified. This codification process not only completed the development of Roman law but also facilitated its transmission to the modern world.

Roman legal history is divided into distinct periods based on the prevailing modes of law-making and the nature and orientation of the legal institutions during different epochs. These periods are as follows:

(i) The archaic period, spanning from the establishment of the city-state of Rome to the mid-third century BC. This period encompasses the Monarchy and the early Republic.
(ii) The pre-classical period, from the mid-third century BC to the early first century AD, largely coinciding with the later part of the Republic.
(iii) The classical period, from the early first century AD to the mid-third century AD, covering most of the initial part of the imperial era, known as the Principate.
(iv) The post-classical period, from the mid-third century AD to the sixth century AD, including the final years of the Principate and the late Empire or Dominate, culminating in the age of Justinian (AD 527–565).

The earliest source of Roman law was unwritten customary law, consisting of norms referred to as *mores maiorum* (the ways of our forefathers). These norms emerged from long-standing usages of the community and from cases resolved by clan patriarchs or the king. Similar to the laws of other primitive societies, early Roman law was characterized by a dominance of religious and formalistic attitudes. Despite the religious significance of these early legal norms, the Romans believed that a distinction between religious law (*fas*) and secular law (*ius*)—the body of man-made norms governing human relations—began as early as the time of the kings. A pivotal event in the archaic period was the codification of customary norms in the Law of the Twelve Tables, enacted around 450 BC. This codification marked the first written record of rules and procedures for the attainment of justice, providing a new source of law alongside unwritten customary law.[1] Following the enactment of the Law of the Twelve Tables, legal development largely relied on the interpretation of its text by priests (pontiffs) and, later, by secular jurists. Additionally, later in this period, the office of praetor was introduced (367 BC), creating a new magistracy entrusted with the administration of private law.

The Romans referred to their own law as *ius civile*, the legal order governing Roman citizens (*cives Romani*). Similar to other ancient civilizations, the Romans adhered to the principle of personality of law, according to which a state's laws applied exclusively to its citizens. Consequently, *ius civile* was the law applicable solely to Roman citizens. However, over time, Roman law experienced significant expansion. As the Roman state grew and legal matters became more complex, Roman jurisprudence incorporated the concept of *ius gentium*: a set of legal institutions and principles common to all people under Roman rule, irrespective of their citizenship (*civitas*). The introduction of *ius gentium* into Roman law significantly broadened its scope. Despite this expansion, certain legal institutions remained exclusive to Roman citizens and were classified under *ius civile*, while others fell under *ius gentium*, being applicable to both citizens and non-citizens alike.

A turning point in the history of Roman law occurred during the late Republican period with the emergence of the first secular jurists (*iurisconsulti* or *iurisprudentes*). These jurists primarily focused on presenting legal advice on complex legal matters to judicial magistrates, judges, and parties at law, as well as drafting of legal documents. Towards the end of this period, the first systematic treatises on civil law appeared, reflecting the influence of Greek philosophy and science on Roman legal thought. The legal history of the Republican period is also marked by the development of the *ius honorarium*, or magisterial law, as a distinct source of law. Early Roman law was rigid, narrow in scope, and resistant to change. However, due to the changes brought about by Rome's expansion, the Romans faced the challenge of adjusting their laws to meet new social and economic conditions. In response, law-dispensing magistrates, especially the praetors, were granted the power to adapt the law in its application. Although these magistrates had no legislative authority, they extensively used their power to regulate the legal process, thereby creating a new body of law that was progressive, flexible, and subject to continual change and development.[2]

---

[1] The Roman historian Livy refers to the Law of the Twelve Tables as "the source of all public and private law" (*fons omnis publici privatique iuris*). (*Ab urbe condita* 3. 34. 6.) Modern reconstructions of the Law of the Twelve Tables include: Warmington (1938), p. 424 ff; Johnson et al. (1961), p. 9 ff; Girard and Senn (1977), pp. 25–73.

[2] According to the classical Roman jurist Marcianus, "the *ius honorarium* is of itself the living voice of the *ius civile*." (D. 1. 1. 8) A parallel may be drawn between the Roman *ius honorarium*, based on the concept of *aequitas*, and English equity. Unlike the English common law and equity,

Roman law reached its full maturity in the early imperial epoch (late first century BC to late third century AD), often referred to as the 'classical' period of Roman law. This development was primarily driven by the creative work of the jurists and their influence on the formulation and application of the law. Early in this period, the emperors customarily granted leading jurists the right to present opinions on legal questions (*ius respondendi*) and deliver them with the emperor's authority. By the latter half of the second century, it was recognized that when jurists who had been granted this right were in agreement, their opinions functioned as authoritative sources of law.[3] In addition to addressing practical legal questions, the jurists were also engaged in teaching law and writing legal treatises. The main body of Roman law as we know it today was established upon the writings of leading jurists from this period.

During the same period, the resolutions of the Roman senate and the decrees of the emperors became recognized as authoritative sources of law. Conversely, the role of the magisterial law (*ius honorarium*) gradually declined as praetorian initiatives became increasingly rare. The final codification of the praetorian edict in AD 130 marked the end of the *ius honorarium* as a distinct source of law. Following the enactment of the *constitutio Antoniniana* (AD 212), an imperial decree that extended Roman citizenship to all inhabitants of the Empire, the old distinction between *ius civile* and *ius gentium* effectively vanished. Every free man within the Empire was now a citizen, subject to the same Roman law.

In the later imperial age (late third century AD to sixth century AD), the only effective source of law was imperial legislation, which was primarily concerned with matters of public law and economic policy. Jurisprudence had ceased to be a living source of law, and earlier juristic works were regarded as a body of settled doctrine. As the body of imperial legislation grew, there emerged a need for the codification of the law. Additionally, there was a requirement for guidance in the use of the classical juridical literature—a vast collection of legal materials spanning hundreds of years of legal development. The codification process began with the publication of two private collections of imperial laws at the end of the third century AD: the *Codex Gregorianus* (AD 291) and the *Codex Hermogenianus* (AD 295). These were followed by the *Codex Theodosianus*, an official codification of imperial laws published in AD 438. In the fifth century, Roman legal scholarship experienced a revival centred around the law schools of the Empire.[4] The study of classical

however, the *ius civile* and *ius honorarium* did not operate as two separate systems administered by different courts but were regarded as two sides of the same legal system.

[3] As the jurist Gaius explains: "The *responsa* of the learned in the law are the decisions and opinions of those to whom it has been permitted to lay down the law. If the decisions of all of these are in accord, that which they so hold has the force of statute. If, however, they differ, the judge is permitted to follow the decision he pleases; and this is expressed in a rescript of [Emperor] Hadrianus." (G. 1. 7.)

[4] The first law school was probably founded in Rome in the late second century and a second such school was later established in Beirut during the third century. As the administrative needs of the Empire grew (especially after Diocletian's reorganization of the administration), new law schools

authorities at the law schools engendered a new type of jurisprudence, focused not so much on developing new legal ideas but on understanding and expounding the classical materials in light of contemporary needs and conditions. Despite its lack of originality, post-classical legal science succeeded in reviving a genuine familiarity with the entire classical inheritance and facilitating its adaptation to the conditions of the times.

The process of codification reached its pinnacle in the mid-sixth century AD with Emperor Justinian's comprehensive codification of Roman law, encompassing both juristic law and imperial enactments. Justinian aimed to create a definite and authoritative compilation of contemporary law based on the legal legacy of the past, to supersede all previous statements of law found in juridical literature and legislation. His objective was to establish a uniform legal system across the empire while preserving the finest elements of classical jurisprudence, thereby eliminating the confusion caused by the previously scattered and extensive legal materials. To achieve this, Justinian appointed commissions of jurists and state officials with three primary goals: (a) collecting and editing all imperial laws issued up to that time for current applicability; (b) gathering and harmonizing the opinions of Roman jurists; and (c) creating a standard textbook that would systematically and clearly introduce the fundamental principles of law to students.

In February 528, Justinian appointed a commission of high officials and jurists to consolidate all valid imperial enactments into a single code. This work, published in April 529 under the name *Codex Iustinianus*, acquired the force of law. However, the extensive new legislation issued by Justinian after 529 soon rendered the Code obsolete, leading to its replacement by a revised edition in 534.

After the publication of the first Code, Justinian focused on systematizing the law derived from the works of the classical jurists. Like the compilers of the Code, the commission members appointed for this task were granted wide discretionary powers. They decided which juristic writings to include or omit as superfluous, imperfect, or obsolete. They could shorten the relevant texts, eliminate contradictions, and update matters considering current legal practice and changes in the law introduced by imperial legislation. The compilation took the form of an anthology of classical jurists' writings with exact references. Despite spanning hundreds of years of legal development, it was devised as a correct statement of the law at the time of its publication and the sole authority for future jurisprudential works and embodied imperial laws. Published under the name *Digesta* or *Pandectae*, it came into force in December 533. From that date, only the juristic writings contained within it were legally binding; references to the original works were deemed superfluous, and the publication of critical commentaries on the Digest was prohibited.

As an authoritative statement of the law, the Digest was intended for use not only by legal practitioners and state officials but also by those engaged in the study of law. However, even before its publication, it became evident that the work was far

---

were established in places such as Alexandria, Caesaria, Athens and Constantinople in the East; and Carthage and Augustodunum in the West.

too lengthy and complex for students, particularly those in their first year of studies. An introductory textbook was needed to help students grasp the basic principles of the law before progressing to the more detailed and complex aspects of legal practice. This necessity inspired Justinian to order the preparation of a new official legal textbook in 533 for use in the empire's law schools. The resulting work, published under the name *Institutiones* or *Elementa*, came into force as an imperial statute alongside the Digest on December 30, 533.

After the publication of the second edition of the Code, Justinian's legislative activity continued unabated as political and social developments necessitated legal adjustments not anticipated by earlier legislation. Most of these new laws, or 'Novels' (*Novellae constitutiones*), primarily addressed administrative and ecclesiastical matters. However, Justinian also introduced significant innovations in private law, particularly in family law and the law of intestate succession. Although these new laws were intended to be officially compiled and published as part of a new edition of the Code, this never occurred. Our knowledge of them comes mainly from three later compilations based on a few private and unofficial collections produced during and after Justinian's reign: the *Epitome novellarum Iuliani*, the *Authenticum*, and the *Collectio Graeca*.

The Code, the Digest, the Institutes, and the Novels constitute the bulk of Justinian's legislative work and are collectively known as the *Corpus Iuris Civilis*.[5]

The influence of Justinian's codification has been immense. In the Byzantine East, it served as the fundamental document for legal evolution until the fall of the empire in the fifteenth century. In Western Europe, it was forgotten for a significant period but rediscovered in the eleventh century. Initially regarded as an object of academic study, it later underwent a profound reception, becoming the common foundation upon which the civil law systems of Continental Europe were built.

7.3 The Later History of Roman Law in the East: The Byzantine Legal Tradition

The sixth-century codification of Emperor Justinian marks the end of the history of Roman law in antiquity and simultaneously heralds the beginning of its 'second life', a phase spanning from the early Middle Ages to modern times. In the Eastern Empire of Byzantium, Justinian's legislation remained in force until the fall of

[5]The term '*Corpus Iuris Civilis*' did not originate in Justinian's time; it was introduced in the late sixteenth century by Dionysius Godofredus (1549–1622), author of the first scholarly edition of Justinian's work, in contradistinction to the codification of the canon law (referred to as *Corpus Iuris Canonici*). The modern standard edition, published from 1888 to 1895, is that of Theodor Mommsen, Paul Krüger, Rudolf Schöll and Wilhelm Kroll, consisting of three volumes: Volume One contains the Institutes (ed. Krüger) and the Digest (ed. Mommsen, revised Krüger); Volume Two elaborates the Code (ed. Krüger); and Volume Three embodies the Novels (ed. Schöll and Kroll).

Constantinople to the Ottomans in 1453. However, the social conditions and intellectual climate of the Greek-speaking Byzantine world necessitated the simplification and popularization of the intricate Roman legal heritage. This led to the development of a new genre of juridical literature, including numerous translations, summaries, paraphrases, and commentaries on Justinian's legal works, as well as several significant legislative enactments designed to adapt the Roman law of Justinian to prevailing conditions and address new social and economic challenges. The post-Justinianic legal developments in the Byzantine East are of tremendous significance to modern jurists, forming a crucial part of the intellectual background of contemporary legal culture, especially in countries once within the orbit of the Byzantine civilization.

7.3.1 The Evolution of Byzantine Law and Jurisprudence During the Post-Justinianic and Isaurian Periods

In the years following the publication of Justinian's law books, Byzantine legal science flourished, particularly at the two preeminent centres of legal learning: the law schools of Constantinople and Beirut. Justinian decreed that only the emperor had the right to interpret the law, forbidding all commentary on his legislation under the threat of punishment. He only sanctioned the creation of content summaries (*indices*) and verbatim (*kata podas*) translations of the Latin texts into Greek. This prohibition aimed to safeguard his legislation from the uncertainties that could arise from disputes concerning the meaning of the legal norms it contained. However, this prohibition soon fell into abeyance, and manuscripts began to circulate that included summaries, commentaries, and interpretations of Justinian's texts, as well as treatises on specific legal topics. Most of these works were written by jurists who taught at the Eastern law schools.[6]

Of the imperial legislation enacted in the early post-Justinianic period, only a very small number of new laws or novels (*novellae constitutiones*) promulgated by Justin II (565–578), Tiberius II (578–582), and Heraclius (610–641) have been preserved. These laws primarily addressed matters of public, ecclesiastical, and private law, especially the law of marriage. Tiberius II's legislation reflects an attempt by the imperial government to curb the excesses of powerful landowners and improve the economic situation of small landholders and free laborers. The four novels from Heraclius's reign deal with the organization of the Eastern Church, including the *privilegium fori*.[7] These enactments represent the last manifestations of lawgiving in

[6] The most distinguished of these law professors (*antecessores*) included Theophilus from the law school of Constantinople, and Dorotheus and Anatolius from the law school of Beirut. Other notable jurists of the same period were Thalelaeus, Cobidas, Stephanus, and Julian.

[7] The concept of *privilegium fori* (choice between different courts) was introduced during the Roman imperial age. From the fourth century, an increasingly complex list of jurisdictional rules evolved whereby certain categories of individuals, including members of the senatorial order,

the Justinianic tradition but, compared to Justinian's work, are of limited significance. Rather, they reflect the emperor's response to specific issues brought to his attention.

This limited scope of legislation is unsurprising given the context of the period: continuous wars against the Avars, Persians, and Arabs took a heavy toll on the empire, and by the end of Heraclius's reign, many eastern provinces had been lost. However, as the imperial boundaries receded, retrenchment led to a comparative strengthening of the state, and the empire acquired the homogeneity that Justinian's policies had failed to produce. The new borders more closely aligned with ethnic and religious lines, as the inhabitants of the empire were now largely Greek-speaking and Orthodox Christian. During these years, the empire fully entered its Byzantine period, embracing the Greek language and displaying a deep orientalization, with Christianity ingrained in its thought and ethos.

By the middle of the seventh century, the production of legal works had largely ceased. During the same period, the disruption of official communications between the capital and the provinces due to war undermined the government's ability to ensure the uniform application of the law throughout the realm. Consequently, local customs began to play a vital role as a source of social regulation. The situation was further exacerbated by the fact that Justinian's legislation was written in a language foreign to many in the empire and contained concepts that both the populace and those involved in the administration of justice found difficult to comprehend. Under these conditions, lawyers and imperial officials struggled to ascertain the exact state of the law. This prompted an urgent need to introduce new legislation that would adapt Justinian's Roman law to the usages actually observed by the inhabitants of the empire and clarify the applicable law in a simple and systematic way. These were the objectives of the compilers of the *Ecloga Legum*, the new legal code enacted in the first half of the eighth century. The enactment of this code attests to the fact that, despite the decline of legal education and scarcity of legal literature, the ideological force of Roman law as a symbol of the state remained strong.[8]

The *Ecloga Legum* (Selection of the Laws) was published in 741 under the authority of Emperor Leo III the Isaurian (717–741) and his son and co-Emperor Constantine V (741–775). A three-member commission, headed by the quaestor Nicetas, prepared the relevant material. Written in Greek, the work consists of a preface and eighteen titles addressing the laws of marriage, succession, tutelage, contracts, and crimes. As stated in the preamble, the *Ecloga* is based on a selection of laws derived from the Institutes, Digest, Code, and Novels of Justinian, modified in accordance with Christian ideas toward greater humanity. The *Ecloga* also incorporated several imperial enactments from the early post-Justinianic era and introduced important innovations reflecting Greek and other Eastern influences. Generally, the work is characterized by its simplicity and its emphasis on Christian

---

Christian bishops, and some clerics, could appeal to specific 'privileged' jurisdictions under certain circumstances as prescribed by imperial legislation. Consider Jones (1964), pp. 284–602.

[8] See on this Haldon (1990), p. 279.

and humanitarian principles.[9] However, as the *Ecloga* fell short of addressing all practical legal needs, gaps in the legislation were often filled by resorting to Justinian's *corpus*.[10]

During the age of the Isaurian emperors, three unofficial compilations emerged, addressing specific branches of the law: the Military Code, the Rural or Farmers' Code, and the Rhodian Maritime Code. The Military Code focused on penal provisions to maintain army discipline.[11] The Rural Code, likely originating in the provinces and based on Justinian's legislation and other early sources, aimed to protect small farmers and tenants from exploitation. In the seventh century, as land concentration among feudal lords increased, small-scale land ownership declined, and rural living conditions deteriorated. The Isaurian emperors sought to curb the power of great landlords and reorganize the rural economy to benefit peasant communities.[12] The Rhodian Maritime Code encapsulated the customary maritime laws of the East from the sixth to the eighth centuries and was widely used throughout the Mediterranean during the Middle Ages. It provided practical regulations for handling ship collisions and addressing issues between ship and cargo owners. Over time, these provisions influenced the early Italian maritime city-states that were closely related to the Byzantines. As Byzantine maritime trade declined from the twelfth century, the Rhodian sea law fell into disuse. However, its key norms persisted, shaping the commercial and maritime practices of Venice, Genoa, Pisa, and other maritime states.[13]

The seventh and eighth centuries witnessed a significant shift: the expansion of canon law and ecclesiastical jurisdiction at the expense of their secular counterparts. This development can be seen as a natural consequence of the conditions of the era. The crisis of the empire disrupted the regular functioning of secular judicial authorities, especially in the provinces where external threats were most acute. Although bishops and other ecclesiastical authorities also faced pressure, their activities were less directly tied to Byzantine political and military administration. Consequently, it is unsurprising that both formal and informal ecclesiastical jurisdiction increasingly assumed the role of secular courts. This shift enhanced the Church's prestige and its law-making functions. In essence, canon law filled the void left by secular law,

[9] In the domain of criminal law, the influence of these principles is reflected in the restrictions imposed on the application of the death penalty. Furthermore, the new code introduced more precision and a degree of individualization in the application of punishment, and placed some limits on inequality before the law. At the same time, the recognition of the penalty of mutilation, which was introduced as a form of punishment for crimes that in the past entailed the death penalty, reflects the strong influence of Oriental practices on Byzantine criminal law.

[10] This led to the creation of a private manual closely connected with the *Ecloga*, now known as the *Appendix Eclogae*, as it is usually found in the same manuscripts. The *Appendix* comprises numerous legal rules derived from various sources, directly or indirectly based on the Justinian's legislation. For a closer look at the *Ecloga* and related sources, see Burgmann (1991), pp. 672–673 and Burgmann (1983). And see Freshfield (1926); Burgmann and Troianos (1979).

[11] Ashburner (1926).

[12] Ashburner (1910, 1912).

[13] For a closer look at the Rhodian Maritime Code see Ashburner (1976); Atkinson (1974).

becoming an integral component of Byzantine society's normative framework and a crucial reference point for its future development.

7.3.2 *Legislation and Juridical Sources in the Middle and Late Byzantine Periods*

The accession of Basil I the Macedonian (867–886) marks the beginning of the most creative period in Byzantine legal history since the reign of Justinian. The legislation of this period is characterized by a renewed emphasis on Justinianic codification as the foundation of the Byzantine legal system. This return to the Roman law of Justinian was part of a broader revival of interest in the classical tradition and reflected the imperial ambition to portray the Byzantine state as the direct heir to the ancient Roman Empire, now reimagined as a Christian empire (*imperium Christianum*). A primary objective of the legislative program initiated by the Macedonian emperors was to restore the substance of Justinianic Roman law. To achieve this, many changes introduced by the Isaurian legislation were reversed, and the precedence of written law over custom was re-established.[14] At the same time, plans to update the legal system were executed by eliminating matters that had become obsolete.

The first in a series of legislative works aimed at a comprehensive revision of the law was the *Eisagoge* ('introduction to the law'), previously known as *Epanagoge* ('return [to the law]'), prepared under the authority of Basil I and his sons Leo and Alexander around 885. This compilation included a selection of laws drawn from the Greek translations of Justinian's codification and consisted of forty titles and a preamble. A notable feature of the *Eisagoge* is its introduction of a system of norms governing the relationship between Church and state, which was significantly different from the previous system. Since the time of Constantine the Great (4th century AD), the prevailing approach had seen Church and state as two aspects of a single, indivisible concept of Christendom. The *Eisagoge* departed from this approach by supporting the theory of the 'two authorities', which viewed the emperor and the patriarch as equally powerful holders of the two highest positions within the state.[15]

A revised edition of the *Eisagoge*, known as the *Procheiros Nomos* or *Procheiron*, was published in the early tenth century by Emperor Leo VI the Wise (886–912). The *Procheiron* comprises extracts from Greek translations and abridgments of Justinian's legislation, along with fragments from the *Ecloga* and enactments of the Macedonian emperors that amended and complemented the existing laws. Like the

---

[14] Although the *Ecloga* was abrogated by the Macedonian emperors, some of its provisions continued to apply in practice, especially in the provinces and among neighboring peoples in the Balkans and Asia Minor (translations of the *Ecloga* have survived in Slavic, Armenian, and Arabic).

[15] For a closer look at the *Eisagoge* see Schminck (1986), p. 4 ff; Troianos (1986), pp. 100–105.

Eisagoge, the materials are divided into forty titles preceded by a preamble. However, the drafters of the *Procheiron* omitted all the titles of the *Eisagoge* that contained provisions on the foundation of the political-ecclesiastical organization, possibly with the aim of eliminating the theory of the 'two authorities.' The *Procheiron* was transmitted through numerous manuscripts and served as the basis of several later law books, including the influential *Hexabiblos* of Harmenopoulos.[16]

As announced in its preamble, the *Eisagoge* was designed to serve as an introduction to a comprehensive new code of law, initially referred to as the 'Revision of the Ancient Laws' (*Repurgatio veterum legum*). Work on this project began under Emperor Basil I and was completed in the late ninth or early tenth century during the reign of his son, Leo VI the Wise. The original title of the new law book appears to have been *Basilica nomima* (Imperial law), but from the eleventh century onwards, it was commonly designated simply as the *Basilica.* As stated in the preamble, the goal of this work was to collect, update, and harmonize the laws contained in Justinian's codification. It consolidates materials from the Code, Digest, Institutes, and Novels into a single body of work. It should be noted that most of the extracts were not drawn from the original Latin text of Justinian's codification but from Greek translations and abridgments by jurists from later periods. The *Basilica* also incorporated the Rhodian Maritime Code mentioned earlier. The materials are arranged into sixty books divided into titles, paragraphs, and themes. The entire work comprises six volumes. The text of the *Basilica* is accompanied by a large number of annotations (*scholia*) that include interpretations, examples, explanations, and references of various kinds. Some of these comments are extracted from the works of sixth century jurists (old *scholia*), while others are derived from juristic works of the post-Macedonian period (new *scholia*).[17]

In the years preceding the publication of the *Basilica*, Emperor Leo VI issued numerous new laws (*novellae constitutiones*). Out of these, 113 were collected and preserved along with four individual enactments. Approximately one-third of these laws focused on ecclesiastical matters, modifying the provisions of civil legislation, primarily those of Justinian, to align them with the requirements of canon law. Some of Leo's novels aimed to resolve apparent contradictions between written law and established customary norms.[18]

Leo VI is rightly regarded as the greatest legislator of the Byzantine era, second only to Justinian in terms of legislative output. Leo viewed Justinian as his role model and aimed to imitate, and even surpass, him as a legislator. By enacting his own novels and the *Basilika* in close association, he aimed to create a coherent legal

---

[16] The *Procheiron* was translated into Slavic in the eleventh century and was particularly influential in the Balkans. For a closer look at the *Procheiron* see Zepos and Zepos (1962), vol. II, pp. 107–228 and 395–410; consider also Freshfield (1928).

[17] Only about two-thirds of the *Basilica* has survived throughout the eras in various manuscripts. Our knowledge on the contents of the missing parts derives from later works, such as the *Tipoukeitos* published in the late eleventh century as a legal repertory. For a modern edition of the *Basilica* see Scheltema et al. (1953–1988). Consider also Scheltema (1955); Lawson (1930, 1931).

[18] For a closer look at Leo's novels see Noailles and Dain (1944).

system that would complete Justinian's work. While Justinian's authority stemmed primarily from his imperial dignity, with God as the source of that dignity, Leo's laws were seen as deriving their authority directly from God. Leo held two views of the law: the noble vision of the law as God's instrument, personified in the emperor, for imposing order on creation; and the pragmatic view that the law must continually provide practical solutions to concrete problems of everyday life, given the 'variety of human affairs', as Leo states at the beginning of the preface to his collection of novels.

In addition to official law collections, several private works by jurists were created for practical and instructional purposes. Notable among these are the *Epitome Legum* (913) and the *Synopsis Basilicorum Maior* (late tenth century). The *Epitome Legum* draws from Justinian's codification, the *Basilica*, the *Procheiron*, and Leo VI's constitutions.[19] The *Synopsis Basilicorum Maior* contains brief abstracts from the *Basilica* arranged in alphabetical order, often accompanied by an appendix with materials from imperial laws of the tenth and later centuries and other sources. Designed to facilitate the application of the *Basilica*, this work circulated in numerous manuscripts and was widely used by legal practitioners and commentators.[20]

Three other works are also noteworthy: the *Experientia Romani* or *Peira* (*c.* 1050), a collection of juristic decisions largely derived from the writings of Eustathius Romanus, a distinguished judge in Constantinople and one of the most prominent middle Byzantine jurists[21] the *Tipoukeitos*, a repertory on the *Basilica* compiled by a judge named Patzes in the late eleventh century;[22] and the *Synopsis Legum* (*c.* 1070), a collection of laws from the codification of Justinian and the *Basilica* prepared by the jurist and philosopher Michael Psellus, dedicated to his pupil, Emperor Michael VII Ducas.[23]

The revival of literary activity in the post-Macedonian period was significantly influenced by the establishment of a new law school in Constantinople around 1045 by Emperor Constantine IX Monomachus (1042–1055). The increasing bureaucratization of the imperial administration in the eleventh century created a growing demand for well-educated officials. In response to this need and the inadequacy of the existing system of legal education, where advocates had to teach themselves or learn from private tutors, Constantine founded the law school and outlined the

---

[19] In the preamble of the *Epitome* its author makes the following statement: "I shall present a history of the ancient origins of [the law], whence it received its beginning and a selection of the laws put into effect by the Romans during particular times." This statement reflects a trend characteristic of law books of the Macedonian and post-Macedonian periods, which often include a brief outline of Roman legal history and portray contemporary legal works as a continuation of the Roman legal tradition. For the text of the *Epitome* see Zepos and Zepos (1962), vol. IV, pp. 261–585 and 596–619. And see Moulakis (1963).

[20] For the text see Zepos and Zepos (1962), vol. V. And see Svoronos (1964).

[21] The *Peira* provides a useful insight into the way in which Byzantine normative sources were applied in actual cases. For the text see Zepos and Zepos (1962), vol. IV, pp. 11–260. And see Simon (1987); Vryonis (1974).

[22] See Ferrini et al. (1914–1957).

[23] Consider Weiss (1977).

conditions for the professors' and students' work. The school's constitution mandated that no person could practice law until they had completed the prescribed courses and received certification of competence from the professors.[24] Admission to the school was open and free of charge. The emperor appointed and paid the professors (*magistri*) as well as the head of the school, who held the office of *nomophylax* (literally 'guardian of the law'), one of the highest state offices. Until the end of the eleventh century, the teaching of law was based directly on the texts of the Justinianic codification with a methodical study and clarification of its contents.[25] The law school of Constantinople appears to have remained operational until the city's capture by the Latins in 1204.

In the thirteenth century, legal culture in the East faced a sharp decline, precipitated by the confusion that ensued from the political disintegration of the Byzantine world following the Latin conquest of Constantinople. After the Byzantines recaptured Constantinople in 1261, the emperors of the Palaeologan dynasty focused on reorganizing the administration of justice. Emperors Andronicus II (1282–1328) and Andronicus III (1328–1341) issued a series of laws aimed at reforming the court system. The earliest of these laws provided for the establishment of a High Court consisting of twelve judges in Constantinople.

Despite some successes in the Paleologi reform program, there was no significant effort to improve the quality of legal education, which had deteriorated after the dissolution of the law school of Constantinople. Legal instruction was now mainly conducted by practitioners in a haphazard and unsystematic manner, based on fragmentary legal sources. Lawyers of this period paid little attention to the codification of Justinian, whose texts were difficult to find, and instead utilized contemporary Greek summaries and adaptations. The most notable of these materials was the *Hexabiblos*, a manual of law in six books compiled around 1345 by Constantine Harmenopoulos, a judge in Thessalonica. Designed for judges and court officials, the *Hexabiblos* drew from sources like the *Procheiron*, the *Synopsis Basilicorum Maior*, the *Peira*, and others. It covered private law in Books 1–5, divided into general principles, property law, obligations, family law, and succession law, while Book 6 addressed criminal law. The text is accompanied by numerous annotations, mostly created by Harmenopoulos.[26]

After the fall of Byzantium, the *Hexabiblos* continued to be utilized throughout the Ottoman period, especially in ecclesiastical courts, significantly contributing to the preservation of the Roman-Byzantine legal tradition in the Balkans. The *Hexabiblos* was also widely known and used in the West, where it underwent several editions during the sixteenth and seventeenth centuries. The existence of a German translation attests to its use in German court practice throughout the Reception period. Similarly, the court use of the *Hexabiblos* in France appears to

---

[24] Lawyers were divided into two categories: *synegoroi* (advocates, barristers) and *taboullarioi* (notaries).

[25] In the twelfth century, the Justinianic codification was increasingly replaced by various abridgments and commentaries in legal studies.

[26] For the text see Heimbach (1969); *Fögen* (1986).

have been equivalent to that in Germany. Additionally, sixteenth century humanist jurists extensively used the *Hexabiblos* as an important basis for the critical reconstruction of the *Corpus Iuris Civilis* and the restoration of the text of the *Basilica*.

During the later Byzantine epoch, the Church played an increasingly significant role in the administration of justice. Since the fourth century, ecclesiastical courts had jurisdiction over cases involving clerics and civil disputes submitted by the relevant parties. By the end of the twelfth century, their competence had expanded to include a variety of civil cases, encompassing matrimonial matters and cases concerning charitable bequests. This trend towards broadening the jurisdiction of Church courts accelerated considerably after the Latin conquest (1204–1261). As ecclesiastical law became more intertwined with civil law, the distinction between civil and ecclesiastical jurisdictions grew increasingly blurred. This development was linked to the general weakening of the Byzantine state and the parallel expansion of the Church's role in civil administration, as the emperors increasingly relied on the Church organization to maintain imperial unity.

As the importance of canon law increased during this period, various compilations emerged that combined both canon and civil law, known as nomocanons (or *Syntagmata*). Notable works include those by Theodore Balsamon, John Zonaras, and Alexios Aristenos in the twelfth century, and Mathaeus Blastares and Constantine Harmenopoulos in the fourteenth century. These materials continued to be produced and utilized by ecclesiastical courts throughout the Ottoman period, significantly contributing to the preservation of the Roman-Byzantine legal tradition in countries formerly within the orbit of the Byzantine civilization.

7.4 The Influence of the Roman-Byzantine Legal Tradition

Byzantine law, whether transplanted in its original form or adjusted to local conditions, exercised a strong influence in the East, particularly on those peoples who inherited their social, political, and ecclesiastical structures from Byzantium. Byzantine law was introduced into the Slavic world through the legislative work of the missionaries Methodius and Cyril and the ninth-century *Zakon Sudnyj Ljudem* ('Law for Judging the People'), a Bulgarian law book corresponding closely to the *Ecloga*.[27] In Serbia, the reception of Byzantine law began with the Nomocanon of St. Sava (early 13th century), a compilation of ecclesiastical law containing the entire *Procheiron*.[28] This reception culminated with the codification of Tsar Stefan Dusan (*Dušanov zakonik*) in 1349, the greatest achievement of the Serbian legal

[27] The original version of the *Zakon Sudnyj Ljudem* primarily addressed matters of criminal law. All of the existing manuscripts come from Russia, where the work was introduced in the late tenth century and was widely used as part of larger legal collections. See Dewey and Kleimola (1977).

[28] St. Sava's law book proved influential far beyond Serbia, becoming the basic constitution of both the Bulgarian and the Russian Church. Furthermore, the rules it contained were also applied to laymen under Church jurisdiction. For a closer view at this work consider Koprivica (2020).

tradition.[29] This codification, which came close to being an all-encompassing constitution, was largely an abridgment of the *Syntagma* of Mathaeus Blastares and was widely used in the Serbian Empire (1346–1371) and the succeeding Despotate of Serbia (1402–1459).

The Russian *Kormčaja kniga* (Book of the Helmsman), a collection of ecclesiastical canons and civil law rules dating from the thirteenth century, contains materials from various Byzantine sources, including the *Ecloga*, the *Procheiron*, and the *Zakon Sudnyj Ljudem*. This work provided the constitutional basis for the relationship between ecclesiastical and secular authorities based on the Byzantine model and served as a primary source of civil law in Russia.[30] Additionally, on the island of Cyprus, Byzantine law remained in force during both the period of the Latin kingdom (1192–1489) and the rule of Venice (1489–1571). Although the *Constitutio Cypria* or *Bulla Cypria*, a papal bull promulgated by Pope Alexander IV in 1260, declared the Latin Church as the official church of Cyprus, the ecclesiastical courts of the Greek Orthodox Church continued to apply the so-called Hellenic law, which was essentially a compilation of Byzantine law, in disputes between Greeks.

After the fall of the Byzantine Empire in the fifteenth century, Byzantine law continued to govern the orthodox Christians within the Ottoman Empire, who were under the spiritual and political leadership of the Patriarchate of Constantinople. In exercising their administrative and judicial functions, the patriarchate and its ecclesiastic authorities applied Byzantine law, derived from various manuscript sources in their original form or in abridged versions. In later times, they also used printed works produced in the West, such as the *Ius Graeco-Romanum* of Johannes Leunclavius (1596) and the *Synodikon* of Guilielmus Beveregius (1672).[31] The various nomocanons of the Ottoman period, which mostly drew directly or indirectly on the last two systematic manuals of Byzantine law—the *Hexabiblos* of Harmenopoulos and the *Syntagma* of Blastares—were of much wider use.[32]

Even outside the Ottoman Empire, in countries tracing their cultural origins to Byzantium, the *Hexabiblos* was often used to address gaps in the law, being regarded as the law that was 'naturally' in force when no other rule could be found. In Russian Bessarabia, this work was officially recognized as the local civil code in the early nineteenth century and remained in force even after the annexation of Bessarabia to Romania in 1918, until Romanian legislation was extended to this region. A Serbian translation of the *Hexabiblos* was also produced for use by the Serb population of

[29] Consider Angelini (2012).

[30] For a closer look at the *Kormčaja kniga* see Zuzek (1964).

[31] The ecclesiastical jurisdiction of the Patriarchate of Constantinople, both in the late Byzantine and Ottoman periods, and its regulatory function in matters of Church interest extended far beyond the boundaries of the Byzantine and Ottoman Empires to the territories of the East ruled by Venice, to the Orthodox Christians of Poland and Ukraine, and to the Orthodox Christians of the diaspora in the West.

[32] The most widely used work of this kind during the Ottoman age was the *Nomocanon* of Manuel Malaxos (late 16th century). Reference may also be made to the *Staff of the Bishops* of Archimandrite James of Ioannina (1645).

the Archdiocese of Karlowitz under Austrian rule, as their own native law. In Greece, the *Hexabiblos* was recognized as an official source of law after its liberation in the early nineteenth century and remained in force until a modern civil code was enacted in 1946.

Furthermore, the Roman-Byzantine legal tradition significantly influenced the development of legal systems in Arab Muslim countries of the Near East. This influence can be traced back to interactions between the Islamic empires and the Byzantine Empire, leading to a blending of legal traditions and the incorporation of certain Byzantine legal practices into the Islamic legal framework. This was especially evident in regions like Syria, Egypt, and Palestine, where Byzantine influence was strong. The Umayyad and Abbasid caliphates adopted and adapted many Byzantine administrative practices, including legal institutions. This adoption included the establishment of a structured tax system and the use of official records, which were crucial for managing the vast and diverse territories under Islamic control. Additionally, certain legal concepts and principles from Roman-Byzantine law, particularly those related to contracts, commerce, and property, were integrated into Islamic jurisprudence.[33] The Byzantine influence is also seen in the judicial procedures of Islamic courts. The use of witnesses, documentation, and formal court sessions in Islamic law reflect practices prevalent in the Byzantine legal system. Overall, while Islamic law remained distinct with its foundation in the Quran and Sunnah, the practical governance and legal administration in Muslim countries of the Near East were significantly shaped by the pre-existing Roman-Byzantine legal traditions. This amalgamation facilitated the management of diverse populations and contributed to the development of a sophisticated legal system in the early Islamic empires.

Byzantine legal science, encompassing both secular and canon law, was regarded by humanist jurists in the West as integral to the Roman legal tradition and an essential source for its reconstruction. Consequently, editions of the *Corpus Juris Civilis* from the sixteenth to the nineteenth century included Novels of Byzantine emperors, particularly those of Leo VI. However, the fragmentation of historical studies and the adaptation of Roman law to local legal traditions, especially in Germany following the Reception, led to the marginalization of Byzantine law. The general disregard for Byzantium during the Enlightenment age furthered this marginalization. Nonetheless, since the mid-nineteenth century, there has been renewed interest in Byzantine law as a distinct branch of legal history, although it still remains somewhat peripheral to the broader history of Roman law.

[33] For example, the concept of *ijara* (leasing) in Islamic law shows similarities to the Roman *locatio conductio*.

7.5 The Revival of Roman Law in Western Europe

The collapse of the Roman state in the West in the fifth century AD led to the replacement of the once universal system of Roman law with a plurality of legal systems. The Germanic conquerors adhered to their own customs, while the Roman population continued to be governed by Roman law. To facilitate the administration of their territories, some Germanic kings ordered the compilation of legal codes containing the personal Roman law that regulated many of their subjects' lives. Notable compilations of Roman law from this period include the *Lex Romana Visigothorum* (AD 506),[34] the *Edictum Theodorici* (late 5th century AD),[35] and the *Lex Romana Burgundionum* (AD 517).[36]

When Justinian reincorporated Italy into the empire in 553, his legislation was introduced there,[37] but it remained valid only briefly as most Byzantine territories in Italy fell to the Lombards in 568. Afterward, Justinian's laws applied only in the regions under Byzantine control. The rest of Italy followed a pattern similar to Gaul and Spain, where Roman law persisted through the application of the principle of personality of the laws. Roman law also survived through the Church, whose laws were imbued with Roman principles and detailed rules.

Over time, as the fusion of the Roman and Germanic elements of the population progressed, the division of people based on national origin began to erode. The system of personal laws was gradually replaced by the concept of law being tied to a particular territory, resulting in a common body of customary norms governing all

---

[34] The *Lex Romana Visigothorum* was promulgated by King Alaric II of the Visigoths, hence it is also known as the Breviary of Alaric (*Breviarium Alarici*). This code contains extracts from the Gregorian, Hermogenian, and Theodosian Codes; a number of post-Theodosian constitutions; an abbreviated version of Gaius' Institutes (*Epitome Gai*); sections of the *Sententiae* by Paulus; and a short *responsum* of Papinianus as a conclusion. Some of these texts are accompanied by interpretations, in the form of paraphrases or explanatory notes, aimed at facilitating their understanding and application. The *Lex Romana Visigothorum* remained in force in Spain until the seventh century, and its application prevailed in Southern France (though no longer as an official code) until the twelfth century.

[35] The *Edictum Theodorici* was enacted by King Theodoric II, ruler of the Visigothic kingdom in Southern France, and was applicable to both Romans and Visigoths. It contains 154 titles and includes materials distilled from the *Sententiae* of Paulus, the Gregorian, Hermogenian, and Theodosian Codes, as well as post-Theodosian legislation.

[36] The *Lex Romana Burgundionum* was composed during the reign of King Gundobad of the Burgundians and was promulgated by his son Sigismund for use by the Roman inhabitants of his kingdom. It is based on the Gregorian, Hermogenian, and Theodosian Codes; a shortened version of the Institutes of Gaius; and the *Sententiae* of Paulus. Unlike the aforementioned Visigothic Code, it does not contain any extracts from the original Roman sources. Instead, the materials are incorporated into a set of newly formulated rules systematically arranged and distributed over forty-seven titles.

[37] Justinian's legislation was introduced in Italy by a special enactment, the *pragmatica sanctio pro petitione Virgilii*, issued on 14 August AD 554 at the request of Pope Virgilius.

residents of a territory.[38] Consequently, Roman law as a distinct system applicable to a specific segment of the population fell into abeyance. The diversity of laws no longer existed as an intermixture of personal laws but as a variety of local customs. However, the customary laws that applied in all regions were a blend of Roman and Germanic elements.[39] By the end of the tenth century, the integration of 'vulgarized' Roman law with Germanic customary law had progressed to such an extent that historians often describe the legal systems of this period as either 'Romanized customary laws' or as 'Germanized Roman laws.' During the same period, Roman law continued to exert a strong influence on the canon law of the Church and shaped the legislation of Germanic rulers, who maintained the Roman provincial administration system for its effectiveness. Despite this influence, the overall picture of early medieval law shows a progressive decline, reflected in the deteriorating standards of legal education. Thus, the transmission of the Roman legal tradition from late antiquity to the early Middle Ages can be described as a process of survival rather than revival.

From the eleventh century onward, transformed political and economic conditions in the West, particularly in Italy, created a more favourable environment for cultural development. The burgeoning enthusiasm for classical antiquity and the economic growth spurred by increased trade and the rise of towns rekindled interest in Roman law.[40] This renewed interest was precipitated by the discovery at Pisa in

[38] During the ninth century, the shift from the principle of personality to that of territoriality was further accelerated by the growth of feudalism. The predominant feature of feudalism was an estate or territory dominated by a great lord (such as a duke, count, baron, or marquis) who was a vassal to an emperor or king. Since the domain of a great lord functioned as a quasi-independent unit both economically and politically, the specific area controlled by a particular lord determined the form of law that would prevail.

[39] A considerable degree of integration of the Roman and Germanic elements first occurred in the Visigothic territory in Spain. In this region, the *Lex Romana Visigothorum* of Alaric ceased to possess any force, and a new code was introduced in 654 under King Recceswinth: the *Lex Visigothorum* (also known as *Forum Iudicum* or *Liber Iudiciorum*: Book of Judicial Actions). The *Lex Visigothorum* follows the structure of the Theodosian Code. It is based on early legislation (especially on a revised edition of Euric's Code issued by King Leovigild) and laws issued by the current monarch, King Recceswinth. Alaric's code continued to be used in southern France, particularly in the territory of the Burgundians, and in some regions north of the Alps.

[40] Among the earliest centres of legal learning was the law school of Pavia, established in the early tenth century. At this institution, Roman law and the customary law of the Lombards were both taught and developed. As the capital of the Lombard Kingdom and the seat of a supreme court with a corps of judges and lawyers, Pavia was a hub of vigorous legal activity. The study of Lombard law was primarily based on the *Liber Papiensis*, a work composed in the early years of the eleventh century. Other significant works from the same period included the *Lombarda*, or *Lex Langobarda*, and the *Expositio ad Librum Papiensem*, an extensive collection of legal commentaries that incorporated materials from both Lombard and Roman sources. The chief source for the study of Roman law was the *Lex Romana Visigothorum*. Pavia was not the only Italian city where law was studied and legal works were produced. In Ravenna, the former centre of the Byzantine Exarchate in Italy, a school of law existed in the eleventh century where Justinian's texts were known and studied. Additionally, Southern Italy remained under Byzantine rule for a considerable period, preserving Roman legal learning through the influence of Byzantine law.

1077 of a manuscript copy of the Digest dating back to Justinian's era. Moreover, the revival of Roman law was influenced by contemporary political conditions: the authoritarian tenor of Justinian's *Corpus* was seen as supportive of the claims to centralized power by emerging dynastic monarchies.[41]

7.5.1 The School of the Glossators

The principal centre of legal revival was the University of Bologna, the oldest in Western Europe. This university became the seat of the School of the Glossators, under the leadership of renowned jurists such as Irnerius,[42] Rogerius, Azo, Accursius, and Odofredus. The jurists of Bologna dedicated themselves to presenting a comprehensive statement of Roman law through meticulous analysis of Justinian's *Corpus*. Their objective was to re-establish Roman law as a science—a systematic body of principles rather than merely a practical tool. However, the ancient texts were unwieldy, containing a vast amount of often poorly organized material and addressing numerous institutions and issues that were no longer relevant. Consequently, the primary task was to accurately reconstruct and explain these texts.[43]

---

[41] The revival of interest in Roman law was significantly influenced by the conflict between the Holy Roman Empire and the Papacy, a clash rooted in competing political theories. Both sides sought justification and support from legal principles. The Papal supporters contended that spiritual authority was superior to secular power, asserting that the Pope was the supreme ruler of all Christendom, with temporal affairs ultimately subject to the Church's control. In contrast, the opponents, drawing on the authoritarian principles of Roman law, argued that the state's power was absolute and could override any internal opposition. Consequently, Roman law was interpreted to support secular absolutism, directly opposing the Papal claims to supremacy. The Holy Roman emperors embraced this interpretation because the doctrine of universal law, based on grand imperial despotism, provided the most robust ideological foundation for the theory that the emperor, as the successor to the Roman emperors, was at the apex of the feudal system.

[42] The law school of Bologna gained its fame largely due to the efforts of the grammarian Irnerius (*c.* 1055–1130), who began lecturing on the Digest and other parts of Justinian's codification around 1088. Although Irnerius is often regarded as the founder of the school, he was not its first teacher. The first public law course at Bologna was delivered in 1075 by the Pavian jurist Pepo (Joseph), who likely taught Irnerius. Irnerius's reputation attracted students from across Europe, and by the mid-twelfth century, the school had around ten thousand students. His success can be attributed to three principal factors: his excellent edition of the Digest, known as *Litera Bononiensis* or the *Vulgata*; a new approach to studying Roman law that treated the *Corpus Iuris Civilis* as living law; and the separation of Roman law studies from rhetoric, canon law, and feudal law.

[43] The most significant aspect of the Glossators' work was the reconstruction of Justinian's Digest. The materials were divided into three parts: the *Digestum Vetus*, which encompassed the first twenty-four books; the *Digestum Novum*, which included the final twelve books, from book 39 to 50; and the *Digestum Infortiatum*, which covered books 25 to 38. These three sections were compiled into three volumes. A fourth volume contained the first nine books of Justinian's Code, while a fifth volume included the Institutes, the remaining three books of the Code, and the Novels as found in the *Authenticum*. Additionally, the fifth volume incorporated several medieval texts, such

The Glossators' interpretative work was closely aligned with their teaching methods and was carried out by means of notes (*glossae*)[44] that clarified difficult terms of phrases in the text, provided necessary cross-references, and reconciled various parts to render the text usable. The extended *glosses* of a single jurist created a cohesive commentary on specific legal topics, leading to the formation of comprehensive collections or apparatuses of *glosses* addressing individual sections or the entirety of Justinian's codification. Utilizing the scholastic reasoning pattern, the Bolognese jurists aimed to reveal the conceptual and logical foundations of various passages and determine the consistency and validity of the underlying legal principles. They began by comparing different passages from Justinian's work on similar issues, resolving inconsistencies, and harmonizing contradictory statements.[45] These processes reflected the medieval *trivium* curriculum progression from grammar and rhetoric to logic or dialectic—first understanding Justinian's works with explanatory notes, then establishing text consistency through dialectical methods. Logic, the cornerstone of medieval education, was based on works like Aristotle's *Organon* and became the dominant technique of medieval scholasticism.[46]

Apart from *glosses*, several other types of juristic literature were developed, partly stemming from the teaching of the *Corpus Iuris Civilis* at law schools. Some works address issues in the order they appear in Justinian's legislation (*ordo legum*), such as the *commenta* or *lecturae*, reports written by assistants or experienced students, sometimes revised by the teacher.[47] Another form of literature is the written record of a *quaestio disputata*, an exercise where a teacher posed a question, either theoretical or derived from legal practice, and students offered opposing views. This

as the *Libri Feudorum* (detailing the fundamental institutions of feudal law), various constitutions of the emperors of the Holy Roman Empire, and the Peace Treaty of Constance (1183). Collectively, these five volumes came to be known as the *Corpus Iuris Civilis*.

[44] These notes were written either in the space between the lines of the original text (*glossae interlineares*) or in the margin of the text (*glossae marginales*).

[45] This method was by no means new; it had been relied upon by earlier medieval scholars and was similar to that used by the jurists of the law schools of Constantinople and Beirut during the later Roman imperial era.

[46] Scholasticism as a system of philosophy was based on the belief that reality exists in the world of abstract ideas, generally independent of the external sensual world. Its chief assumption was that truth is discoverable if pursued according to the norms of formal logic. From this point of view, the only path to wisdom was the avoidance of logical fallacies rather than observation of commonplace nature. The formal logic that was applied was largely based on the work *Sic et Non* ('Yes and No') of the French philosopher Peter Abelard (1079–1142), composed around 1120. In this work Abelard applies the principles of logic, as laid down by Aristotle, to texts of the Church Fathers. The relevant texts are grouped by reference to their similarity (*similia*) or contrariety (*contraria*) and reasoning *per analogiam* or *a contrario* is applied, while distinctions (*distinctiones*) are introduced to explain the differences between the texts. This so-called scholastic method, which could be applied to any authoritative text, whether in the field of theology, philosophy, medicine, or law, prevailed throughout the Middle Ages and remained influential even after the end of this period.

[47] The *commentum* was rather condensed, whilst the *lectura* was a full report on the lecture that included all that was said and done in the lecture hall.

exercise aimed to teach students to analyze legal problems and argue their cases logically and in a structured way. A further type of commentary, which did not originate in the classroom, is the *summa*. The *summae* are synopses or summaries of particular parts or the entirety of Justinian's work.[48] Unlike the *commenta* or *lecturae*, these systematic works do not follow the order of issues in the original texts but establish their own order concerning the fragments within the title they treat.

Other forms of juristic literature included works clarifying conceptual distinctions arising from the texts (*distinctiones*), which involved a series of divisions of a general concept into subcategories that were carefully defined and explained until all the implications of the concept were elucidated; collections of conflicting juristic interpretations (*dissensiones dominorum*—the term *domini* referred to medieval jurists); anthologies of opinions on various legal questions connected with actual cases (*consilia*); cases constructed to exemplify or illustrate difficult points of law (*casus*); collections of noteworthy points (*notabilia*); statements of broad legal principles drawn from the texts (*brocarda* or *aphorismata*); and short monographs or treatises (*summulae* or *tractatus*) on specific legal topics, such as the law of actions and legal procedure.[49]

Among the successors of Irnerius, the most notable were Bulgarus, Martinus Gosia, Jacobus, Ugo (renowned as the 'four doctors of Bologna'), Azo, Rogerius, Placentinus, Vacarius, John Bassianus, Odofredus, and Accursius. Azo became famous for his influential work on Justinian's Code, known as the *Summa Codicis* or *Summa Aurea*.[50] In the late twelfth century, Rogerius, probably in collaboration with Placentinus, founded a law school at Montpellier in France, which became an important center of legal learning. Vacarius, a Lombard, traveled to England around the mid-twelfth century and began teaching civil law at Oxford. In 1149, he composed his famous *Liber pauperum*, a collection of texts from the Code and the Digest of Justinian accompanied by explanatory notes. The aim of this work was to introduce the Roman law of Justinian to poorer students in England.[51] The greatest of the late Glossators was the Florentine Franciscus Accursius, a student of Azo, who dominated the law school of Bologna during the first half of the thirteenth century. Accursius produced the renowned *Glossa Ordinaria* or *Magna Glossa*, an extensive collection (*apparatus*) of *glosses* from earlier jurists covering the entire Justinianic codification and supplemented by his own annotations. The *Glossa*

[48] The *summae* were similar to the *indices* composed by the jurists of the law schools in the East during the late imperial era.

[49] Of particular importance were works dealing with the law of procedure (*ordines iudiciarii*). Since the *Corpus Iuris Civilis* does not contain a comprehensive section on the law of procedure, these works sought to record and compile all the relevant material on legal procedure in general and on specific actions, and to provide guidance on how to initiate a legal claim. One of the best-known works of this kind is the *Speculum iudiciale* of Wilhelmus Durantis (c. 1270).

[50] The importance of Azo's *Summa Codicis* was reflected in the popular saying: '*Chi non ha Azo, non vada a palazzo*', which means that in some places a man could not be admitted as an advocate unless he possessed a copy of Azo's *Summa*.

[51] See De Zulueta (1927).

Ordinaria summarized and rendered obsolete the vast body of glossatorial writings from preceding generations of jurists. It represented the culmination of the Glossators' work and quickly gained acceptance in Italy and other parts of Europe as the standard commentary on Justinian's texts, providing essential guidance for those engaged in the teaching and practice of law.[52] The *Glossa Ordinaria* was regularly published alongside editions of the *Corpus Iuris Civilis*, ensuring their joint reception throughout the Continent. With the publication of Accursius's Great Gloss, the School of the Glossators' contributions to the revival of Roman law ceased, though their methods continued to be applied in the teaching of law at Bologna and elsewhere for many years.

The Glossators' approach to Roman law is characterized by a notable lack of historical perspective. They showed little regard for the fact that Justinian's codification had been compiled over five hundred years earlier or that it comprised extracts from even more ancient sources. Instead, they viewed the *Corpus Iuris Civilis* as an authoritative and self-contained statement of the law, paying scant attention to the considerable differences between the laws in Justinian's codification and the legal system in force during their time. This perspective was bolstered by their support for the theory that the Holy Roman Empire was the successor to the ancient Roman Empire.[53] Additionally, their primary interest in law was academic rather than practical. As true medieval scholars, the Glossators revered Justinian's texts in much the same way that theologians revered the Bible or contemporary scholars viewed Aristotle's works. Just as Aristotle was considered infallible and universally applicable, the Glossators treated Justinian's texts as sacred and the ultimate repository of legal wisdom.

The Glossators have been criticized for neglecting the developing canon law and the statutory law enacted by local political bodies, particularly in the Italian city-states. They were entirely preoccupied with the study of Roman law, which they saw as a more fully developed system of legislation compared to the nascent canon law or contemporary statutory law. Despite this, the Glossators succeeded in reviving genuine familiarity with the entirety of Justinian's codification. Their work laid the groundwork for the practical application of the legal doctrines it contained. Their new insights into Roman law catalysed the development of a true science of law, which had a lasting influence on legal thinking and practice in subsequent centuries.[54]

---

[52] The importance of Accursius's gloss was manifested in the popular saying: '*Quod non adgnovit glossa, non adgnoscit curia*', which means that a rule unknown to the *Glossa Ordinaria* was also not recognized by a court.

[53] This is evidenced by the fact that the Glossators added to the *Codex* constitutions of the German Emperors Frederick Barbarossa and Frederick II.

[54] For more on the school of the Glossators see Robinson et al. (1994), p. 42 ff; Vinogradoff (1929/2001), p. 32 ff; Clarence Smith (1975); Tamm (1997), pp. 203–206; Stein (1999), p. 45 ff; Cortese (1992); Lange (1997); Schlosser (2005), pp. 36–53; Mather (2002).

7.5.2 The Commentators

By the end of the thirteenth century, the jurists' focus had shifted from the purely dialectical analysis of Justinian's texts to addressing issues arising from the application of customary and statute law, as well as conflicts of law emerging from intercity commerce. As the enthusiasm for studying ancient texts, which had drawn many students and scholars to Bologna in the twelfth century, waned, the Glossators were succeeded by a new type of jurist known as the Post-glossators (*post-glossatores*) or Commentators (*commentatores*). This new school, with principal centres at the universities of Pavia, Perugia, Padua, and Pisa, reached its peak in the fourteenth century and remained influential until the sixteenth century.

The rise of the Commentators' school was closely linked to the political and intellectual changes that emerged in the late thirteenth century. Of particular importance was the gradual erosion of the traditional dualism of a universal Church and a universal Empire due to crises affecting both institutions. Concurrently, the growing strength of kingdoms and city-states in Europe allowed these entities to develop their political structures with minimal interference from higher universal authorities. During this period, scholastic philosophy reached its zenith with the work of the Catholic theologian Thomas Aquinas (1225–1274), who synthesized Aristotelian philosophy and Christian theology into a comprehensive philosophical and theological system. This new dialectic extended beyond theological and metaphysical speculation, significantly influencing the study of both public and private law.

Unlike the Glossators, the Commentators were not solely concerned with the literal reading and exegesis of Justinian's texts. Instead, they aimed to construct a comprehensive legal system by adapting Roman law to contemporary needs and conditions. At that time in Italy, the positive law that applied was a blend of Roman law, Germanic customary law, canon law, and the statutory laws of the empire and various self-governing cities. The Commentators endeavoured to integrate these diverse bodies of law into a coherent and unitary system. In executing this task, they moved away from the excessive literalism of the Glossators, focusing on elucidating the general principles of law through rational inquiry and speculative dialectics. This approach allowed them to build an analytic framework, or 'dogmatic construction', of the law.

In their roles as legal consultants and administrators, the Commentators significantly contributed to the development of case law, which in turn provided fertile ground for the refinement and testing of their concepts and analytical tools. Many of their theoretical propositions and dogmatic constructions emerged from the practical pressures of actual cases. However, since the Commentators were primarily focused on the development of contemporary law, they paid less attention to the primary sources of Roman law. The synthesis they achieved was between the non-Roman elements and the Roman law of Justinian as expounded by the Glossators. Systematic treatises and commentaries were written based on this body of law, particularly in areas where new legal principles were needed for practical application.[55]

Among the earliest Commentators was Cino of Pistoia (1270–1336), a student of the French masters Jacques de Revigny and Pierre de Belleperche, who were professors at the Orleans law school in the second half of the thirteenth century. Cino began his teaching career at Siena, following approximately ten years of legal practice, and moved to Perugia in 1326. There, he composed his monumental commentary, the *Lectura super Codice*, which continued to be read and cited for more than a century. Cino's method consisted of several successive stages: (a) the literal rendition of a legislative text (*lectio literae*); (b) the subdivision of the text into its component provisions (*divisio legis*); (c) a summary of the content of the text (*expositio*); (d) examples of practical cases to which the text was relevant (*positio casuum*); (e) significant observations derived from the law (*collectio notabilium*); (f) possible counterarguments (*oppositiones*); and (g) an exposition of potential problems that might arise (*quaestiones*). By applying this method, Cino aimed to subject a legislative enactment to a dialectical process and systematic analysis that would elucidate the rationale behind the law, while being aware that the pursuit of logic could sometimes lead to arguments irrelevant to the law's actual application. At Perugia, Cino taught Bartolus of Saxoferrato, who would become the most influential of the Commentators and one of the greatest jurists of all time.

Bartolus (1314–1357) earned his doctorate at the University of Bologna and later lectured at the universities of Perugia and Pisa, where he also served as a judge. He produced a monumental commentary on the entire *Corpus Iuris Civilis*, which, like Accursius's Great Gloss, was recognized as an authoritative work and widely used by legal practitioners and jurists throughout Western Europe. In addition to his commentaries, Bartolus dictated numerous legal opinions and authored a large number of monographs on diverse subjects. His reputation among his contemporaries was unparalleled, and his writings dominated the universities and courts for centuries. In Italy, under the doctrine of *communis opinio doctorum* (whereby the solution supported by the majority of juristic authorities should be upheld by the courts), Bartolus's opinions were deemed to possess the same weight as the Law of Citations accorded to the works of Papinian.[56] In Portugal, his writings were declared to have the force of law in 1446. Moreover, lectures on his work were established at the University of Padua in 1544 and at the University of Ferrara in 1613. The extent of Bartolus's influence is encapsulated in the saying '*nemo jurista nisi Bartolista*', which means 'no one can be a jurist unless they are a follower of Bartolus'.

---

[55] The increased attention to the needs of legal practice is evidenced in the development of the *quaestio disputata*: from the middle of the thirteenth century onwards, jurists increasingly based their *quaestiones* on local statute law or even local custom, which were then analysed using the methods of civil law.

[56] The Roman emperors Theodosius II (Eastern emperor, AD 408–450) and Valentinian III (Western emperor, AD 423–455) introduced the Law of Citations in AD 426. This law mandated that the writings of the jurists Gaius, Papinianus, Paulus, Ulpianus, and Modestinus were to be considered the primary authorities in legal matters and the only sources that could be cited in lawsuits.

Another influential jurist of this period was Baldus de Ubaldis (*c.* 1327–1400), a pupil of Bartolus. Baldus taught at Bologna, Perugia, and Pavia and was deeply involved in public life. Unlike Bartolus, he was both a canonist and a feudalist, in addition to being a civilian.[57] He was best known for his opinions (*consilia*), which proposed solutions for problems arising from actual cases, particularly those involving conflicts between Roman law and local laws and customs. The *consilium*, advice given by a law professor on a practical problem, evolved as the most important form of legal literature during this period, as judges were often obliged to obtain such advice before delivering their decision. In the *consilia*, problems arising from the interplay between diverse sources of law (local statutes, customs, etc) were addressed using the Roman law jurists' techniques of interpretation and argumentation.

The Commentators demonstrated remarkable flexibility in their interpretation and application of Roman texts, often using these texts to address contemporary issues regardless of their original context. They were willing to apply a text to a current issue, even if they recognized that its real meaning had become obsolete, as long as it could prove useful. However, when they derived arguments from materials that had little or no relation to current affairs, they were not recklessly distorting Roman law to fit their needs. Instead, they were consciously adopting its principles to develop new ideas. This approach partly stemmed from a belief that it was important to support a conclusion by referencing authoritative texts, even if the conclusion was reasonable on its own. The reconciliation of scholarly Roman law with local law achieved though the work of the Commentators resulted in what is known as 'statute theory'. This theory posits that, in legal practice, local statutes were the primary source of law, while Roman and canon law were supplementary. However, despite the primacy of statutory law, Roman law-based civil law could prevail in various ways. Firstly, a statute might explicitly incorporate elements of Roman law, thereby granting Roman law shared primary authority. Secondly, a statute might include technical terms or concepts derived from Roman law, which would almost invariably be interpreted according to civilian legal principles. This is particularly true given the accepted notion that statutory enactments should be interpreted with minimal deviation from civil law. Even when a statute required strict textual interpretation, it was often possible to argue for a declaratory interpretation in light of other available legal sources.

The Commentators succeeded both in adapting Roman law to the needs of their own time and in providing contemporary law with a scientific foundation through the theoretical elaboration of Roman legal concepts and principles.[58] Their

---

[57] Baldus's work includes commentaries on the Decretals of Gregory IX and the *Libri Feudorum*. It should be noted that during the time of Baldus, there was a closer connection between civil law and canon law. It was customary for a student to engage in the study of both subjects and thus become a doctor of both laws (*doctor utriusque iuris*).

[58] In the words of the German jurist Paul Koschaker, "[the Commentators] drew from the treasures of Roman wisdom and legal technique that could be used at the time and made of it a basic part of the law of their time, thus preparing the unification of Italy in the field of private law; they in addi-

contributions were particularly significant in the development of criminal law, commercial law, procedural rules, and the theory of conflict of laws. Notably, the Commentators constructed a legal science and a general theory of criminal responsibility based on Roman criminal law texts. They advanced commercial law in areas such as negotiable instruments and partnerships, articulated the concepts and principles of international private law, and devised the detailed rules of Romano-canonical procedure grounded in the Roman *cognitio* process. Additionally, they formulated doctrines of legal personality for entities other than humans and gave substance to the notion of third-party rights in transactions and the law of agency. The work of the Commentators played a major role in the creation of the *ius commune* and facilitated the reception of Roman law throughout Western Europe in the fifteenth and sixteenth centuries.[59]

7.6 The Reception of Roman Law

The thousands of students from all over Europe who studied at Bologna and other Italian universities brought back the new legal learning based on the revived Roman law to their home countries. Throughout Western Europe, including France, Spain, the Netherlands, Germany, and Poland, universities were established where scholars trained in the methods of the Glossators and Commentators taught civil law using Justinian's texts. Their students formed a new class of professional lawyers who came to occupy significant positions in both the administrative and judicial branches of government. Before the twelfth century, justice was administered by untrained jurors relying on local legal sources. In contrast, justice was now administered by professional judges who applied Roman law when local sources, either customary or statutory, were insufficient. The activities of university-trained judges and jurists facilitated the integration of Roman law, as expounded by the Glossators and Commentators, into the legal life of Continental Europe. This integration led to the development of a common body of law, a common legal language, and a common legal science, a process known as the 'Reception' of Roman law.

The received Roman law, much like the Latin language and the universal Church, acted as a crucial universalizing factor in the West during a period devoid of centralized states and unified legal systems. Instead, this era was characterized by a plethora of overlapping and often competing jurisdictions, including local, feudal, ecclesiastical, mercantile, and royal authorities. The reception of Roman law, however, was complex and marked by significant variation. This complexity stemmed from the diverse local conditions across Europe and, as a result, the actual degree of

tion made of Roman law the substratum of a legal science, which was later to become European legal science." Koschaker (1953), p. 93.

[59] For more on the school of the Commentators see Robinson et al. (1994), p. 59 ff; Stein (1999), pp. 71–74; Tamm (1997), pp. 206–208; Wieacker (1995); Horn (1973); Lange and Kriechbaum (2007).

Roman law's infiltration varied from region to region. In Southern Europe, where Roman law had already been woven into customary law, the reception process can be described as a resurgence, refinement, and enlargement of Roman principles. This was particularly evident in Italy, where Roman law's influence remained strong, and in Southern France, where customary law was heavily Romanized. Conversely, in Northern Europe, Roman law had largely faded, resulting in a prolonged reception process with a more profound impact in some regions during its later stages. The common law (*ius commune*) of Europe that gradually emerged towards the end of the Middle Ages was largely the product of a fusion between the Roman law of Justinian (as elaborated by medieval scholars), the canon law of the Church, and Germanic customary law. Roman law was the dominant element in this mixture, although it underwent significant changes due to the influence of local customs and statutory and canon law.

The universal *ius commune* was juxtaposed with the *ius proprium*, the local laws of the diverse medieval city-states and other political entities. Local law sometimes assumed the form of statute or, especially in earlier times, grew out of custom.[60] However, the universal and local laws were not necessarily antithetical; they were complementary and each interacted with and influenced the other. Statutory enactments born out of the need to address situations not provided for by the *ius commune* were often formulated and interpreted according to the concepts developed by scholars of the *ius commune*. These scholars, concerned with concrete problems of social and commercial life and the need to deal with the law as it actually existed, took local law into consideration. In their roles as judges, lawyers, and officials, jurists trained in Roman law at the law schools regarded local law as an exception to the *ius commune*, thus requiring restrictive interpretation. Furthermore, they tended to interpret local law using concepts and terminology derived from Roman law, thereby harmonizing it with the *ius commune*.[61]

---

[60] The first compilations of city customary law appeared in the second half of the twelfth century in Venice and Bari. These collections were subsequently superseded by statutory enactments, i.e., legislation issued by a local legislative body. An enactment of this kind (*statutum*) was distinguished from a law of theoretical universal application (*lex*), which could be promulgated only by the emperor. In principle, a *statutum* was subordinate and could only supplement but not alter or derogate from a *lex*. In fact, however, local statutes that were irreconcilable with imperial laws often prevailed in the legal practice of the area or city in which they had been enacted. An example of legislation issued by a monarch is the *Liber Constitutionum Regni Siciliae*, also known as *Liber Augustalis*, a legal code for the Kingdom of Sicily promulgated by Emperor Frederick II in 1231. This code remained the principal body of law in the Southern Kingdom until the eighteenth century. Royal legislation was also enacted in the County (later Duchy) of Savoy, the provinces of Sardinia, the Patriarchate of Aquileia, and many other areas. In the domains of the Church, the most important legislative enactment was the *Constitutiones Sanctae Matris Ecclesiae*, also informally known as *Constitutiones Aegidianae*, issued in 1357 by Cardinal Gil of Albornoz, the legate to the papal state during Pope's residence in Avignon.

[61] Even in parts of Europe where Roman law was not received in a normative sense, the conceptual structure created by the Glossators and the Commentators was sometimes employed to give a Roman form to indigenous customary rules. Thus, although the *ius commune* was not adopted in Norway and Hungary, local legislation exhibited a certain Roman influence. For example, the

7.6.1 The Reception of Roman Law in France

Between the sixth and ninth centuries, three bodies of law applied in France: under the system of the personality of laws, the Germanic segments of the population were governed by their own laws and customs, while the Roman inhabitants of the country continued to live according to Roman law. At the same time, everyone in France, regardless of ethnic origin, was bound by the laws promulgated by the Frankish monarchs. In the ninth century, the personal system of laws began to disintegrate, as the blending of different populations made its application nearly impossible, and it was gradually replaced by a territorial system. The transition from the personality-based system to territoriality coincided with the expansion and consolidation of feudal institutions in France. Under this new system, each feudal lord's territory was governed by its own customs, although the customary law in any given area generally reflected the predominant ethnic group. As a result, France came to be divided into two broad regions: the country of the written law (*Pays du Droit écrit*) in the South, where Roman law—preserved in sources like the *Lex Romana Visigothorum* and later editions of the *Corpus iuris civilis*—prevailed; and the country of customary law (*Pays des Coutumes* or *droit coutumier*) in the North, characterized by local customs of a Frankish-Germanic nature. In both regions, the legal systems included elements derived from royal, feudal, and canonical sources.

In the south of France, a region characterized by written law, the common law was essentially rooted in Roman law (despite some local variations). The Roman law of Justinian was swiftly adopted in Southern France, becoming the prevailing legal system. This favourable adoption was facilitated by the revival of Roman law during the late eleventh and twelfth centuries and its dissemination from Bologna to Montpellier and other parts of France. In the early twelfth century, a summary of Justinian's Code, known as *Lo Codi*, was produced in southern France, influenced by the work of the Glossators. The study of Roman law gained renewed momentum with the establishment of new law schools in Toulouse and Orléans in the thirteenth century. In these and other schools that subsequently emerged, civil law was taught based on Justinian's texts.[62]

Norwegian Code of 1274 of King Magnus VI, while intended to be a written statement of ancient Viking custom, reflects the influence of Roman-canonical law in its organization and many of its institutions. Similarly, in Hungary, the spirit of Roman law influenced the structure of Hungarian law and the character and development of legal thought. In areas as far off as the Ukraine and Belarus, where there was no reception, doctrines and practices of Roman law were introduced through the influence of Byzantine law.

[62] The *Ultramontani*, as the jurists at Toulouse, Orléans, and Montpellier were referred to, employed essentially the same methods and produced similar types of legal works as their Italian counterparts in Bologna. The first professors at these universities were Frenchmen who had studied at Bologna, although later there were some, such as Jacques de Revigny and Pierre de Belleperche (both of whom taught at Orléans), who had received their training in France. These later jurists showed greater interest in legal theory than the Italian Glossators and adopted a more historical and liberal approach to studying Roman legal sources. Furthermore, they made significant contributions to non-Roman areas of law, including penal law and private international law.

In the northern regions of France, the country of customary law, a variety of Germanic customs were observed. Some of these customs applied broadly across regions (*coutumes générales*), while others were restricted to specific towns or localities (*coutumes locales*). In total, there were sixty general customs and three hundred special or local customs. In this part of France, Roman law was considered a supplementary system, applied when customary law was silent or ambiguous. Additionally, in certain areas of law, such as contract law and obligations, the Roman system had been adopted and was regarded as superior to customary law, offering a better framework for addressing the new issues arising from expanding economic activity.

The administration of justice fell under the jurisdiction of regional judicial and legislative bodies known as Parliaments (*Parlements*). In areas governed by customary law, the case law established by the Parliament in Paris held particular significance. Advocates associated with this body advanced legal development through intensive literary activity, focusing primarily on the study of case law. Over time, the works of Parisian advocates formed the foundation of an extensive body of jurisprudence, developed through the comparative study of diverse local customs, which also incorporated elements of the great tradition of Roman law in France.

From the beginning of the thirteenth century, the customs of many regions in Northern France began to be documented. Several collections of customary law emerged, written in the vernacular but modelled after Roman law compilations. Some of these works, such as the *Les Livres de Jostice et de Plet* (The Books of Justice and Pleading), composed around 1260, reflect a strong influence of Roman law. In other works, such as the *Coutumes de Beauvaisis* (the customs of the county of Clermont in Beauvaisis), written in the late thirteenth century, the impact of Roman law is much less noticeable. Additionally, some of these compilations were privately produced, while others were issued under the authority of various feudal lords (*chartes de coutumes*). Generally, the purpose of these works was to compile and present clearly the rules of customary law applicable in specific regions, making it easier to prove these rules in courts of law.

To reduce the confusion caused by the multiplicity of customs, King Charles VII ordered the compilation of customs from all regions of France in his Ordinance of Montils-les-Tours in 1453. Although the directive proved largely ineffectual, it was reiterated by subsequent monarchs, and by the end of the sixteenth century, most customary law had been committed to writing. This consolidation of customary law through official publication precluded the wholesale reception of Roman law in Northern France, although elements of Roman legal doctrine entered the fixed body of customary law through interpretation. Additionally, Roman law continued to apply in areas of private law not addressed by customary law. This interaction of Roman and customary sources gave the law that prevailed in Northern France a distinctive character.

Although the publication of the customs helped alleviate much of the confusion caused by local differences, it did not achieve complete legal unity. Significant regional diversity persisted, not only between Northern and Southern France but also within each of these main territorial divisions. Legal unity in France was ultimately established with the introduction of the Napoleonic Civil Code in 1804. In the century and a half leading up to the enactment of the Civil Code, the academic study of Roman law reached its peak – a development closely associated with the writings of jurists like Jean Domat (1625-1695)[63] and Robert Joseph Pothier (1699–1772).[64]

7.6.2 *The Reception of Roman Law in Germany*

During the early Middle Ages, the law that applied in Germany was customary law, which varied regionally due to the shift from the system based on the personality of laws to the one focused on territoriality. Some customs were applicable across entire regions, while others were specific to individual cities, village communities, or manors. Following the establishment of the Holy Roman Empire of the German Nation in the tenth century, imperial law—focused primarily on constitutional matters—served as an additional source of legal authority. Although the German emperors considered themselves successors to the Roman emperors, and imperial legislation was influenced by the idea of a universal empire, there was initially no attempt to make Roman law universally applicable across German regions as a replacement for local customs. In the twelfth and thirteenth centuries, Germans who had studied at law schools in Italy and France introduced Roman law knowledge to Germany. However, the impact of this on local customary laws was limited, as Roman law scholars largely dismissed the local laws, viewing them as primitive in both form and substance and unworthy of serious scholarly attention.

In the thirteenth and fourteenth centuries, several compilations emerged that embodied the customary laws practiced in various regions of Germany. The most significant of these works were the *Sachsenspiegel*, or *Mirror of the Saxons*, composed around 1225 by Eike von Repgow, which contained the territorial customary

[63] Domat's best-known work is *Les loix civiles dans leur ordre naturel*, published in three volumes between 1689 and 1694. After a thorough examination of the entire body of recorded legal material (*droit écrit*) from his region, Auvergne, Domat concluded that it exhibited an internal logic and rationality suggesting the existence of universal or immutable legal principles (*loix immuables*). He observed that these natural principles were most clearly reflected in the norms of private law; public law, by contrast, was composed to a much greater extent of statutory laws that were changeable or arbitrary in nature (*loix arbitraires*). Domat argued that the general principles of Roman law, as codified in Justinian's compilation, met the standards of the *loix immuables* and could be recognized as a coherent system. Furthermore, he claimed that contemporary French was capable of articulating this system with clarity and precision. For a closer look at Domat's work see Sarzotti (1995).

[64] Pothier's major works included *La coutume d'Orléans avec des observations nouvelles* (1740), primarily focused on the customary law of his hometown, and a comprehensive treatise on Roman private law titled *Pandectae Justinianeae in novum ordinem digestae cum legibus codicis et novellis* (1748–1752). See Chap. 2 above.

law observed in parts of Northern Germany;[65] the *Deutschenspiegel*, or *Mirror of the Germans*, published around 1260 in Southern Germany; and the *Schwabenspiegel*, or *Mirror of the Swabians*, a collection of Swabian customs published in the late thirteenth century.[66] These works aimed to lay the foundation for a unified customary law for Germany. However, strong centrifugal forces prevented this unification. The creation of a common law for all of Germany based on Germanic traditions was thwarted by the weakened imperial power, which was further eroded by the political fragmentation of the empire in the late thirteenth century, as well as by the wide variety of local customs. Another barrier to legal unity was the absence of an organized professional class of lawyers committed to developing a cohesive body of law. Legal administration was managed by lay judges, or *schoffen*, who were responsible for identifying the applicable law in each case based on the local customs of each district. Yet, the rulings of the *schoffen* often addressed only specific cases and reflected the personal interpretations of lay judges who were not necessarily guided by consistent rules or principles, thereby contributing to the uncertainty surrounding customary law.

In the fifteenth century, the problems arising from the fragmented legal landscape in Germany became intolerable as commercial transactions increased across various territories. Local customs could no longer accommodate the needs of a rapidly evolving society, and the weakness of the imperial government made unification of customary law through legislation alone unfeasible. Since a common body of law could not be developed from Germanic sources, an alternative system was readily available—Roman law. The acceptance of Roman law in Germany was facilitated by the belief that the Holy Roman Empire of the German Nation was a continuation of the ancient Roman Empire.[67] Thus, Roman law was not seen as a foreign legal system but as a body of law that continued to apply within the empire as its common law. This notion was reinforced by the newly established German universities, where legal education was based exclusively on Roman and canon law,[68] while Germanic customary law was largely overlooked. Like jurists in other countries, German jurists regarded Roman law as superior to native law, recognizing it as valid both as written law (*ius scriptum*) due to the imperial tradition and as written reason (*ratio scripta*) for its inherent value.

At a practical level, the reception of Roman law in Germany was facilitated by the establishment of the Imperial Chamber Court (*Reichskammergericht*) in 1495, through a legislative act of Emperor Maximilian I (1493–1519). This act focused on centralizing the German judicial administration system and was part of Maximilian's broader political agenda to restore monarchical power and secure legal and political

---

[65] The *Sachsenspiegel*, a work of outstanding quality, achieved great prestige and authority throughout Germany. Modern commentators regard it as the beginning of Germanic legal literature.

[66] Both the Mirror of the Germans and the Mirror of the Swabians reflect some influence of Roman law.

[67] The Emperor of the Holy Roman Empire was at the same time king of Germany and of Italy.

[68] The methods of study and the legal materials used were substantially the same as those employed in Italian universities.

unity. The new imperial court, which heard appeals from regional and local courts, was instructed to decide cases according to the imperial and common law, and also according to just, equitable, and reasonable ordinances and customs. Since *doctores iuris* (jurists trained in Roman law) dominated the court's composition, the term 'common law' naturally came to be interpreted as Roman law.

The significance of the 1495 legislation was that it formally recognized Roman law as positive law in Germany. Under this law, judges were required to apply Roman law only when a relevant custom or statutory provision could not be proven. In practice, however, the difficulty in proving an overriding German rule often meant that Roman law effectively became the foundational law across Germany. The model of the Imperial Chamber Court was subsequently adopted by territorial courts of appeal established by local princes in Austria, Saxony, Bavaria, Brandenburg, and other German states. Simultaneously, courts where lay judges presided increasingly relied on the guidance of learned jurists (such as city advocates, state officials, and university professors) for information on both local and Roman law. Over time, the role of lay judges diminished, and the administration of justice became dominated by professional lawyers trained in Roman and canon law at universities.

By the end of the sixteenth century, it had become common practice for judges to seek advice from university professors on complex legal questions arising from actual cases. The opinions rendered were regarded as binding on the court that had requested them. This practice, known as *Aktenversendung*, continued until the nineteenth century, leading to the accumulation of an extensive body of legal doctrine that applied throughout Germany.

By the beginning of the seventeenth century, Roman law had become firmly established as the common law of Germany.[69] Germanic law had largely been set aside in favour of the more advanced Roman system, and German jurisprudence had essentially become Roman jurisprudence. The received Roman law encompassed the Roman law of Justinian, as interpreted and modified by the Glossators and the Commentators. This body of law was further adapted by German jurists to fit contemporary conditions, introducing a Germanic element into what remained a fundamentally Roman structure. In certain regions of Germany, such as Saxony, Germanic customary law persisted, and some institutions of Germanic origin were retained in local princely and municipal legislation. From the sixteenth to the eighteenth century, legal practitioners and jurists undertook the process of merging Roman and Germanic law into a unified system. This process led to the development of a new approach to the analysis and interpretation of Justinianic Roman law, known as *Usus modernus Pandectarum* ('modern application of the Pandects/Digest').[70] This

[69] German scholars use the phrase *Rezeption in complexu*, meaning 'complete reception,' to describe this development.

[70] Although this approach appears externally to be a continuation of the Bartolist method, under the influence of Legal Humanism (see relevant discussion below), it led to a different doctrine concerning the sources of law. While Roman law continued to be regarded as a significant source of law, local law was no longer viewed as an aberration from Roman law but rather as a further devel-

approach continued to be followed in Germany, subject to regional variations, until the introduction of the German Civil Code in 1900.

7.6.3 *The Ius Commune in Italy, the Iberian Peninsula and the Netherlands*

By the close of the fifteenth century, the medieval world of the Italian city-states had evolved into distinct territories: the Kingdom of Naples in the south, the Papal States and Tuscany in central Italy, Piedmont, Lombardy under Milan, the Republic of Venice, and several smaller states.[71] The Kingdom of Naples had developed into a centralized state with a court hierarchy more akin to those of France or Spain than to the rest of Italy. Despite Italy's continued political fragmentation, the application of civil law and court proceedings remained unified, retaining the traditional blend of Roman law as interpreted by the Glossators and Commentators, canonical procedures, and both general and particular customs. The influential medieval treatises of Bartolus and Baldus, in particular, continued to hold great esteem.

The legal literature that emerged from university towns like Bologna, Padua, Pavia, and Naples, while often addressing local concerns, became part of the broader European *ius commune*—a spread facilitated by the invention of the printing press in the late fifteenth century. Italian scholars of the late fifteenth and early sixteenth centuries, such as Giasone del Maino (1435–1519) and Filippo Decio (1454–c. 1535), sought to integrate the tradition of the *ius commune* with the ideals of the new humanist learning.

Following Italy's integration into the Napoleonic state, the French Civil Code was introduced in the country (1806). Although the *ius commune* persisted even after the Italian states were restored following Napoleon's defeat in 1815, an increasing number of states began to establish their own law codes (the so-called *codici preunitari*). The earliest of these, the codes of the Kingdom of Naples (1819) and the Duchy of Parma (1820), were closely modelled on the French Civil Code,

opment of Roman law through custom. Consequently, the *Usus modernus Pandectarum* elevated the importance of local law, which now became the focus of systematic scientific study. Regarding Roman law, the term *Usus modernus Pandectarum* implies that the jurists' intent was to apply Roman legal texts within contemporary legal practice. Although representatives of this approach may have been somewhat influenced by Humanist jurists, they tended to use the Roman texts a historically, treating them as yet another source of legal norms. However, there was no consensus among jurists on which texts were applicable. It should be noted that many French and Dutch jurists adopted the methods of the *Usus modernus* movement. Leading representatives of this movement include Samuel Stryk (1640–1710), a professor at Frankfurt a.d. Oder, Wittenberg and Halle; Georg Adam Struve (1619–1692); Ulric Huber (1636–1694); Cornelis van Bynkershoek (1673–1743); Arnoldus Vinnius (1588–1657); Gerard Noodt (1647–1725); and Johannes Voet (1647–1713). On the *Usus modernus Pandectarum* see Wieacker (1995), p. 159 ff; Tamm (1997), p. 225; Schlosser (2005), pp. 76–83; Voppel (1996).

[71] These included Siena, Ferrara and Mantua.

while the later codes of Piedmont (1837) and Modena (1851) represented a distinctive blend of French influences and traditional local elements. In Lombardy and Venice, which had returned to Austrian rule, the Austrian Civil Code (*ABGB*) of 1811 was implemented.[72]

Any consideration of the development of law in Spain must take into account the fluid relationships among the various peoples who settled in the Iberian Peninsula and the changing fortunes of the diverse states that evolved in medieval times. As noted earlier, in the second half of the fifth century, the Germanic tribe of the Visigoths successfully established permanent rule on the Peninsula. During the period that followed, Roman personal law, as embodied in the *Lex Romana Visigothorum*, coexisted with the laws of the Visigoths, who never constituted more than 5% of the total population. Over time, as the two ethnic groups merged, a territorial law—permeated in both substance and form by Roman law—prevailed. This law was embodied in the *corpus iuris* promulgated for all citizens by the Visigothic king Recceswinth around 654. The new law code, referred to as the *Liber Iudiciorum* or *Lex Visigothorum*, remained the basis of law in Spain until the fifteenth century, governing the Christian population even during the prolonged period of Muslim rule beginning in 711. During the era when Christian forces were pushing back those of Islam, a variety of states of differing sizes and significance emerged in the territory of present-day Spain: Castile (later reunited with León), which included Galicia and the Basque region; Aragon; Catalonia; Navarre; and the Balearic Islands.

The legal development of Castile-León deserves special mention due to the important role this kingdom played in the unification of Spain. In this realm, the king exercised supreme jurisdiction as the natural lord of all his subjects. The growing influence of the *alcades de corte*, or royal court, composed of professional judges, diminished the significance of local customs of largely Germanic origin, known as *fueros* or *usus terrae*. Over the course of the thirteenth and fourteenth centuries, men trained in Roman law at universities (known as *letrados*) became increasingly influential, attaining high office in royal service. A large number of students from Spain attended Bologna, a trend that continued even after the establishment of Spain's first universities in Palencia, Salamanca, Seville, and Lleida in the thirteenth century. These institutions disseminated knowledge of Roman law and the methods of the Glossators and Commentators throughout the Iberian Peninsula. The most significant product of this growth in Roman law studies was the famous *Libro de las leyes*, commonly called *Las Siete Partidas* ('The Seven Parts of the Law'), compiled by order of King Alfonso X the Learned between 1256 and 1265. Drafted largely by jurists from the University of Salamanca, this work contains numerous legal rules on marriage, contracts, inheritance, and procedure, derived from a variety of Roman and canonical sources.[73] The enforcement of *Las*

[72] The *ABGB* combined natural law ideas, especially in the fields of the law of persons and family law, with Roman law concepts and principles.

[73] These sources included the *Corpus Iuris* of Justinian, the *Decretum* of Gratian, the *Decretales* of Gregory IX, and the works of some of the most famous of the Glossators, especially Azo and Accursius on civil law, and Goffredo of Trani and Raymond of Peñafort on canon law.

Siete Partidas as the common law of Spain was delayed due to opposition from Spanish traditionalists, who remained loyal to their local customs. It was only in 1348, with the *Ordenamiento de Alcalá*—a compilation of laws enacted by the courts of Alfonso XI in Alcalá de Henares—that it was promulgated as general law, though it remained subordinate to local custom. However, as local customs needed to be proven in court as actually observed, while a presumption always favoured *Las Siete Partidas*, this later work gradually became established as the official law of Spain. The concurrent reception of the learned law of the *ius commune* was so extensive that monarchs decreed that courts, when faced with gaps in the law, should rely on the authority of the major Glossators and Commentators.[74] Although *Las Siete Partidas* was reorganized at various times as political conditions evolved, it remained the foundation of Spanish law until it was superseded by the *Código Civil* of 1889.

In neighbouring Portugal, the law initially derived from the *Liber Iudiciorum* of the Visigoths, extended in 1054 by King Alfonso V of León, along with local customs. However, over time, the *ius commune* was also received in Portugal, with the universities of Coimbra and Lisbon emerging as principal centres of legal learning. It is therefore unsurprising that the first comprehensive collection of Portuguese laws, the *Ordenações Afonsinas*, enacted by King Alfonso V in 1446, largely incorporated Roman and canon law. This compilation was succeeded by the *Ordenações Manuelinas*, promulgated by King Manuel in 1521, and finally by the *Ordenações Filipinas* in 1603, during the reign of King Philip II. The *Ordenações Filipinas* remained in force until modern times, not only in Portugal but also in its colonies, such as Brazil. These enactments established the principle that Roman law, along with the works of the Glossators and Commentators, constituted the common law of the realm, applicable whenever local legislation or customs were silent or ambiguous.

In the Netherlands, as in much of Western Europe, the revival of Roman law study and application during the High Middle Ages led to a significant reception of Roman legal norms, concepts, and principles. By the end of the sixteenth century, Dutch law had become heavily Romanized. This shift occurred when Holland's material prosperity was growing considerably, largely due to the expansion of trade and commerce, which created a demand for a more sophisticated legal system to meet new societal needs. Roman legal influence was particularly prominent in the areas of property, contract, and delict law, where Roman law was deemed far superior to indigenous Dutch law. However, in fields such as the law of persons and intestate succession, local customary laws largely resisted the Roman influence. Even within property and contract law, Dutch jurists were selective in adopting Roman rules, often rejecting archaic and overly formal concepts. This process

[74] To avoid confusion, in 1427 John II, King of Castile and León, ordained that the courts should not follow, as authorities, the opinions of jurists later that Johannes Andreae (Giovanni d'Andrea) on canon law and Bartolus on Roman law. Later, by a law of 1499, Baldo was also included.

resulted in a hybrid legal system that combined Roman and Dutch elements, ultimately known as Roman-Dutch law.[75]

The University of Leyden, established in 1575, became the principal centre for Roman legal studies in the Netherlands. Following Leyden, other universities were founded in Franeker, Friesland (1585), Groningen (1614), Utrecht (1636), and Harderwijk, Gelderland (1648). In the seventeenth and eighteenth centuries, Dutch legal development was shaped largely by professors, especially those at Leyden, and by High Court judges across the provinces. Together, they created a highly advanced body of law that synthesized legal science and practical application.[76] In 1652, Roman-Dutch law was introduced to South Africa, where Roman and Dutch texts became authoritative sources for South African law.[77]

7.7 The Humanists and the School of Natural Law

The Renaissance and the Reformation ushered in a broader appreciation of intellectual and cultural achievements, liberating human reason from the constraints of traditional faith and dogma. This new outlook and spirit fostered impatience with the narrow pedantry of the old schools of law. The established doctrine of *communis opinio doctorum*, in its extreme form, impeded the logical development of principles by resolving legal problems through the consensus of legal scholars, essentially counting heads. Consequently, during this period, the law schools of Italy, once renowned throughout Europe, came to be seen as bastions of an outdated theory known as *mos italicus*. The influence of the Renaissance gave rise to a new school

[75] The term 'Roman-Dutch law' was introduced in the seventeenth century by the jurist Simon van Leeuwen, who used it as a title in his principal work, *Roomsch Hollandsch Recht* (1664).

[76] The greatest product of the Leyden law faculty was Hugo Grotius, author of the famous work *De Iure Belli ac Pacis*(1625). Grotius also published *An Introduction to the Jurisprudence of Holland* (*Inleidinge tot de Hollandsche Rechtsgeleerdheid*, 1631), in which he addresses the law of Holland as a unique amalgam of Germanic custom and Roman law. Reference should also be made to Arnold Vinnius (1588–1657), a law professor at Leyden, who established Dutch legal science as a blend of Roman, customary, and natural law elements; Johannes Voet (1647–1714), another Leyden professor and author of the influential *Commentarius ad Pandectas*, published in two volumes in 1698 and 1704; and Ulrich Huber (1636–1694), a professor at the University of Franeker, whose works *De Iure Civitatis Libri Tres* (1672) and *Praellectiones Iuris Civilis* (1678–1690) are constructed largely from Roman sources. The widespread influence of these Dutch masters across Europe is evidenced by the numerous foreign editions of their principal works published in the seventeenth and eighteenth centuries.

[77] It should be noted that, unlike Continental European legal systems but similar to English common law, Roman-Dutch law in South Africa was not codified. Consequently, it is unsurprising that law courts and commentators still grapple with the historical sources of the *ius commune* and its Dutch variant. Special attention is given to seventeenth- and eighteenth-century Dutch authorities such as Grotius, Voet, and Vinnius, although works from the entire body of learned literature—from Bartolus to the German Pandectists, and even Roman law sources—are regularly consulted in areas like property, contract, and succession.

of jurists, the Humanists, who infused legal writing with the spirit of the revival of letters.

As previously noted, the school of the Commentators marked a shift in scholarly focus from the dialectical examination of Justinian's texts to the adaptability of Roman law to the needs and conditions of medieval life. However, in their primary interest in developing contemporary law, the Commentators often disregarded the historical framework and primary sources of Roman law. In the fifteenth century, the rising interest in the cultural inheritance of classical antiquity, fuelled by humanistic scholarship, led to a new approach to the study of Roman law. Scholars began to view Roman law as a historical phenomenon, emphasizing the techniques of history and philology for its proper understanding and interpretation. The methods used by the Commentators to study Justinian's texts had led to theories that, from the Humanists' perspective, were unwarranted when ancient texts were considered in their proper historical context. Consequently, these theories were rejected in favour of interpretations based on the true historical sense of the texts.

The chief aim of Humanist scholars was to rediscover the Roman law as it existed during Roman times by applying the historical method rather than the scholastic method of the medieval Commentators, known as *mos italicus*. A significant part of the Humanists' work involved detecting interpolations in the Justinianic codification, which was crucial in uncovering the true character of classical Roman law. An important innovation by the Humanists was their ability to read Greek texts, unlike the medieval jurists. This skill enabled them to utilize Byzantine legal sources, such as the *Basilica*, to reconstruct the texts of Justinian.[78] The Humanists also aimed to provide a more systematic treatment of the contents of Justinian's *Corpus*. While medieval *summae* and other works had introduced systematic treatment for individual works, the Humanists attempted to present the entire *Corpus Iuris Civilis* as

---

[78] The Legal Humanists were responsible for the beginnings of what is known as *palingenesia*: the reconstruction of legal texts that have been altered by editors after they were first issued. With respect to the works of the classical Roman jurists, *palingenesia* benefited from the fact that every fragment in the Digest is accompanied by an *inscriptio* containing the name of the original author and the title and part of the work from which the fragment was taken. This allowed scholars to separate all the fragments contained in the Digest, sort them by jurist, and then, for each jurist, sort them by work and then by book (e.g., Ulpianus, *libro octavo decimo ad edictum*). This approach was initiated by Jacobus Labittus, a sixteenth century Legal Humanist, in his *Index legum omnium quae in Pandectis continentur* [...], published in 1557. In this work Labittus listed the texts of the Digest according to their authors, the works in which they appeared, and the books of those works from which they were excerpted; other Digest texts that cited that jurist; those jurists who were not themselves excerpted in the Digest but who were referred to by other jurists therein; and, finally, those texts in the Codex and Novels that mentioned specific jurists. However, he did not attempt to restore the original order in the works of individual Roman jurists—this was achieved in the nineteenth century by Lenel, author of the more extensive *Palingenesia iuris civilis*, I-II (1889). It should be noted that, as the compilers of Justinian's *Corpus* retained only about 5 per cent of the available texts, a complete reconstruction of the original works was impossible. Nevertheless, with respect to those jurists whose works were extensively used, it is possible to gain a good impression of the scope and structure of a particular work.

a unified system. The Institutes served as an important model because it was the only part of Justinian's codification that contained a true system.[79]

The new school of thought was initiated in France by the Italian Andreas Alciatus (1492–1550), and its effects resonated throughout Europe.[80] The method adopted by the Humanist scholars in France for the study of Roman law became known as *mos gallicus* (in contrast to the *mos italicus* of the Bolognese jurists), also referred to as *Elegante Jurisprudenz*. However, the Humanist movement had a limited impact on the practice of law, as courts in France and other regions continued to adhere to the Bartolist tradition. This persistence was largely because most Humanists focused primarily on the historical analysis of Roman law and gave little attention to practical legal applications or the adaptation of Roman law to contemporary conditions. Nevertheless, the Humanists' approach, treating Roman law as a historical phenomenon, fostered an appreciation among jurists for the differences between Roman law and the laws of their own time. By highlighting the historical and cultural contexts in which law develops, the Humanists laid the groundwork for the eventual displacement of the *ius commune* and the emergence of national legal systems.[81]

In the seventeenth and eighteenth centuries, European legal thought moved in a new direction under the influence of the School of Natural Law.

The concept of natural law, originating in ancient Greek philosophy, was concretized by the Stoic philosophers during the Hellenistic and Roman eras. Influenced by Stoicism, Roman jurists regarded natural law as a universal body of law observed by all peoples, also referred to as *ius gentium* (law of nations in a theoretical sense). Stoic philosophy provided the terminology that enabled the early Church Fathers to formulate the first conceptions of Christian natural law philosophy and disseminate them to their contemporaries.

Aurelius Augustinus (AD 354–430), a prominent Church Father, advocated for the divine origin of law and developed a theory that significantly bridged ancient

---

[79] In this connection, reference should be made to the French Humanist Franciscus Connanus (François de Connan, 1508–1551), who, in his *Commentaria iuris civilis libri decem*, attempted to re-order legal material in a more rational way under the tripartite division of law into persons, things, and actions derived from the Institutes. Hugues Doneau (Donellus), a sixteenth-century French Humanist, in his *Commentarii de iure civili libri viginti octo* (Frankfurt 1595–1597), departed from the traditional approach to law that gave priority to actions and procedures and regarded the rights of the individual as being of greater importance than the methods by which these rights could be defended. This new approach is clearly reflected in the structure of his work. Moreover, Donellus separated the law of obligations from the law of property, both originally considered to constitute aspects of the law of things. See Garnsey (2007), p. 202; Stein (1993).

[80] The centre of the Humanist School was the University of Bourges in France. Among the most important representatives of this school, which included not only jurists but also historians and philologists, were Jacques Cujas (Cuiacius, 1522–1590), Hugues Doneau (Donellus, 1527–1591), Guillaume Bude (Budaeus, 1467–1540), Ulrich Zasius (1461–1535), Antoine Favre (Faber, 1557–1624), Charles Annibal Fabrot (Fabrotus, 1580–1659) and Jacques Godefroy (Godofredus, 1587–1652).

[81] For more on the influence of the Humanist movement see Stein (1999) p. 75ff; Kelley (1970); Robinson et al. (1994), ch. 10; Gilmore (1963); Wieacker (1995), p. 120 ff; Wolff (1951/1976), p. 209 ff.

philosophy and Christian jurisprudence. Augustinus asserted that the *lex naturalis moralis* (natural moral law) is imprinted on the human soul, heart, and mind. However, he acknowledged the necessity of temporal or human positive laws to reveal what sin and vice had obscured.

Thomas Aquinas (1225–1274), a towering figure in medieval theology, synthesized earlier traditions, particularly Aristotle's philosophy[82] and the theology of the early Church Fathers, including Augustinus. In his seminal work, the *Summa Theologiae*, a manual for theology students, Aquinas defined natural law as man's participation in God's eternal law (God's purpose in creation), discoverable through reason. Unlike other entities in the universe, human beings possess freedom of choice, meaning they do not necessarily act in accordance with the eternal law. Consequently, two sources of guidance are provided: divine law and natural law, operating through revelation (God's will in the Holy Scriptures) and reason, respectively.

Aquinas addressed the issue of disputes over fundamental moral issues or differing understandings of right and wrong by explaining the process through which specific natural law precepts are deduced from general principles. He connected this deduction process to human inclination and the nature of reason itself, emphasizing that reasoning about morality is practical rather than speculative. The fact that practical reason's conclusions are not equally known by everyone does not undermine their truth. Furthermore, applying practical reason to various situations may necessitate exceptions to general principles, leading to variations in natural law over time and place. While the primary precepts of natural law (such as promoting good and avoiding evil) are unchanging, the secondary precepts are variable.

Aquinas defined human law as an ordinance of reason for the common good, made by those responsible for the community. He explained the need for human law due to unequal knowledge of natural law and the distinction between knowledge and conduct—people are free to disobey. Human law, therefore, can help train individuals to act according to natural law. Although Aquinas viewed human law as deduced from natural law, he acknowledged that this deduction process, reliant on practical reason, can lead to multiple valid conclusions. Variations in human laws across societies and history are partly due to differences in secondary natural law precepts and partly because the deduction process allows for a degree of freedom and creativity.

The doctrines of Aquinas dominated the theological, philosophical, and intellectual landscape of Western Europe until the sixteenth century, when Humanism, Protestantism, and the discovery of the New World began to challenge traditional ideas about humanity and its relationship with God and the world. From this period, the natural law discourse began to separate itself from scholastic theology and increasingly employed the language of reason. Of particular importance in this development was the work of Hugo Grotius (1583–1645), a Dutch jurist often

[82] Aquinas was able to draw on recently made translations of the works of Aristotle by Willem van Moerbeke (*c.* 1215- *c.* 1286), which had made available works that had not been in circulation until then.

regarded as the founder of modern international law.[83] In his seminal work, *De iure belli ac pacis* (1625), Grotius presented the idea of a secular natural law independent of ecclesiastical authority. He posited that even if one were to assume that God does not exist or is indifferent to human affairs, natural law would still hold validity.[84] This secularization of natural law allowed Grotius to position it outside the contentious religious conflicts of the Reformation and Counter-Reformation. Essentially, he returned to the common rational foundation of all law, a concept recognized by Humanist thinkers through their rediscovery of Stoic philosophy. On this basis, Grotius developed his theory of international law as a system binding all nations by reason.

Grotius's starting point in formulating principles for the mutual relations of states (and, where applicable, individuals) was the notion that humans are inherently sociable: "Among the traits characteristic of man is an impelling desire for society, that is, for the social life – not of any and every sort, but peaceful and organized according to the measure of his intelligence, and with those of his own kind."[85] He asserted that "The maintenance of the social order … which is consonant with human understanding, is the source of law properly so called. To this sphere of law belongs the abstaining from that which is another's, the restoration to another of anything of his which we may have, together with any gain which we may have received from it; the obligation to fulfil promises, the reparation of a loss incurred through our fault, and the infliction of penalties on men according to their deserts."[86] Grotius viewed natural law as fundamentally an injunction to maintain peace by respecting the rights of others.[87] Despite acknowledging that this law originates from humanity's inmost being, he also attributed it to God, whose will places these principles within us.[88] Summarizing his view, Grotius wrote that "natural law is the command of right reason, which points out, in respect of a particular act, depending on whether or not it conforms with that rational nature, either its moral turpitude or its moral necessity; and consequently shows that such an act is either prohibited or

[83] The secularism of the natural law of this era accounts for its relative lack of popularity in Italy, where, especially in the seventeenth century, the cultural environment of the Counter-Reformation tended to stifle new ideas. It is thus unsurprising that the famous Italian scholar Alberico Gentili (1552–1608), regarded as one of the founders of the Natural Law School, came under suspicion for heresy and had to seek refuge in England, where he became Regius Professor of Civil Law at the University of Oxford.

[84] *De iure belli ac pacis, Prolegomena* 11.

[85] *De iure belli ac pacis, Prolegomena*, 6.

[86] *De iure belli ac pacis, Prolegomena*, 8.

[87] According to Grotius, one of the rights derived from the law of nature is the right of self-defence. (*De iure belli ac pacis*, 2. 1. 3) Furthermore, a natural right to punish a wrongdoer must be assumed, for otherwise such a right could not be possessed by the state by cession from its subjects. (*De iure belli ac pacis*, 2. 20. 1–2) The law of nature is also the source of validity of various forms of acquisition, and underpins rights emerging through promises and contractual agreements. (*De iure belli ac pacis*, 2. 3. 4 ff and 2. 11. 4.)

[88] *De iure belli ac pacis, Prolegomena*, 11–12.

commanded by God, the author of that nature."[89] Thus, Grotius's hypothesis played a crucial role in liberating the doctrine of natural law from theological constraints.

Additionally, as noted in Chap. 2, Grotius employed the comparative method to empirically support his natural law doctrine. He believed that the universal propositions of natural law could be demonstrated not only through deduction from reason but also by the fact that certain legal rules and institutions were universally recognized across different legal systems. To illustrate and support his system of natural law, he utilized legal materials from diverse countries and historical periods. This approach allowed him to show that natural law principles were not merely theoretical but had practical manifestations in various legal traditions.

The idea of a rational natural law was further developed by the German philosophers Samuel Pufendorf (1632–1694), Christian Thomasius (1655–1728), and Christian Wolff (1679–1754). Pufendorf posited that natural law is entirely a product of reason, independent of divine revelation. One of his fundamental principles states, "Let no one act towards another in such a way that the latter can justly complain that his equality of rights has been violated."[90] More concrete rules derived from reason and nature include: not harming others and making reparations when harm is caused, treating others as having equal rights due to the dignity of all human beings, assisting others to the best of one's ability, and fulfilling one's obligations.[91] Pufendorf was the first modern philosopher to create a comprehensive system of natural law encompassing all branches of law.[92] His work significantly influenced the structure of later legal codifications, particularly the 'general part' found at the beginning of codes, where basic legal principles are laid down.

Christian Thomasius, like other natural law thinkers, emphasizes the transition from *iurisprudentia divina*, a theological approach to legal study, to a doctrine of law grounded in reason and nature. A central theme in Thomasius's natural law theory is justice (*iustum*), which involves forbidding any transgression against the rights of others and justifies the state's right to exercise coercion. Thomasius treats this as distinct from the demands of honesty (*honestum*) and decency (*decorum*), thereby separating the domain of law from that of morality.[93] Drawing on the works of Leibniz and Pufendorf, Christian Wolff proposed a system of natural law intended to establish law as a rigorously deductive science. His system significantly

[89] *De iure belli ac pacis*, 1. 1. 10. 1–2.

[90] *Elementa jurisprudentiae*, 2. 4. 4.

[91] *De officio hominis et civis*, 1. 3. 9. 6–9.

[92] Pufendorf is best known for his book *De jure naturae et gentium* (on the Law of Nature and Nations, 1672). His earlier work *Elementa jurisprudentiae universalis* (Elements of a Universal Jurisprudence, 1660) led to his being appointed to a chair in the Law of Nature and Nations, which was especially created for him at the University of Heidelberg. As Erik Wolf remarks, "Pufendorf combines the attitude of a rationalist who describes and systematizes the law in the geometrical manner with that of the historian who rummages through the archives and who explores historical facts and personalities." Wolf (1944), p. 298.

[93] Some of Thomasius's key works on natural law include: *Institutiones Jurisprudentiae Divinae* (Institutes of Divine Jurisprudence) (1688); and *Fundamenta Juris Naturae et Gentium* (Foundations of the Law of Nature and Nations) (1705).

influenceed eighteenth and nineteenth- century German codifiers and jurists, as well as legal education in German universities.[94]

The School of Natural Law challenged the supreme authority that medieval jurists had accorded to the codification of Justinian. It argued that the *Corpus Iuris Civilis* was an expression of a specific legal order whose rules, like those of any other system of positive law, must be evaluated against higher, eternal, and universally valid norms—those of Natural law. Natural law was construed as rational in its content, as its norms could be discovered only through the use of reason, logic, and rationality. It was regarded as common to all humankind across all times and possessing a higher moral authority than any system of positive law. From this perspective, Natural Law scholars rejected certain 'irrational' features of the Roman legal system highlighted by the Humanists, such as the remnants of the old Roman formalism in the *Corpus Iuris Civilis*, as being specific to the Roman system of social organization and temporally restricted. However, they acknowledged that Roman law contained many rules and principles that reflected or corresponded to the precepts of natural law—rules and principles they viewed as products of logical reasoning about the nature of man and society rather than expressions of the Roman state's legal development. The Roman doctrines of *ius gentium* and *ius naturale*, in particular, seemed to support their theories. Methodologically, Natural Law scholars relied on deductive reasoning to extract abstract principles of universal application from a small number of general concepts, which could form the basis for developing an orderly and comprehensive legal system. The Natural Law School's system-building approach to law prompted renewed interest in codification as a means of integrating the diverse laws and customs of a national territory into a logically consistent and unitary system.[95]

7.8 The Codification Movement

In the seventeenth and eighteenth centuries, the rise of nationalism and the consolidation of royal power in Europe led to an increased interest in developing national law, which, in turn, precipitated the movement towards codification. The demand for law to be reduced to a code arose from two interrelated factors: the necessity to establish legal unity within the boundaries of a nation-state and the need to develop a rational, systematized, and comprehensive legal system adapted to contemporary conditions. The School of Natural Law, with its rationalist approach to institutional

[94] Wolff's most important works include *Philosophia Rationalis, sive Logica* (Rational Philosophy, or Logic) (1728); *Philosophia Prima sive Ontologia* (First Philosophy or Ontology) (1730); *Philosophia Practica Universalis* (Universal Practical Philosophy) (1738–1739); and *Theologia Naturalis* (Natural Theology) (1736–1737).

[95] On the rise and influence of the School of Natural law see D'Entreves (1970); Robinson et al. (1994), ch.13; Kelly (1992/2013), ch. 6; Wieacker (1995), ch. 15; Stein (1999), pp. 107–110; Tamm (1997), p. 231 ff; Wolff (1951/1976), p. 213 ff.

reform, emphasized the creation of comprehensive legal systems and thus provided the ideological and methodological foundation for the codification movement. The unification of national law through codification resulted in the eventual displacement of the *ius commune*, causing Roman law to cease to exist as a direct source of law. However, as the drafters of the codes relied heavily on the *ius commune*, elements of Roman law were incorporated into the legal systems of Continental Europe in various ways and to varying degrees.

The first national codes aimed at achieving legal unity within a single kingdom were compiled in Denmark (1683)[96] and Sweden (1734).[97] Codification efforts continued into the late eighteenth and early nineteenth centuries with the introduction of codes in Bavaria (1756),[98] Prussia (1794),[99] and Austria (1811).[100] The Natural law philosophy heavily influenced both the content and structure of these codes. However, the most significant codification event of this period was Napoleon's enactment of the French Civil Code (*Code civil des francais*) in 1804. The primary objective of Napoleon's Code was to unify French law by integrating Roman law,

---

[96] Prior to 1683, Denmark and Norway had a fragmented legal system characterized by various regional laws and customary practices. The rise of absolutism under King Frederick III (1609–1670) led to the centralization of power, creating a need for a unified legal system. King Christian V (1646–1699) established a commission to create a comprehensive legal code to standardize and modernize the legal system. The Code of 1683, also known as '*Danske Lov*', was a significant milestone in Danish legal history, marking the establishment of a uniform legal system across Denmark and Norway.

[97] The Code of 1734 (also known as the '1734 års lag'), developed under the reign of King Frederick I (1720–1751), was a comprehensive legal enactment that replaced older regional laws and unified the legal system of Sweden, providing clarity, consistency, and fairness in the administration of justice. It consisted of several books covering various aspects of law, including civil law, criminal law, procedural law, and administrative law. The 1734 code laid the foundation for Sweden's legal system, many parts of which remain influential today.

[98] The Bavarian Civil Code of 1756 (also known as the *Codex Maximilianeus Bavaricus Civilis*), was a comprehensive legal code enacted under the rule of Elector Maximilian III Joseph. It aimed to standardize and modernize the legal system within the region by consolidating various customary laws and legal practices into a single, cohesive document. The code covered a wide range of legal areas, including civil law, property law, and family law, reflecting Enlightenment principles of rationality and uniformity in legal processes. It served as a precursor to later, more extensive codifications in German-speaking territories and influenced subsequent legal reforms in Bavaria and beyond.

[99] The Prussian legal code of 1794 (*Allgemeines Landrecht für die Preußischen Staaten*), was a comprehensive legal code that aimed to provide a clear and unified set of laws for the entire Prussian state. It was one of the most detailed and extensive legal codes of its time, covering various aspects of civil, criminal, and administrative law. The code emphasized rationality, order, and the authority of the state, reflecting Enlightenment ideals.

[100] The Austrian Civil Code of 1811 (*Allgemeines Bürgerliches Gesetzbuch*) was enacted under Emperor Francis I (1804–1835). It is a comprehensive enactment that covers various areas of private law, including personal status, family law, property law, and the law of obligations. Its structure is influenced by Roman law and Enlightenment principles, emphasizing individual rights, legal equality, and the protection of private property. The code is known for its clarity, systematic organization, and progressive elements for its time, such as the recognition of women's rights in certain contexts.

customary law, royal ordinances, and certain laws of the revolutionary period into a comprehensive system. This goal was achieved with remarkable success. The importance of the Code lies not only in its promotion of legal unity within France but also in its widespread adoption, imitation, or adaptation by numerous countries worldwide. This was partly due to its clarity, simplicity, and elegance, which made it an attractive model for exportation, and partly due to France's significant influence in the nineteenth century.

The French Civil Code was drafted by a commission of four eminent jurists: Tronchet, President of the Court of Cassation and former defence counsel for King Louis XVI; Portalis, a lawyer and provincial administrator at Aix-en-Provence and a close supporter of Napoleon; Bigot de Préameneau, government commissioner for the *Tribunal de cassation* and former lawyer at the Parliament in Rennes; and Maleville, formerly a lawyer at the Parliament in Bordeaux and later a judge at the Court of Cassation.[101] The three ideological pillars of the Code were private property, freedom of contract, and the patriarchal family. The Code posited that the primary role of the state was to protect private property, ensure the enforcement of legally formed contracts, and uphold the autonomy of the family.

Regarding private property, the Code consolidated the rejection of feudalism and its institutions achieved by the French Revolution. Through private law mechanisms, such as imposing limitations on the freedom of testation, the drafters sought to dismantle the estates of the once-powerful landowners. The formal division of the Code into three parts—Persons, Property, and the Different Ways of Acquiring Property—mirrored the structure adopted by the drafters of Justinian's Institutes. Each part or book is divided into titles, such as Enjoyment and Loss of Civil Rights, Marriage, Divorce, Domicile, and Adoptions, which are further subdivided into chapters and, in several instances, into sections.

Book One covers matters such as marriage, divorce, the status of minors, guardianship, and domicile; Book Two deals with property, usufruct, and servitudes; and Book Three includes diverse topics such as wills and intestate succession, donations, contracts, torts, matrimonial property settlements, sale, lease, partnership, mortgages, and special contracts. Certain parts of the Code, such as the law of contracts, were heavily based on the Roman or written law of Southern France, while others, such as family law and the law of succession, reflect a stronger influence from the North French customary law of Germanic origin.

The drafters of the Code recognized that a legislator could not foresee all possible applications of a basic legal principle. Therefore, they opted for the flexibility of general rules rather than detailed provisions. As Portalis commented, "we have avoided the dangerous ambition to regulate and foresee everything… The function of the law is to determine in broad outline the general maxims of justice, to establish principles rich in implications, and not to descend into the details of the questions

[101] Portalis, who presented the drafting intentions in the *Discours préliminaire*, was in overall charge. On Portalis' contribution see Plesser (1997); Long and Monier (1997).

that can arise in each subject."[102] From this perspective, he identified the main tasks of judges in a codified system of law as clarifying the meaning of the legal rules in the various circumstances submitted to them, elucidating any obscure facets of the law and filling its gaps, and adjusting the law to the evolution of society.

The new code, reflecting the influence of the middle class, marked a significant departure from the previous legal system, which it was intended to replace. Even the numerous pre-revolutionary rules and institutions incorporated into the code were considered effective solely due to their re-enactment within the new legislation. Despite the formal break with the *ius commune*, the code was of necessity constructed from culturally familiar concepts, institutions, and legal thinking derived from the former system. Consequently, much of the earlier legal tradition, now underpinned by a new ideological basis, was carried over into the code.

In Germany, the French Civil Code garnered significant attention, and as Napoleon extended his rule over Europe, it was adopted in various parts of the country. The rise of German nationalism during the wars of independence prompted many scholars to advocate for the introduction of a uniform code to unite Germany under a modern legal system and facilitate its political unification. In 1814, Anton Friedrich Justus Thibaut, a professor of Roman law at Heidelberg University, expressed this view in his pamphlet "On the Necessity for a General Civil Code for Germany."[103] Thibaut, a proponent of the Natural Law movement, suggested that the existing French, Prussian, and Austrian Civil Codes could serve as valuable models for the German lawmakers.

Thibaut's proposals, however, faced strong opposition from the Historical School,[104] led by the influential jurist Friedrich Carl von Savigny (1779–1861).[105] In his pamphlet "On the Vocation of our Times for Legislation and Legal Science,"[106]

[102] See von Mehren and Gordley (1977), p. 54.

[103] Thibaut (1814a); and see Thibaut (1814b).

[104] The rise of the Historical School was one manifestation of the general reaction to the rationalism of the School of Natural Law and the political philosophy associated with the French Revolution and the regime of Napoleon. Savigny officially founded the School in 1815, together with his Berlin colleague Karl Friedrich Eichhorn (1781–1854). They edited the programmatic journal of the School, the *Zeitschrift für geschichtliche Rechtswissenschaft* – the predecessor of the modern *Savigny-Zeitschrift*.

[105] Savigny was born in Frankfurt am Main and became professor at Marburg University in 1803. After a brief period in Landshut (predecessor of the University of Munich), he became one of the founders of the University of Berlin (1810), where he taught until 1842. Furthermore, he was named Counsellor of the state (*Staatsrat*) in 1829 and held the position of legislative minister in the Prussian cabinet from 1842 to 1848. Notwithstanding his impressive professional career, Savigny's reputation is mainly derived from his academic achievements and their influence on 19th-century German legal and political thought. The focus of his work was Roman law, as preserved in the codification of Justinian. From 1815 to 1831, he dedicated himself to an extensive and in-depth study of Roman law in the Middle Ages, with the view to elucidating the process through which Roman law formed the basis of European legal culture. In his work, special attention is given to the contribution of the glossators of the twelfth and thirteenth centuries to the reception of Roman law as the common law of Continental Europe.

[106] von Savigny (1814).

Savigny argued that law, like ethics, language, and literature, is a product of the history and culture of a people, a manifestation of national consciousness (*Volksgeist*), and cannot be derived from abstract principles of natural law by logical means alone. According to Savigny, the introduction of a German Code should be postponed until the historical circumstances shaping German law were fully understood and the present needs were properly assessed.

A key question Savigny had to address was how the idea that the law emanated from the people could be reconciled with the fact that Roman law, an alien import, operated in Germany. Savigny responded by explaining that at a certain stage in a nation's development, law creation by the people becomes overly complex and technical, necessitating the establishment of a professionally trained class of lawyers and jurists. In Germany, this stage was reached in the fifteenth century, and the jurists responsible for the reception of Roman law during that period were true exponents of the German national spirit. Thus, Roman law, as organically received law, became part of German legal history and contemporary legal life, while also serving as a connecting link between German law and European legal culture.

Early proposals for legal codification in Germany were abandoned primarily due to the influence of the Historical School and the lack of an effective central government. Consequently, scholarly attention shifted from the largely ahistorical Natural Law approach to a historical examination of the two main sources of law in Germany: Roman law and Germanic law. The goal of legal studies was to develop a true science of law.

A group of scholars focused on Germanic law, while others, including Savigny, concentrated on Roman law, delving into the *Corpus Iuris Civilis* and other ancient sources beyond the *ius commune*. These latter jurists, known as Pandectists, aimed to uncover the 'latent system' within Roman that could be adapted to contemporary needs. In this endeavour, they elevated the study of the *Corpus Iuris Civilis*, particularly the Digest, to its highest level, creating an elaborate and systematic body of law known as *Pandektenrecht* for nineteenth-century Germany.[107]

However, the Pandectists, convinced of the superiority and eternal validity of Roman law, eventually adopted a largely ahistorical and doctrinaire approach. Their chief objective was to construct a legal system in which all particular rules could be derived from and classified under clearly formulated juridical categories and abstract propositions. Despite receiving severe criticism from other scholars, especially those in the Germanist branch of the Historical School, the Pandectists played a significant role in the codification of the civil law in Germany. This process began in 1874, three years after the political unification of the country under Otto von Bismarck, President of Prussia and first Chancellor of Germany, and culminated in the promulgation of the German Civil Code (*Bürgerliches Gesetzbuch* or BGB) in 1896, which came into force in 1900. Like the French Code, the German Code has gained wide acceptance beyond Germany's borders.

[107] Leading representatives of the Pandectists were Georg Puchta, Adolf Friedrich Rudorff, Ernst Immanuel Bekker, Alois Brinz, Heinrich Dernburg, Rudolf von Ihering and Bernhard Windscheid.

The German Civil Code is distinguished by two key characteristics: its highly systematic structure and its conceptualism. In both these respects, it owes a great deal to the work of the Pandectists. The Code is divided into five books. The first book contains the general principles of the entire civil law, i.e., the principles that have general application to all legal relations except when special rules are provided. It includes provisions relating to persons (both natural and legal), the nature and classification of things and juristic acts, acting capacity, offer and acceptance, agency and ratification, limitation and prescription, and private means of redressing wrongs and securing rights. The second book is devoted to the law of obligations (*Schuldrecht*), which addresses the legal relations between particular subjects of rights. The third book contains the law of property (*Sachenrecht*), which addresses the rights of persons over things, describing the content, acquisition, loss, and protection of real rights. The fourth book covers family law (*Familienrecht*) and is divided into two parts: the first regulates personal relationships within the family, and the second regulates the property relationships of family members. Finally, the fifth book deals with the law of succession (*Erbrecht*), which regulates the succession to the rights and liabilities of a deceased person. The influence of the Pandectists is reflected in the Code's systematic consistency, succinctness, and conceptual clarity. However, the Code is not designed to be intelligible to the layperson; it is codified jurists' law for jurists, intended to be read and understood by them. This did not pose a problem for judges and legal practitioners, who were familiar with the style and methods of the Pandectists through their university legal training.

Despite their important differences in style and structure, the German and French Civil Codes share significant commonalities. Both codes heavily drew upon common sources of law, particularly the *ius commune* and their respective national laws. The influence of the *ius commune* is especially evident in the law of obligations and the structuring and systematization of materials within these codes. Conversely, native sources of law exerted considerable influence in areas such as family law and the law of succession. Furthermore, both codes share a common ideological foundation, being rooted in nineteenth-century liberalism and embodying the notions of individual autonomy, freedom of contract, and private property.

As societal changes unfolded during the century separating the two codes, the German Civil Code reflects more advanced or contemporary elements than the French one in certain respects. For instance, several key provisions of the German Code acknowledge the relationship between certain private rights and social obligations, recognizing that subjective rights can be misused or abused. In family law, the authority of husbands and fathers is less absolute compared to the French Code, and the definition of family is narrower. Additionally, women possess greater power over their property matters. Certain aspects of contract and tort law in the German Code also reflect the increasing complexity of commercial relationships and the advances of industrialization.

After the enactment of the Civil Code, German scholars concentrated on making the Code applicable in practice. This involved interpreting its complex text and clarifying and developing its concepts and principles. During this period, there was a growing reaction against the excessive formalism and conceptualism of the

Pandectists. Following the First World War, German legal science began to move away from the Pandectists' methods. While maintaining the Pandectists' talent for formulating general concepts, German jurists increasingly emphasized examining detailed facts and the application of legal principles in specific factual situations. This evolution was interrupted by the rise of National Socialism and the subsequent decline of liberal democratic ideas in Germany. Nevertheless, the new approaches to conceptualizing law—associated with legal realism and the sociology of law—were adopted in America and other countries, significantly influencing the development of legal thought in the twentieth century.

7.9 The Civil Law Tradition

Legal scholars use the term 'civil law systems' to describe the legal systems of nations predominantly rooted in the historical tradition derived from Roman law, as transmitted to Continental Europe through the *Corpus Iuris Civilis* of Emperor Justinian. When we refer to civil law systems as belonging to a single legal family, we emphasize their fundamental unity despite considerable national differences. This unity is primarily due to their common derivation from the same sources and their classification of legal institutions according to a universally accepted scheme that predated their own development and was later adopted and adapted. However, it is important to note that, despite their common elements, civil law systems differ in many respects. A civil law lawyer can only fully appreciate the affinity between these systems when comparing them to common law and other legal families. Consequently, contemporary comparative law scholars identify sub-categories within the civil law family, notably the Romanistic-Latin (or French) and the Germanic systems, forming two secondary groupings or sub-families.[108] The distinctive legal codifications and juristic styles of France and Germany have significantly influenced legal systems worldwide, often in overlapping ways. One might argue that the 'typical' civil law systems today are not those of France and Germany but rather those that have undergone a combined influence of both. Nevertheless, in the post-codification period, French law and German legal science have been the two main tributaries to the civil law tradition.

The Romanistic-Latin or French group of countries and territorial units share a private law system rooted in the Napoleonic Civil Code of 1804. During Napoleon's conquests and the subsequent political and administrative reshaping of many European countries, the French Civil Code was introduced into western regions of Germany, the low countries, Italy, Spain, and other parts of Europe. During the nineteenth century, France, as a major colonial power, further extended its legal influence beyond Continental Europe to parts of the Middle East, Northern and

[108] Consider on this matter David and Brierley (1985), p. 35; Zweigert and Kötz (1987), pp. 68–75.

sub-Saharan Africa, Indochina, Oceania, French Guiana, and the French Caribbean islands.

The influence of French law has persisted and extended well beyond the Napoleonic conquests and French colonialism. Today, the French Civil Code, albeit revised, remains in effect in Belgium and Luxemburg. Additionally, the *Code Civil* significantly influenced the Netherlands Civil Code of 1838, which, in turn, impacted the new civil code of the Netherlands enacted in 1992. It also served as a model for the law codes of the Italian federal states prior to 1860 and the first *Codice Civile* of 1865,[109] the Portuguese Civil Code of 1867 (replaced in 1967), the Spanish Civil Code of 1889, the Romanian Civil Code of 1864, and some of the Swiss cantonal codes.[110]

Furthermore, when the Spanish and Portuguese empires in Latin America disintegrated in the nineteenth century, the legislatures of the newly independent nations of Central and South America primarily looked to the French Civil Code for inspiration. This is unsurprising, as the language and concepts of the French code were already familiar due to their affinities with the legal institutions and practices introduced by the Spanish and the Portuguese. Additionally, French culture and the French revolutionary heritage were greatly admired in Latin American countries, and Napoleon's personality served as an example to many of the early statesmen in these countries.[111]

The French legal tradition also persists in territories initially colonized by France but later taken over by Great Britain or other powers with a common law legal system, such as the province of Québec in Canada and the state of Louisiana in the United States of America. Although the local populations in some of these territories were initially promised they could retain their French-inspired law, Anglo-American law gradually gained prominence. This shift occurred largely due to isolation from legal developments in France, the introduction of numerous English-inspired legal amendments, and the transition to English as the language of the courts and daily life. This is particularly evident in the U.S. state of Louisiana, where the positions of both the French language and French law have significantly

---

[109] See on this Ghisalberti (1979), p. 223.

[110] Even after the Congress of Vienna (1815), the French Civil Code remained in effect in German territories on the left bank of River Rhine and also in parts of the Prussian Rhine Province.

[111] The Mexican state of Oaxaca promulgated the first Latin American civil code in 1827, following the French *Code Civil*. Bolivia enacted a civil law code in 1830, also modelled on the French Code. This code remained in force until a new code, based on the Italian Civil Code of 1942, was introduced in 1975. The Chilean Civil Code of 1855 was strongly influenced by the French Civil Code, although its principal drafter, Andrés Bello, was also familiar with the work of the German Historical School. Bello's Código Civil was adopted by Ecuador (1860), Colombia (1873), Nicaragua (1867), Honduras (1880) and El Salvador (1859), and had an impact on the relevant Venezuelan (1862) and Uruguayan (1868) legislation. The Argentinean Civil Code of 1871 (adopted by Paraguay in 1876) and the Brazilian Civil Code of 1916 (completed by Clóvis Beviláqua in 1899) also reflect the concurrent influence of the Napoleonic Civil Code, French nineteenth-century jurisprudence, and the German Historical School. See in general Stoetzer (1966); Guzmán Brito (2000).

weakened. In contrast, the legal system of the Canadian province of Québec, where the French language continues to be used by the overwhelming majority of the population, has substantial legal resources rooted in French legal heritage, making it resistant to common-law influence. In countries that once belonged to the French colonial empire,[112] the current influence of French law varies, depending on the strength of French culture in these countries and the impact of local customs and legal traditions, especially Islamic law.[113]

The Germanic legal family comprises countries that have adopted or been influenced by the German Civil Code of 1896 and the preceding German Pandectist scholarship (*Pandektenwissenschaft*). Although the German Civil Code emerged relatively late in the codification era, and its highly technical language and complex structure made direct transplantation challenging, it significantly impacted the codification of civil law in several countries, including Italy,[114] Greece,[115] Portugal,[116] and Japan.[117] The influence of German civil law also spread to Korea,[118] Thailand, and, to some extent, China,[119] either directly or via Japan.

Furthermore, the legal science that preceded and accompanied the German Code has profoundly influenced legal theory and doctrine in several Central and Eastern European countries, particularly Austria,[120] Hungary, Switzerland, and the former Yugoslavia. German legal influence, especially that of the Historical School, became evident in various legal reforms during the early twentieth century. German legal science had a significant impact in other territories of the Habsburg Empire, especially Hungary, where it led to three civil code drafts (1900, 1911–1915 and 1928).

[112] This group includes Morocco, Algeria and Tunisia in North Africa; Senegal, Togo, Ivory Coast, the Republic of Congo, Cameroon, Guinea, Gabon, Benin and Burkina Faso in West Africa; Mauritania, Mali, Niger, the Central African Republic and Chad in Central Africa; Madagascar and Djibouti in Eastern Africa; as well as the former Belgian colonies of Congo and Rwanda and Burundi.

[113] In combination with Islamic law, French-inspired civil law and jurisprudence remain influential in most North African countries as well as in many Middle Eastern countries.

[114] The German Civil Code was drawn upon by the drafters of the Italian Civil Code of 1942.

[115] The Greek Civil Code of 1940, which came into effect in 1946, was shaped substantially according to the German model.

[116] The drafters of the Portuguese Civil Code of 1967 closely followed the system of the German Civil Code, although individual provisions also reflect French and Italian legal influences.

[117] The Japanese Civil Code of 1898 drew heavily on the first draft of the German Civil Code, but also embodied elements from French and English law. On the codification of civil law in Japan see Ishikawa and Leetsch (1985); Marutschke (2009). And see Chap. 12 below.

[118] The Korean Civil Code, enacted in 1960, was drafted by jurists who had studied at universities in Japan and Germany. See Cho (1980).

[119] German legal science and the various forerunners of the German Civil Code (e.g. the Dresden Draft and the Saxon Civil Code), as well as the Code itself exerted a strong influence on Chinese jurists. This influence is reflected in the Civil Code of 1930, parts of which are still applicable in Taiwan.

[120] Many of the ideas of the German Civil Code found their way into Austrian civil law via the so-called Third Partial Amendment, concerning largely the law of obligations, which came into effect in 1916.

Although none of these drafts attained the status of law, they played an important role in judicial practice. The Swiss Civil Code (*Zivilgesetzbuch*) of 1907, drafted by the jurist Eugen Huber, drew upon German and, to a lesser extent, French sources but was adapted to Swiss circumstances and incorporated significant contemporary reforms.[121]

Even the initial codifications of civil law in the Soviet Union during the 1920s exhibited similarities to the German Civil Code. German jurisprudence, both directly and via the Soviet Union, significantly influenced the legal systems in formerly socialist countries in Central and Eastern Europe. German legal science had a particularly strong impact in the Baltic states of Lithuania, Latvia, and Estonia, where a system of private law developed by Friedrich Georg von Bunge, a professor at the University of Dorpat in Estonia in the late nineteenth century, was adopted by the independent states in 1918. Following World War II, the influence of civil law in Central and Eastern Europe diminished as socialist countries implemented new civil codes. Although these codes retained several traditional civil law features, the fundamentally different public law and significant private law reforms led most contemporary comparative law scholars to classify these legal systems as part of a new socialist legal family. However, with the collapse of socialist regimes, Central and Eastern European nations are once again showing strong affinities to the civil law family.

As previously noted, civil law endures in so-called 'mixed' or 'hybrid' legal systems, which historically represent a blend of legal traditions from two or more families of law. Examples include the civil and common law systems of Quebec, Louisiana, South Africa, Scotland,[122] Puerto Rico, and the Philippines.[123] Civil law is also one of the diverse elements in the complex legal systems of many countries in Asia, such as China, Sri Lanka, Indonesia, Taiwan, Laos, Vietnam, and Cambodia.

7.10 Defining Features of Civil Law Systems

Defining the characteristics of the civil law family of legal systems is challenging without resorting to generalizations that require extensive qualifications to be meaningful. This difficulty arises from the largely abstract nature of the concept of legal family and the insufficient attention often given to the changes that have occurred within individual systems over time. As previously noted, according to Zweigert

[121] In 1926, the Swiss Civil Code was adopted, almost word for word, as the Civil Code of the newly formed Republic of Turkey.

[122] The private law of Scotland still reflects a Roman law influence, although contract law, under the influence of the House of Lords jurisprudence, has borrowed much from English law. It should be noted that in Scotland, just like in South Africa, Roman-based civil law survived in uncodified form.

[123] Zweigert and Kötz (1987), p. 74. Civil law is also one of the many elements in the legal systems of Israel and Lebanon.

and Kötz, the ultimate distinguishing feature of legal families is their 'style' (*Rechtsstil*), a multifaceted concept shaped by the interaction of five principal factors: (a) history; (b) mode of legal thinking; (c) legal institutions; (d) sources of law; and e) ideology.[124] These factors, though varying in their relevance, collectively distinguish the civil law from the common law and other legal families.

The common features of civil law systems can be summarized as follows:

(1) *Codification*: The cornerstone of civil law systems is the comprehensive codification of laws. Legal rules and principles are systematically organized into codes, such as civil codes, criminal codes, and commercial codes.[125] These codes aim to cover all potential scenarios and provide a clear, detailed framework for judges to follow. The tradition of codification is rooted in the rationalist tendencies that dominated European philosophy during the eighteenth and nineteenth centuries. However, its origins can be traced back to the monumental codification of Roman law by the Emperor Justinian in the sixth century AD.
(2) *Primacy of Legislation*: In civil law systems, legislation is the primary source of law. Statutes and legal codes enacted by legislative bodies hold the highest authority. This legislative primacy ensures that the law remains consistent and predictable. Judicial decisions are secondary and are not considered binding precedents.
(3) *The role of the judiciary*: Judges in civil law systems have a more limited role compared to those in common law countries. Their primary function is to apply the law as written in the codes and statutes to the facts of a case. While they do interpret laws, they do not create law, and their decisions do not have a binding effect on other courts. Despite the absence of a formal doctrine of precedent (*stare decisis*), there is a strong tendency among civil law judges to follow precedents, particularly those of the higher courts. One might say that, in practice, the difference between *stare decisis* and what is referred to in France as *jurisprudence constante* (the persuasiveness of judicial trend) is constantly being narrowed.
(4) *Distinction between public and private law*: Civil law systems feature a clear division between public law and private law. Public law governs the relationship between individuals and the state and includes branches such as constitutional, administrative, and criminal law. Conversely, private law regulates relationships between individuals and encompasses civil and commercial law. This distinction ensures specialized legal frameworks for different types of legal relations. Historically, private law has played a dominant role in the development of legal concepts and principles within civil law systems. This dominance is reflected in the fact that the classification of civil law systems focuses primarily on the law outlined in civil codes, namely private law. Other

[124] Zweigert and Kötz (1987), p. 68 ff.

[125] See Stein (1992), pp. 1594–1595. Consider also Glenn (1998).

branches of law, such as public law, developed later and were largely based on concepts and principles derived from private law.

(5) *Distinction between substantive law and legal procedure*: Civil law systems maintain a clear distinction between substantive law and legal procedure. This distinction has its historical origins in the work of the humanist jurists of the sixteenth and seventeenth centuries, who viewed the law as a system of subjective rights derived from substantive law. Legal procedure, in this context, was seen as a supplementary mechanism for the enforcement of these rights. Whenever substantive law recognizes a right, procedural law, as an accessory to substantive law, must provide an appropriate remedy.[126] Modern procedural codes in civil law jurisdictions emphasize the public nature of judicial proceedings and the principle that control of claims and means of evidence primarily belongs to the parties. However, in practice, this principle is limited by the judge's extensive power to supervise and direct the proceedings.

(6) *Legal reasoning*: In civil law systems, legal rules are characterized by optimal generality: they are not overly general, which would complicate the application of law, but general enough for application in specific situations. Consequently, legal reasoning in these systems is primarily deductive. Deductive reasoning proceeds from a broad rule or principle expressed in general terms, followed by consideration of the facts of the particular case and the application of the rule or principle to these facts to arrive at a conclusion. Civil law legal reasoning has a top-down structure, moving from the general to the specific. This prompts civil law lawyers to present legal arguments as if there is only one correct answer to any legal problem, attributing any disagreement over the application of the law to faulty logic. This explains why civil law judges usually do not offer dissenting opinions; every judgment, even in cases decided on appeal, is considered to be the judgment of the court as a whole. Under the deductive approach of civil law, the value of case law is limited, as court decisions are viewed as particular illustrations of, or exceptions to, the law embodied in a general rule or principle. In this respect, the body of law may be construed to form an independent, closed system where, at least in theory, all questions should be answered by interpreting existing legal rules. In civil law systems, the law is regarded as 'found' rather than 'made' in each individual case through the application of deductive reasoning or, if necessary, reasoning *per analogiam* or *a contrario*.[127]

---

[126] In the common law system, by contrast, legal development focused on remedies rather than rights, on forms of action rather than causes of action. As often said, it was with writs and not with rights that the older English law was concerned. The difference is mainly one of emphasis, but it has the important practical consequence that the agent who controls the grant of remedies also controls the development of the law. By creating new forms of action or extending existing forms to deal with new facts, that agent could, in fact, create new rights. See Chap. 8 below.

[127] In contrast, in common law, what is authoritative is what is decided. Law in this system is seen as open-ended, with new extensions to existing rules potentially revealed at any time by the courts. Common law lawyers start by examining the facts to identify the precise legal issue raised by the case and the legal rules that should be applied. They do not view law as a set of given rules that can

(7) *Intellectualism and Conceptualism*: Despite the increasing emphasis on the practical implications of the law in recent times, civil law systems, particularly the German system and those it has influenced, generally approach law as a science. This perspective treats the law as a form of logic, a coherent assembly where everything can be reduced to principles, concepts, and categories. In the domain of legislation, this approach entails using technical and abstract language, leading to a high level of precision in selecting relevant terms and phrases, whose meanings remain fixed throughout the legal text. Regarding the study of law, this scientific approach implies that one cannot rely solely on the study of cases to grasp the essence of the law. The study of cases serves only to illustrate how the law operates in practice, while its essence remains abstract. As Charles Gonthier remarks, civil law is distinguished from common law by "a difference in intellectual approach, in the quest and ordering of [legal] knowledge. Each approach reflects one of the modes of functioning of the human intellect, that is, on the one hand, the empirical mode based on specific instances from which one may eventually draw rules and even identify principles and, on the other, the theoretical approach based on established principles from which concrete consequences and applications are drawn".[128]

(8) *The role of legal scholars and doctrinal writings*: In civil law systems, doctrinal writings by eminent legal scholars are highly respected and can influence the development, interpretation, and application of the law. These scholarly works help elucidate complex legal principles and fill gaps in codified laws. Consequently, legal scholars and academics in civil law countries often enjoy more prestige than judges. The principal task of the civil law judge is to apply the law as expounded by academic writers, positioning the legal scholar as the senior partner and the judge is the junior partner in the legal process.[129] The authority of academic writers in civil law countries has historical roots. When the texts of Justinian's legislation were rediscovered in the High Middle Ages, they were perceived as complicated and difficult to understand, and thus it fell to academic scholars (the glossators and the commentators) to decipher and explain them. As a result, the works of academic commentators acquired as much authority as the texts themselves. Judges began to rely on legal scholars for guidance concerning the interpretation and application of the law. By the end of the sixteenth century, it was common practice for judges in Germany

---

be applied with inexorable logic. When a common law lawyer queries the nature of a case, they contemplate the facts to identify the material circumstances and show that these fall within the scope of one rule rather than another. Conversely, when a civil law lawyer explores the nature of a case, they refer to the legal issues defined in a general and abstract way. See Stein (1992), pp. 1596–1597.

[128] Gonthier (1993).

[129] As Stein remarks, "Traditionally the civil-law judge is a fungible person, one of a group of anonymous, almost colorless, individuals who hide their personality behind the collegiate responsibility of their court. Their duty is to apply the written law, and the meaning of that law is to be discovered from the writings of its academic exponents." Stein (1992), p. 1597.

and other Continental European countries to refer difficult cases to university law faculties and adopt the faculty's collective opinion on questions of law. This practice, which prevailed until the nineteenth century, led to the accumulation of an extensive body of legal doctrine. When systematized in reports and treatises, the scholarly opinions rendered in actual cases were regarded as a kind of case law and an authoritative source of legal interpretations.[130] In contemporary civil law systems, where court decisions play an increasingly important role in shaping the law, an ever-vigilant academic community observes, reviews, and critiques the courts to ensure that any shaping or reshaping of the law remains a controlled activity.

(9) *Legal education*: Legal education in civil law countries typically centres on understanding and interpreting codes and statutory enactments. Law students engage in extensive courses covering various branches of law and are trained in a systematic and structured approach to legal reasoning. This education usually adopts a theoretical approach, emphasizing the comprehension and application of written laws over case analysis. Academic scholars in these systems maintain a tradition of writing authoritative textbooks and treatises in their areas of expertise, which serve as the primary sources of legal knowledge. These works are imparted to students and future legal professionals by scholars. Consequently, in civil law systems, textbooks, rather than casebooks, have traditionally been the principal source of legal knowledge.[131]

(10) *Inquisitorial process*: In civil law systems, there is a relatively greater scope for an inquisitorial model of legal process, especially in criminal cases. In this model, judges take an active role in investigating the facts of the case by questioning witnesses, examining evidence, and seeking out additional information.[132] This contrasts with the adversarial system of common law, where judges act as neutral arbiters between the opposing parties. However, the typical contrast between the inquisitorial approach of the civil law and the adversarial approach of the common law should not be overstated. A closer examination of the trial process in civil law jurisdictions reveals a blend of inquisitorial and adversarial elements. Although the civil law model places greater responsibility on judges for investigating facts, litigators still advance partisan positions from initial pleadings to final arguments. They suggest lines of factual inquiry, participate in the examination of witnesses, urge inferences from facts, discuss and distinguish precedent, interpret statutes, and formulate legal views to further their clients' interests. Generally, the civil law model of legal procedure shows a preference for 'centripetal' decision-making, determinative rules, and a rigid ordering of authority.[133]

---

[130] As John Henry Merryman remarks, if the Common law is the law of the judges, the Civil law is the of the law professors. Merryman (1969), pp. 59–60. And see Dawson (1968), p. 231.

[131] On the differences between the civil law and common law models of legal education see Merryman (1975).

[132] See Stein (1992), pp. 1598–1599.

[133] Consider on this Langbein (1985). Consider also Damaska (1975).

7.11 Concluding Remarks

In this chapter, we have traced the long and intricate process that culminated in the codification of civil law in Europe. The codes mark a new point of departure in the development of the civil law tradition. In the years following their publication, the dynamics of legal change have primarily operated through special legislation, judicial interpretation, code revision, constitutional law, and the harmonization of law at a European or international level. Legislatures in civil law countries have responded to societal and economic changes by excising large areas of law from the domain of the civil codes. They have also created entirely new areas of law, such as employment law, insurance law, competition law, and landlord and tenant law, which fall outside the scope of the codes. Furthermore, legislatures have endeavoured to update the civil codes by modifying their texts. Both the French and German codes have been amended several times since their introduction. Generally, code revision has been more extensive in family law than in other areas. Many family law reforms were precipitated by constitutional provisions introduced after the Second World War and by international conventions promoting new ideas of equality and liberty, which were at variance with the patriarchal family law of the civil codes. In other areas of law, legislatures have often encountered difficulties in forging the necessary changes within the structure of the civil codes. To address this problem, they have resorted to introducing special statutes outside the codes, which can be more easily amended as socio-economic conditions change.

While legislatures have created and developed bodies of law outside the scope of the civil codes, the courts have introduced new rules through the interpretation of these codes' provisions. This judicial adaptation of the codes to new social and economic conditions has resulted in a new body of law based on the expansion of existing legislative texts through interpretation. In some civil law countries, such as France, this process has been facilitated by the structural characteristics of the civil code—its gaps, ambiguities, and incompleteness. The drafters of the French Civil Code did not foresee the litigation-inducing aspects of modern life, such as industrial and traffic accidents, telecommunications, photographic reproduction of images, and mass circulation of publications. Consequently, the modern French law of torts is almost entirely judge-made. For later codes, such as the German Civil Code, judicial adaptation to changing conditions was facilitated by the inclusion of 'general clauses'—provisions that intentionally leave significant discretion to judges. Although traditional civil law theory denies that judges make law or that judicial decisions can be a source of law, contemporary civil law systems increasingly acknowledge the unavoidable dependence of legislation on the judges and administrators who interpret and apply it.

Throughout its development, the civil law tradition has spawned various subtraditions and exported its ideology and legal concepts globally. It has significantly influenced European Union law in terms of structure, style of reasoning, and ethos, and continues to play a crucial role in the harmonization of laws in Europe. Additionally, it has exerted a strong influence on the development of international law. Its focus on codification has shaped the creation of comprehensive international legal codes and treaties.[134] Many principles of international law, such as sovereignty, the equality of states, and the concept of state responsibility, have roots in civil law doctrines. These principles provide a foundation for the legal framework governing state interactions and the resolution of international disputes. The civil law tradition's methodological approach to legal interpretation has permeated international law. Civil law's emphasis on general principles and doctrines aids in interpreting international legal texts consistently, promoting uniformity in their application. Prominent international legal scholars, often trained in civil law systems, have contributed to the development and interpretation of international legal norms through their writings and involvement in international legal institutions. Finally, the civil law tradition's influence is visible in the procedural aspects of international courts and tribunals. The International Court of Justice (ICJ), for example, incorporates elements of civil law procedures, such as written pleadings and inquisitorial processes, reflecting civil law's structured approach to legal proceedings.

As the exchange of ideas among civil law, common law, and other legal systems gains momentum, many of the differences that once separated these systems are diminishing. Nonetheless, significant distinctions remain. The civil law tradition is unique due to its predominant forms of legal reasoning, divisions of law, organization of justice, reliance on statutory and codified precepts, and approaches to legal scholarship and education. The legal landscape has undergone substantial changes in recent decades due to the effects of globalization and regional integration, making it challenging to predict how the civil law tradition will evolve or be characterized by future observers. However, it is reasonable to conclude that this oldest and most influential of Western legal traditions has entered a new phase of development and will continue to adapt to the challenges of an ever-changing world.

References

Angelini P (2012) The Code of Dusan 1349-1354. Leg Hist Rev 80:77–93

Ashburner W (1910) The Farmer's law. J Hell Stud 30:85–108

Ashburner W (1912) The Farmer's law (continued). J Hell Stud 32:68–95

Ashburner W (1926) The Byzantine Mutiny Act. J Hell Stud 46:80–109

Ashburner W (1976) The Rhodian sea-law. Scientia Verlag, Aalen (original work published 1909)

Atkinson KMT (1974) Rome and the Rhodian sea-law. Iura 25:46–98

Burgmann L (1983) Ecloga. Das Gesetzbuch Leons III und Konstantinos V. Löwenklau-Gesellschaft, Frankfurt

Burgmann L (1991) Ecloga. In: The Oxford dictionary of Byzantium I. Oxford University Press, New York, pp 672–673

Burgmann L, Troianos S (eds) (1979) Appendix Eclogae. Klostermann, Frankfurt

Cho K-C (1980) Koreanisches Bürgerliches Gesetzbuch. Metzner, Frankfurt

---

[134] This influence is evident in major international treaties such as the Vienna Convention on the Law of Treaties and the United Nations Convention on the Law of the Sea, which are detailed and systematic.

Clarence Smith JA (1975) Medieval law teachers and writers. University of Ottawa Press, Ottawa
Cortese E (1992) Il rinascimento giuridico medievale. Bulzoni, Rome
Damaska M (1975) Structures of authority and comparative criminal procedure. Yale Law J 84:480–544
David R, Brierley J (1985) Major legal systems in the world today. An introduction to the comparative study of law, 3rd edn. Stevens, London
Dawson JP (1968) The oracles of the law. University of Michigan Press, Ann Arbor
De Zulueta F (ed) (1927) The Liber Pauperum of Vacarius. Selden Society Publications, London
D'Entreves AP (1970) Natural law: an introduction to legal philosophy, 2nd edn. Hutchinson, London
Dewey HW, Kleimola AM (trans.) (1977) Zakon sudnyj ljudem (Court law for the people). Michigan Slavic Materials 14. Dept. of Slavic Languages and Literatures, University of Michigan, Ann Arbor
Ferrini C, Mercati G, Doelger F, Hoermann S (eds) (1914–1957) M. Kritou tou Patze Tipoukeitos. Typis Polyglottis Vaticanis, Rome
Fögen MT (*1986*) *Hexabiblos aucta*. Eine Kompilation der spätbyzantinischen Rechtswissenschaft. Fontes Minores 7:259–333
Freshfield EH (1926) A manual of Roman law: the Ecloga. Cambridge University Press, Cambridge
Freshfield EH (1928) A manual of Eastern Roman law. The Procheiros Nomos. Cambridge University Press, Cambridge
Garnsey P (2007) Thinking about property: from antiquity to the age of revolution. Cambridge University Press, Cambridge
Ghisalberti C (1979) Unità nazionale e unificazione giuridica in Italia. Laterza, Bari
Gilmore MP (1963) Humanists and jurists. Harvard University Press, Cambridge
Girard PF, Senn F (1977) Les lois des Romains. Jovere Editore, Naples
Glenn HP (1998) The grounding of codification. Univ Calif Law Davis Rev 31:765–782
Gonthier CD (1993) Some comments on the common law and the civil law in Canada: influences, parallel developments and borrowings. Canadian Bus Law J 21:323–334
Guzmán Brito A (2000) A La codificación civil en Iberoamérica, Siglos XIX y XX. Editorial Jurídica de Chile, Santiago
Haldon JF (1990) Byzantium in the seventh century: the transformation of a culture. Cambridge University Press, Cambridge
Heimbach GE (ed) (1969) *Constantini Harmenopuli* Manuele legum sive Hexabiblos. Scientia, Aalen (Original work published 1851)
Horn N (1973) Die Legistische Literatur der Kommentatoren und der Ausbreitung des gelehrten Rechts. In: Coing H (ed) Handbuch der Quellen und Literatur der neueren europäischen Privatrechtsgeschichte I: Mittelalter (1100-1500), Die gelehrten Rechte und die Gesetzgebung. Beck, Munich, pp 261–364
Ishikawa A, Leetsch I (1985) Das japanische BGB in deutscher Sprache. Carl Heymanns, Cologne
Johnson AC, Coleman-Norton PR, Bourne FC (1961) Ancient Roman statutes. University of Texas Press, Austin
Jones AHM (1964) The Later Roman Empire 284–602. Basil Blackwell, Oxford
Kelley DR (1970) Foundations of modern historical scholarship: language, law and *history* in the French Renaissance. Columbia University Press, New York
Kelly JM (1992) A short history of Western legal theory. Clarendon Press, Oxford, p 2013
Koprivica M (2020) The political background to the establishment of the Slavic Nomocanon in the thirteenth century. Stud Church Hist 56:78–92
Koschaker P (1953) Europa und das Römische Recht. Beck, Munich
Langbein JH (1985) The German advance in civil procedure. Univ Chic Law Rev 52:823–866
Lange H (1997) Römisches Recht im Mittelalter,1: Die Glossatoren. Beck, Munich
Lange H, Kriechbaum M (2007) Römisches Recht im Mittelalter. Band II, Die Kommentatoren. Beck, Munich
Lawson FH (1930) The Basilica. Law Q Rev 46:486–501

Lawson FH (1931) The Basilica. Law Q Rev 47:536–556
Long M, Monier C (1997) Portalis: l'esprit de justice. Michalon, Paris
Marutschke HP (2009) Einführung in das japanische Recht. Beck, Munich
Mather H (2002) The medieval revival of Roman Law: implications for contemporary legal education. Catholic Lawyer 41:323–362
Merryman JH (1969) The civil law tradition, An introduction to the legal systems of Western Europe and Latin America. Stanford University Press, Stanford
Merryman JH (1975) Legal education there and here: a comparison. Stanf Law Rev 27:859–878
Moulakis CM (1963). Studien zur Epitome Legum. A Schubert, Munich
Noailles P, Dain A (eds) (1944) Les Novelles de Léon VI le Sage. Les Belles Lettres, Paris
Plesser MA (1997) Jean Étienne Marie Portalis und der Code civil. Duncker & Humblot, Berlin
Robinson OF, Fergus TD, Gordon WM (1994) European legal history, 2nd edn. Butterworths, London
Sarzotti C (1995) Jean Domat: Fondamento e metodo della scienza giuridica. Giappichelli, Turin
Scheltema HJ (1955) Über die Natur der Basiliken. Tijdschrift 23:287–310
Scheltema HJ, Van der Wal N, Holwerda D (eds) (1953–1988) Basilicorum Libri LX. J.B. Wolters, Groningen
Schlosser H (2005) Grundzüge der Neueren Privatrechtsgeschichte, Rechtsentwicklungen im europäischen Kontext. Müller, Heidelberg
Schminck A (1986) Studien zu mittelbyzantinischen *Rechtsbuchern*. Lowenklau, Frankfurt
Simon D (1987) Die Melete des Eustathios Rhomaios über die Befugnis der Witwe zur Mordanklage. Zeitschrift der Savigny 104:559–595
Stein P (1992) Roman law, common law, and civil law. Tulane Law Rev 66(6):1591–1604
Stein P (1993) Donellus and the origins of the modern civil law. In: Ankum JA et al. (eds) Mélanges F. Wubbe. Fribourg, pp 448–452
Stein P (1999) Roman law in European history. Cambridge University Press, Cambridge
Stoetzer C (1966) El pensamiento político en la América española durante el período de la emancipación (1789-1825). Inst. de Estudios Politicos, Madrid
Svoronos NG (1964). La Synopsis major des Basiliques et ses appendices. Presses universitaires de France, Paris
Tamm D (1997) Roman law and European legal history. DJOF, Copenhagen
Thibaut AFJ (1814a) Rezension über August Wilhelm Rehberg, Ueber den Code Napoléon und dessen. Einführung in Deutschland (1814). Heidelbergische Jahrbücher der Litteratur 7:1–32
Thibaut AFJ (1814b) Ueber die Nothwendigkeit eines allgemeinen bürgerlichen Rechts für Deutschland. Mohr & Zimmer, Heidelberg
Troianos S (1986) The Sources of Byzantine Law. Sakkoulas, Athens
Vinogradoff P (1929) Roman law in medieval Europe. Clarendon Press, Oxford, p 2001
von Mehren A, Gordley J (1977) The civil law system, 2nd edn. Little, Brown, Boston
von Savigny FC (1814) Vom Beruf unserer Zeit für Gesetzgebung und Rechtswissenschaft. Mohr und Zimmer, Heidelberg
Voppel R (1996) Der Einfluß des Naturrechts auf den Usus modernus: eine Untersuchung anhand der Literatur zum geltenden Recht im 17. und 18. Jahrhundert. Carl Heymanns, Köln
Vryonis S (1974) The Peira as a source for the history of Byzantine aristocratic society. In: Koumjian DK (ed) Near Eastern numismatics, iconography epigraphy and history: studies in honor of G.C. Miles. American University Press, Beirut, pp 279–284
Warmington EH (1938) Remains of old Latin III. Loeb Classical Library, Cambridge
Weiss G (1977) Die "Synopsis legum" des Michael Psellos. V. Klostermann
Wieacker F (1995) A history of private law in Europe: with particular reference to Germany (trans: Weir T). Clarendon Press, Oxford
Wolf E (1944) Grosse Rechtsdenker der deutschen Geistesgeschichte, 2nd edn. Mohr, Tübingen
Wolff H-J (1951) Roman law: an historical introduction. University of Oklahoma Press, Norman, p 1976

Zepos J, Zepos P (eds) (1962) Jus graecoromanum, 8 vols. Scientia, Aalen (original work published 1931)
Zuzek I (1964) Kormčaja kniga: studies on the chief code of Russian canon law. Pontificium Institutum Orientalium Studiorum, Rome
Zweigert K, Kötz H (1987) An introduction to comparative law, 2nd edn. Clarendon Press, Oxford

Chapter 8
Navigating the Duality of Law and Equity in the English Common Law Tradition

8.1 Introduction

The English common law tradition, encompassing several distinct sub-traditions, is one of the two major legal traditions of the Western world. Similar to the civil law tradition, it has exerted a profound global influence, being adopted by numerous countries with diverse social and cultural backgrounds. The reception of English law in such varied settings testifies to its genius and adaptability, especially when this reception was voluntary rather than imposed. Initially, the spread of English common law resulted from British colonization and the political dominance of the British Empire from the eighteenth through the early twentieth century. It was an established principle of English law that settlers in a new colony would bring with them and adhere to the laws of their homeland.

Countries such as Australia, Canada (excluding Quebec), and New Zealand, which were once part of the British colonial empire, inherited the English common law system and continue to apply its legal philosophy and principles in their contemporary legal systems. Other nations that share, to varying extents, the heritage of common law include the United States, Ireland, India, Pakistan, Bangladesh, Malaysia, Singapore, Hong Kong, South Africa, Nigeria, and Kenya. Much of the law in these countries is rooted in old precedents from the time when they were under British rule, although their legal systems have diverged since gaining independence. Remarkably, in many of these countries, this uniquely English set of legal sources, institutions, and norms has co-existed with indigenous cultural, religious, and legal traditions, often resulting in 'hybrid' systems. These hybrid systems reflect a blend of English common law and local customs, creating legal frameworks that are both resilient and adaptable to the specific needs and contexts of each country.

The development of common law in England has unfolded gradually over an extended period. Common law is understood as a system of law that emerged from

G. Mousourakis, *Traversing Legal Traditions*, Springer Textbooks in Law,
https://doi.org/10.1007/978-3-031-94669-1_8

a centralized justice system, becoming uniform across the entire country. This stands in contrast to largely customary local or provincial laws, which were specific to particular areas or regions and predated the establishment of common law. In some cases, these customary laws continued to apply alongside common law.

The administration of common law was predominantly carried out by the monarch and the representative courts. It is primarily characterized as case-based law—a body of legal principles developed through judicial decisions. This system evolved distinctly from statute law, which is comprised of laws enacted by the legislature. While statute law is derived from acts of Parliament, common law is 'judge-made,' arising from courts applying legal principles established in previous cases with similar facts. The operation of this judge-made law hinges on a hierarchical court structure where decisions of higher courts are binding on lower courts, adhering to the doctrine of precedent (*stare decisis*). The term 'common law' in this context refers specifically to case law and the reliance on judicial precedents.

The doctrine of precedent can be understood in two distinct ways. The first interpretation posits that a judge's decision serves as evidence of an already existing law, suggesting that the relevant rule was in place prior to the judicial ruling. This interpretation implies that the same rule should be consistently applied in future cases. Conversely, the second interpretation holds that a judge's decision establishes a new rule that did not previously exist but becomes binding from the moment the decision is issued, thereby affecting future cases. Historically, in earlier centuries, the predominant view was that judicial decisions merely provided evidence of pre-existing laws.[1] During the nineteenth and twentieth centuries, the interpretation that court decisions create law, rather than merely stating it, became prevalent. This interpretation is confirmed by the doctrine of *stare decisis* (Latin for 'to stand by things decided'). The application of *stare decisis*, along with the custom of deciding cases by analogy to previous cases, suggests that common law has developed based on precedents and case law. Consequently, common law legal reasoning is a form of case-based reasoning that identifies similarities and differences between new cases and previously decided cases.

Common law, as it developed through the royal courts from around the twelfth century, is distinct from the body of rules and principles known as equity. Equity emerged from the decisions of the courts of equity, starting around the fourteenth century. Equity aimed to address the rigidities and deficiencies of common law by providing more flexible and fair outcomes.

Over time, the role of statutes and legislation has increased significantly in common law jurisdictions, often taking precedence over judge-made common law. This shift has been driven by the need for clear, consistent, and comprehensive legal frameworks to address the complexities of modern society. Consequently, statutes and legislative enactments are now the primary sources of law, supplemented by common law principles where necessary. This evolution reflects the dynamic nature

[1]As the eighteenth-century English jurist William Blackstone stated, "the decisions of courts of justice are the evidence of what is common law." Blackstone (1825), vol. 1, p. 71.

of law in responding to societal changes. Statutes provide specificity and clarity that common law, which evolves more slowly through judicial decisions, sometimes lacks. Legislatures can quickly address new issues and provide detailed regulations that are essential for governance in areas such as technology, environmental protection, and international trade. Moreover, the democratic process underlying legislative enactments ensures that laws reflect the current values and needs of society. This process involves public participation and debate, resulting in laws that are more aligned with contemporary expectations and norms. As a result, the judiciary often defers to statutory law, interpreting and applying it within the bounds set by legislative intent. While common law continues to play an important role in interpreting and filling gaps in statutes, the primacy of legislation in common law jurisdictions underscores the necessity for a robust and adaptable legal system capable of addressing the demands of an ever-evolving society.

As the above discussion suggests, the term 'common law' can be understood in more than one way. First, common law refers to the universal system of law that developed in England from about the twelfth century onwards. This system emerged from the decisions of the royal courts and became a standardized set of legal principles and practices applicable across the realm, replacing local customs and laws. Secondly, the same term refers to the family of legal systems derived from English law, including those in former British colonies such as the United States, Canada, and Australia. When we say that a legal system belongs to the common law family, we usually refer to the system as a whole, encompassing case law, legislative enactments, and principles originally established by the courts of equity. Within these legal systems, the term 'common law' denotes that part of the law developed by the courts, as contrasted with statute law or the law enacted by Parliament. Additionally, the term differentiates that part of the law created by the common law courts from the body of rules and principles of equity, which were developed separately by the Courts of Chancery to address issues of fairness and justice that common law could not adequately resolve.[2]

8.2 Custom, Royal Justice, and the Rise of the English Common Law

At the end of the eleventh century, the law in England differed little from that in Germany or northern France. Although England had been a Roman province for over three centuries, the invasion of the Angles and Saxons led to the replacement of Roman law with Anglo-Saxon law, a form of Germanic folk-law. The law codes

[2] For a closer look at the defining features and influence of the common law tradition see: De Cruz (1999), p. 99 ff; Bogdan (1994), p. 101 ff; Glenn (2004), p. 222 ff; Baker, (2000); Buckland and McNair (1965); David and Brierley (1985), Pt Three (The Common Law); Eisenberg (1988); Zweigert and Kötz (1998), ch. B.III (The Anglo-American Legal Family).

of *Aethelberht* of Kent (*c.* 600),[3] Ine of Wessex (*c.* 700),[4] and Alfred the Great (*c.* 890)[5] were similar in nature to the Continental *leges barbarorum*. However, unlike the latter, these English codes were written in Anglo-Saxon rather than Latin. In general, the law in England, like elsewhere in northern Europe, primarily consisted of unwritten customary law, which was occasionally supplemented or superseded by canon law.

The country was organized into shires (later known as counties), which were further subdivided into hundreds and vills (small townships). Each shire and hundred had its own court, known as communal courts, in addition to seignorial courts held by local lords for their free tenants. These seignorial courts operated as 'private enterprise' courts, profiting from court fees and providing justice backed by the lord's military power. The shire court convened periodically and was presided over by the sheriff, who acted as the king's representative. In contrast, the hundred courts had jurisdiction over smaller localities and dealt with minor matters compared to those handled by the shire courts. Overall, while the formal structure and jurisdiction of these courts varied, they collectively administered a system of law that was deeply rooted in local customs and the power dynamics of the time.[6]

The immediate effect of the Norman Conquest of England in the latter half of the eleventh century (1066) was a significant intensification of legal particularism. This was marked by an increase in the number of franchise and manorial courts and the reintroduction of the old principle of personality of law, which favoured the Norman segment of the population. However, the strong administrative interests of the

[3]The law code of King Aethelberht of Kent is one of the earliest written legal codes in Anglo-Saxon England, reflecting a blend of Germanic customary law and Christian influences. This code primarily addressed personal injury, property rights, and social order, providing a detailed account of compensations for various offenses. It established a wergild, or man-price, system where specific monetary compensations were prescribed for various injuries and deaths. The amount of compensation varied according to the victim's social status, indicating a stratified society. Nobles, freemen, and slaves each had distinct wergild values, with offenses against higher-status individuals incurring greater penalties. The code shows the influence of Christianity, particularly in its protection of church property and clergy.

[4]The Law Code of Ine consisted of seventy-six sections in the form of 'dooms' or penal judgments. It specifies various crimes, including theft, violence, and other offenses, and their corresponding punishments. Punishments often involved fines or physical penalties, depending on the severity of the crime and the status of the offender. The code also includes regulations concerning land ownership, property rights, and inheritance and outlines procedures for resolving disputes and seeking justice.

[5]The law code of Alfred the Great, known as the 'Doom Book' or 'Code of Alfred', is a comprehensive collection of legal statutes that combined earlier Anglo-Saxon laws with Biblical principles. It is one of the largest and most ambitious legislative enactments to survive from Anglo-Saxon England, reflecting Alfred's aim to create a unified and just legal system in his kingdom. The code incorporates laws from the Bible, particularly the Old Testament, adapting them to fit the Anglo-Saxon context. It includes detailed criminal laws, defining various offenses and their punishments, as well as procedures for the administration of justice. Alfred included laws from earlier rulers, such as Ine of Wessex, to show continuity and respect for established legal traditions.

[6]On the system of justice that prevailed in Anglo-Saxon times see Baker (2019), chapter 1; Sandberg (2023), p. 45 ff; Robinson et al. (1994), pp. 124–129.

Norman kings and their centralization efforts gradually led to the establishment of a strong central government in England, capable of imposing a uniform legal system across the entire country.

Initially, the Norman kings utilized the existing local courts but soon began dispatching their own judges throughout the country to hear cases locally. This practice allowed them to exert more efficient control over their realm and enabled them to compete with local courts for litigants' fees. To attract litigants away from the local courts, the royal courts introduced new and superior methods of trial. These innovations were so successful that eventually, all law courts came under royal control. One significant advantage of having disputes adjudicated by a royal court was the higher likelihood of proper enforcement of the court's judgments, compared to those decided by local courts.[7]

King Henry II (r. 1154–1189), aiming to strengthen royal authority, divided England into regional circuits, or *eyres*, and initiated the regular dispatch of judges throughout the country to hear and decide cases.[8] These judges, known as *justiciae errantes*, were tasked with investigating crimes, addressing negligence and misconduct by officials, resolving private disputes, and enforcing the feudal and other rights of the king. Henry II aimed to build trust among his subjects by resolving disputes fairly in accordance with local customs, administered by the circuit judges. These judges carried out their tasks under specific commissions, of which there were three main types: *gaol delivery*, *Oyer and Terminer*, and *assize*. The commission of gaol delivery empowered the judges to try all persons held in gaols.[9] The commission of Oyer and Terminer, literally meaning 'to hear and determine', authorized judges to try all criminal cases of treason, felony, or misdemeanour committed within the county. The commission of assize empowered judges to try civil cases. Although civil cases were generally tried at Westminster, trials could be held in local courts for the convenience of the parties involved.[10]

In 1160, Henry II introduced the 'petty assizes', a significant legal reform aimed at streamlining the process of resolving land disputes. The petty assizes were legal

---

[7] The Norman kings, especially Henry II, sought to expand the scope of royal jurisdiction not only at the expense of local and feudal authorities but also at the expense of the ecclesiastical courts.

[8] The word *eyre* is French and derived from the Latin *iter*, meaning journey. *Eyres* appear to have existed during the reign of Henry I (1100–1135), but Henry II systematized this practice. In 1166, Henry II appointed Earl Geoffrey de Mandeville and Sir Richard de Lucy to tour the country to enforce royal law. In 1176, the itinerant judges, who numbered between 20 and 30 at a time, were organized into six circuits. According to Milsom, "the conduct of business at an *eyre* epitomized its historical role. The first part, the pleas of the Crown, represents the system of itinerant government, the first stage in institutional centralization… The other part of the eyre's business was the common pleas, ordinary litigation between ordinary people…and since [the central royal court or Court of Common Pleas] became the ordinary forum for such litigation, it is important to emphasize that it was in the eyre that such pleas could first come to royal justice as a matter of routine." Milsom (1981b), pp. 27–29.

[9] It should be noted that during this period, imprisonment was not regarded as a form of punishment.

[10] A case would be formally set down for hearing at Westminster 'unless before' (*nisi prius*) it came up for trial locally. For more on the character of itinerant royal justice see Baker (2019), p. 17 ff.

proceedings involving a panel of neighbours, known as an assize, tasked with determining facts in disputes primarily concerning property and related issues. These panels operated as early forms of juries, with local individuals familiar with the parties and the land in question investigating and providing verdicts based on their knowledge and observations. The term 'assize' originally referred to a session or sitting of a council or court,[11] where judicial or legislative matters were discussed and resolved. Over time, the term 'assize' came to denote the specific enactments, decisions, or laws made during these sessions. Essentially, the meaning evolved from the act of holding a court session to the substantive outcomes of those sessions—namely, the legal judgments and rules issued by the court. The assizes established the practice of trial by inquisition, which over time became synonymous with the term 'assize' itself, referring to a specific legal procedure involving the inquisition of 12 men, known as jurors, who were responsible for investigating and determining the facts of a case.[12] Henry II systematized and expanded this procedure, ensuring that juries were always summoned before royal judges rather than local officials like sheriffs. Furthermore, whereas the relevant procedure (*recognitio*) was initially used only to protect royal and other privileged interests, it was now made available to individual plaintiffs who could use it in various specified civil actions.

Through a series of enactments or 'assizes', Henry II expanded the availability of trial by inquisition across various cases. The Assize of Clarendon, a landmark decree enacted in 1166, established the use of juries for presenting criminal charges. It mandated the formation of grand juries, composed of 12 men from each hundred and 4 men from each township. These juries were tasked with reporting those suspected of serious crimes, such as murder, robbery, arson, theft, counterfeiting, and harbouring criminals, to the king's judges. Jurors faced fines if they concealed an offence or provided false information. Suspects could be subjected to trial by ordeal if the jurors deemed there was sufficient evidence against them.[13] By centralizing

[11] The term 'assize' originates from the Old French word 'assise,' meaning a session or sitting of a court, which itself is derived from the Latin 'assidere,' meaning 'to sit beside.' Over time, the meaning of 'assize' expanded to encompass several related concepts: it came to refer to something akin to an act of parliament, the authorization of specific judicial proceedings, the proceedings themselves, the jurors who played a crucial role in these proceedings, and the sessions held by itinerant judges who oversaw these proceedings.

[12] Early forms of communal justice that served similar functions existed in Anglo-Saxon times. The Anglo-Saxon legal system relied heavily on local communities to maintain law and order. The hundred and shire courts were gatherings where free men of the community came together to settle disputes and administer justice. One key element of this system was the process of 'compurgation', where the accused could be acquitted if a sufficient number of 'oath-helpers' (typically twelve) swore to their innocence. These oath-helpers were not jurors in the modern sense but were character witnesses who vouched for the credibility of the accused. The role of community members in these processes laid the groundwork for the later development of the jury system in England.

[13] Trial by ordeal was a form of trial where the accused had to undergo a physically painful or dangerous test, the outcome of which was believed to be determined by divine intervention. It was based on the belief that God would protect the innocent and reveal the guilty through the ordeal's results. There were several types of ordeals, including ordeal by fire, ordeal by water, and ordeal by combat. In the ordeal by fire, the accused had to walk a certain distance holding a red-hot iron.

judicial processes, the Assize of Clarendon extended the king's authority over criminal justice, reducing the influence of local lords and feudal courts.

Given the scarcity of educated laypeople, it was common for the royal administration, including the judicial system, to rely heavily on clerics. Clerics were typically among the few literate and educated members of society, making them well-suited for the roles of judges and administrators. These clerics possessed the requisite skills in Latin (the administrative language of the time), knowledge of canon law, and experience in record-keeping and legal procedures. Consequently, they were appointed to serve as royal justices and to administer the law throughout the kingdom. Over time, as the legal profession developed and more laypeople became educated, the role of clerics in the judiciary diminished, leading to the establishment of a more secular legal system. By the early fourteenth century, judges were appointed from among the senior advocates who argued cases before the royal courts. These advocates, known by various names over time (such as serjeants-at-law and barristers), formed an elite group of learned lawyers alongside the judges. The development of English law has been significantly influenced by the political, economic, and intellectual environment of this group.

Initially, circuit judges decided cases by applying local customs, which they learned with the help of a jury. The jury, typically composed of local men familiar with the customs and practices of the region, provided the judges with the necessary insights into local traditions and norms. However, circuit judges had the authority to evaluate local customs and could refuse to enforce those they considered unreasonable or unjust. This practice was crucial in ensuring that local customs did not conflict with overarching principles of justice and fairness.

Upon their return to Westminster, judges would engage in discussions about the merits of various customs, approving certain customs and condemning others. By exercising this discretion, the judges eliminated customs deemed inappropriate or outdated and helped to standardize legal practices across different regions. This process contributed to the emergence of a more uniform and coherent body of law throughout England, known as the common law.[14]

If their wounds healed cleanly within a few days, they were considered innocent; if not, they were deemed guilty. There were two forms of ordeal by water: cold water and hot water. In the cold water ordeal, the accused was tied and thrown into a body of water. If they floated, it was believed that the water, a pure element, had rejected them, indicating guilt. If they sank, they were considered innocent. In the hot water ordeal, the accused had to retrieve an object from boiling water. As with the ordeal by fire, the healing of their wounds determined their innocence or guilt. The ordeal by combat was a judicial duel where the accused fought their accuser. It was believed that God would grant victory to the righteous party. These ordeals were administered under the supervision of the church, and it was believed that divine judgment would manifest through the ordeal's outcome. However, the use of trial by ordeal declined after the Fourth Lateran Council in 1215, which forbade clergy from participating in such practices. This eventually led to the development of more rational legal procedures and the decline of ordeals as a means of determining guilt or innocence.

[14]Today, it is common to distinguish judge-made case law from customary law as sources of law. However, this distinction has not always been clearly made. The customary character of customary law partly lies in the fact that judges and other adjudicators follow the custom of applying these

As common law began to take shape, the courts of common law came into existence. The early Norman kings ruled with the assistance of the *Curia Regis* (King's Council), a body composed of the king's chief officers, such as the Chancellor, Treasurer, and Justiciar, as well as leading nobles and clergy.[15] The *Curia Regis* functioned as a legislative, administrative, and judicial body, serving as the supreme central court that handled all the business of the central government. It advised the king on important matters of state, including policy decisions, administration, and lawmaking. As the highest court of appeal in the kingdom, it heard cases involving significant disputes, particularly those concerning land, and could override decisions made by lower courts. The *Curia Regis* also assisted in the administration of the kingdom, including the management of royal lands, collection of taxes, and implementation of the king's orders. Over time, the *Curia Regis* evolved and its functions became more specialized, resulting in the development of distinct institutions such as the Court of Exchequer, the Court of Common Pleas, and the King's Bench. The bulk of English law during this period emerged not from legislation but from the decisions made by these courts, which established legal precedents. Unlike in Continental Europe, where the unification of customs was achieved through codification, England unified its customs through the judicial decisions of its courts.[16]

The first court to separate from the *Curia Regis* was the Court of Exchequer. Established in the twelfth century during the reign of Henry I, it was originally part of the royal household and gradually evolved into a distinct entity. As the Treasury Department of the Monarchy, the primary function of the Exchequer was to manage the royal finances, particularly the collection and auditing of taxes, revenues, and debts owed to the Crown. The court was divided into two main components: the Exchequer of Account (or the Upper Exchequer) and the Exchequer of Pleas (or the Lower Exchequer). The Exchequer of Account dealt with the auditing of accounts and the management of royal revenues. The Exchequer of Pleas, on the other hand, functioned as a court of law handling civil cases involving financial matters, particularly those related to debts owed to the Crown. It adjudicated disputes over payments and levies, ensuring that the Crown's interests were protected.

The Court of Common Pleas, often referred to simply as Common Pleas, was established in the late twelfth century to handle civil litigation between private individuals, as opposed to criminal cases or matters involving the crown, which were addressed by other courts.[17] This court had jurisdiction over a variety of civil

rules. Customary rules can come into being, or are confirmed, if they are actually used in legal decision making.

[15] The Norman *Curia Regis* was similar in constitution and function to the Anglo-Saxon *Witan*—the council of the Anglo-Saxon kings.

[16] Baker (2019), p. 20 ff. Reference should be made here to the introduction of law reporting, probably in the 13th century. This was a significant development that enabled the opinions and decisions of the courts to be recorded for continued reference. Law reporting made possible the consistent development of the law through the doctrine of precedent.

[17] King Henry II appointed five members of his *Curia Regis* to hear disputes between the king's subjects. This measure was probably intended to relieve the *Curia Regis* from some of the burden

disputes, including those related to property, contracts, and debts. Unlike other medieval courts that often travelled with the king, the Court of Common Pleas was based in Westminster Hall, providing a fixed location where individuals could reliably bring their disputes. This stability was essential for fostering a consistent and accessible legal process. As a permanent court whose judges made decisions that set precedents, the Court of Common Pleas played a significant role in the development and consolidation of common law. Additionally, the court contributed to the professionalization of the legal system in England. It was staffed by professional judges, known as justices of the Common Pleas, who possessed significant legal expertise. This professional judiciary helped ensure more consistent and knowledgeable adjudication of cases.

The third court, the Court of King's Bench, was the last of the three courts to break away from the *Curia Regis*. It had the authority to hear serious criminal cases, including treason, murder, and other major felonies. Its jurisdiction extended to cases that threatened the king's peace and stability of the kingdom. While primarily known for its criminal jurisdiction, the King's Bench also handled civil cases, particularly those involving the crown or significant legal principles. The court was theoretically always in the presence of the king, symbolizing its importance and the direct involvement of royal authority in its proceedings. The justices of the King's Bench often travelled on circuit throughout the kingdom, hearing cases in different localities. This practice helped to extend the reach of royal justice beyond the capital and ensured that even remote areas received attention from the highest judicial authority. As a permanent fixture in the English judicial system, the Court of King's Bench set important legal precedents and contributed to the development of common law, influencing legal practices and principles far beyond its original scope.

The separation of these three courts from the King's Council had significant consequences. The establishment of a stationary royal court, functioning independently of the king's personal presence, marks the beginning of the separation between the judiciary and other organs of governance. By the thirteenth century, typical justices were no longer the king's private counsellors and advisers but professional judges employed to administer the law. Nevertheless, medieval judges were regarded as special representatives of the king, serving his interests. During this era, no clear distinction was made between the king, the living individual ruler, and the Crown, the impersonal institution of the monarchy. Additionally, it should be noted that just as the royal courts had previously competed with local and feudal courts for business, the aforementioned courts competed among themselves because the judges and other officials relied on the fees paid by litigants for their incomes.

The royal courts developed a rigid system of rules and principles that extended beyond legal procedures to include the specific actions through which claims could be initiated. An action at common law began with the issuance of a formal document known as a writ.[18] This writ was obtained from the chancery office, headed by

---

of the judicial work, especially where it did not affect the king directly.

[18] The word 'writ' simply denotes a writing and refers to a brief, succinct order.

the Chancellor, the king's chief advisor and principal administrative officer. Originally an administrative device created by the Anglo-Saxon rulers of England, the writ became, under the Norman kings, the chief instrument of both administration and legal development. King Henry II 'judicialized' the writs, transforming them into orders addressed to the sheriff. These orders commanded a defendant to either comply with a specified action or appear before the king's judges to explain why he should not. Essentially, the writ served as an authorization form, permitting common law judges to hear and determine a matter. Consequently, writs became the principal means of initiating legal proceedings.

Initially, writs were issued only in special cases to address exceptional circumstances. When a significant event occurred, the king, through the Chancellor, would issue a written command to a royal official or a lord holding a franchise court, and this command was the writ. Each writ acquired a specific name, and once formulated, it became a precedent. Until the mid-thirteenth century, the Chancellor had the freedom to issue writs as needed without restriction on their wording. However, by the fourteenth century, this practice ended as it was believed that too many grounds for claims had been developed.[19] From that time onwards, the Chancellor could issue writs only when the facts of the case were similar to those of a previous case for which a writ had been issued.

All litigation commenced with a writ that outlined the nature of the plaintiff's claim in the prescribed form. The plaintiff's success or failure depended on their ability to meet the established formal requirements. The existence of a legal remedy was contingent upon the existence of a writ.[20]

There were different writs for various claims, such as the writ of right to recover land, the writ of debt to recover money owed, and the writ of trespass to complain of a breach of peace. Clerks in the chancery office kept precedents of the issued writs, and unless a complainant could frame their complaint within one of the forms of writ recorded in the *Register of Writs*, they had no remedy. Since an action could not be brought without a writ, it became established that the only kinds of harm for which one could seek redress in law were those that could be described within the narrow and unyielding language of some recognized writ.[21]

---

[19] At the time of Glanvill (late twelfth century) there were about 40 writs, whereas during the reign of Edward I (1272–1307) there were more than 400. By the Provisions of Oxford (1258), the Chancery clerks were prohibited in future from sealing unprecedented writs without the permission of the king's council.

[20] Before the introduction of legal procedures based on writs under King Henry II, legal proceedings in secular courts were entirely oral. The law dispensed was based on unwritten customs, and the doctrine of precedent was unknown. Additionally, judges did not present reasoned judgments, and legal rolls rarely recorded principles of jurisprudence. Most cases concluded with a jury verdict, where matters of fact and law were intermingled, or by trial by combat.

[21] A clear illustration of the complexity introduced by this highly technical system can be seen through the following examples of writs available for wrongs against chattels: (a) A damages B's book: *writ of trespass to goods*; (b) A borrows B's book for two weeks but then informs B that he will not return the book until six months later: *writ of detinue*; (c) A borrows B's book and then sells it to another person: *writ of trover*. In each case, a wrong was committed against B's property.

If a plaintiff succeeded in their action, they were typically awarded damages, meaning the defendant had to pay a sum of money determined by the court. There was a limited right to appeal if an error occurred. The common law evolved largely through arguments by lawyers and judges about the nature and scope of the writs, the circumstances under which a writ should be issued, and the remedies it should entail. Indeed, the development of the common law was closely tied to the expansion of the writ system. As with all rudimentary legal systems, procedural institutions, such as those associated with the writ system, preceded substantive law. Thus, each new writ eventually led to the emergence of a substantive law rule.

Lawyers referred to the compartmentalization of law and practice associated with specific writs as 'forms of action'. These forms of action served to formalize, categorize, classify, and eventually ossify diverse actions in accordance with available remedies. In other words, a *cause* of action recognized by the law implies the existence of a *form* of action set out in a specific writ that covers the facts of a plaintiff's case.[22] Generally, the system of writs as a method of pleading was restrictive, and the relevant rules, derived from reported cases, were strictly applied without exception. This rigidity led to significant injustices in the common law.[23] As we will see later, it was in response to these shortcomings that the system of equity was developed.

The writ system was formally abolished around the mid-nineteenth century by the Common Law Procedure Act 1852.[24] This enactment sought to simplify and streamline legal procedures by abolishing the necessity of choosing specific writs for different types of actions. Instead, the Act introduced more flexible and straightforward procedures for commencing legal actions, thus making the legal process more accessible and less prone to technical errors. This reform was part of a broader movement during the nineteenth century aimed at modernizing and rationalizing the English legal system, making it more efficient and fairer. However, the principles of common law, originally structured through the writs, continue to influence case law. While the writ system and its formalism have vanished, much of its substance and spirit persist.

At this point, we might say that three strands of influence can be identified in the early development of English law. The foremost among these is the *Curia Regis*, the king's court, and the courts that evolved from it. These courts played a pivotal role in developing the writ system, unparalleled in the contemporary history of Continental European law. The second influence is the Roman and canon law

---

In example (a), B's enjoyment of his property was unjustifiably interfered with; in example (b), B was deprived of possession of his property; and in example (c), B's right of ownership was denied. Each writ had its own specific procedural rules, including time limits, rules of evidence, and hearing requirements.

[22] See in general, Maitland (1976). And see Baker (2019), p. 60 ff; Sandberg (2023), p. 92 ff.

[23] As a commentator has remarked, "it was better said the judges to suffer a mischief in an individual case than the inconvenience which would follow from admitting exceptions to general rules." Baker (1979), p. 70.

[24] 15 & 16 Vict. Cap. 76.

introduced to England in the twelfth century. The third influence is the customary law that survived the Norman Conquest and continued to be applied by local courts. While the latter two sources significantly shaped private law in much of Continental Europe, their relatively minor impact on English law explains why common law evolved distinctly from civil law. The history of English law is characterized not by the adoption of a foreign legal system and its merger with native customs but by the growth of a body of rules developed by the king's justices and their successors, in which neither Roman law nor customary law was a decisive influence. Instead, the development of common law rules occurred largely through the creation of exceptions to existing rules, which themselves became fixed and rigid. The rigidity of the legal process, the need to conform to the established framework, and the centralized court system all contributed to unifying the diverse local customs and practices into a common law followed by the entire country.

It should be noted, however, that for a century and a half after the Norman Conquest, it was by no means certain that England would develop a distinct legal system. The revival of Roman law studies in Italy during the eleventh century also influenced England, and English students were among those who travelled to Italy to attend lectures at the law schools. Moreover, there were several direct connections between England and some of the prominent Glossators, including Lanfranc, a former law teacher at Pavia, who served as Archbishop of Canterbury from 1070 until his death in 1089. Lanfranc was an accomplished jurist with profound knowledge of civil, canon, and Lombard law. He is recognized for his significant contributions to the administrative and legislative reorganization of England. His efforts included the reformation of church governance, aligning it more closely with continental practices, and the establishment of ecclesiastical courts, which operated alongside the secular courts, thereby creating a dual system of justice. These reforms not only enhanced the efficiency and coherence of the legal system but also ensured a more centralized and organized administration. Lanfranc's influence extended to the drafting of laws and charters, bringing a degree of legal sophistication that had not previously existed in England.

The first known teacher of Roman law in England was the Glossator Vacarius, who arrived around the mid-twelfth century. He was appointed as a teacher at the University of Oxford, where he lectured on Roman law and wrote his most famous work, the *Liber Pauperum* (Book of the Poor), a nine-volume compendium of Roman law based on Justinian's Code and Digest, specifically designed to be accessible to students who could not afford the expensive legal texts from the Continent.[25] However, Vacarius' success alarmed the monarchy, which feared the imposition of Roman law as the law of the land and its implications of imperial sovereignty. The barons, concerned that Roman law might lend support to royal absolutism, also resisted. Consequently, King Stephen prohibited Vacarius from teaching at Oxford, and in 1234, Henry III forbade the teaching of Roman law in London. In 1236, the barons at Merton rejected a proposal by bishops to adopt the Roman law principle

[25] See de Zulueta (1927).

of legitimizing children born before their parents' marriage, asserting they did not wish to change the laws of England (*Nolumus leges Angliae mutare*). This stance reinforced the practice of English courts and encouraged the autonomous development of English law. Nevertheless, Roman law concepts continued to influence English legal doctrine, as reflected in the era's two most significant legal treatises: Glanvill's *Tractatus de legibus et consuetudinibus regni Angliae* (Treatise on the Laws and Customs of the Kingdom of England), written between c. 1187 and 1189, and Bracton's treatise of the same title, written between 1220 and 1240.

Ranulf de Glanvill, also known as Glanvill or Glanville, held several prominent positions during his career. He served as the sheriff of both Lancashire and Yorkshire, where he was responsible for maintaining law and order in these counties. His diplomatic skills were also recognized, leading to his role as an ambassador. Additionally, he acted as a justice in eyre, traveling to various parts of the kingdom to administer royal justice. In 1180, Glanvill was appointed Justiciar (Chief Minister of the Crown) at the court of Henry II, becoming one of the most powerful officials in England. As Justiciar, he played a crucial role in the administration of the kingdom, overseeing the legal system and implementing the king's policies. His aforementioned treatise, one of the earliest and most significant legal texts of medieval England, is divided into fourteen books and records the law laid down by the king's court—the common law, which, according to Glanvill, was only one of the sources of law in England. In this treatise, he outlined the remedies available in the king's court and the manner in which these remedies could be invoked. The work primarily focuses on legal procedure, particularly concerning land issues, and reflects an enduring feature of the common law: its dependence on the writ system.[26] Glanvill's work demonstrates that the author had some knowledge of Roman and canon law. The preface and introductory chapters are modelled on those of Justinian's Institutes, and there is an attempt, albeit not always successful, to assimilate Roman legal concepts into English common law. More importantly, the work shows that Roman law provided a method of reasoning on legal matters and a capacity to create a technical language and forms, enabling the evolution of precise yet general rules from a mass of vague customs and particular cases.[27]

Bracton, formally known as Henry de Bracton (or Bratton) served as one of the king's justices on both the King's Bench and the Assizes. Like many royal judges of his era, he was also an ecclesiastic, holding the position of Chancellor at Exeter Cathedral until his death in 1268. Bracton was a student of Justice William de Raleigh, who was instrumental in the development of several legal writs. Bracton's treatise *Tractatus de legibus et consuetudinibus Angliae*, written during the reign of Henry III (1216–1272), was notably influenced by Roman law, particularly through the Glossator Azo. The work is written in Latin and is divided into two parts: the *Liber Primus*, which parallels Justinian's Institutes, and the *Liber Secundus*,

---

[26] In the time of Glanvill, writs were not fixed in number and the king possessed unlimited power to issue new writs.

[27] Holdsworth (1938), p. 15.

primarily a treatise on some of the writs foundational to English common law.[28] Bracton's treatise incorporates numerous extracts from Justinian's Digest and Code, as well as Azo's *Summae* and the works of other Continental jurists. The scope of his work is akin to the contemporary French texts on customary law, which similarly incorporated elements of Roman law. Bracton enhanced the common law's insufficient rules in areas such as personal property and contract law with Roman legal principles. Additionally, he utilized Roman concepts and distinctions to describe, classify, and explain the writs and actions administered by the royal courts.[29] Bracton's work is a testament to the advancement of English common law, highlighting the introduction of new writs and forms of action, and the significant displacement of local customs by the common law.[30]

The two centuries following Bracton's death witnessed a marked decline in the influence of Roman law in England. Although Roman law continued to be studied at the Universities of Oxford and Cambridge, its impact on the development of common law was minimal. This decline can be attributed to several factors, many of which were political. A key reason was the emergence of a distinct English legal identity that emphasized the autonomy of the common law tradition, which was considered uniquely suited to the English social context. The political climate of the time, characterized by a desire to assert English sovereignty and legal independence, further marginalized Roman law, often associated with the Papacy and foreign influence. The Church's canon law, which was based on Roman law, often conflicted with English common law, creating tension between ecclesiastical courts and royal courts.[31]

---

[28] As the basis of his work, Bracton compiled a notebook in which he collected two thousand cases from the plea rolls of the first 24 years of Henry III's reign. However, the treatise appears to be unfinished; it ends abruptly during the discussion of the writ of right.

[29] As Samuel Thorne observes, "[Bracton] was a trained jurist with the principles and distinctions of Roman jurisprudence firmly in mind, using them throughout his work, wherever they could be used, to rationalize and reduce to order the results reached in English courts." Thorne (1968), p. 33.

[30] It is interesting to note that Bracton agreed with Glanvill when he claimed that a king who wished to rule well needed two things: arms and laws. He declared that, although the king was supreme in his realm, his power was derived from law, which should govern all, king and subject alike. Notwithstanding such claims, Bracton recognized the Roman law concepts of *necessitas* and *utilitas publica*, which provided rulers with justification to override the law to promote or safeguard the public interest. For a closer look at the contribution of Glanvill and Bracton see Baker (2019), p. 185 ff.

[31] From the eleventh century, ecclesiastical courts administered canon law, and their jurisdiction was remarkably extensive. They presided over all matters related to matrimony, wills, and the succession of personal property. Additionally, these courts held disciplinary authority over clergy members, who typically claimed the right to be tried in an ecclesiastical court when accused of offenses, as the penalties imposed by these courts were generally milder than those enforced by secular courts. The Church frequently sought to expand its jurisdiction beyond these areas, leading to disputes with secular authorities. These tensions reached a dramatic climax during the reign of Henry II with the murder of Thomas Becket, *Archbishop* of Canterbury. On the role of the ecclesiastical courts see Baker (2019), chapter 8.

Another significant reason was the structure of legal education in England, where judges and lawyers were trained at the Inns of Court rather than at universities. The Inns of Court—comprising Lincoln's Inn, Inner Temple, Middle Temple, and Gray's Inn—were self-governing societies akin to trade guilds, shaped by the medieval spirit of corporate organization. These Inns served not only as places of residence but also as centres of learning where students of law could live, study, and gain practical experience.[32] Additionally, the Inns of Court acted as professional guilds, controlling the admission of lawyers to the bar and regulating the practice of law, thereby ensuring that only those who had undergone rigorous training and demonstrated competence could practice. The Inns also played a vital social and networking role, allowing aspiring lawyers to build relationships with established members of the legal profession, which was crucial for career advancement in an era when personal connections were often as important as legal knowledge.

Legal education at the Inns was primarily practical. Aspiring lawyers began their training with basic legal instruction at an inn of Chancery before being admitted to one of the Inns of Court. There, they spent approximately seven years as 'inner barristers,' engaging in moots, attending lectures (known as 'readings'), and participating in various practical exercises under the guidance of senior members. Upon completing their training, they could be called to the bar as 'utter' or 'outer barristers.'[33]

Unlike their Continental European counterparts, who studied law at universities, English lawyers acquired their legal knowledge through hands-on experience in the practical world.[34] Universities typically focused on teaching civil and canon law, often excluding municipal law from their curricula, possibly because it was not written in Latin. As a result, common lawyers distanced themselves from the study of these bodies of law.

Once legal training began to be provided at the Inns of Court, the use of earlier legal treatises such as those by Glanvill and Bracton declined. The works that were now in demand were of a more practical nature, written in French—the language of common lawyers. These practical texts primarily served as guides to legal procedure. Alongside these works, 'plea rolls' were compiled, recording actual cases decided by the common law courts. Additionally, Year Books were produced by individual lawyers, containing concise reports of significant arguments and rulings in cases they observed. By around 1400, personal compilations of legal cases were replaced by standardized collections of court pleadings. In the first half of the sixteenth century, the first 'private law reports' emerged, firmly establishing the

[32] Much about their origins is unclear, but they probably began as hostels (*hospicia*: inns).

[33] The term 'barrister' was not used before the middle of the fifteenth century. It derives from the 'bar' or forum where senior students were called upon to argue at the mock courts or moots. Students who did not wish to become barristers, known as 'practitioners under the bar', could become 'pleaders' and later 'equity draftsmen' and 'conveyancers.' On the rise of the legal profession in England see Palmer (1976); Brand (1987); Baker (2019), chapter 10.

[34] It was not until 1828 that the newly established University of London created the first Chair of English Law.

practice of citation. Among the most renowned of these reports are those by Sir Edward Coke, who is widely regarded as the greatest jurist of his time.[35]

The common law during this period exhibited two notable characteristics: first, it became increasingly fixed and rigid in its substance; second, the rules governing legal procedure grew more complex and technical. Legal works from this era predominantly consist of commentaries on the writ system, while the legal education provided in the Inns of Court focused primarily on imparting to students a precise understanding of procedural law, within which substantive law remained deeply embedded. Any introduction of Roman law occurred not through the common law courts but through ecclesiastical and admiralty courts, as well as the Court of Chancery, which itself arose in response to the growing rigidity of the common law. Additionally, the development of forms of action, around which the law of tort and contract later crystallized, ensured that areas of law that had succumbed most readily to Roman law influence on the Continent were preserved within the common law tradition.

The sixteenth century was probably the most crucial period in the history of the common law. During the early part of this century, common law faced significant challenges, with numerous influential figures advocating for its replacement by Roman law, which was being widely adopted in Germany and other parts of Continental Europe.[36] Despite these pressures, common law endured, thanks to four critical factors. First, the Tudor monarchs, rather than dismantling medieval institutions, chose to adapt and modernize them to meet the evolving needs of the era. This can be explained by the fact that the principles of common law also formed the foundation of the constitution. Abolishing them entirely would have been more of a revolution than a resettlement. Furthermore, during the Reformation, when England broke away from the Roman Catholic Church, Roman law was viewed with suspicion as it was linked to the authority of the Pope, whom the English monarchs and many of their subjects viewed as a foreign adversary. Second, the establishment of new courts, particularly the Court of Chancery[37] and the Court of Star Chamber,[38]

[35] Coke's law reports, which began to appear in 1600, comprise 13 volumes. In these reports, the author emphasizes the role of judicial activity in the continuous development and refinement of the law, as well as in declaring its principles and applying them to the cases at hand. Although Coke's reports fall short of what would now be considered accurate reporting and offer only a vague notion of precedent, they serve the author's primary purpose—namely, the defence of the common law—admirably well.

[36] Frederic William Maitland has brilliantly related the story of the sixteenth century pressure of Roman law in England in his *English Law and the Renaissance* (1901).

[37] See Sect. 8.3 below.

[38] The Court of Star Chamber evolved from the king's Council. In 1487, during the reign of Henry VII, this court was established as a judicial body separate from the Council. The court, as structured under Henry VII, had a mandate to hear petitions of redress. Although initially the court only heard cases on appeal, Henry VIII's Chancellor Thomas Wolsey and, later, Thomas Cranmer encouraged suitors to appeal to it straight away, and not wait until the case had been heard in the common law courts. In the Court of Star Chamber (as in the Court of Chancery) all questions were decided by the court itself, and the granting or withholding of relief was in the discretion of the

addressed many of the shortcomings of common law.[39] Third, the Inns of Court played a crucial role in preserving and teaching the tradition of common law, which, as Maitland described, possessed the toughness of a taught tradition. Lastly, the continuity and modernization of common law were ensured by Edward Coke's restatement of its principles in the early seventeenth century.

Edward Coke (1552–1634) was an influential legal scholar and politician whose career and writings profoundly impacted the development of English common law. Born in Norfolk, England, Coke was educated at Trinity College, Cambridge, and later trained at the Inner Temple, one of the four Inns of Court in London. His legal career began in earnest in the 1570s, and he quickly gained a reputation as a formidable lawyer. Coke's rise to prominence was marked by his appointment as Solicitor General in 1592 and later as Attorney General in 1594. In these roles, he prosecuted several high-profile cases, demonstrating skills in formulating rigorous legal arguments and adherence to the letter of the law. In 1606, Coke was appointed Chief Justice of the Court of Common Pleas, a position in which he became a staunch defender of common law principles against the encroachments of royal prerogative. Coke's judicial career was cut short in 1616 when he was dismissed as Chief Justice of the King's Bench due to his opposition to the Crown's attempts to exert influence over the judiciary. Despite this setback, Coke remained a prominent figure in English politics, serving as a Member of Parliament and using his legal expertise to oppose arbitrary rule.

Coke's most enduring legacy lies in his legal writings, particularly his multi-volume work *Institutes of the Laws of England*. The first volume, known as *Coke on Littleton*, is a commentary on Sir Thomas Littleton's treatise on property law and became a foundational text for English law. His other volumes, which cover various aspects of law, were influential in shaping legal thought in England and, later, in other common law jurisdictions. Furthermore, Coke's commitment to the rule of law and his belief in the supremacy of common law over royal prerogative had a lasting impact on the development of constitutional law. Coke asserted that the law the judges declare and apply is unwritten and immemorial, embodying the wisdom of generations—a result not of philosophical reflection but of the accumulations and refinements of experience. What emerges when a judge declares the law is the distilled knowledge of several generations of men, each decision being based on the experience of those before and tested by the experience of those after. Coke regarded the common law as an expression of right reasoning in the service of natural human

court and not regulated by rigid rules of law. The Court of Star Chamber was abolished in 1641, but its better rules were taken over by the King's Bench and became a permanent part of the law of England. See Baker (2019), p. 127.

[39] As Maitland noted, "were we to say that equity saved the common law, and that the Court of Star Chamber saved the constitution, even in this paradox there would be some truth." Maitland (1911), p. 496.

interests. It followed from this that the common law was fundamental and, as such, it must prevail over any statutory enactment that did not conform to its precepts.[40]

Since the time of Coke, the common law in England has never faced a serious threat. However, while there was no formal reception of Roman law, its influence on English law was not entirely absent. For instance, Roman law provided valuable insights to Lord Mansfield (1705–1793) during the development of English commercial law. Judges have occasionally drawn upon Roman law in both equity and common law, particularly when analogies were available. Moreover, certain Roman legal terms were incorporated into English law. Though Roman legal concepts and doctrines have been woven into the fabric of English law, it cannot be said that its corpus or structure is fundamentally Roman. As William Holdsworth has remarked: "We have received Roman law; but we have received it in small homoeopathic doses, at different periods, and as and when required. It has acted as a tonic to our native legal system, and not as a drug or poison. When received it has never been continuously developed on Roman lines. It has been naturalized and assimilated; and with its assistance, our wholly independent system has, like the Roman law itself, been gradually and continuously built up by the development of old and the creation of new rules to meet the needs of a changing civilization …"[41]

In contrast to English law, Scottish law was significantly influenced by the Roman law-based *ius commune*. By the close of the Middle Ages, Scotland had developed a customary law similar to that of England, though considerably less advanced. However, unlike its English counterpart, Scottish law remained receptive to external influences. The most prominent of these influences was the Church, through which Roman law first began to shape Scottish legal practices and procedures via the infusion of canon law. Additionally, Roman law was introduced to Scotland by students who had attended Continental European universities as early as the thirteenth century. In 1532, the establishment of the Court of Session, a permanent court of professional judges, marked a significant development in Scottish law. This court utilized a version of the Continental Romano-canonical procedure. While the court primarily relied on native Scots law, in cases where it was

[40] For a closer look at Coke's career and work see Bowen (1957); Boyer (1997); Boyer (2003); Gest (1909); Berman (1994); Sandberg (2023), p. 236 ff.

[41] Holdsworth (1923), vol. IV, p. 293. According to Roscoe Pound, "History has played a decisive part in the development of systems of law more than once. A taught tradition is a decisive element in a system. Two distinct long traditions, the one going back to the Roman jurisconsults of the classical era, the other to the teaching of the law of the King's Courts by medieval English lawyers, have kept their identity since the Middle Ages. They have put their mark upon the significant features of the respective systems and have set the two systems off as independent however much either may have borrowed from the other at one time or another. Whatever the Continental law borrows it Romanizes...Whatever the Anglo-American law borrows it Anglicizes...From the Middle Ages the Continental lawyer and the English lawyer have had a different bringing up." Pound (1951), pp. 1–2. For more on the origins and historical evolution of the English common law tradition see: Baker (2019); Hudson (1996); Kiralfy (1958); Lobban (1991); Milsom (1981b); Plucknett (1956); van Caenegem (1988); Harding (1966); Keeton (1966); Pollock and Maitland (1978); Turner (1985); Robinson et al. (1994), chapter 8; Sandberg (2023).

inadequate, judges turned to the Romanist *ius commune*. By the end of the sixteenth century, Roman law had permeated many aspects of Scottish law, becoming a dominant feature of the Scottish legal system. However, from the beginning of the eighteenth century, particularly after the Act of Union in 1707, which unified Scotland and England into a single kingdom, English law began to exert a strong influence on Scottish law. Despite this, the close relationship between Scots law and Continental European law persisted.[42]

8.3 Another Path to Justice: The Emergence and Function of Equity

Legal systems often begin with broad rules designed to address the majority of societal disputes. In England, following the Norman Conquest, common law emerged as a body of non-statutory, general rules applied uniformly across the country. By the end of the thirteenth century, the central authority in England had consolidated its power, significantly aided by the centralization of the legal system and the development of common law courts, which evolved from the king's council (*Curia Regis*). Over time, these courts gained institutional autonomy, but this also led to institutional rigidity. The courts became increasingly reluctant to handle cases that did not conform to established forms of action, leaving many wronged individuals without recourse because no appropriate writ existed, or the remedies provided by common law were insufficient. This refusal to address substantive injustices due to procedural and formal constraints resulted in a gap within the legal system. In response to these shortcomings, equity developed in England as a system designed to fill the gaps left by common law, addressing situations where the common law was inadequate in either the rights it recognized or the remedies it provided.[43]

Equity, in its broadest sense, refers to fairness or justice and is therefore considered a fundamental aspect of law, given that the primary characteristic of good law is its just nature. In a more specific context, particularly within legal philosophy, 'equity' is often contrasted with strict law (*ius strictum*). Once a legal rule is established, it is the judge's duty to apply it, without questioning it, as justice requires consistency in the application of the law. However, no legal system can create rules that ensure justice in every possible scenario, since the vast range of circumstances cannot be fully anticipated. A legal rule is designed to have general applicability, meaning it should be binding in all cases that fall within its scope. Yet, as society evolves and becomes increasingly complex, situations arise that the general rules of the legal system cannot adequately address. One approach to resolving this issue is

[42] Consequently, comparative law scholars often regard Scots law as an example of a 'mixed' or 'hybrid' system. For a closer look at the history and character of Scottish law see: Meston et al. (1991); Evans-Jones (1995); Evans-Jones (1999); MacQueen (1993); MacQueen (1999); Rodger (1996); Carey Miller and Zimmermann (1997).

[43] Kitto (2002), p. v.

through the enactment of new legislation. However, legislative changes are not always easily attainable, particularly when a legal system is still in its early stages of development. In such instances, recourse to equity, as distinct from strict law, becomes essential. As Sidney Smith aptly explains:

> A legal principle, in whatever period, aims at establishing a generalisation for an indefinite variety of cases. Uniformity and universality must characterise it and these are essential qualities in it. [The Greek philosopher] Aristotle, in calling attention to the fact, stated that legal rules are necessarily general while the circumstances of every case are particular, and it is beyond the power of human insight to lay down in advance a rule which will fit all future variations and complications of practice. He concluded that law must be supplemented by equity, there must be a power of adaptation and flexible treatment sometimes resulting in decisions which will even be at variance with formally recognised law and yet will turn out to be intrinsically just.[44]

Aristotle described equity (*epieikeia*) not as distinct from justice, but as a superior form of it, defining it as "a correction of the law where [the law] is defective due to its universality."[45] Legal rules are inherently general, whereas the circumstances of individual cases are uniquely specific. It is impossible for human foresight to create rules in advance that can perfectly account for every future variation and complexity. As a result, the law must be supplemented by equity—a mechanism that allows for adaptation and flexible treatment. This approach may sometimes lead to decisions that deviate from established legal norms, yet these decisions ultimately achieve intrinsic justice. An equitable decision is deemed just because it reflects what the lawgiver would have decided under the specific circumstances of the case, had they been present. The concept of equity (*aequitas*), in contrast with strict law (*ius strictum*), played a significant role in the history of Roman law,[46] and there are notable similarities between the English and Roman approaches to equity. Interpreting legal rules in a liberal and humane spirit, modifying strict and formal laws in the interest of justice, supplementing and expanding the scope of existing rules, and preventing the abuse of legal rights and remedies are all fundamental principles of equity that must be integral to any legal system. England, when common law was in its early stages, the law was flexible enough to be modified to meet the demands of justice, thereby eliminating the need to resort to equity as a separate source of law. Even after many legal rules became settled, early common law judges sometimes administered general equity concurrently with the law by mitigating strict legal rules in particular cases. However, as the legal system grew more complex, the difficulties experienced in common law courts, particularly regarding the use of writs and forms of action, led to increasing dissatisfaction with the system.

---

[44] Smith (1933), p. 310.

[45] Aristotle, *Nicomachean Ethics* V, chapter 10.

[46] Cicero's definition of the *ius civile* as 'the equity constituted for those who belong to the same state so that each may secure his own' (*Top*. 2. 9.), and the renowned aphorism of the jurist Celsius '*ius est ars boni et aequi*': 'the *ius* is the art of the good and just' (Digest 1. 1. 1. pr.), are obviously inspired by the concept of equity as an abstract ideal of justice and as a touchstone of the norms of positive law.

The rise of equity can be attributed to four primary shortcomings of the common law system.[47] First, a plaintiff could only pursue legal action if their complaint fell within the scope of an existing writ or form of action. However, the available writs covered a relatively narrow range of situations, leaving many wronged individuals without recourse in the common law courts because no suitable writ existed. Even when a case did fall within the existing framework, the lack of discretionary power in the courts meant that justice was not always achievable. Secondly, the general and inflexible nature of common law could lead to unconscionable or unjust outcomes.[48] Thirdly, the common law courts were perceived by many medieval people as susceptible to influence by the powerful or wealthy. Fourthly, plaintiffs were often denied a remedy due to defendants defying the court or intimidating the jury, injustices to which the common law had no effective response. When faced with such challenges, the only recourse for a wronged individual was to petition the monarch, who was regarded as 'the fountain of justice', to exercise extraordinary judicial powers and provide a remedy. These petitions would typically assert that, due to the aforementioned deficiencies, the petitioner was unable to obtain a remedy at law and would appeal to the king for relief on the grounds of 'conscience' or 'for the love of God and by way of charity.' Some petitioners would specify the desired remedy, such as the discharge of a mortgage, the enforcement of a trust, or the restraint of a stranger attempting to interfere with an executor's possessory rights.

Initially, most petitions were heard by the King himself.[49] Over time, the King began to delegate requests for assistance to the Chancellor, his chief secretary, and a prominent member of the royal council. Early Chancellors were typically senior ecclesiastics, and although they were not professional lawyers, their prominent position in the royal court likely gave them some familiarity with English law. The Chancellor's department, known as the Chancery, was closely connected with the administration of the law, as it was from this office that writs were issued. During the fourteenth century, it became customary for petitioners to approach the Chancellor directly, and eventually, the Chancellor began to be recognized as holding a court. A Statute of 1340[50] mentioned the Court of Chancery alongside other contemporary courts, and by around 1400, petitions explicitly acknowledged the Chancellor's court.[51] By the Tudor period, the Court of Chancery was a

[47] Perell (1990), p. 4.

[48] According to some commentators, certain individuals deliberately employed the common law to achieve unconscionable outcomes. However, it seems more likely that these outcomes were simply the unfortunate result of the strict application of the common law.

[49] Certain classes of petitions were, however, referred to the king's most important official, the Chancellor. One such class involved cases where the alleged wrongdoer was the king himself. For example, this occurred when the king held possession of land that had been seized as an escheat (the term escheat refers to the reversion of property to the king or the state in the absence of legal claimants), but in reality, the late tenant of the land had left an heir. The common law did not provide the heir with a means of recovering the land. To recover it, the heir had to petition, and such petitions were addressed to the Chancellor.

[50] 14 Ed III St 1 c 5.

[51] See Meagher et al. (1984), p. 4.

well-established institution and an integral part of the English legal system. From that time onwards, most Chancellors were trained lawyers. The Chancellor did not act like a regular common law judge; instead, he developed his own distinct body of law known as equity. In earlier times, when Chancellors were ecclesiastics, equity referred broadly to fairness or justice; however, as more Chancellors became lawyers, equity took on a more technical meaning, referring specifically to the rules and principles developed by the Chancery court. Despite these changes, the fundamental distinction between equity and common law remained intact. Over time, several Chancery courts were established, leading to the coexistence of two legal systems in England for several centuries: common law, administered by common law courts, and equity, administered by the Chancery courts.[52]

It is important to emphasize that the Chancellor had jurisdiction in both equity and common law. However, with respect to common law, his jurisdiction was limited to: (a) certain types of writs; (b) cases directly involving the king; and (c) personal actions brought by or against officers of the Court of Chancery. The Chancellor's equitable jurisdiction was significantly broader, encompassing, among other things: (a) the recognition of uses and trusts; (b) the enforcement of contracts on grounds not recognized by common law; (c) relief from the strict enforcement of legal rights that led to unfairness; and (d) the granting of remedies either non-existent or unavailable under common law.

Proceedings in the Court of Chancery differed considerably from those in common law courts. Common law proceedings were initiated by the issuance of a writ, and factual issues were tried by a jury without any direct evidence presented by the parties themselves. If the jury's verdict favoured the plaintiff, the judgment typically awarded damages. In contrast, proceedings in the Court of Chancery were initiated by a petition to the Chancellor. The Chancellor would then issue a writ of subpoena, commanding the defendant to appear before him to respond to the allegations.

When the defendant and plaintiff appeared before the Chancellor, he would closely and thoroughly question them to uncover the truth.[53] If the Chancellor believed that one party was acting against their conscience, he would order them to correct the situation by doing or refraining from doing something. If the party refused to comply, they could be confined in the Chancellor's prison until they decided to clear their conscience and adhere to the Chancellor's order.

The fundamental principle guiding the Chancellor's court was the concept of 'conscience.' Relief was granted based on the Chancellor's individual perception of justice and how the parties' consciences should be bound by it.[54] However, the idea

[52] Baker (2019), p. 105 ff; Sandberg (2023), p. 201 ff.

[53] From the time of King Henry VI (1421–1471), written answers were allowed, and in the sixteenth and seventeenth centuries, a regular course of procedure based on written pleadings was adopted.

[54] As stated by Lord Ellesmere in 1615: "The cause why there is a Chancery is for that men's actions are so divers and infinite, that it is impossible to make any general law which may aptly meet with every act and not fail in some circumstances. The office of the Chancellor is to correct men's consciences for frauds, breach of trusts, wrongs, and oppressions of what nature soever they

that the Chancellor's role was merely to correct the rigidity of common law, guided solely by moral ideals, proved incompatible with the development of consistent legal rules. The lack of constraints on this discretionary power in administering justice led to equity being described as "a roguish thing." As John Selden famously remarked:

> Equity is a roguish thing; for law we have a measure, know what to trust to. Equity is according to the conscience of him that is Chancellor, and as that is larger or narrower, so is equity. [It is] as if they should make the standard for the measure we call a foot a Chancellor's foot; what an uncertain measure would this be! One Chancellor has a long foot, another a short foot, a third an indifferent foot. [It is] the same in the Chancellor's conscience.[55]

However, while the Chancellor undoubtedly possessed a broad degree of discretion, it would be incorrect to assume that his powers were without limits. Beginning in the sixteenth century, the scope of the Chancellor's discretion gradually narrowed, as the arbitrary and discretionary nature of equity was increasingly tempered by adherence to precedent and established principles. This evolution is commonly referred to as the 'systemization of equity.'

8.3.1 The Uneasy Relationship Between Law and Equity

The thirteenth-century records indicate that many remedies granted by the courts of equity were also awarded by other courts, including those of common law. Additionally, it was not uncommon for the Chancellor to either sit with or seek the advice of common law judges.[56] However, this cooperation between the courts of common law and equity did not endure. By the fourteenth century, common law courts began adopting a strictly normative approach to resolving legal disputes (*rigor juris*), which discarded considerations of conscience and equitable discretion.[57] This shift led to a pronounced separation between equity and common law, inevitably resulting in conflict. This conflict arose because, in certain matters, common law and equity had differing views on how issues should be resolved. An example of such a dispute involves the arrangement known as a 'use.'

In some parts of England, when a tenant died, the land passed to his eldest son, who was required to give some money or a farm animal to the landlord. However, if the tenant gave away his rights over the land before his death, nothing had to be given to the landlord. To avoid this obligation, some tenants would transfer their land rights to a friend who promised to allow the son to use the land after the

be, and to soften and mollify the extremity of the law." *Earl of Oxford's Case* (1615) 1 Ch Rep 1; 21 ER 485, at 486.

[55] Pollock (1927), p. 43.

[56] See Meagher et al. (1984), pp. 5–6; Roebuck (1988), p. 73.

[57] By the time of the Tudors and Stuarts, the Chancellor's power to give common law remedies had been removed.

tenant's death, ensuring that the son could benefit from the land without having to pay anything to the landlord. This arrangement was referred to as a 'use.' The common law courts refused to recognize the existence of uses, meaning that, from their perspective, the friend had full rights over the land, while the son had none. However, the Chancery courts took a different stance: they acknowledged the common law rights of the friend but held that these rights had to be exercised according to his conscience. If the friend refused to allow the son to benefit from the land, a Chancery court would imprison him until he 'cleared his conscience' by fulfilling his promise to the deceased father. Consequently, the friend was compelled to honour his promise, leading to the distinction that the friend held a 'legal interest,' while the son had an 'equitable interest.'

At the close of the sixteenth century, the conflict between common law and equity reached a critical point, particularly concerning the Chancellor's practice of issuing injunctions—an equitable remedy intended to prevent successful but dishonest plaintiffs at law from enforcing unconscionable judgments awarded by common law courts. Chief Justice Edward Coke, representing the common law courts, objected to the use of injunctions by the Court of Chancery to prevent actions being pursued in common law courts, arguing that such injunctions undermined the authority of the common law. He held that imprisonment for disobedience of injunction was therefore unlawful.[58] Coke's stance was rooted in his belief that the common law was the supreme law of the land and that no court, including the Chancery, should have the power to interfere with the proceedings of common law courts. In response, Lord Ellesmere, the Chancellor at the time, argued in the *Earl of Oxford's Case*[59] that injunctions did not interfere with common law; instead, their effect was *in personam*, directing the individual concerned that, on equitable grounds, the legal action should not proceed or the judgment should not be enforced. A personal dispute arose between Coke and the Chancellor, leading to an appeal to King James I. Acting on the advice of Francis Bacon and other legal experts, the King ruled that when equity and common law were in conflict, equity should prevail. This decision established the supremacy of the Court of Chancery and significantly increased the importance of equity in the legal system.

While the role of equity remained unchallenged, its application became increasingly regulated through a system of rules and principles based on precedent. This

[58] In *Heath v Rydley* (1614) Cro. Jac. 335 it was stated that "if any Court of equity doth intermeddle with any matters properly triable at the Common law or which concern freehold, they are to be prohibited" (i.e. liable to be subject to the "Writ of Prohibition." And see *Bromage v Genning* (1617) 1 Rolle 368; *Throckmorton v Finch* (1598) Third Institute 124, 125.

[59] *Earl of Oxford's Case* (1615) 1 Ch Rep 1; 21 ER 485. In this landmark case, the specific dispute was between the Earl of Oxford and Magdalene College, Cambridge, concerning the validity of a lease. The common law court ruled in favour of the Earl of Oxford, upholding the lease. However, Magdalene College petitioned the Court of Chancery arguing that the lease was obtained by fraudulent means and should be voided. The Lord Chancellor subsequently granted an injunction to prevent the Earl from enforcing the common law judgment, thereby protecting the College. The ruling solidified the role of the Court of Chancery in providing remedies that were more flexible and just than those available under the common law.

system was gradually developed by a series of Chancellors, who were all lawyers, as opposed to the ecclesiastics of the earlier era. This so-called 'systematization of equity' is evident in several developments, including the classification of trusts,[60] the formulation of the doctrine of specific restitution[61] and the establishment of the doctrine of equity of redemption.[62] In 1673, Lord Nottingham asserted that "the conscience of the Chancellor is not his natural and private conscience but a civil and official one."[63] By the nineteenth century, the systematization process was complete. As Lord Eldon, the last of the great Chancellors involved in this process, declared:

> The doctrines of this court ought to be as well settled, and made as uniform almost as those of the common law, laying down fixed principles, but taking care that they are applied according to the circumstances of each case. I cannot agree that the doctrines of this court are to be changed with every succeeding judge. Nothing would inflict on me greater pain, in quitting this place, than the recollection that I had done anything to justify the reproach that the equity of this court varies like the Chancellor's foot.[64]

In his *Commentaries on the Laws of England*, written in the middle of the eighteenth century, William Blackstone[65] remarked:

> The systems of jurisprudence in our courts both of law and equity are now equally artificial systems, founded in the same principles of justice and positive law; but varied by different usages in the forms and mode of their proceedings: the one being originally derived (though much reformed and improved) from the feudal customs ... the other (but with equal improvements) from the imperial and pontifical formularies, introduced by their clerical chancellors.[66]

The relationship between common law and equity evolved into one of distinct but complementary systems of rules, despite the persistence of certain procedural differences between them. The following statement by Maitland provides a valuable

[60] See Sect. 8.3.2 below.

[61] The doctrine of specific restitution is a legal principle that seeks to restore a party to their original position before a contractual breach or wrongful act occurred. This doctrine aims to undo the wrongful gain by requiring the wrongdoer to give back what was taken, rather than simply compensating the other party with monetary damages. Specific restitution is related to the concept of *restitutio in integrum*. See Sect. 8.3.2 below.

[62] See Sect. 8.3.2 below.

[63] Quoted in Smith (1933), p. 315.

[64] *Gee v Pritchard* (1818) 2 Swan 402, 414.

[65] William Blackstone (1723–1780) was a distinguished jurist, judge, and legal scholar and one of the great legal minds in the history of English common law tradition. He served as a professor of English law at Oxford University, where he was the first to hold the Vinerian Chair of English Law, a position created specifically to teach English law in the context of a university curriculum. Blackstone was later appointed as a judge of the Court of Common Pleas, a position he maintained until his death in 1780. His four-volume work, *Commentaries on the Laws of England*, published between 1765 and 1769, systematically described the common law of England and became a foundational text in the study of law. It provided a comprehensive overview of English law, covering topics such as the rights of individuals, property law, and criminal law. For a closer look at Blackstone's career and work see: Milsom (1981a); Doolittle (2001); Cairns (1984).

[66] Blackstone (1978), III, p. 429 ff.

perspective for understanding how this relationship was perceived in the nineteenth century:

> We ought not to think of common law and equity as of two rival systems. Equity was not a self-sufficient system, [for] at every point it presupposed the existence of common law. Common law was a self-sufficient system. I mean this: that if the legislature had passed a short Act saying "Equity is hereby abolished", we might have got on fairly well; in some respects our law would have been barbarous, unjust, absurd, but still the great elementary rights, the right to immunity from violence, the right to one's good name, the rights of ownership and of possession would have been decently protected and contracts would have been enforced. On the other hand, had the legislature said, "Common Law is hereby abolished", this decree, if obeyed, would have meant anarchy. At every point equity presupposed the existence of common law.[67]

As the statement suggests, equity functioned as a supplement to the common law rather than as a competing or opposing legal system. It was viewed as a "sort of appendix added on to our code, or a sort of gloss written round our code."[68] According to Megarry and Wade, "equity, although it followed the inevitable course towards fixity and dogma, remained in general a more modern and flexible system than the common law. Originally it provided the means, needed in every legal system, of adapting general rules to particular cases, and this character was never entirely lost."[69]

In the previous paragraphs, we observed that English common law was established as a comprehensive and autonomous legal system. Equity, in contrast, evolved as a mechanism to address the deficiencies within the common law, inherently assuming the existence of the latter system. Initially, equity was understood to embody the fundamental principles of justice and fairness. However, by the nineteenth century, it had transformed into a rigid set of rules that operated parallel to those of common law, but was administered by a separate set of courts.

8.3.1.1 The Judicature Acts of 1873 and 1875 and the Administrative Fusion of Law and Equity

The nineteenth century was a period of significant law reform in England. The administration of justice had many unsatisfactory aspects at this time. The jurisdictions of the various courts overlapped; the procedures used in the common law courts were outdated; and the Courts of Chancery were overburdened with cases and very slow in carrying out their work. In the 1850s, Parliament attempted to improve the situation through legislation, but these measures achieved only limited success.

One of the primary challenges arising from the division between common law and equity was equity's lack of jurisdiction to resolve disputes involving legal

[67] Brunyate (1936), pp. 18–19.

[68] Brunyate (1936), p. 18.

[69] Megarry and Wade (1984), pp. 111–112.

rights, titles, and interests. This limitation meant that equitable relief could not be obtained until or unless: (a) a legal right was admitted; (b) a legal right had already been established by a prior judgment at law; or (c) the case had been referred to the common law courts for trial by jury. This difficulty was remedied by the Chancery Regulation Act 1862, also known as Rolt's Act.[70] The purpose of the act was to mandate that the Court of Chancery resolve all issues of fact or law necessary for the final determination of a case, thereby eliminating the practice of referring specific issues in Chancery cases to the common law courts for resolution. Consequently, in an action for specific performance, a court of equity could decide whether there was a contract or not. In an action to restrain a trespasser, it could determine who had title to the land. Furthermore, in an action for an injunction to prevent an infringement of copyright, the courts of equity could decide whether or not copyright existed.

Another difficulty stemmed from equity's lack of power to award damages in the manner they were granted at common law. While equity could award monetary compensation on a restitutionary basis for the infringement of an equitable right, a plaintiff could not obtain damages if they failed to establish the title to the equitable remedy sought. This also led to uncertainty regarding whether the Court of Chancery could award damages in support of a purely legal right. The Chancery Amendment Act, also known as Lord Cairns' Act of 1858,[71] granted the courts of equity the power to award damages in lieu of or in addition to an injunction or an order for specific performance.[72] The Act also introduced several procedural reforms to the Chancery courts, most notably granting them the authority to summon a jury and empowering the Lord Chancellor to amend the courts' practice regulations. By enabling the Chancery courts to award damages, the Act effectively narrowed the gap between common law and equity courts.

It is also important to note that common law did not provide the interlocutory remedies available in equity. Therefore, to obtain an order for discovery, interrogatories, or other interlocutory steps in a suit commenced at law, a litigant had to turn to the courts of equity. Furthermore, common law courts lacked the power to grant specific performance, declarations, or common injunctions. Although the Common Law Procedure Act of 1854[73] empowered the common law courts to grant injunctions—a remedy that was traditionally within the jurisdiction of the equity courts—in addition to damages for breaches of contractual obligations or torts, it did not extend this power to granting injunctions against infringements of equitable rights. As a result, there remained no remedy for the common law's refusal to recognize equitable interests.

In addition to the aforementioned difficulties, litigants faced the real risk of initiating their action in the wrong court. For instance, if a contract contained an error,

[70] Chancery Regulation Act 1862, 25 & 26 Vict., c. 42.

[71] Chancery Amendment Act 1858, 21 & 22 Vict., c. 27.

[72] On the equitable remedy of specific performance see Sect. 8.3.2 below.

[73] *Common Law Procedure Act 1854*, 17 & 18 Vict. c.125.

that mistake might be correctable through legal construction, allowing the plaintiff to safely pursue damages. However, it might have been necessary first to seek rectification in equity, followed by a legal claim for damages. Similarly, when a public body failed to perform a statutory duty, it was often unclear whether to request a writ of *mandamus* in law[74] or an injunction in equity. Moreover, parties frequently had to first establish liability under common law and then turn to equity for any equitable defences. This was particularly true in cases involving the breach of a contract for the sale of land, where equity provided the remedy of specific performance.[75] It also applied in cases where the breach concerned a stipulation regarding the timing of contract performance. While common law required strict adherence to such time stipulations, equity provided relief unless time had been expressly made the essence of the contract.

The challenges associated with the separation between law and equity eventually led to calls for reform of the English court system. In the latter half of the nineteenth century, after a series of legislative reforms primarily addressing procedural matters,[76] significant changes were recommended by the UK Judicature Commission in 1869. The Commission proposed the creation of a unified Supreme Court, consolidating the jurisdictions previously exercised by the superior courts of law, equity, probate, admiralty, and divorce. This recommendation was inspired by changes implemented in the State of New York two decades earlier. In 1848, New York had merged its separate systems of law and equity into a unified system of procedure and courts, though no substantive changes to the law were made.

The recommendations of the Judicature Commission led to the enactment of the Supreme Court of Judicature Acts of 1873–1875. This legislation reorganized the English court system by merging the separate jurisdictions of common law and equity into a unified court system, known as the Supreme Court of Judicature. Under this new structure, the three original royal courts—the Court of Queen's Bench for criminal cases, the Court of Common Pleas for civil disputes, and the Court of Exchequer for revenue matters—were converted into three divisions within a newly established High Court of Justice. These divisions continued to deal primarily with common law matters but were now integrated into a single judicial hierarchy. In addition to these three divisions, the Court of Chancery, which historically handled equity matters separately from common law, became the fourth division of the High Court. This change allowed both legal and equitable remedies to be administered by the same court, streamlining the judicial process. A fifth division was also created to handle cases that did not strictly fall within the domains of common law or equity. This division encompassed the Probate, Divorce, and Admiralty jurisdictions, dealing with matters such as wills, matrimonial disputes, and maritime issues. An Order

[74] A prerogative order from a higher court instructing a lower tribunal or other public body to perform a specified public duty related to their responsibilities, such as addressing a particular dispute.

[75] But this was not the case for contracts for the sale of goods, as equity did not provide the remedy of specific performance for such contracts.

[76] The Common Law Procedure Acts of 1852, 1854, and 1860, and the Chancery Amendment Act of 1858.

in Council in 1880 further consolidated these changes by merging the three royal courts into the Queen's Bench Division, leaving the High Court with three divisions: Queen's Bench, Chancery, and Probate, Divorce, and Admiralty.

The Judicature Acts established on a statutory foundation the earlier principle that when a conflict arises between the rules of equity and the rules of common law concerning the same matter, the rules of equity shall prevail. This legislation also empowered all courts to administer both the rules of common law and equity, granting the appropriate remedies as required by the cases before them. Consequently, litigants seeking relief under both common law and equity could obtain such relief within the same court. This arrangement led many to believe that the two systems had merged. However, as commentators have noted, the enactment of the Judicature Acts did not eliminate the distinction between equity and common law, nor between equitable and legal rights, interests, and titles. There was nothing in this legislation that attempted to codify law and equity as a single subject matter or to sever the fundamental conceptual distinctions between them.[77] The fusion of law and equity brought about by the Judicature Acts can be described as procedural, as no substantive merger of the two bodies of rules was effected.[78]

Nonetheless, subsequent legal developments suggest a gradual coalescence of the two streams in areas of common concern. Sir Anthony Mason observed that "by providing for the administration of the two systems of law by one system of courts and by prescribing the paramountcy of equity, the Judicature Act freed equity from its position on the coat-tails of the common law and positioned it for advances beyond its old frontiers."[79] It is important to note that the abolition of the distinction between law and equity, and between legal and equitable rights, interests, and titles, need not be absolute. Lord Selborne, in introducing the Judicature Act to Parliament, acknowledged this when he described the distinction between law and equity as "real and natural" but only "within certain limits."[80] These statements support the view that common law and equity are increasingly fusing, with their remedies and procedures becoming more intertwined. For instance, it has been argued that common law remedies, such as damages, may be awarded for the violation of an equitable obligation, or that a common law defence may be raised against an equitable claim. However, it is important to note that the notion of a full merger of law and equity remains highly controversial in some common law jurisdictions.[81]

---

[77] See, e.g., Meagher et al. (1984), p. 45; Baker (1977), p. 531.

[78] As has been pointed out, "The two streams of jurisdiction [that is, law and equity], though they run in the same channel, run side by side and do not mingle their waters." Browne (1933), p. 18. This approach seems to gain support from the exclusive jurisdictions left to the Queen's Bench and Chancery divisions. In fact, the work previously conducted by the Court of Chancery is now handled by the Chancery division. A Chancery case remains distinct from a common law case, and this distinction also applies to procedural matters.

[79] Mason (1993), p. 10.

[80] Hansard (1830–1891), 3rd Series, vol. 214, 339.

[81] For example, in Australia, the prevailing position is that the doctrines and remedies of equity are clearly distinct from those of the common law. Indeed, some authors refer to the notion of the

8.3.2 *Equitable Principles and Remedies: A Brief Overview*

As previously noted, individuals wronged by others often found it difficult or impossible to seek redress through the common law courts. This could be due to flaws in the law, such as the absence of an appropriate remedy, or because the remedies provided by common law, typically in the form of damages, were inadequate. Equity emerged to address these shortcomings. Unlike the rigid and narrowly defined rules of common law, equity is considered more flexible, relying on a set of fundamental principles articulated in general terms. These principles are rooted in concepts such as conscience, justice, and fairness, which helps prevent conflicts between them. Despite the rigidity that characterized equity by the nineteenth century, the principles of fairness and good conscience continue to influence contemporary common law systems, cutting through the complexities of legal rules and procedures.

Among the many equitable principles developed by the Court of Chancery to guide the exercise of equitable jurisdiction, a few key ones are outlined here:

(i) *A person who seeks equity must do equity.* This principle means that a person who asks the court for equitable relief must themselves act fairly and justly. One cannot seek an equitable remedy if they have engaged in unethical or unfair behaviour related to the matter at hand. This principle emphasizes that equity is a two-way street: to receive fairness, one must also demonstrate fairness and integrity in their conduct.[82]

(ii) *Equity will not suffer a wrong without a remedy.* This principle allows equity to intervene where a legal technicality may prevent a right from being enforced under the law. It underpins the development of law through judicial interpretation, ensuring that justice can prevail even when legal remedies are inadequate. In practice, this principle empowers courts to provide fair solutions in situations where legal remedies might be inadequate or unavailable, ensuring that justice is served in a broader sense.

(iii) *A person who comes to equity must come with 'clean hands.'* This means that equity, when addressing a claim, will consider whether the claimant has acted fairly and without malice in the matter for which relief is sought. If the claimant has acted in bad faith, a remedy will be denied. The rationale behind this principle is that the court should not assist those who have acted in bad faith

---

fusion of law and equity the 'fusion fallacy'. See on this matter Meagher et al. (2002), p. 54. In contrast, the Court of Appeal New Zealand has adopted the view that, with respect to remedies, it is now settled that equity and common law are merged. Consider, e.g., *Mouat v Clark Boyce* [1992] 2 NZLR 559. This means that the courts can apply equitable principles and remedies even in cases where the issues traditionally would have been dealt with under common law. In practical terms, this allows the courts to provide remedies such as injunctions, specific performance, or equitable damages in situations where common law remedies like damages might be inadequate or inappropriate.

[82] For example, if someone requests the court to enforce a contract under equity, but they themselves have not fulfilled their obligations under that contract or have acted in bad faith, the court may deny their request.

or have themselves contributed to the problem they are asking the court to resolve. It is not required that the person seeking relief be perfect, but their behaviour in the specific matter must be free from significant inequity or bad faith.

(iv) *Equity acts in personam.* Equitable proceedings and remedies are directed against a specific individual rather than an object or piece of property. These proceedings require a party to act or refrain from acting in a particular way. For example, if a court orders someone to perform a specific action, such as completing a contract, the order applies directly to that individual. Failure to comply with the court's order can result in penalties, including fines, imprisonment for contempt of court, or confiscation of their assets.

(v) *Equity regards as done that which ought to have been done.* When parties have created an enforceable obligation, equity treats them as if the obligation has already been fulfilled. For example, in a contract for the sale of land, if the buyer has fulfilled all their obligations and the only thing left is for the seller to formally transfer the title, equity will treat the buyer as the rightful owner of the property even before the formal transfer has taken place. This is because the transfer of title is something that 'ought to have been done.' This maxim ensures that the principles of fairness are upheld, by treating the intended outcome as if it has been achieved, thereby preventing someone from being unjustly deprived of their rights due to technicalities or procedural delays.

(vi) *Delay defeats equity.* An equitable remedy may be denied if not requested promptly. This principle discourages unreasonable delays in presenting claims and enforcing rights. This concept is closely related to the doctrine of 'laches,' where a court may refuse to grant an equitable remedy if the claimant's delay in bringing the action has prejudiced the defendant or made it inequitable to grant relief.

(vii) *Equity follows the law.* Equity does not replace common law or statutory law but operates alongside them. When a court of equity is asked to provide a remedy, it will respect and adhere to legal principles and statutes. Equity steps in to provide justice in situations where the law may be too rigid or does not offer an adequate remedy, but it does so without disregarding legal rules. For example, if a legal rule clearly applies to a situation, an equitable remedy will not be granted in a way that negates or conflicts with that rule.

(viii) *Where the equities on both sides are equal, the law prevails.* When two parties in a legal dispute have equal standing in terms of equity, the court will resolve the matter by applying the established law rather than trying to achieve a more equitable outcome through the application of discretionary or equitable principles. In other words, if both parties have equally valid claims or defences based on fairness, the court will default to applying the strict rules of law. This principle underscores the idea that equity cannot override the law when both sides are equally justified. The law, in such cases, serves as the final arbiter.[83] This maxim reinforces the idea that equity complements, but does not replace, the law.

(ix) *Equity looks to intent rather than the form.* In determining whether to grant a remedy, equity considers the substance and intent of the transaction rather than its formal structure. This principle implies that in situations where strict adherence to legal forms or technicalities might result in an unjust outcome, equity intervenes to prioritize the true intentions behind the actions or agreements of the parties involved. This principle is especially important in cases involving trusts, wills, and contracts, where the rigid application of legal rules might not accurately reflect the actual wishes or agreements of those involved.[84]

(x) *Equity is equality.* There is a presumption of equal division where two or more people can establish an interest in the same piece of property. It should be noted, however, that while they are related, equity and equality have distinct meanings and applications, particularly in social and economic contexts. Equality refers to treating everyone the same, providing the same resources or opportunities to all individuals regardless of their needs, circumstances, or starting points. Equity, on the other hand, takes into account the varying needs, circumstances, and disadvantages of individuals or groups. It is about fairness, which may require providing different levels or types of support to achieve an equal outcome. Equity recognizes that people have different starting points and seeks to level the playing field by addressing systemic barriers and inequalities.

(xi) *Where equities are equal, the first in time prevails.* This principle essentially means that when two or more parties have equal, valid claims to the same property or right, the party that acquired their interest first will have the superior claim. This rule is often applied in situations involving priority disputes, such as when two creditors have claims against the same asset, or when multiple parties claim an interest in the same piece of property. If both claims are of equal merit and the law does not favour one over the other based on the nature of the claims, the tie is broken by looking at the timing of when each party's interest was established. The party whose interest was first in time will be given precedence. This principle helps maintain order and predictability in the law by establishing a clear rule for determining which claim should prevail in cases of equal equity.

(xii) *Equity will not decree a vain thing.* Equity focuses on achieving practical, substantive justice, avoiding judgments that cannot or will not be implemented.

---

[83] For example, if two parties claim ownership of a piece of property, and both have equal equitable interests in the property (e.g., both paid for it equally and contributed to its upkeep), the court would look to the legal title to determine who the rightful owner is, rather than trying to further balance the equities.

[84] For example, if a contract is poorly worded or lacks certain formalities but clearly reflects the genuine intentions of the parties, a court of equity may enforce the contract according to what the parties intended rather than dismissing it on technical grounds.

> In other words, equity will not make a ruling or order that serves no meaningful or just purpose. The concept underscores the idea that equitable decisions should be grounded in reason, purpose, and fairness, rather than being mere formalities or empty gestures.

The above maxims underscore that equity is rooted in principles of fairness and natural justice. Although these maxims have diminished in significance over time, judges may still invoke them when deciding whether to exercise equitable jurisdiction.[85]

Based on our discussion, three key qualitative differences between common law and equity can be identified:

1. The flexible and discretionary nature of equity's doctrines and remedies.
2. Equity's ability to impose terms and conditions tailored to the specific circumstances of a case.
3. Equity's ability to override common law in certain situations to achieve fairness.

Equitable doctrines and remedies are characterized by their flexibility and discretion, as judges take into account all the circumstances of a case according to established criteria to determine whether equity demands a remedy. Consequently, even if a plaintiff meets the basic requirements of an action, they may still be denied a remedy due to the application of an equitable maxim or defence. For instance, the discretionary nature of equity is evident in cases involving an alleged breach of contract where the remedy of specific performance is sought. Although the elements necessary to establish a breach of contract may be present, the equitable defence of laches (excessive delay) may prevent the granting of specific performance. The laches defence applies when the plaintiff has delayed bringing their action to such an extent that they are deemed to have: (a) acquiesced in the defendant's conduct; (b) caused the defendant to alter their position in reasonable reliance on the plaintiff's acceptance of the status quo; or (c) allowed a situation to develop that would be unjust to disturb. Courts consider several factors when applying the doctrine of laches, including the length of the delay, the reason for the delay, whether the defendant suffered any prejudice due to the delay, and whether the plaintiff had a valid excuse for nor bringing the claim sooner. Additionally, if the plaintiff's conduct has been improper, the equitable maxim "He who comes into equity must come with clean hands" will bar the remedy of specific performance. In contrast, common law generally lacks such discretionary criteria in awarding remedies, which can lead to outcomes that are less equitable.[86]

---

[85] On the principles of equity see Martin (1993), p. 26.

[86] It should be noted, however, that common law has evolved to allow some discretion regarding remedies in certain cases. One example occurs in the context of judicial review of administrative actions. The common law remedy of certiorari, which is a remedy where the High Court orders decisions of lower courts, tribunals, and administrative authorities to be brought before it and quashes them if they exceed the powers conferred on them or show an error of law on the face of the record, may be denied on the grounds of misconduct by the applicant. See, e.g., *R v Stephens, ex parte Callendar*, [1956] CLY 2160, The Times, October 26, 1956.

The power of equity to impose terms and conditions on both the plaintiff and defendant when granting a remedy is a natural extension of its aim to achieve justice in the specific circumstances of each case. A notable example of this is the equitable remedy of rescission, which nullifies a contract and treats it as if it never existed. This remedy is typically sought when a contract is found to be voidable due to issues such as misrepresentation, mistake, undue influence, fraud, or lack of capacity. In such cases, *restitutio in integrum*, which aims to restore the parties to their pre-contractual state, may be ordered. When the court orders *restitutio in integrum*, it seeks to reverse any unjust enrichment that may have resulted from the contract, returning any benefits or profits one party may have gained at the expense of the other, as if the contract had never existed. However, merely returning the parties to their original positions may not always suffice to achieve true fairness or equity. For instance, if one party has profited from the contract in a way that leaves them better off even after the contract is voided, equity may require further measures. This is where the concept of ordering an 'account of profits' comes into play. An account of profits is an equitable remedy requiring the party who has profited from the contract to account for and possibly return those profits to the other party. This remedy ensures that the party who benefited from the contract does not retain any unjust gains that would result in an unfair advantage. For example, if a party has used resources obtained under a voided contract to generate additional profits, equity may require that those profits be accounted for and returned to the other party, to ensure that both parties are genuinely returned to their pre-contractual positions.

A third significant qualitative difference between equity and common law lies in equity's dominance over common law in areas where both had concurrent jurisdiction.[87] The concept of concurrent jurisdiction stems from Justice Story's classification of equity's jurisdiction into three categories: exclusive, concurrent, and auxiliary.[88] Exclusive jurisdiction refers to cases where only equity has the authority to grant relief, such as matters involving trusts and fiduciary relationships. Concurrent jurisdiction pertains to cases where both common law and equity courts have the authority to grant relief, for instance, in cases of fraud or mistake. Auxiliary jurisdiction involves situations where equity provides support to parties seeking to assert legal rights more effectively or conveniently than they could in a common law court. Examples include *quia timet* injunctions, which prevent irreparable harm before a legal decision is made,[89] and bills for discovery or the perpetuation of testimony, which are designed to aid legal proceedings. Equity's dominance over common law is particularly evident in its ability to issue common injunctions, restraining actions or judgments in common law courts under certain conditions.[90] This

[87] As previously noted, equity's dominance with respect to the concurrent jurisdiction was settled in the *Earl of Oxford's Case*.

[88] Story (1892), pp. 19–20.

[89] The court will only grant such a remedy if the applicant can show that there is imminent danger of a substantial kind or that the injury, if it occurs, will be irreparable.

[90] For some examples see Jones (1967), pp. 442–443.

dominance is rooted in equity's jurisdiction being *in personam* and its origins as a court of conscience.

Other differences between equity and common law relate to the treatment of property ownership and property-related interests. Equity, acting *in personam*, recognizes property rights in individuals beyond those acknowledged by common law. For example, equity protects the rights of a *bona fide* purchaser of a legal title in property where a third party holds an equitable interest. As long as the purchase is made for valuable consideration and without notice of the equitable interest, the *bona fide* purchaser's rights will be upheld.[91] In contrast, common law, acting *in rem*, regards legal ownership as a universal and enforceable right against all others, and in this respect, offers protection to a *bona fide* purchaser only as an exception to this rule. Equitable property interests not fully recognized by common law include restrictive covenants[92] and the mortgagor's equity of redemption.

Equity has significantly enriched the legal system by introducing a range of alternative actions, principles, and remedies. One of the most notable legal constructs that emerged from the courts' equitable jurisdiction is the *trust*, which has become an integral part of property law. A trust is a unique arrangement where one person (the trustee) holds property on behalf of and for the benefit of one or more individuals (the beneficiaries). The settlor (also known as the grantor, trustor, or donor) creates the trust by transferring assets into it and outlining its terms, including how the assets will be managed, who the beneficiaries will be, and under what conditions they will receive benefits from the trust. The settlor appoints the trustee to manage the trust according to these terms for the benefit of the beneficiaries.[93] Due to the

---

[91] See e.g. *Pilcher v Rawlins* (1872) LR 7 C App 259.

[92] A restrictive covenant in equity law refers to a promise in a deed or contract that limits the use of land or property, often to maintain certain standards or prevent specific activities. These covenants are usually imposed by a landowner or developer and are enforceable in equity, meaning that they can be enforced by a court even if they are not enforceable at common law. Equitable remedies for breach of a restrictive covenant can include an injunction to prevent or stop the prohibited activity or damages for the breach.

[93] Trusts are classified into several categories based on their purpose, creation, beneficiaries, and the nature of their terms. These include: private trusts, created for the benefit of specific individuals or classes of individuals; charitable or public trusts, established for purposes that benefit the public or a significant segment of it, such as education or poverty relief; express trusts, formed intentionally by the settlor through explicit declaration or documentation, such as a trust deed or will; implied trusts, established by law based on the circumstances, often arising from the conduct of the parties; fixed trusts, where beneficiaries and their interests are clearly defined by the settlor; discretionary trusts, where the trustee has the power to decide which beneficiaries will receive benefits and to what extent; bare trusts, where the trustee holds the property in name only for the beneficiary, who has an absolute right to the trust's assets; revocable trusts, in which the settlor retains the right to revoke or alter the trust; irrevocable trusts, which cannot be revoked or altered without the beneficiaries' consent once established; protective trusts, designed to protect the beneficiary's interest from creditors or the beneficiary's own imprudence; spendthrift trusts, which restrict the beneficiary's ability to alienate or pledge their interest in the trust property; domestic trusts, governed by the laws of the settlor's home country; and offshore trusts, established in jurisdictions with favourable tax or legal conditions. Each of these classifications serves a different legal and practical purpose, catering to the diverse needs and intentions of the settlor and beneficiaries.

special nature of the trust relationship, the law imposes stringent fiduciary duties on the trustee, requiring them to always act in the best interests of the beneficiaries and to avoid any conflicts between their own interests and those of the beneficiaries. Given that a trustee manages property belonging to another, there are strict regulations governing how this property must be handled. The trustee's powers are typically outlined in a legal document known as the *trust instrument*, which generally includes the authority to sell, purchase, repair, and invest the property. However, unlike when managing their own property, a trustee is not permitted to take risks. Failure to adhere to the duties specified in the trust instrument constitutes a breach of trust, for which the trustee is liable for any resulting loss.

Furthermore, equity recognized the mortgage as a means of borrowing money secured by real property. The borrower who provides the security is known as the *mortgagor*, while the lender who offers the funds is referred to as the *mortgagee*. Equity introduced the concept of the 'equity of redemption,' a fundamental principle in property law. This doctrine allows the mortgagor to reclaim their property after defaulting on a mortgage, provided they can pay off the full amount of the debt, including any accrued interest and costs, before the foreclosure is completed. Historically, this doctrine developed to mitigate the harsh consequences of strict foreclosure practices, where lenders could immediately take ownership of the property upon the borrower's default.

Of the new remedies developed by equity, injunctions and specific performance are considered the most important. At common law, the primary remedy for a breach of contract was damages—a monetary payment awarded as compensation for the loss suffered. However, equity recognized that monetary compensation often did not provide adequate relief for many claimants. As a result, equity introduced the remedies of injunction and specific performance to address these shortcomings.

An injunction is a court order that requires a party to either do or refrain from doing a specific act, often to prevent a breach of legal obligations. Equity introduced injunctions to provide preventative and protective relief, ensuring that a party could be restrained from acting in a way that would cause irreparable harm or breach of rights.[94] There is a distinction between prohibitory injunctions, which prevent a person from doing or continuing to do a certain act, and mandatory injunctions, which compel a person to carry out a specific act. Other types of injunctions include temporary, preliminary, and permanent injunctions, each serving to maintain the status quo, prevent harm, or enforce legal rights depending on the circumstances of the case. A person who fails to abide by the terms of an injunction can be found guilty of contempt of court.

Specific performance, another equitable remedy, is an order from the court requiring a party to fulfil their contractual obligations rather than simply paying damages for breach. Common law typically awarded damages when a contract was

[94] For example, if Thomas sells his business to Alice and agrees not to compete, but later opens a shop next door, Alice may find monetary compensation insufficient, especially since her actual losses might be difficult to quantify. In such a case, equity would allow her to obtain an injunction compelling Thomas to close his shop.

breached, which might not always be adequate, particularly in cases involving unique goods or property where monetary compensation would not suffice. Equity stepped in with the remedy of specific performance, ensuring that the party in breach must fulfil their contractual duties, especially in cases involving real estate or rare items, where the subject matter of the contract is unique and damages would not provide a just outcome. This remedy is granted only when monetary compensation would not adequately remedy the situation, following the principle that 'equity follows the law.'

There are several other remedies developed by equity that have a significant impact on substantive rights. Among these are the right to have a contractual document corrected through a process known as 'rectification' and the right to rescind or withdraw from a contract. Traditionally, written contractual documents were considered conclusive of the parties' legal rights. However, if a court of equity was convinced that such a document misstated the parties' true intentions, it would 'rectify' the document to reflect the accurate agreement. Additionally, while common law often disregarded whether an agreement was unfair or harsh, courts of equity would 'rescind'—that is, annul—an agreement on the grounds of 'unconscionability'. For instance, under common law, the general principle was that an innocent misrepresentation—a false statement made without any intent to deceive—did not render a contract voidable. This was because common law primarily focused on the presence of fraud or deliberate deception when determining whether a contract could be invalidated. However, equity recognized that even an innocent misrepresentation could lead to unfairness if one party entered into a contract based on incorrect information provided by the other party, even if that misinformation was not intentionally deceptive. Therefore, equity would grant rescission, a remedy that allows the contract to be undone or cancelled, effectively putting the parties back in the position they were in before the contract was formed. This equitable intervention ensured that parties were not bound by contracts that were formed based on false information, thus preventing unjust outcomes that could arise under the rigid application of common law principles.

8.4 Concluding Remarks

The role of equity in the development of the English common law tradition is profound and cannot be overstated. Equity represents a system of general rules and principles, organically developed by courts over time, that successfully addressed many of the manifest injustices inherent in the common law legal system. Initially, this system appeared too vague to administer objective justice; however, it evolved into a framework of principles that, while flexible, were sufficiently concrete to support a system of justice increasingly characterized by predictability and uniformity.

Every legal system must balance the need for certainty, stability, and predictability with the demands for flexibility, fairness, and justice in individual cases. The English common law tradition uniquely institutionalized these often competing values within the dual systems of law and equity. However, it is important to recognize that equity eventually struggled to maintain its flexibility. The pursuit of stability and order led to the establishment of rules, principles, and guidelines that constrained equity's discretion, thereby making it more certain and predictable.

In modern times, in England and other common law jurisdictions, the explicit invocation of equity and its maxims has gradually diminished. This shift can be attributed to the increasing complexity of the legal system and the extensive body of court precedents that have integrated equitable principles into the interpretation of the law. Moreover, lawmakers now draft legislation with these principles in mind, aiming to ensure that enacted laws align with the spirit of equity. However, when conflicts arise between the letter of the law and equitable principles, the latter continue to hold significant normative force.

Society requires certainty in the law so that its members can organize their behaviour around established standards of conduct. However, the development of substantive law should not be constrained by the rigid application of legal rules. While the importance of legal certainty cannot be overlooked, it must be balanced with the need for a robust and adaptive body of substantive law. Therefore, although the principle of precedent is crucial, it should not prevent courts from examining the real purpose and function of the law in specific areas. The law should evolve based on principles and in accordance with established precedents. In this context, historical distinctions between common law and equity that serve no useful purpose or detract from addressing the substantive issues in a particular legal field should not be considered obstacles. When rules traditionally classified under different categories seem to conflict or compete, the legal system's essential function is to resolve, reconcile, or rationalize such conflicts, not to exacerbate or perpetuate them.

References

Baker JH (1979) An introduction to English legal history, 2nd edn. Butterworths, London

Baker JH (2000) The common law tradition: lawyers, books, and the law. Hambleton Press, London

Baker JH (2019) An introduction to English legal history, 5th edn. Oxford University Press, Oxford

Baker PV (1977) The future of equity. Law Quart Rev 93:529–540

Berman H (1994) The origins of historical jurisprudence: Coke, Selden, and Hale. Yale Law J 103:1651–1738

Blackstone W (1825) Commentaries on the Laws of England, 16th edn. A. Strahan for T. Cadell and J. Butterworth and Son, London (Original work published 1765–1769)

Blackstone W (1978) Commentaries on the Laws of England. Garland Publishers, New York. (Original work published 1765-1769)

Bogdan M (1994) Comparative law. Kluwer, Deventer

Bowen CD (1957) The lion and the throne: the life and times of Sir Edward Coke(1552–1634). Little, Brown & Co, Boston, repr. 1990

Boyer A (1997) Understanding, authority, and law: Sir Edward Coke and the Elizabethan origins of judicial review. Boston Coll Law Rev 39:43–93

Boyer A (2003) Sir Edward Coke and the Elizabethan age. Stanford University Press, Stanford

Brand PA (1987) The origins of the English Legal Profession. Law Hist Rev 5(1):31–50

Browne D (ed) (1933) Ashburner's principles of equity, 2nd edn. Butterworth, London

Brunyate J (ed) (1936) Equity, a course of lectures by FT Maitland, 2nd edn. Cambridge University Press, Cambridge
Buckland W, McNair AD (1965) Roman law and common law: a comparison in outline, 2nd edn. Cambridge University Press, Cambridge
Cairns JW (1984) Blackstone, an English institutist: legal literature and the rise of the nation state. Oxf J Leg Stud 4:318–360
Carey Miller D, Zimmermann R (eds) (1997) The civilian tradition and Scots law. Dunker and Humblot, Berlin
David R, Brierley JEC (1985) Major legal systems in the world today, 3rd edn. Stevens, London
De Cruz P (1999) Comparative law in a changing world, 2nd edn. Cavendish, London
De Zulueta F (ed) (1927) The Liber Pauperum of Vacarius. Selden Society Publications, London
Doolittle IG (2001) William Blackstone, a biography. Maney Publishing, Leeds
Eisenberg M (1988) The nature of the common law. Harvard University Press, Cambridge
Evans-Jones R (ed) (1995) The civil law tradition in Scotland. The Stair Society, Edinburgh
Evans-Jones R (1999) Roman law in Scotland and England and the development of one law for Britain. Law Quart Rev 115:605–630
Gest CM (1909) The writings of Sir Edward Coke. Yale Law J 18:504–532
Glenn HP (2004) Legal traditions of the world: sustainable diversity in law, 2nd edn. Oxford University Press, Oxford
Hansard TC (1830–1891) Hansard's parliamentary debates, 3rd Series. TC Hansard, United Kingdom
Harding A (1966) A social history of English law. Penguin Books, London
Holdsworth WS (1923) A history of English law. Methuen, London
Holdsworth WS (1938) Some makers of English law. Cambridge University Press, Cambridge
Hudson J (1996) The formation of the English common law: law and society in England from the Norman conquest to Magna Carta. Longman, London and New York
Jones WJ (1967) The Elizabethan Court of Chancery. Clarendon Press, Oxford
Keeton LW (1966) The Norman conquest and the common law. Barnes and Noble, New York
Kiralfy AKR (1958) Potter's historical introduction to English law and its institutions, 4th edn. Sweet and Maxwell, London
Kitto F (2002) Foreword to Meagher RP, Heydon JD, Leeming MJ, Meagher, Gummow and Lehane's equity: doctrines and remedies, 4th edn. Butterworths Lexis Nexis, Sydney
Lobban M (1991) The common law and English jurisprudence 1760–1850. Clarendon Press, Oxford
MacQueen H (1993) Common law and feudal society in medieval Scotland. Edinburgh University Press, Edinburgh
MacQueen H (1999) Scots law and the road to the new ius commune. Law Librarian 30(1):19–25
Maitland FW (1901) English law and the Renaissance. Cambridge University Press, Cambridge, repr. Union N.J. 2000
Maitland FW (1911) The collected papers of F.W. Maitland. Cambridge University Press, Cambridge
Maitland FW (1976) The forms of action at common law. Cambridge University Press, Cambridge (originally published 1936)
Martin JE (1993) Hanbury and Martin: modern equity, 14th edn. Sweet and Maxwell, London
Mason A (1993) The place of equity and equitable doctrines in the contemporary common law world. Second International Symposium on Trusts, Equity and Fiduciary Relationships, University of Victoria, British Columbia
Meagher RP, Gummow WMC, Lehane JRF (1984) Equity: doctrines and remedies, 2nd edn. Butterwrorths, Sydney
Meagher RP, Heydon JD, Leeming MJ (2002) Meagher, Gummow and Lehane's equity: doctrines and remedies, 4th edn. Butterworths Lexis Nexis, Sydney
Megarry R, Wade HWR (1984) The law of real property, 5th edn. Sweet and Maxwell, London
Meston M, Sellar W, Cooper L (1991) The Scottish legal tradition. The Saltire Society and The Stair Society, Edinburgh

Milsom SFC (1981a) The nature of Blackstone's achievement. Selden Society, London
Milsom SFC (1981b) Historical foundations of the common law. Butterworths, London
Palmer RC (1976) The origins of the legal profession in England. Irish Jurist 11(1):126–146
Perell PM (1990) The fusion of law and equity. Butterworths, Toronto
Plucknett TFT (1956) A concise history of the common law, 5th edn. Little, Brown, London
Pollock F (ed) (1927) Table talk of John Selden. Selden Society, London
Pollock F, Maitland FW (1898) The history of English law before the time of Edward I, 2nd edn. Cambridge University Press, Cambridge, repr. 1978
Pound R (1951) Philosophy of law and comparative law. Univ Pa Law Rev 100(1):1–19
Robinson OF, Fergus TD, Gordon WM (1994) European legal history, 2nd edn. Butterworths, London
Rodger A (1996) Thinking about Scots law. Edinburgh Law Rev 1:3–24
Roebuck D (1988) The background of the common law. Oxford University Press, Oxford
Sandberg R (2023) A historical introduction to English law: genesis of the common law. Cambridge University Press, Cambridge
Smith S (1933) The stage of equity. Canadian Bar Rev 11(5):308–316
Story J (1892) Commentaries on equity jurisprudence, 2nd edn. Stevens and Haynes, London, repr. The Lawbook Exchange, 2006
Thorne SE (trans) (1968) Bracton on thc laws and customs of England. Harvard University Press, Cambridge, Mass
Turner RV (1985) The English judiciary in the age of Glanvill and Bracton, c. 1176-1239. Cambridge University Press, Cambridge
Van Caenegem RC (1988) The birth of the English common law, 2nd edn. Cambridge University Press, Cambridge
Zweigert K, Kötz H (1998) An introduction to comparative law, 3nd edn. Clarendon Press, Oxford

Chapter 9
Continuity, Diversity, and Change in the Islamic Legal Tradition

9.1 Introduction

Islamic law, known as Shari'a (meaning 'path' or 'way' in Arabic), is a comprehensive set of rules that reflects the religious faith and aspirations of the Muslim community. At its core is the fundamental principle of Islam: total and unreserved submission to the will of Allah, the one true God and master. Islamic law defines Allah's will as a complete code of conduct that governs all aspects of human life, guiding Muslims toward the fulfillment of their religious obligations in this life and the promise of reward in the hereafter.[1]

Islamic law provides an example of a system where law and religion are inextricably linked. Unlike Western law, which distinctly separates the religious and secular spheres, Islamic law addresses both the regulation of an individual's religious life and with the regulation of society.[2] In Islam, the obligation to obey the law is not an obligation owed to the state or another individual but to Allah.[3] It is the duty of

---

[1] Islam is translated into English as 'submission' or 'surrender'—specifically, the submission or surrender of individuals to the will of God. Shari'a provides the path that Muslims are to follow to achieve salvation. See Esposito (2003), p. 144; Esposito (1988), p. 14. Lombardi (1998), p. 91. And see Yamani (1979).

[2] As Bernard Weiss has remarked, "it is something of an oversimplification to equate the Shari'a with law. The Shari'a may indeed be said to contain law, but one must also recognize that it embraces elements and aspects that are not, strictly speaking, law." Weiss (1992), p. 1. According to Mohammed Iqbal, "In Islam it is the same reality which appears as Church looked at from one point of view and State from another. It is not true to say that Church and State are two sides or facets of the same thing. Islam is a single unanalyzable reality which is one or the other, as your point of view varies." Iqbal (2009), p. 181.

[3] As Noah Feldman explains: "Shariah, properly understood, is not just a set of legal rules. To believing Muslims, it is something deeper and higher, infused with moral and metaphysical purpose. At its core, Shariah represents the idea that all human beings—and all human governments—are subject to justice under the law. … The word "Shariah" connotes a connection to the divine, a

G. Mousourakis, *Traversing Legal Traditions*, Springer Textbooks in Law,
https://doi.org/10.1007/978-3-031-94669-1_9

Muslims to live in accordance with the tenets of Islam and maintain harmony with God. God created human beings with the ability to ascertain divine dictates, as Islam teaches that human beings are distinguished from other creations of God by their unique capacity for rational thinking.[4]

A further difference between the Western concept of law and Islamic law is that the latter, like God Himself, is eternal and immutable—not in letter but in spirit. While human interpretations of Islamic law may vary, the essence of the law remains constant.[5] As an expression of the divine will, Islamic law exists independently of human structures and cannot be altered by human action, such as parliamentary enactment or government decree. This notion was long ago abandoned in the West, where the law was secularized and became the concern of the state rather than the church. Furthermore, the main focus of Islamic law is on the responsibilities of individuals, rather than on the protection of personal or property rights and interests.

Like other legal systems, the Islamic legal system is dynamic and has evolved over its long history to meet the needs of the diverse societies it serves. The principles and mechanisms for its renewal are rooted in divine revelation, enabling the system to adapt to changing social conditions. Since the advent of Islam in the early seventh century AD, Islamic jurists have continuously re-examined the application of Islamic law to ensure it remains a living and workable system.[6] Over time, these jurists developed an extensive body of doctrine, and by the end of the tenth century, Shari'a had been clearly formulated in legal texts. Throughout the Middle Ages, this foundational doctrine was elaborated and systematized in legal manuals and commentaries, producing a vast body of literature regarded as the authoritative expression of Shari'a law. As the embodiment of the ideal Islamic way of life, this traditional Shari'a doctrine remains central to any inquiry into Islamic law.

However, it should be noted that medieval legal texts do not provide a complete picture of the laws governing Muslim communities today for two primary reasons. First, law in the contemporary Islamic world is not exclusively religious. In Islamic countries, there has inevitably been a degree of tension between the idealism of religious doctrine and the practical demands of social, political, and economic realities. Consequently, Islamic states and societies have adopted and implemented laws that do not fully correspond to the religious doctrine found in medieval legal

---

set of unchanging beliefs and principles that order life in accordance with God's will." Feldman (2008), p. 46.

[4]Consider on this issue Chan et al. (1969), p. 309.

[5]See Kamali (1989), pp. 216–217 & 230. According to Zweigert and Kötz, "Islamic law is in principle immutable, for it is the law revealed by God. Western legal systems generally recognize that the content of law alters as it is adapted to changing needs by the legislator, the judges, and all other social forces which have a part in the creation of law, but Islam starts from the proposition that all existing law comes from Allah who at a certain moment in history revealed it to man through his prophet Muhammad." Zweigert and Kötz (1998), p. 304.

[6]On the concepts of renewal (*tajdid*) and reform (*islah*) in the Islamic tradition consider Voll (1983). And see Ramadan (2009), pp. 12–13.

manuals. In most Islamic countries today, a significant portion of legal relations is governed by rules and principles derived from foreign, particularly European, sources.

Second, the medieval Shari'a texts can no longer be regarded as complete authorities in the context of modern law because many Muslim countries now enforce laws that differ from traditional authorities' dictates, yet still claim to represent a legitimate version of Allah's law. This is further complicated by significant religious divisions within the Islamic world, such as the division between Sunni and Shia Islam.[7] Despite this complex diversity in contemporary legal practices, Shari'a stands as a symbol of the ideological unity of all Islamic communities and, insofar as it is applied, can be regarded as the 'common law' of the Islamic world. As Asaf Fyzee has pointed out:

> Islamic law is not a systematic code, but a living and growing organism; nevertheless there is amongst its different schools a large measure of agreement, because the starting point and the basic principles are identical. The differences that exist are due to historical, political, economic and cultural reasons, and it is, therefore, obvious that this system cannot be studied without a proper regard to its historical development.[8]

Islamic law is a comprehensive legal system that governs various aspects of life, including personal, moral, social, and political matters. At its core, it draws from a structured framework of sources (*al-masadir*), guiding principles (*al-usul*), and legal evidence (*al-adilla*), all working cohesively to provide jurisprudential rulings. Additionally, legal maxims (*al-qawa'id*) and underlying objectives (*al-maqasid*) shape its dynamic and adaptive legal theory, ensuring ethical integrity and promoting societal welfare.

The primary sources (*al-masadir*) of Islamic law are the Qur'an and the Sunnah, the recorded practices and sayings of the Prophet Muhammad. The Qur'an is regarded as the ultimate divine authority, providing general commands and prohibitions, while the Sunnah offers practical applications and clarifications of these directives. Secondary sources, such as *ijma* (the consensus of scholars) and *qiyas* (analogical reasoning), enable jurists to extend legal principles to situations not explicitly addressed in the primary texts. For instance, jurists employ *qiyas* to draw parallels between contemporary issues and rulings established in the Qur'an and Sunnah, ensuring that Islamic law remains dynamic and relevant to modern contexts.

---

[7] The schism between Shia and Sunni branches of Islam originated from a fundamental disagreement over the rightful successor to the Prophet Muhammad as the leader of the Islamic community. Shia Muslims believed that leadership should remain within the Prophet's family, specifically supporting Ali, his cousin and son-in-law, as the rightful successor. In contrast, Sunni Muslims believed that the leader, or Caliph, should be chosen from among the Prophet's companions based on consensus rather than familial lineage. This disagreement set the stage for the enduring division between the two branches, with the Shia emphasizing the significance of the Prophet's bloodline in religious and political leadership, while the Sunnis prioritized a broader, community-based approach to selecting leaders. Consider on this issue Donner (1999), p. 1.

[8] Fyzee (1964), p. 1.

The guiding principles (*al-usul*) of Islamic legal theory are articulated through *usul al-fiqh* (principles of jurisprudence), which establish the methods for interpreting the primary texts and applying them to evolving contexts. Central to these principles is the emphasis on understanding divine intent while ensuring consistency and coherence in the application of legal rulings.

Legal evidence (*al-adilla*) encompasses the various forms of textual and rational evidence used by Islamic jurists to derive legal rulings. Explicit textual evidence from the Qur'an or Sunnah (*Nass*) is prioritized, while reasoning, analogy, and consensus act as supplementary forms of evidence. Jurists are expected to weigh these forms of evidence carefully to arrive at conclusions that align with divine will and justice.

Legal maxims (*al-qawa'id*) further contribute to the interpretative framework by offering broad, universally applicable principles derived from centuries of legal practice. These maxims, rooted in the Qur'an and established through scholarly consensus, form an essential part of *usul al-fiqh*. They provide overarching guidelines that embody the spirit of Islamic law, promoting consistency and coherence.[9] By distilling the extensive and sometimes complex corpus of *usul al-fiqh* into concise theoretical statements, they simplify legal rulings and enhance judicial consistency, particularly in ambiguous or unprecedented cases.

Lastly, the objectives of Islamic law (*al-maqasid*) play a pivotal role in guiding its application. These objectives, as articulated by scholars, emphasize five key areas: the preservation of religion, life, intellect, lineage, and property. Collectively, these goals aim to balance individual rights with communal welfare, ensuring that the implementation of Shari'a promotes justice, compassion, and the overall well-being of society.

As the abode discussion suggests, Islamic law originates from two fundamental sources: divine revelation (*wahy*) and human reason (*'aql*). Divine revelation encompasses the Qur'an, regarded as the ultimate and infallible word of God, and the Sunnah, the traditions and practices of the Prophet Muhammad. Human reason (*'aql*) plays a crucial role in interpreting and applying these divine sources through methods such as *ijtihad* (independent reasoning) and *qiyas* (analogical reasoning). These tools enable scholars to derive rulings on matters that did not exist during the time of the Prophet or remain ambiguous in scripture. The balance between *wahy* and *'aql* is foundational to Islamic jurisprudence, ensuring adherence to divine guidance while maintaining adaptability to evolving contexts.

[9] For example, the maxim 'actions are judged by their intentions' (*Al-umoor bi-maqasidiha*) helps jurists assess legal responsibility and ethical considerations based on the underlying intent behind actions. Similarly, the maxim 'hardship begets ease' (*Al-mashaqqah tajlibu al-taysir*) allows for flexibility in the application of legal rulings during times of difficulty, reflecting the balance between divine law and practical life.

9.2 Historical Origins and Evolution of Islamic Law

The first Muslim community was established in Medina, a city in Arabia, under the leadership of the Prophet Muhammad in AD 622. For these early Muslims, Islam meant obedience to the will of Allah as conveyed through His messenger, the Prophet Muhammad, in a series of revelations. These revelations, which occurred throughout Muhammad's lifetime, were collected and written down in the Qur'an (or Koran), the Muslim holy book.[10] A number of scholars assert that Muhammad composed the Qur'an himself and recognize that the existing text is genuine and unaltered; that is, it is written exactly as it was dictated to the Prophet's scribes.[11] In the eyes of Muslims, the Qur'an is the actual verbatim revelation from Allah, sent down upon Muhammad through the agency of the angel Gabriel, as Muhammad was illiterate and could not have composed the work himself.[12] Muslims regard the Qur'an as the last revelation that God sent to mankind and as the culmination of a long evolutionary process of revelation.[13]

As the very word of Allah, the Qur'an is historically and ideologically the primary expression and source of Islamic law.[14] However, the Qur'an is not a legislative document; it can only be used, in combination with other sources, as a basis for constructing a body of law.[15] The Qur'an lays down guidelines, moral precepts, and general principles aimed at realizing an ideal civilized society. It describes certain acts as prohibited, obligatory, recommended, and discouraged. Among other things, it commands the believers to pray, fast during the month of Ramadan, return property held in trust to its rightful owner, and duly discharge one's contractual obligations. It also commands the believers to abstain from consuming wine, gambling, and committing adultery. Polygamy is allowed (a husband could have up to four wives at the same time), provided that the husband treats his wives with equal respect. However, nothing is said about the precise legal significance of this norm or about the remedies that may be available to a wife in the event of its violation. In general, most of the rules in the Qur'an were concerned with providing practical solutions to concrete problems and were intended to modify or reform the customary tribal law of Arabia rather than replace that law with an entirely new system. It

[10] The Qur'an is divided into 30 main parts of approximately equal length, which together contain 114 chapters, or surahs, which in turn are divided into more than 6616 verses, or ayahs, of a few lines each. See Faruqi and Faruqi (1986), p. 100.

[11] See Muir (1923), p. xxviii.

[12] See Donner (1999), pp. 6–7.

[13] This process encompasses a series of revelations sent to earlier prophets, such as the Psalms of David, the Torah of Moses, and the Bible of Jesus. See Donner (1999), p. 7.

[14] Hasan (1970), pp. 12–20.

[15] Only about 3 percent of the Qur'an deals with matters considered in the West to be related to law. Family relationships are regulated in 70 verses; private and commercial transactions are covered in about 70 verses; matters relating to crime and punishment are addressed in 30 verses; constitutional and fiscal matters are touched upon in 20 verses; and about the same number of verses can be considered to be related to international law. See Kamali (1999), pp. 119–120.

could be said that the existing institutions of customary law were subjected to new moral standards—standards that were directed primarily at the individual's conscience.

Until around AD 660, the community of Medina remained the center of Muslim activity. During his lifetime, Muhammad served not only as the spiritual and temporal leader of the community but also as its supreme judge and arbiter, offering solutions to legal problems as they arose by interpreting the relevant revelations in the Qur'an.[16] Muhammad also extensively consulted with his companions and community elders in formulating legal opinions and providing advice. After the Prophet's death in AD 632, judicial power was assumed by his companions, who extrapolated, inferred, and deduced legal norms from their knowledge of the foundational principles of the Islamic belief system, particularly those derived from the Qur'an and the Sunnah—the precedents, practices, and sayings of Prophet Muhammad that explain and expand upon the postulates of the Qur'an.[17] Among them were the four caliphs[18] who succeeded Muhammad in political leadership. These caliphs, referred to in the Islamic tradition as the 'Rightly Guided Caliphs,' were Abu Bakr (reigned AD 632–634), Umar ibn al-Khattab (reigned AD 634–644), Uthman ibn Affan (reigned AD 644–656), and Ali ibn Abi Talib (reigned AD 656–661). The era of these caliphs is regarded as the Golden Age of Islam.[19] The teaching and decisions of the Prophet's companions and the caliphs marked the beginning of the development of a vast body of legal norms that supplemented and expanded upon the general precepts of the Qur'an.

A fundamental problem facing Muhammad and his successors in their judicial capacity was precisely determining the relationship between the rules of the Qur'an and the traditional norms and standards of Arab customary law. As scholars have observed, Qur'anic law was not a legislative revolution that sought to eliminate the entire body of norms known and applied by the Arabs before its emergence. Quite the opposite, the Prophet, in his capacity as Islam's supreme judge, issued numerous

[16] See Fyzee (1964), pp. 31–32; Faruqi and Faruqi (1986), p. 274.

[17] Consider Hasan (1970), p. xiv; Kamali (1999), p. 111. In pre-Islamic Arabia, the term Sunnah referred to established, ancestral customs or practices passed down through generations. These customs held significant importance, as they were considered the guiding principles of daily life, social conduct, and tribal law. The Sunnah of a tribe was central to its identity, distinguishing it from other tribes and serving as a source of collective pride and cohesion. Since tribal life in pre-Islamic Arabia was largely organized around kinship and loyalty, adherence to these customs reinforced communal bonds and preserved social order. The opposite of Sunnah is *bid'ah*: innovation or lack of precedent and continuity with the past. In Islamic jurisprudence, scholars categorize *bid'ah* into various types, ranging from permissible innovations (such as new methods of teaching the Qur'an) to harmful ones (such as distorting religious rituals). This tension between Sunnah and *bid'ah* highlights the emphasis in Islam on preserving orthodoxy while navigating the challenges of societal change.

[18] The term Khalifa Rasoul Allah or simply Khalifa denotes the successor of the messenger of God.

[19] See Kamali (1999), pp. 111–112. Omar Bin Al-Khattab, the second of the aforementioned caliphs, designated the legal opinions of some of the Prophet's companions as an additional source to be drawn upon by later jurists. Faruqi and Faruqi (1986), p. 275. Bosworth (1996), pp. 1–2.

rulings on diverse legal issues, recognizing and legalizing Arab customary practices.[20] In the domain of family law, especially in matters of marriage and divorce, the Prophet approved one of several systems that were known to the Arabs before the rise of Islam, while other systems were disapproved and consequently declared illegal. For example, under the patriarchal customary law of Arabia, a husband's right to end his marriage at will by simply repudiating his wife was well established. Qur'anic law does not attempt to deprive the husband of this power; instead, it urges the husband not to abuse it, advocating for 'releasing wives with prudence' and 'making a fair provision' for wives who are repudiated.

One of the key areas where the conflict between Qur'anic law and Arab customary law became evident was in matters of inheritance. In pre-Islamic Arab tribal society, tribes were patriarchal and patrilineal, with tribal solidarity based on the kinship ties among male members who traced their descent through male ancestors. In this system, inheritance was traditionally restricted to male agnate relatives. However, the Qur'an introduced a significant shift by emphasizing the close family ties between parents and children, advocating for a family unit in which women held a higher and more responsible position within Muslim society. Consequently, the Qur'an granted inheritance rights to certain close female relatives—such as the wife, daughter, mother, and sister—by specifying fixed fractional portions of the property as their entitlement.

The Qur'an's silence on the inheritance rights of male agnate relatives led to challenges in reconciling the traditional heirs with the new heirs designated by the Qur'an. Given that inheritance rights were closely linked to the structure of family ties and responsibilities, and that the influx of new wealth from military conquests heightened concerns about wealth distribution rules, these issues were particularly significant. The decisions made by Muhammad and the early caliphs in related cases illuminate the early development of legal principles in this area. From these decisions emerged what is often referred to as the golden rule of Islamic inheritance law: those relatives designated by the Qur'an were to receive their prescribed portions first, with the male agnates inheriting what remained. This approach effectively integrated the new Islamic heirs with the traditional customary law heirs into a unified system of succession. To illustrate this point, reference may be made to the case of Sa'd, a close companion of the Prophet Muhammad, who died in battle defending Islam. Sa'd's widow appeared before the Prophet and complained that she and her daughters had no means to support themselves, as her husband's entire estate had gone to his brother in accordance with the customary law that prevailed at that time. Under divine inspiration, the Prophet determined that Sa'd's widow was entitled to one-eighth of the estate, the two daughters to two-thirds, and Sa'd's brother to the remaining share of the estate.[21]

It is important to note that, in cases of uncertainty, early Islamic authorities often interpreted Qur'anic principles in light of accepted customary law standards. Thus,

[20] Consider on this matter Mahmood (1965), pp. 102–106.

[21] Consider Coulson (1969), pp. 10–11.

the Qur'anic heirs were superimposed onto the customary system, limited to the portions prescribed by the Qur'an.[22] This restrictive interpretation of Qur'anic provisions, along with the continued influence of traditional customary law, was not confined to inheritance law but was a central aspect of legal development in the early Islamic era. In this context, references to the early evolution of Islamic criminal law can also provide valuable insights.

The norms of pre-Islamic customary law relating to crimes allowed the victim's tribe to exact blood revenge against the tribe of the alleged offender (*talio* or *lex talionis*).[23] Retaliation for murder was death; for theft, amputation of the hand; and for adultery, stoning to death or flogging. The form of retaliation varied depending on the relative social status of the tribes involved: a socially superior tribe could impose a more severe penalty on an inferior one. This system of blood revenge often resulted in escalating cycles of retaliation and tribal violence. Although the parties could choose to arbitrate the dispute and address the grievance through mutually agreed-upon compensation, arbitration was usually a last resort after a protracted conflict.[24] The norms and practices of Arab customary law provided the basis for much of the Qur'anic criminal law and justice system. However, Qur'anic law introduced significant reforms: blood revenge was abolished, and uniform criminal offences, procedures, and penalties were established,[25] which emphasized individual rather than collective responsibility.[26]

During the late seventh and eight centuries, under the leadership of the Umayyad dynasty (AD 661–750), Islam evolved from a small, closely-knit community in Medina into a vast military empire with its central government in Damascus. The Umayyad Dynasty, the first dynasty to hold the title of Caliphate, was established in AD 661 by Muawiya ibn Abi Sufyan, who had previously served as the governor of Syria. After the death of the fourth caliph, Ali, Muawiya took control and founded the Umayyad Caliphate. Under the Umayyads, the empire expanded significantly, encompassing regions such as North Africa, Spain, parts of the Indian subcontinent,

---

[22] On the rules governing succession in Islamic law see generally Khan (2007); Powers (1986); Powers (1993); Hussaini (2007); Coulson (2008).

[23] *Lex talionis*, commonly referred to as the law of retaliation, is a concept rooted in ancient legal systems. The term originates from the Latin *lex* (law) and *talio* (retaliation), which embodies the idea that the punishment for a crime should correspond directly to the offense committed. This principle is often associated with the idea of retributive justice, where the response to a wrong should be proportional to the harm caused. The concept of *lex talionis* appears in various ancient legal codes, such as the Babylonian Code of Hammurabi, the Torah in the Old Testament, and Roman law. In these contexts, the principle served as a guideline to ensure that punishments were fair and proportional rather than excessive. Over time, the strict application of *lex talionis* was tempered by more nuanced forms of justice, such as monetary compensation or other penalties, which could be considered more humane and practical.

[24] Sharif (1972), pp. 7–10.

[25] New forms of criminal wrongdoing and related penalties were introduced, e.g., the penalty of flogging for illicit sexual intercourse (the same penalty was imposed for an unsubstantiated charge of such an offence).

[26] Consider in general Khadduri (1984).

and several Mediterranean islands. The dynasty was known for its effective rule and strong political authority, which helped to consolidate and manage the vast territories under its control.[27] Governors were appointed to manage the affairs of the conquered provinces, and it became common practice for them to delegate their judicial powers to officials known as *qadis*, or judges.[28] The role of the *qadis* was limited to resolving conflicts among Muslims within their territorial jurisdiction, while non-Muslim communities were subject to their own laws and court systems.

The *qadis'* decisions were based on 'sound opinion' (*ra'y*) derived from the precepts of the Qur'an, the rulings handed down by earlier religious leaders, administrative regulations, and local customs and laws. The *qadis* had a duty to render judgments consistent with fundamental Qur'anic principles. Although there was no appeal from a *qadi*'s decision, a defendant found guilty in a criminal case could appeal to the ruler after the execution of the sentence. If it was determined that the defendant was wrongfully punished, the *qadi* was dismissed from office, and the same penalty which was wrongfully imposed on the defendant was inflicted upon him; additionally, the defendant was be compensated.[29] Each case was judged on its own merits, with no systematic effort made to develop a consistent methodology or meticulously follow precedent.

The activities of the *qadis* contributed to increasing diversity in Islamic legal practice, as the extent to which decisions were based on the Qur'an or early precedents varied according to the knowledge and piety of each individual *qadi*. Furthermore, the interpretation of relevant rules often led to differences of opinion, even among judicial authorities within the same region.[30] Another factor contributing to this diversity was that *qadis* saw themselves as representatives of local customary law, which varied significantly from place to place.[31] This recognition of local norms and standards facilitated the incorporation of elements from Byzantine Roman law and Persian law into Islamic legal practice in the lands conquered by the Arabs.[32] As a result of these diverse influences and local variations, Islamic legal

[27] For more on the history of the Umayyad Dynasty see Bosworth (1996), pp. 3–5; Saunders (1978), chapter 5; Hawting (2000); Marsham (2024).

[28] See Shapiro (1980), p. 364.

[29] See al-Saleh (1982), p. 84.

[30] For example, Ibn Hujayra, who was *qadi* of Cairo from AD 680 to 702, considered the Qur'anic rule requiring husbands to make a 'fair provision' for the wives they repudiated as obligatory and fixed the relevant amount at three dinars. In AD 733, another *qadi* of Cairo, Tawba ibn Namis, ruled that the Quranic injunction was directed only at the individual's conscience and that a husband who refused to pay compensation could not be compelled to do so. However, under Tawba's successor, the payment once again became legally obligatory.

[31] For example, in Medina, where society had retained the traditional standards of Arab tribal law, no woman could marry without the express permission of her guardian. In the more cosmopolitan Iraqi region of Kufa, on the other hand, women could marry without the intervention of their guardians.

[32] When the Umayyads came to power, they inherited vast territories that were previously part of the Byzantine Empire, including regions such as Syria, Palestine, and Egypt. These regions had long-standing legal traditions rooted in Roman-Byzantine law, which inevitably influenced the

practice during the late seventh and eighth centuries lost much of the unity and cohesion it had enjoyed during the early Medinan period.

The eighth century witnessed a growing discontent against the Umayyad regime, which was perceived as having strayed from the core tenets of Islam. This dissatisfaction found a particular outlet in the realm of legal thought. Muslim scholars of the time, critical of the Umayyad courts for not upholding the essence of the Qur'an, began to articulate ideas that aligned more closely with authentic Islamic ethics. These scholars, often organized into informal groups, laid the groundwork for what would become the early schools of Islamic jurisprudence, or *fiqh*. Their influence became even more pronounced with the rise of the Abbasid dynasty in the mid-eighth century,[33] as the Abbasids supported these legal schools and appointed scholars, or *faqih*, as qadis and legal advisors. These scholars were instrumental in developing a coherent legal doctrine, which would form the foundation of the Abbasid state's legal and social systems.[34]

Fiqh literally means profound understanding. In a broader sense, this term refers to the process of deducing and applying the principles and rules of Shari'a law in real or hypothetical situations. Furthermore, the term is sometimes used to denote the entire body of laws derived from the Shari'a through the use of *fiqh* methodologies. The principal difference between *fiqh*-based rules and Shari'a-based rules is that the latter are immutable and non-negotiable, whereas the former are flexible and can be adjusted according to different circumstances and customs, as long as those customs do not contradict Shari'a. *Fiqh*'s objective is to demonstrate the practical application of Shari'a in all fields of social life and law, including religion, politics, civil relationships, criminal wrongdoing, the administration of justice, and

emerging Islamic legal system. One significant area of influence was in administrative law and governance. The Byzantine provincial administration system, which was highly organized and bureaucratic, served as a model for the Umayyads. They adopted and adapted many of these administrative practices, including tax collection methods and legal procedures for managing provincial affairs. This adoption was not merely pragmatic but also helped legitimize Umayyad rule by presenting a continuity of legal order, which was important for maintaining stability in newly conquered territories. In terms of private law, such as contracts and family law, there is evidence that early Islamic law was shaped by existing Byzantine practices. This cross-pollination of legal ideas contributed to the development of Islamic legal concepts, particularly in areas where Islamic law was not yet fully codified or where local practices were deeply entrenched. However, it is crucial to note that while Byzantine law influenced early Islamic law, Islamic jurists also sought to distinguish Islamic law from the laws of the previous empires. The Umayyads, while borrowing administrative and legal practices, emphasized the Islamic nature of their rule, leading to the gradual development of a distinct Islamic legal identity.

[33] The Abbasid dynasty, founded in AD 750, led a large portion of the Muslim community for five centuries from its capital in Baghdad. The early Abbasid period (eighth–ninth centuries) is often referred to as the Islamic Golden Age. Caliphs like Harun al-Rashid (r. 786–809) and Al-Ma'mun (r. 813–833) are considered among history's greatest patrons of the arts and sciences. Under their rule, Baghdad became the world's most important center for science, philosophy, medicine, and education. For a closer look at the history of the Abbasid Dynasty see Bosworth (1996), pp. 6–10; Saunders (1978), chapter 6; El-Hibri (2021); Kennedy (2016).

[34] Consider Kamali (1999), pp. 110–116.

the conduct of war. According to classical Islamic scholars, *fiqh* has two aspects: (a) the science of jurisprudence (*usul al-fiqh*: the roots of *fiqh*), concerned with the primary sources from which the rules of human conduct are derived and the methods and principles of interpretation used in discovering the rules of law;[35] and (b) the changeable rules of positive law governing social activities and the actual decisions deriving from the application of the *usul al fiqh* (*furu' al-fiqh*).[36]

Among the many schools of law (*madhabs*) that existed during the early Islamic period, particularly under the Umayyad and Abbasid caliphates,[37] the most influential were the *Hanafi* School, established by Abu Hanifa (AD 699–767) in Kufa (Iraq),[38] and the *Maliki* School, established by Malik ibn Anas (AD 711–795) in Medina.[39] The ultimate goal of these schools was the same: to formulate the ideal

[35] *Usul al-fiqh* encompasses a systematic approach that clarifies how texts should be interpreted and applied in various legal contexts. One of its core functions is to provide scholars with the tools to distinguish between speculative (*zanni*) texts and definitive (*qat'i*) texts. Speculative texts are those open to interpretation, often based on ambiguous or non-explicit wording, while definitive texts are clear, unambiguous, and not subject to reinterpretation. Additionally, *usul al-fiqh* guides scholars in differentiating between general (*amm*) texts and specific (*khas*) ones. General texts encompass broad categories or rules applicable to a wide range of cases, whereas specific texts narrow down the scope by applying conditions, exceptions, or particular contexts. This distinction ensures that rulings are applied correctly and proportionately, considering both broad legal principles and specific cases. Another critical aspect of *usul al-fiqh* is its ability to separate literal (*haqiqi*) meanings from metaphorical (*majazi*) ones. The literal meaning refers to the primary, conventional understanding of a word or phrase, while the metaphorical meaning involves figurative interpretation when context suggests that the literal meaning is not intended. This differentiation is vital in cases where a literal interpretation may contradict overarching principles or lead to impractical outcomes. Finally, *usul al-fiqh* enables scholars to understand the implications (*dalalat*) of a given text. *Dalalat* refers to the various levels of meaning derived from a text, including explicit meanings (*dalalat al-'ibara*), implicit implications (*dalalat al-ishara*), contextual inferences (*dalalat al-nass*), and logical deductions (*dalalat al-iqtida*). Mastering these implications ensures that the legal rulings align with the intent of the Lawgiver and cover both explicit commands and implicit guidelines, thereby allowing comprehensive application of Shari'a law in diverse contexts.

[36] Abdal-Haqq (2002), p. 50; Kamali (1999), p. 110; Bassiouni and Badr (2002), pp. 135–137. And see Hallaq (1992).

[37] According to the Islamic jurist Muhammad Iqbal, "[F]rom about the middle of the first century (late seventh–early eighth century AD) up to the beginning of the fourth (early tenth century AD) not less than nineteen schools of law and legal opinion appeared in Islam. This fact alone is sufficient to show how incessantly our early doctors of law worked in order to meet the necessities of a growing civilization." Iqbal (2011), p. 131.

[38] The Hanafi School is known for its emphasis on reason and opinion (*ra'y*) in the application of Islamic law. Abu Hanifa and his students developed a systematic legal methodology that included the use of analogical reasoning (*qiyas*) and juristic discretion (*istihsan*), allowing for flexibility in legal judgments. The Hanafi school's adaptability to diverse cultural contexts and its emphasis on rational legal interpretation contributed to its widespread acceptance.

[39] The Maliki School is characterized by its reliance on the practices of the people of Medina as a source of law. Malik ibn Anas viewed the customs and practices of Medina's inhabitants, who were considered to be close to the Prophet Muhammad's traditions, as a crucial source of Islamic law. The Maliki School is also known for its conservative approach, giving precedence to established practices over new interpretations. The School's emphasis on the practice of the early Muslim community in Medina made it particularly respected for its perceived authenticity.

form of Islamic law. Legal institutions and practices were systematically reviewed in the light of the fundamental principles enshrined in the Qur'an and early precedents, and were either approved or rejected on that basis. Islamic scholars embraced the view that humanity's understanding of the Shari'a, as the revealed word of God, is imperfect and fallible. According to them, the role of human reason is to rectify humanity's faulty understanding of these revealed truths.[40] However, because individual jurists were free to exercise their personal reasoning within the limits set, and because their thinking naturally depended on the social environment in which they lived, the legal doctrine developed in the school of Medina differed in some important respects from that of Kufa. Thus, apart from the common ground established by the express provisions of the Qur'an and the precedents of the early authorities, local customs influenced legal thought and doctrine, just as they had influenced the judgments of the *qadis* during the Umayyad era.

The mutual tolerance of the various schools' divergent views was ensured by their common recognition of the four basic sources from which the rules of Islamic law could be derived: the Qur'an, the *Sunnah*, the consensus of the scholars (*ijma*), and analogical reasoning (*Qiyas*). These sources of law were complemented by local custom (*urf*)[41] and the independent reasoning or intellectual endeavor (*ijtihad*) of individual jurists to extract solutions to problems not explicitly addressed in the primary sources.[42] The unity of the Islamic legal system was based on an agreement among the schools about the sources of law and an acceptance of a diversity of doctrine. It should be noted that judicial decisions were not recognized as a source of Islamic law, ensuring that the development of the law remained grounded in theological and intellectual consistency rather than considerations of social utility.

In the late eighth and ninth centuries, special attention was given by jurists to the question of the authority of doctrine and the sources from which it came. This jurisprudential debate led to significant conflicts and differences of opinion both between and within the various schools of thought. At its core, the debate centered on the extent to which personal reasoning (*ijtihad*) should be allowed in the jurists' efforts to discern and elucidate the will of Allah. The initial acceptance of speculative reasoning in the absence of explicit divine texts began to be challenged. Many argued that reasoning should be more disciplined and based on deduction by analogy (*qiyas*) from established norms.

A particularly radical stance was taken by the so-called 'Defenders of Traditions' (*Ahl al-Hadith*). This group of scholars argued that legal reasoning in any form was both unwarranted and unnecessary. They insisted that, aside from the Qur'an, the only true source of legal injunctions was the recorded words and actions of the

[40] Consider Faruqi and Faruqi (1986), p. 265.

[41] Custom is defined as a body of unwritten norms formed by the recurrence of certain practices over a long period of time. These norms are incorporated into the law through judicial decisions and the consensus of scholars (*ijma*). As indicated earlier, Islamic jurisprudence treats local custom as a source of law only when it does not contradict Islamic rules and principles derived from the primary sources. For a closer look at the role of custom consider Libson (1997); Shabana (2010).

[42] See Bassiouni and Badr (2002), pp. 140–141.

Prophet Muhammad (*Sunnah*), who was the chosen instrument of Allah and the only person qualified to interpret and explain Allah's will.[43] The *Sunnah*, which was initially transmitted orally, was memorized and passed down until the third century of Islam (AD 816–913), when it was compiled into collections of traditions known as *ahadith* (singular, *hadith*), documenting what the Prophet said or did on specific occasions. These *ahadith* relied on oral transmissions through a chain of named narrators, tracing back to reliable witnesses of the Prophet's actions or sayings. They were ranked according to their presumed degree of reliability and authenticity as sound (*sahih*), good (*hasan*) and weak (*daif*).[44]

The task of the jurist, according to the 'Defenders of Traditions,' was to uncover the Sunnah through the study of *ahadith*, rather than engage in speculative reasoning about what Allah's law might be. The conflict between speculative jurisprudence (*ra'y*) and the 'Defenders of Traditions' was closely linked to a fundamental issue in Islamic jurisprudence: the relationship between divine revelation and human reason in the realm of law. It was during this period that the renowned jurist Mohammed Al-Shafi'i (AD 767–820)—arguably the most significant figure in the history of Islamic jurisprudence—emerged as a key player in shaping the field.[45] Al-Shafi'i is best known for his work in systematizing the principles of Islamic jurisprudence (*usul al-fiqh*). His most famous work, *Al-Risala*, is considered the first treatise on *usul al-fiqh* and laid the foundation for a systematic approach to Islamic law. Al-Shafi'i's contributions were pivotal in reconciling differences between the earlier schools of thought and providing a more structured framework for Islamic jurisprudence.

Al-Shafi'i was the first jurist to systematically and unequivocally articulate the principle that certain knowledge of Allah's law could only be obtained through divine revelation. He argued that, apart from the Qur'an, the only other legitimate source of legal norms was the *Sunnah* of the Prophet Muhammad, which encompasses everything the Prophet did, said, or consented to during his lifetime.[46] In cases involving issues not clearly resolved by the Qur'an or the *Sunnah*, Al-Shafi'i acknowledged the necessity of reasoning, but only in the strictly disciplined and subsidiary form of reasoning by analogy (*Qiyas*), and the role of scholarly consensus (*Ijma*). According to him, the function of jurisprudence was not to create new laws but to discover the law from the substance of divine revelation and, where necessary, to apply its principles to new cases through analogical reasoning. By

[43] Schacht (1982), pp. 34–36.

[44] In the course of time, six *ahadith* collections were recognized as the most authoritative (*sihah Sittah*), namely, those of *al-Bukhari, Muslim, Abu Dawud, al-Tirmidhi, al-Nasa'i, and Ibn Majah*. See Ruthven (1984), pp. 148–156; Faruqi and Faruqi (1986), p. 114.

[45] Al-Shafi'i is one of the four great Imams of Sunni Islam and the founder of the Shafi'i school of thought, one of the four major Sunni legal schools. Born in Gaza, Palestine, Al-Shafi'i was a descendant of the Prophet Muhammad's family through his grandfather. He studied under several renowned scholars of his time, including Imam Malik, the founder of the Maliki school. For a closer look at Al-Shafi'i's career and work see Weeramantry (1988), p. 52 ff; Ali (2011).

[46] See Esposito (2003), p. 305.

formulating a general theory about the sources of law, Al-Shafi'i introduced a degree of uniformity to Islamic jurisprudence that was lacking in earlier periods. As mentioned earlier, legal diversity had resulted from the recognition of local and personal criteria in early jurisprudence and legal practice. Al-Shafi'i replaced these local and limited elements with concepts of universal validity and application.[47]

Following Al-Shafi'i's approach, scholars devoted themselves to the task of documenting the *Sunnah* (the practices of Muhammad) by collecting and systematizing the traditions (*ahadiths*). After Al-Shafi'i's death, two new schools of law were established in addition to the existing ones. Those who accepted the exact terms of Al-Shafi'i's doctrine unconditionally formed the Shafi'i School. In contrast, jurists who sought to push the doctrine of the authority of the Hadiths to even more rigid extremes formed the Hanbali School. The founder of the latter school, Ahmad ibn Hanbal (ninth century AD), rejected the role of human reason in any form, including reasoning by analogy, in the legal process, insisting that every legal rule must be supported by an authority found only in the Qur'an or the *Sunnah*.

Over time, however, the jurists of the Hanbali School gradually modified their original position and came to recognize that analogical reasoning was a necessary tool for the elaboration of law. Earlier schools of thought, such as the Maliki and Hanafi Schools, also managed to reconcile their approaches to law with the fundamental tenets of Al-Shafi'i's doctrine. By the end of the ninth century, Islamic jurisprudence as a whole had absorbed Al-Shafi'i's teaching in a form acceptable to all the major schools (*mathhabs*).[48]

The four principal schools of Islamic jurisprudence—Hanafi, Maliki, Shafi'i, and Hanbali—exerted a strong influence on legal thought and practice, with courts in various regions of the Islamic world gradually adopting the doctrines or approaches of one school or another. The Hanafi school prevailed in the Middle East and the Indian subcontinent, the Maliki School was particularly influential in North, West, and Central Africa, and the Shafi'i School played a dominant role in East Africa, parts of the Arabian Peninsula, Malaysia, and Indonesia. By the eighteenth century, the doctrine of the Hanbali School had been accepted and applied by the courts in most of the Arabian Peninsula.[49]

---

[47] The following is an extract from Shafi'i's *Risala*, a work he composed in Cairo at the beginning of the ninth century AD: "On all matters concerning which God provided clear textual evidence in His Book or [a sunna] uttered by the Prophet's tongue, disagreement among those to whom these [texts] are known is unlawful. As to matters that are liable to different interpretations or derived from analogy, so that he who interprets or applies analogy arrives at a decision different from that arrived at by another, I do not hold that [disagreement] of this kind constitutes such strictness as that *arising from textual* [evidence]." See Khadduri (1961), p. 333.

[48] George Makdisi observes that the scholastic method of disputation and instruction developed by Islamic scholars in the ninth century was later employed by jurists in the universities of Bologna, Paris, Oxford and other early European universities. See Makdisi (1985a). And see Makdisi (1981).

[49] On the schools of Islamic jurisprudence see in general Kamali (1999), pp. 112–113; Cornell (1999), pp. 94–95; Bearman et al. (2005).

The process of endeavouring to comprehend the commands of divine law and construct rules consistent with the first principles of Islam is called *ijtihad*.[50] In determining the course that this process should follow, Muslim jurists adhered to Al-Shafi'i's doctrine. The *mujtahid*—the scholar exercising *ijtihad*—must first seek the solution to a legal problem in the Qur'an or *Sunnah*. If no solution can be found there, the *mujtahid* must use the method of reasoning by analogy (*qiyas*). *Qiyas* was defined as the process of reasoning from a known injunction to a new injunction. By applying this method, jurists could extend the rulings of the Qur'an and *Sunnah* to new problems, provided that the earlier case or precedent and the new problem shared the same operative or effective cause.[51] *Qiyas* encompasses argument *a fortiori*,[52] *reductio ad absurdum*,[53] and induction.[54] When exercising *ijtihad*, a scholar must consider the six higher purposes or objectives of the Shari'a (*maqasid al shari'a*), namely, the preservation of life, property, family, religion, honour or dignity, and reason.[55] In regulating the effect of *ijtihad* and assessing its results, jurists extended Al-Shafi'i's doctrine by incorporating the doctrine of *ijma*. *Ijma*, as defined by classical jurists, is the agreement of qualified scholars in a given generation on issues for which neither the Qur'an nor *Sunnah* provides guidance. A consensus of opinion is accepted to produce certain knowledge of Allah's will. True consensus presupposes (a) participation of a reasonable number of qualified scholars, (b) a unanimous decision, and (c) an unequivocal statement of agreement by each jurist.[56] However, where no consensus is reached, differing views are recognized as equally valid attempts to discover the divine will.

It should be noted that since the time of the Prophet and his companions, achieving a universal consensus has proven impossible due to the social and political divisions within the Muslim world. Although a universal *ijma* cannot be attained, a limited consensus can be reached within a particular geographic area or school of thought (*madhhab*). Islamic jurisprudence recognizes the existence of different versions of Shari'a law, depending on the diversity of changing circumstances. This is said to be based on the Prophet Muhammad's alleged saying, "Difference of opinion within my community is a sign of the bounty of Allah."

---

[50] On the role of *ijtihad* see Bassiouni and Badr (2002), p. 173.

[51] See Makdisi (1985a). On the nature and role of *qiyas* see generally Hasan (1980); Hallaq (1985).

[52] Argument *a fortiori* is a form of argument that draws upon another argument that is so strong as to make it unanswerable. This kind of argument has two versions, namely, argument *a maiore ad minus*, and argument *a minore ad maius*. The argument *a maiore ad minus* describes an argument from the bigger or more general to the smaller ore more specific. The argument *a minore ad maius*, on the other hand, claims that what is true on a small or specific scale is true on a larger or more general scale.

[53] The refutation of a proposition by showing that the conclusion to which it would logically lead would be absurd.

[54] *Induction* is a method of *reasoning* from a part to a whole, from the specific to the general, or from the individual to the universal.

[55] Kamali (1989), pp. 224 & 229.

[56] See Schacht (1982), p. 30. On the concept of *ijma* consider also Freamon (1998); Nyazee (2000), pp. 182–194.

Reference should also be made to the concept of *Istihsan*, which is defined as the process of selecting one alternative solution to a problem over another because the chosen solution is more suitable for the case at hand, even if the rejected solution may be technically more correct. *Istihsan* allows jurists a measure of flexibility in interpreting the law by prioritizing the spirit or essence of the law over its letter. In this sense, it can be understood as equity, fairness, or a departure from the strict letter of the law to promote public welfare. *Istihsan* is sometimes referred to as 'hidden *qiyas*,' in contrast to the 'apparent *qiyas*,' which requires the strict application of the law.[57]

As previously noted, the doctrines of the four major schools of Islamic jurisprudence were regarded as equally legitimate under the doctrine of *ijma*, or consensus. However, *ijma* also served as a restrictive and exclusive principle. Once *ijma* extended its infallible authority over not only the points of consensus but also the existing divergent opinions, the situation was considered irrevocably settled, and any alternative views were deemed contrary to *ijma*—the infallible expression of God's will. Those who held differing opinions were thus accused of heresy. Consequently, the practice of *ijtihad*, or independent reasoning to determine Islamic law, began to decline. By the end of the tenth century, Islamic jurisprudence acknowledged that the creative potential of *ijtihad* had been exhausted. This so-called 'closing of the door of *ijtihad*' marked the beginning of the era of *taqlid*, or imitation. From that point onward, jurists no longer possessed the right to *ijtihad* but were expected to be mere 'imitators,' obligated to adhere to the doctrines established by their predecessors. As Joseph Schacht has noted:

> The point had been reached when the scholars of all schools felt that all essential questions had been thoroughly discussed and finally settled, and a consensus gradually established itself to the effect that from that time onwards no one might be deemed to have the necessary qualifications for independent reasoning in law, and that all future activity would have to be confined to the explanation, application, and, at the most, interpretation of the doctrine as it had been laid down once and for all.[58]

By the end of the fourteenth century, various legal texts had emerged, representing the authoritative statement of the law for each school, validated by the doctrine of consensus (*ijma*). Through this doctrine, every legal rule was identified with a command from Allah. Consequently, classical jurisprudence eventually obscured the true origins of much of the Shari'a doctrine, which, as previously discussed, lay in local customs and the personal reasoning of individual scholars. Law was now perceived as something imposed on society from above, rather than as something that developed from social conditions and customs. Knowledge of true values and standards of behavior could not be attained through human reason and experience but only through divine revelation. Actions were considered good or evil solely because Allah had designated them as such. Moreover, the law of Allah, as outlined

---

[57] See Makdisi (1985b), pp. 73 & 92.

[58] Schacht (1982), pp. 70–71. According to some commentators, however, Islamic scholars may still rely on *ijtihad* in addressing legal problems. See, e.g., Hallaq (1986).

in the authoritative Shari'a texts, was seen as an immutable system, for after the death of the Prophet Muhammad, there could be no further communication of the divine will to humanity. In essence, the law, as articulated in the Shari'a texts, was regarded as a divinely ordained, comprehensive, and eternally valid code of conduct binding on all Muslim communities.

Regarding the administration of justice, by the time of the Abbasid dynasty, the *qadis* had become full-time judicial officials, who, in principle, could carry out their duties free from governmental interference. In practice, however, they were subject to dismissal by the central government, which also supervised their jurisdiction and was responsible for enforcing their judgments. Although the Shari'a was considered the official law of the state, in reality, the jurisdiction of the Shari'a courts was always subject to the limitations set by the political sovereign. When conflicts arose between the terms of the Shari'a and the interests of the sovereign, the latter could restrict the powers of the Shari'a courts and recognize alternative jurisdictional bodies. A significant limitation to the practical efficiency of the Shari'a courts was related to the limited scope of Qur'anic law and the rigid system of procedure and evidence, in both civil and criminal cases, to which they were bound.[59] Since political rulers could not tolerate the cumbersome nature of Shari'a procedures, the authority to try cases within certain areas of the law was delegated to officials other than the *qadis*. This led to the development of a new form of jurisdiction, known as *Mazalim* (complaints) jurisdiction, with concurrent authority over Shari'a crimes and supplementary jurisdiction over newly introduced secular offenses. Exercised by an official called the *Sahib al-Mazalim*, this jurisdiction grew to the point where it became a serious competitor to the Shari'a courts, creating a clear division in Islamic legal practice. Although all the functions of the Islamic state were theoretically religious in nature, the distinction between the *Mazalim* and Shari'a jurisdictions came close to resembling a division between secular and religious courts. The *qadi* was regarded as the representative of Allah's law, while the *Sahib al-Mazalim* was seen as the exponent of the ruler's law. By the end of the Abbasid period in the thirteenth century, the *Mazalim* courts adjudicated most legal matters, while the jurisdiction of the Shari'a courts was restricted primarily to issues relating to marriage, divorce, and the devolution of property.[60] The secular law applied by the

[59] The burden of proof was strict, and the party bearing it, usually the plaintiff, was required to produce two adult male Muslim witnesses whose moral integrity and religious devotion were unquestionable, to testify orally based on their direct knowledge of the truth of his claim. If the plaintiff or accuser failed to meet this burden, the defendant was offered the oath of denial. When properly sworn on the Qur'an, such an oath secured judgment in his favor. If the defendant failed to take the oath, the judgment would go in favor of the plaintiff or accuser, provided that, in some cases, they also took the oath. This system of procedure made it challenging for Shari'a courts to administer justice in certain areas of the law.

[60] With respect to civil law, judicial power was delegated to several officials: the Inspector of the Marketplace (*Muhtasib*) had summary jurisdiction over minor commercial disputes and could impose immediate punishment on thieves and other minor offenders; the Master of Complaints (*Sahib al-Mazalim*) had jurisdiction over matters concerning real property; and the Master of the Treasury was responsible for tax-related issues. Additionally, secular criminal jurisdiction was

Mazalim tribunals was an amalgam of Shari'a law, customary law, administrative decrees, and principles derived from other legal systems.[61]

9.3 The Influence of Islamic Law on Modern Legal Systems

By the early sixteenth century, three powerful Muslim empires had emerged: the Sunni Ottoman Empire in Western Asia, North Africa, and Eastern Europe; the Shia Safavid Empire in Persia; and the Sunni Mughal Empire in the Indian subcontinent. Although Shari'a law continued to be regarded as the official law of these empires, its jurisdiction was largely restricted to family and inheritance matters, while most other cases were adjudicated by the *Mazalim* tribunals.

During the nineteenth and twentieth centuries, the influence of the West on Islamic society led to significant changes in many areas of the law, particularly the law governing civil and commercial transactions.[62] European law codes were often applied in disputes between Muslims and Westerners, and over time, Islamic jurists and lawyers became increasingly familiar with foreign legal systems. Expanding commercial and political relations between Europe and the Middle East gradually led to the widespread adoption of European legal models.[63] This shift was largely due to the fact that Shari'a law concerning civil obligations was based on the relatively simple system of commercial relations that prevailed in early Arab society, which included a strict prohibition on all forms of interest on capital investment, making it incompatible with modern systems of trade and economic development. Equally untenable in the context of a modern state was much of Shari'a criminal law. Firstly, the prescribed penalties for certain offenses, such as hand amputation for theft and stoning to death for adulterous wives, were no longer acceptable on humanitarian grounds. Secondly, under Shari'a law, homicide is treated more like a civil tort than a crime, as the prosecution of the offense depends on the wishes of the victim's relatives. The relatives can either demand the death of the perpetrator as retribution, request a sum of money as compensation, or forgive him completely. While this approach to homicide may make sense in a tribal society—a similar approach was adopted in the West during the Middle Ages—it does not fit the framework of a modern state. Finally, apart from the six specified offenses, namely wine-drinking, fornication, theft, slander, highway robbery, and apostasy, Shari'a law allows the judge almost unlimited discretion in defining and punishing offenses.

overseen by an official called the *Wali al-Jara'im* (official in charge of crimes). The relevant court was not bound by Qur'anic standards of evidence, procedure, and punishment but was empowered to take measures as deemed necessary to uncover the truth. See Coulson (1964), pp. 127–128.

[61] Schacht (1982), pp. 76–85.

[62] The influence of Western law was first felt through a series of treaties known as capitulations, which allowed European citizens residing in the Ottoman Empire to be governed by the laws of their own countries.

[63] Coulson (1964), pp. 149–151.

Such arbitrary judicial power was deemed unacceptable in many Islamic states influenced by Western models of criminal justice. As a result, during the nineteenth and twentieth centuries, Shari'a criminal law and the law of civil transactions were abrogated or limited in scope and replaced by new laws largely based on European models.

A far-reaching reception of European legal concepts and rules occurred in the Ottoman Empire during the nineteenth century. French law codes served as the model for the 1850 Ottoman Commercial Code, which provided for the payment of interest, and for the 1858 Ottoman Penal Code, which ended most of the harsh Qur'anic punishments. The French codes of commercial procedure and maritime commerce were adopted in 1861 and 1863, respectively, and a new system of secular civil courts was introduced in the latter half of the nineteenth century. Furthermore, through a series of legislative enactments beginning in 1875, Egypt adopted the French Penal, Civil, Commercial, and Maritime codes and instituted a system of secular courts to apply the relevant rules. Over time, French, German, Italian, English, and Swiss law codes spread throughout the Middle East, limiting the application of Shari'a law to family law, inheritance law, charitable endowment (*waqf*), and matters of personal status. Outside the Middle East, Western law spread primarily through colonialism to many countries in Africa and Asia. The French implemented their civil and penal codes in Algeria, and a similar policy was followed by the Dutch in Indonesia. In India and parts of Africa, the British initially preserved the indigenous legal systems, but over time, they introduced the English common law system. The coexistence of Islamic and English laws led to the development of unique 'hybrid' legal systems, such as the Anglo-Muhammadan law, which was applied in British colonial India between the eighteenth and twentieth centuries. As a result of these processes, laws of European origin today form an integral part of the legal systems in many contemporary Muslim states.

Nevertheless, there are still a number of countries, such as Saudi Arabia, Qatar, the United Arab Emirates, Iran, and Afghanistan, where Shari'a law remains formally supreme in most areas of law. In general, with respect to Shari'a law, what is tolerated by the state varies from one Islamic country to another. Some of these countries, such as Turkey, Albania, Kazakhstan, and Uzbekistan, are effectively secular, even though Islam is the predominant religion. These countries often have laws and policies that promote the separation of religion from political and governmental matters, even though Islam may play a significant cultural and social role in their societies. At the opposite extreme are countries like Saudi Arabia, Iran, and Afghanistan, where the state is viewed as completely subservient to religion, functioning as a mere tool for its implementation. In these countries, Shari'a rules are automatically enforced by the state. Between these two extremes, there are countries where the government applies secular law, although practicing Muslims may still choose to bring familial and financial disputes to Shari'a courts for resolution. This approach prevails in the majority of Islamic countries, including Malaysia, Lebanon, Jordan, and Morocco, although the precise reach of the Shari'a courts' jurisdiction varies from country to country. In most Islamic nations, Islam is declared the state religion; however, this simply means that the state has the authority to decide if, when, and how Shari'a is to be implemented.

It should be noted that, within the recognized limits of their jurisdiction, Shari'a courts may deviate to some extent from the strict doctrines of Shari'a texts for reasons of social or economic necessity. Despite its perceived rigidity, Islamic law can actually be a flexible system of rules, provided that the court or authority applying it aims to achieve flexibility. This flexibility arises from the fact that many of its rules are broadly worded. Moreover, in some instances, the courts employ specific mechanisms to circumvent the strict rules of Shari'a doctrine that have proven to be impractical in practice, without formally abolishing them.

For example, a well-known rule stipulates that a marriage can be dissolved unilaterally by the husband by pronouncing "I divorce you" three times. However, in some Islamic countries, this form of divorce is only recognized if a court or relevant authority has examined the circumstances and basis of the action. In theory, the purpose of this investigation is to ensure that the husband's request for divorce is both voluntary and serious.

Another example involves polygamy, the right of a man to marry multiple women simultaneously. While polygamy is currently banned in many Islamic countries, this has been achieved without contravening Shari'a law. Islamic law does not mandate polygamy but merely permits it, provided that the husband treats all his wives fairly and equally—an expectation that, according to certain sources, is beyond the capabilities of any man. Furthermore, it is acknowledged that, in the marriage contract during the first marriage, the husband can voluntarily renounce his right to enter into subsequent marriages.

A further example relates to the prohibition in Islamic law against taking interest, which is equated with usury. One common method used to circumvent this ban involves engaging in a fictitious sale and repurchase transaction.

Additionally, reasoning by analogy (*qiyas*) plays a crucial role in addressing situations not directly covered by the primary sources. In such cases, an analogy is drawn to a similar situation for which guidance exists. For example, the prohibition of alcohol in Islamic law is derived by analogy from the Qur'anic prohibition of drinking wine, and this ban has been further extended by analogy to include certain hard narcotics.[64]

9.4 Concluding Remarks

The question to be addressed at this point is this: how much has the influence of Islamic law been affected by the reception of Western legal ideas in Islamic countries? As previously indicated, a general answer to this question is difficult to provide due to the differences that exist among these countries. Scholars have observed

[64] See Makdisi (1985b), p. 63 ff.

that most Islamic countries have successfully merged the various aspects of their existing laws, whether of traditional or Western origin, in a manner consistent with the traditions and mentality of their peoples. Concepts and institutions borrowed from Western legal systems have been, and continue to be, synthesized with methods of reasoning and an outlook shaped by the Islamic legal tradition. It is worth remembering what happened in the former Soviet Union: a systematic attempt was made to repudiate or eliminate tradition to build an entirely new socio-political order, and legal system. However, experience has shown that the past cannot be erased with the stroke of a pen. While a different system of law governed by a different ideology may have been introduced, people's attitudes towards law and their traditional ways of thinking and acting remained largely unaffected. It is therefore unsurprising that Islamic law has experienced a revival and is exerting considerable influence on the legal systems of some states that emerged after the breakup of the Soviet Union, as several of these countries have overwhelmingly Muslim populations. Experience in other Islamic countries suggests a similar outcome. New branches of law based on Western models may have been introduced, and there may be varying degrees of deviation from the core orthodox tenets of Islam, in some cases even to the point of secularizing or abandoning fundamental concepts of Islamic law. However, the law of Islamic countries cannot be said to have fully assimilated with Western law. Beyond considerations of the substance and structure of the law, jurists in these countries tend to adhere to their traditional ways of reasoning and thinking, which are deeply rooted in the society and culture in which they live.

In the last several decades, the Islamic world has been witnessing a resurgence of Islamic fundamentalism.[65] While the majority of Muslim people participate in some facets of today's globalizing world without abandoning their own cultural practices and values, there are also those who attempt to isolate themselves from global Western influences to protect their culture from external forces that might change or 'contaminate' it.[66] According to Benjamin Barber, the global pressures for uniformity produce cultural and political forces of resistance, which he terms 'jihad.' In contrast to the homogenizing forces of uniformity, jihad is a fragmenting force that

---

[65] For a general account of this phenomenon see Jansen (1979); Tibi (1998); Kepel (2003).

[66] Scholars use the term 'cultural differentialism' to emphasize the notion that individual cultures possess a real and lasting uniqueness that can persist independently of globalization. This concept is explored in Samuel Huntington's famous work, *The Clash of Civilizations*. Huntington employs the term 'civilizations' to describe coherent cultural identities that exist globally, identifying eight such cultures: Western, Sino/Confucian, Japanese, Islamic, Hindu, Slavic-Orthodox, Latin American, and (possibly) African. According to him, "The great divisions among humankind and the dominating source of conflict will be cultural. Nation states will remain the most powerful actors in world affairs, but the principal conflicts of global politics will occur between nations and groups of different civilizations. The clash of civilizations will dominate global politics. The fault lines between civilizations will be the battle lines of the future." Huntington (1993), p. 22. The Islamic, Confucian and Hindu civilizations are identified in direct relation to the dominant religion of their members. In general, Huntington emphasizes the continued importance of religion as the principal force that motivates and mobilizes people.

pits culture against culture and rejects any kind of interdependence and cooperation.[67]

A central tenet of Islamic fundamentalist movements is the rejection of the secularism and corruption of contemporary Muslim regimes and the creation of a social order based on fundamental Qur'anic principles. These movements maintain that when the government fails to observe these principles, the obligation of political obedience withers away and is replaced by a duty of disobedience and defiance.[68] Fundamentalists argue that only a return to the true values of Islam will safeguard Muslims against the influence of Western mass media, consumerism, economic exploitation, and nationalism, all of which threaten to submerge the Islamic world under a wave of "conspicuous consumption and the cult of economic growth, hedonism, and permissiveness."[69] According to them, the solution lies neither in nationalism nor in pan-Arabism but in the creation of a community of believers united by the Islamic faith and a revived Shari'a law.[70]

Contemporary regimes across the Muslim world find themselves under increasing pressure to respond to these popular calls for Islamization. This poses significant challenges for legal practice and scholarship, as certain aspects of Shari'a law are arguably incompatible with international human rights standards. In response to this, some commentators have argued that international human rights standards should be construed and applied in light of domestic cultural and religious values, norms, and practices.[71] Others are willing to acknowledge that certain rights may be overridden on the grounds of cultural relativism—the theory that norms and values are specific or relative to a particular culture and cannot be judged according to the standards of another culture.[72] However, several scholars have argued that care

[67] Barber (1992). Barber regards both Jihad and the forces pushing for integration and uniformity (McWorld) as antidemocratic forces that undermine civil liberties. He advocates for a form of governance that protects and supports local communities while helping them become more tolerant and participatory. It should be noted that scholars have differing opinions regarding the effects of cultural globalization. These disagreements are partly due to the complexity of cultural flows, which result in uneven and contradictory outcomes. In some contexts, local cultures may be largely replaced by Western cultural products; in others, global pressures may lead to a resurgence of local cultures; and in still others, cultural exchanges give rise to new forms of cultural hybridity.

[68] As Edward Mortimer remarks, the history of Islam "is full of movements that sought simultaneously to restore what they saw as the true doctrine of Islam and to overthrow the existing political order." Mortimer (1982), p. 40.

[69] See Sivan (1985), p. 45.

[70] As Sivan notes, "The linchpin of this reformatory enterprise is the slogan of the 'application of Muslim law' *(tatbiq al-Shari'a)*, or in its up-to-date, and somewhat pared-down form, 'codification of Muslim Law' *(taqnin al-Shari'a)*." Sivan (1985), p. 143.

[71] From this point of view, it has been argued that human rights are a Western cultural construct and should not be imposed on regions of the world that do not share the culture and values of the West. An expression of this perspective can be found in the 'Statement on Human Rights' of the American Anthropological Association (1947), which stressed the need to study and honor the values of other cultures and warned against the making of a Universal Declaration of Human Rights that reflects only Western values. On this issue see in general Renteln (1985).

[72] Consider Donnelly (1984).

should be taken not to overstate the force of the cultural relativist argument, as it opens the door to abuse and the subordination of individuals by oppressive regimes cynically cloaking themselves in the guise of Islamic traditionalism.[73] Despite the profound differences between Islam and the West, the repudiation or curtailment of human rights on the basis of religious ideology or doctrine is too high a price to pay in the name of cultural relativism.[74]

As Islamic societies continue to evolve and face new challenges in an ever-changing world, law will undoubtedly remain a central element in the ongoing ideological and political struggle between traditionalism and modernism, shaped by Western, international, and transnational legal frameworks. The legitimacy and acceptability of the outcomes of this process will depend on how well these outcomes are grounded in the universal and eternal values of Islam, while also being adapted to diverse social and cultural contexts. Upholding these values will help shield the resulting changes in law and society from inevitable attacks by extremist elements, who are likely to denounce them as foreign or Western impositions.

References

Abdal-Haqq I (2002) Islamic law: an overview of is origin and elements. J Islam Law Cult 7(1):27–81

Ali K (2011) Imam Shafi'i: scholar and saint. Oneworld Publications, Oxford

al-Saleh OA (1982) The right of the individual to personal security in Islam. In: Bassiouni C (ed) The Islamic criminal justice system. Oceana Publications, New York, pp 55–90

Barber BR (1992) Jihad vs. McWorld. Artlantic Monthly 269(3):53–65

Bassiouni MC, Badr GM (2002) The Shari'ah: sources, interpretation, and rule- making. J Islam Near Eastern Law 2(1):135–181

Bearman P, Peters R, Vogel F (eds) (2005) The Islamic school of law: evolution, devolution and progress. Harvard University Press, Cambridge

Bosworth CE (1996) New Islamic dynasties: a chronological and genealogical manual. Edinburgh University Press, Edinburgh

Chan W-T et al (1969) The great Asian religions: an anthology. Macmillan, New York

Cornell VJ (1999) Fruit of the tree of knowledge: the relationship between faith and practice in Islam. In: Esposito JL (ed) The Oxford history of Islam. Oxford University Press, Oxford, pp 63–106

Coulson NJ (1964) A history of Islamic law. Edinburgh University Press, Edinburgh

Coulson NJ (1969) Conflicts and tensions in Islamic jurisprudence. University of Chicago Press, Chicago

---

[73] Consider Howard-Hassmann (1983). And see generally Wright (2001).

[74] The cultural relativist critique exemplifies the so-called naturalistic fallacy, which assumes that the way things are now (people holding different values) determines how things should be (that they should always continue to hold these values). However, one can argue that even if it were true that human rights are a Western cultural construct, this does not mean that people from other parts of the world cannot culturally embrace and benefit from them. The term 'naturalistic fallacy' was coined by G.E. Moore in his work *Principia Ethica*, published in 1903 by Cambridge University Press. On the naturalistic fallacy consider, in general: Prior (1956), chapter 1; Sinclair (2019); Crisp (1996).

Coulson NJ (2008) Succession in the Muslim family. Cambridge University Press, Cambridge
Crisp R (1996) Naturalism and non-naturalism in ethics. In: Lovibond S, Williams SG (eds) Identity, truth and value. Blackwell Publishers, Malden, pp 113–129
Donnelly J (1984) Cultural relativism and universal human rights. Hum Rights Q 6(4):400–419
Donner FM (1999) Muhammed and the Caliphate: political history of the Islamic empire up to the Mongol conquest. In: Esposito JL (ed) The Oxford History of Islam. Oxford University Press, Oxford, pp 1–62
El-Hibri T (2021) The Abbasid Caliphate: a history. Cambridge University Press, Cambridge
Esposito JL (1988) Islam: the straight path. Oxford University Press, New York
Esposito JL (ed) (2003) The Oxford dictionary of Islam. Oxford University Press, Oxford
Faruqi IR, Faruqi LL (1986) The cultural atlas of Islam. Macmillan, London
Feldman N (2008) Why Shariah? New York Times Magazine, Mar. 16, pp 46–51
Freamon BK (1998) Slavery, freedom, and the doctrine of consensus in Islamic jurisprudence. Harv Hum Rights J 11(1):1–64
Fyzee AAA (1964) Outlines of Muhammadan law. Oxford University Press, London
Hallaq W (1985) Legal reasoning in Islamic law and the common law: logic and method. Cleveland State Law Rev 34:79–96
Hallaq W (1986) On the origins of the controversy about the existence of Mujtahids and the Gate of Ijtihad. Studia Islamica 63:129–144
Hallaq W (1992) Usul Al-Fiqh: beyond tradition. J Islam Stud 3(2):172–202
Hasan A (1970) The early development of Islamic jurisprudence. Islamic Research Institute, Islamabad
Hasan A (1980) The definition of Qiyas in Islamic jurisprudence. Islam Stud 19(1):1–28
Hawting GR (2000) The first dynasty of Islam: The Umayyad Caliphate AD 661-750, 2nd edn. Routledge, London
Howard-Hassmann R (1983) The full-belly thesis: should economic rights take priority over civil and political rights? Evidence from Sub-Saharan Africa. Hum Rights Q 5(4):467–490
Huntington S (1993) The clash of civilizations? Foreign Aff 72(3):22–49
Hussaini SS (2007) The laws of inheritance in Islam, 2nd edn. Outskirts Press, Denver
Iqbal M (2009) The reconstruction of religious thought in Islam. Dodo Press, Gloucestershire UK (originally published 1930)
Iqbal M (2011) The reconstruction of religious thought in Islam. Iqbal Academy Pakistan, Lahore (originally published 1930)
Jansen GH (1979) Militant Islam. Harper & Row, New York
Kamali MH (1989) Sources, nature and objectives of Shari'ah. Islam Q 33(4):215–236
Kamali MH (1999) Law and society: the interplay of revelation and reason in the Shariah. In: Esposito JL (ed) The Oxford history of Islam. Oxford University Press, Oxford, pp 107–153
Kennedy H (2016) The early Abbasid Caliphate: a political history. Routledge, New York
Kepel G (2003) Muslim extremism in Egypt: the Prophet and Pharaoh. University of California Press, Berkeley
Khadduri M (trans) (1961, repr 1997) al-Shafii's Risala: treatise on the foundation of Islamic jurisprudence, 2nd edn. Islamic Texts Society, Cambridge
Khadduri M (1984) The Islamic conception of justice. Johns Hopkins University Press, Baltimore
Khan H (2007) The Islamic law of inheritance. Oxford University Press, Oxford
Libson G (1997) On the development of custom as a source of law in Islamic law. Islam Law Soc 4(2):131–155
Lombardi CB (1998) Islamic law as a source of constitutional law in Egypt: the constitutionalization of the Sharia in a modern Arab state. Columbia J Transnatl Law 37(1):81–123
Mahmood T (1965) Custom as a source of Law in Islam. J Indian Law Inst 7(1/2):102–106
Makdisi G (1981) The rise of colleges: institutions of learning in Islam and the West. Edinburgh University Press, Edinburgh
Makdisi G (1985a) The guilds of law in medieval legal history: an inquiry into the origins of the inns of court. Cleveland State Law Rev 34(3):3–18

Makdisi J (1985b) Legal logic and equity in Islamic law. Am J Comp Law 33(1):63–92
Marsham A (2024) The Umayyad Empire. Edinburgh University Press, Edinburgh
Mortimer E (1982) Faith and power: the politics of Islam. Random House, New York
Muir W (1923) The life of Mohammad. John Grant, Edinburgh
Nyazee IAK (2000) Islamic jurisprudence. International Institute of Islamic Thought, Islamabad
Powers DS (1986) Studies in Qurʾān and Ḥadīth: the formation of the Islamic law of inheritance. University of California Press, Berkeley
Powers DS (1993) The Islamic inheritance system: a socio-historical approach. Arab Law Q 8(1):13–29
Prior AN (1956) Logic and the basis of ethics. Clarendon Press, Oxford
Ramadan T (2009) Radical reform: Islamic ethics and liberation. Oxford University Press, New York
Renteln AD (1985) The unanswered challenge of relativism and the consequences for human rights. Hum Rights Q 7(4):514–540
Ruthven M (1984) Islam in the world. Oxford University Press, New York
Saunders JJA (1978) A history of medieval Islam. Routledge, London & New York
Schacht J (1982) An introduction to Islamic law. Oxford University Press, New York
Shabana A (2010) Custom in Islamic law and legal theory: the development of the concepts of ʻUrf and ʻĀdah in the Islamic legal tradition. Palgrave Macmillan, New York
Shapiro M (1980) Islam and appeal. Calif Law Rev 68(2):350–381
Sharif M (1972) Crimes and punishment in Islam. Institute of Islamic Culture, Lahore
Sinclair N (ed) (2019) The naturalistic fallacy. Cambridge University Press, Cambridge
Sivan E (1985) Radical Islam: medieval theology and modern politics. Yale University Press, New Heaven
Tibi B (1998) The challenge of fundamentalism: political Islam and the new world disorder. University of California Press, Berkeley
Voll JO (1983) Renewal and reform in Islamic history: Tajdid and Islah. In: Esposito JL (ed) Voices of resurgent Islam. Oxford University Press, New York, pp 32–47
Weeramantry C (1988) Islamic jurisprudence: an international perspective. Macmillan, Basingstoke
Weiss B (1992) In search of God's law: Islamic jurisprudence in the writings of Sayf al-Dīn al-Āmidī. University of Utah Press, Salt Lake City
Wright R (2001) Sacred rage: the wrath of militant Islam. Simon & Shuster, New York & London
Yamani AZ (1979) The eternal Sharia. N Y Univ J Int Law Polit 12(2):205–212
Zweigert K, Kötz H (1998) An introduction to comparative law, 3rd edn. Clarendon Press, Oxford

Chapter 10
The Enduring Legacy of Indigenous Legal Traditions

10.1 The Concept of Indigenous People

The term 'indigenous peoples' entered the vocabulary of the United Nations in the post-WWII period and gradually replaced earlier terms such as 'aboriginal', 'native', and 'Indian', although these terms are still used in some domestic legal systems. While there is no universal agreement on the precise meaning of 'indigenous peoples,' the most frequently cited definition is likely the one provided by José Martínez Cobo, the UN Special Rapporteur of the Sub-Commission on Prevention of Discrimination and Protection of Minorities, in his *Study on the Problem of Discrimination Against Indigenous Populations*. This definition reads as follows:

> Indigenous communities, peoples and nations are those which, having a historical continuity with pre-invasion and pre-colonial societies that developed on their territories, consider themselves distinct from other sectors of the societies now prevailing on those territories, or parts of them. They form at present non-dominant sectors of society and are determined to preserve, develop and transmit to future generations their ancestral territories, and their ethnic identity, as the basis of their continued existence as peoples, in accordance with their own cultural patterns, social institutions, and legal systems. ... On an individual basis, an indigenous person is one who belongs to these indigenous populations through self-identification as indigenous (group consciousness) and is recognized and accepted by these populations as one of its members (acceptance by the group). This preserves for these communities the sovereign right and power to decide who belongs to them, without external interference.[1]

Cobo's definition contains several key elements: historical continuity, ethnic distinctiveness, a non-dominant position in society, the special significance of ancestral lands, and the collective will to preserve ethnic identity and self-determination.

[1] United Nations Workshop on Data Collection and Disaggregation for Indigenous people, *The Concept of Indigenous Peoples*, New York, UN, 19–21 January 2004, p. 2. Consider also Kingsbury (1998), pp. 419–420.

G. Mousourakis, *Traversing Legal Traditions*, Springer Textbooks in Law,
https://doi.org/10.1007/978-3-031-94669-1_10

It has been argued that the element of historical continuity should not be understood as applying only to pre-invasion and pre-colonial societies, as this would limit the definition of 'indigenous people' to populations that were invaded and conquered by Western or other distant nations, thus excluding those who were subjugated by neighbouring enemies.[2] Additionally, it has been suggested that placing excessive emphasis on the importance of preserving and passing down ancestral lands may overlook the fact that some ethnic groups, either through coercion or voluntarily, left their ancestral homelands without abandoning their traditional ways of life, customs, and social behaviours.[3] Moreover, it has been pointed out that while the non-dominant position included in Cobo's definition accurately reflects the situation of most indigenous peoples worldwide, it does not account for those indigenous groups that have, in more recent times, achieved a dominant position within their nation-states, such as the indigenous inhabitants of the Fiji Islands in the Western Pacific.[4] Despite its noted limitations, Cobo's definition remains one of the most widely used and continues to provide a valuable framework for discussions and inquiries into the nature of indigenous peoples or ethnic groups.[5]

Reference should also be made to the definition of the term 'indigenous people' adopted by the International Labour Organization (ILO), one of the most active UN specialized agencies in promoting the rights of indigenous peoples. Article 1, paragraph 1 of the ILO's 1957 Indigenous and Tribal Populations Convention (No. 107) states that "members of tribal or semi-tribal populations in independent countries [are those] whose social and economic conditions are at a less advanced stage than the stage reached by the other sections of the national community, and whose status is regulated wholly or partially by their own customs or traditions or by special laws or regulations; members of tribal or semi-tribal populations in independent countries [are those] who are regarded as indigenous on account of their descent from the populations which inhabited the country, or a geographical region to which the country belongs, at the time of conquest or colonisation and who, irrespective of

[2] Colonialism is an age-old phenomenon that has existed throughout human history. History is filled with examples of societies expanding by incorporating neighbouring territories and settling their people in newly conquered lands. However, beginning in the sixteenth century, colonialism underwent significant transformations due to technological advancements in navigation, which enabled Europe to establish connections with distant parts of the world. As a result, the term '*colonialism*' came to denote the process of European settlement and political domination over nations and peoples in Africa, the Americas, and the Asia-Pacific region. On different approaches to the definition of colonialism see Wiessner (1999), p. 111; Kingsbury (1998), pp. 420–421, 454; van de Fliert (1994), p. 4; Hannum (1988), pp. 663–664.

[3] See Mills (2002), p. 58; Wiessner (1999), p. 111.

[4] Consider on this issue Wiessner (1999), p. 111; Brownlie (1992), p. 60.

[5] According to E.I. Daes, former Chairperson and Rapporteur of the United Nations Working Group on Indigenous Populations (WGIP), Cobo's definition, in conjunction with WGIP's experience, provides sufficient criteria for determining when an individual may be considered a member of an indigenous community or group. See WGIP, Report of the Working Group on Indigenous Populations on its eleventh session, E / CN.4 / Sub.2 / 1993 / 29, 23 August 1993, par. 44; E / CN.4 / Sub.2 / AC.4 / 1995 / 3, par. 11. And see Kingsbury (1998), p. 419.

their legal status, live more in conformity with the social, economic, and cultural institutions of that time than with the institutions of the nation to which they belong."[6] The content of this definition was partially amended by the ILO's 1989 Indigenous and Tribal Peoples Convention (No. 169), which, in Article 1, paragraph 1, defines "tribal peoples in independent countries" as those "whose social, cultural, and economic conditions distinguish them from other sections of the national community, and whose status is regulated wholly or partially by their own customs or traditions or by special laws or regulations." The same Article defines "indigenous peoples in independent countries" as those "who are regarded as indigenous on account of their descent from the populations which inhabited the country, or a geographical region to which the country belongs, at the time of conquest or colonisation or the establishment of present state boundaries, and who, irrespective of their legal status, retain some or all of their own social, economic, cultural, and political institutions." Furthermore, Article 1, paragraph 2 of the same Convention states that "Self-identification as indigenous or tribal shall be regarded as a fundamental criterion for determining the groups to which the provisions of this Convention apply."[7]

According to Erica-Irene Daes, former Chairperson and Rapporteur of the United Nations Working Group on Indigenous Populations (WGIP), the addition in the 1989 Convention of the element of descent from populations that inhabited the country at the time of the establishment of present state borders as a condition for recognizing a population as indigenous minimizes the differences between the concepts of 'indigenous' and 'tribal', since both concepts are now largely defined by the extent to which the group in question constitutes a distinct social and cultural unit. In other words, the principal objective criterion for determining the 'indigenous' or 'tribal' character of a group is its distinctiveness, while the remaining criterion is subjective: the group's choice to be and remain distinct, which constitutes an expression of self-determination.[8]

Reference should finally be made to the definition of 'indigenous people' adopted by the World Bank, a UN specialized agency that provides technical and financial support to developing countries with the goal of reducing poverty and promoting sustainable development. In Operational Directive OD 4.20 of September 1991, paragraph 3, it is stated that "The terms 'indigenous peoples,' 'indigenous ethnic minorities,' 'tribal groups,' and 'scheduled tribes'[9] describe social groups with a

[6] In para. 2 of the same Article it is noted that "the term *semi-tribal* includes groups and persons who, although they are in the process of losing their tribal characteristics, are not yet integrated into the national community."

[7] Consider Shaw (1990), p. 41; Wiessner (1999), pp. 111–112; Kingsbury (1998), p. 440; Brownlie (1992), pp. 60–61; Mills (2002), p. 61; Wolfrum (1999), pp. 372 and 379.

[8] *Working Paper on the Concept of "Indigenous Peoples"*, E / CN.4 / Sub.2 / AC.4 / 1996 / 2, pars. 22, 28, 29, 30, 31, 72. And see Berman (1988), pp. 48–57; Mills (2002), pp. 58–59; Wiessner (1999), p. 112.

[9] The term 'scheduled tribe' is used to describe a tribal community in India lying outside the established caste system and officially regarded as socially disadvantaged.

social and cultural identity distinct from the dominant society, making them vulnerable to being disadvantaged in the development process. For the purposes of this directive, 'indigenous peoples' is the term that will be used to refer to these groups."[10] As can be seen, the term 'indigenous people' also encompasses the concepts of 'indigenous ethnic minorities' and 'tribal groups.' The same Directive emphasizes that, due to the varied and evolving contexts in which indigenous people live, no single all-encompassing definition can fully capture their diversity. Furthermore, it notes that indigenous peoples, who often belong to the poorest strata of the population, can be identified by the presence, in varying degrees, of certain characteristics, such as: (a) a close attachment to ancestral lands and the natural resources in these lands; (b) self-identification and recognition by others as members of a culturally distinct group; (c) the use of an indigenous language, often different from the national language; (d) the presence of customary social and political institutions; and (e) a largely subsistence-oriented production process.[11]

To summarize, United Nations bodies, including the International Labour Organization and the World Bank, along with international law scholars, rely on four key criteria to distinguish indigenous peoples: (a) they live on or are attached to geographically distinct ancestral lands; (b) they maintain distinct social, economic, and political institutions within their territories; (c) they seek to remain culturally and institutionally distinct rather than fully assimilate into national society; and (d) they self-identify as indigenous or tribal. Despite these common elements, there is no universal definition of indigenous peoples that fully captures their diversity. In general, self-identification as indigenous or tribal is regarded as a fundamental criterion for determining indigenous status—often claimed by politically marginalized ethnic groups that view themselves as culturally distinct from the majority populations of the states in which they reside. Scholars have noted that the unique relationship indigenous peoples have with their ancestral lands forms an essential basis for their cultural identity, social well-being, and survival.[12] For the vast majority of indigenous peoples, land is not merely an economic asset or property, as it is in the Western market economy; rather, it is a central element of their collective identity, encompassing diverse cultural, spiritual, social, political, and economic dimensions.[13]

---

[10] See Plant (1998), p. 10.

[11] Consider Kingsbury (1998), p. 420; van de Fliert (1994), p. 5; Hitchcock (1994), p. 4.

[12] Davis and Partridge (1996), p. 42; Hannum (1988), p. 666. See also UN, Report of the Working Group on Indigenous Populations on its eighteenth session, E / CN.4 / Sub.2 / 2000 / 24, 17 August 2000, παρ. 59, 104.

[13] As stated by the Inter-American Court of Human Rights: "Among indigenous peoples there is a communitarian tradition regarding a communal form of collective property of the land, in the sense that ownership of the land is not centered on an individual but rather on the group and its community. Indigenous groups, by the fact of their very existence, have the right to live freely in their own territory; the close ties of indigenous people with the land must be recognized and understood as the fundamental basis of their cultures, their spiritual lives, their integrity and their economic survival. For indigenous communities, relations to the land are not merely a matter of possession and production but a material and spiritual element which they must fully enjoy, even to preserve their

10.2 Indigenous Legal Traditions: Foundations and Contemporary Approaches

Indigenous legal traditions have garnered significant attention from academics and policymakers over the past several decades. Most studies in this area focus on the theory of legal pluralism, which posits that law is generated in diverse contexts that are not necessarily tied to or dependent upon the state. Before examining how legal pluralism applies to indigenous laws, it is crucial to first provide a general understanding of the sources of indigenous legal traditions and related issues.

Laws emerge as a result of interpersonal social interactions that give rise to expectations of proper behaviour. Indigenous communities develop their legal systems similarly, drawing from multiple sources, including sacred traditions, natural law, deliberation, and authority-based rules.[14]

Laws are considered sacred when they originate from a supreme creator, creation stories, or revered ancient teachings that have endured over time. Such laws are often viewed as mystical or spiritual, commanding the highest level of respect.[15]

Laws derived from nature are considered timeless and are discovered through observing both the physical and spiritual realms. In this context, it is important to consider how the interconnectedness of living beings with their natural environment benefits not only humans but all forms of life.[16]

Another source of indigenous legal norms arises from processes of deliberation, dialogue, council, and persuasion. While sacred and natural laws often provide the backdrop for debate, most indigenous laws evolve through discussions of concrete problems and the lived experiences of the community. The deliberative nature of many indigenous laws implies that these laws are subject to continuous re-examination and revision to remain relevant in the contemporary world.[17]

A further source of indigenous law consists of proclamations, teachings, and axioms that are considered binding and regulate people's behaviour. Legal rules derived from this source do not necessarily rely on appeals to a creator deity, the natural environment, or deliberative processes to gain their force. Instead, their authority comes from the fact that they originate in proclamations made by individuals or groups deemed authoritative by a significant portion of the community. These individuals often include hereditary chiefs, clan or tribal elders, and other

---

cultural legacy and transmit it to future generations." See 'The case of the Mayagna (Sumo) Awas Tigni Community v. Nicaragua, Judgement of August 31, 2001', *Arizona Journal of International and Comparative Law*, vol. 19, 2002, pp. 395–442 at p. 430. And see Arsanjani (1996), p. 88. And see UN, Commission on Human Rights, Sub-Commission on the Promotion and Protection of Human Rights, Indigenous peoples and their relation to land: Final working paper prepared by the Special Rapporteur, Mrs. Erica - Irene A. Daes, E / CN.4 / Sub.2 / 2001 / 21, 11 June 2001, παρ. 13, 20, 121.

[14] See Borrows (2010), p. 51; Napoleon (2013).

[15] Borrows (2010), pp. 53 ff.

[16] Borrows (2010), pp. 60 ff.

[17] Borrows (2010), pp. 73 ff.

influential community leaders. As circumstances change, some rules that were once based on sacred, natural, or deliberative sources may now be observed because they have been pronounced by individuals or groups who have accumulated enough power to ensure compliance.[18]

The perceived source of a rule influences both its content and the form in which it is expressed—whether orally, in writing, or in a combination of the two. Even if indigenous peoples choose to borrow concepts and tools from Western legal traditions, this does not diminish the indigenous nature or authority of their laws. When defining indigenous law, the most important aspect is not its form, but its authorship—the fact that it has been created by indigenous peoples or communities. This perspective emphasizes the essential link between indigenous law-making and self-determination, as it recognizes that each legal tradition determines for itself what constitutes law.[19]

Western jurists typically define law as a body of formally enacted and enforced rules established by the state to institute and maintain order in society. From this perspective, the principal characteristic that distinguishes law from other normative systems, such as morality or religion, is that legal rules are created, applied, and enforced by state institutions. A rule that has been formally enacted belongs to what is referred to as 'positive law'.[20]

According to Professor Hart, early societies were governed by obligation-imposing primary rules—rules that prohibited behaviours to which humans are naturally inclined, such as violence, theft, and deception, but which must be suppressed to enable coexistence in society. As societies grew more complex, state-regulated procedures for dispute resolution and institutions for authoritatively making decisions developed. Simultaneously, certain morally approved social practices became further institutionalized through their incorporation into judicial adjudication. In this view, law becomes distinct from morality through its special institutionalization.

For Hart, a society governed solely by primary rules would not possess a legal system; it would only have a set of social or moral rules. This is because primary rules alone suffer from three main deficiencies: (a) uncertainty, as there is no clear method of identifying the rules; (b) static nature, since there is no mechanism for changing or updating primary rules; and (c) inefficiency, because violations of

[18] Borrows (2010), pp. 96 ff.

[19] See Glenn (2014), p. 62.

[20] The word 'positive' in this context is derived from the Latin *positus*, which literally means 'laid down'. In a narrow sense, positive law refers to law that has been formally created or established by a competent legislator. In a broader sense, positive law includes not only law that has been explicitly laid down but also law that exists because it is recognized as such by state authorities. This broader category includes indigenous law as well as case law in countries where the principle of precedent, or *stare decisis*, which directs courts to follow previous judicial decisions, does not apply. Legal positivism is the view that law is equivalent to positive law: all positive laws are valid, and there is no valid law outside the realm of positive law.

primary rules cannot be addressed by any official authority and are instead left to individuals or the community as a whole.

To address these deficiencies, Hart introduces three types of what he calls 'secondary rules.' To resolve uncertainty, a *rule of recognition* is needed, allowing for the identification of sovereign authority and, consequently, valid law. To overcome the static nature, a *rule of change* is required, enabling the amendment of primary rules or the creation of new ones. To remedy inefficiency, *rules of adjudication* are necessary to empower officials to handle breaches of primary rules and to enforce sanctions.

Hart argues that a normative system must reach a certain level of institutional development to qualify as law, stating that "the introduction into society of rules enabling legislators to change and add to the rules of duty, and judges to determine when the rules of duty have been broken, is a step forward as important to society as the invention of the wheel … a step from the pre-legal to the legal world."[21]

When the Western positivist conception of law is applied to indigenous legal systems, which are often decentralized and non-professionalized, non-legal terms such as 'oral history', 'indigenous perspective', or 'indigenous normative framework' are frequently used to describe them.[22] In Western legal literature and domestic sources like legislation and court decisions, the term 'customary law' is sometimes employed to describe indigenous legal orders or rules. Customary law refers to a body of norms considered binding within a community, generated through repeated interactions that, over time, lead to commonly accepted standards of behaviour. Importantly, the norms of customary law are not merely the result of past repetition; they also reflect the life experiences and evolving reasoning of the broader community. In this way, the norms and practices historically developed by indigenous groups to maintain social harmony continue to shape their legal reasoning today.

According to the nineteenth-century positivist jurist John Austin, a custom is a rule of conduct observed spontaneously by the governed, not because it is set by a political superior. A custom is transmuted into positive law when it is adopted by the sovereign or a court acting in the sovereign's name, and when judicial decisions based on it are enforced by the power of the state. In this way, the status of the custom as law results from an act resembling legislation. Before it is adopted by the courts and given legal sanction, it remains merely a rule of positive morality: a rule generally observed by citizens or subjects, with its authority derived only from the general disapproval directed at those who violate it.[23] Austin asserts that the rules of positive morality are shaped by a convergence of popular attitudes and supported by informal social pressures. In contrast, the rules of positive law are laid down by political superiors. For Austin, a centralized authority issuing explicit commands accompanied by sanctions is necessary for a legal system to exist.

[21] Hart (1994), p. 41 ff.

[22] Consider on this matter Napoleon (2013).

[23] Austin (1995), p. 176.

Hart accepts that a primary function of law is to regulate human conduct by directing people on what to do and threatening them with sanctions in cases of non-compliance. This regulatory function corresponds to what he terms 'obligation-imposing' or 'primary rules.' However, he argues that there are additional laws within the legal system that cannot be explained by Austin's framework. He points out that there are rules which "provide individuals with facilities for realizing their wishes by conferring legal powers upon them to create by certain specified procedures and subject to certain conditions, structures of rights and duties within the coercive framework of law."[24] Furthermore, Hart criticizes Austin's approach to customary law. He argues that customary rules do not necessarily lack legal status until they are employed in litigation. Just as courts recognize the binding principle that legislative enactments constitute law, there is also no reason why they should not recognize the principle that certain types of customs are valid law even before they are presented in court.[25] This approach to custom suggests that, insofar as custom is regarded as a subordinate source of law to statute, the legislator's failure to explicitly revoke the legal status of a customary rule may be interpreted as an indication of its acceptance.

Critics of the Western positivist perspective on law argue that applying its definition of customary law to indigenous peoples can perpetuate false stereotypes about these peoples and their societies. Specifically, the view that indigenous customary law reflects 'primitive' or 'less civilized' societies due to its perceived lack of Western legal characteristics has been rejected as a serious mischaracterization. As Professor Lon Fuller has remarked,

> If, in an effort to understand what [indigenous] customary law is and what lends moral force to it, we consult treatises on jurisprudence, we are apt to encounter some such explanation as the following …: "Customary law expresses the force of habit that prevails so strongly in the early history of the race. One man treads across an area previously unexplored, following a pattern set by accident or some momentary purpose of his own, others then follow the path until a path is worn." [This approach to the matter] presents, I believe, a grotesque caricature of what customary law really means in the lives of those who govern themselves by it.[26]

Fuller distinguishes between two kinds of law: enacted or authoritatively declared law (positive law) and customary law. He describes customary law as a 'language of interaction' that people rely on to engage meaningfully in effective social behaviour. This language of interaction enables the creation of social contexts where people's behaviours fall into predictable patterns.[27] Similarly, Roberto Unger defines customary law as a "recurring mode of interaction among individuals and groups, together with the more or less explicit acknowledgment by these groups and individuals that such patterns of interaction produce reciprocal expectations of conduct

[24] Hart (1994), pp. 27–28.

[25] Hart (1994), p. 46.

[26] Fuller (1968–1969), pp. 537–538.

[27] Fuller (1969), pp. 1–2. Jeremy Webber has adopted the notion of 'tacit deliberation' to explain the process through which custom acquires its binding force. See Webber (2009).

that ought to be satisfied." He contrasts this with what he calls bureaucratic or regulatory law: a body of explicit rules established and enforced by an identifiable government. Such law, he explains, is "limited to situations in which the division between state and society has been established, and some standards of conduct have assumed the form of explicit prescriptions, prohibitions, or permissions, addressed to more or less general categories of persons and acts." Unger introduces a third type of law: 'legal order' or 'legal system', which he regards as being autonomous, general, public, and positive. These three forms of law represent different stages of legal evolution: regulatory law is preceded by customary law, and the autonomous legal order is preceded by regulatory law.[28]

Like other legal systems, indigenous laws are deeply ingrained in indigenous legal traditions, passed down through generations. As previously noted, a legal tradition is rooted in a specific culture and value system and cannot be easily separated from it.[29] Understanding indigenous laws within the context of the broader traditions to which they belong poses considerable challenges for Western legal scholars, who are trained primarily in civil and common law traditions and have limited opportunities to engage with indigenous cultures and systems of social order. These challenges give rise to a range of issues, particularly those of 'detachment' and 'misrepresentation'.

Detachment occurs when a non-indigenous scholar attempts to incorporate an element of an indigenous legal tradition within the framework of Western legal reasoning. In such cases, the indigenous element is often separated from its cultural and linguistic context, expressed in terms that only approximate its original meaning. When indigenous legal concepts and norms are isolated from the legal tradition in which they are rooted, they lose connection to the network of meanings that defines the tradition.

Misrepresentation often arises because information about indigenous legal traditions is frequently conveyed by non-indigenous individuals, typically Western social scientists and historians. Consequently, descriptions of these traditions are often laden with generalizations and stereotypes. Furthermore, the tendency to perceive and describe indigenous legal norms and practices through the categories of Western law can blur concepts and overlook important differences between

[28] See Unger (1976), p. 49 ff. In this work, Unger, drawing on Max Weber's theory of law, seeks to situate the development of legal systems within a broad historical and comparative framework. He argues that law reflects the normative structure of social reality. Unger distinguishes between two competing forms of normative integration: consensual and instrumental. The former embodies and expresses the shared value system of a group, reflecting a stable structure of social interaction; the latter pertains to regulatory law, which maintains social control through a system of positive rules enacted by a political authority. Unger describes autonomous law as both consensual and instrumental, contending that sacred and natural law provide the context within which instrumental norms are legitimized. In an autonomous legal order, instrumental rules apply universally, allowing individuals to pursue their chosen goals within the limits set by law. In this type of order, the principles of law require further legitimation, with consensus derived from the social contract and agreement on standards of substantive justice.

[29] Consider Napoleon (2013).

indigenous and Western legal systems. Additionally, the authority given to judicial decisions and academic works may overshadow the role of indigenous knowledge keepers, ultimately undermining the authority of indigenous law.

It is essential to recognize that, like all legal traditions, indigenous legal traditions are in a continuous process of change and are subject to external influences.[30] One significant aspect of this evolution pertains to fundamental human rights and freedoms enshrined in domestic constitutions and international legal instruments. Many indigenous groups have embraced norms that protect these fundamental rights, while relinquishing traditions that conflict with such rights.[31] This suggests that authenticity is a problematic notion when applied to legal traditions, including indigenous ones. Assessing authenticity by referring to a distant past may lead to the assumption that indigenous legal traditions are static. Alternatively, defining authenticity by an idealized 'authentic' content risks imposing Western stereotypes. Thus, it is crucial to acknowledge that, in the process of making legal traditions more authentic—i.e., more aligned with indigenous culture and worldviews—the responsibility lies with indigenous peoples themselves to determine, through internal deliberation, which aspects of their past should inform their future. Western jurists should resist the temptation to impose their own criteria for authenticity on indigenous laws and instead accept that it is for indigenous communities to define what they consider authentic.[32]

10.3 Indigenous Legal Traditions and Legal Pluralism

Sometimes, diverse legal traditions can coexist within a single state or political community, a phenomenon known as *legal pluralism*.[33] This is particularly evident in countries with a colonial history, where the legal system imposed by former colonial powers often exists alongside indigenous or customary legal systems.[34] The scope of legal pluralism is broad, encompassing both formal and informal systems,

[30] See Glenn (2014), pp. 23–27.

[31] Consider on this issue Borrows (2010), p. 45.

[32] Borrows (2010), pp. 38–39.

[33] See Simpson (1988), pp. 53–82; Friedman (1975), p. 196. John Gilissen's *Le pluralisme juridique* (1971) stands as a pioneering work that laid the foundation for the study of legal pluralism and introduced the term itself. Gilissen defined legal pluralism as the coexistence of multiple legal systems within a specific geographical and temporal context. Building on this groundwork, Barry Hooker broadened the scope of inquiry by examining the dynamic interactions and relationships between these overlapping legal systems, enriching the conceptual framework of legal pluralism. See Thomas (2017), pp. 27–28.

[34] The concept of legal pluralism emerged significantly from the study of law during the colonial period, yet its scope extends far beyond this historical context. The examination of the interplay between 'imported' European legal frameworks and 'customary law' during colonial rule served as a foundational point of departure. This initial focus evolved into a broader inquiry into the coexistence and interaction of multiple legal systems within a single geographic or societal space.

including traditional and modern practices.[35] It is not limited to the coexistence of laws but also includes their interactions and overlaps.[36] Legal pluralism characterizes many of the world's legal orders, where civil law, common law, religious law, and indigenous legal traditions coexist and manage conflict and dispute resolution in distinct yet sometimes intersecting ways. Recognizing multiple legal systems can foster cultural diversity and respect for minority groups, providing justice that is more relevant and accessible to local communities. However, legal pluralism also presents challenges related to legal coherence, human rights standards, and the administration of justice.[37]

Most theories of legal pluralism have been developed to analyse and elucidate the complex relationships that emerge when state and non-state legal systems coexist within the same societal or institutional framework. These theories seek to understand the dynamics of interaction, collaboration, conflict, and negotiation that arise as diverse legal systems, such as customary, religious, or indigenous laws, operate alongside formal state laws. By examining these interconnections, scholars aim to reveal how these systems influence each other, reshape power structures, and impact individuals and communities navigating multiple legal orders. Furthermore, these theories often investigate broader implications for justice, governance, and the recognition of cultural diversity within pluralistic legal landscapes.

Lawrence Freedman distinguishes between *horizontal legal pluralism*, where subcultures or subsystems hold equal status and legitimacy (as seen, for example, in a federal state), and *vertical legal pluralism*, where subcultures or subsystems are organized hierarchically (as in colonial or imported legal systems).[38] In the latter case, each socio-legal entity engages in an internal struggle to maintain and reshape its legal traditions within an integrating national legal order.[39] If existing socio-legal entities fail to assert themselves, they may gradually retreat until they vanish, leading to legal assimilation or acculturation.[40] Conversely, if socio-legal entities successfully adapt to the new legal environment, they may coexist with the dominant legal order, often under the guise of informal law or custom. Under certain

[35] Legal pluralism predates its formal conceptualization, as is often the case with terms and the phenomena they describe. Before the rise of modern nation-states and their centralized legal systems, the Western legal landscape was inherently pluralistic. As discussed in Chap. 7, from the fall of the Roman Empire to the nineteenth century, multiple and parallel legal orders coexisted within the same geographical regions and historical periods. These included the *ius commune*, various local legal systems, the *lex mercatoria*, and the canon law of the Roman Catholic Church. Significantly, this coexistence of legal systems was predominantly characterized by non-state laws, underscoring the fact that law did not originate with the state but evolved independently of it.

[36] See Tamanaha (2008), pp. 375–411.

[37] On the concept of legal pluralism see in general: Hooker (1975); Griffiths (1986); Merry (1988).

[38] Friedman (1975), p. 197.

[39] Consider on this issue Chiba (1991).

[40] See on this matter Manai (1993), p. 3. According to this author, acculturation is a dynamic and global process, which has two complementary aspects: the heterogeneousness of the cultures that come into contact with one another, and the prevalence of one of them over the others. Consider also Alliot (1968), p. 1181.

conditions, these entities may even prevail over the imported legal system, which might then fall into disuse, or, through integration with it, create new forms of legal hybridity. The strength of each legal tradition lies not in its adherence to historical origins or original forms, but in its capacity to evolve and remain relevant in changing contexts.

Legal pluralism can be further categorized into antagonistic, tolerant, and integrated forms.[41]

Antagonistic legal pluralism describes a situation where state and non-state systems are overtly hostile and opposed to one another. When their normative foundations are incompatible, each seeks to weaken, undermine, and ultimately replace the other. This form of legal pluralism often emerges in countries experiencing active insurgency or separatist movements, particularly where post-conflict state-building efforts have failed to achieve their objectives.[42]

In *tolerant legal pluralism*, the general authority of the state is not challenged; however, non-state actors retain a degree of autonomy and the right to maintain order by applying their own justice systems within their communities. This form of legal pluralism is often prevalent in many developing countries and is particularly common in post-conflict settings, where tensions between state and non-state parties persist, and state legal institutions remain fragile.[43] In such contexts, both state and non-state actors respect each other's right to exist and, at least in principle, are willing to engage with one another to avoid conflict.[44]

Integrated or state legal pluralism refers to a situation in which non-state legal systems are subordinated to the state, whose normative legitimacy and capacity to enforce its mandates are undisputed.[45] In such a setting, non-state actors operate under the authority of the state and lack substantial autonomy to override or reject state decisions.[46] It is the state that decides whether competing legal systems will be permitted to coexist, at least in an official capacity.[47]

State legal pluralism operates within the framework of state legal systems, where state authorities regulate and interact with non-state laws. This regulation can manifest in several distinct forms:

a. *Formal Recognition*: Non-state laws are acknowledged by the state legal system as legitimate and valid, allowing them to coexist with state laws.

---

[41] For a closer look at the different forms of legal pluralism and their policy implications see Swenson (2018), p. 442 ff.

[42] Under such circumstances, non-state justice constitutes a key element of a separatist movement. See on this issue Mampilly (2011).

[43] Tamanaha (2008).

[44] Consider Baker and Scheye (2007).

[45] See, e.g., Woodman (1999), p. 8 ff.

[46] See on this issue Ellickson (1991).

[47] It is argued that only this form of legal pluralism allows for the full implementation of the rule of law and, specifically, the principle that the law should be applied equally to all. Consider Carothers (1998).

b. *Full Integration*: Non-state laws are fully absorbed into the state legal system, effectively becoming part of the formal legal framework.
c. *Recognition with Exclusive Jurisdiction*: Non-state laws are formally recognized, and exclusive authority is granted to their governing bodies within specific areas of law or community practice.

This form of legal pluralism is rooted in a hierarchical system in which state laws are considered superior, whereas non-state laws are relegated to a subordinate status. The integration of alternative legal orders into the state system precludes their recognition as truly autonomous. Consequently, references to legal expressions outside the state framework are often described using the term 'semi-autonomous social domains.'[48]

The theory of state legal pluralism is grounded in the belief that nothing is truly just unless it is recognized by the state. This perspective extends the Western notion that law exists only in conjunction with the state, reflecting an ethnocentric approach to legal pluralism. Consequently, the theory has faced significant criticism for presenting a narrow and limited interpretation of legal pluralism, wherein legal centralism continues to dominate as the prevailing paradigm. Moreover, the characterization of this coexistence of laws as legal pluralism has been challenged. Jacques Vanderlinden, for instance, argues that pluralism controlled by the state cannot constitute genuine pluralism, describing it instead as 'pseudo-pluralism.'[49] Others have taken a more moderate stance, referring to it as 'weak,' 'minimal,' or 'mild' legal pluralism.[50] These descriptions may better capture the phenomenon in question, as the unequal treatment of laws does not entirely negate the reality of their coexistence.

Unlike state legal pluralism, which begins its analysis with the state as the central reference point, critical legal pluralism adopts a fundamentally different approach. It rejects the notion of the state as the primary or exclusive source of legal authority and instead focuses on the diverse, overlapping, and dynamic legal orders that exist within and beyond state structures. By shifting the analytical lens, critical legal pluralism emphasizes the agency of individuals and communities in creating, interpreting, and practicing their own normative frameworks. This perspective acknowledges that law can emerge from a variety of sources—such as social practices, cultural traditions, and grassroots movements—challenging the traditional monopoly of the state in defining legality and legitimacy. Through this broader and more decentralized view, critical legal pluralism aims to capture the complexity and fluidity of how law operates in everyday life.[51]

[48] Sally Falk Moore defines a semi-autonomous social field as a domain possessing the authority to establish rules and enforce compliance. However, it is also embedded within a larger social framework that both influences and interacts with it. This external influence may occur either through the deliberate engagement of individuals within the field or independently, as the broader social network exerts its influence at will. Falk Moore (2000), p. 56.

[49] Vanderlinden (1998).

[50] See, e.g., Grammond (2010), p. 57.

[51] Kleinhans and Macdonald (1997). And see Vanderlinden (1989); Dupret (2007); Tamanaha (2001), p. 166 ff.

According to the theory of critical legal pluralism, every society possesses a legal system. Law exists as long as there is a human need for the administration of justice. This theory emphasizes the free and equal coexistence of multiple legal orders. Notably, similar theories have emerged over time that, while not necessarily grounded in the study of the individual as a normative agent, nonetheless advocate for an egalitarian approach to diverse legal frameworks.[52] While this perspective is often recommended for understanding various legal phenomena, it is not entirely supported by legal experience. Nevertheless, its emphasis on recognizing the individual as a normative agent and positioning them as the focal point of study is highly significant, particularly in understanding legal forms that develop independently of the state.

As previously noted, legal pluralism often originates in colonial history, where colonial powers imposed their legal systems on indigenous populations, leading to a blend of laws and practices. Consequently, it is unsurprising that post-colonial states frequently exhibit legal pluralism, as indigenous and imported legal systems continue to coexist—sometimes in conflict, sometimes in harmony.[53] There have been periods in recent history when governments sought to enforce cultural and legal uniformity through state-mandated assimilation policies, at times resorting to coercive measures against indigenous groups within their borders. However, many states today have embraced multiculturalism in an effort to foster peaceful relations between different communities and have adopted policies and legislative frameworks designed to guarantee and protect indigenous people's rights. Multiculturalism acknowledges and addresses cultural diversity within a society, especially concerning indigenous or minority groups. It recognizes the presence and contributions of various cultures, races, and ethnicities within a dominant political culture. Multiculturalism can be defined as a state of cultural pluralism or diversity within a society or as a doctrine or policy that promotes this state of affairs. From a liberal perspective, multiculturalism is often said to emphasize the importance of cultural membership, viewing it as essential for individual autonomy and self-identity.[54] It should be noted, however, that the interaction between legal pluralism and indigenous law is a complex and dynamic field, reflecting the ongoing struggle to balance respect for cultural diversity and traditional practices with the demands of a modern, often globalized, legal framework.

Over the past few decades, awareness has grown across much of the globe of the significant role indigenous legal traditions play within a country's pluralistic society and legal system. Indigenous laws and justice systems have proven particularly influential and effective in areas such as land and natural resource allocation, dispute settlement, and conflict prevention and resolution. This influence is partly due

---

[52] Consider, e.g., Griffiths (1986), p. 5; Woodman (1999), pp. 5 & 10.

[53] See Tamanaha (2000).

[54] Will Kymlicka argues that cultural groups provide 'contexts of choice' for individuals, offering meaningful frameworks within which they can pursue their goals. He adds that respect for a person's group is intimately connected to their sense of self-respect and identity. Kymlicka (1989). See also Kymlicka (1995, 2001, 2007).

to the inherent community acceptance of indigenous law and the fact that such law, by its nature, has evolved to suit the communities in which it operates. However, despite this growing recognition of indigenous law's importance, many states remain reluctant to grant it formal recognition. Even in countries where it has been recognized, conflicts often arise between established statutory regimes and indigenous legal norms. This resistance may partly stem from concerns that indigenous law could challenge national sovereignty. Additionally, the historical reluctance of many Western legal scholars to accept indigenous law as a valid form of law has reduced its chances of recognition by policymakers. Since the legitimacy of indigenous law ultimately derives from its acceptance by those governed by it, indigenous communities are often more inclined to view it as having greater legitimacy in cases of conflict with statutory law and may continue to uphold it.

10.4 Constitutional Recognition of Indigenous Legal Traditions: Global Perspectives on Legal Pluralism

The constitutional recognition of indigenous legal orders is particularly significant, as in many states, statutory law generally takes precedence over any conflicting indigenous law unless the latter is protected by the constitution. Nevertheless, states can incorporate indigenous law within their domestic law and policy even without constitutional entrenchment. The doctrine of Native Title, whereby states with limited constitutional recognition of indigenous law still acknowledge the land rights of original inhabitants, serves as an example of this approach.

The highest level of state recognition of indigenous customary law is likely found in African constitutions, both in terms of the number of states incorporating relevant clauses and the breadth of indigenous law areas they address.[55] Many African constitutions include provisions aimed at safeguarding indigenous traditions and cultures, alongside obligations for the state to preserve and promote indigenous cultural practices and a broader right to cultural or traditional identity. Frequently, these rights and obligations are subject to a condition that indigenous traditions or cultures must align with the constitution and the fundamental human rights it guarantees.[56] Furthermore, several African constitutions contain general

[55] Some constitutions have adopted a definition of law as including unwritten or customary law. For example, s 7(e) of the *Constitution of the Republic of The Gambia 1997* states that: 'the laws of The Gambia consist of ... (e) Customary law so far as concerns members of the communities to which it applies'. And see *Constitution of the Republic of Ghana 1992 (rev. 1996)*, art 11(2); *Constitution of Sierra Leone 1991*, s 171; *Constitution of the Kingdom of Swaziland 2005*, s 261; *Constitution of Zimbabwe 2018*, s 332.

[56] For example, art 91(1) of the *Constitution of the Federal Democratic Republic of Ethiopia 1995* provides that: "[The] Government shall have duty to support, on the basis of equality, the growth and enrichment of cultures and traditions that are compatible with fundamental rights, human dignity, democratic norms and ideas, and the provisions of the Constitution." Similarly, Art 4 of the *Constitution of the Republic of Mozambique* of 2004 (rev. 2007), titled 'Legal Pluralism', states:

provisions recognizing indigenous law and the role of customary authorities in relation to it, as well as more detailed provisions establishing specific bodies with specialized functions related to indigenous law.[57] Instead of creating separate traditional institutions, some constitutions provide for indigenous representation within existing government bodies.[58] Additionally, several constitutions include provisions on the role of indigenous customary law in the justice system. Some legal systems maintain, establish, or permit special courts dedicated to applying indigenous law, while others delineate the jurisdiction of regular courts over customary law matters.[59] It is also notable that the jurisdiction of customary law is sometimes explicitly limited to civil matters, excluding criminal cases.[60] Many constitutions prioritize statutory law over indigenous customary law, prohibiting the application of customary norms that conflict with constitutionally protected human rights, statutory law, natural justice, or public order.[61] Furthermore, some constitutions stipulate that laws

---

"The State recognises the different normative and dispute resolution systems that co-exist in Mozambican society, insofar as they are not contrary to the fundamental principles and values of the Constitution." S 32 of the *Constitution of the Republic of The Gambia 1997* declares: "Every person shall be entitled to enjoy, practice, profess, maintain and promote any culture, language, tradition or religion subject to the terms of this Constitution and to the condition that the right protected by this section do not impinge on the rights and freedoms of others or the national interest, especially unity." And according to s 31(1) of the *Constitution of the Republic of South Africa 1996*, "Persons belonging to a cultural, religious or linguistic community may not be denied the right, with other members of that community *(a)* to enjoy their culture, practise their religion and use their language; and *(b)* to form, join and maintain cultural, religious and linguistic associations and other organs of civil society." S 31(2) adds that "The rights in subsection (1) may not be exercised in a manner inconsistent with any provision of the Bill of Rights." Consider also *Constitution of the Republic of Benin 1990*, arts 10 &11*; Constitution of Cote d'Ivoire 2000*, art 7; *Constitution of the Republic of Ghana 1992*, art 26(1).

[57] Consider, e.g., *Constitution of the Republic of Angola 2010*, arts 223–225; *Constitution of the Democratic Republic of the Congo 2005 (rev. 2011)*, art 207; Constitution *of the Republic of Mozambique 2004 (rev. 2007)*, art 118; *Constitution of the Republic of South Africa 1996*, ss185 & 212; *Constitution of the Republic of Uganda 1995 (rev. 2017)*, art 246; *Constitution of the Republic of Namibia 1990 (rev. 2010)*, art 102(5); *Constitution of Zambia 1996*, arts 130 & 131.

[58] See, e.g., *Constitution of Kenya 2010*, arts 56 &100; *Constitution of the Republic of Angola 2010*, art 213.

[59] Consider, for example, *Constitution of the Federal Democratic Republic of Ethiopia 1995*, art 78(5); *Constitution of the Federal Republic of Nigeria 1999*, ss265 & 280; *Constitution of Sierra Leone 1991 (rev. 2008)*, s 120(4); *Constitution of the Republic of South Africa 1996*, schedule 6, s 16; *Constitution of the Democratic Republic of the Congo 2005 (rev. 2011)*, art 153; *Constitution of the Republic of Liberia 1986*, art 65.

[60] See, for example, *Constitution of the Republic of Malawi 1994 (rev. 2017)*, s 110(3); *Constitution of the Republic of Chad 2018*, art 27; *Constitution of the Federal Republic of Nigeria 1999*, s 282. The Nigerian constitution requires that some justices of the Supreme Court and Court of Appeal must be learned in customary law (ss 237(2)(b) & 288). Art 159 of the *Constitution of Kenya 2010* recognizes the need for courts to take into consideration traditional dispute resolution mechanisms.

[61] See, e.g., *Constitution of the Republic of Angola 2010*, art 7; *Constitution of the Democratic Republic of the Congo 2005 (rev. 2011)*, art 207; *Constitution of the Federal Democratic Republic of Ethiopia 1995*, art 35(4); *Constitution of the Republic of Ghana 1992 (rev. 1996)*, art 26(2); *Constitution on Kenya* 2010, s 2; *Constitution of the Republic of Liberia 1986*, art 2; *Constitution*

should not be viewed as discriminatory if they permit the application of traditional customary law to its respective communities.[62]

Similar to African constitutions, those of Central and South American countries include provisions on indigenous customary law. However, few explicitly address the broader preservation of indigenous culture.[63] Several constitutions grant rights to autonomy and self-administration,[64] recognizing that indigenous communities may apply their own laws as long as these do not conflict with the constitution, national law, basic human rights, or public order.[65] The constitutions of Mexico, Peru, Bolivia, and Ecuador specifically address the role of customary law in the judicial process. In Mexico, while the constitution does not grant jurisdiction to indigenous courts, it provides protection (*amparo*)[66] in cases contesting actions that dispossess indigenous groups of their ancestral lands.[67] The Peruvian constitution mandates that, where the law is silent or ambiguous, general legal principles and customary law should serve as guiding frameworks.[68] Bolivia's constitution recognizes the legitimacy of indigenous dispute resolution methods, affirming that indigenous leaders may adjudicate according to their cultural norms, provided

---

of the Republic of Namibia 1990, art 66(1); *Constitution of the Republic of Uganda 1995 (rev. 2017),* art 2(2).

[62] Consider, e.g., *Constitution of the Republic of The Gambia 1997,* s 33(5)(d); *Constitution of Sierra Leone 1991 (rev. 2008),* s 27(4); *Constitution of Zambia 1996,* art 23(4)(d).

[63] Reference should be made here to the constitution of Paraguay, which requires the state to respect cultural heritage and protect indigenous people against economic exploitation, alienation and threats to their natural environment. See *Constitution of the Republic of Paraguay 1992 (rev. 2011),* art 66. Similar provisions can be found in the constitutions of Bolivia, Ecuador, Guatemala, Honduras, El Salvador and Nicaragua.

[64] See, e.g., *Political Constitution of Peru 1993 (rev. 2021),* art 89; *Republic of Bolivia Constitution of 2009,* arts 2, 269, 289, 290, 291–296, 303, 304; *Constitution of the Republic of Paraguay 1992 (rev. 2011),* art 63; *Political Constitution of the Republic of Nicaragua 1987 (rev. 2014),* art 181.

[65] Consider *Constitution of Colombia 1991 (rev. 2015),* art 246; *Political Constitution of Peru 1993 (rev. 2021),* art 149; *Constitution of the Bolivarian Republic of Venezuela 1999 (rev. 2009),* art 260. Some constitutions also provide for the participation of indigenous peoples in the political process and institutions that make government policies in accordance with their own customary norms and practices. See on this matter *Constitution of the Republic of Paraguay 1992 (rev. 2011),* art 65; *Republic of Bolivia Constitution of 2009,* arts 2, 11, 26, 30, 146, 147; *Republic of Ecuador Constitution of 2008* art 57. And see Gomez Isa (2014), pp. 722–755.

[66] The *amparo* procedure is a legal process designed to protect individuals' constitutional rights and freedoms. It is a fundamental component of the Mexican legal system and serves as a powerful mechanism for safeguarding fundamental rights against violations by the government or other public authorities. This procedure can be initiated by individuals or legal entities who believe their constitutional rights have been or are at risk of being violated by acts or omissions of authorities, including laws, decrees, regulations, and other governmental actions. *Amparo* can be directed against any authority, not just the federal government, and encompasses local and state governments as well. These proceedings are characterized by formal rigor, requiring specific legal arguments to demonstrate how an individual's constitutional rights have been infringed upon. For a closer look at the *amparo* procedure see Zamora et al. (2005), chapter 8.

[67] *Constitution of Mexico 1917 (rev. 2015)* art 107(II).

[68] *Political Constitution of Peru 1993 (rev. 2021)* art 139(8).

fundamental rights guaranteed by the constitution are respected.[69] Additionally, Bolivian state laws recognize the jurisdiction of indigenous judicial bodies as equal to that of state courts. Ecuador's constitution adopts a more limited approach, recognizing indigenous authority only over disputes within indigenous territories.[70]

Land tenure is a particularly prominent subject in Latin American constitutions. Many acknowledge rights to traditionally occupied land, communal properties, or reserves, often specifying that these rights are inalienable.[71] Mexico's constitution safeguards the territorial integrity of indigenous communities and mandates laws governing the communal use of land, water, and forests.[72] Venezuela's and Paraguay's constitutions secure the right of indigenous populations to cultivate their identity in connection with their habitat, thus linking cultural protection to land rights.[73] The Peruvian constitution states that indigenous communities have self-governance over their lands and the freedom to manage them independently, while also providing that indigenous lands are imprescriptible and immune from state seizure.[74] Paraguay's constitution prohibits the expulsion of indigenous communities from their lands without their explicit consent, as does the Brazilian constitution with some exceptions.[75] Brazil's constitution defines 'lands traditionally occupied' as areas inhabited and used for productive activities, or those essential for preserving natural resources vital to indigenous populations. Indigenous people who traditionally inhabit these lands have rights to the wealth of the soil, rivers, and lakes, with restrictions on mining activities on these lands.[76]

In North America, Canada's constitution is unique in its comparatively robust acknowledgment of customary law. Rather than specifying particular Indigenous rights, the Canadian constitution provides a broad recognition of these rights,

[69] *Republic of Bolivia Constitution of 2009* arts 179, 190. Moreover, The Bolivian constitution mandates that indigenous peoples are represented on the country's Plurinational Constitutional Court. This court's responsibilities encompass resolving disputes between indigenous and other jurisdictions. See *Republic of Bolivia Constitution of 2009* arts 197, 202. And see Barrera (2012), p. 380.

[70] *Republic of Ecuador Constitution of 2008 (rev. 2021)* art 171. See Barrera (2012), p. 373.

[71] *See, e.g., Republic of Bolivia Constitution of 2009* art 394; *Constitution of the Federative Republic of Brazil 1988 (rev. 2017)* art 231; *Republic of Ecuador Constitution of 2008* art 57; *Political Constitution of the Republic of Nicaragua 1987 (rev. 2014)* arts 89 & 180; *Constitution of the Bolivarian Republic of Venezuela 1999 (rev. 2009)* art 119.

[72] *Constitution of Mexico 1917 (rev. 2015)* art 27.

[73] *Constitution of the Bolivarian Republic of Venezuela 1999 (rev. 2009)* art 119; *Constitution of the Republic of Paraguay 1992 (rev. 2011)* arts 63, 64.

[74] *Political Constitution of Peru 1993 (rev. 2021)* art 89. And see *Constitution of Colombia 1991 (rev. 2015)* art 63.

[75] *Constitution of the Republic of Paraguay 1992 (rev. 2011)* art 64(2); *Constitution of the Federative Republic of Brazil 1988 (rev. 2017)* art 231(6).

[76] *Constitution of the Federative Republic of Brazil 1988 (rev. 2017)* art 231. Consider also *Republic of Bolivia Constitution of 2009* arts 30, 374, 388, 403.

affirming and protecting all established Aboriginal and treaty rights, including land claims.[77]

Indigenous customary law holds a significant level of constitutional recognition across Asia; however, most relevant provisions primarily affirm a general right to culture, with only a few detailing institutional frameworks or land ownership rights.[78] The greatest diversity and strongest safeguards for indigenous personal legal systems are typically found in countries that were once part of the British Empire, such as Bangladesh, India, Pakistan, and Malaysia. Under British rule, the colonial administration acknowledged the existence of multiple legal systems within various communities, differentiated by religious beliefs (such as Muslim and Hindu law) or ethnic backgrounds (including tribal law). The Indian Constitution's recognition of the customary laws of the indigenous Naga and Mizo peoples in north-eastern India, covering personal laws and resource rights, represents one of the most significant examples of formal acknowledgment for customary law.[79]

In other countries, the official recognition of indigenous customary laws may not reach the prominence given to the Nagas and Mizos in India but still receives explicit constitutional acknowledgment. For instance, the current Constitution of the Philippines includes provisions that recognize and advocate for indigenous rights, including protections for ancestral lands.[80] The Federal Constitution of Malaysia establishes the duty of the King of Malaysia to safeguard the unique status of indigenous peoples in the states of Sabah and Sarawak, while also mandating specific quotas for these groups in employment and licensing.[81] Pakistan's Constitution expressly recognizes custom and usage within the legal framework, though it invalidates any custom that contradicts the Constitution.[82] In Thailand, indigenous groups

---

[77] *Constitution of Canada 1982* ss 25, 35.

[78] As with other constitutions around the world, a number of Asian constitutions include definitions of law that recognize customary law. See, e.g., *Constitution of the People's Republic of Bangladesh 1972* art 152; *Constitution of India 1949* art 13(3)(a); *Constitution of Malaysia 1957* art 160(2).

[79] The Indian government has enacted a law that acknowledges the authority and legal frameworks of communities traditionally residing in forests. The Forest Rights Act of 2006 validates the power of Indigenous customary bodies to define the scope and details of both individual and communal rights in their territories. See on this matter Deva Prasad and Suchithra Menon (2020), pp. 79 & 87.

[80] *Constitution of the Philippines 1987*, Article II, Section 22; Article XII, Section 5.

[81] *Constitution of Malaysia 1957*, Articles 153(1 & 2), 161, 161A, 161B and 161E. It should be noted, however, that in Malaysia, while the official constitution appears to offer protections for the social and cultural integrity of indigenous communities, including their traditional laws, the implementation of these protections has been largely insufficient in upholding all indigenous peoples' rights and the safeguards on indigenous peoples' customary laws vary throughout the country.

[82] *Constitution of the Islamic Republic of Pakistan 1973 (rev. 2018)* arts 8, 203B. Reference should be made to the Jirga system, a traditional method of dispute resolution that has been practiced for centuries in many rural areas of Pakistan. The Jirga serves as a communal institution typically composed of esteemed male elders, including tribal chiefs, as well as religious and political figures within the community. It functions as a deliberative body for resolving disputes, relying on established customs and traditions. Decisions rendered by the Jirga carry binding authority and are generally upheld through communal consensus. This system is predominantly observed among Pashtun communities in Pakistan and Afghanistan, though it also exists under varying names and

possess robust customary law practices, typically focused on personal or family law. The 2007 Thai Constitution tasks the state with protecting indigenous cultures, including cultural rights to governance, preservation, and the sustainable use of natural resources and the environment.[83]

The provisions governing the interaction between customary and statutory law in Asia vary considerably. In India, for example, the Constitution specifies that statutory laws affecting customary laws are inapplicable in certain regions unless determined otherwise by the region's legislative assembly.[84] Likewise, Timor-Leste maintains that customs are upheld unless they conflict with the Constitution or specific legislation related to customary law.[85]

Several Pacific nations' constitutions include provisions pertinent to customary law, with a particular focus on institutional structures and land matters.[86] Additionally, a significant number of these provisions address the judiciary's role in customary law, with some establishing specialized courts that hold authority over cases related to customary law.[87] The constitution of Micronesia mandates that all judicial rulings align strictly with the customs and traditions of Micronesia.[88] Similarly, the constitution of Papua New Guinea allows courts to take any measures deemed suitable when a normally binding decision conflicts with relevant customary practices.[89] The Constitution of Vanuatu mandates that in cases where no relevant law exists, courts

---

forms in Punjab, Balochistan, and other regions of Pakistan. The Jirga system is deeply embedded within the social and cultural fabric of the communities that employ it and is often regarded as a legitimate and effective means of conflict resolution and maintaining social harmony. It provides a platform for dialogue, negotiation, and compromise, underscoring the importance of interpersonal relationships and community bonds in resolving disputes. Furthermore, the Jirga acts as a vital conduit for preserving traditions and cultural values, facilitating their transmission from one generation to the next. However, despite its integral role, the Jirga system has faced criticism for perpetuating inequalities and biases, particularly against women and marginalized individuals. Despite these drawbacks, the Jirga continues to play a significant role in the social and cultural life of many rural communities in Pakistan and is frequently viewed as a more accessible and efficient means of dispute resolution than the formal judicial system. For a closer look at the Jirga system see Yousufzai and Gohar (2012); Mahmood et al. (2018), Ullah and Ali (2021).

[83] *Constitution of the Kingdom of Thailand 2007* s 66.

[84] *Constitution of India 1949* arts 371A, 371G.

[85] *Constitution of the Democratic Republic of East Timor 2002* s 2(4). Consider also the *Constitution of the Republic of Indonesia 1945* art 18B(2).

[86] The most comprehensive definition of customary law is found in the Papua New Guinean constitution, which defines custom as "the customs and usages of indigenous inhabitants of the country existing in relation to the matter in question at the time when and the place in relation to which the matter arises, regardless of whether or not the custom or usage has existed from time immemorial." *Constitution of the Independent State of Papua New Guinea 1975* Schedule 1.2. It is notable that this provision does not require the existence of a long-standing custom.

[87] *Constitution of the Republic of the Marshall Islands 1979 (rev. 1995)* art VI, s 4; *Constitution of the Independent State of Samoa 1960 (rev. 2016)* art 103; *Constitution of the Republic of Vanuatu 1980 (rev. 2013)* art 52.

[88] *Constitution of the Federated States of Micronesia 1975/1978 (rev. 1990)* art XI, s 11.

[89] *Constitution of the Independent State of Papua New Guinea 1975 (rev. 2014)* schedule 2.10(1).

must resolve issues in accordance with traditional customs.[90] Furthermore, it allows for the inclusion of individuals with expertise in customary law in judicial appointments and requires Parliament to establish procedures for defining customary law.[91]

The interaction between statutory and customary law in Oceanic nations presents a unique dynamic, distinct from other regions. For instance, Palau's constitution mandates a balance between statutory laws and traditional customs, affirming their equality. It stipulates that in cases of conflict, statutory law takes precedence but only if it does not violate the core principles of traditional law.[92] Similarly, the constitutions of the Solomon Islands and Papua New Guinea recognize customs as part of the legal framework, provided that these customs do not conflict with the constitution, statutory law, or basic principles of humanity.[93] Both also affirm the primacy of customary law, accepting the common law and equity of England only insofar as they align with customary law.[94] The Constitution of Micronesia requires that local traditions be considered when determining crimes and punishments.[95] It also asserts that safeguarding Micronesian traditions is a substantial societal interest, particularly in legal challenges against laws meant to protect traditions, based on constitutional rights.[96] In the Solomon Islands, the constitution mandates that Parliament must respect and consider traditional customs and practices,[97] while in the Marshall

---

[90] *Constitution of the Republic of Vanuatu 1980 (rev. 2013)* art 47(1).

[91] *Constitution of the Republic of Vanuatu 1980 (rev. 2013)* art 51.

[92] *Constitution of the Republic of Palau 1979/1981 (rev. 1992)* art V, s 2.

[93] *Constitution of the Solomon Islands 1978 (rev. 2018)* sch 3 s 3; *Constitution of the Independent State of Papua New Guinea 1975* sch 2.1.

[94] *Constitution of the Independent State of Papua New Guinea 1975* sch 2.2(1); *Constitution of the Solomon Islands 1978 (rev. 2018)* sch 3 s 2. And see *Constitution of the Republic of Vanuatu 1980 (rev. 2013)* art 95(2), (3). Papua New Guinea's Underlying Law Act 2000 sought to cultivate a distinct legal foundation or common law for the country. This initiative seeks to merge customary law with British common law to form an underlying law or common law (developed in courts) that is uniquely tailored to Papua New Guinea. Section 6 of the Underlying Law Act outlines the hierarchy of legal authorities to be applied in cases. It establishes that written and underlying laws, developed from earlier cases, are to be applied first, followed by customary law. Should these sources prove insufficient for resolving the matter at hand, the court is then permitted to turn to British common law for guidance. The Underlying Law Act not only gives precedence to customary law over British common law, but it also specifies that whether a rule of customary law exists or what it entails is a matter of legal interpretation rather than a factual issue. Furthermore, the act allows courts to officially recognize customary laws without the need for formal proof. Furthermore, the Underlying Law Act provides guidelines to assist courts in deciding if specific customary laws are applicable in a given situation. See *Underlying Law Act 2000*, Act no 13 of 2000, ss. 3, 6, 7, 15(1), 16, 17.

[95] *Constitution of the Federated States of Micronesia 1975/1978 (rev. 1990)* art IX, s 2(p). Vanuatu seems to tacitly recognize traditional criminal law, forbidding the retroactive application of crimes according to both written and customary legislation. See *Constitution of the Republic of Vanuatu 1980 (rev. 2013)* art 5(2)(f).

[96] *Constitution of the Federated States of Micronesia 1975/1978 (rev. 1990)* art V, s 2.

[97] *Constitution of the Solomon Islands 1978 (rev. 2018)* s 75.

Islands, a customary authority known as the Council of Iroij has the right to request a review of legislative proposals affecting traditional law.[98]

In New Zealand, Māori customary law, known as Tikanga Māori, plays a significant and evolving role in the legal system. Tikanga Māori, encompassing the customs, practices, and values of the Māori people,[99] has been increasingly recognized and integrated into New Zealand's legal framework. This integration reflects New Zealand's commitment to the principles of the Treaty of Waitangi, signed in 1840 between the British Crown and Māori chiefs, which serves as the foundational document governing the rights and responsibilities of the Māori and the Crown. The Waitangi Tribunal, established in 1975 as a permanent commission to investigate claims by Māori regarding breaches of the Treaty by the Crown, has led to the recognition of Tikanga Māori in various areas of law and policy.[100] Today, several New Zealand statutes explicitly reference Tikanga Māori and principles from the Treaty of Waitangi, requiring their consideration in decision-making, including in environmental protection, fisheries management, and the justice system, where Māori perspectives are increasingly integrated. However, challenges remain in the application and interpretation of Tikanga principles and in balancing them with other legal considerations, making it an area of ongoing debate and development.

10.5 Concluding Remarks

When contemplating indigenous legal traditions, it is helpful to consider the essence and concept of law itself. Certain definitions of law are limited, focusing solely on rulings or laws that come from official agencies, such as courts or legislative bodies. However, a broader perspective is essential when discussing indigenous law. This perspective recognizes law in the processes by which members of a society legitimately and authoritatively address issues, make decisions, ensure safety, and sustain or mend relationships. Understanding indigenous law necessitates an awareness of the unique significance of relationships within each indigenous community. All legal systems, including those of indigenous peoples, originate from one or several centres of authority. The foundations or origins of indigenous law are intricately connected to the social, historical, political, biological, economic, and spiritual

[98] *Constitution of the Republic of the Marshall Islands 1979 (rev. 1995)* art III, s 2.

[99] See Mead (2003). See also Durie (1996).

[100] The Waitangi Tribunal operates with approximately equal representation of Māori and Pākehā (settler) members, following both Māori and Western legal procedures. Initially, the tribunal's jurisdiction was limited to hearing claims from 1975 onward, which constrained its social and political impact. However, in 1985, its jurisdiction was expanded to include state actions and omissions dating back to the signing of the Treaty in 1840. This change subjected New Zealand's historical record of state–Māori relations to in-depth scrutiny. Further amendments to the Treaty of Waitangi Act increased the tribunal's membership and expanded its capacity for research, hearings, and report writing. See in general Kawharu (2008).

contexts of different indigenous groups and communities. A person's ability to utilize indigenous legal resources is influenced by their prior knowledge, immersion in the culture, connections within the community, and proficiency in various methods of engaging with specific resources. Although engagement with indigenous law predates the existence of many modern states, it is only recently that legal professionals and scholars are beginning to recognize their duty to earnestly engage with indigenous law as a legitimate body of law and to explore the interactions between indigenous and state legal systems.

Most contemporary literature suggests that indigenous law, as a dynamic and evolving phenomenon, serves as a crucial resource for indigenous communities in addressing present-day challenges. Given its deep connection with broader indigenous values and perspectives, strengthening the role of indigenous law simultaneously supports the preservation and resilience of indigenous cultures. The resurgence of indigenous legal systems is closely linked to indigenous peoples' empowerment to reclaim autonomy over their affairs in ways consistent with their traditional values. Increasingly, indigenous communities worldwide are actively exploring and promoting the use of their own standards and perspectives, both in internal administration and in their interactions with external entities on ancestral lands. Developing innovative approaches to revitalize indigenous legal systems represents a significant step toward achieving reconciliation and fostering better relationships between indigenous and non-indigenous peoples, as well as with state authorities. Although the primary responsibility for reviving indigenous legal traditions rests with indigenous communities, all levels of government should contribute by recognizing the authority of indigenous peoples to apply their own legal norms and justice mechanisms in conflict resolution. In this context, the role of legislative bodies and courts is especially vital in enhancing the recognition and integration of indigenous laws within broader legal frameworks.

As noted in the previous section, numerous countries worldwide have enacted laws that recognize indigenous legal systems. These include several nations across Africa, Central and South America, and the Asia-Pacific region, where such recognition is embedded within constitutions and, in some cases, further detailed through specific legislation. In some countries, even without explicit constitutional acknowledgment or protection for indigenous legal systems, laws have been enacted that recognize traditional customs and practices. Recognizing and integrating indigenous legal traditions offers significant benefits for both indigenous communities and the broader society. Allowing these traditions to thrive and be practiced empowers indigenous communities to advance socially, economically, and politically in ways that align with their unique cultural values. This process not only supports the revival of indigenous cultures but also promotes the development of legal systems and institutions that are culturally appropriate and respected, thereby strengthening the rule of law. Additionally, the coexistence of diverse legal traditions within a legal system is beneficial, as it allows for the integration of multiple perspectives in addressing legal issues.

References

Alliot M (1968) L'acculturation juridique. In: Poirier J (ed) Encyclopédie de la Pléiade – Ethnologie générale. Gallimard, Paris, pp 1180–1246

Arsanjani MH (1996) Environmental rights and indigenous wrongs. Saint Thomas Law Rev 9(1):85–92

Austin J (1995) The province of jurisprudence determined, 2nd edn. Cambridge University Press, Cambridge. (original work published 1832)

Baker B, Scheye E (2007) Multi-layered justice and security delivery in post-conflict and fragile states. Conflict Secur Dev 7(4):503–528

Barrera A (2012) Turning legal pluralism into state-sanctioned law: assessing the implications of the new constitutions and laws in Bolivia and Ecuador. In: Schilling-Vacaflor A, Nolte D (eds) New constitutionalism in Latin America: promises and practices. Taylor & Francis Group, Abingdon, pp 371–390

Berman HR (1988) The International Labour Organization and indigenous peoples: revision of ILO Convention No.107 at the 75th Session of the International Labour Conference 1988. Int Comm Jurists Rev 41:48–57

Borrows J (2010) Canada's indigenous constitution. University of Toronto Press, Toronto

Brownlie I (1992) Treaties and indigenous peoples. Oxford University Press, New York

Carothers T (1998) The rule of law revival. Foreign Aff 77(2):95–106

Chiba M (1991) Legal pluralism in and across legal cultures. In: Sack P, Carl Wellman P, Yasaki M (eds) Monismus oder Pluralismus der Rechtskulturen? Anthropologische und ethnologische Grundlagen traditioneller und moderner Rechtssysteme/Monistic or Pluralistic Legal Culture? Anthropological and Ethnological Foundations of Traditional and Modern Legal Systems, *Rechtstheorie*: *Zeitschrift* für *Logik*, *Methodenlehre*, *Kybernetik* und *Soziologie* des *Rechts*. Duncker & Humblot, Berlin, Beiheft 12, pp 283–306

Davis S, Partridge W (1996) Promoting the development of indigenous people in Latin America. In: Iturralde D, Krotz E (eds) Indigenous development: poverty, democracy and sustainability. Inter-American Development Bank, Washington DC, pp 41–45

Deva Prasad M, Suchithra Menon C (2020) Indian forest rights legislation: significance of recognizing the legal pluralism for indigenous peoples' rights. Statute Law Rev 41(1):78–88

Dupret B (2007) Legal pluralism, plurality of laws, and legal practices: theories, critiques, and praxiological re-specification. Eur J Leg Stud 1:296–318

Durie E (1996) Will the settlers settle? Cultural conciliation and the law. Otago Law Rev 8(4):449–465

Ellickson R (1991) Order without law: how neighbors settle disputes. Harvard University Press, Cambridge

Falk Moore S (2000) Law as process. An anthropological approach. LIT Verlag, Hamburg

Friedman LM (1975) The legal system: a social perspective. Russell Sage Foundation, New York

Fuller L (1968–1969) The law's precarious hold on life. Ga Law Rev 3:530–545

Fuller L (1969) Human interaction and the law. Am J Jurisprud 14(1):1–36

Glenn HP (2014) Legal traditions of the world: sustainable diversity in law, 5th edn. Oxford University Press, Oxford

Gomez Isa F (2014) Cultural diversity, legal pluralism, and human rights from an indigenous perspective: the approach by the Colombian Constitutional Court and the Inter-American Court of Human Rights. Hum Rights Q 36(4):722–755

Grammond S (2010) La réception des systèmes juridiques autochtones au Canada. In: Breton A, Des Ormeaux A, Pistor K, Salmon P (eds) Le Multijuridisme. Manifestations, Causes et Conséquences. Editions ESKA, Paris, pp 54–86

Griffiths J (1986) What is legal pluralism? J Leg Plur Unoff Law 18(24):1–55

Hannum H (1988) New developments in indigenous rights. Va J Int Law 28:649–678

Hart HLA (1994) The concept of law, 2nd edn. Oxford University Press, Oxford

Hitchcock K (1994) Robert, 'International Human Rights, the Environment and Indigenous Peoples'. Colo J Int Environ Law Policy 5:1–22
Hooker MB (1975) Legal pluralism: an introduction to colonial and neo-colonial laws. Clarendon Press, Oxford
Kawharu IH (2008) Biculturalism and inclusion in New Zealand: the case of Orakei. Anthropologica 50(1):49–56
Kingsbury B (1998) "Indigenous peoples" in international law: a constructivist approach to the Asian controversy. Am J Int Law 92(3):414–457
Kleinhans M-M, Macdonald R (1997) What is critical legal pluralism. Can J Law Soc 12:25–46
Kymlicka W (1989) Liberalism, community, and culture. Oxford University Press, Oxford
Kymlicka W (1995) Multicultural citizenship: a liberal theory of minority rights. Oxford University Press, Oxford
Kymlicka W (2001) Politics in the vernacular: nationalism, multiculturalism, and citizenship. Oxford University Press, Oxford
Kymlicka W (2007) Multicultural Odysseys: navigating the new international politics of diversity. Oxford University Press, Oxford
Mahmood A, Ullah S, Ashfaq S (2018) The evolution of Jirga system: a conflict resolution mechanism in FATA. Lib Arts Soc Sci Int J 2(1):21–28
Mampilly Z (2011) Rebel rulers: insurgent governance and civilian life during war. Cornell University Press, Ithaca
Manai D (1993) Acculturation. In: Arnad A-J (ed) *Dictionnaire* encyclopédique de théorie et de sociologie du droit, 2nd edn. LGDJ, Paris, p 3
Mead HM (2003) Tikanga Maori: living by Maori values. Huia Publishers, Wellington
Merry SE (1988) Legal pluralism. Law Soc Rev 22(5):869–896
Mills JA (2002) Legal constructions of cultural identity in Latin America: an argument against defining "Indigenous Peoples.". Tex Hisp J Law Policy 8:49–78
Napoleon V (2013) Thinking about indigenous legal orders. In: Provost R, Sheppard C (eds) Dialogues about human rights and legal pluralism. Springer, Dordrecht, pp 229–246
Plant R (1998) Issues in indigenous poverty and development. Inter-American Development Bank, Washington DC
Shaw M (1990) The definition of minorities in international law. Israel Yearb Hum Rights 20:13–43
Simpson AWB (1988) Invitation to law. Basil Blackwell, Oxford
Swenson G (2018) Legal pluralism in theory and practice. Int Stud Rev 20:438–462
Tamanaha B (2000) A non-essentialist version of legal pluralism. J Law Soc 27(2):296–321
Tamanaha B (2001) A general jurisprudence of law and society. Oxford University Press, Oxford
Tamanaha B (2008) Understanding legal pluralism: past to present, local to global. Sydney Law Rev 30(3):375–411
Thomas MS (2017) The challenge of legal pluralism. Local dispute settlement and the Indian-state relationship in Ecuador. Routledge, London & New York
Ullah S, Ali R (2021) The mechanism of tribal Jirga system: challenges and prospects. Central Asia J 88:73–87
Unger RM (1976) Law in modern society: toward a criticism of social theory. Free Press, New York
Van de Fliert L (1994) Introduction. In: van de Fliert L (ed) Indigenous peoples and international organizations. Spokesman, Nottingham, pp 1–10
Vanderlinden J (1989) Return to legal pluralism. Twenty years later. J Leg Plur Unoff Law 21(28):149–157
Vanderlinden J (1998) Villes africaines et pluralisme juridique. J Leg Plur Unoff Law 30(42):245–274
Webber J (2009) The grammar of customary law. McGill Law J 54(4):579–626
Wiessner S (1999) Rights and status of indigenous peoples: a global comparative and international legal analysis. Harv Hum Rights J 12:57–128
Wolfrum R (1999) The protection of indigenous peoples in international law. Heidelberg J Int Law 59:369–382

Woodman G (1999) The idea of legal pluralism. In: Dupret B, Berger M, al-Zwaini L (eds) Legal pluralism in the Arab world. Kluwer Law International, The Hague, pp 3–19
Yousufzai HM, Gohar A (2012) Towards understanding Pukhtoon Jirga. Sang-e-Meel Publications, Lahore
Zamora S et al (2005) Mexican law. Oxford University Press, Oxford

Chapter 11
Indigenous Legal Traditions and Legal Pluralism in Africa

11.1 The Struggle for Recognition

One fundamental question about African law relates to its place among the legal systems of the world. Although this expression has always been used as a popular descriptor, the question whether African law exists *per se* or, contrariwise, encompasses the plurality of its legal traditions has always been controversial among comparative scholars.[1] Consequently, the answers to this question have varied over time depending on legal, temporal and historical contexts.

African law started gaining formal, albeit limited, recognition in the colonial era. This was somewhat triggered by the 'West African Conference' in Berlin (1884–1885), which led to both the partition of the Continent and the establishment of European formal empires. The first attempts to define African law date back to this period: the expression designates a set of legal rules applicable to groups and communities and, within them, to individuals. African law comprises the totality of legal institutions and refers to both public and private law: law-making, marriage, kinship, family, civil and public wrongs, law of obligations, evidence and land law fall under this wide-ranging legal descriptor.[2]

European colonial approaches towards African law varied enormously. France's colonial policy, for example, pursued social and legal uniformity: its *mission*

This chapter was contributed by Matteo Nicolini, Professor of Comparative Law, Law Department, Verona University; Visiting Lecturer, Newcastle Law School, Newcastle University, UK; External partner of the Centre for the Study of Law in Theory and Practice (LTAP), Liverpool John Moores University, UK. ORCID ID: http://orcid.org/0000-0002-4614-4478. Email: matteo.nicolini@univr.it.

---

[1] On the debate African law/African laws see the pivotal essay by Allott (1959). The debate has recently been revived by Mancuso (2023).

[2] See Driberg (1935), p. 231.

G. Mousourakis, *Traversing Legal Traditions*, Springer Textbooks in Law,
https://doi.org/10.1007/978-3-031-94669-1_11

civilisatrice endeavoured to assimilate African natives by deliberately propagating 'the best of French culture along with the rationalist and libertarian values deriving from the Enlightenment and French revolution'.[3] It also forged the *indigénat*: originally established in Algeria in 1881, this policy was applied across all French colonies and eventually abolished in 1946. The *indigénat* neither recognised indigenous legal systems nor recollected customary law; it created a legal (mainly criminal) regime; it was derogatory to French law inasmuch as it listed offenses that only natives could actually commit.[4]

In South Africa, the Boer Republics of Transvaal and Orange Free State recognised customary law in 1885. The creation of the Union of South Africa (1910) resulted in even more conflicting approaches: there was 'complete non-recognition in the Cape, limited application in the Transvaal and full recognition and application in Natal and the Transkeian territories'.[5] Odd as it may seem, African customary law obtained full recognition with the implementation of apartheid; the *South African Native Administration Act* (Act No 38 of 1927) recognised customary law and established a separate system of courts for Africans with the main purpose of fostering separateness among the different races living within the Dominion.

African indigenous law was granted limited application in tropical Africa. In British colonies—and, to a lesser extent, in Spanish colonies—, this was facilitated by the indirect rule, i.e. a method of administration whereby natives were associated to colonial governance.[6]

The limited recognition of African legal systems is usually traced back to its intrinsic features. Not only does African law comprise a variety of systems of law, but it is also handed down by means of oral transmission: law-making is a communal performance, the output of which is collective legal wisdom. As, for example, s 3(3)(c) *Traditional Authorities Act 25 of 2000* (Namibia) states, 'In the performance of its duties and functions [...] a traditional authority may [...] make customary laws'. Hence, legislators act as 'poets and singers' on behalf of the whole society.[7]

These features hardly squared with the Western legal mentality and colonial policies. Since oral transmission might well have favoured contrasting interpretations of customary law, in dispute resolutions colonial agents depended on native assessors, i.e. 'reliable informants' on customary law.[8] Furthermore, local variations in customary law were reduced through legislative action and restatement, whereby

[3] Sharkey (2013), pp. 153–154. For a critical evaluation of French colonial policy see Harris Sir (1912), p. 97.

[4] See Merle (2002), p. 80 and Mann (2009), p. 336.

[5] Grant (2006), pp. 1, 13. See Himonga and Thandabantu (2024), Chapter 1.

[6] See the seminal book by Lugard (1922), pp. 192–213. See also Mann and Roberts (1991), p. 20.

[7] Leman (2009), pp. 30, 109.

[8] Ubink (2010), p. 96. On native assessors see e.g., s 48 *Indian Evidence Act*, 1872; s 19 *Supreme Court Ordinance* 1876 (Ghana); s 8 *Swaziland High Court Proclamation* 1938; S11 *Proclamation of 10 June 1891*, S1 *Special Court Proclamation (Amendment) Making Provision for Native Assessors* (Amendment 22 of 1935), and *Amendment 22 of 1935* (Botswana); and s 222 *Criminal Procedure Act of Northern Rhodesia* 1939.

customary rules were recollected in written form and accommodated to the colonial legal framework. In addition, European colonial authorities established legal dualism (or pluralism), where European law was applied alongside customary law. Their mutual interactions were arranged upon a hierarchical scale: according to the repugnancy clauses appended to restated law, African law was applied to the extent that it was not 'contrary to justice and humanity'.[9] In the event of inconsistency between European law and African law, the former prevailed.

A new approach emerged in the 1950s and 1960s in the wake of decolonisation. As they gained independence, African countries addressed the topic within the broader framework of the dualistic (often pluralistic) legal regime they had received during the colonial era. It was not just a matter of defining African law; the application of customary law posed methodological problems. There was continuity between the colonial past and independent Africa. At the same time, however, the study of African law entailed a full understanding of its cultural underpinnings: it became a cross-disciplinary field of research for legal scholars, anthropologists, and legal anthropologists.[10]

The winds of democratic change, which blew over Africa after the dismantlement of apartheid and the end of the Cold War, favoured the transition of several states from authoritarian rule to democratic regimes; the adoption of new constitutions soon followed.[11] This also led to the revival of customary law and African legal systems. Their institutions and rules, which had been displaced by Western legal paradigms for decades, gained new ground; under African constitutionalism, 'living' customary law became the subject of renewed legislative and judicial actions.

11.2 The Biases of Comparative Law

The recognition of African law did not have any significant bearing on comparative legal research. The question whether African legal traditions constitute either an undivided legal tradition or a family or a group of legal systems remains unsettled. Although scholars now acknowledge that one of Africa's distinctive features is its intrinsic legal pluralism,[12] what we term as 'African law' is still located at the margins of comparative legal studies.

---

[9] See, among others, s 12(1)(a) *Local Courts Act* 1966, Act No. 20 of 1966 (Zambia); art. 52 of the *The Native Courts Regulations*, Order in Council No. 15 of 189 (East Africa); sect. 10 of the Nigerian Native Courts Ordinance of 1933.

[10] Roberts (1979); Vanderlinden (1996); Eberhard and Vernicos (2006).

[11] See the articles published in *Journal of African Law* 35 (1991) 1/2, issue on 'Recent Constitutional Developments in Africa'; and Richard (1997), pp. 3, 363.

[12] Allott (1959), p. 351 (African legal pluralism as 'unité dans la diversité'); Rambaud (2017), pp. 257–258; David et al. (2016), p, 483 et seq.; Sacco (2009); Vanderlinden (2000), p. 279.

Although scholars uphold that the study of African legal traditions is both 'desirable' and 'methodologically defensible',[13] the pluralistic social, political, and legal mosaic which is Africa still represents a challenge—and a hindrance—to the understanding and knowledge of how legal traditions has been accommodated within this extremely diverse continent. I am not denying that comparative lawyers are genuinely interested in African legal systems: besides some monographs, several handbooks dedicate chapters to them. My point is this: such an interest is usually affected by a methodological bias: legal scholarship still exhibits a colonial attitude towards non-Western conceptions of the law. Concealed under a benign approach towards them, there is an unconscious ethnocentric bias that still presupposes the superiority of Euro-Atlantic legal paradigms. This is evidently a legacy of colonialism, when European powers shaped African legal cartography and superimposed their own spatiality of law onto the continent. Peoples, communities, territories, and collective legal wisdom still bear the consequences of colonial domination.

The consequences are threefold. Firstly, the methodological bias explains why, despite the increasing interest in customary law, comparative law still focuses on the similarities between former African colonies and Western legal systems. By emphasising legal-colonial links, scholars rank French, Spanish, Portuguese and Italian former colonies among the civil-law legal systems; former British colonies and protectorates are ascribed to the common-law legal tradition, whereas Southern African countries, Mauritius, and the Seychelles join the mixed jurisdictions.[14]

Secondly, ethnocentrism entails that inferior systems do not have anything to teach superior systems. The Ethnocentric, and colonial, attitude towards African conceptions of the law has often resulted in a lack of reference to them;[15] even when handbooks cover African legal traditions, the analysis is usually limited in range and scope and are confined within either classifications of the legal systems or micro-comparative analyses.[16] The bias is apparent even when scholars suggest the adoption of new taxonomies. For example, Glenn advocates the establishment of the chthonic legal tradition, into which several pre-colonial legal traditions (i.e. African, Asian, Polynesian, and Inuit) coalesce.[17] However, the legal descriptor does not account for the rich variety of 'non-Eurocentric conceptions of the law': within the chthonic milieu, African law loses its own legal-specific features.

---

[13] This particularly true also in the field of constitutional law: Dixon et al. (2022), p. 2.

[14] See Bamodu (1994), p. 127; Zimmermann and Visser (1996), pp. 7–8. On African mixed jurisdictions see Palmer (2012), p. 625; du Plessis (2019), pp. 484–486.

[15] Zweigert and Kötz (1996) and Valcke (2018) omit references to African law, whereas Siems (2022), pp. 95–97 analyses Asian and African legal systems together.

[16] See Fombad (2024), p. 367; Ragone and Smorto (2023), pp. 43–44; Ajani et al. (2023); Bennett, (2019); Kischel (2019); Rambaud (2017); David et al. (2016); Sacco (2012); Gambaro and Sacco (2009); Menski (2006); Ntampaka (2005). As for monographs see Vanderlinden (1983); Sacco (2006); Mancuso (2023).

[17] Glenn (2014), p. 62. The term derives from the ancient Greek *kthonos* ('earth'); hence mod. English 'autochthonous'. See Goldsmith (1992), xvii.

Ethnocentrism also affects how African legal systems are arranged in manuals: these systems are usually succinctly outlined, and these outlines are also superficial and often inaccurate. Both Africa and its legal traditions are depicted as an indistinct whole: scholars usually refer to them as either 'The sub-Saharan legal tradition' or 'African law' or 'The African family of legal systems'.[18] There is only a clear precinct separating 'customary' African law from Northern Africa (and its Islamic legal tradition): the Sahel region marks the transition between Africa's tropical areas to the south from and the lands located to the north of the sand belt. The precinct is geographical rather than legal, and therefore its cultural and linguistic connotation is not applicable when demarcating African legal traditions. Nor are political yardsticks of any practical use: as almost all African states are members of the African Union (AU)—which replaced the Organisation of African Unity (OAU) in 2001—, the geopolitical alignment reinforces the predicament according to which Africa is an 'indistinct whole', which evidently draws a veil over the varieties of its legal systems.

Thirdly, according to this legal-colonial attitude, 'superior' European systems had the duty to nurture changes in African 'inferior' law. European colonial law promoted 'social engineering', i.e. the economic development, modernisation and transformation of indigenous African societies.[19] For this purpose, colonial agents forged new institutions whereby African societies could be both governed and 'civilised': chiefs, tribes and customary courts are 'invented traditions', which 'became in themselves realities through which a good deal of colonial encounter was expressed'.[20]

Modernisation was also achieved by backing official customary law, the development of which required the 'unification' of native customary law, that is, the progressive amalgamation of its local variations. Its unification was achieved by fostering either 'codification' or 'restatement'. Whereas codification incorporates customary law and, at the same time, abolishes it in the fields which it covers, restatement does not entail any legislative activity: it merely rearranges, in written form, the existing law, thus offering a 'comprehensive account of a branch of the law which is unwritten or is scattered between a variety of sources'.[21] The results are particularly interesting: in Madagascar (1957), Senegal and Tanganyika (1961), Kenya (1968–1969) and Malawi (1970–1971), restatement altered, i.e. modernised, 'native' customary law. This brought pervasive legal and cultural changes in native customary law, the aim of which was the preservation of both groups and their intrinsic social inequalities. Within the group, native customary law 'lawfully' discriminated against people on the grounds of rank and lineage (for accession to

[18] See M'Baye (1976), p. 138; (1968); Sacco (2012); Fombad (2013), p. 48. On such inaccuracy see Vanderlinden (2006), p. 1187.

[19] Allott (1968), p. 55; Mar (1960), p. 447; Eisenstadt (1965), p. 453.

[20] Ranger (1983), pp. 211, 212. See also Joireman (2001).

[21] Prinsloo (1987), p. 411. See also Bennett and Vermeulen (1980). For codification, see, among others, the Civil Code of Ethiopia (1960) and the 1964 Land Tenure Law (*Loi sur le Domain National*) (Senegal).

positions of power), status (low status people were excluded from enjoying some fundamental liberties), age and sex (older male members had more authority than the younger generations). Restatement mitigated the strictures of native customary law by infusing European values, such as individualism and liberalism, into the traditional systems, which favoured the relaxation of social inequalities of group-centred traditional societies.

Like social engineering, restatement of 'liberal' customary law is a legacy of the colonial era. The first attempts to modernise it date back to the early twentieth century: Germany started restating Tanganyikan family law in 1907—and the process was subsequently carried on by the United Kingdom in the 1940s.[22] The 'School of Oriental and African Studies' (SOAS) of London fostered its own *Restatement of African Law Project* in 1959: this was a comprehensive pattern for the study and restatement of African customary law of 16 Anglophone countries in the fields of land tenure, succession, family law and status of women. The colonial legacy is apparent, because the project was delivered in London. In the aftermath of decolonisation, the task of modernising African law was resumed by the *Law and development* movement, whereby European and U.S. legal and economic assistance aimed to develop African countries by imposing their own legal paradigms.[23]

Likewise, the bias is also apparent when it comes to that special form social engineering, which is usually styled as constitutional transition. For those comparativists who aim to emancipate the African continent from the colonial perspective, this approach is not particularly rewarding. It still applies a concept of transition elaborated in the Americas and Europe, where nineteenth- and twentieth-century constitutional transitions have always supposed to be 'democratic'.[24] Consequently, transitions taking place in Africa must also be democratic and adopt constitutional texts similar in principle to that enacted in the West. The separation of powers, the independence of the judiciary and the protection of rights become constitutionally indefectible contents, real benchmarks for the scrutiny of the text adopted at the end of the transition.

Yet, the reality is more complex: with the exception of Botswana—to which we may add Senegal—the transplantation of Western constitutionalism into Africa has resulted in the collapse of democratic experiments in several African states. The reasons are said to ultimately lie in the failure of African communities to metabolise Western constitutionalism. Metabolisation, it should be added, is often hampered by the specificities of the social, political, and cultural context, as well as the continued application of non-Western conceptions of law that appear difficult to reconcile with Western constitutionalism

Like in the case of the colonial links between former colonial powers and their former colonies, the benchmarks were 'manufactured in Europe not Africa' after the constitutional traditions of the Global North. This agenda must be realised even at

[22] Sippel (1998), p. 378.

[23] Merryman (1977), p. 457.

[24] See e.g. Okubasu (2022).

the cost of forcing reality: not only was the dream 'manufactured in Europe', but it 'took no cognisance either of contemporary African realities, nor, more important and less forgivable, of the legacy of colonial rule'.[25] What lies beneath such a predicament is the implicit assumption that the Western conception of constitutional law is a universal legal paradigm 'superior' to the African constitutional paradigms.

Africa is also experiencing new forms of legal unification, which stem from supranational integration and trigger the creation of 'African transnational law'. Among them, there is the *Organisation for the Harmonisation in Africa of Business Law* (*Organisation pour l'Harmonisation en Afrique du Droit des Affaires*—OHADA), a supranational union founded in 1993 by French-speaking countries which mimics the EU. Like the OHADA, the *Common Market for Eastern and Southern Africa* (COMESA) is a process of supranational integration with economic and legal implications, among which the harmonisation of commercial law, in general, and contract law, in particular. Legal harmonisation is also the objective of several regional integration processes, such as the *East African Community* (EAC), the *Southern Africa Development Community* (SADC) and the *Economic Community of West African States* (ECOWAS). Harmonisation entails the convergence of both state and customary laws in order to stimulate business and economic development.[26]

11.3 Ranking African Legal Systems

Modernisation of customary law may be attributed to the ethnocentric attitude that still saturates scholarly comparative research. However, the methodological bias is both procedural—i.e. it considers how comparative legal method is applied to African law—and substantive. To this extent, the study of African legal systems and institutions discloses a vast array of colonial underpinnings, which reflect the narratives of superiority and domination, as well as the production of legal spaces, that European powers manufactured in the last few decades of the nineteenth century. As the processes of socio-legal engineering mentioned above uphold, domination and colonialism have common features: the latter is a species of the broader concept of domination, which endeavoured to impose 'superior' legal orders to the subordinate African legal systems.[27]

The changes in the law fostered by spatial production also account for how some scholars have answered the question whether African law constitutes a family of legal systems. Due to the relaxation of traditional societies triggered by liberalism

[25] Crowder (1987), p. 10.

[26] See Mancuso (2007), p. 165; Shumba (2015), p. 127; Kamala and Lipimile (2021).

[27] For more on these issues see Nicolini (2022), p. 103 et seq.

and by the pervasiveness of Western legal paradigms, 'the days of African customary law as a fully-fledged legal system are gone'.[28]

The idea of development also has a huge impact on classifications. How the varieties of legal systems are ranked depends, *inter alia*, on their evolution and performativity. We take for granted that the Western legal tradition is dominant across the globe. Like Western societies, African societies might attain the same level of development provided that they evolve through various stages of development that are universal and lead to the same stage of superiority envisaged by European comparative legal traditions.[29]

Such a narrative of superiority is apparent as regards both 'native' African systems and 'received', i.e. European, systems. Not only did mixed jurisdictions replace the customary law substrate in Southern Africa, Mauritius and the Seychelles, but these 'received' laws are also deemed to be inferior to European legal systems. Suffice it here to say that, in Africa, 'common law of the land' designates only the legal systems derived from the English common law, thus disregarding the fact that, 'In South Africa, the term "common law" [...] denotes the systems of Roman-Dutch and English law that were imported during the colonial period'.[30] The same linguistic connotations of the legal systems evidently share the epistemologies and hierarchies underpinning the colonial attitude.

This ranking approach to legal systems is also applied within 'native' African law. According to the majority of comparative legal scholars, African law is a complex legal reality where several strata overlap and each layer is superimposed onto the others: these are the traditional (or pre-colonial) stratum, the religious stratum, the colonial and the post-colonial strata.[31]

Stratification entails that African law has progressively evolved through various stages with the Western legal paradigm as the natural end point. It should be argued, however, that the post-colonial or independence stratum—which stands above all other layers—does not only imitate European legal paradigms (such as constitutionalism, rule of law, enforcement of rights), but also embeds the revival of African traditional legal values. Such a revival also characterises supranational legal harmonisation: OHADA's Uniform Acts on Contract Law and on General Commercial Law refer to custom, which, within the African context, also styles customary law as a source of obligations.[32]

---

[28] Oba (2010), p. 79.

[29] See Nicolini (2024).

[30] Bennett (2011), p. 710 fn 4.

[31] Among others, see Seidman (1979), p. 17; Oba (2010), p. 58; Sacco (2012), p. 314; Mancuso (2023), Chapter 2.

[32] See Art 194 of OHADA Uniform Act on Contract Law and Arts 238–239 of OHADA Uniform Act on General Commercial Law.

11.4 Stratification and Evolution of African Law

The interweaving of modern and traditional legal strata discloses other substantive effects of Ethnocentrism. Stratification makes it possible to discretely analyse the different strata and, within the pre-colonial layer, to study legal arrangements prior to the contact with other civilisations. This also makes it possible to detect commonalities among different pristine African legal systems. This is not to deny that African societies followed divergent politico-legal patterns: comparative scholars and legal anthropologists usually draw a distinction between acephalous societies, which lacked a centralised political power (such as the Pygmies and the Wala people in Upper Ghana), and those communities (the Akan or the Birim-Volta, for example), whose societal arrangements were highly structured and possibly influenced by Northern African civilisations.[33] Legal anthropological research focuses on how supernatural and magico-religious beliefs forged socio-legal relationships in pre-colonial African law, thus playing a major role as far as laws relating to kinship, evidence and inheritance were concerned.[34] Supernatural entities also give a reason for the role ancestors were granted within family groups and settlements: they were (and still are) part of the community, and therefore actively engaged in both lawmaking and dispute resolution. Not only does it enhance the role of kinship, but it also emphasises the centrality of the group over individuals and explains the relevance of marriage settlements (e.g. the bride price) when it comes to constituting bonds between families—or among families, as far as polygamous marriages are concerned.[35]

The search for commonalities among the diverse African legal systems might be of practical help for didactic purposes; yet it conceals the Ethnocentric attitude prevalent in scholarly comparative studies. African legal systems certainly share common features; by emphasising their unifying traits, however, scholars keep under wraps Africa's pluralistic mosaic and mask its diatopic variation. Despite the superimposition of homogeneous colonial and post-colonial strata, it is not an easy task to universalise legal concepts when it comes to African law: its variety entails 'that there is almost an exception to any generalization somewhere.'[36]

Like the tiles of a roof, then, the different strata are so imbricated that is impossible to disentangle—and therefore study—the 'African lawscape' as if it were in watertight compartments.[37] Due to the interaction between customary law and European legal paradigms, the line between pristine customary laws and the colonial stratum is constantly blurred: in *Lewis v Bankole* [1909] NLR 100, for example,

[33] 'Screened by a tropical forest from the north and facing the Gulf of Guinea, the region remained isolated from external influences [...] creating specific systems of state law': Sinitsina (1987).

[34] Elias (1955), pp. 228–238; Sacco (2012), p. 315.

[35] The role of individuals depends on their position in the group to which they belong: see Rambaud (2017), p. 258; David et al. (2016), Mancuso (2023), p. 195.

[36] Woodman (2010), p. 9. See aslo Njuguna (2020). See also Siems (2022), p. 114 et seq.

[37] Mancuso (2023), p. 135 et seq.

it was stated that courts must enforce 'existing native law and custom and not that of bygone days'.

The interweaving of the different strata is particularly apparent when it comes to considering statehood as the major legacy Europeans handed over to African communities. Boundaries were unfamiliar to African conceptions of the law; they were also incompatible with traditional societal organisation, which was primarily built upon family settlements and non-territorial arrangements. However, colonial policy disregarded borderless, communal arrangements: since they were divided among different states, communities were arbitrarily separated and subsequently merged with other groups with the aim of creating political entities based on territorial jurisdictions. Odd as it may seem, when the representatives of the newly independent African states met in Addis Ababa in 1963 in order to create the OAU, they immediately conformed to the status quo.

Contemporary African legal systems should be assessed, taking into consideration that their full understanding entails a full understanding of all the variables which may have some bearing on them. Hence, scholars must examine customary law by considering how it has evolved through interaction between the different strata.

Interactions between traditional and colonial strata often cross the public-private divide. This is apparent as far as African land law is concerned: the African land tenure system was mainly communal and governed by both supernatural entities and the group; therefore, there was no room left for Western possessive individualism. The rise of trade pushed for its suppression—or, at least, reduction—, 'because the land market could not fit with ideas regarding the communal nature of African land tenure'.[38] In the aftermath of decolonisation, Western, i.e. individual, land titles were retained and colonial laws regarding customary lands were adapted to the African context: land acts transformed former communal lands into public lands, such as in Tanzania and Ghana. Like in England, Tanzanian legislation assigns the land to the Head of State (the President), who acts as trustee on behalf of all citizens: the latter "cannot own land, but they can own rights over the land," which 'may be bought or sold, and inherited, and can thus be seen as (limited) decision-making rights'. The 1992 Constitution of Ghana does the same: 'All public lands in Ghana shall be vested in the President on behalf of, and in trust for, the people of Ghana'; whereas 'stool lands', which the communal soul (the stool) granted to its own people, are vested 'in the appropriate stool on behalf of, and in trust for, the subjects of the stool in accordance with customary law and usage'.[39]

Supernatural entities and societal structures are also relevant when it comes to settling disputes or performing the most relevant legal deeds. Marriage, divorce, adoption, guardianship, inheritance, acknowledgment of either cession or

[38] Joireman (2010), p. 298.

[39] ss 255(1) and 167(1) of the 1992 Constitution (Ghana); *Loi* no 034-2009/AN du 16 juin 2009 *portant régime foncier rural* (Burkina Faso); URT, *Land Act* (No. 4), sec. 7 and URT, *Village Land Act* (No. 5), sec. 8(1), 12(1) (Tanzania). On the supernatural see Hamer (1998), p. 311. In Nigeria, Sect. 1 Land Use Act 1990 vests state land in the Governor.

acquisition of rights over the land, and other acts made or taken are considered legal, valid and binding provided that they are performed before the whole community. In Madagascar, for example, Malagasy law and custom (*fomba*) has always been part of its dualistic legal system together with French-derived law. In the wake of the revival of customary law, the Preamble to the 2010 Constitution enshrines both traditional law and the system of village councils (*Fokon'olona*), where men and women that are descendants of a single ancestor and live within the same territory (*Fokon'tany*) gather. Acting as a notary, the community embodies the local rule-making process (*Dina*) and secures the validity of the most relevant legal deeds; these thus become part of the collective legal wisdom and are handed down to future generations.[40]

Unlike continental customary laws, Malagasy law thus tolerates limited forms of women's participation in communal rule-making processes. We have already noticed that customary law tends to preserve social inequality by 'lawfully' discriminating against people on the grounds of sex. Indeed, African societies see women 'as adjuncts to the group to which they belong, such as a clan or tribe, rather than equals'.[41] This is evident when it comes to marriage, i.e. a communal engagement where economic aspects merge with societal considerations: due to the overwhelming importance of the group, it constitutes an agreement between families and clans rather than a spousal union. To this extent, modernisation has not favoured any improvement in women's antenuptial conditions: national legislation, which enables Africans to enter into a statutory marriage, usually does not prescribe any forms for the solemnisation of customary-law marriages. Nor does legislation set any age for such a solemnisation but leaves it to customary law. As polygamous marriages are allowed under customary law, national legislation merely presupposes their existence, the continuance of which impedes contracting any valid statutory marriage.[42]

African customary tort law and law of contract have a broader scope if compared to their civil-law and common-law counterparts. On the one hand, tort law protects individuals and groups, as well as their name, integrity and interests—such as familial unity and marital relationships—also from mere vulgar abuse. On the other hand, the law of contract, which also has knowledge of consideration and requires formalities for contractual performances, gives prominence to the group, thus curbing individuals' freedom of contract.[43]

---

[40] Blanc-Jouvan (1964), p. 7; Molte (1967), p. 123.

[41] Ndulo (2011), p. 89.

[42] See s 34 *Marriage Act* 1963 (Zambia); s 1(2) *Marriages Act* 1964 (Eswatini). For example, Nigeria legislation does not set any age for such solemnisation: see the *Marriage Act* 1990 (Nigeria). Namibia, South Africa, Togo, Rwanda and Niger and few other countries explicitly recognise customary marriages. See, among others, s 4(3)(b) Constitution of Namibia; *Recognition of Customary Marriages Act*, 1998 (Act No. 120 of 1998) (South Africa).

[43] For more on African family, contract, and land law see Mancuso (2023), Chapter 4.

11.5 From African Law to African Legal Traditions

With its critical and subversive approach comparative law has allowed us to detect how several methodological biases affect the study of African law. When it comes to its legal systems and institutions, comparative legal research still displays noticeable colonial underpinnings. It is an intertwining of both inherited colonial attitudes and a truly Ethnocentric approach, which still percolates through the scholarly examination of the different legal strata. This approach is based on the assumption that African law has progressively evolved through various stages with the Western legal paradigm as the natural end point.

Being subversive means that comparative law may display its own strategies, which aim to revise the study of African law. Like post-colonial studies—which examine history through the lenses of the peripheries of the colonial empires—, our view is that comparative law has to give voice to legal systems which have been traditionally disregarded by 'official', i.e. mainstream, comparative legal research. The re-examination of African law in the light of post-colonial legal studies is pivotal. We noticed above that African law is considered 'inferior' to Western law, and therefore has been set at the ostensible margins of comparative studies. Comparative law aims to overturn this perspective and unveils colonial methodological legacies; by adopting the point of view of 'marginalised' legal systems, it endorses Africa's 'disengagement from the whole colonial syndrome'.[44]

The aim of comparative law is to subvert the established mainstream narrative, which shares the European perspective on African law and conceives of Africa as a peripheral 'family' of sundry legal systems. Adopting such a perspective means challenging the assumption according to which Africa is a sort of an indistinct legal whole. The assumption, it goes without saying, is still part of the legal mindset. When enquiring into its legal institutions, scholars regularly point to the commonalities among systems rather than delve into a closer analysis of their specific constitutive traits.[45]

Comparative law must critically examine the idea that African law is an indistinct whole, a miscellaneous 'family' into which heterogeneous legal systems coalesce. To put it differently: within post-colonial comparative legal research, the study of African law moves towards the examination of different 'African legal systems.' Scholars might recover Africa's legal pluralism provided that they take into account the variety of legal substrates, each of which is dominant in a specific area of the continent. The most relevant substrates are: Cape colonial law in Southern Africa; customary law in tropical Africa; Malagasy law in Madagascar. The Islamic legal tradition coexists with customary law in Somalia and in the Barbary states and is the 'traditional' substrate north of the Sahel region.[46]

---

[44] Hulme (1995), p. 120.

[45] Allott (1959), p. 351.

[46] On Islamic law as variety of customary law see Anderson (1962), p. 617.

Due to its insularity, it is easy to demarcate the Malagasy legal tradition. When it comes to African continental legal systems, however, the demarcation process must be complemented with several criteria. The Sahel region, which marks the transition from Northern Africa to tropical Africa, also denotes a linguistic transition (from Afroasiatic languages in the north to Nilo-Saharian and Niger-Kordofanian languages in the south) and an ethnic transition. Consequently, these criteria supplement the legal criterion, i.e. the boundaries between the countries situated north of the Sahel and those located south of it. Boundaries also mark the transition from tropical Africa and Southern Africa, whose legal substrate is the Cape colonial law, i.e., the jurisdiction stemming from the mixture of Roman-Dutch law and English common law which was applied in the Cape Colony in the nineteenth century. This explains, for example, why Zimbabwe and South Africa share a common legal substrate, but, at the same time, Zimbabwe has strong political ties with Zambia and Malawi, whose legal substrate complements customary law with common law. From 1953 to 1963, indeed, the former British colonies of Nyasaland (Malawi), Northern Rhodesia (Zambia) and Southern Rhodesia (Zimbabwe) joined the Federation of Rhodesia and Nyasaland, that is, a quasi-federal dominion created within the British Empire.

Not only does the variety of substrates reflect the pluralistic mosaic which embeds African legal traditions, but it also accounts for the different legal-historical narratives of Southern Africa, tropical Africa and Madagascar. With the disembarkment of the Dutch flotilla and the creation of a supply base in the Cape peninsula (1652), Roman-Dutch law became the common law of Southern Africa. After the British occupation (1795), the Dutch handed over the Cape colony to the United Kingdom (1806). The 1828 *First Charter of Justice* abolished the civil-law Court of Justice and established a judiciary styled after the English common-law courts: this favoured the blending of Roman-Dutch law and English common law, and Cape colonial law became the legal substrate of both the Boer Republics and Southern African colonies and protectorates.[47] Within the Cape legal tradition, Lesotho is unique in that its customary law was codified. British colonial authorities promoted a codification process which led to the promulgation of the *Laws of Lerotholi*: the code collects Basotho customary law and covers several subject matters, which range from public law to private law. In Lesotho, its status and authority are relevant, albeit subordinate to Western law.[48]

---

[47] See *De Grondwet* 1854 (Orange Free State); *Royal Charter of Natal* 1856 (Natal); *De Grondwet Der Zuid-afrikaansche Republiek*, alson known as The Thirty-Three Articles (*Drie en Dertig Artikelen*) of 1844–1849 (Transvaal). On Cape colonial law as the common law of Southern African protectorates territories see: *Order in Council* 3 November 1871 and s 2 *General Law Proclamation 2B of 1884* (Basutoland-Lesotho); *Order in Council* 9 May 1891, *Proclamation* 10 June 1891 and *General Law Proclamation* 1909 (Bechuanaland-Botswana); *Order in Council* 20 October 1898 (Southern Rhodesia-Zimbabwe); *General Administration Act No. 11 of 1905* and *General Law and Administration Proclamation No. 4 of 1907* (Swaziland-Eswatini); *Proclamation No 21 of 1919* which granted the *Roman-Dutch law* "as existing and applied in the Province of the Cape of Good Hope" to South-West Africa-Namibia.

[48] See, among others, Juma (2011).

Like Lesotho, Madagascar experienced the restatement of Malagasy law, which was promoted by Queen Ranavalona I (1828–1861) before French protectorate (1884) and colonisation (1895–1897).[49] The establishment of the Kingdom of Madagascar (1824) as a highly centralised independent state undoubtedly favoured the adoption of these pre-colonial collections, which restate pre-colonial customary law in written form.

Finally, in tropical Africa the legal substrate consists of customary law, which coexists alongside 'received' European, i.e. mainly French- and English-derived, legal systems.

11.6 Pluralism in African Legal Systems

Within the variety of African legal traditions, customary-law substrate is *per se* a pluralistic mosaic: it combines manifold legal arrangements, which are usually inseparable from their societal contexts. National constitutions and legislation also entrench customary law. In so doing, not only do they reflect the variety of native laws, but they also provide them with a flexible legal frame within which 'official', i.e. restated, customary law might be revitalised by local and communal variations of 'living' customary law.

Constitutional and statutory provisions on customary law operate as conflict of law rules whereby lawyers and judges might determine the law applicable to a specific community or ethnic group. Between contrasting norms, indeed, conflict-of-law rules make a renvoi not only to official customary law, but also to living customary laws enacted by the collective legal wisdom. This allows native law to flourish and vary throughout African communities; it also fits the requirements set by the 'superior' Eurocentric legal framework, because customary law, when applicable, is considered as if it were the law of a different legal system. This also accounts for the transnational character of customary law, which is inherent to African legal systems. Seldom does it reflect colonial borders; as 'it grows and evolves for and with that [specific] group', it does not reflect a specific territory, but 'the group that obeys it'.[50]

Throughout the whole of Africa, judicial dispute resolution plays a meaningful role in allowing 'living' customary law to prosper. This is particularly apparent

[49] The first code was promulgated by Queen Ranavalona in 1828; Queen Radama II enacted a second code in 1862. Queen Rasoherina promulgated two codes in 1863; Queen Ranavalona II issued a Malagasy-law criminal code in 1869. Two more codes where enacted in 1868 and 1881.

[50] See, *inter alia*, Art. 162 of the 2018 Chad Constitution; Art. 211 of the 1996 South African Constitution; Art. 11(3) 1992 Ghana Constitution (customary law comprises 'rules of law which by custom are applicable to particular communities in Ghana'); s 68 *Courts (Amendment) Act* 1967 (Malawi) (conflict of law rule for determining the applicable customary); s 2(b) *Customary Law and Local Courts Act* 1990 (Zimbabwe) ('customary law' means the customary law of the people of Zimbabwe, or of any section or community of such people'); s 258(1) *Evidence Act* 2011 (Nigeria) ('Custom' is a rule which, in a particular district, has, from long usage, obtained the force of law'). On the impact of traditional institutions on constitutional texts see Erk (2022).

when we consider how constitutions and primary legislation accommodate the interweaving of the different legal strata. Firstly, customary courts are often integrated into the European-oriented judicial system, in order to 'preserve as much of the traditional customary laws principles as possible, whilst extending the perceived benefits of the received laws'. Secondly, European-oriented judicial systems usually act as reflective judiciaries, and therefore resort to 'indigenous reasonable test' which reflect community standards and rules.[51] This means paving the way to a kind of 'legal syncretism', i.e. a process whereby the '*adoption, rejection, invention, and transformation of diverse and seemingly opposite legal rules, principles, and practices' is reinvented 'into a constitutional state with imperial or colonial legacies'*.[52]

Thirdly, the proof of living customary law is usually a matter of fact. When, however, a court takes judicial notice of a custom, customary law ceases to be considered as a matter of fact: it is noticed as a matter of law and therefore acts as a binding precedent.

Finally, judicial proceedings consent to expand the scope of customary law. Suffice it to consider Sect. 20(2) of South Africa's *Black Administration Act* 1927, which was replaced by Sect. 7 of the *Traditional Courts Act* (No 9 of 2022), according to which 'The procedure at any proceedings ... must be in accordance with customary law and custom'. This also allows state law to be infused with traditional communal African socio-legal conceptions; among them, *ubuntu*, which comprises traditional key values, such as 'restorative justice', 'reconciliation', and 'humaneness'.[53]

When it comes to African law, 'So great is the ascendency' of procedural law 'that substantive law has at first the look of being gradually secreted in the interstices of procedure', as Henry Sumner Maine stated in his *Dissertations on Early Law and Custom* (1883) with regard to English law. Not only do 'native' legal proceedings make living customary law flourish;[54] but Sumner Maine's predicament also allows us to draw up an intriguing equation between the 'superior' English legal system and the 'inferior' African customary law. In England, the forms of actions played a pivotal role in the development of the legal system. With a hint of irony, like 'superior' English law, native law and custom also adapts through judicial application and enforcement. To put it another way: both common law and African legal systems evolve through the depositaries of their respective collective legal wisdom irrespective of their ranking.

---

[51] On the integration of customary courts into the received legal system see Fombad (2013), p. 113. See also *Common Law and Customary Laws Act* 1969 (Botswana). On indigenous standards see Oba (2010), pp. 76–78.

[52] Gebeye (2021), p. 10.

[53] Jordaan (2017), pp. 2, 402. See Himonga et al. (2013), p. 369 and Mancuso (2023), p. 251 et seq.

[54] See Van der Wall (2004), p. 113: 'Benefits [...] include the fact that the customary courts are more open ("like democracy") because all adults can participate in them, they are public and they keep traditions alive. A lawyer is not needed since the system is not professionally driven and the fines are not high. The emphasis is on social outcomes rather than on individualizing outcomes'.

References

Ajani G et al (2023) Diritto comparato. 3. Le tradizioni giuridiche asiatiche e africane. Giappichelli, Turin

Allott AN (1959) L'unité du droit Africain. Présence Africaine 27(28):343–358

Allott N (1968) African law. In: Derrett JDM (ed) An introduction to legal systems. Sweet & Maxwell, London, pp 131–156

Anderson JND (1962) The future of Islamic law in British Commonwealth territories in Africa. Law Contemp Probl 27:617–631

Bamodu G (1994) Transnational law, unification and harmonization of international commercial law in Africa. J Afr Law 38:125–143

Bennett TW (2011) An African doctrine of equity in South African public law. Loyola Law Rev 57:709–726

Bennett TW (2019) Comparative law and African customary law. In: Reimann M, Zimmermann R (eds) The Oxford handbook of comparative law, 2nd edn. Oxford University Press, Oxford, pp 652–680

Bennett TW, Vermeulen T (1980) Codification of customary law. J Afr Law 24:206–219

Blanc-Jouvan X (1964) Development of a new law code in Madagascar. Afr Today 11:7–9

Crowder M (1987) Whose dream was it anyway? Twenty-five years of African independence. Afr Aff 86:7–24

David R et al (2016) Les grands systèmes de droit contemporains, 12th edn. LGDJ, Paris

Dixon R, Ginsburg T, Abebe A (2022) Introduction to comparative constitutional law in Africa. In: Dixon R, Ginsburg T, Abebe A (eds) Comparative constitutional law in Africa. Edward Elgar, Cheltenham and Northampton, pp 1–4

Driberg JH (1935) The African conception of law. J R Afr Soc 136:230–246

Du Plessis J (2019) Comparative law and the study of mixed legal systems. In: Reimann M, Zimmermann R (eds) The Oxford handbook of comparative law, 2nd edn. Oxford University Press, Oxford, pp 474–501

Eberhard C, Vernicos G (eds) (2006) La quête anthropologique du droit: autour de la démarche d'etienne le roy. Karthala, Paris

Eisenstadt SN (1965) Social change and modernization in African societies south of the Sahara. Cahiers d'études africaines 5:453–471

Elias O (1955) The nature of African customary law. Manchester University Press, Manchester

Erk J (2022) Traditional kingdoms and modern constitutions: parochialism, patriarchy, and despotism vs. indigenous safeguards against absolutism. In: Dixon R, Ginsburg T, Abebe A (eds) Comparative constitutional law in Africa. Edward Elgar, Cheltenham and Northampton, pp 328–359

Fombad CM (2013) The Botswana legal system. Lexis Nexis, Durban

Fombad CM (2024) Sub-Saharan Africa. In: Siems M, Yap PJ (eds) The Cambridge handbook of comparative law. Cambridge University Press, Cambridge, pp 367–384

Gambaro A, Sacco R (2009) Sistemi giuridici comparati, 2nd edn. UTET, Turin

Gebeye BA (2021) A theory of African constitutionalism. Oxford University Press, Oxford

Glenn HP (2014) Legal traditions of the world: sustainable diversity in law, 5th edn. Oxford University Press, Oxford

Goldsmith E (1992) The way: an ecological world view. Rider, London

Grant E (2006) Human rights, cultural diversity and customary law in South Africa. J Afr Law 50:2–23

Hamer M (1998) "Stool rights" and modern land law in Ghana: a geographical perspective on the transformation of tradition. Afr Spectr 33:311–338

Harris Sir J (1912) Dawn in darkest Africa. Smith, Elder & Co., London

Himonga C, Thandabantu N (eds) (2024) African customary law in South Africa. Post-Apartheid and living law perspectives, 2nd edn. Oxford University Press Southern Africa, Cape Town

Himonga H et al (2013) Reflections on judicial views of ubuntu. Potchefstroomse Elektronies Regsblad 16:372–429
Hulme P (1995) Including America. ARIEL: Rev Int English Lit 26:117–123
Joireman SF (2001) Inherited legal systems and effective rule of law: Africa and the colonial legacy. J Mod Afr Stud 39:571–596
Joireman SF (2010) Entrapment or freedom: enforcing customary property rights regimes in common-law Africa. In: Fenrich J-M et al (eds) The future of African customary law. Cambridge University Press, Cambridge, pp 295–311
Jordaan DW (2017) The open society: what does it really mean. De Jure 50:396–405
Juma L (2011) The laws of Lerotholi: role and status of codified rules of custom in the kingdom of Lesotho. Pace Int Law Rev 23:92–145
Kamala D, Lipimile G (2021) Harmonization and integration in Africa: the case of competition law and policy. In: Amao O, Olivier M, Magliveras KD (eds) The emergent African Union law: conceptualization, delimitation, and application. Oxford University Press, Oxford, pp 65–86
Kischel U (2019) Comparative law. Oxford University Press, Oxford
Leman P (2009) Singing the law: Okot p'Bitek's legal imagination and the poetics of traditional justice. Res Afr Lit 40:109–128
Lugard FD (1922) The dual mandate in British tropical Africa. William Blackwood and Sons, Edinburgh
M'Baye K (1976) The African conception of the law. In: David R (gen ed) International encyclopedia of comparative law, volume II, The legal systems of the world. Their comparison and unification. J.C.B. Mohr, Tübingen
Mancuso S (2007) Trends on the harmonisation of contract law in Africa. Annu Surv Int Comp Law 13:157–178
Mancuso S (2023) African law(s). Comparative insights on the African lawscape. Brill-Nijhoff, Leiden-Boston
Mann G (2009) What was the "Indigénat"? The "Empire of Law" in French West Africa. J Afr Hist 50:331–353
Mann K, Roberts R (eds) (1991) Law in colonial Africa. Heinemann-James Currey, Portsmouth, NH, and London
Mar LP (1960) Social change in Africa. Int Aff 36:447–456
Menski WF (2006) Comparative law in a global context: the legal systems of Asia and Africa. Cambridge University Press, Cambridge
Merle I (2002) Retour sur le régime de l'indigénat : genèse et contradictions des principes répressifs dans l'Empire français. French Polit Cult Soc 20:77–97
Merryman JH (1977) Comparative law and social change: on the origins, style, decline and revival of the law and development movement. Am J Comp Law 25:457–491
Molte L (1967) Sources et tendances du droit moderne à Madagascar. Can J Afr Stud/Revue Canadienne des Études Africaines 1:123–134
Ndulo M (2011) African customary law, customs, and women's rights. Ind J Global Leg Stud 18:87–120
Nicolini M (2022) Legal geography. Comparative law and the production of space. Springer, Cham
Nicolini M (2024) The land, the sea, and the colonial production of space within the Anglo/British Empire. Legalities 4:43–67
Njuguna C (2020) African customary law: assessing its status and effects today. Lexington Books, Lanham, Maryland
Ntampaka C (2005) Introduction aux systèmes juridiques africains. Presses Universitaires de Namur, Namur
Oba AA (2010) The future of customary law in Africa. In: Fenrich J-M et al (eds) The future of African customary law. Cambridge University Press, Cambridge, pp 58–80
Okubasu DM (2022) Democratic constitutional transitions in Sub-Saharan Africa. In: Dixon R, Ginsburg T, Abebe A (eds) Comparative constitutional law in Africa. Edward Elgar, Cheltenham and Northampton, pp 137–156

Palmer VV (ed) (2012) Mixed jurisdictions worldwide, 2nd edn. Cambridge University Press, Cambridge
Prinsloo MW (1987) Restatement of indigenous law. Comp Int Law J South Afr 20:411–420
Ragone S, Smorto G (2023) Comparative law: a very short introduction. Oxford University Press, Oxford
Rambaud T (2017) Introduction au droit comparé, 2nd edn. Presses Universitaires de France, Paris
Ranger T (1983) The invention of tradition in colonial Africa. In: Hobsbawm E, Ranger T (eds) The invention of tradition. Cambridge University Press, Cambridge, pp 211–262
Richard J (1997) Democratization in Africa after 1989: comparative and theoretical perspectives. Comp Polit 29:363–382
Roberts S (1979) Order and dispute: an introduction to legal anthropology. Penguin, London
Sacco R (2006) Il diritto africano. UTET, Turin
Sacco R (2009) Le droit africain: anthropologie et droit positif. Dalloz-Sirey, Paris
Sacco R (2012) The sub-Saharan legal tradition. In: Bussani M, Mattei U (eds) The Cambridge companion to comparative law. Cambridge University Press, Cambridge, pp 313–343
Seidman RB (1979) Law and stratification: the African case. Contemp Crises 3:17–39
Sharkey HJ (2013) African colonial states. In: Reid R, Parker J (eds) The Oxford handbook of modern African history. Oxford University Press, Oxford, pp 151–170
Shumba T (2015) Revising legal harmonisation under the Southern African Development Community Treaty: the need to amend the Treaty. Law Democr Dev 19:127
Siems M (2022) Comparative law, 3rd edn. Cambridge University Press, Cambridge
Sinitsina I (1987) African legal tradition: J.M. Sarbah, J.B. Danquah, N.A. Ollennu. J Afr Law 31:44–57
Sippel H (1998) Customary family law in colonial Tanganyika: a study of change and continuity. Comp Int Law J South Afr 31:373–383
Ubink J (2010) The quest for customary law in African state courts. In: Fenrich J-M et al (eds) The future of African customary law. Cambridge University Press, Cambridge, pp 83–102
Valcke C (2018) Comparing law. Comparative law as reconstruction of collective commitments. Cambridge University Press, Cambridge
Van der Wall KCS (2004) Formal and informal dispute resolution in the Limpopo Province, South Africa. Anthropol South Afr 27:111–121
Vanderlinden J (1983) Les systèmes juridiques africains. Presses Universitaires de France, Paris
Vanderlinden J (1996) Anthropologique juridique. Dalloz, Paris
Vanderlinden J (2000) Les droits africains entre positivisme et pluralisme. Bulletin de séances de l'Académie royale de sciences d'Oute-Mer 46:279–292
Vanderlinden J (2006) Ex Africa Semper. Revue internationale de droit comparÉ 58:1187–1202
Woodman GE (2010) A survey of customary laws in Africa in search of lessons for the future. In: Fenrich J-M et al (eds) The future of African customary law. Cambridge University Press, Cambridge, pp 9–30
Zimmermann R, Visser D (1996) Introduction. South African law as a mixed legal system. In: Zimmermann R, Visser D (eds) Southern Cross: civil law and common law in South Africa. Clarendon Press, Oxford, pp 1–30
Zweigert K, Kötz H (1996) Einführung in die Rechtsvergleichung auf dem Gebiete des Privatrechts, 3rd edn. J.C.B. Mohr Siebeck, Tübingen

Chapter 12
Legal Transplantation and the Evolution of the Japanese Legal Tradition

12.1 The Dynamics of Legal Transplantation

The development of transnational legal traditions is intimately tied to the phenomenon of legal transplanting. Legal transplanting occurs when one legal system integrates a specific legal rule, institution, or concept from another legal system. This process may extend to the adoption or reception of an entire legal system, which is often executed in a centralized or systematic manner. To understand the phenomenon of legal transplantation, one must examine the historical context and specific motivations behind the introduction of foreign law in any given instance. According to Alan Watson, comparative law, as a distinct intellectual discipline, primarily focuses on examining the historical relationships between legal systems and traditions and the trajectories of legal transplants across various countries. Through this lens, one can identify the factors that drive changes or maintain continuity within legal frameworks.[1] Watson argues that comparative law offers valuable insights for those involved in law reform, helping them to better comprehend their historical role and responsibilities. It provides a clearer perspective on whether, and to what extent, it is appropriate to adopt elements from other legal systems, which systems

[1] Watson (1993), p. 6. To illustrate his point, Watson mentions a set of rules concerning matrimonial property, which travelled "from the Visigoths to become the law of the Iberian Peninsula in general, migrating then from Spain to California, [and] from California to other states in the western United States." He adds that if one considers a range of legal systems over the long term, "the picture that emerge[s] is of continual massive borrowing of rules." On this basis, he concludes that the movement of a rule or system of law from one country to another has been shown to be the most fertile source of legal development, as most changes in most systems are the result of borrowing. Watson (1993), pp. 107–108. And see Watson (1978), pp. 313–315 and 332. According to Rodolfo Sacco, "borrowing and imitation is of central importance to understanding the course of legal change" … "the birth of a rule or institution is a rarer phenomenon than its imitation." Sacco (1991), pp. 394 and 397.

G. Mousourakis, *Traversing Legal Traditions*, Springer Textbooks in Law,
https://doi.org/10.1007/978-3-031-94669-1_12

are most suitable for borrowing, and whether foreign legal rules and institutions can be incorporated with or without modification.

Legal transplantation can occur in both voluntary and involuntary settings. In voluntary transplantation, a nation or jurisdiction actively chooses to adopt external legal models to achieve specific objectives, such as modernization, economic reform, or alignment with international standards. In contrast, involuntary legal transplantation occurs under conditions of conquest, colonization, or external imposition, where a dominant power enforces its legal framework on the subordinated territory. This often disregards the cultural, social, or traditional practices of the local population. While voluntary transplantation typically involves adaptation to local needs, involuntary transplantation often leads to resistance, legal pluralism, or the marginalization of local legal traditions.

Notably, territorial expansion via military conquest did not universally result in the imposition of the conqueror's laws on subjugated populations. For instance, under Roman, Germanic, and Islamic rule, subject populations often retained their own legal systems, according to the 'principle of the personality of law'. This principle allowed different groups within the same territory to be governed by their respective laws based on identity or community affiliation rather than territorial jurisdiction. In some situations, however, direct imposition of the conqueror's laws did occur, as exemplified by the introduction of Spanish law in South America following colonization. Additionally, there were cases where the conquering nation's legal system was implemented partially or indirectly. During British and French colonial expansions, for example, the colonial powers often incorporated elements of their own legal frameworks into the legal systems of the territories they controlled, creating hybrid systems that, while adapted to local conditions, remained heavily influenced by the legal principles and structures of the colonial powers' metropolitan systems. This selective or adapted approach reflects a nuanced form of legal transplantation, which could combine metropolitan legal concepts with local norms to varying degrees, often serving the administrative and economic interests of the colonial rulers.

Voluntary legal transplantation can be initiated by any branch of government, including legislatures, courts, or administrative bodies. Legislative actions hold significant potential for legal transplantation due to the legislature's extensive authority to enact and implement legal reforms. Perhaps the most striking examples of legal transplantation via legislation occur during transitional periods in a nation's history, when political-legal systems undergo profound transformation and legislation becomes the primary instrument for change. A nation in the process of enacting a new constitution is particularly susceptible to external influences, often due to a desire to abandon norms associated with overthrown political regimes or a disappointing constitutional past. For example, after World War II, both Germany and Japan adopted new constitutions drafted with the assistance and under the guidance of the victorious powers, particularly the United States. Similarly, legislative transplantation has accompanied the establishment of legal systems in countries emerging from colonialism or, later, from communist regimes.

For example, the legal systems of Latin American countries post-independence were significantly shaped by European legal frameworks, with the French and German civil codes serving as primary models. As these nations sought to modernize and establish cohesive legal systems, they looked to established European codes to ensure their laws would be comprehensive, structured, and aligned with Western legal standards.[2] In the 1960s, many newly independent nations adopted legal systems modelled on those of their former colonial rulers. This Western legal framework was promoted as a key factor for the development and modernization of these states, offering a structured legal foundation seen as integral to economic and social progress. However, this adoption has faced substantial criticism, as the Western legal models often failed to align with the unique socio-cultural contexts of the recipient countries. The critique highlights that legal systems must be culturally sensitive and adaptable to be effective, rather than a one-size-fits-all solution transplanted from entirely different legal and cultural environments.[3]

Following the fall of communist regimes in Eastern Europe, transitioning former communist states underwent substantial legal transformations, implementing extensive reforms in both public and private law. In public law, the focus was predominantly on constitutional reform, aiming to establish democratic governance structures, safeguard human rights, and promote checks and balances within the government. These new constitutions typically embodied principles of rule of law, transparency, and accountability, with many countries adopting a separation of powers among the executive, legislative, and judicial branches to counter the concentration of power characteristic of their former regimes. Meanwhile, in private law, reforms targeted the creation of legal frameworks that could support a market economy. This included revising property rights, contract law, and corporate regulations to facilitate private ownership, foreign investment, and free enterprise. The combined reforms were instrumental in transitioning these countries from centrally planned economies to market-driven ones, aligning their legal systems more closely with those of Western democracies and supporting their aspirations to integrate with international organizations, such as the European Union.[4]

In the 1980s and 1990s, China pursued extensive legislative reforms to modernize its legal infrastructure, aligning it with its rapidly transitioning market-oriented economy. This shift was crucial as China opened up to foreign investments and integrated more deeply into the global economy. These reforms primarily focused on creating a stable legal environment that could attract and reassure foreign investors, thus facilitating sustained economic growth. By drawing insights from international standards and working closely with foreign legal experts, China was able to craft laws that encouraged foreign direct investment and streamlined business

[2] See, in general, Mirow (2000, 2001, 2004).

[3] See Berkowitz et al. (2003).

[4] Consider, e.g., Ajani (1995).

regulations, providing clearer property rights, contractual protections, and dispute resolution mechanisms.[5]

The tendency to borrow foreign legal concepts and institutions varies according to the socio-cultural and political context, as well as the specific subject matter of the legislation. In particular, legal areas where a system encounters novel challenges—lacking relevant prior experience—tend to be more susceptible to borrowing from foreign systems. For example, technological innovations such as artificial intelligence and new reproductive technologies often prompt legislators to seek models from other jurisdictions. Additionally, economic competition between countries frequently drives the search for legal inspiration abroad, especially in fields like tax legislation and special investment laws, which are crucial for competitive economies.[6] Another form of externally influenced legislation arises from the requirements of international treaties that mandate or encourage contracting parties to adopt harmonized laws. Finally, some legislative acts are motivated by the desire to facilitate global or regional legal harmonization, aiming to reduce disparities in national laws and address conflicts in areas such as intellectual property rights or internet law.

A legislator's willingness to adopt a foreign legal rule is often influenced by considerations of economic efficiency. As Ugo Mattei observes, the adoption of foreign legal rules usually results from a competition in which each legal system offers distinct solutions to a specific problem. In this 'market of legal culture', where rule providers aim to satisfy demand, the most efficient rule ultimately prevails.[7] According to Mattei, from the perspective of a particular legal system, 'efficiency' refers to whatever improves the system's functionality by reducing transaction costs. Mattei's approach, which exemplifies a recent trend toward combining comparative law and economics, may be seen as a narrower version of functionalism. Rather than focusing on social functions in general, it emphasizes a specific function: the economic efficiency of a legal rule or institution. However, Mattei recognizes that diversity in legal systems does not necessarily imply inefficiency. Legal systems may reach varying solutions to a common legal issue, yet these approaches can be equally valid without affecting the efficiency of outcomes. This implies that the effectiveness of a legal response is not always bound to a singular method; multiple pathways can lead to satisfactory, functional results. By allowing alternative solutions, legal systems retain flexibility and adaptability, demonstrating that efficiency in law isn't solely a product of uniformity but can also emerge from context-specific adaptations.

As noted in Chap. 4, judges occasionally turn to foreign legal systems for guidance, particularly when facing complex or unprecedented cases. However, since judges are typically expected to apply existing legal frameworks rather than create new ones, the use of foreign legal materials is generally limited to interpreting

[5] See Seidman and Seidman (1996).

[6] Consider on this issue Avi-Yonah (2000); Charny (2000).

[7] See Mattei (1994). Consider also Mattei and Pulitini (1991).

current laws amid legal ambiguities caused by conflicting rulings. In other words, judges are not permitted to engage in legal transplantation that would necessitate institutional reform or lack a foundation in established, binding norms within the domestic legal system. Constitutional norms, especially those related to individual or collective rights, are particularly susceptible to judicial interpretation through reference to international and foreign legal standards due to their often vague wording and the expectation of alignment with international human rights conventions.[8] Additionally, when courts encounter novel issues—those beyond the scope of both existing legislation and judicial precedent—they frequently turn to foreign law resources for guidance. Generally, courts find it easier to draw on precedents from legal systems that belong to the same legal tradition as their own. However, a potential concern with judicial transplantation of legal norms is that it requires broad judicial discretion regarding when and from which jurisdictions to borrow.

The practice of legal transplantation by the executive branch is an important yet frequently overlooked aspect of contemporary comparative law. While administrators are traditionally not considered lawmakers, they play a role in generating new legal norms through two primary channels: by introducing legislation that originates from executive initiatives and by adopting administrative models from other countries. Notably, significant legislative reforms are often proposed and drafted by the executive's professional staff, who may incorporate foreign legal materials they consider beneficial. Indirect transplantation also occurs when government agencies introduce new governance methods—such as outsourcing, privatization, and other administrative innovations—from abroad. Although these initiatives are technically administrative decisions and lack explicit normative content, they are frequently accompanied by a tendency to import the legal frameworks developed in the donor country to support the respective administrative model. A key concern with transplantation through administrative channels is its potential conflict with democratic principles, as administrative decisions often lack transparency and are generally exempt from public scrutiny.

The process of legal transplantation may be either interrupted or accelerated by revolutionary change. A revolution can be defined as a profound historical event that redefines the identity of a socio-political system, primarily by reshaping the ideological foundations upon which its legitimacy rests and thus reorienting its direction. A shift in legitimacy due to revolutionary change represents the most radical transformation a socio-political system can experience.[9] When such a change drives

[8] Consider on this matter Neuman (2004).

[9] Legitimacy represents the foundation upon which a socio-political system's authority is justified and accepted within a specific place, time, and community. This legitimacy can arise from various sources, reflecting the values and beliefs that support the system's power. In democratic systems, legitimacy is typically based on social consensus and the will of the people, while in theocratic states, it may derive from a divine or transcendental command, viewed as an unassailable source of authority. In other cases, legitimacy might even rest on coercion or arbitrary enforcement, where power is maintained through oppression rather than broad acceptance. The orientation of a system, meanwhile, reflects its ideological direction, which can range from a laissez-faire, open-ended approach—favoring minimal state intervention—to a centrally planned, communist model, or

the transformation of a country's legal system, it may cause that system to diverge from or converge with others, depending on the ideological alignments and disparities between nations' socio-political and economic structures as reflected in their legal frameworks.[10]

As the above discussion suggests, legal transplantation is more widespread and multifaceted than often assumed. While it is commonly thought to involve only lawmakers and judges, this practice also extends to the executive branch and administrative officials, who play a significant role in adopting and integrating foreign legal elements. Consequently, focusing research solely on legislation and judicial writings could yield an incomplete understanding of the dynamics behind legal changes. A comprehensive approach that encompasses the roles of diverse governmental actors beyond the legislative and judicial branches, as well as the impact of socio-political changes, is crucial for a deeper understanding of how legal systems evolve and adapt under external influences.[11]

Transplant bias, a core concept in Watson's theory that legal change largely arises from the adoption or imitation of external norms, refers to a legal system's receptivity to foreign laws independent of an exhaustive evaluation of all possible alternatives. This receptivity varies among legal systems and is influenced by factors such as shared linguistic traditions with a potential donor system, the educational backgrounds and experiences of legal professionals within the recipient system, and, most importantly, the general prestige of the donor system.[12] The wholesale adoption of a foreign legal code exemplifies transplant bias most clearly. Watson posits that juristic doctrine—the academic and theoretical underpinnings of

numerous hybrids in between. This orientation defines the system's economic, social, and political goals and its methods of governance. Efficiency, on the other hand, refers to the overall effectiveness of the system in achieving its objectives, maintaining order, and ensuring stability. For a system to remain stable over time, the underlying basis of its legitimacy and the direction of its orientation must be durable and resilient. Gradual, non-revolutionary changes—such as policy adjustments or minor reforms—are generally conducted within the bounds of the existing legitimacy framework, so they do not undermine the system's fundamental authority. In these cases, any shifts in orientation must be aligned with the established legitimacy criteria, ensuring continuity and preserving stability. However, revolutionary change can occur when there is a profound crisis that disrupts either the authority or efficiency of a system. Such a collapse might stem from a drastic failure in governance, economic breakdown, or widespread public discontent, causing a loss of confidence in both the system's legitimacy and its ability to function effectively. This rupture opens the way for significant transformation, often involving a complete redefinition of legitimacy and orientation in the wake of systemic failure.

[10] On the role of revolution as a factor explaining the divergence or convergence of legal systems see Rodière (1979), p. 21.

[11] See on this matter Siems (2007).

[12] According to Watson, in addition to the authority and prestige of the legal system from which rules are borrowed, several factors influence which rules are likely to be adopted from other legal systems: (a) accessibility, meaning the rule is documented in a way that is easy to locate, understand, and readily available; (b) habit, where a legal system repeatedly used as a reference becomes a habitual source, encouraging further borrowing even if the rule adopted is not entirely appropriate; and (c) chance, such as a particular source being available in a specific library or lawyers from one country being trained in another's legal system.

law—is particularly susceptible to external influence because it often draws heavily from comparative studies, historical models, and the prestige of foreign legal traditions. This openness stems from the theoretical nature of doctrine, which is not immediately constrained by the practical demands of the domestic legal system. In contrast, judicial precedent, being grounded in practical adjudication and case law, is typically less influenced by foreign transplant bias. Judges, tasked with resolving real disputes, tend to critically evaluate foreign legal rules before adopting them, ensuring their relevance and compatibility with the domestic legal framework. Watson suggests that this evaluative process often filters out incongruous elements, as judicial decisions must consider local legal principles, societal norms, and the overarching coherence of the legal system. This dynamic illustrates the interplay between legal theory and practice, showing how foreign influence can permeate differently depending on the context—freely in doctrine and more cautiously in judicial precedent.

The perceived quality and prestige of a donor legal system play a crucial role in its adoption and integration across diverse societies because these attributes significantly influence how the recipient society views the legitimacy and utility of the foreign legal framework. A donor legal system that is associated with successful governance, economic prosperity, or historical influence often gains prestige, making it more attractive for emulation or adoption. Moreover, the quality of the legal system—reflected in its coherence, adaptability, and fairness—affects its practical implementation within the recipient society. Roman law serves as a prime example, with its enduring impact largely attributed to its codification under Emperor Justinian in the sixth century AD. This codification, known as the *Corpus Iuris Civilis*, became a cornerstone of Western legal tradition, providing a sophisticated legal structure adaptable across diverse socio-economic contexts. Throughout the Middle Ages and Renaissance, most of Continental Europe embraced Roman law, including vast areas of Germany, where it remained an active source of legal authority until the late nineteenth century. The endurance of Roman law is remarkable, spanning Catholic, Calvinist, and Lutheran regions, agricultural societies, mercantile hubs, and eventually industrialized nations. This legal tradition, initially adopted in Europe, spread globally to regions such as South America, Quebec, Louisiana, and parts of Asia and Africa, either directly or through European-influenced codes. One primary reason for Roman law's adoption was its comprehensive structure and established authority, which offered a compelling alternative to the fragmented legal systems of the medieval period, where centralized governments and fully developed legal frameworks were often absent. Additionally, the *Corpus Iuris Civilis* inspired a codification trend among emerging nation-states, aligning with the ambitions of jurists who sought to systematize and modernize their own legal studies to reflect this respected model. Ultimately, Roman law's conceptual framework, characterized by its logical organization and internal coherence, provided a foundation for Western legal systems that continues to serve as a *tertium comparationis*—a shared point of reference for structuring legally organized social relationships.

According to Watson, transplant bias interacts with multiple factors, including the source of law, pressure forces, opposition forces, law-shaping lawyers, the discretion factor, the generality factor, inertia, and felt needs.[13] The evolution of a legal system is shaped by the primary source of law, whether custom, statute, judicial precedent, or juristic doctrine. Generally, precedent-based law evolves more slowly than statutory law, as it relies on real events, particularly litigated cases, to drive change.[14] The term 'pressure force' refers to organized groups who believe they would benefit from a legal change. Watson argues that the power of such groups to effect legal change depends on their social and economic standing and their ability to influence the relevant source of law. Legislative development is typically more responsive to pressure forces than judicial precedent. In contrast, 'opposition force' represents groups who fear that a legal change would harm their interests. These groups often resist change out of concern for a potential loss of power, prestige, or wealth. 'Law-shaping lawyers' are the legal elite who, through their expertise, imagination, training, and experience, significantly influence legal changes. Watson notes that lawyers are well-positioned to act as both pressure and opposition forces, given their intimate knowledge of how the legal system operates and how changes in the law impact their interests.[15] The 'discretion factor' involves the implicit or explicit latitude to enforce or withhold enforcement of the law, or to assert or refrain from asserting one's legal rights. Watson describes this factor as reflecting "the extent to which the rules permit variations, or can be evaded, or need not or will not be invoked."[16] Some level of discretion is, according to Watson, inherent in any mature legal system. The 'generality factor' refers to the degree to which legal rules apply to multiple groups, transactions, or factual situations. Watson observes that the broader the scope of a legal rule, the harder it is to tailor the rule precisely to the circumstances of each regulated entity or event. The broader the scope of a proposed legal change, the more challenging it becomes to secure consensus on the new rule, thus complicating legal reform. 'Inertia' reflects the absence of a strong and sustained drive within society and its ruling elites to achieve the most 'satisfactory' rule. For legal change to happen, a sufficiently powerful impulse, typically driven by a pressure force acting on a source of law, must overcome this inertia. Lastly, 'felt needs' are the objectives recognized and deemed appropriate by a pressure force seeking legal change. Watson acknowledges that understanding felt needs can be complex and requires examining words, actions, and outcomes: what the pressure force claims is needed, its actions before and after the legal change, and how the change ultimately impacts its interests.

Watson argues that history demonstrates three key points: (i) transplanting legal rules between systems is socially feasible, even when there are substantial material and cultural differences between the donor and recipient societies; (ii) no area of law is particularly resistant to transformation through foreign

[13] For a closer view at this issue see Watson (1978).

[14] Watson (1978), p. 323.

[15] On the role of the culture of the legal elite in shaping law's internal development, see Watson (2001), p. 264.

[16] Watson (1978), p. 330.

influence—challenging sociologically oriented arguments that culturally rooted laws are more resistant to change than laws seen as merely instrumental;[17] and (iii) recipient legal systems do not need to understand the original context or development of transplanted laws.[18] Social, economic, and political factors influence the shape of the resulting laws only to the extent that these factors are within the consciousness of lawmakers—specifically, the lawyers and jurists who control the mechanisms of legal change.[19] While societal pressures may increase lawmakers' awareness of these factors, the lawmakers' responses remain conditioned by legal tradition, guided by their expertise and knowledge of both domestic and foreign laws.[20] Societal pressures may prompt legal change, but new legal rules are typically adopted from familiar systems and modified, often without a full appreciation of local conditions. Watson emphasizes that law largely functions at the ideological level, existing as an autonomous discipline that is often resistant to external influences. Nevertheless, he acknowledges the intrinsic connection between law and society, despite a considerable discord between the law society ideally envisions for itself and the law it actually possesses. Legal theory, particularly when grounded in comparative law, aims to illuminate this relationship and, more specifically, to clarify the discrepancies between the law as it currently stands and the ideal law that would align with societal demands or those of its dominant groups.[21]

According to Otto Kahn-Freund, there are varying 'degrees of transferability' among legal rules. All legal rules can, to some extent, be detached from their

---

[17] See on this issue Levy (1950).

[18] Watson (1976), pp. 80–81.

[19] According to Watson, "It should be obvious that law exists and flourishes at the level of idea, and is part of culture. As culture it operates in at least three spheres of differing size, one within another. The spheres are: the population at large, lawyers and lawmakers. By 'lawmakers' I mean the members of that elite group who in a particular society have their hands on the levers of legal change, whether as legislators, judges, or jurists. For a rule to become law it must be institutionalized. It must go through the stages required for achieving the status of law. Because lawyers and lawmakers are involved in all those processes a rule cannot become law without being subject to legal culture'. Watson (1983), pp. 1152–1153.

[20] Watson speaks of an 'internal legal logic' or 'the internal logic of the legal tradition' governing legal development. See Watson (1985), pp. 21–22. In contrast to Watson's view of law as developing autonomously through the influence of legal elites, proponents of autopoiesis theory, like Niklas Luhmann, perceive law as evolving independently as a self-referential system. Autopoiesis theory suggests that law is a functionally unique communication system that operates by processing legal communications and reproducing itself within its own framework. Rather than being shaped primarily by external actors or social elites, law is seen to evolve according to its own internal logic and rules, creating and maintaining boundaries that distinguish legal discourse from other social systems. This self-sustaining mechanism allows law to function as a separate sphere that selectively interacts with society, yet operates through its specialized language and norms. On the autopoiesis theory see, in general, Luhmann (1995); Teubner (1993); Priban and Nelken (2001). On the implications of the autopoiesis theory for comparative law see Teubner (1998).

[21] Watson's theory of legal transplants has been subjected to strong criticism by scholars who insist on functional-sociological explanations of law. See, in general, Abel (1982); Legrand (1997, 2001); Wise (1990); Nelken (2003). On the view that law is the result of the social needs of a given society see, in general, Friedmann (1972); Damaska (1986).

socio-political contexts, making legal transplants across different socio-political environments theoretically possible. However, because laws become disconnected to differing degrees, some are more likely to endure and adapt to new contexts than others. Kahn-Freund further argues that socio-political and institutional factors shape the extent of integration between law and society. These factors include the ideological function of law, the distribution of state power, and pressures from non-state interest groups. For transplanted laws to be effective, they must align with the host country's dominant political-legal ideology, conform to its legal frameworks and power structures, and attract sufficient support from key interest groups, such as market-supporting organizations (e.g., banks, trade unions, and political parties).[22]

Examining the fates of legal transplants across diverse socio-cultural, economic, and political contexts is essential for assessing the desirability and applicability of these transplants in legislative and judicial practices. While it may be true that socio-cultural and other differences between exporting and importing countries do not necessarily prevent the successful transplantation of legal rules and institutions, this process is not straightforward. Legal rules can indeed be adapted as models for development in societies with very different contexts. However, one must remember that an imported legal norm is often 'indigenized' to take on a unique local meaning, shaped by the host culture's intrinsic capacity to reinterpret foreign elements. Even if there is little difference in the formal wording of a legal rule between a donor and a recipient country, it does not follow that the practical legal realities or everyday practices in both countries will be identical or even similar. The legal realities in the host country may differ substantially in how individuals—including judges and legal practitioners—interpret, construe, and apply the law, as well as in the reasoning behind judicial decisions.[23] Furthermore, the role of statutory law in the recipient country may be less prominent than in the exporting country, with customary practices holding greater influence. In practice, this means that socio-cultural norms may deter individuals from pursuing legal claims or even from utilizing a court decision that supports such claims. Consequently, it is unwise to evaluate a borrowed legal rule or institution from the perspective of one's own legal culture, as this approach risks creating a misleading impression of similarity between the legal systems that may not, in fact, exist. A contextual and culturally sensitive

[22] Kahn-Freund (1974), pp. 12–14. Consider also Stein (1977).

[23] For example, consider the complexities involved in interpreting the concept of individual freedom as it appears in international human rights treaties. In Western societies, individual freedom is often rooted in Enlightenment ideals, emphasizing autonomy, personal rights, and self-expression. Conversely, in China and other Asian cultures, the idea of freedom is deeply influenced by a collectivist framework, which prioritizes social harmony, family duties, and community over individual desires. This divergence goes beyond political systems and reflects fundamental cultural ideologies. It reveals the challenge of applying universal human rights principles in a way that respects these distinct cultural values, underscoring that 'freedom' may not be universally understood or valued in the same way.

approach is therefore essential to accurately understand the impact and functionality of legal transplants in foreign settings.[24]

12.2 Legal Transplants and the Meeting of Traditions: A Short History of Japanese Law

Japan's legal system is frequently regarded as *sui generis* in comparative legal studies due to its distinctive fusion of indigenous traditions and foreign influences, adapted to its unique cultural and societal context. Historically, Japan's legal culture was profoundly influenced by Chinese Confucian principles and legal norms, which emphasized moral governance and the maintenance of societal harmony. During the Meiji era (1868–1912), Japan undertook a deliberate modernization of its legal system, adopting a civil law framework modelled on Continental European systems, particularly those of Germany and France. This period marked a transformative effort to align with Western legal standards while preserving national identity. Following World War II, Japan underwent sweeping reforms under Allied occupation, led predominantly by the United States, which introduced elements of the Anglo-American legal tradition into its legal system. Despite these substantial changes, Japanese law retains characteristics that reflect its societal values, such as an emphasis on harmony and social order, which often prioritize informal dispute resolution over litigation. This ability to synthesize indigenous traditions with foreign legal frameworks, while maintaining a cohesive and functional legal order, highlights Japan's distinctive position in the global legal landscape. This section adopts a historical approach to contextualize Japanese law, aiming to illuminate the intricate relationship between diverse legal influences and the country's social and cultural norms.

12.2.1 Divisions in Japanese Legal History

Japanese legal development is traditionally divided into distinct periods, marked by three major receptions of foreign legal influence: the Chinese reception (702), the European reception (1868), and the Anglo-American reception (1945).[25]

The extensive period between 702 and 1868 is further subdivided into two significant phases. The first is the early Chinese reception period (702–1185), during

---

[24] As Alan Watson has remarked, "except where the systems are closely related, the differences in legal values may be so extreme as to render virtually meaningless the discovery that systems have the same or a different rule". Watson (1993), p. 5. And see Ewald (1995). On the topic of legal transplantation see, in general, Siems (2018), p. 231 ff; Graziadei (2009, 2019); Örücü (2002); Gillespie (2001).

[25] Oda (2021), p. 90. Consider also Dean (2002), pp. 55–56.

which Chinese legal principles and administrative structures were introduced and adapted to Japan's socio-political context. The second phase, known as the feudal or harmonization period (1185–1868), represents a gradual integration of these imported legal frameworks with indigenous Japanese customs and practices. This phase coincides with Japan's feudal era and is further divided into three sub-periods: the Shikimoku period (1185–1467), encompassing the Kamakura and Muromachi regimes and characterized by the development of the legal codes that established foundational laws for the feudal samurai society; the Kokuho period (1467–1603), often referred to as the Sengoku or 'Warring States' period in Japanese history, marked by the decentralization of laws and the emergence of domain-specific regulations to govern local territories amid political fragmentation; and the Tokugawa period (1603–1868), during which Japan implemented a highly centralized legal structure, with codified laws reinforcing order and control over the feudal hierarchy.[26] This trajectory highlights the dynamic evolution of Japanese law, from external influences to localized adaptations and codifications, reflecting the broader cultural and political transformations of each era.

12.3 The Chinese Reception Period

Before the seventh century, Japanese society was organized around a clan- and tribe-based system known as the *uji* system. The *uji* were familial clans, each headed by a patriarch who acted as the leader. These clans were hierarchical and held both political and religious power within their respective regions.[27] Law was predominantly unwritten, relying on customary practices and clan-based traditions, and it was closely linked to the Shinto religion.[28] The administration of justice likely revolved around arbitration rooted in kinship ties and established norms, supplemented by ad hoc political commands when necessary. This approach provided a rudimentary framework for rule without the need for formalized written or institutional laws.[29]

[26] Henderson (1952), p. 88.

[27] In the late fourth to early fifth century AD, the Yamato clan emerged as the dominant power among the various clans in Japan, with its chieftain being recognized as the supreme leader. Over time, the authority of this leader was formalized, and the chieftain came to be regarded as the Emperor of Japan (*Tennō*).

[28] Shinto, an indigenous religion of Japan, centres around the worship of kami—gods or spirits believed to dwell in natural objects such as mountains, trees, and rocks, or manifest in phenomena like wind and thunder. Given the profound reliance of early Japanese society on the rice harvest, the development of a nature-centric religion seems almost inevitable. Notably, it is believed that the role of emperor originated as that of Shinto's chief priest, underscoring the deep connection between the faith and Japan's early societal structure. See, in general, Mason and Caiger (1997), pp. 32–34.

[29] See Haley (1991b), p. 29.

The introduction of Buddhism to Japan in the mid-sixth century, brought from the Korean Peninsula, marked a transformative period in the country's cultural and spiritual development. Actively supported by the ruling elite, Buddhism was seen as a tool to centralize power and bolster state authority. Alongside Buddhism, the adoption of the Chinese written script profoundly influenced Japanese administration, literature, and communication. Additionally, Confucian ethics and Taoist principles enriched Japan's philosophical and political foundations. This era thus established a syncretic blending of indigenous Shinto beliefs with imported religious and philosophical traditions, shaping the trajectory of Japanese culture and governance.

While Shinto and Buddhism came to jointly shape rituals and beliefs, Confucianism, with its emphasis on hierarchy, filial piety, and governance through moral virtue, provided the structural underpinnings for Japan's administrative and legal frameworks.[30] In 604 AD, Prince Shotoku, serving as Regent to Empress

[30] Confucianism is an ethical and philosophical system rooted in the teachings of Confucius (551–479 BC), a Chinese philosopher and educator. It encompasses a complex system of thought that integrates moral principles, social norms, political theories, and philosophical ideas, with elements that have sometimes been regarded as quasi-religious. One of the cornerstones of the Confucian worldview is the concept of 'cosmic harmony'—a universe that is harmoniously ordered and well-balanced. Individuals are expected to maintain this harmony by avoiding mutual conflicts and adhering to their societal roles. They should conscientiously follow the ethical rules of conduct specific to their position, which are rooted in established customs. These rules are intricate and tailored to the diverse relationships and situations between individuals. Confucianism emphasizes governance through moral rules (*li*) rather than legal rules enforced by state authority (*fa*). Confucius viewed statutes and courts of law as a necessary evil to address criminal behaviour but deemed them unnecessary for regulating relationships among virtuous individuals. This suggests that criminal law is indispensable for punishing wrongdoers, whereas private law is superfluous. According to Confucian thought, if everyone adhered to moral principles, disputes and conflicts would naturally be avoided. In essence, Confucianism asserts that social order is best achieved not through rigid legal enforcement and coercion, but through the collective recognition and practice of appropriate and ethical behaviour. In this respect, the appropriate basis for resolving disputes lies in conciliation and compromise, guided by ethical principles rooted in both human sentiment and reason. The resolution of disputes aims to restore harmony, ensuring that no one is left feeling like either a winner or a loser. In the Confucian scheme, moral education through ritual is an ideal form of social regulation. Through ritual formalized behaviour becomes progressively internalized and individual desires are channelled. Shaping rituals in a way that leads to a healthy society is a chief purpose of Confucian philosophy. Human relationships are central to Confucianism. Particular duties arise from one's situation in relation to others. Social harmony—the ultimate goal of Confucianism—results in part from each individual knowing their place in the social order and fulfilling their role effectively. Confucius never explicitly stated whether man is born good or evil. Instead, he observed that "by nature, men are similar; by practice, they are set apart." This suggests that Confucius perceived all men as having intrinsic similarities at birth but believed that individuals are shaped and differentiated through study and social practices. The concept of humaneness (*rén*) forms the foundation of Confucian political theory. It presupposes an autocratic ruler who refrains from acting inhumanely toward his subjects. An inhumane ruler risks losing the 'Mandate of Heaven', the divine right to rule. A ruler who loses this mandate is no longer entitled to obedience. Conversely, a ruler who governs humanely and prioritizes the well-being of the people must be strictly obeyed, as his benevolence demonstrates that he has been granted the Mandate of Heaven. While Confucius himself said little about the will of the people, his prominent

Suiko, introduced the Seventeen-Article Constitution, widely regarded as Japan's first attempt at a nationwide codification of legal and ethical principles. Rather than a legal code in the modern sense, this document functioned as a moral and political guideline aimed at promoting harmony and good governance within the court and among officials. It emphasized Confucian and Buddhist ideals, such as the importance of harmony (*wa*), respect for hierarchical authority, and proper conduct among officials.[31] Notably, it reflected a move toward centralization and the development of a more structured governmental system under imperial authority. This constitution is a foundational document in Japanese history, marking the early influence of Chinese philosophical and administrative ideas on Japan.

The Taika Reforms, initiated around the middle of the seventh century, were a series of political and administrative changes aimed at consolidating imperial authority in Japan. These reforms sought to centralize power around the emperor by weakening the influence of regional authorities, particularly the clan-based aristocracy, and implementing a more structured governance system. Heavily inspired by the administrative and legal frameworks of the T'ang Dynasty (AD 619–906) in China, the Taika Reforms laid the groundwork for a centralized state, including reforms related to land ownership and taxation.[32] Although these measures were not codified as a formal legal code, they significantly influenced the development of later legal codes.[33] The reforms were implemented progressively over several years and represented a transformative period in Japan's history, aligning its governance more closely with Chinese bureaucratic models.[34]

In AD 702, Emperor Monmu promulgated a formal written code of law known as the *Taihō Ritsuryō* or *Taihō Code*. This legal framework combined two elements: *ritsu*, which refers to penal law, and *ryō*, which pertains to administrative law.[35] Heavily influenced by Chinese legal sources, particularly those of the T'ang Dynasty, the *Taihō Code* also reflected Confucian and Buddhist principles. However, significant adaptations were made to suit the unique socio-political structure and cultural context of Japan at the time.

In AD 718, the *Taihō* Code was updated and amended by the *Yōrō* Code (*Yōrō Ritsuryō*), which officially came into force in AD 757. While the *Taihō* Code laid

---

follower Mencius asserted on one occasion that the people's opinions on certain significant matters should be considered. Confucianism has profoundly influenced the cultural, social, and political development of East Asian countries, including China, Korea, Japan, and Vietnam, shaping their values, governance, and interpersonal relationships over centuries. For a closer look at Confucian philosophy see, in general, Gardner (2014); Littlejohn (2011); Yao (2000). And see Gardner (2007).

[31] See de Bary et al. (2001), pp. 40–42; Sansom (1974), pp. 73–74; Mason and Caiger (1997), pp. 40–42.

[32] Port (1996), p. 20.

[33] For a closer look at the Taika reforms see Mason and Caiger (1997), p. 42 ff.

[34] The central government in Japan adopted Chinese doctrines to unify the country, similar to how English kings used Norman law. However, while Japan's adoption was inspired by admiration for China's advanced culture, the Normans imposed their legal system on the Saxons through conquest. See Haley (1991b), p. 29.

[35] Sansom (1974), p. 111.

the foundation of the *ritsuryō* legal system, the *Yōrō* Code is particularly significant because much of it has been preserved, providing valuable insights into the legal and administrative framework of early Japan.[36] The *Yōrō* Code presents several intriguing facets. While it was rooted in Chinese models, it incorporated significant adaptations reflective of Japanese culture. For example, the severity of punishments prescribed by the law was reduced compared to those in Imperial China's legal system. The relatively light punishments in the Japanese *ritsuryō* system, compared to their Chinese counterpart, may be attributed to the strong Buddhist influence on Japanese officials and the fear of angry spirits (*goryō*), a concept influenced by native *Shinto* beliefs.[37] Another important difference between the Japanese system and its Chinese antecedents was the role of women. The status of women in the traditional Chinese Confucian system, as reflected in the laws of the T'ang Dynasty, was oppressive. In China at that time, women could not inherit property and lost all status in their ancestral clan upon marrying into their husband's clan. In Japan, however, women had inheritance rights, both as daughters and as spouses, and their family of origin continued to play a role in their lives after marriage.[38] Additionally, the Chinese political philosophy of the 'Mandate of Heaven', which allowed for the possibility of an emperor losing legitimacy, was not compatible with Japanese beliefs. In Japan, the emperor was considered to descend from an unbroken lineage tracing back to the founding deities of the nation, making such a concept unacceptable. The principles and structures outlined in the *Yōrō* Code influenced Japanese governance and legal practices for centuries, enduring in various forms until the Meiji Restoration in the late nineteenth century.[39]

Within two centuries of its promulgation, the *Yōrō Ritsuryō* Code began to lose its relevance as an increasing portion of the population came under the control of powerful and wealthy families, clans, and military leaders who acquired estates and offices through force and influence.[40] The *ritsuryō* system established a hereditary bureaucracy that served and supported a hereditary nobility, which in turn was sustained financially through taxes levied on land and agricultural production. This structure necessitated a system for identifying and managing productive farmland. Under the *ritsuryō* framework, farmers were allocated plots of land and granted what might today be considered ownership or usage rights. However, agricultural productivity often failed to increase at the same rate as taxation demands. As a result, many farmers struggled to meet their tax obligations, leading to widespread

---

[36] Sansom (1974), p. 115; Haley (1991b), pp. 29–30.

[37] One aspect of the Confucian system of punishments retained from China was that the relative status of the offender and the victim played a significant role in determining criminal sanctions. For example, it was far more reprehensible for a son to assault his father than the reverse, which might not have been considered an offense at all.

[38] Polygamy existed in both societies, particularly among the wealthy. In China, however, second wives were often treated as property and could be sold. In contrast, in Japan, second wives were not regarded as chattels; they had inheritance rights and were afforded legal protections.

[39] See Haley (1991b), pp. 29–30; Sansom (1974), p. 115.

[40] Mason and Caiger (1997), pp. 74–75.

financial hardship. This situation forced numerous farmers into a legal arrangement wherein landholdings became privatized and were placed under the protection of powerful aristocratic or religious institutions, effectively bypassing the *ritsuryō* taxation system. These private estates, known as *shōen* (manors), rapidly grew in power and influence, and their unchecked development significantly undermined the authority of the monarchy, contributing to political instability. The *shōen* system allowed farmers to avoid direct taxation from the central government, as the responsibility for taxes fell to the landowning lords. However, this arrangement often reduced farmers to the status of permanent, hereditary tenants, bound to the land they worked. This hierarchical structure, characterized by the farmers' dependency on their lords, persisted for centuries and significantly influenced Japan's feudal social and economic systems, with some elements extending into the modern era.[41]

While many Japanese adhered to the Buddhist principle of non-violence, the necessity of protecting *shōen* estates from attacks by neighbouring clans led to the rise of private soldiers. Over time, these soldiers evolved into a distinct and powerful social class known as the *samurai*, whose role in maintaining order and defending territories became integral to the socio-political landscape of Japan.

Interestingly, while *samurai* often operated outside formal legal frameworks and resisted governmental authority, their actions were guided by an internal moral and ethical code known as *bushidō*. This 'personal customary law' dictated principles of honour, chivalry, and a strong sense of duty and responsibility, ensuring their conduct adhered to specific ideals even in the absence of external legal enforcement. *Samurai* loyalty, or fealty, to their overlord was deeply embedded in a system of mutual obligations. Overlords secured their *samurai*'s loyalty through tangible rewards, typically land or monetary stipends, which ensured their service and allegiance. In return, *samurai* were bound by the principle of *on*—a concept deeply rooted in Japanese culture, signifying an obligation to repay the benevolence received from superiors. This reciprocal relationship of duty and reward not only reinforced the hierarchical structure of *samurai* society but also shaped broader Japanese societal values, promoting loyalty and duty to one's superiors as paramount virtues. This system became a cornerstone of social order and cohesion, influencing relationships far beyond the *samurai* class.[42]

As the centralized authority of the imperial government waned during the twelfth century, local lords, or *daimyō*, supported by private *samurai* armies, began asserting control over their territories. This decentralization of power led to frequent conflicts among these lords, plunging the realm into widespread insecurity. The feudal system evolved to address this instability. This period also saw the rise of the shogunate, a military government headed by the *shogun*,[43] which gradually became the

[41] On the *shōen* system see, in general, Sansom (1990), pp. 110–111; Haley (1991b), pp. 33–34.

[42] Hane and Perez (2013), pp. 3 and 23–24.

[43] The *shogun* was originally a military rank awarded only to individuals in the upper echelons of the military hierarchy. Prior to 1192, the holder of this rank was authorized to wage war against the Ainu, the indigenous people of Japan, as part of campaigns to capture their territory. This rank was typically revoked once the campaign was completed. However, in 1192, Minamoto no Yoritomo

de facto ruling authority, relegating the imperial court to a largely ceremonial role. The resulting political structure could best be characterized as a decentralized network of landed and familial authorities, each maintaining its own independent system of governance encompassing order, discipline, and dispute resolution. These systems were enforced through localized power structures, which relied on the principle of obedience to maintain control over their members, servants, and protégés. This feudal structure shaped Japan's unique fusion of military governance and aristocratic tradition, enduring until the Meiji Restoration in the late nineteenth century.

12.3.1 The Feudal Period

The history of Japanese feudalism reflects a unique synthesis of external influences and indigenous traditions. Initially, Japan adapted the sophisticated administrative framework and codified legal systems of China, blending these with its native clan-based society. These laws primarily focused on regulating land tenure, taxation, and governance, reflecting China's significant cultural and institutional impact. However, native Japanese traditions gradually reasserted themselves, leading to the erosion of purely Chinese influences. This shift became evident by the late twelfth century when Japan experienced a transformative civil war between the Minamoto and Taira clans. The Minamoto victory, led by Yoritomo, established a military government grounded in feudal principles, a model that shaped Japan's governance until its Westernization in the nineteenth century.[44] This government was headed by the *Shogun*, a military generalissimo, who nominally ruled under the Emperor but operated as the *de facto* ruler.

From 1185 to 1333, the Minamoto family consolidated power at Kamakura, successfully defending Japan from external threats such as Kublai Khan's Mongol invasions. This period also epitomized Japan's characteristic preference for indirect rule, as the *Shogun* himself was often managed by a regent.[45] The Kamakura era ended when the Ashikaga family assumed control, marking the beginning of a new phase in Japan's feudal history, known as the Muromachi or Ashikaga era (1333–1573).

Under the Ashikaga shoguns, Japan experienced significant cultural and economic growth. The arts flourished, and Japanese maritime trade expanded to keep pace with European developments, indicating a vibrant and outward-looking

---

was appointed as *shogun* with a broader mandate—not just to lead military campaigns but also to govern and maintain peace across Japan. This marked a significant shift, as the position of *shogun* became hereditary, transforming it into the cornerstone of a military government known as the *bakufu* (shogunate).

[44] Mason and Caiger (1997), p. 128 ff.

[45] Goodman (2003), pp. 11–12.

society. However, from around 1500, Japan's focus shifted inward due to nearly continuous civil war, which distracted its leaders from external affairs.[46]

The *Kokuhō* period (1467–1603), often referred to as the *Sengoku* or 'Warring States' period in Japanese history, was characterized by political fragmentation and the decentralization of authority. Central power, traditionally held by the Ashikaga shogunate, weakened significantly, leading to the rise of regional *daimyo* or feudal lords who established domain-specific regulations to maintain order and govern their territories effectively.[47] These local laws were tailored to address the specific needs and challenges of their regions, reflecting the practical necessities of self-governance in the absence of a strong central authority. This legal decentralization allowed each domain to develop its administrative structures and policies, often emphasizing agricultural productivity, military readiness, and local justice systems. The period thus represents a shift from a unified legal framework to a more fragmented, regionally autonomous legal landscape.

In the early seventeenth century, Japan embarked on a distinctive historical path that set it apart from other nations. After a series of civil wars, the Tokugawa family consolidated power in 1603 when Tokugawa Ieyasu was appointed as *Shōgun*. Ieyasu established the military capital in Edo (modern-day Tokyo), while the imperial capital remained in Kyoto. To secure loyalty, he distributed land and prime domains to *daimyo* who supported his regime. Concerned that Christian missionaries might pave the way for European colonization, Ieyasu and his successors enacted stringent measures to suppress Christianity, expel most foreigners, and enforce a policy of national seclusion (*sakoku*).[48] This era of isolation, known as the Tokugawa or Edo period, lasted over 250 years and brought enduring internal peace and stability to Japan. This was achieved through centralized feudal control, with the *daimyo* subordinated to the shogunate and the *samurai* transitioning to administrative roles rather than engaging in active warfare. This prolonged peace deeply influenced Japanese society, economy, and culture, creating a foundation that would later support the country's modernization efforts in the late nineteenth century.[49]

During the feudal era, the *ritsuryō* system technically remained in place but gradually diminished in importance as imperial authority weakened. This decline

---

[46] The mid-sixteenth century marked a pivotal moment with Japan's first encounters with the West, particularly through Portuguese traders and Jesuit missionaries. By the century's end, the influence of these missionaries, led by St. Francis Xavier, was profound, with over 300,000 Japanese converts to Christianity. This period reflects both the openness of Japanese society to external influences and the beginnings of significant cultural and religious exchanges that would shape Japan's interactions with the world.

[47] Goodman (2003), p. 12.

[48] Japan's isolationist policy involved (a) banning Christianity; (b) progressively limiting foreign ships' access to Japanese ports; (c) prohibiting Japanese citizens from traveling abroad, a crime punishable by death; and (d) reducing and eventually ceasing diplomatic and trade relations with most foreign nations. Limited trade was permitted with the Dutch and Chinese, restricted to Dejima, a small artificial island in Nagasaki, where interactions were closely monitored. See Hane and Perez (2013), p. 18; Mason and Caiger (1997), p. 202 ff.

[49] Mason and Caiger (1997), p. 190 ff.

coincided with the rise of a military feudal system, which introduced its own rules and localized governance structures. The shogunate system consolidated this new order, effectively bypassing the centralized control envisioned under *ritsuryō* law and prioritizing military and regional governance over the decrees of the imperial court. Additionally, Buddhist temples and monasteries played an increasingly prominent role during this period. These religious institutions not only shaped Japan's cultural and spiritual life but also wielded considerable economic and political power. Many large temples developed their own internal legal systems to govern monastic communities and manage their extensive landholdings. These internal legal frameworks further fragmented Japan's legal landscape, diminishing the relevance of the *ritsuryō* system.

During the Kamakura period, the Hōjō clan, acting as regents for the shoguns, significantly solidified the centralized governance structure that had begun under the Minamoto clan. By around 1225, they enhanced this structure by establishing the *Hyōjōsho* (High Court of Justice), a judicial institution designed to handle legal disputes and administrative matters. Shortly thereafter, a lower court system was also instituted, broadening the reach and effectiveness of Kamakura's judicial authority. To ensure efficiency and expertise, the Hōjō clan actively recruited skilled bureaucrats and legal scholars from Kyoto, the imperial capital, whose expertise also trickled down to the courts of local warlords.

The Hōjō Institutes of Judicature (also known as *Goseibai Shikimoku* or *Joei Shikimoku*) of 1232 represents a landmark in the legal history of feudal Japan. This code was composed of 51 articles designed to serve as moral and procedural guidelines for feudal magistrates. Rather than supplanting existing customary private laws, the *Goseibai Shikimoku* was intended to complement them by standardizing judicial practices and ensuring fair governance within the *samurai* class. Its hortative nature emphasized moral integrity, justice, and practical governance, reflecting the Confucian and Buddhist principles that influenced Kamakura-era jurisprudence. The articles focused on resolving disputes, land management, and ethical behaviour among *samurai*, aiming to maintain stability and order in a society transitioning from aristocratic to *samurai* dominance. The code underscores the feudal ethos of the time, balancing the preservation of tradition with the necessity for a structured legal framework to address the complexities of feudal administration.[50]

After Ashikaga Takauji's victory over the Hojo Shogunate at Kamakura,[51] the *Kemmu Shikimoku* was promulgated in 1336 not as a replacement for the well-established Hojo Code but as a supplementary set of regulations. The *Kemmu Shikimoku*, emphasizing administrative discipline and morality among *samurai*, is particularly noteworthy as the final major codified precedent influencing the Tokugawa legal system, which would later formalize many of these feudal principles into a highly structured governance system.[52]

[50] Henderson (1952), p. 90; Hall (1906).

[51] Mason and Caiger (1997), p. 138 ff.

[52] Henderson (1952), p. 90; Hall (1908).

The written laws of Tokugawa Japan can be categorized into four primary sources. First, the *Kuge Hoshiki* (1615), a code established for the Imperial Court Nobles.[53] Second, the *Buke Shohatto* (1615), which provided governance for the ruling warrior classes, later amended and republished in 1635, 1663, and 1683,[54] alongside the *Shoshi Hatto* (1632), aimed specifically at lesser warriors.[55] Third, the *Kosatsu*, starting in 1711, comprised public prohibitions and instructions displayed in Edo's public spaces for the common people.[56] Lastly, the *Kujikata Osadamegaki* (Written Rules of Procedure), enacted in 1742 under Shōgun Tokugawa Yoshimune, served as a seminal legal code for the Tokugawa shogunate. It comprised two volumes: the first focused on administrative laws, while the second, known as *Osadamegaki Hyakkajō*, contained approximately 100 articles detailing criminal laws and procedures.[57] The *Osadamegaki Hyakkajō* was particularly significant as it codified judicial precedents and outlined appropriate judgments and punishments, thereby standardizing legal practices across the shogunate's territories.[58]

The Tokugawa legal system, despite having structured courts and codified laws, operated without a nationwide unified legal code.[59] Furthermore, the Tokugawa Shogunate's legal philosophy reveals a deliberate effort to restrict public knowledge of the law to maintain societal harmony and control. Dissemination of the law beyond official circles was actively discouraged, encapsulated in the saying: "The people do not need to know the law, but they must obey it." This approach underscored the Shogunate's belief that a well-governed society thrived on obedience and moral order rather than legal contention. While officials were expected to understand the law, the Shogunate deemed it undesirable for the general populace—or even legal aides—to fully grasp the legal rules. This aligns with the Tokugawa

[53] Hall (1912), pp. 272–285.

[54] Hall (1912), p. 288.

[55] Hall (1912), p. 309.

[56] Hall (1912), p. 320.

[57] See Henderson (1952), p. 90; Noda (1976), pp. 35–36; Dean (2002), pp. 58–59.

[58] It should be noted that the Edo period criminal law system was marked by its harshness and the widespread use of physical punishments. Execution was a frequent outcome even for relatively minor offenses, reflecting the era's strict societal order. Mutilation, such as cutting off noses or ears, and severe beatings served as public and physical markers of criminality, intended both as punishment and as deterrence. Torture was also a sanctioned method, utilized to extract confessions or testimonies, which underscores the lack of procedural safeguards for the accused and witnesses. The influence of Chinese legal practices was evident in the introduction of tattooing criminals, a form of stigmatization abolished in 1872 during the Meiji reforms. An interesting dynamic in Edo justice was the differential treatment of social classes. Samurai, as the ruling class, were held to stricter moral and legal standards. Crimes committed by samurai often carried penalties of greater severity, including the expectation of seppuku for certain offenses—a punishment symbolizing atonement and honor restoration. In contrast, farmers, who occupied a lower social rung, might face milder consequences for the same infractions. This reflects the Confucian-influenced hierarchical ethos of the time, where accountability was proportional to one's social status and expected role in maintaining societal order. For a closer look at criminal justice during the Edo era see Botsman (2005).

[59] Goodman (2003), pp. 14–15.

neo-Confucian governance framework, which prioritized harmony as the hallmark of good leadership. Litigation, viewed as a public display of discord, was seen as antithetical to this ideal. By limiting access to legal knowledge, the authorities sought to suppress disputes and reinforce the perception of an orderly, harmonious society.[60]

Tokugawa society, deeply influenced by Confucian philosophy, operated under a rigid hierarchical class system reinforced by geographical limitations.[61] This structure, which emphasized relationships between classes over individuals, was sustained by the legal system. For instance, although no formal restrictions existed until the mid-eighteenth century, individuals from lower social classes could rarely sue those of higher status, except under very limited circumstances. Social identity was determined by one's class and family, as individuals lacked legal standing outside these frameworks.[62] The family unit served as the cornerstone of society, extending outward to the self-governing *mura* (villages), where approximately 80% of the population lived. Villages relied on custom rather than formal law to resolve disputes, emphasizing harmony and conciliation.[63] Social cohesion was vital for survival in emergencies and under heavy taxation, but non-compliance with group values often resulted in ostracism—a practice that persists in contemporary Japan.[64] This societal stasis, coupled with geographical and political isolation, discouraged legal reform, leaving Tokugawa laws virtually unchanged.

While the prolonged peace and growth of commerce during the Edo period led to some procedural uniformity, the Tokugawa government never established a legal system grounded in universal rules or justiciable rights.[65] Authority was discretionary and authoritarian, with legal processes focused on maintaining order rather than granting rights. Relief was viewed as an act of grace rather than an entitlement, reflecting the absence of the concept of legal rights in Japanese traditional thought. The legal framework of the Edo period primarily served the shogunate's governance objectives rather than protecting individual rights or promoting social equity. Law functioned as a tool of control, ensuring the stability of the feudal hierarchy and reinforcing the centralized power of the Tokugawa regime. It was less about justice in the modern sense and more about maintaining order and compliance.[66] This

---

[60] See on this issue Henderson (1952), p. 106.

[61] This period in Japan is commonly characterized by a Confucian-inspired four-tiered class system, with merchants at the bottom, followed by artisans, then farmers, and samurai at the top (replacing scholars found in the Chinese model). However, in practice, the key distinction—particularly a legal one—was between samurai and non-samurai. See, in general, Gordon (2019), pp. 9 and 14 ff; Mason and Caiger (1997), p. 220 ff; Henderson (1952), p. 92 ff.

[62] Goodman (2003), pp. 231–232; Hall (1974).

[63] Wren (1968), p. 222.

[64] Haley (1982), p. 275 ff; Gibbons (1990), p. 109; Haley (1991a), p. 447.

[65] Goodman (2003), p. 14.

[66] As George Sansom has observed, during the Tokugawa era "law was nothing but the expression of the will of a dominant chieftain in a state of war…it was in essence martial law continued into times of peace." Sansom (1962), pp. 458–459. In the words of Yoshiyuki Noda, during the Edo

authoritarian legal culture fostered a preference for informal dispute resolution methods, such as conciliation within social groups.[67] These processes were guided by contextual and adaptable norms influenced by group dynamics and social pressures, rather than strict, universal legal principles.[68] This approach reflected Japan's historical prioritization of harmony and group cohesion, favouring collaborative resolutions over adversarial legal proceedings.[69]

12.4 The European Reception Period

Japan's self-imposed isolation (*sakoku*) ended abruptly in 1853 with the arrival of Commodore Matthew Perry and his fleet of four U.S. warships. Perry carried a letter from President Millard Fillmore, demanding that Japan reopen its borders to international trade and diplomatic relations. By 1858, Japan had signed a series of commercial treaties with the United States, Great Britain, Russia, the Netherlands, and France. Collectively known as the Ansei Treaties, these agreements were highly unequal, placing Japan in a politically and economically vulnerable position. Key

---

period "the law for most Japanese meant little else than the means of constraint used by the authorities to achieve government purposes." Noda (1976), p. 37.

[67] In the Confucian value system prominent in Japan, harmonious relationships were deeply significant as they were seen as the pathway to achieving *jen* (also spelled *ren*), described as 'a state of consciousness reflecting the individual's compassion'. This principle held such prominence that it was considered paramount, even in resolving disputes. The prioritization of harmony extended beyond personal interactions and played a vital role in governance. Village leaders, for example, were judged on their capacity to restore and maintain harmony within their communities. This ability was not merely a moral virtue but a critical determinant of their reputation and influence, directly affecting their standing. Such emphasis underscores the interplay between Confucian ethics and socio-political structures in historical Japan, where social cohesion was both a personal and institutional imperative. See Berat (1992), p. 130; Henderson (1952), pp. 98–99.

[68] As Takeyoshi Kawashima has remarked, "the notion that a justice measured by universal standards can exist independent of the wills of the disputants is apparently alien to the traditional habit of the Japanese people." Kawashima (1963), p. 50.

[69] The interplay between *giri* and *ninjo* in Japanese interpersonal relations reflects a nuanced cultural framework for navigating conflicts and social obligations. *Giri,* translated as social obligation or duty, represents the external expectations and societal pressures individuals face, often tied to hierarchical relationships, honour, and the maintenance of social harmony. Conversely, *ninjo*, embodying human emotions or compassion, signifies the personal, heartfelt responses that may conflict with *giri*. This tension between societal duties and personal feelings is a recurring theme in Japanese culture, highlighting a delicate balance between conforming to societal norms and honouring individual emotional impulses. The interconnectedness of *giri-ninjo* suggests that actions and attitudes in traditional Japanese thinking are often shaped by the need to reconcile these conflicting forces. This dynamic often informs attitudes towards conflict and dispute resolution, where considerations of duty, honour, shame, and human emotions interplay to guide behaviour. The discussion of *giri-ninjo* also intersects with *Nihonjinron*—the discourse on Japanese national and cultural identity—because these concepts are seen as uniquely Japanese, forming part of the cultural self-perception. Consider, in general, Noda (1976), pp. 174–183; Benedict (1967), p. 175 ff.

provisions included the opening of Japanese ports to foreign trade and the imposition of fixed low import-export duties. Additionally, the treaties granted extraterritorial rights to Western powers, allowing foreign nationals accused of crimes to be tried in consular courts staffed by foreign judges, rather than under Japanese jurisdiction. Commercial and civil disputes involving Japanese and foreign nationals were similarly handled in these courts. These measures reflected the Western powers' lack of confidence in Japan's legal system and underscored the Tokugawa Shogunate's inability to protect Japan's sovereignty. The revision of these 'unequal treaties', widely regarded as a precursor to potential colonization by foreign powers, became the nation's top priority.[70]

The unequal treaties and the shogunate's failure to resist foreign pressure fueled widespread discontent among samurai and intellectuals. By 1867, the Tokugawa Shogunate had collapsed, allowing the Emperor, whose ancestors had been only of symbolic and not political importance for several centuries, to reclaim full governmental authority. This ushered in a transformative period in Japan's history known as the Meiji Restoration.[71] Named after Emperor Meiji, this era saw the centralization of political power, rapid industrialization, and the adoption of Western military, legal, and educational systems. However, in the immediate aftermath of the Meiji Restoration, Japan's new leaders faced numerous challenges: external threats, internal unrest often erupting into open conflict, and an uneasy, shifting alliance among the ruling factions. A significant hurdle was establishing their legitimacy as the leaders of a unified modern nation rather than a fragmented collection of feudal domains.

To address these challenges, the new government issued the *Charter Oath* in 1868, proclaimed in the Emperor's name.[72] This foundational document outlined five key principles:

1. Deliberative assemblies shall be widely established and all matters decided by open discussion.
2. All classes, high and low, shall be united in vigorously carrying out the administration of affairs of state.
3. The common people, no less than the civil and military officials, shall all be allowed to pursue their own calling so that there may be no discontent.
4. Evil customs of the past shall be broken off and everything based upon the just laws of Nature.
5. Knowledge shall be sought throughout the world so as to strengthen the foundation of imperial rule.

The fifth tenet is particularly noteworthy, as it set the stage for Japan to embrace the advanced technological and industrial expertise of Western powers. Concurrently,

---

[70] Goodman (2003), pp. 16–17; Dean (2002), p. 57.

[71] Noda (1976), pp. 41–42; Nakamura (1964), p. 25; Mason and Caiger (1997), p. 258 ff; Sansom (1990), p. 444 ff; Goodman (2003), pp. 19–20.

[72] Dean (2002), p. 61.

the Emperor's divine lineage and religious significance were leveraged to unify the population under a politicized version of Shinto, imposed by the state to consolidate authority and national identity.

In a strict sense, the Meiji period refers to the reign of Emperor Meiji, which lasted from his formal enthronement in 1868 until his death in 1912. At the start of this era, Edo, later renamed Tokyo ('Eastern City'), became the official capital of Japan. Day-to-day governance was conducted by a select group of advisors, known as the *genro*, prominent men who had played key roles in the Meiji Restoration. Under the new government, the *samurai* class lost most of their traditional privileges, while the feudal lords (*daimyo*) were stripped of their domains, leading to the establishment of a centralized prefectural system. The feudal social hierarchy (*shinokosho*) was dismantled, and individuals previously classified as samurai, farmers, artisans, and merchants were collectively designated as 'commoners.' Simultaneously, as Japan's economy expanded and modern industries emerged, the government supported the rise of powerful family-run conglomerates known as *zaibatsu*. These organizations became vertically integrated monopolies, dominating key sectors of the economy. However, questions about Japan's international standing persisted, and by the late nineteenth century, a 'colonize or be colonized' mindset began to take root among the new ruling elite. This was driven by a desire to secure Japan's position on the global stage and avoid subjugation by Western powers. Japan's military successes in the First Sino-Japanese War (1894–1895) and the Russo-Japanese War (1904–1905), combined with rapid domestic industrialization, fostered a growing sense of national confidence. By this time, many Japanese believed their nation had achieved the social, economic, and technological advancements necessary to be recognized as equals by Western powers. The Meiji period officially ended with Emperor Meiji's death in 1912 and the ascension of Emperor Taisho. In the years that followed, the influence of the elder statesmen (*genro*) diminished as party politics began to dominate. This shift in political power is often referred to as the era of Taisho democracy.

The Meiji period witnessed a series of ground-breaking legal reforms, heavily inspired by European civil law models. Despite its long-standing isolationist policy, some European political and legal ideas were already known to the Japanese during the Tokugawa Shogunate, primarily through the Dutch. After Japan reopened its borders, both the *daimyo* and the Tokugawa government began sending young Japanese students abroad to study law. Following the fall of the Tokugawa regime, the Meiji government, striving to modernize the nation, faced a growing demand for lawyers well-versed in Western legal systems. To address this, the government invited European professors to Japan to serve as advisors and educators. By the early 1870s, a precursor to the Ministry of Justice had established a school specializing in French law. At the same time, the Tokyo Kaisei School (which later became the University of Tokyo) recruited English lawyers to teach law. Across the country, private law schools also emerged, offering education in both French and English legal systems.[73] Similar to medieval students who studied Roman law in Bologna and disseminated it across Europe, a generation of Japanese judges, officials, lawyers, and academics trained exclusively in European legal traditions began to shape the nation's legal landscape.

The process of 'Europeanization' of the Japanese legal system advanced significantly through the translation and adaptation of foreign legal codes, particularly those from France, whose legal system was considered one of the most advanced of its time. The French Civil Code, in particular, renowned for its clarity, brevity, and anti-feudal principles, aligned with Japan's ambitions to modernize and dismantle its feudal structure. Furthermore, The Code was grounded in claims of universal reason—claims that Japanese bureaucrats, influenced by Neo-Confucianism, found familiar.

In 1870, Japan established a commission to translate the French Civil Code into Japanese, marking the beginning of systematic legal reform in the country. Two French legal experts, Gustave-Emile Boissonade and Georges Bousquet, played pivotal roles in adapting French legal principles to the Japanese context.[74] Boissonade's efforts culminated in the drafting of Japan's first modern Criminal Code and Code of Criminal Procedure in 1880. These codes, heavily influenced by the French legal system and supplemented by elements from Belgian and Italian codes, came into force in 1882.[75] They were widely accepted, facing little opposition or dissent. This lack of resistance can be attributed to two key factors: for the government and ruling elite, the codes symbolized a return to the *ritsuryō* system of ancient imperial Japan, while for the general populace, unfamiliar with the principle of legality in crime and punishment, there was neither the knowledge nor the opportunity to question them. Nevertheless, the introduction of these codes marked a significant turning point in Japan's transformation from a feudal legal system to a modern, codified one.

The Criminal Code introduced the inquisitorial system, which was prevalent across much of Western Europe, and established the concept of personal responsibility as opposed to collective responsibility. Furthermore, it adopted the French classification of offences into three categories: '*crime*', '*délit*', and '*contravention*'. Most notably, the Code enshrined the legality principle of *nullum crimen, nulla poena sine lege* (no crime and no punishment without law).[76] This principle, which stipulates that an individual cannot be punished for an act unless it was defined as a crime under the law at the time it was committed, significantly restricted judicial discretion but ensured legal certainty in the administration of justice. The 1880 Criminal Code remained in effect for over two decades until it was replaced in 1907 by a revised, German-inspired code. This new code abandoned the classification of offenses and allowed for greater judicial discretion. The Criminal Procedure Code

[73] Oda (2021), p. 98.

[74] Noda (1976), p. 45; Oda (2021), p. 97.

[75] Noda (1976), p. 45; Oda (2021), p. 97; Port (1996), p. 27; Dean (2002), pp. 63–65.

[76] Noda (1976), p. 207.

remained in force until 1890, when it was replaced by a new code that closely resembled its predecessor. In 1922, another Code of Criminal Procedure was introduced, which retained significant French influences. This code was extensively revised during the post-World War II period.[77]

Boissonade was also tasked with preparing a draft Civil Code, which, after extensive study and debate, was adopted by the government in 1888 and enacted into law in 1890, set to take effect at the beginning of 1893.[78] However, the new code sparked intense controversy among lawyers, statesmen, and the general public. The newly established parliament, formed under the German-inspired Constitution of 1889, insisted on having a say in the matter. A significant number of its members opposed the code's implementation, as did many lawyers and jurists trained in German and English legal traditions. Conservatives—representing a parliament elected solely by the wealthy, as the poor had no voting rights at the time—objected to the code's relatively individualistic provisions regarding family, marriage, and inheritance. They favoured imposing the kinship structures prevalent among the upper classes on the entire population. Additionally, lawyers criticized the code for its lack of a General Chapter containing definitions, leading to numerous repetitions throughout the text.

According to Nobushige Hozumi, the debate between the supporters and opponents of the code bore significant similarities to the conflict between the Historical School and the School of Natural Law.[79] English-educated lawyers, in particular—steeped in the ideas of Bentham, Austin, and Maine, and committed to legal positivism—rejected Boissonade's assertion that the universal and eternal principles of justice embodied in the French Civil Code were applicable to all nations.[80] While they acknowledged the necessity of a civil code, they contended that laws evolve organically within each society and argued for the inclusion of traditional Japanese social norms, particularly in family law and the law of succession. At the same time, for economically significant areas of law—such as contracts, land, commercial law, and personal property—they advocated considering other historically developed European legal systems in addition to the French model.[81]

The dispute between supporters and opponents of the Civil Code persisted for some time until a bill was introduced in the Diet proposing that the Code, as originally adopted, should not be enforced. Instead, its implementation was to be postponed pending a comprehensive revision. Subsequently, a codification commission was established, comprising representatives from the parliament, legal profession, commerce, industry, and academia.[82] This commission included jurists from various

[77] Noda (1976), pp. 209–210.

[78] Oda (2021), p. 98; Sansom (1990), pp. 444–445.

[79] Hozumi (1904).

[80] Takayanagi (1963), p. 25.

[81] On the debates surrounding Boissonade's civil code see Noda (1976), pp. 46–48; Dean (2002), pp. 65–66; Ono (1996).

[82] Particularly noteworthy was the contribution of three law professors who had studied in various European countries: Hozumi, well-versed in both English and German legal systems; Tomii, who

foreign schools of jurisprudence. The new draft of the Civil Code prepared by the commission was heavily influenced by the recently adopted German Civil Code, while also incorporating elements from several other European legal systems.[83] The revised Code received majority approval in Parliament and was enacted into law in 1898.[84] The Code of Civil Procedure, modelled on the German Code of Civil Procedure of 1877, was introduced earlier, in 1890, leading to a notable irony in Japanese legal history: the procedural code was established before the substantive provisions were codified.[85] As a result, it was not fully aligned with the new Civil Code, necessitating a significant revision of the procedural code in 1926. Additionally, the Commercial Code was promulgated and came into effect in 1899.[86] This code drew inspiration not only from German law but also from English law, incorporating a dedicated chapter on company law.[87] By this time, French influence on Japanese legal development had significantly waned, and the shift toward German law and jurisprudence was well underway.[88]

To explain why the German model eventually gained favour, several factors must be considered:

1. The German Civil Code was perceived as the most mature and sophisticated example of European legislative art.
2. The French Code, in contrast, was outdated in certain respects and suffered from technical flaws.
3. German conceptualism and systematic exposition held significant appeal for Japanese scholars.

Additionally, Imperial Germany's political history resonated with the Japanese government. Germany had recently and successfully transitioned away from feudalism without abandoning militarism. It had surpassed France both on the battlefield and as an industrial power. Furthermore, Germany's constitutional monarchy, where the Kaiser exercised significant autonomy from parliamentary control, aligned closely with Japanese governance preferences. This partially explains why the Meiji Constitution was deliberately modelled after the German system.

The Japanese Civil Code is divided into five books: (1) General Provisions, (2) Real Property, (3) the Law of Obligations, (4) Family Law, and (5) the Law of Succession. This structure was chosen in part because it allowed for the

---

had studied law in France; and Ume, who had pursued legal studies in both Germany and France.

[83] Other systems that were considered included Austria, Belgium, California, the Netherlands, Portugal, Russia and Spain. See, in general, Noda (1976), pp. 50–52.

[84] Sansom (1990), pp. 445–446.

[85] Oda (2021), p. 97. See also Dean (2002), p. 67; Nakamura (1971), p. 82.

[86] Dean (2002), pp. 66–67.

[87] The Commercial Code is organized into four sections: (1) General Provisions, (2) Company Law, (3) Commercial Transactions, and (4) Maritime Commercial Transactions. For a closer look at the Commercial Code and its evolution see Noda (1976), p. 202 ff. See also Blakemore and Yazawa (1953), p. 13.

[88] Port (1996), p. 27.

incorporation of provisions based on traditional Japanese law, particularly in the sections on succession and family law. The first book, General Provisions, established foundational principles that apply across the entire code, making the overall framework more streamlined and concise.

Perhaps the most striking feature of the new Japanese Civil Code is its incorporation of a key principle of modern European law, introducing an entirely new concept into Japanese legislation: the concept of *right*, as contrasted with *obligation*. This marks a clear and distinct instance of direct Western influence on Japanese culture. The notion of *right* was entirely foreign to the jurisprudence Japan adopted from China in the seventh century, which served as the foundation for much of its subsequent legal framework. Historically, both Japan's laws and customs were deeply rooted in the idea of duty, to the near exclusion of the concept of individual rights.[89] Indeed, the concept of individual *right* was so unfamiliar in traditional Japanese thought that no term in classical Japanese legal writing corresponded closely to the Western notion of *right*—something owed to an individual or something an individual could claim. Similarly, everyday Japanese vocabulary lacked a word to express this idea. To address this gap, a new term, *kenri*, was coined. This term combines *ken* (meaning 'power' or 'influence') with *ri* (meaning 'interest').[90]

However, it is important to emphasize that the legislation of the Meiji period not only introduced modern legal principles but also acknowledged and preserved certain traditional aspects of Japanese social life. This is particularly evident in the provisions of the Civil Code concerning the institution of the family. The legislature took care to avoid excessive interference with the age-old and deeply rooted customary sentiments embodied in the family system, which was regarded as a cornerstone of social stability. Balancing this preservation with the recognition of Western principles of individual rights was a delicate and challenging task, as these principles often stood in tension with indigenous beliefs and practices.

Consider the institution of the family, for example. The principal feature of the Japanese family system is the emphasis on the *house* as a legal entity, originally founded on ancestor worship, in contrast to the broader family, which is an indeterminate group of blood relatives loosely associated. The *house* consists of the head of the house and its members, who are subject to his authority. These members may include not only blood relatives but also individuals who are not related by blood but have joined the house with the head's consent. This customary arrangement was so fundamental that, when national registration was introduced in 1871, the unit of registration adopted was the *house*, rather than the family or the individual. At the same time, the state, having adopted the principle of individual rights, was compelled to acknowledge that a person could not be regarded solely as a member of a *house* in certain aspects of life. Individuals were also recognized as members of a family and as autonomous subjects with rights and obligations beyond the authority

[89] Henderson (1952), p. 105.

[90] See Sansom (1990), p. 446. The newly created word 'kenri' sparked some controversy, as its connotations of 'power' and 'selfishness' appeared to contradict the Confucian principle of subordinating personal interests. Consider Rahn (1990), p. 85.

of the head of the *house*. As a result, the new legal code required modifications to customary practices. One of the simplest changes was the provision for registering individual status separately from *house* or family membership. This was addressed through the Law of National Registration (1898), enacted as a complement to the Civil Code.[91]

A challenging question arose regarding the succession of House members to property. Traditionally, authority over the House and its property was vested in the House head, as inheritance was primarily seen as a means to ensure the perpetuation of ancestor worship within the House. While the Civil Code upheld the principle that the House head succeeded to this role to maintain continuity of worship, it also distinguished between succession to House headship and succession to property. Simultaneously, the law implemented safeguards to prevent the extinction of a House—and the associated termination of worship—through measures such as legally recognizing adoption and imposing restrictions on the legal heir's ability to renounce succession or inheritance.

The provision in the new Civil Code allowing a House member to own, inherit, or bequeath property as an individual marked a complete departure from tradition. Prior to 1868, House members had no personal property rights; whatever they possessed was held not as personal owners but with the permission of the House head. The Meiji-era legislation gradually dismantled this traditional system, as it conflicted with the evolving economic realities of the time. A distinctive aspect of the Civil Code is that, while it preserved the traditional family system in terms of function, it adopted Western concepts and practices regarding property rights, reflecting the pressures of modernization and the influence of Western legal principles.[92]

It is important to note that the departure from tradition was significantly motivated by changes in the country's economic structure, which began as early as, or even before, the establishment of the Meiji government. One of the primary forces driving the Restoration was the ambition of samurai, particularly those of lower rank and limited financial means, to channel their talents and energies into public service and to establish independent careers as statesmen, officials, or military officers. In the early years, many of these individuals acquired substantial sums of money through grants, pensions, or annuities awarded as compensation for their efforts. This represented a new form of property which, along with official salaries, was deemed inappropriate to classify as the income of the House to which they belonged. As a result, a new category of independent ownership of property by House members as individuals emerged. Similar developments occurred due to the

[91] The law established a comprehensive system for maintaining *koseki* (family registers), which were vital for regulating the legal status of individuals in accordance with the Civil Code. The *koseki* system recorded births, deaths, marriages, divorces, and adoptions, linking individuals to family units rather than recognizing them as wholly autonomous legal entities. The system also reflected broader state-building goals, facilitating population control, taxation, and conscription. For a closer look at the Japanese family system see Fukutake (1982), Chapter 3; Hendry (1995), Chapter 2.

[92] Sansom (1990), pp. 447–450.

rapid expansion of property in forms such as bonds, stocks, bank deposits, and title deeds during the early Meiji era. These assets were registered in the names of individuals and, therefore, could not be controlled or disposed of by the House head. Moreover, the House head was no longer held accountable for debts incurred through private transactions by individual House members. This shift necessitated a modification of the traditional practice by which property left by a deceased House member reverted to the House. The new legal code stipulated that such property should instead pass to the member's descendants in equal shares, irrespective of the House to which they might belong at the time.

The introduction of Western commercial and financial institutions inevitably brought significant changes to long-established Japanese customs. Numerous examples illustrate that, among the various forms of Western influence—whether direct or indirect—it was the economic transformations beginning in the mid-nineteenth century that triggered the most profound and lasting changes in Japanese society. A thorough and meticulous analysis of Meiji-era legislation across all areas of law reveals countless instances of cultural conflict between Western and Eastern traditions. These instances highlight the compromises that were necessary as Japanese society adapted to the demands of an emerging industrial economy, reshaping its social structures and practices to align with the needs of modernization.

While the legal codes were fundamental to the modernization of Meiji Japan, the introduction of a constitution was equally pivotal. Its development and adoption marked a significant transition from feudal rule by might to a constitutional monarchy. Just as Western influence was instrumental in shaping the legal codes, it also played a crucial role in the drafting of the Meiji Constitution. However, unlike the codes, which were often authored by Western experts, the constitution was primarily a product of Japanese research and scholarship, albeit heavily inspired by Western models.[93] Largely modeled after the Prussian constitution,[94] the document, titled *The Constitution of the Empire of Japan*, came into effect on November 29, 1890, and comprised 76 articles. In a notable departure from the Tokugawa shogunate's governance, the constitution allowed the Emperor to confer rights upon citizens who had previously been denied them. However, it simultaneously affirmed the Emperor's divinity, re-establishing him as a supreme sovereign leader with no direct accountability to the populace.[95]

The Meiji Constitution granted significant sovereign power to the state while deliberately excluding the people, rooted in the belief that entrusting political authority to the masses would undermine the state's strength at a time when national

---

[93] The Meiji Constitution was essentially drafted by Kowashi Inoue, Miyojo Ito, Kentaro Kaneko, and led by the man who became the first Prime Minister, Hirobumi Ito. Another senior government official Tomomi Iwakura had been sent to Europe to study various constitutions and on his return drew up a set of principles together with a commentary supporting a Prussian style monarchical constitution. Carl Friedrich Hermann Roesler, a prominent German jurist, political theorist, and economist, also played a significant role in the process. See Akita (1967), p. 63.

[94] Port (1996), p. 29.

[95] Oda (2021), pp. 203–204.

unity and power were paramount. Although the constitution introduced a judiciary along with executive and legislative branches, it departed from the Western principle of separation of powers. Instead, these institutions functioned in a way that consolidated authority within the state, further entrenching its dominance. Consequently, the powers of the Diet (parliament) were severely restricted, with legislative authority vested in the Emperor. The judiciary, subordinated to the Ministry of Justice, operated merely as an extension of the executive, whose supremacy was enshrined in the constitutional framework.

While undeniably authoritarian and absolutist in its origins and ideology, the Meiji Constitution marked the beginning of a transformative journey toward modernization and democratization. In retrospect, it is easy to dismiss the constitution as conservative, fundamentally undemocratic, and largely symbolic. However, it was, in its time, a remarkable and even revolutionary document. Representing a significant leap forward, it succeeded in transitioning Japan from a feudal society to a constitutional monarchy. Moreover, it struck a delicate balance between preserving tradition, embodied in the Emperor's divine right to rule, and embracing modernity, reflected in the newly established governmental structures.[96]

An overhaul of the court system followed swiftly after the adoption of the 1890 Constitution, with the court structure modelled after the German system. Notably, the *Daishinin* (Supreme Court) had already been established in 1875, and the Court Organisation Law, drafted by the German jurist Otto Rudolph, came into force in 1890. Despite the introduction of a well-organized court system and a proficient judiciary, the general populace continued to prefer traditional conciliatory methods for resolving civil disputes.[97] These methods were regarded as less expensive, more convenient, and quicker than the formal court system, which often could not guarantee timely or satisfactory outcomes. In response, the Justice Ministry promoted the use of conciliation through the introduction of the *kankai* procedure, drawing inspiration from Tokugawa-era practices. Furthermore, measures introduced in 1875 stipulated that Tokugawa customs would govern civil suits in the absence of applicable laws. Additional conciliation procedures were introduced by the Diet in 1922 to address conflicts between the regulation of landlord-tenant relationships under formal property law and traditional socio-cultural norms.[98] This development further underscored the enduring relevance of informal normative mechanisms in the regulation of legal relationships.

The Meiji Restoration marked a pivotal moment in Japanese history, signifying the nation's transformation from feudalism under the Tokugawa shogunate to modernization and centralization under imperial rule. A cornerstone of this transformation was the comprehensive reform of Japan's legal system, which aimed to align with Western standards to fortify the country's sovereignty and international

---

[96] On the Meiji Constitution see Noda (1976), pp. 55–57 and 190–197; Oda (2021), p. 92 ff; Goodman (2003), pp. 28–30; Dean (2002), pp. 68–70 and 445–447; Takayanagi, (1963), p. 6 ff. See also Minear (1970).

[97] Consider See (1982), p. 345.

[98] Berat (1992), p. 141.

standing. The adoption of Western legal models during this era profoundly influenced Japanese law, shaping its structure, substance, and application.[99] However, this adoption was not a wholesale importation but rather a process of selective integration and adaptation. Customary law, deeply rooted in Japanese traditions, continued to play a significant role, particularly in areas such as family law and inheritance. The interaction between received and indigenous legal traditions often revealed tensions and negotiations. Reformers sought to modernize Japan and pre-empt Western encroachment by adopting foreign legal frameworks but also recognized the need to ground legal reforms in Japan's unique societal values. Across various legal domains, this interplay between Western and Japanese values highlighted the challenges of adapting an industrial society to the demands of modernization while preserving cultural identity. The resulting legal framework blended Western rationality with Japanese cultural norms, ensuring functionality within the nation's socio-political context.

12.5 The Anglo-American Reception Period

With a new legal system, constitution, and set of codes, Japan sought to redefine its interaction with the rest of the world by portraying itself as a modern, Western-oriented nation. Japan entered World War I in August 1914 at the request of Great Britain, seizing German-held territories in China. This role earned Japan a seat on the Council of the League of Nations, solidifying its status as an emerging global power. However, Japan's efforts to establish equality with the major Western powers were largely unsuccessful, fuelling the rise of ultra-nationalist movements and widespread resentment toward Western nations among its populace.

The 1930s marked a period of intense political upheaval, during which right-wing factions with strong military ties increasingly gained influence. In 1931, Japan invaded Manchuria, disregarding international condemnation, and began expanding its territorial control in China. In 1932, the Kwantung Army—a division of the Imperial Japanese Army tasked with overseeing occupied Manchuria—formally established the puppet state of Manchukuo, with the last Chinese emperor installed as its nominal leader. Facing mounting criticism from other members of the League of Nations, Japan withdrew from the organization in 1933, signalling its shift toward isolation from Western diplomacy and its pursuit of imperial expansion.

In 1940, Japan formally joined the Axis powers alongside Germany and Italy. In response, the United States and Britain imposed an embargo on oil shipments to Japan, a critical blow to a nation with limited natural resources. To secure access to oil and other resources, Japan launched an aggressive campaign to capture the resource-rich Dutch East Indies (modern-day Indonesia) and initiated war against the United States and Great Britain. Within months, key locations such as Hong

[99] See Haley (2006), pp. 30–32.

Kong, Manila, and Singapore fell to the Japanese Imperial Army as it advanced across the region. However, from mid-1942 onward, the tide of the war began to shift. Japan's navy suffered a series of significant defeats, and the Japanese mainland faced increasingly devastating air raids. On the morning of August 6, 1945, the United States dropped an atomic bomb on Hiroshima, followed by a second atomic bombing on Nagasaki three days later. Faced with unprecedented destruction, Emperor Shōwa announced Japan's surrender on August 14, 1945, bringing World War II in the Pacific to an end.

The Occupation period following the Second World War (1945–1952) brought sweeping reforms to Japan's political, economic, and legal systems. Led by General Douglas MacArthur, the Supreme Commander for the Allied Powers,[100] the Occupation combined both civilian and military elements from its inception. Its objectives, initially outlined in the Potsdam Declaration (1945) and later clarified in the Initial Post-Surrender Policy, focused on dismantling Japan's capacity for future military aggression and promoting democratic governance as a means to achieve lasting peace.[101] The Occupation operated through the Japanese government, implementing its reforms with increasing precision over time. Given that the Occupation forces were predominantly American, these reforms were heavily influenced by American political ideals and practices.[102] The process recognized and accommodated Japan's unique social and cultural conditions, ensuring that indigenous traditions were integrated in a manner that aligned with the overarching principles of reform rather than conflicting with them.

The reforms initiated by the Allied Powers during this period dismantled autocratic structures, renounced war, promoted gender equality, encouraged the growth of trade unions, restructured the education system, liberalized the economy, and reformed the rural landholding system to address severe inequities in land distribution. Among the most significant reforms was the Emperor's renunciation of his divine status, a central tenet of State Shinto. This marked the disassembly of the Shinto-based ideological framework that had played a critical role in mobilizing Japan's populace for war.[103] More broadly, the notion of 'rule by law' under the Meiji Constitution was replaced by the concept of the 'rule of law' (*ho no Shihai*), as developed in Anglo-American jurisprudence.[104]

The reform measures were embodied in the new Japanese Constitution (*Nihon Koku Kenpō*), which was promulgated on 3 November 1946 and came into effect on 3 May 1947. The Constitution contains 103 articles organized into a preamble and 11 chapters. The chapters address various aspects such as the Emperor, the rights and duties of the people, the Diet, the Cabinet, and the judiciary, among others. It

---

[100] Tanaka and Smith (1976), p. 249.

[101] Oda (2021), p. 100. For a closer look at the Occupation period see Mason and Caiger (1997), p. 354 ff.

[102] In the words of a commentator, "[these reforms brought] together American constitutional principles and Western European-derived institutions and legal concepts." Dean (2002), p. 71.

[103] Oda (2021), p. 100.

[104] Oda (2021), pp. 109–110.

rests on three fundamental pillars: popular sovereignty (art. 1), pacifism (art. 9), and safeguard of fundamental human rights (art. 11).[105]

The first fundamental principle underpinning the Constitution is that sovereignty resides in the people. Prior to the constitutional changes, the Emperor (*Tenno*) wielded significant political and social authority, justified by claims of divine right. However, the new Constitution shifted sovereignty from the Emperor to the people, effectively ending legal obligations of loyalty to the Emperor and reducing his role to a purely symbolic one. The Emperor now represents 'the unity of the people' and engages in state affairs in a ceremonial capacity, such as convening the National Diet, but these actions require the advice and approval of the Cabinet. This shift underscores Japan's transition to a constitutional monarchy, where the Emperor's authority is no longer political but representative, aligning with democratic principles.[106]

The second fundamental principle of the Constitution is pacifism. Article 9 declares that "the Japanese people forever renounce war as a sovereign right of the nation and the threat or use of force as means of settling international disputes" and that "land, sea, and air forces, as well as other war potential, will never be maintained."[107] Following this principle, the Law on the Maintenance of Public Security was abolished,[108] the armed forces were dismantled, suspected war criminals were prosecuted, and political prisoners were released. Individuals responsible for promoting the war were removed from their positions, and Shintoism, which had been established as the state religion during the war and was believed to have significantly supported the war effort, was formally separated from the state.

The third fundamental principle of the Constitution is respect for fundamental human rights. Chapter III serves as a Bill of Rights, modelled after provisions in the United States Constitution. Article 11 states that "fundamental human rights guaranteed to the people by this Constitution shall be conferred upon the people of this and future generations as eternal and inviolate rights."[109] These rights include not only civil liberties such as freedom of speech, the free exercise of religion, and several procedural protections for the accused, but also a right to welfare under Article 25.[110]

---

[105] Oda (2021), pp. 101 and 112–113.

[106] Oda (2021), p. 115.

[107] Oda (2021), p. 115.

[108] This legislation was enacted in Japan in 1925 during the Taishō era, primarily aimed at curbing political dissent and suppressing movements perceived as threats to the state and the existing social order.

[109] Oda (2021), pp. 116 and 205 ff.

[110] Article 25 declares that "All people shall have the right to maintain the minimum standards of wholesome and cultured living." However, the concrete content of this right is thought to depend on the welfare policy of the government, so welfare recipients are not entitled to claim that a particular welfare policy is unconstitutional.

The Constitution adopts the separation of powers as a guiding principle for the governmental system.[111] Legislative power is vested in the Diet (Chapter IV), which consists of the lower House of Representatives (*shugi-in*) and the upper House of Councillors (*Sangi-in*). The former holds greater significance than the latter in most respects. Members of both Houses are elected, and all citizens over the age of twenty are eligible to vote. An important reform was that laws enacted by the Diet must now be followed by the State, which previously had considerable power over the Diet.

The Constitution further establishes the executive branch of government, centred on the Prime Minister and their Cabinet, with duties outlined in Chapter V. The position of Prime Minister, created in 1885—four years before the Meiji Constitution—must be held by a member of the Diet and is typically occupied by the president of the majority party in power.

The judiciary, as outlined in Chapter VI of the Constitution, constitutes the third branch of government. The judicial system is vested in the Supreme Court and such inferior courts as established by law. The Supreme Court serves as the court of last resort, possessing the authority to determine the constitutionality of laws, orders, and official acts.[112]

Japan underwent significant reforms in its criminal justice system as part of the broader democratization and modernization process led by the Allied Occupation. These reforms aimed to align Japan's legal framework with democratic values and human rights principles. Of particular importance were the revisions to the Criminal Code of 1907, carried out in 1947, which brought the Code into conformity with the new Constitution.[113] Several provisions related to wartime offenses were abolished, and the lèse-majesté offenses—concerned with acts deemed insulting or disrespectful toward the Emperor or the imperial family—were removed, as they were considered incompatible with the Emperor's changed constitutional role.[114]

Furthermore, articles in the Penal Code that permitted or tacitly endorsed physical punishment or torture, especially during police investigations, were repealed or replaced to comply with Article 36 of the 1947 Constitution, which explicitly prohibits torture and cruel punishment. Provisions were also added or amended to

[111] Oda (2021), p. 118.

[112] For a closer look at the 1947 Constitution see, in general, Noda (1976), p. 190 ff; Oda (2021), pp. 151–152; Goodman (2003), pp. 30–33 and 35 ff; Dean (2002), p. 447 ff.

[113] Noda (1976), pp. 208–209.

[114] These offenses were primarily codified during the Meiji era, reflecting the state's emphasis on reverence for the emperor as the symbol of national unity and divine authority. Under the Criminal Code of 1907, these offenses included acts such as physical harm, threats, or insults directed toward the emperor, empress, crown prince, or regent. Punishments ranged from imprisonment to the death penalty for severe offenses, such as attempted assassination. Propaganda, speech, or publications perceived as undermining the emperor's dignity were also subject to legal penalties. During wartime, lèse-majesté laws became even stricter, with Japan's government equating criticism of the emperor or imperial policies with treason. Although lèse-majesté offenses are no longer recognized under modern Japanese law, respect for the emperor remains culturally significant, and disparaging remarks about the imperial family can still provoke strong public reactions.

address gender discrimination in the Penal Code, reflecting broader societal reforms initiated during the occupation. For instance, crimes related to sexual violence were revised to emphasize the protection of women and align with international norms. Additionally, some prewar moral offenses, such as adultery, were decriminalized to reflect modern social values and the emphasis on individual freedoms. Criminal penalties related to censorship, suppression of political activity, and restrictions on press freedom were similarly abolished. While capital punishment remained in the Penal Code, efforts were made to limit its application by introducing more rigorous procedural safeguards and narrowing the scope of crimes eligible for the death penalty.

The Criminal Procedure Code of 1948 replaced earlier laws that were remnants of the authoritarian pre-war legal system. It incorporated many rules of Anglo-American origin, particularly those designed to guarantee the liberty and dignity of accused persons.[115] A cornerstone of the code is the principle that a defendant is presumed innocent until proven guilty. Additionally, the code adopted a more adversarial style of procedure, drawing from Anglo-American legal systems at key points. This approach contrasted with the earlier inquisitorial system, where judges played a dominant role, and bias and a presumption of guilt were common. Reflecting Article 31 of the Constitution, the code enforces protections against arbitrary arrest and detention, requiring warrants issued by impartial judges. Defendants are granted the right to legal representation, including access to court-appointed lawyers if they cannot afford one. The code also ensures that no one is compelled to testify against themselves, aligning with constitutional guarantees. Prosecutorial authority is centralized, granting prosecutors significant power to investigate crimes, decide on charges, and represent the state in court. To prevent abuse of power, police investigations are subject to judicial oversight. Furthermore, the code establishes strict rules for evidence collection, emphasizing admissibility and reliability to ensure fair trials. Sentencing guidelines are aligned with constitutional protections against cruel or disproportionate punishment, and defendants are guaranteed the right to appeal their convictions, ensuring opportunities for judicial review.

Despite the strong Anglo-American influence, the Japanese criminal justice system retained elements of Continental European legal traditions, blending adversarial and inquisitorial traits along with uniquely Japanese practices.[116] Over time, the Criminal Procedure Code has been amended to address evolving societal needs, such as incorporating victim participation in trials and adapting to technological advancements in evidence gathering.

One of the most significant and far-reaching reforms carried out during the Occupation period was the promotion of gender equality, which profoundly impacted Japanese society, particularly the family and inheritance systems. Before the war, these systems were rooted in a patriarchal, hierarchical structure that

---

[115] Noda (1976), p. 210.

[116] Traditional aspects are still evident in provisions such as Article 297, which empowers the court to determine and modify the scope, order, and method of evidence examination after considering the opinions of both the public prosecutor and the defendant.

perpetuated gender inequality. Article 24 of the new Constitution explicitly guaranteed gender equality in matters of family and marriage, significantly influencing civil law provisions. The Civil Code of 1948, a comprehensive revision of the earlier 1898 Civil Code, incorporated numerous amendments based on principles of equality under the law, the protection of personal rights, and gender equity.

To advance gender equality specifically, the Civil Code's sections on family and succession underwent extensive revisions, eliminating provisions that reinforced patriarchal control. The traditional Japanese household system, which prioritized the authority of the male head of the house, was abolished in favor of a legal framework aligned with the Western concept of family and the principle of equality between husband and wife. Restrictions that denied women legal capacity were removed, and parental authority, previously vested solely in the father, was redefined as a shared responsibility between both parents. Furthermore, equal inheritance rights were granted to all children, irrespective of gender, and provisions ensured that non-lineal family members, such as spouses, were also entitled to a share of the estate.[117]

These landmark changes not only restructured familial and inheritance systems but also expanded political rights for women, who were granted suffrage for the first time, enabling them to participate in the 1946 general elections.

The Code of Civil Procedure, originally enacted in 1890 and heavily influenced by German law, underwent significant amendments to align with democratic principles and modern procedural norms.[118] These reforms emphasized the right to a fair trial, ensuring that procedural rules adhered to the ideals of due process outlined in the postwar Constitution. Key changes included guaranteeing judicial impartiality and improving equitable access to courts.

While preserving its civil law tradition, the Japanese legal system incorporated certain features of the adversarial system, influenced by Anglo-American law, to provide both parties with equal opportunities to present their cases. This shift enhanced transparency and participation in judicial proceedings. Additionally, procedural rules were streamlined to minimize delays and ensure the efficient resolution of disputes, with reforms targeting evidence submission processes and procedural timelines for swifter adjudication of civil cases.

To improve accessibility for ordinary citizens, measures were introduced to simplify procedural requirements and reduce the financial burden on litigants. These included lowering court fees and implementing mechanisms to assist indigent parties in pursuing claims. Furthermore, the reforms reinforced the principle of separation of powers by clearly delineating judicial authority from administrative influence. Judges were granted greater independence, enabling them to adjudicate cases based solely on law and evidence, free from external interference.

The judicial reforms of this period also included the introduction of conciliation procedures to facilitate dispute resolution. A special pre-trial process known as

[117] Noda (1976), pp. 201–202.

[118] Noda (1976), pp. 204–207.

wakai (conciliation) was established, which often proved effective in resolving disputes. If conciliation failed, the parties retained the right to pursue regular court proceedings.

In addition to the aforementioned legal reforms, numerous laws were enacted during or immediately after the Occupation period to complement the principal codes and the Constitution. These included the Supreme Court Rules of 1948, which established procedural and organizational guidelines for the Japanese judiciary; the Juvenile Law of 15 July 1948, which addressed issues concerning juvenile delinquents; the Law of 28 March 1948, which regulated penal institutions and outlined the treatment of inmates and detainees; and the Probation Law of 1 April 1954, which introduced provisions for probation. Reference should also be made to the Minor Offences Law of 1948, which compiled minor offences previously handled by police courts, and to the Law of 21 July 1952, aimed at preventing subversive activities and repressing political violence.

During this period, three major labour laws were enacted, heavily influenced by American labour legislation, each designed to protect workers and foster a fairer labour environment. The Labour Union Law (1945) ensured workers' rights to form and join unions, engage in collective bargaining, and participate in industrial actions such as strikes. This law was modelled after the Wagner Act (National Labour Relations Act) of 1935 in the United States. The Labour Standards Law (1947), inspired by the Fair Labour Standards Act of 1938 in the U.S., established minimum standards for working conditions, including limits on working hours, minimum wage requirements, paid leave entitlements, and protections against unfair treatment.[119] Lastly, the Labour Relations Adjustment Law (1946), influenced by the Taft-Hartley Act (1947) in the United States, aimed to mediate labour disputes and promote industrial harmony. This legislation reflected the occupation authorities' dual objective of empowering labour unions while ensuring economic stability during recovery. American lawyers played a pivotal role in drafting these transformative laws.

The democratization of Japan's economy was pursued through the dissolution of large business conglomerates (*zaibatsu*) that had previously dominated the market. To ensure fair competition and prevent monopolization, anti-monopoly legislation was introduced, alongside supervisory laws to regulate the stock market and share issuance. The 1947 Anti-Monopoly Law, strongly influenced by American legal frameworks, became a cornerstone of this economic transformation.[120] The law explicitly prohibited cartels, private monopolization, and unfair trade practices, aiming to establish a competitive market structure. Over the years, it has undergone amendments to adapt to evolving economic conditions while upholding its foundational principles of economic fairness and competition.

---

[119] Despite the constitutional guarantee of equality under the law and the prohibition of gender discrimination, the Labour Standards Law was unable to effectively challenge societal attitudes and adequately address discrimination against women.

[120] Oda (2021), p. 100.

The Court Organization Law of 1947 stands as a cornerstone of Japan's post-war judicial reform, embodying principles of democratic governance and judicial independence introduced under the new Constitution of 1947. This legislation abolished the pre-war dual court system, which included general courts and specialized administrative courts, and established a unified judiciary under the Supreme Court's oversight. The law emphasized the separation of the judiciary from the executive branch, a critical shift from the Meiji-era system where courts were heavily influenced by the government. By doing so, it sought to prevent undue political interference in legal matters and enhance public trust in judicial impartiality. Under the Court Organization Law, the Supreme Court was positioned as the apex of the judicial system, with powers to oversee lower courts and adjudicate constitutional matters. Below the Supreme Court, a hierarchy of lower courts—High Courts, District Courts, Family Courts, and Summary Courts—was established. Each level of the judiciary was assigned specific jurisdictions, ensuring a streamlined and accessible system for resolving disputes ranging from minor infractions to complex constitutional questions. The Court Organization Law also introduced measures to improve court administration, including standardized training for judges and the establishment of a court clerk system. These reforms were aimed at enhancing the efficiency and professionalism of the judiciary.

The liberalization and democratization of education were among the major reforms recommended by the Allied Powers during the Occupation era. The Fundamental Law of Education, enacted in 1947, emphasized the principles of peace, justice, and respect for individual dignity.[121] As part of these reforms, education based on Shintoism and Confucian ethics was abolished.

It is important to note that while the aforementioned reforms brought significant changes to Japan's legal system, they did not have a corresponding impact on unofficial or 'living' law. This living law encompasses longstanding practices, customs, and informal social norms rooted in Japan's indigenous legal traditions. Its practical application by government authorities, courts, and citizens often creates a gap between the written law and how it is enforced and practiced daily. The integration of indigenous legal norms with received law and Western-derived jurisprudence is complex and sometimes uneasy. Indigenous norms can supplement, modify, or even undermine formal law, influencing its overall effectiveness. While such norms may seem inconsistent with positivist theories, which assert that only the state can create law, secondary sources like custom (*kanshū*) and equitable principles of natural reason (*jori*) are often used to address gaps in the legal system.[122] In this context, it

[121] Oda (2021), p. 100.

[122] The word *jori* is believed to originate from the term *dori*, which appeared in the laws and decisions of feudal Japan. *Dori* referred to common sense and ordinary reason—justice based on prevailing moral principles rather than the strict letter of the law. The concept of *jori* is related to broader principles like equity in Western legal traditions but is rooted in the unique cultural and historical context of Japanese jurisprudence. It reflects Japan's emphasis on harmony and the societal balance of interests in legal proceedings. On the role of custom and the concept of *jori* see Noda (1976), pp. 217–224; Oda (2021), pp. 144–145; Dean (2002), pp. 133–135.

is fair to assert that Western-inspired laws operate within a society whose values are deeply rooted in an enduring cultural tradition.

Both imperial authority and the traditional family system continued to function as elements of unofficial law, alongside the persistence of certain aspects of shrine law. Moreover, conciliation remains the predominant method of dispute resolution, despite the introduction of a Western-style court system.

In the post-WWII period, the values and practices of ordinary Japanese citizens often lagged behind the newly implemented legal framework. Consequently, the Emperor continued to receive—and still receives, both officially and unofficially—utmost reverence, with his symbolic role extending far beyond what was anticipated by post-war legislation. Moreover, large sections of the population were unprepared to fully embrace the changes introduced to family law and made little effort to understand their implications. While developments in Japan since the Occupation period demonstrate that the ideals of the new civil law—particularly the principle of equality—have significantly influenced family relationships, political forces continue to advocate for the preservation of traditional norms from the old family system. Although efforts to legally reinstate these traditional family structures have been unsuccessful, some Japanese people still adhere to the practices of the former system.

The laws relating to Japan's shrine system were reorganized by both the Meiji and post-WWII reforms.[123] However, within local communities, the customary laws and practices associated with shrine worship have persisted as unofficial shrine law, rooted in tradition and long-standing community involvement. These customs typically govern local rituals, the selection of priests, and the observance of festivals. While these customs do not have formal legal standing under national law, they continue to shape the practices and management of community shrines, reflecting a deep respect for cultural continuity.

As previously noted, in traditional Confucian ethics, harmony and social order are highly valued. This has historically influenced Japanese society's preference for avoiding direct confrontation and litigation, which are often perceived as disruptive to relationships and societal harmony. Instead, Japanese people have tended to rely on extra-judicial methods such as negotiation, mediation, and conciliation to settle private disputes.[124] During the Tokugawa period, formal legal proceedings among commoners were often discouraged, with disputes typically resolved within community frameworks or by village elders acting as mediators. This tradition persisted

[123] During the Meiji era, Japan's shrine system underwent significant reorganization as part of the government's efforts to create a centralized and unified state. The Meiji government established State Shinto, formalizing and integrating Shinto shrines into a state-controlled framework to promote national identity and loyalty to the emperor. Post-World War II reforms dismantled State Shinto as part of efforts to separate religion from the state. The 1947 Constitution guaranteed freedom of religion, and Shinto shrines were privatized, removing them from government control. This reform allowed shrines to operate independently, governed by their respective shrine organizations.

[124] Kim and Lawson (1979). And see Goodman (2003), pp. 238–239 and 259–263; Dean (2002), pp. 356–361.

into the modern era, even after the adoption of Western-style legal codes during the Meiji period and the Allied Occupation.

Confucian ethics discourage the resolution of conflicts in public, operating on the assumption that disputes should ideally not arise and, when they do, should be resolved through mutual understanding. Resorting to legal action to protect individual interests is traditionally viewed as 'shameful,' with the concept of shame forming a cornerstone of traditional Japanese culture. Instead, social order is maintained through adherence to the principles of *giri*, which encompass one's duties and obligations toward their community. These principles emphasize reciprocity and the pursuit of harmony. The demands of *giri* increase with social status, placing greater expectations on individuals in positions of higher standing. However, even for those of lower status, the psychological sanctions—such as the loss of 'honour' or 'face'—can be equally severe.

Today, while Japan has a highly developed and accessible court system, cultural preferences for extra-judicial dispute resolution remain evident. Alternative dispute resolution methods, such as arbitration and mediation, are widely used. Moreover, many disputes are resolved informally through negotiation before reaching the courts. The court system itself often encourages settlements and compromises during legal proceedings, reflecting this cultural inclination. However, it would be incorrect to suggest that the Japanese exclusively rely on extra-judicial methods. Over time, there has been an increase in the use of the court system, particularly in areas such as consumer rights, labour disputes, and intellectual property. This reflects a gradual shift in attitudes as Japan's legal system has modernized and become more aligned with global standards. Thus, while Confucian ethics continue to influence Japanese dispute resolution practices, they coexist with and complement the formal Western-based legal system. This duality reflects the adaptability of Japanese society in integrating traditional values with modern legal structures.

12.6 Concluding Remarks

Legal transplantation refers to the process by which legal norms, institutions, or systems from one jurisdiction are adopted, adapted, or integrated into another. This phenomenon is a cornerstone of comparative law and significantly influences the evolution of legal systems worldwide. Its primary objective is to modernize, harmonize, or enhance a recipient jurisdiction's legal framework by drawing on the perceived strengths of foreign legal traditions. However, while legal transplants aim to bring about improvements, they may encounter resistance when the imported laws clash with deeply rooted cultural values or established legal traditions. This tension underscores the critical importance of contextual adaptation. For example, the transplantation of Western legal systems into former colonies often created a duality, where indigenous customary laws coexisted uneasily with imposed legal frameworks. In many cases, this coexistence led to hybrid systems that blended local traditions with received laws, as observed in numerous African and Asian legal systems.

The success of legal transplantation hinges on the alignment between the transplanted legal norms and the recipient culture's social, economic, and political context. Alan Watson, as previously noted, argues that legal transplants often succeed not because they are inherently culturally compatible but because legal actors and institutions can adapt and reinterpret foreign norms to fit local realities. In contrast, some scholars contend that laws are deeply embedded in their cultural contexts, making meaningful transplantation difficult and calling for greater sensitivity to cultural particularities. Legal transplantation, therefore, functions both as a tool for legal development and as a potential source of cultural tension. Its outcomes depend on the extent to which transplanted norms resonate with or are effectively integrated into the recipient society's traditions. This interplay between received laws and indigenous cultures highlights the importance of balancing innovation with cultural preservation to ensure the legitimacy and functionality of transplanted legal systems.

Legal transplantation is a central theme in Japanese legal history. Japan's experiences reveal the intricate challenges and adaptations that come with this process, reflecting the tension between external influence and local cultural, political, and societal factors. Historically, Japan has undergone multiple waves of legal transplantation. The most notable examples include the adoption of Chinese legal principles during the pre-feudal and feudal periods, which were based on Confucian and Buddhist ideologies, and the later influence of Western legal systems during the Meiji era. Each instance involved not just the introduction of foreign legal concepts but also significant modifications to align them with Japan's unique societal structures and values.

During the Meiji era, Japan incorporated elements of European legal systems, particularly the French and German models, as part of its modernization efforts. This strategic decision aimed to demonstrate Japan's readiness to join the ranks of modern, 'civilized' nations and to address the pressures imposed by Western powers. However, these transplanted legal concepts were not adopted wholesale; instead, they were carefully adapted to align with Japan's traditions, including its hierarchical social structure and communal values.

One of the primary challenges of legal transplantation in Japan was the risk of superficiality—laws could be adopted in form but not in substance. This issue was evident in the Meiji Constitution, which, while introducing Western-style governance structures such as a parliament and legal protections, retained authoritarian power dynamics rooted in Japan's centralized feudal heritage. The process of legal transplantation in Japan also highlights the dynamic interplay between law and society. For example, the post-World War II reforms initiated by the Allied Occupation involved the adoption of American legal principles, culminating in a new constitution that emphasized democracy, human rights, and the rule of law. While these principles represented a dramatic departure from pre-war authoritarianism, they faced resistance and required decades of gradual integration to become embedded in Japanese society.

Japan's legal history demonstrates that legal transplantation is not a straightforward process of borrowing and implementing foreign laws. Rather, it involves complex negotiations to harmonize imported legal concepts with indigenous traditions and values. The Japanese experience highlights that successful transplantation depends on the ability to adapt and contextualize legal frameworks to align with the unique characteristics of the recipient society, thereby ensuring that the transplanted laws gain legitimacy and functionality.

References

Abel R (1982) Law as lag: inertia as a social theory of law. Mich Law Rev 80(4):785–809
Ajani G (1995) By chance and prestige: legal transplants in Russia and Eastern Europe. Am J Comp Law 43(1):93–117
Akita G (1967) Foundations of Constitutional Government in Modern Japan, 1868–1900. Harvard University Press, Cambridge
Avi-Yonah R (2000) Globalization, tax competition and the fiscal crisis of the welfare state. Harv Law Rev 113(7):1573–1676
Benedict R (1967) The chrysanthemum and the sword: patterns of Japanese culture. Meridian Books, Cleveland
Berat L (1992) The role of conciliation in the Japanese legal system. Am Univ Int Law Rev 8(1):125–154
Berkowitz D, Pistor K, Richard J-F (2003) The transplant effect. Am J Comp Law 51:163–203
Blakemore T, Yazawa M (1953) Japanese Commercial Code revisions concerning corporations. Am J Comp Law 2(1):12–24
Botsman DV (2005) Punishment and power in the making of modern Japan. Princeton University Press, Princeton
Charny D (2000) Regulatory competition and the global coordination of labor standards. J Int Econ Law 3(2):281–302
Damaska M (1986) The faces of justice and state authority: a comparative approach to the legal process. Yale University Press, New Haven
de Bary WM et al (2001) Sources of Japanese tradition: from earliest times to 1600, vol 1, 2nd edn. Columbia University Press, New York
Dean M (2002) Japanese legal system, 2nd edn. Cavendish Publishing, London
Ewald W (1995) Comparative jurisprudence (II): the logic of legal transplants. Am J Comp Law 43(4):489–510
Friedmann W (1972) Law in a changing society, 2nd edn. Penguin, Harmondsworth
Fukutake T (1982) The Japanese social structure: its evolution in the modern century. University of Tokyo Press, Tokyo
Gardner DK (2007) The Four Books: the basic teachings of the later Confucian tradition. Hackett Publishing Co, Indianapolis
Gardner DK (2014) Confucianism: a very short introduction. Oxford University Press, New York
Gibbons DJ (1990) Law and the group ethos in Japan. Int Leg Perspect 3:98–126
Gillespie J (2001) Globalisation and legal transplantation: lessons from the past. Deakin Law Rev 6(2):286–311
Goodman CF (2003) The rule of law in Japan: a comparative analysis. Kluwer Law International, The Hague
Gordon A (2019) A modern history of Japan: from Tokugawa times to the present. Oxford University Press, New York

Graziadei M (2009) Legal transplants and the frontiers of legal knowledge. Theor Inq Law 10(2):723–743
Graziadei M (2019) Comparative law, transplants and receptions. In: Reimann M, Zimmermann R (eds) The Oxford handbook of comparative law, 2nd edn. Oxford University Press, Oxford, pp 442–473
Haley JO (1982) Sheathing the sword of justice in Japan: an essay on law without sanctions. J Jpn Stud 8:265–281
Haley JO (1991a) Dispute resolution in Japan: lessons in autonomy. Canada-US Law J 17(2):443–447
Haley JO (1991b) Authority without power: law and the Japanese paradox. Oxford University Press, New York
Haley JO (2006) The spirit of Japanese law. The University of Georgia Press, Athens
Hall JC (1906) Japanese feudal law: the Institutes of Judicature. The Asiatic Society of Japan, Tokyo
Hall JC (1908) Japanese feudal law Part II: the Ashikaga Code. The Asiatic Society of Japan, Tokyo
Hall JC (1912) Japanese feudal law Part III: the Tokugawa legislation. The Asiatic Society of Japan, Tokyo
Hall JW (1974) Rule by status in Tokugawa Japan. J Jpn Stud 1(1):39–49
Hane M, Perez LG (2013) Modern Japan: a historical survey, 5th edn. Westview Press, Boulder
Henderson DF (1952) Some aspects of Tokugawa law. Wash Law Rev 27(1):85–109
Hendry J (1995) Understanding Japanese society, 2nd edn. Routledge, London
Hozumi N (1904) The New Japanese Civil Code, as Material for the Study of Comparative Jurisprudence. A paper read at the International Congress of Arts and Sciences, at the Universal Exposition, Saint Louis, 1904. Tokyo Printing Co. Ltd, Tokyo
Kahn-Freund O (1974) On uses and misuses of comparative law. Mod Law Rev 37(1):1–27
Kawashima T (1963) Dispute resolution in contemporary Japan. In: von Mehren AT (ed) Law in Japan: the legal order in a changing society. Harvard University Press, Cambridge, pp 41–72
Kim C, Lawson CM (1979) The law of the subtle mind: the traditional Japanese conception of law. Int Comp Law Q 28(3):491–513
Legrand P (1997) The impossibility of legal transplants. Maastricht J Eur Comp Law 4:111–124
Legrand P (2001) What "legal transplants"? In: Nelken D, Feest J (eds) Adapting legal cultures. Hart Publishing, Oxford, pp 55–69
Levy E (1950) The reception of highly developed legal systems by peoples of different cultures. Wash Law Rev 25:233–245
Littlejohn RL (2011) Confucianism: an introduction. IB Tauris, London
Luhmann N (1995) Social systems. Stanford University Press, Stanford
Mason RHP, Caiger JG (1997) A history of Japan. Tuttle Publishing, Tokyo
Mattei U (1994) Efficiency in legal transplants: an essay in comparative law and economics. Int Rev Law Econ 14(1):3–19
Mattei U, Pulitini F (1991) A competitive model of legal rules. In: Breton A et al (eds) The competitive state: Villa Colombella papers on competitive politics. Kluwer Academic Publishers, Dordrecht, pp 207–219
Minear R (1970) Japanese tradition and western law: Emperor, state and law in the thought of Hozumi Yatsuka. Harvard University Press, Cambridge
Mirow M (2000) The power of Codification in Latin America: Simón Bolívar and the Code Napoléon. Tulane J Int Comp Law 8:83–116
Mirow M (2001) Borrowing private law in Latin America: Andres Bello's use of the Code Napoleon in drafting the Chilean Civil Code. La Law Rev 61:291–329
Mirow M (2004) Latin American law: a history of private law and institutions in Spanish America. University of Texas Press, Austin
Nakamura K (1964) The formation of modern Japan as viewed from legal history. The Centre for East Asian Cultural Studies / East West Center Press, Tokyo
Nakamura H (1971) Die Rezeption des deutschen Rechts in Japan: insbesondere auf dem Gebiete des Zivilprozessrechts. Zeitschrift für Zivilprozess 84(1):74–90

Nelken D (2003) Comparatists and transferability. In: Legrand P, Munday R (eds) Comparative legal studies: traditions and transitions. Cambridge University Press, Cambridge, pp 437–466
Neuman G (2004) The uses of international law in constitutional interpretation. Am J Int Law 98(1):82–90
Noda Y (1976) Introduction to Japanese Law. University of Tokyo Press, Tokyo. (originally published 1966)
Oda H (2021) Japanese law, 4th edn. Oxford University Press, Oxford
Ono S (1996) Comparative law and the civil law of Japan (1). Hitotsubashi J Law Polit 24:27–45
Örücü E (2002) Law as transposition. Int Comp Law Q 51:205–223
Port K (1996) Comparative law: law and the legal process in Japan. Carolina Academic Press, Durham, North Carolina
Priban J, Nelken D (eds) (2001) Law's new boundaries: the consequences of legal autopoiesis. Ashgate/Dartmouth, Aldershot
Rahn G (1990) Rechtsdenken und Rechtsauffassung in Japan: Dargestellt an der Entwicklung der modernen japanischen Zivilrechtsdogmatik. Beck, Munich
Rodière R (1979) Introduction au droit comparé. Dalloz, Paris
Sacco R (1991) Legal formants: a dynamic approach to comparative law II. Am J Comp Law 39(2):343–401
Sansom GB (1962) Japan: a short cultural history. Appleton Century Crofts, New York
Sansom GB (1974) A history of Japan to 1334. Charles E. Tuttle Company, Vermont and Tokyo
Sansom GB (1990) The western world and Japan: a study in the interaction of European and Asiatic Cultures. Charles E. Tuttle Company, Tokyo
See H (1982) The judiciary and dispute resolution in Japan: a survey. Florida State Univ Law Rev 10(3):339–368
Seidman A, Seidman RB (1996) Drafting legislation for development: lessons from a Chinese project. Am J Comp Law 44:1–44
Siems M (2007) The end of comparative law. J Comp Law 2:133–150
Siems M (2018) Comparative law, 2nd edn. Cambridge University Press, Cambridge
Stein E (1977) Uses, misuses and nonuses of comparative law. Northwest Univ Law Rev 72:198–216
Takayanagi K (1963) A century of innovation: the development of Japanese law, 1868-1961. In: von Mehren AT (ed) Law in Japan: the legal order in a changing society. Harvard University Press, Cambridge, pp 5–40
Tanaka H, Smith M (1976) The Japanese legal system. University of Tokyo Press, Tokyo
Teubner G (1993) Law as an autopoietic system. Blackwell, Oxford
Teubner G (1998) Legal irritants: good faith in British law or how unifying law ends up in new divergences. Mod Law Rev 61(1):11–32
Watson A (1976) Legal transplants and law reform. Law Q Rev 92:79–84
Watson A (1978) Comparative law and legal change. Camb Law J 37(2):313–336
Watson A (1983) Legal change: sources of law and legal culture. Univ Pa Law Rev 131(5):1121–1157
Watson A (1985) The evolution of law. Blackwell, Oxford
Watson A (1993) Legal transplants: an approach to comparative law, 2nd edn. University of Georgia Press, Athens, Georgia
Watson A (2001) The evolution of Western private law. John Hopkins University Press, Baltimore
Wise EM (1990) The transplant of legal patterns. Am J Comp Law 38:1–22
Wren HG (1968) The legal system of pre-Western Japan. Hastings Law J 20(1):217–244
Yao X (2000) An introduction to Confucianism. Cambridge University Press, Cambridge

Selected Bibliography

Aarnio A (1979) Denkweisen der Rechtswissenschaft. Springer, Vienna
Abdal-Haqq I (2002) Islamic law: an overview of is origin and elements. J Islam Law Cult 7(1):27–81
Abel R (1982) Law as lag: inertia as a social theory of law. Mich Law Rev 80(4):785–809
Abel RL, Lewis PSC (eds) (1995) Lawyers in society: an overview. University of California Press, Berkeley
Abou El Fadl K (2012) The Islamic legal tradition. In: Bussani M, Mattei U (eds) Cambridge companion to comparative law. Cambridge University Press, Cambridge
Adam L, Trimborn H (1958) Lehrbuch der Völkerkunde, 3rd edn. Enke, Stuttgart
Adams M, Bomhoff J (2012) Comparing law: practice and theory. In: Adam M, Bomhoff J (eds) Practice and theory in comparative law. Cambridge University Press, Cambridge
Adams M, Van Hoecke M (eds) (2021) Comparative methods in law, humanities and social sciences. Elgar, Cheltenham
Agostini E (1988) Droit comparé. P.U.F., Paris
Ainsworth JE (1996) Categories and culture: on the 'rectification of names' in comparative law. Cornell Law Rev 82:19–42
Ajani G (1995) By chance and prestige: legal transplants in Russia and Eastern Europe. Am J Comp Law 43(1):93–117
Ajani G et al (2018) Diritto comparato. Lezioni e materiali. Giappichelli, Turin
Ajani G et al (2023) Diritto comparato. 3. Le tradizioni giuridiche asiatiche e africane. Giappichelli, Turin
Akita G (1967) Foundations of Constitutional Government in Modern Japan, 1868–1900. Harvard University Press, Cambridge
Ali K (2011) Imam Shafi'i: scholar and saint. Oneworld Publications, Oxford
Allen CK (1964) Law in the making. Oxford University Press, Oxford
Alliot M (1968) L'acculturation juridique. In: Poirier J (ed) Encyclopédie de la Pléiade – Ethnologie générale. Gallimard, Paris, pp 1180–1246
Allot AN (1959) L'unité du droit Africain. Présence Africaine 27(28):343–358
Allott AN (1968) African law. In: Derrett JDM (ed) An introduction to legal systems. Sweet & Maxwell, London, pp 131–156
Allott A (1980) The limits of law. Butterworths, London
al-Saleh OA (1982) The right of the individual to personal security in Islam. In: Bassiouni C (ed) The Islamic criminal justice system. Oceana Publications, New York, pp 55–90

G. Mousourakis, *Traversing Legal Traditions*, Springer Textbooks in Law, https://doi.org/10.1007/978-3-031-94669-1

Amoo SK, Warikandwa TW, Kariseb K (2024) Comparative law and jurisprudence in Namibia: functions, methods and perspectives from selected jurisdictions. University of Namibia Press, Namibia
Ancel M (1981) Le comparatiste devant les systèmes (ou "familles") de droit. In: Bernstein H, Drobnig U, Kötz H (eds) Festschrift fur Konrad Zweigert. CB Mohr, Tübingen, pp 355–362
Ancel M (1982) Le probléme de la comparabilité et la méthode fonctionelle en droit compare. Festschrift für Imre Zajtay. Mohr Siebeck, Tubingen, pp 1–6
Andenas M, Fairgrieve D (eds) (2015) Courts and comparative law. Oxford University Press, Oxford
Anderson JND (1962) The future of Islamic law in British Commonwealth territories in Africa. Law Contemp Probl 27:617–631
Anscombe GEM (1958) On brute facts. Analysis 18(3):69–72
Aoki H (2001) Nobushige Hozumi: a skillful transplanter of Western legal thought into Japanese soil. In: Riles A (ed) Rethinking masters of comparative law. Hart Publishing, Oxford, pp 129–150
Arminjon P, Nolde B, Wolff M (1950) Traité de droit comparé, vol 1. Librairie Générale de Droit et de Jurisprudence, Paris
Arnad A-J (ed) (1993) Dictionnaire Encyclopédique de Théorie et de Sociologie du Droit, 2nd edn. LGDJ, Paris
Arnaud A-J (1975) Les Juristes face à la société du XIXe siècle à nos jours. PUF, Paris
Arvind TT (2010) The "transplant effect" in harmonization. Int Comp Law Q 59:65–88
Assiez-Andrieu L (1996) Le droit dans les sociétés humaines. Nathan, Paris
Atiyah RS, Summers RS (1987) Form and substance in Anglo-American Law, a comparative study of legal reasoning, legal theory, and legal institutions. Clarendon Press, Oxford
Auby J-B (2017) Globalisation, law and the state. Hart, Oxford
Austin J (1995) In: Rumble WE (ed) The province of jurisprudence determined. Cambridge University Press, Cambridge. (original work published 1832)
Avenarius M (2014) Fremde Traditionen des römischen Rechts. Wallstein, Göttingen
Ayittey G (1991) Indigenous African Institutions. Transnational Publishers, New York
Baker PV (1977) The future of equity. Law Q Rev 93:529–540
Baker JH (2000) The common law tradition: lawyers, books, and the law. Hambleton Press, London
Baker JH (2019) An introduction to English legal history, 5th edn. Oxford University Press, Oxford
Bamodu G (1994) Transnational law, unification and harmonization of international commercial law in Africa. J Afr Law 38:125–143
Barak A (2006) The judge in a democracy. Princeton University Press, Princeton
Barber BR (1992) Jihad vs. McWorld. Artlantic Monthly 269(3):53–65
Barnard A (2000) History and theory in anthropology. Cambridge University Press, Cambridge
Barone-Adesi G (1992) L'età della Lex Dei. Jovene, Naples
Barreau H (1995) L' épistémologie, 3rd edn. Presses Universitaires de France, Paris
Barrera A (2012) Turning legal pluralism into state-sanctioned law: assessing the implications of the new constitutions and laws in Bolivia and Ecuador. In: Schilling-Vacaflor A, Nolte D (eds) New constitutionalism in Latin America: promises and practices. Taylor & Francis Group, Abingdon, pp 371–390
Barton J (1971) Roman law in England. Giuffrè, Milan
Bassiouni MC, Badr GM (2002) The Shari'ah: sources, interpretation, and rule- making. J Islam Near Eastern Law 2(1):135–181
Baxter LG (1983) Pure comparative law and legal science in a mixed legal system. Comp Int Law J South Afr 16(1):84–99
Bearman P, Peters R, Vogel F (eds) (2005) The Islamic school of law: evolution, evolution and progress. Harvard University Press, Cambridge
Bell J (1994) Comparative law and legal theory. In: Krawietz W, MacCormick N, von Wright GH (eds) Prescriptive formality and normative rationality in modern legal systems, Festschrift for RS Summers. Duncker and Humblot, Berlin, pp 19–31
Bell J (1995) English law and French law – not so different? Curr Leg Probl 48:63–101

Bellomo M (1995) The common legal past of Europe, 1000–1800. Catholic University of America Press, Washington DC
Benedict R (1967) The chrysanthemum and the sword: patterns of Japanese culture. Meridian Books, Cleveland
Bennett TW (2019) Comparative law and African customary law. In: Reimann M, Zimmermann R (eds) The Oxford handbook of comparative law, 2nd edn. Oxford University Press, Oxford, pp 652–680
Bennett TW, Vermeulen T (1980) Codification of customary law. J Afr Law 24:206–219
Benson RL, Constable G (eds) (1982) Renaissance and renewal in the twelfth century. Harvard University Press, Cambridge
Benton L (2002) Law and colonial cultures. Cambridge University Press, Cambridge
Bergel J-L (1989) Théorie générale du droit, 2nd edn. Dalloz, Paris
Berkowitz D, Pistor K, Richard J-F (2003) The transplant effect. Am J Comp Law 51:163–203
Berlin I (2000) Three critics of the enlightenment: Vico, Hamann, Herder. Pimlico, London
Berman HJ (1974) The interaction of law and religion. SCM Press, London
Berman H (1994) The origins of historical jurisprudence: Coke, Selden, and Hale. Yale Law J 103:1651–1738
Berman H (2003) Law and revolution II: the impact of protestant reformations on the western legal tradition. Harvard University Press, Cambridge
Bernhöft F (1878) Über Zweck und Mittel der vergleichenden Rechtswissenschaft. Zeitschrift für vergleichende Rechtswissenschaft 1:1–38
Beudant R et al (1914) L'Oeuvre juridique de Raymond Saleilles. Rousseau, Paris
Bevilaqua C (1897) Resumo das licções de legislação comparada sobre o direito privado, 2nd edn. Bahia, Magalhães
Biddulph S, Nicholson P (2008) Expanding the circle: comparative legal studies in transition. In: Nicholson P, Biddulph S (eds) Examining practice, interrogating theory: comparative legal studies in Asia. Martinus Nijhoff, Leiden, pp 9–23
Bierling ER (1894) Juristische Prinzipienlehre I. Mohr, Freiburg im Br/Leipzig
Bitas BC (2016) Comparative legal systems. LexisNexis, Singapore
Blackstone W (1825) Commentaries on the Laws of England, 16th edn. A. Strahan for T. Cadell and J. Butterworth and Son, London (Original work published 1765-1769)
Blackstone W (1978) Commentaries on the Law of England. Garland Publishers, New York. (Original work published 1765-1769)
Blakemore T, Yazawa M (1953) Japanese Commercial Code revisions concerning corporations. Am J Comp Law 2(1):12–24
Blanc-Jouvan X (2001) Centennial world congress on comparative law: opening remarks. Tulane Law Rev 75(4):859–864
Blankenburg E (1994) The infrastructure for avoiding civil litigation – comparing culture of legal behaviour in the Netherlands and West Germany. Law Soc Rev 28(4):789–809
Blankenburg E, Bruinsma F (1991) Dutch legal culture. Kluwer Publishers, Deventer
Bodenheimer E (1974) Jurisprudence: the philosophy and method of the law. Harvard University Press, Cambridge
Boele-Woelki K, Grosheide FW, Hondius EH, Steenhoff GJW (1994) Comparability and evaluation. Martinus Nijhoff Publishers, Dordrecht
Bogdan M (1978) Different economic systems and comparative law, comparative law yearbook. Sijthoff, Leiden
Bogdan M (1994) Comparative law. Kluwer, Deventer, repr. 2000
Bogdan M (2013) Concise introduction to comparative law. Europa Law Publishing, Groningen
Bonell MJ (ed) (2006) The UNIDROIT principles in practice: caselaw and bibliography on the UNIDROIT principles of international commercial contracts, 2nd edn. Transnational Publishers, Ardsley
Borrows J (2010) Canada's indigenous constitution. University of Toronto Press, Toronto

Bosworth CE (1996) New Islamic dynasties: a chronological and genealogical manual. Edinburgh University Press, Edinburgh

Bothe M, Ress G (1980) The comparative method and international law. In: Butler WE (ed) International law in comparative perspective. Sijthoff & Noordhoff, Alphen aan den Rijn, pp 49–66

Botsman DV (2005) Punishment and power in the making of modern Japan. Princeton University Press, Princeton

Bowen CD (1957) The lion and the throne: the life and times of Sir Edward Coke (1552–1634). Little, Brown & Co, Boston, repr. 1990

Boyer A (1997) Understanding, authority, and law: Sir Edward Coke and the Elizabethan origins of judicial review. Boston Coll Law Rev 39:43–93

Boyer A (2003) Sir Edward Coke and the Elizabethan age. Stanford University Press, Stanford

Bozeman A (1971) The future of law in a multicultural world. Princeton University Press, Princeton

Brand O (2007) Conceptual comparisons: towards a coherent methodology of comparative legal studies. Brooklyn J Int Law 32:405–466

Braun A (2006) Giudici e Accademia nell'Esperienza Inglese. Il Mulino, Bologna

Browne D (ed) (1933) Ashburner's principles of equity, 2nd edn. Butterworths, London

Brownlie I (1992) Treaties and indigenous peoples. Oxford University Press, New York

Brundage JA (1995) Medieval canon law. Longman, London

Brunyate J (ed) (1936) Equity, a course of lectures by FT Maitland, 2nd edn. Cambridge University Press, Cambridge

Buckland W, McNair AD (1965) Roman law and common law: a comparison in outline, 2nd edn. Cambridge University Press, Cambridge

Bussani M, Mattei U (eds) (2003) The common core of European private law. Kluwer Law International, The Hague

Bussani M, Mattei U (eds) (2012) The Cambridge companion to comparative law. Cambridge University Press, Cambridge

Bussani M, Sebok AJ (eds) (2015) Comparative Tort law. Global perspectives. Edward Elgar, Cheltenham

Butler WE (ed) (1980) International law in comparative perspective. Sijthoff & Noordhoff, Alphen aan den Rijn

Butler WE (1989) On the history of international law in England and Russia. In: Butler WE (ed) The non-use of force in international law. Martinus Nijhoff, Dordrecht, pp 3–15

Cain M, Harrington CB (eds) (1994) Lawyers in a postmodern world; translation and transgression. Open University Press, Buckingham

Cairns JW (1984) Blackstone, an English institutist: legal literature and the rise of the nation state. Oxf J Leg Stud 4:318–360

Cairns JW (2013) Watson, Walton and the history of legal transplants. Ga J Int Comp Law 41:637–696

Cannata CA (1989) Histoire de la jurisprudence européenne. Giappichelli, Turin

Cardozo B (1925) The nature of the judicial process. Yale University Press, New Haven

Carey Miller D, Zimmermann R (eds) (1997) The civilian tradition and Scots law. Dunker and Humblot, Berlin

Carothers T (1998) The rule of law revival. Foreign Aff 77(2):95–106

Carr EH (1964) What is history? Penguin Books, Harmondsworth

Cavinet G, Andenas M, Fairgrieve D (eds) (2004) Comparative law before the courts. BIICL, London

Chan W-T et al (1969) The great Asian religions: an anthology. Macmillan, New York

Charny D (2000) Regulatory competition and the global coordination of labor standards. J Int Econ Law 3(2):281–302

Chen J (2016) Chinese law: context and transformation. Brill Nijhoff, Leiden

Cheng B (1953) General principles of law as applied by international courts and tribunals. Stevens & Sons, London, repr. (2006)

Chiba M (1989) Legal pluralism. Toward a general theory through Japanese legal culture. Tokai University Press, Tokyo
Chiba M (1991) Legal pluralism in and across legal cultures. In: Sack P, Carl Wellman P, Yasaki M (eds) Monismus oder Pluralismus der Rechtskulturen? Anthropologische und ethnologische Grundlagen traditioneller und moderner Rechtssysteme/Monistic or Pluralistic Legal Culture? Anthropological and Ethnological Foundations of Traditional and Modern Legal Systems, Rechtstheorie: Zeitschrift für Logik, Methodenlehre, Kybernetik und Soziologie des Rechts. Duncker & Humblot, Berlin, Beiheft 12, pp 283–306
Cho K-C (1980) Koreanisches Bürgerliches Gesetzbuch. Metzner, Frankfurt
Clarence Smith JA (1975) Medieval law teachers and writers. University of Ottawa Press, Ottawa
Clark DS (1990) Comparative and private international law. Duncker & Humblot, Berlin
Clark DS (2001) Nothing new in 2000? Comparative law in 1900 and today. Tulane Law Rev 75(4):871–912
Clark DS (ed) (2007) Encyclopedia of law and society: American and global perspectives. Sage Publications, Thousand Oaks
Clark DS (2014) Comparative law and society. Edward Elgar, Cheltenham
Cocks R (1988) Sir Henry Maine: a study in Victorian jurisprudence. Cambridge University Press, Cambridge
Coing H (1956) Das deutsche Schuldrecht und die Rechtsvergleichung. Neue Juristische Wochenschrift 569
Coing H (1977) Handbuch der Quellen und Literatur der neueren europäischen Privatrechtsgeschichte. II: Neuere Zeit (1500–1800), 1. Teilband, Wissenschaft. Beck, Munich
Collins R (1991) Early medieval Europe 300–1000. MacMillan, London
Collins H (1996) Marxism and law. Oxford University Press, Oxford
Constantinesco LJ (1971) Rechtsvergleichung I. Heymanns, Köln
Constantinesco LJ (1974) Traité de droit comparé, II, La méthode comparative. Librairie générale de droit et de jurisprudence, Paris
Constantinesco LJ (1979) Über den Stil der 'Stiltheorie' in der Rechtsvergleichung. Zeitschrift für vergleichende Rechtswissenschaft 78:154–172
Constantinesco LJ (1981) Die Kulturkreise als Grundlage der Rechtskreise. Zeitschrift für Rechtsvergleichung 22:161–178
Constantinesco LJ (1983) Rechtsvergleichung III Die rechtsvergleichende Wissenschaft. Heymanns, Köln
Cooper J, Nettler RL, Mahmoud M (2000) Islam and modernity. Tauris Publishers, New York
Cornell VJ (1999) Fruit of the tree of knowledge: the relationship between faith and practice in Islam. In: Esposito JL (ed) The Oxford history of Islam. Oxford University Press, Oxford, pp 63–106
Cortese E (1992) Il rinascimento giuridico medievale. Bulzoni, Rome
Cortese E (1995) Il diritto nella storia medievale, vol 2. Il cigno Galileo Galilei, Rome
Cotterrell R (1989) The politics of jurisprudence. Butterworth, London
Cotterrell R (2006) Law, culture and society: legal ideas in the mirror of social theory. Ashgate, Aldershot
Cotterrell R (2007) Sociology of law. In: Clark DS (ed) Encyclopedia of law and society: American and global perspectives. Sage, Thousand Oaks, pp 1413–1420
Cotterrell R (2016) Living law. Studies in legal and social theory. Routledge, London & New York
Coulson NJ (1964) A history of Islamic law. Edinburgh University Press, Edinburgh
Coulson NJ (1969) Conflicts and tensions in Islamic jurisprudence. University of Chicago Press, Chicago
Coulson NJ (2008) Succession in the Muslim family. Cambridge University Press, Cambridge
Crisp R (1996) Naturalism and non-naturalism in ethics. In: Lovibond S, Williams SG (eds) Identity, truth and value. Blackwell Publishers, Malden, pp 113–129
Crowder M (1987) Whose dream was it anyway? Twenty-five years of African independence. Afr Aff 86:7–24

Cuche D (2004) La notion de culture dans les sciences sociales, 3rd edn. Le Decouverte, Paris
D'Entreves AP (1970) Natural law: an introduction to legal philosophy, 2nd edn. Hutchinson, London
Damaska M (1975) Structures of authority and comparative criminal procedure. Yale Law J 84:480–544
Damaska M (1986) The faces of justice and state authority: a comparative approach to the legal process. Yale University Press, New Haven
Dannemann G (2019) Comparative law: study of similarities or differences? In: Reimann M, Zimmerman R (eds) The Oxford handbook of comparative law, 2nd edn. Oxford University Press, Oxford, pp 390–422
Danner RA, Bernal M-LH (1994) Introduction to foreign legal systems. Oceana Publications, New York
Darian-Smith E (2013) Laws and societies in global contexts: contemporary approaches. Cambridge University Press, New York
Dauchy S, Martyn G, Musson A et al (eds) (2016) The formation and transmission of Western legal culture. Springer, Cham
David R (1950) Traité élémentaire de droit civil comparé: Introduction à l'étude des droits étrangers et à la méthode comparative. Librairie générale de droit et de jurisprudence, Paris
David R (1971) Livre du Centenaire de la Societé de la Legislation Comparé, vol 2. Librairie générale de droit et de jurisprudence, Paris
David R (chief editor) (1976) International Encyclopedia of comparative law, vol II, The legal systems of the world. Their comparison and unification. Tübingen et al., J.C.B. Mohr
David R (1988) Les grands systèmes de droit contemporains, 9th edn. Dalloz, Paris; 12th edn. LGDJ, Paris, 2016
David R, Brierley J (1985) Major legal systems in the world today. An introduction to the comparative study of law, 3rd edn. Stevens, London
Davis S, Partridge W (1996) Promoting the development of indigenous people in Latin America. In: Iturralde D, Krotz E (eds) Indigenous development: poverty, democracy and sustainability. Inter-American Development Bank, Washington DC, pp 41–45
Dawson JP (1968) The oracles of law. University of Michigan Press, Ann Arbor
de Bary WM et al (2001) Sources of Japanese tradition: from earliest times to 1600, vol 1, 2nd edn. Columbia University Press, New York
de Boer TM (1994) The missing link: some thoughts on the relationship between private international law and comparative law. In: Boele-Woelki K, Grosheide FW, Hondius EH, Steenhoff GJW (eds) Comparability and evaluation: essays on comparative law, private international law and international commercial arbitration. Martinus Nijhoff Publishers, Dordrecht, pp 15–25
de Boer TM (1996) Facultative choice of law, the procedural status of choice-of-law rules and foreign law. Recueil des cours 257:223–427
de Cruz P (1993) A modern approach to comparative law. Kluwer, Deventer
de Cruz P (1999) Comparative law in a changing world, 2nd edn. Cavendish Pub, London
de Sola Cañizares F (1954) Iniciación al derecho comparado. Consejo Superior de Investigaciones Científicas, Barcelona
de Zulueta F (ed) (1927) The Liber Pauperum of Vacarius. Publications of the Selden Society, London
Dean M (2002) Japanese legal system, 2nd edn. Cavendish Publishing, London
del Vecchio G (1950) L' unité de l' esprit humain comme base de la comparaison juridique. Revue internationale de droit comparé 2(4):686–691
del Vecchio G (1960) Les bases du droit comparé et les principes généraux du droit. Revue internationale de droit compare 12:493–499
Demleitner N (1998) Challenge, opportunity and risk: an era of change in comparative law. Am J Comp Law 46(4):647–655
Demleitner N (2019) Comparative law in legal education. In: Reimann M, Zimmermann R (eds) The Oxford handbook of comparative law, 2nd edn. Oxford University Press, Oxford, pp 320–344

Derrett JDM (ed) (1968) An introduction to legal systems. Sweet & Maxwell, London
Descamps O (2019) Robert-Joseph Pothier: (1699-1772). In: Descamps O, Domingo R (eds) Great Christian jurists in French history. Cambridge University Press, Cambridge
Deva Prasad M, Suchithra Menon C (2020) Indian forest rights legislation: significance of recognizing the legal pluralism for indigenous peoples rights. Statute Law Rev 41(1):78–88
Diamond A (ed) (2006) The Victorian Achievement of Sir Henry Maine: a centennial reappraisal. Cambridge University Press, Cambridge
Dibadj R (2008) Panglossian transnationalism. Stanford J Int Law 44:253–299
Dixon R, Ginsburg T, Abebe A (2022) Introduction to comparative constitutional law in Africa. In: Dixon R, Ginsburg T, Abebe A (eds) Comparative constitutional law in Africa. Edward Elgar, Cheltenham and Northampton, pp 1–4
Doe N (2018) Comparative religious law: Judaism, Christianity, Islam. Cambridge University Press, Cambridge
Domingo R (2018) Roman law: an introduction. Routledge, London
Donahue C (1979) Review of St German's Doctor and Student, eds. T.F.T Plucknett and J.L. Barton. Leg Hist Rev 47(2):182–186
Donahue C (2019) Comparative law before the Code Napoléon. In: Reimann M, Zimmermann R (eds) The Oxford handbook of comparative law, 2nd edn. Oxford University Press, Oxford, pp 3–28
Donlan SP, Mair J (eds) (2020) Comparative law: mixes, movements, and metaphors. Routledge, Abingdon
Donnelly J (1984) Cultural relativism and universal human rights. Hum Rights Q 6(4):400–419
Donner FM (1999) Muhammed and the Caliphate: political history of the Islamic empire up to the Mongol conquest. In: Esposito JL (ed) The Oxford history of Islam. Oxford University Press, Oxford, pp 1–62
Doolittle IG (2001) William Blackstone, a biography. Maney Publishing, Leeds
Drew KF (1988) Law and society in early medieval Europe. Studies in legal history. Variorum, London
Driberg JH (1935) The African conception of law. J Roy Afr Soc 136:230–246
Drobnig U, Dopffel P (1982) Die Nutzung der Rechtsvergleichung durch den deutschen Gesetzgeber. Rabels Zeitschrift für ausländisches und internationals Privatrecht 46:253–307
Drobnig U, van Erp JHM (eds) (1999) The use of comparative law by courts. Kluwer Law International, The Hague
du Plessis PJ (2015) Borkowski's textbook on roman law, 5th edn. Oxford University Press, Oxford
du Plessis J (2019) Comparative law and the study of mixed legal systems. In: Reimann M, Zimmermann R (eds) The Oxford handbook of comparative law, 2nd edn. Oxford University Press, Oxford, pp 474–501
Dubber MD, Tomlins C (eds) (2018) The Oxford handbook of legal history. Oxford University Press, Oxford
Dupret B (2007) Legal pluralism, plurality of laws, and legal practices: theories, critiques, and praxiological re-specification. Eur J Leg Stud 1:296–318
Durie E (1996) Will the settlers settle? Cultural conciliation and the law. Otago Law Rev 8(4):449–465
Dworkin R (1986) Law's Empire. Harvard University Press, Cambridge
Eberhard C, Vernicos G (eds) (2006) La Quête Anthropologique du Droit: Autour de la Démarche d'Étienne le Roy. Karthala, Paris
Eberle EJ (2009) The method and role of comparative law. Wash Univ Global Stud Law Rev 8(3):451–486
Ehrmann HW (1976) Comparative legal cultures. Prentice-Hall, Englewood Cliffs
Eisenberg M (1988) The nature of the common law. Harvard University Press, Cambridge
Eisenstadt SN (1965) Social change and modernization in African societies south of the Sahara. Cahiers d'études africaines 5:453–471
El-Hibri T (2021) The Abbasid Caliphate: a history. Cambridge University Press, Cambridge

Elias O (1955) The nature of African customary law. Manchester University Press, Manchester

Emon AM, Ahmed R (2018) The Oxford handbook of Islamic law. Oxford University Press, Oxford

Endicott T (1989) The conscience and the king: Christopher St German and Thomas More and the development of English equity. Univ Toronto Law Rev 47(2):549–569

Engelbrekt AB, Nergelius J (eds) (2010) New directions in comparative law. Edward Elgar Pub, Cheltenham

Erk J (2022) Traditional kingdoms and modern constitutions: parochialism, patriarchy, and despotism vs. indigenous safeguards against absolutism. In: Dixon R, Ginsburg T, Abebe A (eds) Comparative constitutional law in Africa. Edward Elgar, Cheltenham and Northampton, pp 328–359

Esmein A (1905) Le droit comparé et l'enseignement du droit comparé. In: Congrès international du droit comparé tenu à Paris du 31 juillet au 4 août 1900, Procès- verbaux des séances et documents I. Librairie générale de droit de jurisprudence, Paris 445

Esmein A (1909) Éléments de droit constitutionnel français et comparé. Sirey, Paris

Esposito JL (1988) Islam: the straight path. Oxford University Press, New York

Esposito JL (ed) (2003) The Oxford dictionary of Islam. Oxford University Press, Oxford

Evans J (1994) Aristotle's theory of equity. In: Krawietz W, MacCormick N, von Wright GH (eds) Prescriptive formality and normative rationality in modern legal systems: Festschrift for Robert S. Summers. Duncker and Humblot, Berlin, pp 225–244

Evans-Jones R (ed) (1995) The civil law tradition in Scotland. The Stair Society, Edinburgh

Evans-Jones R (1999) Roman law in Scotland and England and the development of one law for Britain. Law Q Rev 115:605–630

Ewald W (1995a) Comparative jurisprudence (1): what was it like to try a rat? Univ Pa Law Rev 143:1889–2149

Ewald W (1995b) Comparative jurisprudence (II): the logic of legal transplants. Am J Comp Law 43(4):489–510

Ewald W (1998) The jurisprudential approach to comparative law: a field guide to 'rats'. Am J Comp Law 46:701–707

Faruqi IR, Faruqi LL (1986) The cultural atlas of Islam. Macmillan, London

Fauvarque-Cosson B (2001) Comparative law and conflict of laws: allies or enemies? New perspectives on an old couple. Am J Comp Law 49:407–423

Feaver G (1969) From status to contract: a biography of Sir Henry Maine 1822–1888. Longmans Green, London

Feldman N (2008) Why Shariah? New York Times Magazine, Mar. 16, pp 46–51

Fenrich J, Galizzi P, Higgins T (2010) The future of African customary law. Cambridge University Press, Cambridge

Ferrari V (1990) Socio-legal concepts and their comparison. In: Oeyen E (ed) Comparative methodology: theory and practice in international social research. Sage, London, pp 63–80

Fezer KH (1986) Teilhabe und Verantwortung. Beck, Munich

Fikentscher W (1995) Modes of thought: a study in the anthropology of law and religion. Mohr, Tübingen

Fletcher GP (1998) Comparative law as subversive discipline. Am J Comp Law 46:683–700

Fombad CM (2013) The Botswana legal system. Lexis Nexis, Durban

Fombad CM (2024) Sub-Saharan Africa. In: Siems M, Yap PJ (eds) The Cambridge handbook of comparative law. Cambridge University Press, Cambridge, pp 367–384

Frankenberg G (1985) Critical comparisons: re-thinking comparative law. Harv Int Law J 26(2):411–455

Frankenberg G (2016) Comparative law as critique. Edward Elgar Publishing, Cheltenham

Franklin M (1954) The influence of Savigny and Gans on the development of the legal and constitutional theory of Christian Roselius. Festschrift Rabel 1:141

Freamon BK (1998) Slavery, freedom, and the doctrine of consensus in Islamic jurisprudence. Harv Hum Rights J 11(1):1–64

Friedman LM (1973) A history of American law. Simon & Schuster, New York

Friedman L (1975) The legal system: a social science perspective. Russell Sage Foundation, New York
Friedman L (1977) Law and society: an introduction. Prentice Hall, Englewood Cliffs
Friedman LM (1994) Is there a modern legal culture? Ratio Juris 7(2):117–131
Friedmann W (1972) Law in a changing society, 2nd edn. Penguin, Harmondsworth
Friedrich CJ (ed) (1954) The philosophy of Hegel. Random House, New York
Friedrich CJ (1963) The philosophy of law in historical perspective. University of Chicago Press, Chicago
Fukutake T (1982) The Japanese social structure: its evolution in the modern century. University of Tokyo Press, Tokyo
Fulbeck W (1600) A direction or preparative to the study of the law. Thomas Wight, London
Fulbeck W (1601) A parallele or conference of the civil law, the canon law, and the common law of this realme of England. Thomas Wight, London
Fuller L (1968–1969) The law's precarious hold on life. Ga Law Rev 3:530–545
Fuller L (1969a) The morality of law. Yale University Press, New Haven
Fuller L (1969b) Human interaction and the law. Am J Jurisprud 14(1):1–36
Fyzee Asaf AA (1964) Outlines of Muhammadan law. Oxford University Press, London
Gagarin M (1989) Early Greek Law. University of California Press, Berkeley and Los Angeles
Gambaro A, Sacco R (2009) Sistemi guridici comparati, 2nd edn. UTET, Turin
Gans E (1824–1835) Das Erbrecht in weltgeschichtlicher Entwicklung. Maurer, Berlin
Gardner DK (2007) The Four Books: the basic teachings of the later Confucian tradition. Hackett Publishing Co, Indianapolis
Gardner DK (2014) Confucianism: a very short introduction. Oxford University Press, New York
Garnsey P (2007) Thinking about property: from antiquity to the age of revolution. Cambridge University Press, Cambridge
Gaudemet E (1912) Raymond Saleilles 1855-1912. Revue bourguignonne de l'Université de Dijon 22:161–263
Gebeye BA (2021) A theory of African constitutionalism. Oxford University Press, Oxford
Geertz C (1973) Interpretation of cultures. Basic Books, New York
Geertz C (1983) Local knowledge: fact and law in comparative perspective. In: Local knowledge: further essays in interpretive anthropology. Basic Books, New York
Gerber DJ (2001a) Globalization and legal knowledge. Tulane Law Rev 75:949–975
Gerber DJ (2001b) Sculpting the agenda of comparative law: Ernst Rabel and the facade of language. In: Riles A (ed) Rethinking the masters of comparative law. Hart Publishing, Oxford, pp 190–208
Gessner V, Hoeland A, Varga C (1996) European legal cultures. Dartmouth, Aldershot
Gest CM (1909) The writings of Sir Edward Coke. Yale Law J 18:504–532
Ghisalberti C (1979) Unità nazionale e unificazione giuridica in Italia. Laterza, Bari
Gibbons DJ (1990) Law and the group ethos in Japan. Int Leg Perspect 3:98–126
Gillespie J (2001) Globalisation and legal transplantation: lessons from the past. Deakin Law Rev 6(2):286–311
Gilmore MP (1963) Humanists and jurists. Harvard University Press, Cambridge
Ginsburg T, Dixon R (eds) (2011) Comparative constitutional law. Elgar, Cheltenham
Ginsburg T, Monateri PG, Parisi F (2014) Classics in comparative law. Edward Elgar, Cheltenham
Girard PF, Senn F (1977) Les lois des Romains. Jovere Editore, Naples
Glanert S (2014) Comparative law: engaging translation. Routledge, Abingdon
Glasson E-D (1879) Le mariage civil et le divorce dans les principaux pays de l'Europe, précédé d'un aperçu sur les origines du droit civil moderne : Études de législation comparée. Pedone-Lauriel, Paris
Glendon MA, Carozza PG, Picker C (2014) Comparative legal traditions: texts, materials and cases on Western law. West Academic Publishing, St. Paul
Glenn HP (1987) Persuasive authority. McGill Law J 32:261–299
Glenn HP (1998) The grounding of codification. Univ Calif Law Davis Rev 31:765–782

Glenn HP (2001) Comparative law and legal practice: on removing the borders. Tulane Law Rev 75:977–1002
Glenn HP (2014) Legal traditions of the world: sustainable diversity in law, 5th edn. Oxford University Press, Oxford
Glenn HP (2019) Comparative legal families and comparative legal traditions. In: Reimann M, Zimmermann R (eds) The Oxford handbook of comparative law, 2nd edn. Oxford University Press, Oxford, pp 423–441
Goff R, Jones G (1986) The law of restitution, 3rd edn. Sweet and Maxwell, London
Goldberg JCP, Smith HE, Turner PG (eds) (2019) Equity and law: fusion and fission. Cambridge University Press, Cambridge
Goldsmith E (1992) The way: an ecological world view. Rider, London
Gomez Isa F (2014) Cultural diversity, legal pluralism, and human rights from an indigenous perspective: the approach by the Colombian Constitutional Court and the Inter-American Court of Human Rights. Hum Rights Q 36(4):722–755
Gonthier CD (1993) Some comments on the common law and the civil law in Canada: influences, parallel developments and borrowings. Can Bus Law J 21:323–334
Goodman CF (2003) The rule of law in Japan: a comparative analysis. Kluwer Law International, The Hague
Gordley J (2001) Comparative law and legal education. Tulane Law Rev 75:1003–1014
Gordley J (2019) Comparative law and legal history. In: Reimann M, Zimmermann R (eds) The Oxford handbook of comparative law, 2nd edn. Oxford University Press, Oxford, pp 754–771
Gordon A (2019) A modern history of Japan: from Tokugawa times to the present. Oxford University Press, New York
Gorla G (1963) Intérêts et problèmes de la comparaison entre le droit continental et la Common Law. Revue internationale de Droit comparé 15:5–18
Grammond S (2010) La réception des systèmes juridiques autochtones au Canada. In: Breton A, Des Ormeaux A, Pistor K, Salmon P (eds) Le Multijuridisme. Manifestations, Causes et Conséquences. Editions ESKA, Paris, pp 54–86
Grande E (2000) Imitazione e Diritto: ipotesi sulla circolazione dei modelli. Giappichelli, Turin
Grant E (2006) Human rights, cultural diversity and customary law in South Africa. J Afr Law 50:2–23
Graziadei M (2003) The functionalist heritage. In: Legrand P, Munday R (eds) Comparative legal studies: traditions and transitions. Cambridge University Press, Cambridge, pp 100–128
Graziadei M (2009) Legal transplants and the frontiers of legal knowledge. Theor Inq Law 10(2):723–743
Graziadei M (2019) Comparative law, transplants and receptions. In: Reimann M, Zimmermann R (eds) The Oxford handbook of comparative law, 2nd edn. Oxford University Press, Oxford, pp 442–473
Griffiths J (1986) What is legal pluralism? J Leg Plur Unoff Law 18(24):1–55
Grossfeld B (1990) The strength and weakness of comparative law. Oxford University Press, New York
Grossfeld B, Eberle EJ (2003) Patterns of order in comparative law: discovering and decoding invisible powers. Tex Int Law J 38:291–316
Grossfeld B, Grosswald Curran V (2005) Core questions of comparative law. Carolina Academic Press, Durham
Grossfeld B, Wilde M (1994) Josef Kohler und das Recht der deutschen Schutzgebiete. Rabels Zeitschrift 58:59–75
Grosswald Curran V (1998a) Dealing in difference: comparative law's potential for broadening legal perspectives. Am J Comp Law 46(4):657–668
Grosswald Curran V (1998b) Cultural immersion, difference and categories in U.S. comparative law. Am J Comp Law 46(1):43–92
Guarnieri A (2020) Lineamenti di diritto comparator, 9th edn. Cedam, Padua
Gutteridge HC (1938) The comparative aspects of legal terminology. Tulane Law Rev 12:401–411

Gutteridge HC (1946) Comparative law: an introduction to the comparative method of legal study and research. Cambridge University Press, Cambridge. repr. 2015
Gutteridge HC (1953) Le droit comparé, Introduction à la méthode comparative dans la recherche Juridique et l'étude du droit. Librairie générale de droit et de jurisprudence, Paris
Guzmán Brito A (2000) A La codificación civil en Iberoamérica, Siglos XIX y XX. Editorial Jurídica de Chile, Santiago
Hage JC (2014) Comparative law as method and the method of comparative law. Hart, Oxford
Hakim N (2002) L'autorité de la doctrine civiliste française au XIX siècle. LGDJ, Paris
Haldon JF (1990) Byzantium in the seventh century: the transformation of a culture. Cambridge University Press, Cambridge
Haley JO (1982) Sheathing the sword of justice in Japan: an essay on law without sanctions. J Jpn Stud 8:265–281
Haley JO (1991a) Dispute resolution in Japan: lessons in autonomy. Canada-US Law J 17(2):443–447
Haley JO (1991b) Authority without power: law and the Japanese paradox. Oxford University Press, New York
Haley JO (2006) The spirit of Japanese law. The University of Georgia Press, Athens
Hall JC (1906) Japanese feudal law: the Institutes of Judicature. The Asiatic Society of Japan, Tokyo
Hall J (1963) Comparative law and social theory. Louisiana State University Press, Baton Rouge
Hall JW (1974) Rule by status in Tokugawa Japan. J Jpn Stud 1(1):39–49
Hallaq W (1985) Legal reasoning in Islamic law and the common law: logic and method. Cleveland State Law Rev 34:79–96
Hallaq W (1986) On the origins of the controversy about the existence of Mujtahids and the Gate of Ijtihad. Studia Islamica 63:129–144
Hallaq W (1992) Usul Al-Fiqh: beyond tradition. J Islam Stud 3(2):172–202
Hallaq W (2004) The formation of Islamic law. Ashgate, Burlington
Hamer M (1998) "Stool rights" and modern land law in Ghana: a geographical perspective on the transformation of tradition. Afr Spectrum 33:311–338
Hane M, Perez LG (2013) Modern Japan: a historical survey, 5th edn. Westview Press, Boulder Col
Hannum H (1988) New developments in indigenous rights. Va J Int Law 28:649–678
Harding A (1966) A social history of English law. Penguin Books, London
Harding A (2002) Medieval law and the foundations of the state. Oxford University Press, Oxford
Harding A, Örücü E (eds) (2003) Comparative law for the 21st century. Kluwer, Hague
Harmathy A (1999) Comparative law and changes of the law. Acta Juridica Hungarica 40:159–167
Harris J (1912) Dawn in darkest Africa. Smith, Elder & Co, London
Hart HLA (2012) The concept of law, 3rd edn. Oxford University Press, Oxford. (original work published 1961)
Hartley TC (1996) Pleading and proof of foreign law: the major European systems compared. Int Comp Law Q 45(2):271–292
Hasan A (1980) The definition of Qiyas in Islamic jurisprudence. Islam Stud 19(1):1–28
Hawting GR (2000) The first dynasty of Islam: The Umayyad Caliphate AD 661-750, 2nd edn. Routledge, London
Heck P (1914) Gesetzesauslegung und Interessenjurisprudenz. Archiv für die civilistische Praxis 112:1–318
Hegel GWF (2008) Outlines of the philosophy of right (trans: Knox TM). Oxford University Press, Oxford
Heimbach GE (ed) (1969) Constantini Harmenopuli Manuele legum sive Hexabiblos. Scientia, Aalen (Original work published 1851)
Henderson DF (1952) Some aspects of Tokugawa law. Wash Law Rev 27(1):85–109
Hendry J (1995) Understanding Japanese society, 2nd edn. Routledge, London
Herzog T (2018) A short history of European law: the last two and a half millennia. Harvard University Press, Cambridge
Hesselink MW (2001) The new European legal culture. Kluwer, Devender

Himonga C, Thandabantu N (eds) (2024) African customary law in South Africa. Post-Apartheid and living law perspectives, 2nd edn. Oxford University Press Southern Africa, Cape Town
Hobsbawm E, Ranger T (eds) (1983) The invention of tradition. Cambridge University Press, Cambridge
Hoeflich MH (2002) Translation and the reception of foreign law in the antebellum United States. Am J Comp Law 50(4):753–775
Hohfeld WN (1917) Fundamental legal conceptions as applied in judicial reasoning. Yale Law J 26(8):710–770
Holdsworth W (1915) The early history of equity. Mich Law Rev 13(4):293–301
Holdsworth WS (1923) A history of English law. Methuen, London
Holdsworth W (1938) Some makers of English law. Cambridge University Press, Cambridge
Holdsworth W (1956–1966) A history of English law, 7th edn. Sweet and Maxwell, Methuen
Holmes OW (1881) The common law. Little, Brown, & Co., Boston
Holmes OW (1897) The path of the law. Harv Law Rev 10:457–478
Honsell H (2002) Römisches Recht, 5th edn. Springer, Berlin; 8th edn 2015
Hooker MB (1975) Legal pluralism: an introduction to colonial and neo-colonial laws. Clarendon Press, Oxford
Horn N (1973) Die Legistische Literatur der Kommentatoren und der Ausbreitung des gelehrten Rechts. In: Coing H (ed) Handbuch der Quellen und Literatur der neueren europäischen Privatrechtsgeschichte. I: Mittelalter (1100-1500), Die gelehrten Rechte und die Gesetzgebung. Beck, Munich, pp 261–364
Howard-Hassmann R (1983) The full-belly thesis: should economic rights take priority over civil and political rights? Evidence from Sub-Saharan Africa. Hum Rights Q 5(4):467–490
Hozumi N (1904) The New Japanese Civil Code, as Material for the Study of Comparative Jurisprudence. A paper read at the International Congress of Arts and Sciences, at the Universal Exposition, Saint Louis, 1904. Tokyo Printing Co. Ltd, Tokyo
Hudson J (2016) The formation of English common law: law and society in England from the Norman conquest to Magna Carta. Routledge, London
Hug W (1932) The history of comparative law. Harv Law Rev 45(6):1027–1070
Hulme P (1995) Including America. ARIEL: Rev Int English Lit 26:117–123
Huntington S (1993) The clash of civilizations? Foreign Aff 72(3):22–49
Husa J (2015) A new introduction to comparative law. Hart, Oxford
Husa J (2022) Interdisciplinary comparative law: Rubbing shoulders with the neighbours or standing alone in a crowd. Elgar, Cheltenham
Husa J (2023) Introduction to comparative law, 2nd edn. Hart, Oxford
Husa J (ed) (2024) A research agenda for comparative law. Elgar, Cheltenham
Hussaini Sohail S (2007) The laws of inheritance in Islam, 2nd edn. Outskirts Press, Denver
Iqbal M (2011) The reconstruction of religious thought in Islam. Iqbal Academy Pakistan, Lahore (originally published 1930)
Ishikawa A, Leetsch I (1985) Das japanische BGB in deutscher Sprache. Carl Heymanns, Cologne
Jamin C (2000) Le vieux rêve de Saleilles et Lambert revisité: À propos du Congres international de droit comparé de Paris. Revue internationale de droit comparé 52(4):733–751
Jamin C (2002) Saleilles' and Lambert's old dream revisited: on the occasion of the centennial of the international congress of comparative law, Paris 1900. Am J Comp Law 50(4):701–718
Jansen GH (1979) Militant Islam. Harper & Row, New York
Jansen N (2019) Comparative law and comparative knowledge. In: Reimann M, Zimmermann R (eds) The Oxford handbook of comparative law, 2nd edn. Oxford University Press, Oxford, pp 291–319
Janssen H (2000) Die Übertragung von Rechtsvorstellungen auf fremde Kulturen am Beispiel des englischen Kolonialrechts: ein Beitrag zur Rechtsvergleichung. Mohr Siebeck, Tübingen
Jayme E (2000) Rechtsvergleichung und Fortschrittsidee in Rechtsvergleichung – Ideengeschichte und Grundlagen von Emerico Amari zur Postmoderne. Miller, Heidelberg
Jessup P (1956) Transnational law. Yale University Press, New Haven

Johnston D (1999) Roman law in context. Cambridge University Press, Cambridge
Joireman SF (2001) Inherited legal systems and effective rule of law: Africa and the colonial legacy. J Mod Afr Stud 39:571–596
Joireman SF (2010) Entrapment or freedom: enforcing customary property rights regimes in common-law Africa. In: Fenrich J-M et al (eds) The future of African customary law. Cambridge University Press, Cambridge, pp 295–311
Jolowicz HF (1957) Roman foundations of modern law. Clarendon Press, Oxford
Jolowicz HF, Nicholas B (1972) Historical introduction to the study of roman law, 3rd edn. Cambridge University Press, Cambridge, repr. 2008
Jones AHM (1964) The Later Roman Empire 284–602. Basil Blackwell, Oxford
Jones WJ (1967) The Elizabethan Court of Chancery. Clarendon Press, Oxford
Jordaan DW (2017) The open society: what does it really mean. De Jure 50:396–405
Juma L (2011) The laws of Lerotholi: role and status of codified rules of custom in the kingdom of Lesotho. Pace Int Law Rev 23:92–145
Kahn-Freund O (1965) Comparative law as an academic subject. Clarendon Press, Oxford
Kahn-Freund O (1966) Comparative law as an academic subject. Law Q Rev 82:40–61
Kahn-Freund O (1974) On uses and misuses of comparative law. Mod Law Rev 37(1):1–27
Kakouris CN (1999) L'utilisation de la méthode comparative par la Cour de justice des Communautés européennes. In: Drobnig U, van Erp S (eds) The use of comparative law by courts. Kluwer Law International, The Hague, pp 97–111
Kamala D, Lipimile G (2021) Harmonization and integration in Africa: the case of competition law and policy. In: Amao O, Olivier M, Magliveras KD (eds) The emergent African Union law: conceptualization, delimitation, and application. Oxford University Press, Oxford, pp 65–86
Kamali MH (1989) Sources, nature and objectives of Shari'ah. Islam Q 33(4):215–236
Kamali MH (1991) Principles of Islamic jurisprudence, revised edn. Islamic Texts Society, Cambridge
Kamali MH (1999) Law and society: the interplay of revelation and reason in the Shariah. In: Esposito JL (ed) The Oxford history of Islam. Oxford University Press, Oxford, pp 107–153
Kamali MH (2008) Shariah Law: an introduction. Oneworld Publications, Oxford
Kamba WJ (1974) Comparative law: a theoretical framework. Int Comp Law Q 23:485–519
Kaser M (1971) Das römische Privatrecht, 2nd edn. Beck, Munich
Kaser M (1976) Römische Rechtsgeschichte. Vandenhoeck & Ruprecht, Göttingen
Kawashima T (1963) Dispute resolution in contemporary Japan. In: von Mehren AT (ed) Law in Japan: the legal order in a changing society. Harvard University Press, Cambridge, pp 41–72
Kawharu IH (2008) Biculturalism and inclusion in New Zealand: the case of Orakei. Anthropologica 50(1):49–56
Keeton LW (1966) The Norman conquest and the common law. Barnes and Noble, New York
Kegel G (1990) Ernst Rabel – Werk und Person. Rabels Zeitschrift für ausländisches und internationales Privatrecht 54:1–23
Kelley DR (1970) Foundations of modern historical scholarship: language, law and history in the French Renaissance. Columbia University Press, New York
Kelly JM (1992) A short history of Western legal theory. Clarendon Press, Oxford; repr, p 2013
Kennedy H (2016) The early Abbasid Caliphate: a political history. Routledge, New York
Kepel G (2003) Muslim extremism in Egypt: the Prophet and Pharaoh. University of California Press, Berkeley
Khadduri M (trans) (1961, repr 1997) al-Shafii's Risala: treatise on the foundation of Islamic jurisprudence, 2nd edn. Islamic Texts Society, Cambridge
Khadduri M (1984) The Islamic conception of justice. Johns Hopkins University Press, Baltimore
Khan H (2007) The Islamic law of inheritance. Oxford University Press, Oxford
Kiesow RM (1997) Das Naturgesetz des Rechts. Suhrkamp, Frankfurt am Main
Kiikeri M (2012) Comparative legal reasoning and European law. Springer, Dordrecht
Kim C, Lawson CM (1979) The law of the subtle mind: the traditional Japanese conception of law. Int Comp Law Q 28(3):491–513

King M (1997) Comparing legal cultures in the quest for law's identity. In: Nelken D (ed) Comparing legal cultures. Aldershot, pp 119–134
Kingsbury B (1998) "Indigenous peoples" in international law: a constructivist approach to the Asian controversy. Am J Int Law 92(3):414–457
Kiralfy AKR (1958) Potter's historical introduction to English law and its institutions, 4th edn. Sweet and Maxwell, London
Kisch G (1955) Humanismus und Jurisprudenz. Der Kampf zwischen mos italicus und mos gallicus an der Universität Basel. Helbing & Lichtenhahn, Basel
Kisch G (1972) Studien zur humanistischen Jurisprudenz. De Gruyter, Berlin
Kischel U (2019) Comparative law. Oxford University Press, Oxford
Kiss AC (1980) Comparative law and public international law. In: Butler WE (ed) International law in comparative perspective. Sijthoff and Noordhoff, Alphen aan den Rijn, pp 41–48
Kitto F (2002) Foreword to Meagher RP, Heydon JD, Leeming MJ, Meagher, Gummow and Lehane's equity: doctrines and remedies, 4th edn. Butterworths Lexis Nexis, Sydney
Kleinhans M-M, Macdonald R (1997) What is critical legal pluralism. Can J Law Soc 12:25–46
Kleinheyer G, Schröder J (1983) Deutsche Juristen aus fünf Jahrhunderten. Eine biographische Einführung in die Geschichte der Rechtswissenschaft, 2nd edn. CF Müller Juristischer Verlag, Heidelberg
Knapp V (1991) Základy srovnávací právni vedy. Alcko, Praha
Knieper R (1996) Rechtsimperialismus? Zeitschrift für Rechtspolitik 29:64–67
Kohler J (1887) Über das Recht der Australneger. Zeitschrift für vergleichende Rechtswissenschaft 7:321–368
Kohler J (1895) Das Recht der Azteken. Zeitschrift für vergleichende Rechtswissenschaft 11:1–111
Koopmans T (1996) Comparative law and the courts. Int Comp Law Q 45:545–556
Koschaker P (1953) Europa und das Römische Recht. C. H. Beck, Munich
Koskenniemi M, Leino P (2002) Fragmentation of international law? Postmodern anxieties. Leiden J Int Law 15:553–579
Krawietz W, MacCormick N, von Wright GH (eds) (1995) Prescriptive formality and normative rationality in modern legal systems. Duncker & Humblot, Berlin
Kritzer HM (2002) Legal systems of the world: a political, social, and cultural Encyclopedia. ABC-CLIO, Santa Barbara
Krygier M (1986) Law as tradition. Law Philos 5:237–262
Krygier M (1991) Thinking like a lawyer. In: Sadurski W (ed) Ethical dimensions of legal theory. Rodopi, Amsterdam, pp 67–90
Kunkel W (1973) An introduction to Roman legal and constitutional history, 2nd edn. Clarendon, Oxford
Kunkel W, Schermaier M (2001) Römische Rechtsgeschichte. Cologne, Böhlau
Kymlicka W (1989) Liberalism, community, and culture. Oxford University Press, Oxford
Kymlicka W (1995) Multicultural citizenship: a liberal theory of minority rights. Oxford University Press, Oxford
Kymlicka W (2001) Politics in the vernacular: nationalism, multiculturalism, and citizenship. Oxford University Press, Oxford
Kymlicka W (2007) Multicultural Odysseys: navigating the new international politics of diversity. Oxford University Press, Oxford
Langbein JH (1985) The German advance in civil procedure. Univ Chic Law Rev 52:823–866
Lange H (1997) Römisches Recht im Mittelalter, 1: Die Glossatoren. C. H. Beck, Munich
Lange H, Kriechbaum M (2007) Römisches Recht im Mittelalter, Band II, Die Kommentatoren. Beck, Munich
Langrod G (1957) Quelques réflexions méthodologiques sur la comparaison en science juridique. Revue internationale de droit compare 9(2):353–369
Launay R (2001) Montesquieu: the specter of despotism and the origins of comparative law. In: Riles A (ed) Rethinking the masters of comparative law. Hart, Oxford, pp 22–38

Lawson FH (1953) A common lawyer looks at the civil law. University of Michigan Press, Ann Arbor; repr. William S. Hein & Company, Buffalo, 1988
Lawson FH (1977) The comparison: selected essays. North-Holland Publishing Co, Amsterdam
le Moigne J-L (1999) Les epistimologies constructivistes, 2nd edn. Presses universitaires de France, Paris
Leão DF, Rhodes PJ (2015) The laws of Solon: a new edition with introduction, translation and commentary. IB Tauris, London and New York
Legrand P (1996) European systems are not converging. Int Comp Law Q 45:52–81
Legrand P (1996–1997) Uniformity, legal traditions and law's limits. Juridisk Tidskrift 2:306–322
Legrand P (1997) The impossibility of legal transplants. Maastricht J Eur Comp Law 4:111–124
Legrand P (1999) Le droit comparé. P.U.F., Paris
Legrand P (2001) What "legal transplants"? In: Nelken D, Feest J (eds) Adapting legal cultures. Hart Publishing, Oxford, pp 55–69
Legrand P (2023) Comparative law and the task of negative critique. Routledge, Abingdon
Legrand P, Munday R (eds) (2003) Comparative legal studies: traditions and transitions. Cambridge University Press, Cambridge
Lepaulle P (1922) The function of comparative law with a critique of sociological jurisprudence. Harv Law Rev 35:838–858
Lesaffer R, Arriens J (2009) European legal history: a cultural and political perspective. Cambridge University Press, Cambridge
Levasseur AA (1999) The use of comparative law by courts. In: Drobnig U, van Erp JHM (eds) The use of comparative law by courts. Kluwer Law International, The Hague, pp 315–334
Levi L (1850–1852) Commercial law, its principles and administration, or, The mercantile law of Great Britain: compared with the codes and laws of commerce of the following mercantile countries: Anhalt, Austria ... Wurtemburg, and the Institutes of Justinian. W. Benning, London
Levi L (1854) Commercial law of the world. Smith Elder and Co, London
Levi-Strauss C (2001) Race et histoire. Albin Michel, Paris
Levy E (1950) The reception of highly developed legal systems by peoples of different cultures. Wash Law Rev 25:233–245
Lévy-Ullmann H (1923) Observations générales sur les communications relatives au droit privé dans les pays étrangers. In: Les transformations du droit dans les principaux pays depuis cinquante ans (1869–1919). Livre du cinquantenaire de la Société de législation comparée, Librairie Générale de Droit et de Jurisprudence, Paris, pp 85–111
Lewis JD (2007) Early Greek lawgivers. Bristol Classical Press, London
Lewis ADE, Ibbetson DJ (1994) The roman law tradition. Cambridge University Press, Cambridge
Libson G (1997) On the development of custom as a source of law in Islamic law. Islam Law Soc 4(2):131–155
Littlejohn RL (2011) Confucianism: an introduction. IB Tauris, London
Lobban M (1991) The common law and English jurisprudence 1760-1850. Clarendon Press, Oxford
Lombardi Clark B (1998) Islamic law as a source of constitutional law in Egypt: the constitutionalization of the Sharia in a modern Arab state. Columbia J Transnatl Law 37(1):81–123
Long M, Monier C (1997) Portalis: l'esprit de justice. Michalon, Paris
Lugard FD (1922) The dual mandate in British tropical Africa. William Blackwood and Sons, Edinburgh
Luhmann N (1974) Rechtssystem und Rechtsdogmatik. W. Kohlhammer, Stuttgart
Luhmann N (1982) The differentiation of society. Columbia University Press, New York
Luhmann N (1995) Social systems. Stanford University Press, Stanford
Luhmann N (2004) Law as a social system. Oxford University Press, Oxford
Lupoi M (2000) The origins of the European legal order. Cambridge University Press, Cambridge
Lyall A (2008) Early German legal anthropology: Albert Hermann Post and his questionnaire. J Afr Law 52(1):114–138

M'Baye K (1976) The African conception of the law. In: David R (gen ed) International encyclopedia of comparative law, volume II, The legal systems of the world. Their comparison and unification. J.C.B. Mohr, Tübingen
MacCormick N, Weinberger O (1986) An institutional theory of law: new approaches to legal positivism. Reidel, Dordrecht
MacQueen H (1993) Common law and feudal society in medieval Scotland. Edinburgh University Press, Edinburgh
MacQueen H (1999) Scots law and the road to the new ius commune. Law Libr 30(1):19–25
Maffei D (1956) Gli inizi dell'umanesimo giuridico. Giuffrè, Milan
Mahmood T (1965) Custom as a source of Law in Islam. J Indian Law Inst 7(1/2):102–106
Mahmood A, Ullah S, Ashfaq S (2018) The evolution of Jirga system: a conflict resolution mechanism in FATA. Lib Arts Soc Sci Int J 2(1):21–28
Mahoney P (2004) The comparative method in judgments of the European Court of Human Rights: reference back to national law. In: Cavinet G, Andenas M, Fairgrieve D (eds) Comparative law before the courts. British Institute of International and Comparative Law, London, pp 135–150
Maine HS (2017) Ancient law. Routledge, Abingdon
Maitland FW (1901) English law and the renaissance. Cambridge University Press, Cambridge
Maitland FW (1911) Collected papers. Cambridge University Press, Cambridge
Maitland FW (1976) The forms of action at common law. Cambridge University Press, Cambridge
Mak E (2011) Why do Dutch and UK judges cite foreign law? Camb Law J 70(2):420–450
Makdisi G (1981) The rise of colleges: institutions of learning in Islam and the West. Edinburgh University Press, Edinburgh
Makdisi G (1985a) The guilds of law in medieval legal history: an inquiry into the origins of the inns of court. Cleveland State Law Rev 34(3):3–18
Makdisi J (1985b) Legal logic and equity in Islamic law. Am J Comp Law 33(1):63–92
Maldonado DB (2021) Legal Barbarians: identity, modern comparative law and the Global South. Cambridge University Press, Cambridge
Malinowski BK (1945) The dynamics of culture change: an inquiry into race relations in Africa. Yale University Press, New Haven
Malmström A (1969) The system of legal systems, notes on a problem of classification in comparative law. Scand Stud Law 13:127–149
Mampilly Z (2011) Rebel rulers: insurgent governance and civilian life during war. Cornell University Press, Ithaca
Manai D (1993) Acculturation. In: Arnad A-J (ed) Dictionnaire encyclopédique de théorie et de sociologie du droit, 2nd edn. LGDJ, Paris, p 3
Mancuso S (2007) Trends on the harmonisation of contract law in Africa. Annu Surv Int Comp Law 13:157–178
Mancuso S (2023) African law(s). Comparative insights on the African lawscape. Brill-Nijhoff, Leiden-Boston
Mann G (2009) What was the "Indigénat"? The "Empire of Law" in French West Africa. J Afr Hist 50:331–353
Mann K, Roberts R (eds) (1991a) Law in colonial Africa. Heinemann/James Currey, Portsmouth/London
Mann K, Roberts R (eds) (1991b) Law in colonial Africa. Heinemann-James Currey, Portsmouth, NH, and London
Mar LP (1960) Social change in Africa. Int Aff 36:447–456
Markesinis B (1990) Comparative law in search of an audience. Mod Law Rev 53:1–21
Markesinis BS (1994) The gradual convergence: foreign ideas, foreign influences, and English law on the eve of the 21st century. Oxford University Press, Oxford
Markesinis BS (2001) Always on the same path, essays on foreign law and comparative methodology II. Hart, Oxford
Markesinis BS (2003) Comparative law in the courtroom and in the classroom: the story of the lest thirty- five years. Hart, Oxford

Marsham A (2024) The Umayyad Empire. Edinburgh University Press, Edinburgh
Martin JE (1993) Hanbury and Martin: modern equity, 14th edn. Sweet and Maxwell, London
Martinez-Paz E (1934) Introducción al estudio del derecho civil comparado. Imprenta de la Universidad, Córdoba Argentina
Martinico G, Pollicino O (2010) The national judicial treatment of the ECHR and EU laws: a comparative constitutional perspective. Europa Law Publishing, Groningen
Marutschke HP (2009) Einführung in das japanische Recht. Beck, Munich
Mason A (1993) The place of equity and equitable doctrines in the contemporary common law world. Second International Symposium on Trusts, Equity and Fiduciary Relationships, University of Victoria, British Columbia
Mason RHP, Caiger JG (1997) A history of Japan. Tuttle Publishing, Tokyo
Mather H (2002) The medieval revival of Roman Law: implications for contemporary legal education. Cath Law 41:323–362
Mattei U (1994) Efficiency in legal transplants: an essay in comparative law and economics. Int Rev Law Econ 14(1):3–19
Mattei U (1997a) Comparative law and economics. University of Michigan Press, Ann Arbor
Mattei U (1997b) Three patterns of law: taxonomy and change in the world's legal systems. Am J Comp Law 45(1):5–44
Mattei U (2004) Il Modello di Common law. Giappichelli, Turin
Mattei U, Pulitini F (1991) A competitive model of legal rules. In: Breton A et al (eds) The competitive state: Villa Colombella papers on competitive politics. Kluwer Academic Publishers, Dordrecht, pp 207–219
Maududi SAA (1997) The Islamic law and constitution (trans: Arhmad K) (ed), 12th edn. Islamic Publications, Lahore
Mayda J (1978) Francois Geny and modern jurisprudence. Louisiana State University Press, Baton Rouge
McDougal MS (1980) The comparative study of law for policy purposes: value clarification as an instrument of democratic world order. In: Butler WE (ed) International law in comparative perspective. Sijthoff & Noordhoff, Alphen aan den Rijn and Germantown, Maryland, pp 191–226
McKnight J (1977) Some historical observations on mixed systems of law. Jur Rev 22:177–186
Mead HM (2003) Tikanga Maori: living by Maori values. Huia Publishers, Wellington
Meagher RP, Gummow WMC, Lehane JRF (1984) Equity – doctrines and remedies, 2nd edn. Butterworths, Sydney
Meagher RP, Heydon JD, Leeming MJ (2002) Meagher, Gummow and Lehane's equity: doctrines and remedies, 4th edn. Butterworths LexisNexis, Sydney
Megarry R, Wade HWR (1984) The law of real property, 5th edn. Stevens and Sons, London
Mehren von A (1971) An academic tradition for comparative law? Am J Comp Law 19(4):624–632
Menski WF (2006) Comparative law in a global context: the legal systems of Asia and Africa. Cambridge University Press, Cambridge; 2nd edn. 2009
Merle I (2002) Retour sur le régime de l'indigénat : genèse et contradictions des principes répressifs dans l'Empire français. French Polit Cult Soc 20:77–97
Merry SE (1988) Legal pluralism. Law Soc Rev 22(5):869–896
Merryman J (1969) The civil law tradition: an introduction to the legal systems of Western Europe and Latin America. Stanford University Press, Stanford; 2nd ed. 1985; 3rd edn 2007
Merryman JH (1975) Legal education there and here: a comparison. Stanford Law Rev 27:859–887
Merryman JH (1977) Comparative law and social change: on the origins, style, decline and revival of the law and development movement. Am J Comp Law 25:457–491
Merryman JH (1998) Comparative law scholarship. Hastings Int Comp Law Rev 21(4):771–784
Merryman J, Clark D (1978) Comparative law: Western European and Latin American legal systems. Bobbs-Merrill, Indianapolis
Meston M, Sellar W, Cooper L (1991) The Scottish legal tradition. The Saltire Society and The Stair Society, Edinburgh

Michaels R (2002) Im Westen nichts Neues? 100 Jahre Pariser Kongreß für Rechtsvergleichung - Gedanken anläßlich einer Jubiläumskonferenz in New Orleans. Rabels Zeitschrift für ausländisches und internationales Privatrecht 66(1):97–115
Michaels R (2019) The functional method of comparative law. In: Reimann M, Zimmermann R (eds) The Oxford handbook of comparative law, 2nd edn. Oxford University Press, Oxford, pp 345–389
Migdal JS (2001) State in society: studying how states and societies transform and constitute one another. Cambridge University Press, Cambridge
Mills JA (2002) Legal constructions of cultural identity in Latin America: an argument against defining "Indigenous Peoples". Tex Hisp J Law Policy 8:49–78
Milsom SFC (1981a) Historical foundations of the common law. Butterworths, London
Milsom SFC (1981b) The nature of Blackstone's achievement. Selden Society, London
Minear RH (1970) Japanese tradition and Western law: emperor, state, and law in the thought of Hozumi Yatsuka. Harvard University Press, Cambridge
Mirow M (2000) The power of Codification in Latin America: Simón Bolívar and the Code Napoléon. Tulane J Int Comp Law 8:83–116
Mirow M (2001) Borrowing private law in Latin America: Andres Bello's use of the Code Napoleon in drafting the Chilean Civil Code. La Law Rev 61:291–329
Mirow M (2004) Latin American law: a history of private law and institutions in Spanish America. University of Texas Press, Austin
Mommsen T (1887) Romisches Staatsrecht. S. Hirzel, Leipzig
Mommsen WJ, de Moor JA (eds) (1992) European expansion and law: the encounter of European and Indigenous law in the 19th and 20th century Africa and Asia. Berg Publishers, Oxford
Monateri PG (ed) (2012) Methods of comparative law. Edward Elgar, Cheltenham
Monateri PG (2023) Comparative law and the style of legal systems. In: Zander LA, Kramp-Seidel N (eds) Europe in law and literature, transdisciplinary voices in conversation. Walter de Gruyter, Berlin & Boston, pp 15–26
Moore CA (ed) (1967) The Japanese mind: essentials of Japanese philosophy. University Press of Hawaii, Honolulu
Moore SF (2000) Law as process. An anthropological approach. LIT Verlag, Hamburg
Mortimer E (1982) Faith and power: the politics of Islam. Random House, New York
Mousourakis G (2007) A legal history of Rome. Routledge, New York
Mousourakis G (2012) Fundamentals of roman private law. Springer, Berlin
Mousourakis G (2015) Roman law and the origins of the civil law tradition. Springer, Cham
Muir W (1923) The life of Mohammad. John Grant, Edinburgh
Muir Watt H (2019) Globalization and comparative law. In: Reimann M, Zimmermann R (eds) The Oxford handbook of comparative law, 2nd edn. Oxford University Press, Oxford, pp 599–623
Muir-Watt H (2000) La fonction subversive du droit comparé. Revue internationale de droit comparé 52:503–527
Mulgan RG (1977) Aristotle's political theory: an introduction for students of political theory. Clarendon Press, Oxford
Nadelmann K, von Mehrin A, Hazard JN (eds) (1961) XXth century comparative and conflicts law: legal essays in honour of Hessel E. Yntema. A.W. Sythoff, Leiden
Nader L (2002) The life of the law: anthropological projects. University of California Press, Berkeley
Nafziger JAR (ed) (2017) Comparative law and anthropology. Elgar, Cheltenham
Nakamura K (1964) The formation of modern Japan as viewed from legal history. The Centre for East Asian Cultural Studies / East West Center Press, Tokyo
Nakamura H (1971) Die Rezeption des deutschen Rechts in Japan: insbesondere auf dem Gebiete des Zivilprozessrechts. Zeitschrift für Zivilprozess 84(1):74–90
Napoleon V (2013) Thinking about indigenous legal orders. In: Provost R, Sheppard C (eds) Dialogues about human rights and legal pluralism. Springer, Dordrecht, pp 229–246

Ndulo M (2011) African customary law, customs, and women's rights. Ind J Global Leg Stud 18:87–120
Nelken D (ed) (1997) Comparing legal cultures. Dartmouth, Brookfield; repr. Routledge, London, 2016
Nelken D (2003) Comparatists and transferability. In: Legrand P, Munday R (eds) Comparative legal studies: traditions and transitions. Cambridge University Press, Cambridge, pp 437–466
Nelken D, Feest J (eds) (2001) Adapting legal cultures. Hart, Oxford
Neuman G (2004) The uses of international law in constitutional interpretation. Am J Int Law 98(1):82–90
Nicholas B (1962) An introduction to roman law. Clarendon Press, Oxford; repr. 1991
Nicholson P, Biddulph S (eds) (2008) Examining practice, interrogating theory: comparative legal studies in Asia. Martinus Nijhoff, Leiden
Nicola FN, Frankenberg G (2024) Comparative law: Introduction to a critical practice. Elgar, Cheltenham
Nicolini M (2022) Legal geography. Comparative law and the production of space. Springer, Cham
Nicolini M (2024) The land, the sea, and the colonial production of space within the Anglo/British Empire. Legalities 4:43–67
Njuguna C (2020) African customary law: assessing its status and effects today. Lexington Books, Lanham, Maryland
Noda Y (1976) Introduction to Japanese Law. University of Tokyo Press, Tokyo (originally published 1966)
Northrop FSC (1959) The complexity of legal and ethical experience, studies in the methods of normative subjects. Little, Brown, Boston
Ntampaka C (2005) Introduction aux systèmes juridiques africains. Presses Universitaires de Namur, Namur
Nyazee IAK (2000) Islamic jurisprudence. International Institute of Islamic Thought, Islamabad
Oba AA (2010) The future of customary law in Africa. In: Fenrich J-M et al (eds) The future of African customary law. Cambridge University Press, Cambridge, pp 58–80
Oda H (2021) Japanese law, 4th edn. Oxford University Press, Oxford
Oeyen E (1990) Comparative methodology. Sage, London
Okubasu DM (2022) Democratic constitutional transitions in Sub-Saharan Africa. In: Dixon R, Ginsburg T, Abebe A (eds) Comparative constitutional law in Africa. Edward Elgar, Cheltenham and Northampton, pp 137–156
Ono S (1996) Comparative law and the civil law of Japan (1). Hitotsubashi J Law Polit 24:27–45
Orianne P (1990) Apprendre le droit: Eléments pour une pédagogie juridique. Éd. Frison-Roche, Paris
Örücü E (1996) Mixed and mixing systems: a conceptual search. In: Örücü E, Attwooll E, Coyle S (eds) Studies in legal systems: mixed and mixing. Kluwer Law International, London, pp 335–352
Örücü E (2002) Law as transposition. Int Comp Law Q 51:205–223
Örücü E (2004) The Enigma of comparative law. Springer, Dordrecht; repr. 2013
Örücü E (2006) Methodological aspects of comparative law. Eur J Law Reform 8(1):29–42
Örücü E, Nelken D (eds) (2007) Comparative law: a handbook. Hart, Oxford
Örücü E, Attwooll E, Coyle S (eds) (1996) Studies in legal systems: mixed and mixing. Kluwer Law International, London
Osakwe C (1986) Louisiana legal system: a confluence of two legal traditions. Am J Comp Law 34:29–45
Oto-Peralía D, Romero-Ávila D (2017) Legal traditions, legal reforms and economic performance. Theory and evidence. Springer, Wien
Padoa-Schioppa A (2017) A history of law in Europe: from the early middle ages to the twentieth century. Cambridge University Press, Cambridge
Palmer VV (2012) Mixed jurisdictions worldwide, 2nd edn. Cambridge University Press, Cambridge

Pargendler M (2012) The rise and decline of legal families. Am J Comp Law 60(4):1043–1074
Paton GW (1972) A textbook of jurisprudence. Clarendon Press, Oxford
Pearce D (1987) Roads to commensurability. D. Reidel Pub. Co., Dordrecht
Pearl D (1979) A text book on Muslim law. Croom Helm, London
Peat D (2019) Comparative reasoning in international courts and tribunals. Cambridge University Press, Cambridge
Perell PM (1990) The fusion of law and equity. Butterworths, Toronto
Pescatore P (1980) Le recours, dans la jurisprudence de la Cour de Justice des Communautés européennes, à des normes déduites de la comparaison du droit des États members. Revue internationale de droit comparé 32:337
Péteri Z (2002) Teaching of comparative law and comparative law teaching. Acta Juridica Hungarica 43:243–261
Phillips DD (2013) The law of ancient Athens. University of Michigan Press, Ann Arbor
Picken GN (2011) Islamic law. Routledge, London
Plant R (1998) Issues in indigenous poverty and development. Inter-American Development Bank, Washington DC
Plesser MA (1997) Jean Étienne Marie Portalis und der Code civil. Duncker & Humblot, Berlin
Plucknett TFT (1956) A concise history of the common law, 5th edn. Little, Brown, London
Plucknett TFT, Barton JL (eds) (1974) Christopher St German's Doctor and Student. Selden Society Series, London, vol 91
Pollock F (1903) The history of comparative jurisprudence. J Soc Comp Legis 5(1):74–89
Pollock F (ed) (1927) Table talk of John Selden. Selden Society, London
Pollock F, Maitland FW (1898) The history of English law before the time of Edward I, 2nd edn. Cambridge University Press, Cambridge, repr. 1978
Port K (1996) Comparative law: law and the legal process in Japan. Carolina Academic Press, Durham, North Carolina
Posner R (2008) How judges think. Harvard University Press, Cambridge
Pospisil L (1971) Anthropology of law: a comparative theory. Harper & Row, New York
Pound R (1911–1912) The scope and purpose of sociological jurisprudence. Harv Law Rev 24 (June 1911):591–619; 25 (December 1911):140–168; 25 (April 1912):489–516
Pound R (1951) Philosophy of law and comparative law. Univ Pa Law Rev 100(1):1–19
Powers DS (1986) Studies in Qurʾān and Ḥadīth: the formation of the Islamic law of inheritance. University of California Press, Berkeley
Powers DS (1993) The Islamic inheritance system: a socio-historical approach. Arab Law Q 8(1):13–29
Priban J, Nelken D (eds) (2001) Law's new boundaries: the consequences of legal autopoiesis. Ashgate/Dartmouth, Aldershot
Prinsloo MW (1987) Restatement of indigenous law. Comp Int Law J South Afr 20:411–420
Prior AN (1956) Logic and the basis of ethics. Clarendon Press, Oxford
Puchta GF (1841) Cursus der Institutionen I. Breitkopf & Härtel, Leipzig
Rabel E (1919) Das Institut für Rechtsvergleichung an der Universität München. Zeitschrift für Rechtspflege in Bayern 15:2–6
Rabel E (1924) Aufgabe und Notwendigkeit der Rechtsvergleichung. Rheinische Zeitschrift für Zivil- und Prozessrecht 13:279–301
Rabel E (1925) Aufgabe und Notwendigkeit der Rechtsvergleichung. Max Hueber, Munich
Rabel E (1931) Das Problem der Qualifikation. Rabels Zeitschrift für ausländisches und internationales Privatrecht 5:241–288
Rabel E (1937) Die Fachgebiete des Kaiser-Wilhelm-Instituts für ausländisches und internationales privatrecht (gegründet 1926) 1900-1935. In: 25 Jahre Kaiser-Wilhelm- Gesellschaft zur Förderung der Wissenschaften 3: Die Geisteswissenschaften. Springer, Berlin, pp 77–190
Rabello AM (2000) Montesquieu et la codification du droit privé (le code Napoléon). Revue internationale de droit comparé 52(1):147–156
Radding CM (1988) The origins of medieval jurisprudence. Yale University Press, New Haven

Ragone S, Smorto G (2023) Comparative law: a very short introduction. Oxford University Press, Oxford
Rahn G (1990) Rechtsdenken und Rechtsauffassung in Japan: Dargestellt an der Entwicklung der modernen japanischen Zivilrechtsdogmatik. Beck, Munich
Ramadan HM (2006) Understanding Islamic law: from classical to contemporary. Rowman & Littlefield, Lanham
Ramadan T (2009) Radical reform: Islamic ethics and liberation. Oxford University Press, New York
Rambaud T (2017) Introduction au droit comparé, 2nd edn. Presses Unversitaires de Frances, Paris
Ranger T (1983) The invention of tradition in colonial Africa. In: Hobsbawm E, Ranger T (eds) The invention of tradition. Cambridge University Press, Cambridge, pp 211–262
Reid R, Parker J (eds) (2013) The Oxford handbook of modern African history. Oxford University Press, Oxford
Reimann M (1995) Conflict of laws in Western Europe, a guide through the jungle. Transnational Publishers, Irvington
Reimann M (2001) Beyond national systems: a comparative law for the international age. Tulane Law Rev 75:1103–1120
Reimann M (2012) Comparative law and neighbouring disciplines. In: Bussani M, Mattei U (eds) The Cambridge companion to comparative Law. Cambridge University Press, Cambridge, pp 13–34
Reimann M (2019) Comparative law and private international law. In: Reimann M, Zimmermann R (eds) The Oxford handbook of comparative law, 2nd edn. Oxford University Press, Oxford, pp 1339–1370
Reitz JC (1998) How to do comparative law. Am J Comp Law 46(4):617–636
Renteln AD (1985) The unanswered challenge of relativism and the consequences for human rights. Hum Rights Q 7(4):514–540
Reyntjens F (1991) Note sur l'utilité d'introduire un système juridique 'pluraliste' dans la macro-comparison des droits. Revue de Droit Internationale et Droit Comparé 68:41–50
Rheinstein M (1938) Teaching comparative law. Univ Chic Law Rev 5(4):615–624
Rheinstein M (1956) In Memory of Ernst Rabel. Am J Comp Law 5:185–196
Rheinstein M (1987) Einführung in die Rechtsvergleichung. Beck, Munich
Richard J (1997) Democratization in Africa after 1989: comparative and theoretical perspectives. Comp Polit 29:363–382
Riles A (2001) Rethinking the masters of comparative law. Hart, Oxford
Riles A (2019) Comparative law and socio-legal studies. In: Reimann M, Zimmerman R (eds) The Oxford handbook of comparative law, 2nd edn. Oxford University Press, Oxford, pp 772–804
Roach Anleu SL (2000) Law and social change. Sage Publications, Thousand Oaks
Roberts S (1979) Order and dispute: an introduction to legal anthropology. Penguin, London
Robertson R (1992) Globalization: social theory and global culture. Sage, London
Robinson OF, Fergus TD, Gordon WM (2000) European legal history: sources and institutions, 3rd edn. Butterworths, London
Rodger A (1996) Thinking about Scots law. Edinburgh Law Rev 1:3–24
Rodière R (1979) Introduction au droit comparé. Dalloz, Paris
Roebuck D (1988) The background of the common law. Oxford University Press, Oxford
Röhl W (2005) History of law in Japan since 1868. Brill, Leiden
Rokumoto K (1994) Sociological theories of law. New York University Press, New York
Rosen L (2002) The Justice of Islam: comparative perspectives on Islamic law and society. Oxford University Press, Oxford
Rothacker E (1957) Die vergleichende Methode in den Geisteswissenschaften. Zeitschrift für vergleichende Rechtswissenschaft 60:13–33
Rotondi M (1968) Technique du droit dogmatique et droit compare. Revue internationale de droit comparé 20(1):5–18
Rouland N (1994) Legal anthropology. Stanford University Press, Stanford

Ruthven M (1984) Islam in the world. Oxford University Press, New York

Sabbioneti M (2019) Raymond Saleilles: (1855-1912). In: Descamps O, Domingo R (eds) Great Christian jurists in French history. Cambridge University Press, Cambridge, pp 324–341

Sacco R (1991a) Legal formants: a dynamic approach to comparative law. Am J Comp Law 39(1):1–34

Sacco R (1991b) La comparaison juridique au service de la connaissance du droit. Economica, Paris

Sacco R (2000) L'avenir du droit comparé: un défi pour les juristes du nouveau millénaire. SLC, Paris

Sacco R (2001) One hundred years of comparative law. Tulane Law Rev 75:1159–1176

Sacco R (2006) Il diritto africano. UTET, Turin

Sacco R (2009) Le droit africain: anthropologie et droit positif. Dalloz-Sirey, Paris

Sacco R (2012) The sub-Saharan legal tradition. In: Bussani M, Mattei U (eds) The Cambridge companion to comparative law. Cambridge University Press, Cambridge, pp 313–343

Sadurski W (ed) (1991) Ethical dimensions of legal theory. Rodopi, Amsterdam

Saidov AC, Butler EW (2003) Comparative law. Wildy, Simmonds & Hill, London

Saleilles R (1900) Rapport presente a la commission d'organisation sur l'utilite, le but et le programme du Congres. Bull. de la societe 29:228–236

Saleilles R (1902) Ecole historique et droit naturel. Revue trimestrielle de droit civil 1:80–112

Saleilles R (1905) Rapport sur la conception et l'objet de la science du droit compare. Congrès international de droit comparé tenu à Paris du 31 juillet au 4 août 1900. Société de législation comparée, LGDJ, Paris, p 68

Samuel G (1998) Comparative law and jurisprudence. Int Comp Law Q 47(4):817–836

Samuel G (2014) An introduction to comparative law theory and method. Hart, Oxford

Sandberg R (2023) A historical introduction to English law: genesis of the common law. Cambridge University Press, Cambridge

Sansom GB (1962) Japan: a short cultural history. Appleton Century Crofts, New York

Sansom GB (1974) A history of Japan to 1334. Charles E. Tuttle Company, Vermont and Tokyo

Sansom GB (1990) The western world and Japan: a study in the interaction of European and Asiatic Cultures. Charles E. Tuttle Company, Tokyo

Sarat A, Kearns TR (eds) (2000) Law in the domains of culture. The University of Michigan Press, Ann Arbor

Sarzotti C (1995) Jean Domat: Fondamento e metodo della scienza giuridica. Giappichelli, Turin

Saunders JJA (1978) A history of medieval Islam. Routledge, London & New York

Sauser-Hall G (1913) Fonction et méthode du droit comparé, Leçon inaugurale faite à l'Université de Neuchâtel le 23 octobre 1912. A Kündig, Genève

Sawer G (1975) "The Western conception of law", International Encyclopedia of comparative law, vol II. Mohr, Tubingen

Scarciglia R (2023) Methods and legal comparison. Edward Elgar, Cheltenham

Schacht J (1982) An introduction to Islamic law. Oxford University Press, New York

Schacht J (2012) An introduction to Islamic law. Clarendon Press, Oxford

Schadbach K (1998) The benefits of comparative law: a continental European view. Boston Univ Int Law J 16:331–422

Schauer F (2015) The force of law. Harvard University Press, Cambridge & London

Scheltema HJ (1955) Über die Natur der Basiliken. Tijdschrift 23:287–310

Scheltema HJ, Van der Wal N, Holwerda D (eds) (1953–1988) Basilicorum Libri LX. J.B. Wolters, Groningen

Scherpe JM (2004) Ausnahmen vom Erfordernis eines strikten Kausalitätsnachweises im englischen Deliktsrecht. Zeitschrift für Europäisches Privatrecht 12:164

Schiller AA (1978) Roman Law: mechanisms of development. Mouton, Hague and New York

Schlesinger RB (1957) Research on the general principles of law recognized by civilised nations. Am J Int Law 51:734–753

Schlesinger RB (1968) Formation of contracts: a study of the common core of legal systems. Oceana Publications, New York

Schlesinger RB (1970) Comparative law. Cases – texts – materials, 3rd edn. Foundation Press, Mineola New York
Schlesinger R (1995) The past and future of comparative law. Am J Comp Law 43(3):477–481
Schlesinger RB, Baade HW, Damaska MR, Herzog PE (1988) Comparative law: cases, text, materials, 5th edn. Foundation Press, New York
Schlesinger RB, Mattei U, Ruskola T, Gidi A (2009) Schlesinger's comparative law: cases, text, materials, 7th edn. Foundation Press, New York
Schlosser H (2005) Grundzüge der Neueren Privatrechtsgeschichte, Rechtsentwicklungen im europäischen Kontext. Müller, Heidelberg
Schminck A (1986) Studien zu mittelbyzantinischen Rechtsbuchern. Lowenklau, Frankfurt
Schnitzer AF (1961) Vergleichende Rechtslehre I. Verlag für Recht und Gesellschaft, Basel
Searle JR (1969) Speech acts. Cambridge University Press, Cambridge
See H (1982) The judiciary and dispute resolution in Japan: a survey. Florida State Univ Law Rev 10(3):339–368
Seidman RB (1979) Law and stratification: the African case. Contemp Crises 3:17–39
Seidman A, Seidman RB (1996) Drafting legislation for development: lessons from a Chinese project. Am J Comp Law 44:1–44
Seong-Hak Kim M (2021) Custom, law, and monarchy: a legal history of early modern France. Oxford University Press, Oxford
Shabana A (2010) Custom in Islamic law and legal theory: the development of the concepts of 'Urf and 'Ādah in the Islamic legal tradition. Palgrave Macmillan, New York
Shapiro H (ed) (1971) Man culture and society, 2nd edn. Oxford University Press, New York
Shapiro M (1980) Islam and appeal. Calif Law Rev 68(2):350–381
Shapiro M (1993) The globalization of law. Ind J Global Leg Stud 1:37–64
Sharif M (1972) Crimes and punishment in Islam. Institute of Islamic Culture, Lahore
Sharkey HJ (2013) African colonial states. In: Reid R, Parker J (eds) The Oxford handbook of modern African history. Oxford University Press, Oxford, pp 151–170
Shaw M (1990) The definition of minorities in international law. Israel Yearb Hum Rights 20:13–43
Shaw MN (2008) International law, 6th edn. Cambridge University Press, Cambridge
Shumba T (2015) Revising legal harmonisation under the Southern African Development Community Treaty: the need to amend the Treaty. Law Democr Dev 19:127
Siems M (2007) The end of comparative law. J Comp Law 2:133–150
Siems M (2018) Comparative law, 2nd edn. Cambridge University Press, Cambridge
Siems M (2022) Comparative law, 3rd edn. Cambridge University Press, Cambridge
Siems M, Yap PJ (eds) (2024) The Cambridge handbook of comparative law. Cambridge University Press, Cambridge
Simon D (1987) Die Melete des Eustathios Rhomaios über die Befugnis der Witwe zur Mordanklage. Zeitschrift der Savigny 104:559–595
Simpson AWB (2015) Invitation to law. Blackwell Publishing, Oxford (first published 1988)
Sinclair N (ed) (2019) The naturalistic fallacy. Cambridge University Press, Cambridge
Sinitsina I (1987) African legal tradition: J.M. Sarbah, J.B. Danquah, N.A. Ollennu. J Afr Law 31:44–57
Sivan E (1985) Radical Islam: medieval theology and modern politics. Yale University Press, New Heaven
Slaughter A-M (2004) A new world order. Princeton University Press, Princeton
Smith S (1933) The stage of equity. Can Bar Rev 11(5):308–316
Smith JC, Weisstub DN (1983) The Western idea of law. Butterworth, London
Smits JM (2014) Elgar Encyclopedia of comparative law, 2nd edn. Edward Elgar, Cheltenham
Smits JM (2019) Comparative law and its influence on national legal systems. In: Reimann M, Zimmermann R (eds) The Oxford handbook of comparative Law, 2nd edn. Oxford University Press, Oxford, pp 502–523
Stammler R (1922) Lehrbuch der Rechtsphilosophie. W. de Gruyter, Berlin
Steger M (2003) Globalization: a very short introduction. Oxford University Press, Oxford

Stein E (1977) Uses, misuses and nonuses of comparative law. Northwest Univ Law Rev 72:198–216
Stein P (1988) The character and influence of the roman civil law. Hambledon, London, repr 2003
Stein P (1992) Roman law, common law, and civil law. Tulane Law Rev 66(6):1591–1604
Stein P (1993) Donellus and the origins of the modern civil law. In: Ankum JA et al (eds) Mélanges F. Wubbe. Fribourg, pp 448–452
Stein P (1999) Roman law in European history. Cambridge University Press, Cambridge
Steyn L (2006) The challenge of comparative law. Eur J Law Reform 8(1):3–11
Stoetzer C (1966) El pensamiento político en la América española durante el período de la emancipación (1789 - 1825). Inst. de Estudios Politicos, Madrid
Stoffel WA (2001) Enlightened decision making. Tulane Law Rev 75:1195–1214
Stolleis M (1998) Nationalität und Internationalität: Rechtsvergleichung im öffentlichen Recht des 19. Jahrhunderts. Steiner, Stuttgart
Stone J (1966) Social dimensions of law and justice. Stevens & Sons, London
Story J (1892) Commentaries on equity jurisprudence, 2nd edn. Stevens and Haynes, London
Swenson G (2018) Legal pluralism in theory and practice. Int Stud Rev 20:438–462
Takayanagi K (1963) A century of innovation: the development of Japanese law, 1868-1961. In: von Mehren AT (ed) Law in Japan: the legal order in a changing society. Harvard University Press, Cambridge, pp 5–40
Tamanaha B (2000) A non-essentialist version of legal pluralism. J Law Soc 27(2):296–321
Tamanaha B (2001) A general jurisprudence of law and society. Oxford University Press, Oxford
Tamanaha B (2008) Understanding legal pluralism: past to present, local to global. Syd Law Rev 30(3):375–411
Tamm D (1997) Roman law and European legal history. DJOF, Copenhagen
Tanaka H, Smith M (1976) The Japanese legal system. University of Tokyo Press, Tokyo
Tanzi A (1990) François Gény tra scienza del diritto e giurisprudenza, G. Giappichelli, Torino
Tarde G (1890) Les Lois de l'Imitation. Alcan, Paris
Tarde G (1905) Le droit comparé et la sociologie. In: Congrès international de droit comparé tenu à Paris du 31 juillet au 4 août 1900, Procès-Verbaux des Séances et Documents. Librairie générale de droit de jurisprudence, Paris, pp 439–440
Tate JC, de Lima Lopez JR, Botero-Bernal A (eds) (2019) Global legal history: a comparative law perspective. Routledge, Abingdon
Taupitz J (1993) Europäische Privatrechtsvereinheitlichung heute und morgen. Mohr, Tübingen
Teitel RG (2002) Transitional justice. Oxford University Press, Oxford
Teubner G (1993) Law as an autopoietic system. Blackwell, Oxford
Teubner G (1997) Global law without a state. Dartmouth, Aldershot
Teubner G (1998) Legal irritants: good faith in British law or how unifying law ends up in new divergences. Mod Law Rev 61(1):11–32
Thieme J (1986) Ernst Rabel (1874-1955): Schriften aus dem Nachlass. Rabels Zeitschrift für ausländisches und internationales Privatrecht 50:251–281
Thirlway H (2014) The sources of international law. Oxford University Press, Oxford
Thomas MS (2017) The challenge of legal pluralism. Local dispute settlement and the Indian-state relationship in Ecuador. Routledge, London & New York
Thorne SE (1968) (transl.) Bracton on the laws and customs of England. Harvard University Press, Cambridge
Tibi B (1998) The challenge of fundamentalism: political Islam and the new world disorder. University of California Press, Berkeley
Troianos S (1986) The Sources of Byzantine Law. Sakkoulas, Athens
Tur R (1977) The dialectic of general jurisprudence and comparative law. Jur Rev 22(2):238–249
Turner RV (1985) The English judiciary in the age of Glanvill and Bracton, c. 1176-1239. Cambridge University Press, Cambridge
Twining W (2000) Globalisation and legal theory. Butterworths, London
Tylor EB (2010) Primitive culture. Cambridge University Press, Cambridge

Ubink J (2010) The quest for customary law in African state courts. In: Fenrich J-M et al (eds) The future of African customary law. Cambridge University Press, Cambridge, pp 83–102
Ullmann W (1975) Law and politics in the middle ages. Cambridge University Press, Cambridge
Ullmann W (1980) Jurisprudence in the middle ages. Variorum, London
Unger RM (1976) Law in modern society: toward a criticism of social theory. Free Press, New York
Vago S, Barkan SE (2018) Law and society, 11th edn. Routledge, New York
Valcke C (2018) Comparing law. Comparative law as reconstruction of collective commitments. Cambridge University Press, Cambridge
Van Caenegem RC (1973) History of European civil procedure. In: Cappelletti (ed) International encyclopedia of comparative law, vol 16. Mohr, Tübingen, chapter 2
Van Caenegem RC (1987) Judges, legislators and professors: chapters in European legal history. Cambridge University Press, Cambridge
Van Caenegem RC (1988) Birth of the English common law, 2nd edn. Cambridge University Press, Cambridge
Van Caenegem RC (1991) Legal history: a European perspective. Hambledon Press, London
Van Caenegem RC (2002) European law in the past and the future: unity and diversity over two millennia. Cambridge University Press, Cambridge
Van de Fliert L (1994) Introduction. In: Van de Fliert L (ed) Indigenous peoples and international organizations. Spokesman, Nottingham, pp 1–10
Van den Berg P (2007) The politics of European codification. A history of the unification of Law in France, Prussia, the Austrian monarchy and the Netherlands. Europa Law Publishing, Groningen
Van der Wall KCS (2004) Formal and informal dispute resolution in the Limpopo Province, South Africa. Anthropol South Afr 27:111–121
Van Hoecke M (2004) Epistemology and methodology of comparative law. Hart, Oxford
van Hoecke M, Warrington M (1998) Legal cultures, legal paradigms and legal doctrine: towards a new model for comparative law. Int Comp Law Q 47:495–536
Vanderinden J (1983) Les Systèmes juridiques africains. Presses Universitaires de Frances, Paris
Vanderlinden J (1989) Return to legal pluralism. Twenty years later. J Leg Plur Unoff Law 21(28):149–157
Vanderlinden J (1996) Anthropologique juridique. Dalloz, Paris
Vanderlinden J (1998) Villes africaines et pluralisme juridique. J Leg Plur Unoff Law 30(42):245–274
Vanderlinden J (2000) Les droits africains entre positivisme et pluralisme. Bulletin de séances de l'Académie royale de sciences d'Oute-Mer 46:279–292
Vanderlinden J (2006) Ex Africa Semper. Revue internationale de droit comparé 58:1187–1202
Varga C (2012) Comparative legal cultures. Szent Istvan Tarsulat, Budapest
Verdirame G (2007) The divided West: international lawyers in Europe and America. Eur J Int Law 18(3):553–580
Vinogradoff P (1929) Roman law in medieval Europe. Clarendon Press, Oxford; repr. 2001
Visegrády A (2001) Legal cultures in the European Union. Acta Juridica Hungarica 42:203–217
Voll JO (1983) Renewal and reform in Islamic history: Tajdid and Islah. In: Esposito JL (ed) Voices of resurgent Islam. Oxford University Press, New York, pp 32–47
von Jhering R (1877) Der Zweck im Recht. Breitkopf & Härtel, Leipzig
von Jhering R (1884) Scherz und Ernst in der Jurisprudenz. Breitkopf & Härtel, Leipzig
von Jhering R (1955) Des Geist des Römischen Rechts auf den verschiedenen Stufen seiner Entwicklung I, 9th edn. Scientia-Verlag, Aalen
von Mehren A (1978) The contribution of comparative law to the theory and practice of private international law. Am J Comp Law 26:31–41
von Mehren A (2001) The rise of transnational legal practice and the task of comparative law. Tulane Law Rev 75:1215–1224
von Mehren A, Gordley J (1977) The civil law system, 2nd edn. Little, Brown, Boston

von Savigny FC (1814) Vom Beruf unserer Zeit für Gesetzgebung und Rechtswissenschaft. Mohr und Zimmer, Heidelberg
Voppel R (1996) Der Einfluß des Naturrechts auf den Usus modernus: eine Untersuchung anhand der Literatur zum geltenden Recht im 17. und 18. Jahrhundert. Carl Heymanns, Köln
Vranken M (1997) Fundamentals of European civil law. The Federation Press, Leichhardt
Wahl E (1973) Influences climatiques sur l'évolution du droit en Orient et en Occident. Contribution au régionalisme en droit compare. Revue internationale de droit compare 25(2):261–276
Wang G, Mo J (1999) Chinese law. Kluwer Law International, The Hague
Warmington EH (1938) Remains of old Latin III. Loeb Classical Library, Cambridge
Watson A (1974) Legal transplants: an approach to comparative law, 2nd edn. Scottish Academic Press, Edinburgh (University of Georgia Press, Athens Georgia, 1993)
Watson A (1976) Legal transplants and law reform. Law Q Rev 92:79–84
Watson A (1978) Comparative law and legal change. Camb Law J 37(2):313–336
Watson A (1981) The making of the civil law. Harvard University Press, Cambridge
Watson A (1983) Legal change: sources of law and legal culture. Univ Pa Law Rev 131(5):1121–1157
Watson A (1984) Sources of law, legal change, and ambiguity. University of Pennsylvania Press, Philadelphia
Watson A (1985) The evolution of law. Blackwell, Oxford
Watson A (1991a) Roman law and comparative law. University of Georgia Press, Athens
Watson A (1991b) Legal origins and legal change. Hambledon Press, London
Watson A (1995) The spirit of roman law. University of Georgia Press, Athens
Watson A (2001) The evolution of Western private law. Johns Hopkins University Press, Baltimore
Watt G (2021) Equity and trusts law directions, 7th edn. Oxford University Press, Oxford
Webber J (2009) The grammar of customary law. McGill Law J 54(4):579–626
Weber M (1954) Law in economy and society (trans: Shils E, Rheinstein M). Harvard University Press, Cambridge
Weber M (1978) In: Roth G, Wittich C (eds) Economy and society: an outline of interpretive sociology. University of California Press, Berkeley
Weeramantry C (1988) Islamic jurisprudence: an international perspective. Macmillan, Basingstoke
Weiss A (1900) Rôle, fonction et méthode du Droit comparé dans le domaine du Droit civil. Bulletin de la Société de législation comparée 12:417
Weiss G (1977) Die "Synopsis legum" des Michael Psellos. V. Klostermann
Weiss B (1992) In search of God's law: Islamic jurisprudence in the writings of Sayf al-Dīn al-Āmidī. University of Utah Press, Salt Lake City
Welzel H (1962) Naturrecht und materiale Gerechtigkeit, 4th edn. Vandenhoeck & Ruprecht, Göttingen
Werro F (2001) Notes on the purpose and aims of comparative law. Tulane Law Rev 75:1225–1233
West R (1993) Narrative, authority and law. The University of Michigan Press, Ann Arbor
White JB (1973) The legal imagination. Studies in the nature of legal thought and expression. Little Brown, Boston
White AA (2001) Max Weber and the uncertainties of categorical comparative law. In: Riles A (ed) Rethinking the masters of comparative law. Hart Publishing, Oxford, pp 40–57
Whitman JQ (2009) Western legal imperialism: thinking about the deep historical roots. Theor Inq Law 10(2):305–332
Wieacker F (1995) A history of private law in Europe: with particular reference to Germany (trans: Weir T). Clarendon Press, Oxford
Wiessner S (1999) Rights and status of indigenous peoples: a global comparative and international legal analysis. Harv Hum Rights J 12:57–128
Wigmore JH (1917) Nova Methodus discendae docendaeque Jurisprudentiae. Harv Law Rev 30(8):812–829
Wigmore JH (1928) A panorama of the world's legal systems I–III. West Publishing Co, Chicago
Windscheid B (1891) Lehrbuch des Pandektenrechts I, 7th edn. Literarische Anstalt Bütten & Loening, Frankfurt

Winroth A (2000) The making of Gratian's Decretum. Cambridge University Press, Cambridge
Winterton G (1975) Comparative law teaching. Am J Comp Law 23(1):69–118
Wise EM (1990) The transplant of legal patterns. Am J Comp Law 38:1–22
Wolf E (1944) Grosse Rechtsdenker der deutschen Geistesgeschichte. Mohr, Tübingen
Wolff H-J (1951) Roman law: an historical introduction. University of Oklahoma Press, Norman; repr. 1976
Wolfrum R (1999) The protection of indigenous peoples in international law. Heidelberg J Int Law 59:369–382
Woodman G (1999) The idea of legal pluralism. In: Dupret B, Berger M, al-Zwaini L (eds) Legal pluralism in the Arab world. Kluwer Law International, The Hague, pp 3–19
Woodman G (2010) A survey of customary laws in Africa in search of lessons for the future. In: Fenrich J-M et al (eds) The future of African customary law. Cambridge University Press, Cambridge, pp 9–30
Wormald P (1999) The making of English law: King Alfred to the Twelfth Century. Blackwell, Oxford
Wren HG (1968) The legal system of pre-Western Japan. Hastings Law J 20(1):217–244
Wright R (2001) Sacred rage: the wrath of militant Islam. Simon & Shuster, New York & London
Yamani AZ (1979) The eternal Sharia. N Y Univ J Int Law Polit 12(2):205–212
Yao X (2000) An introduction to Confucianism. Cambridge University Press, Cambridge
Yntema HE (1956) Comparative legal research: some remarks on 'looking out of the cave'. Mich Law Rev 54(7):899–928
Yntema HE (1958) Le droit comparé et l' humanisme. Revue internationale de droit comparé 10(4):693–700
Youngs R (2014) English, French and German comparative law, 3rd edn. Routledge, Abingdon
Zamora S et al (2005) Mexican law. Oxford University Press, Oxford
Zaphiriou GA (1982) Use of comparative law by the legislator. Am J Comp Law 30:71–95
Zepos J, Zepos P (eds) (1962) Jus graecoromanum, 8 vols. Scientia, Aalen (original work published 1931)
Zimmerman R (1995a) 'Common law' und 'civil law', Amerika und Europa. In: Zimmerman R (ed) Amerikanische Rechtskultur und europäisches Privatrecht. Mohr Siebeck, Tübingen, pp 1–10
Zimmerman R (1995b) Amerikanische Rechtskultur und europäisches Privatrecht. Mohr, Tübingen
Zimmerman R (2001) In der Schule von Ludwig Mitteis: Ernst Rabels rechtshistorische Ursprünge. Rabels Zeitschrift 65:1–38
Zimmerman A, Tomuschat C, Oellers-frahm K (eds) (2006) The statute of the international court of justice, a commentary. Oxford University Press, Oxford
Zimmermann R (1996) The law of obligations: roman foundations of the civilian tradition. Clarendon Press, Oxford
Zimmermann R (2001) Roman law, contemporary law, European law: the civilian tradition today. Oxford University Press, Oxford
Zimmermann R, Visser D (1996a) Introduction: South African law as a mixed legal system. In: Zimmermann R, Visser D (eds) Southern Cross: civil law and common law in South Africa. Clarendon Press, Oxford, pp 1–30
Zimmermann R, Visser D (1996b) Southern cross: civil law and common law in South Africa. Clarendon Press, Oxford
Zweigert K (1961) Zur Lehre von den Rechtskreisen. In: 20th century comparative and conflicts law. Legal essays in honor of Hessel E. Yntema. Sythoff, Leyden, pp 42–55
Zweigert K (1966) Des solutions identiques par des voies différentes. Revue internationale de droit comparé 18:5–18
Zweigert K, Kötz H (1977) An introduction to comparative law. North Holland Publishing, Amsterdam

Zweigert K, Kötz H (1987) An introduction to comparative law, 2nd edn. Clarendon Press, Oxford (3rd ed., 1998, repr. 2011)
Zweigert K, Kötz H (1996) Einführung in die Rechtsvergleichung auf dem Gebiete des Privatrechts, 3rd edn. J.C.B. Mohr Siebeck, Tübingen

Index

G. Mousourakis, *Traversing Legal Traditions*, Springer Textbooks in Law,
https://doi.org/10.1007/978-3-031-94669-1

M

T

U

The manufacturer's authorised representative in the EU is Springer Nature Customer Service Centre GmbH, Europaplatz 3, 69115 Heidelberg, Germany. If you have any concerns regarding our products, please contact ProductSafety@springernature.com

Printed and bound by CPI Group (UK) Ltd, Croydon, CR0 4YY
01/10/2026
02225950-0015